Ersel Hickey

THE ROLLING STONE ILLUSTRATED HISTORY OF ROCK & ROLL

Edited by
Jim Miller

Designed by
Robert Kingsbury

Rolling Stone Press
Random House
New York

Library of Congress Cataloging in Publication Data
Main entry under title:
The Rolling Stone illustrated history of rock & roll.
Includes index.
1. Rock music—History and criticism.
I. Miller, Jim, 1947-
ML3561.R62R6   784   76-14190
ISBN 0-394-40327-4
ISBN 0-394-73238-3 pbk.
Manufactured in the United States of America
2 4 6 8 9 7 5
Cover design by Roger Black

Grateful acknowledgment is made to the following for permission to reprint previously published material:

The Village Voice: "Elton John" by Robert Christgau originally appeared in a different version in *The Village Voice* as "Elton John, the Little Hooker that Could," November 24, 1975. Copyright © 1975 by The Village Voice, Inc.

The Real Paper: "Sexy, Safe and Out of Sync/On the Road with Al Green" by Robert Christgau. Reprinted from *The Real Paper*, March 26, 1975. Copyright © 1975 by *The Real Paper*, Cambridge, Mass.

Simon and Schuster, Inc.: Selected quotes from the book *Elvis Presley: A Biography* by Jerry Hopkins. Copyright © 1971 by Jerry Hopkins. These selections appear in the chapter "Elvis Presley" by Peter Guralnick.

Straight Arrow Publishers, Inc.: "Otis Redding" by Jon Landau. Reprinted from *It's Too Late To Stop Now: A Rock & Roll Journal.* Copyright © 1972 by Jon Landau. Originally printed in *Eye* magazine.

LYRIC CREDITS

INTRODUCTION: "I Shall Be Released" by Bob Dylan Copyright © 1967, 1970 Dwarf Music; used by permission; all rights reserved. **ROCK BEGINS:** "Run Old Jeremiah" traditional. "Pan American Boogie" by Alton Delmore and Rabon Delmore Copyright © 1949 Fort Knox Music Co. **RHYTHM AND GOSPEL:** "Baby, Don't Do It" by Lowman Pauling Copyright © 1952 Bess Music Co. "Work With Me Annie" by Henry Ballard Copyright © 1954 Armo Music Corp.; copyright assigned to Fort Knox Music Co.; used by permission; all rights reserved. "Annie Had a Baby" by Lois Mann and Henry Grover Copyright © 1954 Jay-Cee Music Co. "Annie's Answer" by Al Smith and Bobby Prince Copyright © 1954 Conrad Publishing Co. "Annie Pulled a Humbug" by Melvin, copyright information unavailable. **ELVIS PRESLEY:** "Good Rockin' Tonight" by Roy Brown Copyright © 1948 Fort Knox Music Co. "Hound Dog" by Jerry Leiber and Mike Stoller Copyright © 1953 Lion Publishing Co. Inc. and Elvis Presley Music. **THE SOUND OF NEW ORLEANS:** "Junker's Blues" by Jack Dupree Copyright © 1959 Progressive Music Publishing Co. Inc. "The Fat Man" by Antoine Domino and Dave Bartholomew Copyright © 1950 Travis Music Co. "Let the Good Times Roll" by Leonard Lee Copyright © 1956 Travis Music Co. and Atlantic Music Co. "Sea Cruise" by Huey P. Smith Copyright © 1966 Lancer Music Inc. and Cotillion Music Inc. "Mother-In-Law" by Allen Toussaint Copyright © 1961 Minit Music Co. "I Like It like That" by Chris Kenner Copyright © 1961 Thursday Music Inc. "Ya Ya" by Lee Dorsey and Morgan Robinson Copyright © 1961 Frost Music Corp. **FATS DOMINO:** "The Fat Man" by Antoine Domino and Dave Bartholomew Copyright © 1950 Travis Music Co. "Goin' Home" by Antoine Domino and Alvin E. Young Copyright © 1956 Travis Music Co. **LITTLE RICHARD:** "Tutti-Frutti" by Richard Penniman, Dorothy LaBostrie and Joe Lubin Copyright © 1956 Venice Music Inc. "Ain't That Good News" by Raymond Taylor Copyright © 1953 Lion Publishing Co. Inc. "Long Tall Sally" by Richard Penniman, Robert Blackwell and Enotris Johnson Copyright © 1956 Venice Music Inc. "I'm Quittin' Show Business" by Richard Penniman, copyright information unavailable. **CHUCK BERRY:** "School Day" by Chuck Berry Copyright © 1957 Arc Music Corp. "It Hurts Me Too" by Elmore James Copyright © 1965 Bob-Dan Music Co.; used by permission; all rights reserved. "Tulane" by Chuck Berry Copyright © 1970 Isalee Music Publishing Co. "Have Mercy Judge" by Chuck Berry Copyright © 1970 Isalee Music Publishing Co. **ROCKABILLY:** "Woman Love" by Jack Rhodes Copyright © 1957 Central Songs Inc. **JERRY LEE LEWIS:** "Great Balls of Fire" by Otis Blackwell and Jack Hammer Copyright © 1957 Unichappell Music Inc. and Anne Rachel Music Corp. "Whole Lot of Shakin' Going On" by Sunny David and Dave Williams Copyright © 1957 Rosarita Music Inc. and Pic Music Corp. "Little Queenie" by Chuck Berry Copyright © 1959 Arc Music Corp.; used by permission. **THE EVERLY BROTHERS:** "That's Old Fashioned" by Bill Giant, Bernie Baum and Florence Kaye Copyright © 1962 Aberbach Inc. and Egap Music Inc.; Unichappell Music Inc., Administrator; International Copyright Secured; used by permission; all rights reserved. "I Wonder if I Care as Much" by Don Everly and Phil Everly Copyright © 1957 Acuff-Rose Publications Inc.; used by permission; all rights reserved. **BUDDY HOLLY:** "American Pie" by Don McLean Copyright © 1971 Mayday Music Inc. and Yahweh Tunes Inc. "Crying, Waiting, Hoping" by Buddy Holly Copyright © 1959 Peer International Corp. "Rock Around with Ollie Vee" by Sonny Curtis Copyright © 1957 Unichappell Music Inc. "Peggy Sue" by Buddy Holly, Norman Petty and Jerry Allison Copyright © 1957 MPL Communications Inc.; used by permission; all rights reserved. "Not Fade Away" by Norman Petty and Charles Hardin Copyright © 1957 MPL Communications Inc. "Take Your Time" by Norman Petty and Buddy Holly Copyright © 1958 MPL Communications Inc.; used by permission; all rights reserved. "I'm Gonna Love You Too" by Joe Mauldin, Niki Sullivan and Norman Petty Copyright © 1957 MPL Communications Inc.; used by permission; all rights reserved. "Well All Right" by Buddy Holly, Jerry Allison, Norman Petty and Joe Mauldin Copyright © 1958 MPL Communications Inc. "You're the One" by Buddy Holly, Slim Corbin and Waylon Jennings Copyright © 1961 Peer International Corp.; used by permission. "Peggy Sue Got Married" by Buddy Holly Copyright © 1961 Cousins Inc. and Shoe-String Music Inc.; used by permission. "Barbara Ann" by Fred Fassert Copyright © 1961 Cousins Inc. and Shoe-String Music Inc.; used by permission. **DOO-WOP:** "I Love You So" by Viola Ethel Watkins and William R. Davis Jr. Copyright © 1953 Viola Ethel Watkins and William R. Davis Jr. **THE TEEN IDOLS:** "Swingin' School" by Cal Mann, Bernie Lowe and Dave Appell Copyright © 1960 Columbia Pictures Music Corp. "Diana" by Paul Anka Copyright © 1957 Pamco Music Inc.; Copyright © assigned 1963 to Spanka Music Corp.; used by permission; all rights reserved. **SAM COOKE:** Were You There When They Crucified My Lord?" traditional. **BRILL BUILDING POP:** "Calendar Girl" by Neil Sedaka and Howard Greenfield Copyright © 1961 Screen Gems-Columbia Music Inc.; used by permission; all rights reserved. "Up On the Roof" by Carole King and Gerry Goffin Copyright © 1962, 1963 Screen Gems-Columbia Music Inc.; used by permission; all rights reserved. **ROY ORBISON:** "Bye Bye Love" by Felice Bryant and Boudleaux Bryant Copyright © 1957 House of Bryant Publications. **ITALO-AMERICAN ROCK:** "Looking for an Echo" by Richard Reicheg Copyright © 1974 WB Music Co. **THE SOUND OF CHICAGO:** "Gypsy Woman" by Curtis Mayfield Copyright © 1961 Warner-Tamerlane Publishing Co. **PHIL SPECTOR:** "Black Pearl" by Phil Spector, Toni Wine and Irwin Levine Copyright © 1969 Irving Music Inc. and Pocket Full of Tunes Music Inc. **THE GIRL GROUPS:** "Beechwood 4-5789" by George Gordy, William Stevenson and Marvin Gaye Copyright © 1962 Jobete Music Co. Inc. "Da Doo Ron Ron" by Phil Spector, Ellie Greenwich and Jeff Barry Copyright © 1963 Mother Bertha Inc. and Trio Music Co. Inc. "A Fine Fine Boy" by Phil Spector, Ellie Greenwich and Jeff Barry Copyright © 1963 Mother Bertha Inc. and Trio Music Co. **THE BEACH BOYS:** "In My Room" by Brian Wilson and Gary Usher Copyright © 1964 Irving Music Inc. (BMI); used by permission; all rights reserved. "I Get Around" by Brian Wilson Copyright © 1964 Irving Music Inc. "Don't Worry Baby" by Brian Wilson and Roger Christian Copyright © 1964 Irving Music Inc. "When I Grow Up (to Be a Man)" by Brian Wilson Copyright © 1964 Irving Music Inc. "That's Not Me" by Brian Wilson and Tony Asher Copyright © 1966 Irving Music Inc. "Caroline, No" by Brian Wilson and Tony Asher Copyright © 1966 Irving Music Inc. "Busy Doin' Nothing" by Brian Wilson Copyright © 1968 Irving Music Inc. **THE BRITISH INVASION:** "(I Can't Get No) Satisfaction" by Mick Jagger and Keith Richard Copyright © 1965 Abkco Music Inc. **THE BEATLES:** "With a Little Help from My Friends" by John Lennon and Paul McCartney Copyright © 1967 Maclen Music Inc. "A Day in the Life" by John Lennon and Paul McCartney Copyright © 1967 Maclen Music Inc. "Lovely Rita" by John Lennon and Paul McCartney Copyright © 1967 Maclen Music Inc. "Lucy in the Sky with Diamonds" by John Lennon and Paul McCartney Copyright © 1967 Maclen Music Inc. "Money (That's What I Want)" by Berry Gordy and Janie Bradford Copyright © 1959 Jobete Music Co. Inc.; used by permission; all rights

Contents

*The Five Satins, who made rock and roll history
with "In the Still of the Nite" ('Record Exchanger')*

Introduction
by Jim Miller

Bob Dylan's Rolling Thunder Revue, 1975 (Grinnell A. Talbot)

There was a moment in Bob Dylan's Rolling Thunder Revue, which crisscrossed the northeastern United States in the fall of 1975, that summarized for me what rock has been all about. Dylan and Joan Baez opened the second half of the concert singing duets: "Blowin' in the Wind," "Wild Mountain Thyme" and, finally, "I Shall Be Released." They had sung together last in the mid-Sixties, and the image of them at Newport in 1963 haunted the stage: another place, another time, Dylan on the verge of his "conversion" to rock, a conversion that would take him beyond political lyrics, the folk circuit and its appreciative audience which idolized him as a poet of the people.

Then he had merely been the outstanding voice of the folk music revival. By mid-1965, he had become a rock and roll star played on Top 40 radio stations—the voice of a generation.

But here, ten years later, he had surrounded himself, not only with a new rock band, but also, in a calculated gesture, with old friends from the folkie days. And to see him with Joan Baez, and to hear them sing "Blowin' in the Wind," which might have been only an exercise in nostalgia, seemed more a statement of belief reborn, a sentiment crystallized in "I Shall Be Released." Baez, after all these years able to joke about being the folkie's "madonna," sang head to head with Dylan:

> They say everything can be replaced
> They say every distance is not near
> So I remember every face
> Of every man who put me here.
> I see my light come shining
> From the West down to the East
> Any day now
> Any day now
> I shall be released.

They sang as if they believed it, and I believed it too: that was one of the promises of rock, a promise redeemed in what followed on the Rolling Thunder Revue, by Roger McGuinn singing "Eight Miles High," by Baez singing "Diamonds and Rust"

(her retrospective love song to Dylan), and by Dylan singing "Mr. Tambourine Man," "Hurricane," "Just like a Woman," "Sara," "Knockin' on Heaven's Door." . . .

It was all there: the social statements (again), the drug anthems, the personal confessions, the evocation of an heroic American past, and this kaleidoscope of folk music past and future, amplified through the medium of rock, epitomized for me the music's magic, the reason why I have listened to it since the first time I heard Elvis Presley on the radio, the reason why rock has defined more than one generation's sensibility, style of life, and fantasies.

Of course, in the aftermath the realization dawned that this tour had been lofted on a mass of hype and hot air; that Dylan loved indulging in self-conscious mythologizing; that he reveled in the obsequious prose pumped out by such latter-day acolytes as Allen Ginsberg; that the whole tour had been conceived, at least in part, as a glorified scam and mise-en-scène for a movie that would finance itself. As for the question: is this for real, for fun, or for money—well, it was for all three, and that's rock and roll. It was *all* there.

Simple entertainment? Around the time the Rolling Thunder Revue toured America, the following items appeared:

FLORIDA MINISTER, FLOCK, FIGHT ROCK

Tallahassee, Florida—Reverend Charles Boykin has a bone to pick with rock and roll, and he's not satisfied with just talking about it. So on November 26th, Brother Charlie and his Lakewood Baptist Church youth group gathered over $2000 worth of records, stacked them in a couple of garbage cans outside the church and set them on fire. What's wrong with them, according to Brother Charlie, is their appeal to the flesh; a sensuous slithering quality that apparently sends youngsters scrambling for the bedroom. In fact, he adds, of 1000 girls who became pregnant out of wedlock, 984 committed fornication while rock music was being played. (ROLLING STONE)

This kind of aphrodisiac doesn't come cheap, though.

PROMOTER SAYS BEATLES OFFERED $30 MILLION

Los Angeles—Hollywood promoter Bill Sargent said yesterday he had offered the Beatles $30 million to do a minimum of 20 minutes on closed-circuit television next July 5th anywhere they want in the world. Sargent, who is already promoting a March 9th "battle to the death" between a great white shark and a scuba diver to be televised worldwide from Samoa, said of the offer, "I haven't heard yes and I haven't heard no. It's a natural sellout."(ASSOCIATED PRESS)

Not that being a rock star is all sweetness and light.

IT'S ELVIS THE NIGHTSTALKER

Vail, Colorado—Elvis Presley has been spotted in seclusion in this jet-set ski resort, emerging from his luxury chalet at 3 a.m. Already carrying a potbelly, he looked even paunchier under the bulky snowsuit as he strolled to a fleet of snowmobiles awaiting him. Elvis's weird night life follows persistent reports that his chronic eye trouble is getting worse. The glare of the snow in daytime is believed to have forced the king of rock into his vampire-type world, only venturing out once the sun is down. Elvis broke out of his seclusion only once—to go on a $70,000 car-buying spree for friends. Even then, he donned a white woolen ski mask when he went into Kumpf Motors in Denver to authorize the purchases. (The *Star*)

At the outset, rock 'n' roll was a succès de scandale, an outrage to an older generation's aesthetic and sexual tastes. With the Beatles, it became fashionable to take the music seriously, just as with Dylan and groups like the Jefferson Airplane it became fashionable to value rock, not simply as an affront, but also as a calculated political gesture, protesting the rigidities of the prevailing culture. In both eras, rebellion (whether repudiated or admired) was the byword. Today, on the other hand, rock is first and foremost a member in good standing of the American entertainment industry, welcome in Las Vegas and Hollywood, on the screen and over the air, in homes and theaters, despite the glum warnings of Reverend Boykin. Rock gossip sells newspapers; rock concerts pack stadiums; rock records dominate the radio. No one much worries about artistic respectability anymore, and the question of political commitment has died a quiet death.

Which is not to say that rock has become irrelevant. Too many generations have grown up with the music: the ultimate product of an ephemeral culture, it has nevertheless dated our lives and supplied us with myths, slang, and heroes, becoming America's most visible export (with the possible exceptions of the army, Coca-Cola and Charles Bronson). I recently met a 27-year-old student who had been born and raised in Poland before moving to Germany in 1962; to him, rock represented a total release from the constraints of the old country. A music "above ideology," it promised fun, immediate gratification, instant glamour. For these reasons, he and his friends, while despising American imperialism, followed rock avidly: it seemed a bright moment in an otherwise bleak reality.

And the music lives on, even if its "golden age" has passed. Rock's lore and legends are now self-consciously preserved, created anew with calculated foresight. Few mysteries remain—and that may be why the music no longer seems quite as magical as it did 20 or even ten years ago. Once few people knew who Mick Jagger was, or how Elvis Presley recorded his first songs; today the answers are readily available.

In this sense, a history of rock cannot help but violate the music's essence. As quick kicks, rock should be as disposable as a paper plate. That it isn't may reflect the kind of ersatz historical tug that masks America's empty sense of tradition; then again, it may be that rock really does represent a lasting cultural statement, a popular expression that will survive its moment, either as artifact or artwork.

The following history chronicles that moment and its music. It cannot be complete: there is no mention of many glorious one-shot hits, from Phil Phillips's "Sea of Love" to Billy Swan's "I Can Help." It does, on the other hand, provide a relatively comprehensive overview. The reader will find here a story told from several perspectives, touching on performers, producers, locales, idioms, even the dubious business practices that rock has promoted. Above all, the reader will find a story told by fans as well as critics, by people who love this music and have grown up with it.

The essays in the book speak for themselves, but the discographies require some comment. They were designed, not as consumer guides—most of the records listed have long been out of print—but as historical references. No attempt has been made to be exhaustive; instead, a sample of the prime work of an artist, genre or locale is presented in chronological order. Each single and album is listed with its original label and catalog number, an indication of how well it did on the *Billboard* charts and its year of release. Thus the following entry:

Elvis Presley, "Don't Be Cruel" b/w "Hound Dog"
(RCA Victor 47-6604; c☆1, r☆1, ☆1, 1956)

indicates that Elvis's two-sided hit got to Number One on the rhythm and blues and country-western as well as pop charts in 1956.

Acknowledgment is due a number of colleagues who helped make this book possible. Madeline Pober heroically copy edited the manuscripts with discretion and professionalism; Monica Suder, our photo editor, located many rare pictures, and Susan Brenneman helped check the facts. Heading up the research department was the indefatigable Linda Ross, who caught many a subtle error and tracked down any number of performers, producers, and criminal records, all in a never-ending quest for strict accuracy.

Finally, a special word of thanks to Greil Marcus, who helped keep this project on course in his capacity as coordinating editor, San Francisco liaison, Berkeley bon vivant, and the once and future king of rock raconteurs. He has made numerous suggestions and criticisms incorporated into the text and structure of the book; he has offered editorial advice on many of the chapters; and he has given generously of his time in seeing the work through its various stages. Without his encouragement and assistance, this book would never have been completed.

Rock Begins

by Robert Palmer

Several dozen black dancers shuffled around the floor of the tiny rural church, stamping out a steady rocking beat on the floorboards and clapping their hands in complex cross-rhythms. A hoarse-voiced leader shouted out one-line phrases in a kind of singsong, the dancers answering with whiplash responses. When the song leader fell back on a bench, overcome by the shuddering rhythms, the heat, and the furious pace of the singing, a second leader took over, half-singing, half-gurgling in an unknown tongue.

> *O my Lord*
> *O my Lordy*
> *Well, well, well*
> *I've gotta rock*
> *You gotta rock*
> *Wah wah ho*
> *Wah wah wah ho*

In a corner of the church, two white folklorists, John Lomax and his son Alan, sat transfixed as their bulky portable recording rig transcribed the music onto an aluminum disc. The year was 1934, and the Lomaxes had stumbled upon a survival of one of the oldest varieties of Afro-American religious song, a genuine backcountry ring shout. But they had also stumbled upon the future. The rhythmic singing, the hard-driving beat, the bluesy melody, and the improvised, stream-of-consciousness words of this particular shout—eventually issued by the Library of Congress as "Run Old Jeremiah"—all anticipate key aspects of rock 'n' roll as it would emerge some 20 years later.

The Lomaxes were just beginning to record folk music on location in the rural South in 1934, but rock prototypes were already abundant. In Mississippi, the sedate spiritual singing of earlier generations was being replaced by a new style, emphasizing the deliberate rhythms of the archaic ring shouts. The style was called "rocking and reeling," and it probably originated in the maverick Sanctified or Holiness churches, where guitars, drums, and horns were as acceptable as the piano or the organ, and more easily afforded. Moreover, it was a style that was already beginning to influence secular music. The Graves brothers of Hattiesburg, Mississippi, who had recorded "rocking and reeling" spirituals for Paramount in 1929, made several blues records as the Mississippi Jook Band in 1936. Their "Barbecue Bust" and "Dangerous Woman" featured fully formed rock and roll guitar riffs and a stomping rock and roll beat.

It is possible, with the help of a little hindsight, to find rock roots at almost every stratum of American folk and popular music during the mid-Thirties. In Chicago, transplanted Southern bluesmen like Tampa Red and Big Bill Broonzy were taming irregular rural forms to the demands of urban accompaniment, often including horns, piano, bass and drums. In the Midwest, jump bands were keeping their fans dancing with hard-riffing instrumental blues, featuring gruff-toned tenor saxophone solos and a four-to-the-bar walking rhythm that was an urban descendant of the down-home sanctified stomp. In Nashville, two white hillbillies named Alton and Rabon Delmore were entertaining radio audiences with their hit, "Brown's Ferry Blues," a black influenced two-guitar dance tune as redolent of things to come as the music of the Mississippi Jook Band. In Texas and Oklahoma, large, white western swing bands like Bob Wills and his Texas Playboys and Milton Brown's Musical Brownies were mixing big band jazz, black blues, and white country music into a heady brew.

Rock 'n' roll was an inevitable outgrowth of the social and musical interactions between blacks and whites in the South and Southwest. Its roots are a complex tangle. Bedrock black church music influenced blues, rural blues influenced white folk song and the black popular music of the Northern ghettos, blues and black pop influenced jazz, and so on. But the single most important process was the influence of black music on white. Rock might not have developed out of a self-contained Afro-American tradition, but it certainly would not have developed had there been no Afro-Americans.

In a very real sense, rock was implicit in the music of the first Africans brought to North America. This transplanted African music wasn't exactly boogie-woogie or jazz, but it did have several characteristics which survive in American music today. It was participatory; often a song leader would be pitted against an answering chorus, or a solo instrument against an ensemble, in call-and-response fashion. It sometimes attained remarkable polyrhythmic complexity, and always had a kind of percussive directionality or rhythmic drive. Vocal quality tended to be hoarse or grainy by European standards, though there was also considerable use of falsetto. Melodies fell within a relatively narrow range and often incorporated flexible pitch treatment around certain "blue notes." There was some improvisation, but always within the limits of more or less traditional structures.

All these characteristics are evident in quite a few rock 'n' roll records. For example, in "What'd I Say," Ray Charles calls out a lead melody while a chorus responds, and riffing horns answer his piano figures. His band's rhythm section drives relentlessly, and superimposes fancy accent patterns over the basic beat. His voice has a hoarse, straining quality, with occasional leaps into falsetto. His melody is narrow in range and blueslike, and the improvisations which occur never threaten the continuity of the song's gospel-derived metric and harmonic structure.

One shouldn't conclude from these similarities that pure African music was somehow transformed into rock 'n' roll. Music

Clockwise from top: (1) John Lomax Jr. with Texas songster Mance Lipscomb; (2) Bob Wills, King of western swing; (3) The Delmore Brothers, circa 1950; (4) Bob Wills and His Texas Playboys, 1937. (1, Chet Flippo collection; Country Music Foundation Library; 3, John Edwards Memorial Foundation)

in Africa was always flexible, ready to accommodate new influences from the next village or from foreign cultures, and in America plantation owners and preachers tried to stamp it out entirely. Accordingly, it adapted. The traits that survived without much alteration tended to be of two kinds. Some were musical imponderables like vocal quality or rhythmic drive, aspects of style so basic to the culture they were rarely considered consciously and were therefore immune to conscious change. Others—blues scales, call-and-response forms—were close enough to some varieties of European folk music to be assimilated and perpetuated by whites.

The acculturation of black Americans to mainstream musical values proceeded more and more rapidly as the 20th century gathered momentum, but pockets of tradition remained. In 1940, when Charlie Christian and T-Bone Walker were already playing modern jazz and blues on electric guitars, a team of interviewers in the Georgia Sea Islands found elderly residents who still knew songs in African languages and knew how to make African drums. Elsewhere, the bedrock African culture persevered most tenaciously in the black church, just as in Africa itself religion, magic, and music had been closely linked in a kind of composite cultural focus. This is why the most African-sounding rock 'n' roll has always come from the church, from gospel-inspired blues shouters like Ray Charles or from former gospel singers like the Isley Brothers, whose "Shout" was an old-fashioned ring shout done up with band accompaniment.

But there is more to rock 'n' roll than this single primordial strain. The roots of "What'd I Say" and "Shout" are not necessarily identical to the roots of Chuck Berry's "Johnny B. Goode" or of Carl Perkins's "Blue Suede Shoes." It would take at least one book, if not a library, to trace these various kinds of rock 'n' roll back through their myriad sources. Here we can only indicate some of the most important contributors and trace a few of the most prominent developmental processes.

The music brought to America by European settlers determined most of the forms in which both old and new song materials would be set. Song stanzas of four and eight bars were a heritage of European epic poetry and narrative ballads; there are examples of such things in some traditional African music, but only as one formal scheme among many. The narrative ballad itself, with its objective performer who comments on but does not become involved in the action, was a European product very foreign to the mainstream of black tradition. A ballad vogue among blacks during the late 19th century did produce memorable songs such as "Stagger Lee" and "Frankie and Johnny," several of which were revived by early rockers. But the 1880s and 1890s were the years when white music's influence on blacks was at its strongest.

In isolated rural areas, particularly Appalachia and the Ozarks, traditional English, Scotch, and Irish dance music survived, along with folk fiddling. But even there the African banjo became as popular as the fiddle. The guitar, which had been derived by the Spanish and Portuguese from the African Moors, came later. During the late 19th and early 20th centuries, white country musicians developed a tradition of virtuosity on all these instruments. Their repertoires retained many old-time folk ballads, dance tunes, and hymns, but black-influenced minstrel tunes, blueslike ballads, and camp meeting songs were also popular.

Afro-Americans had developed their own distinctive and diverse body of folk music by 1900, alongside the relatively pure African strains which survived in some church music and in the work songs sung by gang laborers. The black creations which whites knew best were minstrel songs—lively, often humorous tunes which tended to resemble Anglo-American jigs and reels. Many minstrel songs were composed by whites like Dan Emmett (composer of "Dixie") and Thomas D. Rice ("Jump Jim Crow"), but all of them were inspired ultimately by the black plantation orchestras which had regaled visitors in the antebellum South. Both the black groups and their white imitators consisted of banjos, fiddles (an instrument with numerous West African precedents), and various percussion instruments, notably tambourines, triangles, and bone clappers. The earliest plantation orchestras had probably played African dance music like that performed by the lute- and fiddle-playing *griots* of the African savanna today; but by the time we heard of them, they had learned enough European dance tunes to satisfy their white patrons, and the fiddlers were paying some attention to European musical standards. The white minstrels, who

copied black playing styles and tunes as closely as they could, became the rage of America and Europe during the years just before the Civil War. For the first time, an essentially black music had found favor with a large white audience, albeit in diluted form. Oddly enough, many popular minstrel songs were absorbed back into black tradition following the war. They turned up in the repertoires of black banjo- and guitar-playing minstrels, or songsters, well into the 20th century.

During the first decades of the century a new kind of black secular song emerged. The songs were originally known as "one-verse songs" because they repeated a single line several times. Gradually an *aab* stanza form replaced the older *aaa* and the songs began to be called blues. They may have represented an attempt by rural blacks to accommodate the demands of guitar accompaniment within the free-flowing strains of their field cries and work songs. In any case, the blues spread rapidly, first through the tent show performances of vaudeville singers like Gertrude "Ma" Rainey, then through the polished, blues-based compositions of W. C. Handy, and finally, after 1926, through recordings by authentic rural bluesman like Blind Lemon Jefferson. Along with blues recordings, which were popular among Northern blacks as well as in the South, came records of singing black preachers and of holy dance music from the Sanctified churches.

The rise of the recording industry in the Twenties accelerated musical syntheses. For the first time, white guitar players from Kentucky were able to listen carefully to the music of black bluesmen from Texas, and rural medicine-show entertainers could hear the latest cabaret hits from New York. Early recordings documented musical changes rather than determining them, but by the mid-Thirties records were the primary source of inspiration for many musicians.

In white country music, the largely traditional repertoires of performers like Uncle Dave Macon became outmoded as younger musicians popularized their own hybrid material. Among the most influential of these were Jimmie Rodgers, the "singing brakeman" from Meridian, Mississippi, and the Alabama-born Delmore Brothers; both acts recorded black-influenced blues and blueslike dance tunes. The Monroe Brothers, Bill and Charlie, popularized a more Anglo-American brand of country music. In a sense they helped preserve white folk traditions by dressing them up with a new vocal intensity and unprecedented instrumental flash. But even mandolinist Bill Monroe, who went on to become the "father of bluegrass," injected a great deal of blues feeling into his playing. Early in his career he had been impressed by a black guitarist and fiddler named Arnold Schultz, who reportedly exercised a decisive influence on Ike Everly and Merle Travis as well. In the West, western swing bands took the country music of the Monroe Brothers, applied it to black-oriented repertoires of musicians like the Delmores and Jimmie Rodgers, and added yet another element—horns

and drums—from another black musical source, jazz.

Jazz itself was growing in several different directions, but in the Southwest it was heavily indebted to vocal blues. Bands like Count Basie's ("the band that plays the blues") concentrated on the 12-bar blues form almost exclusively, and often played "head" arrangements: blues riffs developed by the musicians on the spur of the moment. Rhythmically, Basie and the other Southwestern bands played a danceable, even, four-to-the-bar pulse which gradually replaced the jerky 2-4 associated with Dixieland. The bluesiness, the riffing horns, the tough tenor saxophone solos, and the driving rhythm of these groups had a profound impact on western swing—which led in turn to country boogie and rockabilly—and on black popular music—which led to rhythm and blues and rock 'n' roll.

As rural bluesmen moved to urban centers, their music lost much of its delicacy and lilt. Rhythms became heavier, more insistent, and faster, in keeping with the pace of city life. The first indications of this shift came from Memphis as early as the Twenties. There, several two-guitar teams worked out a characteristic differentiation of parts in which one played lead lines while the other provided bass notes and chords. (Earlier country-blues guitar duets had tended toward a more intricate, more democratic counterpoint.) Memphis blues rhythms were already harder and steadier than those of the surrounding countryside.

Big Bill Broonzy, a Mississippian who relocated in Chicago, took these ideas a step further by working with washtub and string bassists and with the percussive washboard of Washboard Sam. During the Thirties Broonzy and his Chicago friends, among them Sam and Tampa Red, became America's most popular blues performers. Harmonically they were increasingly influenced by jazz, while rhythmically they favored the easy, relaxed swing of the Southwestern bands. When horns, drums, and piano were added to their accompaniments, these ties to jazz became even more apparent.

Meanwhile, Southwestern blues and jazz musicians were experimenting with a revolutionary new instrument, the electric guitar. Eddie Durham seems to have recorded the first solos on the amplified instrument in 1938 with the Kansas City Five and Six, groups recruited from the Basie band. In 1939, Charlie Christian, an Oklahoman, recorded on electric guitar with Benny Goodman. His virtuoso, hornlike single-string lines and the deep, bluesy character of his playing set standards for jazz guitar playing which have yet to be superseded. But Christian was a former country bluesman. As a youngster he performed with an older guitarist, Aaron "T-Bone" Walker, who had recorded country blues (as Oak Cliff T-Bone) as early as 1929.

If Christian invented modern jazz guitar—and helped to invent modern jazz, for his work was as progressive as Charlie Parker's before the two Southwesterners met—it was T-Bone Walker who invented modern blues, setting the style which

14

almost all subsequent blues and rock lead guitarists would follow, from B.B. King through Eric Clapton. The jazzy flash of Walker's work was not in itself revolutionary. While the Memphis bluesmen were developing early lead guitar styles within a relatively simple framework, Eddie Lang and Lonnie Johnson were working as jazz soloists, playing single-note lines on their acoustic guitars on recordings by Bix Beiderbecke, Duke Ellington, and other prominent figures. Their techniques were exemplary, and necessarily so, for they had to fill with their virtuosity the spaces left by their instrument's rapidly decaying notes and relatively thin sound. Christian continued their style of rapid runs. But it took Walker to really exploit electricity. By using his amplifier's volume control to sustain pitches, and combining this technique with the string-bending and finger vibrato practiced by traditional bluesmen, Walker in effect invented a new instrument. He was able to reproduce both the linear urgency of jazz saxophonists and the convoluted cry of blues and gospel singers. In addition, he developed a chordal style on fast numbers, a pumping guitar shuffle which led eventually to the archetypal rock 'n' roll guitar style of Chuck Berry.

Jazz, which was a popular music with mass appeal throughout the Thirties, continued to produce occasional pop hits during the Forties. But the slicker, more sophisticated black bands did not appeal to a significant number of urban Afro-Americans, most of whom were either born in the country or only a generation removed from it, and a raunchier, more down-home jazz style emerged to cater to their tastes, a kind of rhythm-and-jazz. Lionel Hampton, a vibraharpist who had worked with Benny Goodman, produced the definitive record in the new genre in 1942. It was "Flying Home," and it became a national hit, due largely to the grainy sound and shrieking intensity of its concluding saxophone solo. The saxophonist, Texan Illinois Jacquet, blew even harder than Louis Jordan, an Arkansan whose Tympany Five was one of the more popular black recording groups of the Forties. After the success of "Flying Home," Jordan began to feature his own gritty saxophone solos more prominently, and his cheerful novelty records grew more and more bluesy. Soon saxophone-dominated band blues, usually with Walker-style guitar leads and shouted vocals like those of Southwesterners Jimmy Rushing and Joe Turner, became a dominant strain in black popular music. The music's most popular practitioners included Roy Milton and Roy Brown, whose cavernous voice and crying style was later reflected in the work of Bobby "Blue" Bland and Wynonie Harris.

Even black vocal harmony groups were affected by the emergence of band blues. Many of these groups had roots in the quartet singing which had been an important part of black religious music since the Twenties, but rather than base their styles on those of the more abandoned sanctified singers, they usually emulated the smooth pop harmonies of the Ink Spots. During the mid-Forties, however, the Spots's popularity waned, and some of the vocal groups adopted a harder approach which was much closer to Southern blues and gospel.

In some cases this was the result of suggestions by white record producers. Independently operated record companies like Savoy, Aladdin, Atlantic, Modern, Imperial, and King recorded a majority of the black music popular after World War II (for the most part, the "majors," like Columbia and Victor, either concentrated on middle-of-the-road pop or continued to issue "race" discs by prewar favorites). The independents were successful in part because they were run by men who knew black music. Many of the producers were collectors of blues, jazz, and gospel records, and even when they were working with Northern musicians and singers they attempted to give their records a Southern flavor.

Around 1950, both rhythm and blues and country and western began to go boogie mad. The term "boogie" has obscure origins, but its first musical application had to do with a variety of two-fisted piano blues which developed in the North from sources in Southern logging- and turpentine-camp piano playing. As practiced by Meade Lux Lewis, Albert Ammons, and other boogie-woogie masters in Chicago and New York, it was a deliberate, steady rocking music, with the pianist's right hand plunking out treble runs and rhythmic arpeggios while his left pumped a steady four-to-the-bar bass.

White and black boogie were somewhat different, but both were heavily rhythmic band music, designed for dancing. In 1950 Louis Jordan had a Number One rhythm and blues hit with his "Blue Light Boogie," and Tennessee Ernie Ford's "Shotgun Boogie" was a C&W Number One. But these were records with melodic hooks and novelty appeal; they represented little more than the tip of a boogie iceberg. Virtually every black blues performer had his own variant, usually with a title like "Dr. Ross Boogie" or, perhaps, "T-Bone Shuffle." (Shuffles were more relaxed. Compared to hardcore Southern boogie they were positively lilting.) White performers were more creative when it came to naming their tunes. Oklahoma's Jack Guthrie had the "Okie Boogie," the stomping pianist Moon Mullican (from Texas) did the "Cherokee Boogie," and the Delmore Brothers carried on with their "Pan American Boogie" (the subject was a train that ran "from Cincinnati all the way to New Orleans") and "Mobile Boogie"; the influential C&W guitarist Merle Travis did "Blue Smoke" in a similar vein. Those numbers were all very black influenced. They had driving rhythms, gospelish piano, bluesy guitar, and melodies and stanza forms derived from gospel and blues.

Memphis produced the rawest black boogie. This postwar Memphis rhythm and blues usually featured a heavily amplified harmonica, relatively crude, distorted guitar, and thud-

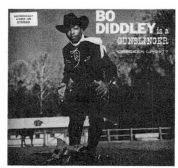

ding, animalistic drumming. (Memphis musician Jim Dickinson fondly refers to it as "gorilla music.") The prototype for the bands working in this rural but very electric idiom was Sonny Boy Williamson's King Biscuit Entertainers, whose broadcasts over a Helena, Arkansas, radio station were sponsored by the King Biscuit Company. Howlin' Wolf, who had a radio show of his own in West Memphis at the beginning of the Fifties, assembled a group that emulated the Biscuit Boys' style. The Beale Streeters, a band which featured Bobby "Blue" Bland, Johnny Ace, Junior Parker and, sometimes, B.B. King, made its early records in an only slightly more refined idiom; it was only later that Bland, Ace and Parker made their reputations as urbane R&B balladeers.

Ike Turner, a young Mississippian who was acting as a talent scout for the Modern and RPM labels of Los Angeles, produced the first recordings by Wolf and the Beale Streeters. Around the same time in 1951, he produced a single which has often been cited as the first rock 'n' roll record. It was "Rocket '88'" by Jackie Brenston—actually it was by Turner's band, with Brenston, its saxophonist, singing lead—and it became a Number One R&B hit that year. It wasn't really a revolutionary record. Everything about it suggested the influence of local boogie bands, with the exception of Brenston's Wynonie Harris-like vocal. But the lengthy saxophone solo on "Rocket" was wilder than anything Louis Jordan or even Illinois Jacquet had put on record. The player, presumably Brenston, growled, honked, and screamed in a style which later became identified with rock 'n' roll. And the song's words seized on a series of sexual/automotive metaphors, an idea which was at least as old as Robert Johnson's 1936 "Terraplane Blues" but which was destined to flower fully in the classic car songs of Chuck Berry.

"Rocket '88'" was an unusually accurate indicator of the course rock 'n' roll would take, but it was not the only indicator. Rufus Thomas, a Memphis disc jockey with a medicine show background, cut several prophetic singles. His "Ain't Gonna Be Your Dog" included a unison horn line which would become a rock and roll cliché, and although it was basically a blues it had a singsong melody and a clever refrain that should have made it a national hit. Another Thomas opus from the early Fifties, "Bear Cat," took Willie Mae Thornton's hit "Hound Dog" and made it into a rock 'n' roll number, several years before Elvis Presley did much the same thing. But Sam Phillips, who recorded both Thomas and Presley for his Sun label, only gradually developed a nationwide distribution network which could adequately disseminate his product.

A music that was recognizably rock 'n' roll had begun in the Memphis area during the early Fifties; "Rocket '88'" was simply the record that broke through. In 1951, it was a ringer on the charts: the year's other R&B hits were either vocal group novelties, urban band blues, or "crying blues" in the gospel-tinged style pioneered by Roy Brown.

Opposite, from top: (1) The Delta Rhythm Boys; (2) The Johnny Otis Band, Newark, New Jersey, 1947; (3) Hank Williams. Above, l to r: (1) John Doe, Ira Louvin of the Louvin Brothers, John Doe II, Chet Atkins, Merle Travis, Charlie Louvin; (2) Little Junior Parker; (3) Etta James; (4) LaVern Baker, Nat "King" Cole, Della Reese and Erskin Hawkins, the mid-Fifties. Overleaf: (8) Bill Haley and his Comets. (1 & 6, Michael Ochs Archives; 2 & 8, Popsie/N.Y.; 3, Gleason collection; 4, John Edwards Memorial Foundation; 5, Peacock Records; 7, John Goddard collection)

But America's musical tastes were changing across the board. Guitarist Les Paul, who had been among the first to use the electric instrument, was beginning to revolutionize pop music with his multitracked guitar overdubs. His wife, Mary Ford, sang sweetly enough, but Paul had been a friend of Charlie Christian's and his playing was blues and jazz oriented. Johnnie Ray's "Cry," a record so emotionally bluesy it virtually parodied itself, was a pop and R&B hit in 1951. But by this time, urban R&B had begun to make way for the Southern sound. The 1952 R&B hits included Eddie Boyd's "Five Long Years" and Little Walter's "Juke," both Mississippi delta blues played in the Memphis boogie style by musicians who had only recently moved to Chicago. The Caribbean-tinged rhythms of New Orleans were featured on two more R&B hits, Fats Domino's "Goin' Home" and Lloyd Price's "Lawdy Miss Clawdy" (with Domino on piano). B.B. King, the Beale Street Blues Boy, combined Southern intensity with T-Bone Walker's guitar style on his "3 O'Clock Blues" (which according to sideman Willie Mitchell was recorded in a Memphis living room) and "You Know I Love You." Many of the hits produced in the North, among them records by Ruth Brown and Willie Mabon, emulated Southern music or had themes and imagery rooted in the south. Billy Ward and the Dominoes' hits resembled secularized gospel shouts.

By 1954, the music on the R&B charts was even rawer. Guitar Slim's "The Things That I Used to Do" combined superamplified lead guitar with a vocal so country many urban listeners probably had trouble understanding the diction. The Midnighters' "Work with Me Annie" was a thinly disguised sexual metaphor; Etta James's similar "Roll with Me Henry" roared along in a raucous sanctified vein. Both records had followups. James's "Hey Henry" resembled its predecessor, while the Midnighters' "Annie Had a Baby" left no doubt as to what the "working" in their earlier hit had been about. These records were widely attacked by white ministers and disc jockeys. Abandoned singing and suggestive lyrics were nothing new to black listeners, but black music was beginning to reach a sizable audience of white adolescents.

In 1954, the Crew-Cuts' version of the Chords' R&B hit "Sh-Boom" was the most successful of many white "covers" of black material. A year later, Bill Haley and his Comets made Number One on the pop charts with "Rock around the Clock," which was introduced to many Americans through the film *The Blackboard Jungle.* This was the first original rock 'n' roll hit by a white artist, although the music and overall style of the group were a somewhat crude copy of the Southern-influenced New York R&B sound exemplified by Joe Turner's "Shake, Rattle and Roll" (which Haley covered). That same year, Elvis Presley scored his first C&W Number One with "I Forgot to Remember to Forget" b/w the black-influenced "Mystery Train" on Sun, while Chuck Berry (with his classic automotive epic "Maybellene") and Fats Domino both had Number One R&B hits. By 1956, Presley, Berry and Domino, along with newcomer Little Richard, had crossed over to the pop charts. The rock 'n' roll era had begun.

Each of these early rock 'n' rollers was firmly rooted in the music of earlier years. The white rockabilly stars groomed by Sun Records' owner Sam Phillips were raised on white country music, country and western, and hillbilly boogie. It was Phillips who urged them to listen to black bluesmen and to affect black singing styles, though Presley at least had already been listening to bluesmen like Arthur Crudup. Carl Perkins's classic "Blue Suede Shoes" and his other work was closer to the mainstream of country and western music, though his "Matchbox" was a 12-bar blues with lyrics which had been popularized by Blind Lemon Jefferson. Jerry Lee Lewis's piano style was not very different from that of Moon Mullican, but Mullican's stomping boogie rhythms had never quite locked into step with his accompanists, while the Sun rhythm section's Memphis boogie perfectly complemented Jerry Lee.

Chuck Berry's guitar work was redolent of the Delmore Brothers and of the fast shuffle playing of T-Bone Walker; it was his unique talent as a lyricist which made him one of the most original of the early rock 'n' rollers. Fats Domino had been making R&B records since 1949 and he did little to change his style. It was his astute producer and bandleader, Dave Bartholomew, who added vocal groups, guitar solos, and other effects, and who wrote many of the songs which Domino made into rock 'n' roll hits. Little Richard, who was backed by Bartholomew's band on many of his early recordings, simply sang novelty blues with the no-holds-barred enthusiasm of a particularly unabashed sanctified vocalist. Bo Diddley, the most primitive of the early black rock 'n' rollers, built his hits on blues and folk materials from backcountry Mississippi and on the Latinlike "hambone" beat.

Without Presley, Berry, and the rest, rock 'n' roll might have turned out differently. But throughout musical history there have been innovators who failed to leave an imprint on succeeding generations, or who simply passed on their styles to a select few. Rock 'n' roll was able to flourish and, eventually, to become the dominant popular music of the Western world precisely because it was firmly rooted in, and sustained by, the fertile soil of the South and Southwest.

Discography

Number One Hits, 1950 to "Don't Be Cruel"

1950

Rhythm and Blues

Ivory Joe Hunter, "I Almost Lost My Mind" **Johnny Otis**, "Double Crossing Blues" **Johnny Otis**, "Mistrustin' Blues" **Joe Liggins**, "Pink Champagne" **Roy Brown**, "Hard Luck Blues" **Louis Jordan**, "Blue Light Boogie" **Lowell Fulson**, "Blue Shadows" **Joe Morris**, "Anytime, Anyplace, Anywhere" **Percy Mayfield**, "Please Send Me Someone to Love" **Ruth Brown**, "Teardrops from My Eyes" **Amos Milburn**, "Bad, Bad Whiskey"

Pop

Andrews Sisters, "I Can Dream, Can't I?" **Ames Brothers**, "Rag Mop" **Red Foley**, "Chattanoogie Shoe Shine Boy" **Teresa Brewer**, "Music! Music! Music!" **Eileen Barton**, "If I Knew You Were Comin' I'd've Baked a Cake" **Anton Karas**, "The Third Man Theme" **Nat "King" Cole**, "Mona Lisa" **Gordon Jenkin and the Weavers**, "Goodnight Irene" **Sammy Kaye**, "Harbor Lights" **Phil Harris**, "The Thing" **Patti Page**, "The Tennessee Waltz"

Country and Western

Red Foley, "Chattanoogie Shoe Shine Boy" **Moon Mullican**, "I'll Sail My Ship Alone" **Hank Williams**, "Long Gone Lonesome Blues" **Red Foley**, "Birmingham Bounce" **Hank Williams**, "Why Don't You Love Me" **Hank Snow**, "I'm Movin' On" **Ernest Tubb and Red Foley**, "Goodnight, Irene" **Hank Snow**, "Golden Rocket" **Tennessee Ernie Ford**, "Shotgun Boogie"

1951

Rhythm and Blues

Charles Brown, "Black Night" **Jackie Brenston**, "Rocket 88" **Dominoes**, "Sixty Minute Man" **Dominoes**, "Don't You Know I Love You" **Five Keys**, "Glory of Love" **Clovers**, "Fool, Fool, Fool" **Tab Smith**, "Because of You" **"Peppermint" Harris**, "I Got Loaded" **Earl Bostic**, "Flamingo"

Pop

Perry Como, "If" **Mario Lanza**, "Be My Love" **Les Paul and Mary Ford**, "How High the Moon" **Nat "King" Cole**, "Too Young" **Rosemary Clooney**, "Come On-a My House" **Tony Bennett**, "Because of You" **Tony Bennett**, "Cold, Cold Heart" **Eddy Howard**, "Sin" **Johnnie Ray**, "Cry"

Country and Western

Eddy Arnold, "There's Been a Change in Me" **Hank Snow**, "Rhumba Boogie" **Eddy Arnold**, "Kentucky Waltz" **Lefty Frizzell**, "I Want to Be with You Always" **Eddy Arnold**, "I Want to Play House with You" **Lefty Frizzell**, "Always Late" **Pee Wee King**, "Slow Poke" **Carl Smith**, "Let Old Mother Nature Have Her Way"

1952

Rhythm and Blues

Johnnie Ray, "Cry" **B.B. King**, "3 O'Clock Blues" **Roscoe Gordon**, "Booted" **Jimmy Forest**, "Night Train" **Ruth Brown**, "5-10-15 Hours" **Fats Domino**, "Goin' Home" **Dominoes**, "Have Mercy Baby" **Lloyd Price**, "Lawdy Miss Clawdy" **Clovers**, "Ting-a-Ling" **Johnny Ace**, "My Song" **B.B. King**, "You Know I Love You" **Little Walter**, "Juke" **Eddie Boyd**, "Five Long Years" **Willie Mabon**, "I Don't Know"

Pop

Kay Starr, "Wheel of Fortune" **Leroy Anderson**, "Blue Tango" **Al Martino**, "Here in My Heart" **Percy Faith**, "Delicado" **Vera Lynn**, "Auf Wiederseh'n Sweetheart" **Jo Stafford**, "You Belong to Me" **Patti Page**, "I Went to Your Wedding" **Johnny Standley**, "It's in the Book" **Joni James**, "Why Don't You Believe Me" **Jimmy Boyd**, "I Saw Mommy Kissing Santa Claus"

Country and Western

Carl Smith, "Don't Just Stand There" **Eddy Arnold**, "Easy on the Eyes" **Hank Thompson**, "Wild Side of Life" **Kitty Wells**, "It Wasn't God Who Made Honky Tonk Angels" **Hank Williams**, "Jambalaya" **Webb Pierce**, "Back Street Affair" **Red Foley**, "Midnight" **Hank Williams**, "I'll Never Get out of This World Alive"

1953

Rhythm and Blues

"5" Royales, "Baby, Don't Do It" **Ruth Brown**, "(Mama) He Treats Your Daughter Mean" **Willie Mae Thornton**, "Hound Dog" **Willie Mabon**, "I'm Mad" **"5" Royales**, "Help Me Somebody" **Johnny Ace**, "The Clock" **Orioles**, "Crying in the Chapel" **Faye Adams**, "Shake a Hand" **Clyde McPhatter and the Drifters**, "Money Honey"

Pop

Perry Como, "Don't Let the Stars Get in Your Eyes" **Teresa Brewer**, "Till I Waltz Again with You" **Patti Page**, "The Doggie in the Window" **Percy Faith**, "Song from Moulin Rouge" **Eddie Fisher**, "I'm Walking Behind You" **Les Paul and Mary Ford**, "Vaya Con Dios" **Stan Freberg**, "St. George and the Dragonet" **Tony Bennett**, "Rags to Riches" **Eddie Fisher**, "Oh! My Pa-Pa"

Country and Western

Eddy Arnold, "Eddy's Song" **Hank Williams**, "Kaw-Liga" **Jim Reeves**, "Mexican Joe" **Hank Williams**, "Take These Chains from My Heart" **Webb Pierce**, "It's Been So Long" **Carl Smith**, "Hey, Joe" **Jean Shepard and Ferlin Husky**, "Dear John Letter" **Davis Sisters**, "I Forgot More than You'll Ever Know" **Webb Pierce**, "There Stands the Glass"

1954

Rhythm and Blues

Faye Adams, "I'll Be True" **Guitar Slim**, "The Things That I Used to Do" **Roy Hamilton**, "You'll Never Walk Alone" **Midnighters**, "Work with Me Annie" **Clyde McPhatter and the Drifters**, "Honey Love" **Ruth Brown**, "Oh What a Dream" **Midnighters**, "Annie Had a Baby" **Faye Adams**, "Hurts Me to My Heart" **Ruth Brown**, "Mambo Baby" **Charms**, "Hearts of Stone"

Pop

Doris Day, "Secret Love" **Jo Stafford**, "Make Love to Me!" **Perry Como**, "Wanted" **Kitty Kallen**, "Little Things Mean a Lot" **Crew-Cuts**, "Sh-Boom" **Rosemary Clooney**, "Hey There" **Rosemary Clooney**, "This Ole House" **Eddie Fisher**, "I Need You Now" **Chordettes**, "Mr. Sandman"

Country and Western

Webb Pierce, "Slowly" **Hank Snow**, "I Don't Hurt Anymore" **Webb Pierce**, "More and More" **Carl Smith**, "Loose Talk"

1955

Rhythm and Blues

Penguins, "Earth Angel" **Johnny Ace**, "Pledging My Love" **Little Walter**, "My Babe" **Roy Hamilton**, "Unchained Melody" **Fats Domino**, "Ain't It a Shame" **Chuck Berry**, "Maybellene" **Platters**, "Only You" **Jay McShann**, "Hands Off" **Platters**, "The Great Pretender"

Pop

Joan Weber, "Let Me Go Lover" **Fontane Sisters**, "Hearts of Stone" **McGuire Sisters**, "Sincerely" **Bill Hayes**, "The Ballad of Davy Crockett" **Perez Prado**, "Cherry Pink and Apple Blossom White" **Bill Haley and His Comets**, "Rock around the Clock" **Mitch Miller**, "The Yellow Rose of Texas" **Four Aces**, "Love Is a Many Splendored Thing" **Roger Williams**, "Autumn Leaves" **Tennessee Ernie Ford**, "Sixteen Tons" **Dean Martin**, "Memories Are Made of This"

Country and Western

Webb Pierce, "In the Jailhouse Now" **Webb Pierce**, "I Don't Care" **Eddy Arnold**, "The Cattle Call" **Elvis Presley**, "I Forgot to Remember to Forget" b/w "Mystery Train" **Webb Pierce**, "Love, Love, Love" **Tennessee Ernie Ford**, "Sixteen Tons" **Red Sovine and Webb Pierce**, "Why, Baby, Why?"

1956

Rhythm and Blues

Frankie Lymon and the Teenagers, "Why Do Fools Fall in Love" **Little Richard**, "Long Tall Sally" **Fats Domino**, "I'm in Love Again" **Little Willie John**, "Fever" **Little Richard**, "Rip It Up" **Bill Doggett**, "Honky Tonk" **Elvis Presley**, "Don't Be Cruel"

Pop

Platters, "The Great Pretender" **Platters**, "My Prayer" **Kay Starr**, "Rock and Roll Waltz" **Les Baxter**, "The Poor People of Paris" **Elvis Presley**, "Heartbreak Hotel" **Gogi Grant**, "The Wayward Wind" **Pat Boone**, "I Almost Lost My Mind" **Elvis Presley**, "Don't Be Cruel"

Country and Western

Elvis Presley, "Heartbreak Hotel" **Elvis Presley**, "I Want You, I Need You, I Love You" **Ray Price**, "Crazy Arms" **Elvis Presley**, "Don't Be Cruel"

(Compiled from Joel Whitburn's *Record Research*, based on *Billboard* charts.)

Thanks a million —
Two, in fact!
Vaya Con Dios
'n' Mary

Rhythm and Gospel
by Barry Hansen

R ock and roll has always been a hybrid music, and before 1950, the most important hybrids in pop were interracial. Black music was influenced by white sounds (the Ink Spots, Ravens and Orioles with their sentimental ballads) and white music was intertwined with black (Bob Wills, Hank Williams and two generations of the honky-tonk blues). Rhythm and gospel, the first great hybridization of the Fifties, happened entirely within black music. Though this hybrid produced a clutch of hits in the R&B market in the early Fifties, only the most adventurous white fans felt its impact at the time; the rest had to wait for the coming of soul music in the Sixties to feel the rush of rock and roll sung gospel-style.

"Rhythm and gospel" was never so called in its day: the word "gospel" was not something one talked about in the context of such salacious songs as "Honey Love" or "Work with Me Annie." Yet these records, and others by groups like the Dominoes and the Drifters, first introduced the electrifying singing style of postwar black gospel to the world of secular music, paving the way for such soul singers of the Sixties as James Brown, Otis Redding and Wilson Pickett.

The combination of gospel singing with the risqué lyrics and all-around hard playing that marked the R&B of the Fifties was not taken lightly either inside or outside the R&B community. When Sam Cooke launched his pop career in 1957, after six brilliant years of singing pure gospel with the Soul Stirrers, the resulting schism among Cooke's fans was deeper and longer lasting than the divisions among Bob Dylan's partisans after he went electric in 1965. On the other hand, the introduction of gospel vocal style to the R&B vocal-group idiom in the early Fifties transfixed nearly everyone who heard it.

At the time gospel music was dominated by vocal groups, which were always called "quartets" regardless of the number of singers. Such quartets as the Pilgrim Travelers, the Dixie Hummingbirds and the Soul Stirrers were quick to adapt the intense and melismatic style of singing popularized in the late Forties by Mahalia Jackson and other gospel soloists including Alex Bradford and Brother Joe May. Quartets were also very big in R&B during the late Forties, thanks to the Ink Spots and their avian followers: the Robins, the Orioles and Ravens. All of these groups sang love songs sweetly and lightly, and would never have been confused with such free-shouting messengers of God as the Soul Stirrers.

Enter Billy Ward. Billy Ward wasn't much of a singer, but he was a good musician and a better talent manager. In 1950, Ward organized a vocal group called the Dominoes and had the perspicacity to engage as its lead singer 17-year-old Clyde McPhatter, who had been brought up in the church and knew only one way to sing, the gospel way.

Clyde sang lead on one side of the group's first record, "Do Something for Me." Musically, it's a gospel song, the slow tempo allowing for numerous melismas; lyrically, on the other hand, it's a proposition. McPhatter was opening a courtship with magical incantations previously reserved for the good Lord. (The Dominoes weren't entirely given over to the rhythm-gospel idea; the group's biggest hit, later in 1951, featured Ravens-style bass singer Bill Brown on the ribald "Sixty Minute Man," which was straight R&B.)

In 1952, however, the Dominoes produced the definitive fast rhythm and gospel record, "Have Mercy Baby," one of the best-selling R&B discs of that year. The title summarizes the whole rhythm and gospel idea: "Baby" is interchangeable with "Lord." In fact, the entire lyric could be transformed back into a gospel prayer with very little effort.

Clyde and the other singers trade two-bar phrases throughout the record, echoing the familiar call-and-response device of gospel quartets. Melodically and harmonically, though, it's a straight 12-bar blues—a form that gospel singers had always avoided like the plague.

In the first chorus, McPhatter sticks close to the simple melody. From there on he improvises freely, much as a gospel singer might. Often he strings out a phrase so that it overlaps the background singers' response. The melismas are short (due to the fast tempo), but very abundant and often spectacular. While Clyde shouts his gospel-funk, the backup band takes special care of the rhythm. The tenor sax solo that was de rigueur in those days is here stretched out for two choruses, while screams and some most sensual *yeah*s from the vocalists help establish "Have Mercy" as a disco classic of its time. For the coup de grace, Clyde breaks down in tears during the fadeout.

Indeed, McPhatter wept all the way through his next great record with the Dominoes, "The Bells," cut in late 1952. Here is the absolute apotheosis of sob rock: Clyde's melismas alternate with wrenching wails, while an R&B tenor sax honks rather unsteadily alongside a gospel organ; the accompanying harmonies steer an extremely curious middle course between gospel and blues changes.

By this time, the group was being billed on disc labels as "Billy Ward and his Dominoes." Considering Ward's lack of vocal contribution, McPhatter could hardly be blamed for feeling the wrong man's name was being billed above that of the group, so in 1953, he took a little gamble. He left the security of the now prestigious Dominoes (where his place was taken by Jackie Wilson) to join a group just being organized. The new group was to be called the Drifters because (according to an early press release) "the members had done a lot of drifting from one group to another." This might not have seemed like the most promising premise for a new group, but there was a recording contract waiting for the Drifters at Atlantic Records, which had already established itself as one of the steadiest ports in the R&B storm thanks to Joe Turner, Ruth Brown and a group called the Clovers, whose early records—"Don't You

Clyde McPhatter in 1953 (Popsie/N.Y.)

Clockwise from top: (1) Billy Ward, at the piano, with his Dominoes, auditioning at King Records in 1950; (2) Hank Ballard and the Midnighters onstage circa 1957; (3) The Ravens; (4) Hank Ballard and the Midnighters, 1955; (5) The Clovers. Center left: (6) The "5" Royales; center right: (7) The Dixie Hummingbirds. (1, Popsie/N.Y.; 2 & 4, John Goddard collection; 3 & 5, Ralph J. Gleason collection; 6, Michael Ochs collection; 7, Peacock Records)

Know I Love You," and "Fool, Fool, Fool"—nearly matched the Dominoes' success in synthesizing rhythm and blues with gospel.

Not only that, but Atlantic offered Clyde the instant glory of his own name on the label along with the group's. Clyde was destined to make only six records with the Drifters before Uncle Sam got him in 1954, but every one of the first four was a smash. First came "Money Honey," later a hit for Elvis. Then, after the torrid "Such a Night" came the outrageous "Honey Love," whose gasps, grunts and sighs made radio executives even more uptight than would the drug lyrics of 1967. For hit number four, the Drifters mended fences with a strutting version of "White Christmas."

By the time McPhatter left the army in 1956, the barriers between R&B and pop music were breaking down; he went solo (one of the first group members to do so) and enjoyed substantial if intermittent success for the next decade, with "A Lover's Question" (1958) and "Lover Please" (1962) as highlights. His style was prettier and less passionate than it had been, however, and next to an Otis Redding (who might have had a much rougher road to the top without McPhatter), McPhatter sounded dated and tame. He died, washed up at 38, on June 13th, 1972. (The Drifters, of course, went on to great success in the early Sixties; but the group's composition—and style—had radically changed by then.)

The Drifters and Dominoes were among the very few groups with the vocal equipment, skill and desire to sing in the true rhythm-gospel style; most preferred the much easier task of imitating the Ink Spots. Several other groups from the early Fifties, however, did achieve popularity singing in a gospel vein. The "5" Royales are best remembered today for such later hits as "Think" and "Dedicated to the One I Love," but their 1953 blazers, "Baby, Don't Do It" (with the inspirational verse "If you leave me pretty baby/I'll have bread without no meat") and "Help Me Somebody," remain fine examples of rhythm and gospel.

And then there are the Royals. After a string of edifying flops on Okeh and Federal, this group struck it rich in 1954 with "Work with Me Annie." Right in the middle of the song's lengthy chart run, the Royals were forced to change their name—to avoid confusion with the aforementioned "5" Royales, who presumably hadn't noticed the Royals before their hit. The switch might have confused the fans, but there was no confusion about the intent of the lyrics sung by the newly named Midnighters: "Work with me Annie . . . let's get it while the gettin' is good/Annie please don't cheat . . . gimme all my meat/Let's get it while the gettin' is good."

Hot on the heels of "Work" came the first of its many sequels—"Annie Had a Baby" ("Can't work no more . . . that's what happens when the gettin' gets good"). Sequels soon flowed in from everywhere, most notably Etta James's "The Wallflower," the record that launched her long career. "The Wallflower" was better known as "Roll with Me Henry" (as in Henry Ballard); those outside the range of R&B stations may remember Georgia Gibbs's bowdlerized "Dance with Me Henry," the only song of the "Annie"/"Henry" cycle to penetrate the pop consciousness of 1955.

R&B initiates, meanwhile, smirked at "Annie's Answer" ("I ain't had no baby") by Al Smith's Combo with Hazel McCollum and the El Dorados. Berkeley's Music City label chimed in with "Annie Pulled a Humbug" ("That's not my kid . . . can't be mine 'cause he's got a bald head") by the Midnights. A label note in very small type said: "Not to be confused with the Midnighters recordings." The Midnighters themselves, meanwhile, pursued the idea far past the point of diminishing returns with sequels-to-sequels like "Annie's Aunt Fannie" and "Henry's Got Flat Feet (Can't Dance No More)." One of these followups deserves a morsel of immortality for its title alone: "Switchie Witchie Titchie."

Hank Ballard went on to new fame in the Sixties with such early soul dance hits as "Finger Poppin' Time" and "Let's Go, Let's Go, Let's Go." Dancers remember him best, though, for a simple little tune he composed in 1959 to fill the back side of "Teardrops on Your Letter," something called "The Twist." Chubby Checker's cover of this song, not as nicely sung but more danceably produced and tirelessly promoted, achieved the unique feat of being Number One on the pop charts two separate times, more than a year apart.

But Hank Ballard got less credit for "The Twist" than he deserved. With the exception of Jackie Wilson, the other rhythm-gospel pioneers had even less luck in the Sixties, a decade that belonged to a new generation of gospel-influenced black singers. There was one very big difference: the hybrid was no longer nameless. And I sometimes wonder what the course of rock and roll might have been if someone had dreamt up the name "soul music" while Clyde McPhatter was still in his prime.

Discography

Dominoes, "Do Something for Me" (Federal 12001; r☆6, 1951). **Dominoes,** "Sixty Minute Man" (Federal 12022; r☆1, 1951). **Dominoes,** "I Am with You" (Federal 12039; r☆8, 1951). **Dominoes,** "That's What You're Doing to Me" (Federal 12059; r☆7, 1952). **Dominoes,** "Have Mercy Baby" (Federal 12068; r☆1, 1952). **Billy Ward and His Dominoes,** "I'd Be Satisfied" (Federal 12105; r☆8, 1952). **Billy Ward and his Dominoes,** "The Bells" (Federal 12114; r☆6, 1953). **"5" Royales,** "Baby, Don't Do It" (Apollo 443; r☆1, 1953). **"5" Royales,** "Help Me Somebody" b/w "Crazy, Crazy, Crazy" (Apollo 446; r☆1, 1953). **Billy Ward and His Dominoes,** "These Foolish Things Remind Me of You" (Federal 12129; r☆5, 1953). **"5" Royales,** "Too Much Lovin' " (Apollo 448; r☆4, 1953). **Drifters,** "Money, Honey" (Atlantic 1006; r☆1, 1953). **Billy Ward and His Dominoes,** "Rags to Riches" (King 1280; r☆3, 1953). **Drifters,** "Such a Night" b/w "Lucille" (Atlantic 1019; r☆5, 1954). **Midnighters,** "Work with Me Annie" (Federal 12169; r☆1, 1954). **Drifters,** "Honey Love" (Atlantic 1029; r☆1, 1954). **Midnighters,** "Sexy Ways" (Federal 12185; r☆3, 1954). **Midnighters,** "Annie Had a Baby" (Federal 12195; r☆1, 1954). **Drifters,** "Bip Bam" (Atlantic 1043; r☆7, 1954). **Midnighters,** "Annie's Aunt Fannie" (Federal 12200; r☆10, 1954). **Drifters,** "White Christmas" (Atlantic 1048; r☆2, 1954). **Drifters,** "What'cha Gonna Do" (Atlantic 1055; r☆3, 1955).
(Chart positions taken from Joel Whitburn's *Record Research,* compiled from *Billboard* Rhythm and Blues chart.)

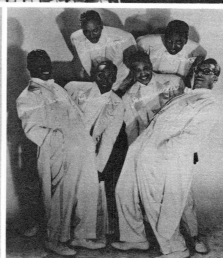

Elvis Presley
by Peter Guralnick

"Have you heard the news?
...There's good rockin' tonight."
> —Elvis Presley, the Hillbilly Cat, in his
> recording of the Roy Brown song, 1954

"The pure products of America go crazy."
> —William Carlos Williams,
> "Spring and All," 1923

The world was not prepared for Elvis Presley. The violence of its reaction to him ("unspeakably untalented," a "voodoo of frustration and defiance") more than testifies to this. Other rock 'n' rollers had a clearer focus to their music. An egocentric genius like Jerry Lee Lewis may even have had a greater talent. Certainly Chuck Berry or Carl Perkins had a keener wit. But Elvis had the moment. He hit like a Pan American flash, and the reverberations still linger from the shock of his arrival.

In some ways the reaction may seem to have been out of proportion, for Elvis Presley was in retrospect merely one more link in a chain of historical inevitability. His ducktail was already familiar from Tony Curtis, the movie star whose pictures Elvis haunted at the Suzore No. 2 in Memphis; the hurt, truculent expression we had seen before in Marlon Brando's motorcycle epic, *The Wild One.* His vulnerability was mirrored by James Dean, whose first movie, *East of Eden,* was released in April 1955, just as Elvis's own career was getting under way. ("He knew I was a friend of Jimmy's," said Nicholas Ray, director of Dean's second film *Rebel without a Cause,* "so he got down on his knees before me and began to recite whole pages from the script. Elvis must have seen *Rebel* a dozen times by then and remembered every one of Jimmy's lines.") His eponymous sneer and the whole attitude which it exemplified—not derision exactly but a kind of scornful pity, indifference, a pained acceptance of all the dreary details of square reality— was foreshadowed by Brando, John Garfield, the famous picture of Robert Mitchum after his 1948 pot bust. Even his music had its historical parallels, not just in the honky-tonk clatter of Bill Haley and His Comets but in the genuine popular success which singers like Frankie Laine and Johnnie Ray—and Al Jolson, Mildred Bailey, even Bing Crosby in an earlier era—had enjoyed in bringing black vocal stylings to the white marketplace.

None of it seemed to matter somehow. To anyone who was alive at the time, Presley was, and remains, a truly revolutionary force. Country singer Bob Luman, a near-contemporary, described in Paul Hemphill's *Nashville Sound* what might almost be considered a typical first reaction. "This cat came out in red pants and a green coat and a pink shirt and socks, and he had this sneer on his face and he stood behind the mike for five minutes, I'll bet, before he made a move. Then he hit his guitar a lick, and he broke two strings. I'd been playing ten years, and I hadn't broken a *total* of two strings. So there he was, these two strings dangling, and he hadn't done anything yet, and these high school girls were screaming and fainting and running up to the stage, and then he started to move his hips real slow like he had a thing for his guitar. That was Elvis Presley when he was about 19, playing Kilgore, Texas. He made chills run up my back, man, like when your hair starts grabbing at your collar. For the next nine days he played one-nighters around Kilgore, and after school every day me and my girl would get in the car and go wherever he was playing that night. That's the last time I tried to sing like Webb Pierce and Lefty Frizzell."

It was the same for countless fans and for other performers, too. To Waylon Jennings he was "like an explosion, really." To Buddy Holly, "Without Elvis none of us could have made it." As for Elvis Presley, the center of the storm, it was something over which he professed to have no control. Repeatedly over the years he has refused to speculate on the reasons for his success, putting it down to luck, blind instinct, anything but conscious design. "I don't know what it is," he said to C. Robert Jennings of the *Saturday Evening Post* in 1956. "I just fell into it, really. My daddy and I were laughing about it the other day. He looked at me and said, 'What happened, El? The last thing I can remember is I was working in a can factory, and you were driving a truck.' We all feel the same way about it still. It just . . . caught us up."

There it all is: the modesty, the deferential charm, the soft-spoken assumption of commonsense virtues (in this version even the tireless twitching and suggestive pelvic action are seen as involuntary reflex) that became the official Elvis. In many ways I am sure that this portrait is true, and it undoubtedly conforms to the image Elvis Presley has of himself. It tends to leave something out, however. What it leaves out is the drive and consuming ambition of the 19-year-old Elvis Presley, who possessed a sweeping musical intelligence, energies that could barely be contained, and a ferocious determination to escape the mold which had seemingly been set for him at birth. Even more, it ignores the extent to which his rebellion, his surly refusal of responsibility, his reaction to the stifling conformity of the time, could stand for an entire generation, taking in a social base of which he could scarcely have been aware, much less directly known. Most of all, though, this explanation, or lack of it, overlooks the music itself, a music which expressed a kind of pure joyousness, a sense of soaring release that in such self-conscious times as ours seems unlikely ever to be recaptured.

He was born Elvis Aron Presley on January 8th, 1935, in Tupelo, Mississippi, a child of hard times but an only child, adored and pampered by a mother who would walk him to school until he was in his teens. His twin, Jesse Garon, died at birth, and he was always to be reminded of this absence ("They say when one twin dies, the other grows up with all the quality

The solid gold rocker: Elvis, in his gold suit, about 1957, at the peak of his career. (ROLLING STONE)

of the other, too. . . . If I did, I'm lucky"), as if he were somehow incomplete, even down to his matching name. His first picture shows a little boy in overalls, sober in an oversize soft-brimmed hat similar to his father's. He is flanked by parents who regard the camera with touching blank-faced looks that reflect neither expectation nor disappointment. His mother's hand rests on his father's shoulder; she is still young and pretty. And the child looks lost, waiflike, with that strange, familiar hurt look in his eyes, that unmistakable, unfathomable curl to his lips.

He grew up, schooled in all the classic virtues of small-town America: diffident, polite, sirring and ma'aming his elders, hungry with an unfocused yearning that would have been impossible for him—or anyone of his background and generation—either to explicitly admit or implicitly deny. "My daddy was a common laborer," he said. "He didn't have any trade, just like I didn't have. He mostly drove trucks, and when he used to bring the truck home from the wholesale grocery, I used to sit in it by the hour." The car radio was his first exposure not to music necessarily but to the world outside.

Music, to begin with, came from the Pentecostal First Assembly of God church. "We were a religious family, going around together to sing at camp meetings and revivals. Since I was two years old all I knew was gospel music; that was music to me. We borrowed the style of our psalm singing from the early Negroes. We used to go to these religious singings all the time. The preachers cut up all over the place, jumping on the piano, moving every which way. The audience liked them. I guess I learned from them. I loved the music. It became such a part of my life it was as natural as dancing, a way to escape from the problems and my way of release."

There is another picture of Elvis and his parents, taken in 1956 after the phenomenal early success. In this picture Elvis is playing the piano; the mouths of all three are open, their eyes half-shut. They hold themselves stiffly and are evidently singing with fervent emotion. Both parents have put on weight; Vernon is still handsome in a beefy sort of way, but Gladys has taken on the bloated, starch-fed appearance of so many poor Southern whites and blacks. She is 44, but will die in only two years' time, to her son's eternal and heartfelt sorrow ("I think of her nearly every single day," he said nearly five years later. "If I never do anything really wrong, it's all because of her. She wouldn't let me do anything wrong"). I can remember to my embarrassment the reaction which my friends and I had when we first saw the picture. We thought it was a joke. We thought that Elvis was putting us on; it seemed so clearly at odds with Elvis's rebel image and the mythology which, impossible to construct from our own lives, we had erected around a pop idol. Today it is easier to recognize that out of this seeming contradiction (newness vs tradition, rebellion vs authority, sacred

vs profane) arose the tension that was rock 'n' roll. Such thinking was at that time beyond the scope of our experience—and probably Elvis's—as well.

He won a singing prize at ten, when his grammar school principal sponsored his appearance at the Mississippi-Alabama Fair and Dairy Show. The song he sang, "Old Shep," was a bathetic C&W ballad about a boy and his dog which Red Foley had popularized and Elvis would record for RCA some ten years later. It is not difficult to imagine the towheaded little boy standing on a chair so he could be seen, and singing, unaccompanied, with that same throbbing emotion for which he would one day become famous. "I wore glasses, no music, and I won, I think it was fifth place. I got a whipping the same day, my mother whipped me for something, I thought she didn't love me."

At 11, his parents got him a guitar ("I wanted a bicycle"). Teachers and relatives remember him carrying the guitar around with him everywhere he went. Elvis later compared his guitar playing to "someone beating on a bucket lid." He listened to the *Grand Ole Opry,* Roy Acuff, Eddy Arnold, Jimmie Rodgers's early records, and Bob Wills. He idolized the Blackwood Brothers, and the Statesmen Quartet, all prominent white gospel groups. Billy Eckstine, Bill Kenny and the Ink Spots were his favorite rhythm and blues performers. And he absorbed the blues from the radio and the pervasive contact which a poor white family like the Presleys, always living on the edge of town and respectability, would necessarily have with blacks. "I dug the real lowdown Mississippi singers, mostly Big Bill Broonzy and Big Boy Crudup. Although they would scold me at home for listening to them." When he was 13, his family moved to Memphis. "We were broke, man, broke, and we left Tupelo overnight. Dad packed all our belongings in boxes and put them on top and in the trunk of a 1939 Plymouth. We just headed for Memphis. Things had to be better."

Memphis in the late Forties and early Fifties was a seedbed of musical activity. Never really much of a center for commercial country music, it had a raw hillbilly style and a distinguished blues tradition that went back to the Twenties. In 1950 Howlin' Wolf and Sonny Boy Williamson were broadcasting on station KWEM from West Memphis; WDIA, the "mother station of the Negroes" and the first black-operated radio outlet in the South, featured B.B. King and Rufus Thomas spinning records and performing daily. On Beale Street and in W.C. Handy Park you could hear all manner of blues singers and entertainers. And at 706 Union Avenue an ex-radio engineer and announcer from Florence, Alabama, named Sam Phillips had opened the Memphis Recording Service for "Negro artists in the South who wanted to make a record [but] just had no place to go."

It sounds a little disarming, but Phillips in fact recorded Howlin' Wolf, Walter Horton, Bobby "Blue" Bland, Little Junior Parker and B.B. King, all at the beginning of their careers.

Elvis, out of character, in an Isotta, not a Cadillac, or a Rolls, or a Ferrari . . . ('Nashville Banner'; Bill Goodman, photographer)

To begin with he leased his sides to the Biharis's West Coast RPM label and to the Chess brothers in Chicago. It was not until 1952 that he started his own Sun label. In the meantime, though, a quiet revolution was taking place. Many of the small independent producers were becoming aware of it, and in Memphis, where there had long been a relaxed social, as well as musical, interchange, it was particularly noticeable. White kids were picking up on black styles—of music, dance, speech and dress. "Cat clothes" were coming in; be-bop speech was all the rage; and Elvis Presley, along with Carl Perkins, Jerry Lee Lewis, Charlie Rich, and all the other Southern children of the Depression who would one day develop the rockabilly style, was seeking his models in unlikely places.

"I knew Elvis before he was popular," blues singer B.B. King has said. "He used to come around and be around us a lot. There was a place we used to go and hang out at on Beale Street. People had like pawnshops there, and a lot of us used to hang out in certain of these places, and this was where I met him."

In other ways Memphis was an oppressively impersonal urban dream for an only child, shy and strangely insecure, living in a city project, working jobs after school, going off by himself to play the guitar. High school was a fog. He went out for football and ROTC but failed to distinguish himself in this or any other way. He majored in shop, grew his hair long, carefully slicked it down, and tried to grow sideburns from the time he started shaving, because, he said, he wanted to look like a truck driver. Which may or may not have gotten him kicked off the football team. Dressed anomalously in pink and black, he called attention only to his personal colorlessness and lived out typical adolescent fantasies of rebellion in teenage anonymity. "Nobody knew I sang, I wasn't popular in school, I wasn't dating anybody. In the 11th grade at school they entered me in another talent show. I came out and did my two songs and heard people kinda rumbling and whispering. It was amazing how popular I was in school after that."

Whether he was in fact popular even then is doubtful. For memories of rejection have been inevitably clouded in the aftermath of success. Indeed it is as if in later years he set out deliberately to erase the loneliness of that time by gathering around him all the popular figures—football heroes, high school politicians, well-established Memphians—who would barely even speak to him then. For 20 years now, as the so-called Memphis Mafia, they have made up his personal retinue, subject to his every whim, devoted only to their chief. When he graduated from Humes High School in 1953, he was perceived by one schoolmate as an individual with "character, but he had no personality, if you know what I mean. Just acted kind of goofy, sitting in the back of class, playing his guitar. No one knew that he was ever going to be *any*thing." When he got a job as a driver for Crown Electric, it seemed as if his life pattern was set.

One year later he had a record out, and everything was changed.

One of Sam Phillips's more lucrative sidelights was a custom recording service where anyone could go in and make a record for two dollars a side. Sometime in the summer after graduation Elvis went in and cut two sides, "My Happiness" and "That's When Your Heartaches Begin," stylized ballads which had been popular for the Ink Spots. He came back again in January 1954 to cut another two sides, once again two sentimental ballads, and to see if Sam Phillips might be interested in recording him professionally for the Sun Records label. Phillips put him off, though Elvis evidently made enough impression for Phillips to hold on to his address and a neighbor's phone where he could be reached. Elvis was not singing professionally, but he had his mind on music at the time. He was always going to the all-night gospel sings at the Memphis Auditorium and that spring almost joined the Songfellows, a junior division of the renowned Blackwood Brothers Quartet.

Around April, Phillips called him to try out a demo on "Without You," still another ballad which met with minimal success. Phillips was more or less undeterred. He put Elvis in contact with Scotty Moore, a 21-year-old guitar player who had been hanging around the studio and was in the process of persuading Phillips to record his own group, Doug Poindexter's Starlight Wranglers, in one of the earliest gropings toward a rockabilly style. Elvis showed up at Scotty's apartment wearing, says Scotty, "a pink suit, white shoes and the ducktail. I thought my wife was going to go out the back door." Bill Black, the bass player for the Starlight Wranglers, wandered in and out, as they ran down song after song, country, ballads, blues on that Sunday afternoon in late spring or early summer of 1954. What they were looking for no one seemed quite sure of. What they got everybody knows.

"Over and over," said Marion Keisker, Sam Phillips's secretary, "I remember Sam saying, 'If I could find a white man who had the Negro sound and the Negro feel, I could make a billion dollars.'" With Elvis, Phillips apparently found the key.

"That's All Right," a traditional blues by Arthur "Big Boy" Crudup, was the first number that actually jelled in July of 1954. According to legend it was worked out during a break between ballads. According to Elvis in a British interview, "'You want to make some blues?' he [Phillips] suggested over the phone, knowing I'd always been a sucker for that kind of jive. He mentioned Big Boy Crudup's name and maybe others, too. All I know is, I hung up and run 15 blocks to Mr. Phillips's office before he'd gotten off the line—or so he tells me. We talked about the Crudup numbers I knew—'Cool Disposition,' 'Rock Me Mama,' 'Hey Mama,' 'Everything's All Right,' and others, but settled for 'That's All Right,' one of my top favorites."

Marion Keisker remembers months of rehearsal and hard work; according to Scotty Moore, though, the initial recording date took place only days after Scotty first met Elvis. "It wasn't intended to be a session at all. That was the reason only Bill and I were in the studio, Sam just wanted to see what would happen on tape. First thing he did was 'I Love You Because.' Then he did a couple of those country oriented things. Little while later we were sitting there drinking a Coke, shooting the bull, Elvis picked up his guitar, started banging on it and singing 'That's All Right Mama.' Just jumping around the studio, just acting the fool. And Bill started beating on his bass and I joined in. The door to the control room was open, and Sam come running out and said, 'What in the devil are you doing?' We said, 'We don't know.' He said, 'Well, find out real quick and don't lose it.'"

It was a turning point in the history of American popular music.

"That's All Right" was at first glance an unlikely song to create such a transformation. A conventional blues put out by a very pedestrian blues singer (if any bluesman deserves the charge of monotony, it is Arthur "Big Boy" Crudup, who rarely escaped from one key and possessed a singular ineptitude on guitar), it consists of a string of traditional verses set to a totally undistinguished melody. Perhaps the very mediocrity of the original is what drew Elvis and other white singers to artists like Arthur Crudup and Jimmy Reed in the first place; unlike great bluesmen like Muddy Waters and Howlin' Wolf or even B.B. King, they could be imitated without an excess of strain. In any case the copy in this instance bore little resemblance to the original. For if the record was not worked out during a break, but was in fact the product of months of hard work, trial and error, and direct calculation, that isn't the way that it comes across at all.

It sounds easy, unforced, joyous, spontaneous. It sounds as if the singer has broken free for the first time in his life. The voice soars with a purity and innocence. There is a crisp authority to Scotty Moore's lead guitar, Elvis's rhythm is ringing and clear, the bass gallops along in slap-heavy fashion. The record sparkles with a freshness of conception, a sharpness of design, a total lack of pretentiousness, an irrepressible enthusiasm. Like each of the ten sides eventually released on Sun—evenly divided between blues and country—"That's All Right" has a timeless quality which was just as striking and just as far removed from trends of the day as it is from contemporary fashion. The sound is clean, without affectation or clutter. And there remains in the conventional lyrics, easing their way into a scat verse which was in Crudup's original leaden and pedestrian, a sense of transformation, both dizzying and breathtaking, an emotional transcendence, which, if only because of the burden of knowledge, could never happen again.

And yet this is not quite literally true either. It is perhaps another self-sustaining myth, with the reality at once more straightforward and more paradoxical. The B side of "That's All Right" was Bill Monroe's classic bluegrass tune, "Blue

tionship with his nonrelative Sam, played the record 30 times one night.

By the time the record came out there was a back order of 5000 copies, and Elvis and Sun Records were well on their way.

Largely on the strength of this success (the record went on to sell 20,000 copies and even made Number One briefly on the Memphis C&W charts) Elvis was named eighth most promising new hillbilly artist in *Billboard*'s annual poll at the end of the year. Almost immediately he began to appear around Memphis, sitting in with the Starlight Wranglers at the Bel Air and Airport Inn, playing with Scotty and Bill (very briefly billed as the Blue Moon Boys) at the Eagle's Nest, debuting at a big country show at the Overton Park Shell, even opening a shopping center. In September he appeared on the *Grand Ole Opry,* where he was advised to go back to truck driving. According to Gordon Stoker of the Jordanaires he cried all the way home. He met with more success on the *Louisiana Hayride,* where he signed on as a regular after his second appearance, and where he picked up a drummer, D.J. Fontana. And he began touring, through Texas and Mississippi, performing at schoolhouses and dance halls, traveling in a succession of secondhand Lincolns and Cadillacs which were sometimes driven until exhausted and then abandoned on the side of the road.

Everywhere the reaction was the same—a mixture of shock and wild acclaim. No one knew what to make of him. "I recall one jockey telling me that Elvis Presley was so country he shouldn't be played after 5 a.m.," said Sam Phillips. "And others said he was too black for them."

Nonetheless the records continued to sell ("Good Rockin' Tonight," the second release, cut in September 1954, made Number Three on the Memphis C&W charts); teenagers turned out in droves to hear the so-called Hillbilly Cat, the King of Western Bop (his titles alone betray the cultural schizophrenia with which he was greeted); and they came away with the same dazed reaction as Bob Luman in Kilgore, Texas. He did splits, kneedrops, and crawled to the edge of the stage, only to leap back from clutching hands. "He threw everything into it," says Bob Neal, his first manager, "trying to break that audience down, trying to get it with him. He'd always react to audience reaction, and in the rare instances where he'd be placed on the show early, I always felt he kind of outdid himself, making it tough for the next guy to follow."

The records followed, one after another, although according to Marion Keisker, "Every session came hard." Each came out sounding like some kind of inspired accident: the unexpected falsetto with which Little Junior Parker's "Mystery Train" trails off, the bubbly hiccuping beginning to "Baby, Let's Play House," the wailing lead-in to "Good Rockin' Tonight," the too perfect beautiful slow intro to blues singer Kokomo Arnold's "Milkcow Blues Boogie" which Elvis interrupts to declare portentously, "Hold it, fellas. That don't *move* me. Let's get real, real gone for a change."

Moon of Kentucky," recorded at the same sessions and taken at something like breakneck tempo in the released version. An unreleased alternate take exists, however, available on *Good Rockin' Tonight,* a Dutch bootleg LP of Sun masters. It indicates that "Blue Moon of Kentucky" at any rate started out its rockabilly life in a slower, bluesier version, more direct emotionally and more ornate vocally, much in the manner of "She's Gone," an alternate take from a later session of the innocuous enough "I'm Left, You're Right, She's Gone." Both contain surprising intimations of what is to come, with hints of the familiar vibrato, the smoky drop to a bass register, the lazy crooning style, all hallmarks, I would have thought, of a later decadent period. In fact it is a style with which Elvis is distinctly more at home than the more frantic rockabilly mold, giving vent to all the smoldering passion that was to be so conspicuously absent from his later efforts. "Fine, fine, man," Sam Phillips declares, as the bluegrass number disintegrates into nervous laughter and edgy chatter. "Hell, that's different. That's a pop song now, little guy. That's good!"

"Blue Moon of Kentucky" and "That's All Right" were cut on July 5th and 6th, 1954. A dub was delivered on almost the same day to Dewey Phillips, host of the popular *Red Hot and Blue* show, which was a kind of Memphis Moondog matinee: rhythm and blues and hipster talk for a young white audience. Phillips, who enjoyed a long and presumably profitable rela-

Well, he got gone. The records picked up in sales, though never on a scale larger than a relatively tiny independent company like Sun could expect. The bookings increased. The cars and the clothes got fancier; the money did, too. A year after his Sun debut, in July of 1955, "Baby, Let's Play House" made the national C&W charts. By the end of the year Elvis Presley was named most promising new C&W artist. But by then, of course, he was a proven commercial commodity, for he had signed with RCA Records.

"He was greatly anxious for success," said Bob Neal, with whom he signed in January 1955, and with whom he went to New York for the first time for an unsuccessful audition with Arthur Godfrey's *Talent Scouts*. "He talked not in terms of being a moderate success. No—his ambition and desire was to be big in movies and so forth. From the very first he had ambition to be nothing in the ordinary but to go all the way. He was impatient. He would say, 'We got to figure out how to do this, we got to get ahead.' "

Sometime in the summer of 1955 Colonel Tom Parker, scion of the Great Parker Pony Circus, manager formerly of Eddy Arnold and then of Hank Snow, heir to the whole medicine show tradition, entered the picture. Through Snow, then one of the nation's top country stars, Parker had developed Hank Snow Jamboree Attractions into one of the major booking agencies in the South, and working through Neal at first, the Colonel began booking Elvis. In November 1955 Bob Neal was eased into a secondary position. On November 22nd, Colonel Tom Parker produced a document which entitled him to represent Elvis Presley exclusively, and signed a contract with RCA. Sun Records received $35,000 plus $5000 in back royalties for Elvis. It was an unheard-of sum for the time.

There were many cogent reasons for such a move. For Sun Records the deal provided much-needed capital, and Sam Phillips has always staunchly defended his decision, citing the subsequent success of Carl Perkins, Johnny Cash, and Jerry Lee Lewis on his label as proof. For Elvis Presley the benefits became obvious immediately. On January 10th, 1956, he entered RCA's Nashville studio and recorded "Heartbreak Hotel." The rest, I think, is history. As for the Colonel, he soon divested himself of all other interests and devoted himself to advancing his boy, a devotion which has taken such forms as the decline of all Presidential and nonremunerative invitations, the hawking and retrieving of souvenir programs at concerts, the personal dispensation of Elvis calendars at the fabled Las Vegas debut in 1970—in short a steadfast refusal to cheapen his product. "When I first knew Elvis," the Colonel has frequently remarked, "he had a million dollars' worth of talent. Now he has a million dollars."

I don't know what there is to say about the success. There are, of course, the hits: "Heartbreak Hotel," with its bluesy country feel, metallic guitar and dour bass; "Hound Dog," with its reversed sexual imagery, savage musical ride, and spewed out lyric ("Well, they said you was high class, well that was just a lie"); "Jailhouse Rock," with its frenetic pace and furiously repeated drum roll; "Love Me Tender," "Love Me," "Loving You"; the scornful ease of "Don't Be Cruel," the mnemonic pop of "All Shook Up." There was the impact of hit after hit after hit, 14 consecutive million-sellers, RCA claimed, simultaneously topping pop, country, and R&B charts; the phenomenal explosion of both the mode and the music over a period of 27 months until his March 1958 induction into the army; the elevation to socio/mytho/psychological status, as Elvis Presley unwittingly became a test of the nation's moral fiber.

The peculiar thing is that in retrospect it is all irrelevant. Not just in the wake of Presley's success but as the inevitable consequence of the almost total acceptance which rock and roll has come to enjoy. When Elvis Presley was first recorded by Sam Phillips, he was an unmarketable commodity, an underground hero on the fringes of society and artistic respectability. Today, like every trend and tidal wave which comes along in our consumer oriented society, with its voracious appetite for novelty and its pitiless need to reduce what it does not understand, his achievement has been subsumed, his art has been converted to product, and rock and roll itself has become part of the fabric of corporate America. And the music—what of the music?

For some reason Elvis Presley never again recaptured the spirit or the verve of those first Sun sessions. When I say "never," I don't mean to imply that all of his output for the last 20 years has been worthless, nor do I mean to set up some arbitrary, pure-minded standard by which to measure, and dismiss, his popular achievement. Many of the songs he recorded, from "Hound Dog" to such extravagant items as "Don't," "Wear My Ring around Your Neck," "A Fool Such as I," were still classic performances, despite their musical excesses and pronounced air of self-parody (the clear, hard tenor had yielded to tremulous vibrato, dramatic swoops from high to low, and lighthearted groans). They were also fundamentally silly records, a charge which could never be leveled at the Sun sides, which, whatever else they might appear to be, were seriously, passionately, joyously in earnest. You are left with the inescapable feeling that if he had never recorded again, if Elvis Presley had simply disappeared after leaving the little Sun studio for the last time, his status would be something like that of a latter-day Robert Johnson: lost, vulnerable, eternally youthful, forever on the edge, pure and timeless.

Not that RCA would not have liked to duplicate the Sun sound. At the beginning there is little question that they tried. Still, even RCA was aware of the difference. It was "a new sound," according to Steve Sholes, Elvis's RCA discoverer, because Elvis had evolved so rapidly in the months following his RCA signing. The fact is, I think, that Elvis was too well suited

From left: (1) Here, Elvis has just received the rarely granted Bing Crosby Award of the National Academy of Recording Arts and Sciences—does he look impressed? (2) Elvis at ease in the army; (3) Elvis arrives late for a game show, registers shock that it could have begun without him.

to success. He was intelligent, adaptable, ambitious, and sure of his goals. He wanted to break loose, and music was only his vehicle for doing so.

He soon settled in fact on a fairly comfortable and formulaic approach which took advantage of his wide-ranging musical background, facility in a number of styles, real talent as a quick study, and almost total lack of taste. With the addition of the Jordanaires, a popular quartet present from the first RCA session, the sound quickly took on the trappings of the gospel and pop groups which Elvis had always admired. With the almost inexhaustible demand for material brought on by the unprecedented dimensions of the Presley success, professional songwriters were called in and invited to submit their compositions for approval (and publication, under the Gladys or Elvis Presley Music imprint). Whereas a song like "Hound Dog," although already part of the stage act, required as many as 30 takes, after a while vocals were merely patterned on the demos which were submitted, and while no session could be complete without the warmups and inevitable gospel sings which remain a feature of Elvis Presley's musical life even today, the loose feel of the Sun studio was gone.

Events moved too rapidly even to try to comprehend. Million sellers, national tours, the triumph over Ed Sullivan's stuffy personal pronouncements (Presley will never appear on my show, said Sullivan, just weeks before he signed Elvis for a $50,000 series of appearances), instant celebrity, the promise of immortality, the rush of success. Record making in fact became something of a subsidiary interest once Elvis went to Hollywood in the summer of 1956. By the time he entered the army in 1958 he was what Sam Phillips had said he would become: a genuine pop singer. A pop singer of real talent, catholic taste, negligent ease, and magnificent aplomb, but a pop singer nonetheless.

I can remember the suspense my friends and I felt when Elvis came out of the army in 1960. By this time we were growing sideburns of our own, and in some ways his fate, like that of any other icon, seemed inextricably linked with ours. What would he be like? Would he declare himself once again? Would he keep the faith? We hadn't long to wait for the answers.

His first release, "Stuck on You," followed the familiar formula of "All Shook Up," "Too Much," "Teddy Bear," innocuous enough rock 'n' roll fare but still rock 'n' roll. The second release was the monumental best-seller, "It's Now or Never," still reputedly Elvis's favorite song and loosely based on the "O Sole Mio" of Mario Lanza, one of Elvis's favorite operatic tenors. The first, and last, paid public appearance was a Frank Sinatra TV special, in tails. Frank Sinatra! After that he retreated from the world for nearly a decade to make movies.

We forgave him his apostasy, just as we forgave him all his lapses and excesses: his self-parodying mannerisms; his negligible gift for, or interest in acting; his corporeal puffiness; his indifference to the material he recorded; his apparent contempt for his own talent; his continuing commercial success in the face of all these fallings-away. The spectacle itself of the bad boy made good.

Because that is what I think gratified us most of all. Elvis's success, flying as it did not only in the face of reason but of good taste as well, seemed in a way a final judgment on the world which had scorned him and which, by the sheer magnitude of his talent, he had transformed. We took it as a cosmic joke. We speculated endlessly on the life that Elvis must be leading, and the laughs he must be having, behind the locked gates of Graceland, his Memphis mansion. Every fact which is presented in this essay was a mystery then, the subject for painstaking detective work, an intricately assembled collage which has since been exploded by knowledge. Most of all we labored happily in the wilderness, self-mocking but earnest, possessors of a secret knowledge shared only by fellow fans: Elvis Presley was to be taken seriously.

There are only two footnotes to this long and continuing saga of perfect decline.

The first is the TV special which ended Presley's eight-year slumber in Hollywood. This came about quite simply because by 1968 Elvis had exhausted his audience, as well as himself, with movies which were no longer drawing, records which, devoid of even a semblance of commitment, were no longer selling. The Beatles, the Rolling Stones, and Dylan had eclipsed their one-time mentor. Elvis was beginning to look dated. And so the Colonel, who has always avowed that it is his patriotic duty to keep Elvis in the 90% tax bracket, decided that it was time for his boy to step out. Seizing the moment with customary astuteness, he wangled a remarkable financial deal for a special to be shown at Christmastime. What could be more appropriate, the Colonel argued, than the star's appearance in a kind of formal Christmas pageant, singing a medley of Christmas carols and hymns. For the first time in his career Elvis seems to have put his foot down. Or perhaps that is merely what the Colonel would like us to believe. In association with the show's youngish producer/director, Steve Binder, he determined to appear in live performance, doing his old songs in taped segments in front of a somewhat handpicked but real, live, breathing audience. A good chunk of the special was still choreographed, it's true, and some big production numbers remained, but the core of the show was just Elvis, alone on the stage with his guitar and such old musical friends as Scotty Moore and D.J. Fontana.

I'll never forget the anticipation with which we greeted the announcement and then the show itself, having the opportunity to see our idol outside his celluloid wrappings for the very first time, knowing that we were bound to be disappointed. The credits flashed, the camera focused on Elvis, and to our utter disbelief there he was, attired in black leather, his skin glistening, his hair long and greasy, his look forever young and cal-

From left: (1) Elvis slicked up; (2) Elvis with dad, Vernon, in Las Vegas, 1969; (3) An early shot, just before the first sessions at Sun. Below: (4) Elvis meets the press before his first appearance in New York City in 1972. (1 & 2, Frank Edwards—Vista Photo Features; 4, Jeff Albertson)

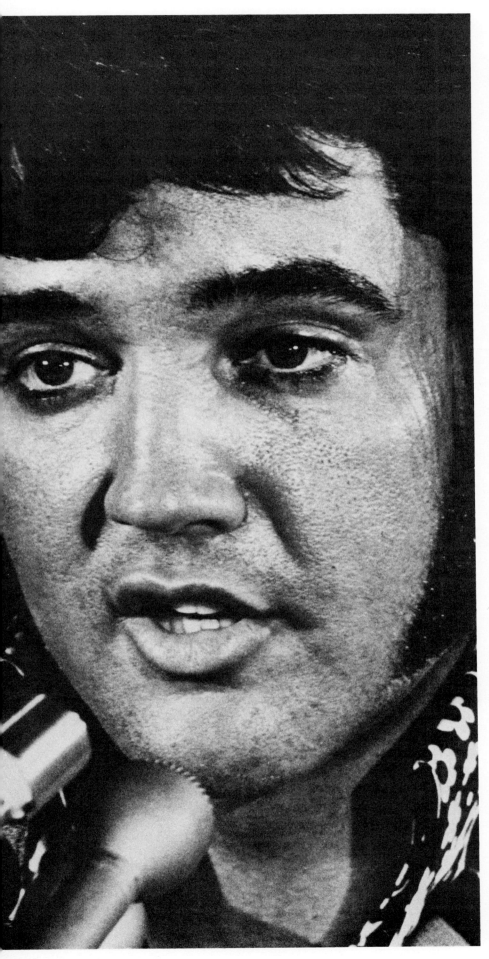

low. "If you're looking for trouble," he announced, "you've come to the right place."

I don't know if I can convey how transcendent, how thrilling a moment it was. Here were all our fantasies confirmed—the look, the sound, the stance, the remarkable appositeness of the selection. The voice took off, it soared, it strained, and then to our vast surprise Elvis is sweating. He is unsure of himself, he is ill at ease, he is uncertain of our reaction, and it seems clear for the first time that Elvis is trying, and trying very hard, to please us. He needs to have our attention, and it comes as something of a shock after all this time to discover that a hero whom we had set up to feel only existential scorn, a hero who was characterized by a frozen sneer and a look of sullen discontent, should need us in the end.

I say that this is a footnote, but maybe it is more than that. Because to my mind at least it gave rise to the second brief flourishing of the art of Elvis Presley, a flourishing that could not have taken place without all that went before but which can stand on its own nonetheless as a real and significant artistic achievement. On the strength of the success of the TV show, and the subsequent sales of "If I Can Dream," the inspirational single which concluded it, he went back to Memphis to record for the first time in nearly 14 years. The singles ("Suspicious Minds," "Kentucky Rain," "Don't Cry Daddy") and initial album, *From Elvis in Memphis*, which came out of these sessions are true reflections of the passion and soul which Elvis invested in that rare moment of unease in an otherwise uninterrupted career. There continues to be that same sense of tension, the atmosphere remains nervous and almost self-effacing, there is that strange anxiety to please and constriction in the voice which seems a million years away from the perfect self-assurance of the 19-year-old "natural" who first recorded for Sun so very long ago.

What happened after that everybody knows. Amid much hoopla Elvis returned to live performing, first in Las Vegas where a flock of critics were flown out to the historic opening, to come back with tales of vitality undimmed, robust roots, and disarming charm. We are all fans. When it became obvious from the relative unsuccess of *Elvis: That's the Way It Is*, a documentary of the Vegas act, that movies were no longer a viable commercial formula, the Colonel hustled his product back out on the road, where he appeared in coliseums, hockey rinks, the Astrodome, and Madison Square Garden. There was a great deal of money made very quickly, and very soon the burst of involvement which had so briefly galvanized Elvis dissipated, the act was reduced to total self-parody and Elvis to practicing his karate kicks onstage. It didn't matter; none of it mattered. When I finally saw him in person at the Boston Garden in 1971, it was like going to a gathering of the faithful, grown middle-aged, perhaps, in pantsuits and double-knits, but faithful nonetheless. I sat as far away from the stage as you can sit in a big arena, but even from there you could see that he was the perfect artifact, preserved like the great woolly mammoth in a block of ice, suspended, Greil Marcus has suggested, in a perpetual state of grace, all his illusions and mine intact.

Since then, sadly, the ice has melted. When Elvis turned 40, the media had a field day. He was fat, and depressed about it, and didn't get out of bed all day. It seems to be a continuing battle against creeping mortality, and Elvis is not winning. His hair is dyed, his teeth are capped, his middle is girdled, his voice is a husk, and his eyes film over with glassy impersonality. He is no longer, it seems, used to the air and, because he cannot endure the scorn of strangers, will not go out if his hair isn't right, if his weight—which fluctuates wildly—is not down. He has tantrums onstage and, like some aging politician, is reduced to the ranks of the grotesque.

Don't feel sorry for him. For Elvis is merely a prisoner of the same fantasies as we. What he wanted he got. What he didn't he deliberately threw away. There is a moment in *Elvis on Tour*, another recent film documentary, in which Elvis yields the stage to J.D. Sumner and the Stamps, the gospel group in his entourage. He has just finished singing "You Gave Me a Mountain," a Marty Robbins song which tells in a series of dramatic crescendos a tale of separation from an only child. It could just as easily be "My Boy" or "Separate Ways" or even "Mama Liked the Roses," all dramas of broken marriage and separation from loved ones (Elvis's daughter, whom he is said to adore, was born nine months to the day after his 1967 marriage, which subsequently ended when his wife took up with her karate instructor). These are the only songs which he sings with conviction nowadays, painful substitutes for self-expression, artful surrogates for real life. In the film he introduces the gospel group, enlists the audience's attention ("I don't sing in this. Just listen to them, please. It's a beautiful song") and for the first time is at rest, expression pensive, eyes uplifted, mouthing the words and shaking his head with a smile, carried outside of himself. It is as if it is intended in expiation, and it probably is. Then the music starts up, the show begins again, he launches into "Lawdy Miss Clawdy" without so much as a blink, and Elvis Presley is once again encapsulated in the gauze-like world from which he will never emerge.

It's all right, you want to say to him impertinently. It's all right. You did all right, even if your greatest talent did turn out to be for making money.

Earlier in the same film there are moving images from *The Ed Sullivan Show* of 1956, where youth is forever captured, forever joyous, with a swivel of the hip, a sneer of the lip, and the full confidence and expectation that nothing will ever go wrong. "My daddy knew a lot of guitar players," recalls Elvis in one of the film's interview segments, "and most of them didn't work, so he said, 'You should make your mind up to either be a guitar player or an electrician, but I never saw a guitar player that was worth a damn!' " Elvis smiles. Elvis laughs. His face fills the screen. "When I was a boy," you can hear Elvis Presley

saying, "I was the hero in comic books and movies. I grew up believing in that dream. Now I've lived it out. That's all a man can ask for."

Jerry Hopkins's biography, Elvis, *has been an invaluable source of information. Several unattributed quotes have been taken from the book.*

Discography

"That's All Right" b/w "Blue Moon of Kentucky" (Sun 209; 1954). "Good Rockin' Tonight" b/w "I Don't Care if the Sun Don't Shine" (Sun 210; 1954). "Milkcow Blues Boogie" b/w "You're a Heartbreaker" (Sun 215; 1955). "Baby, Let's Play House" b/w "I'm Left, You're Right, She's Gone" (Sun 217; c☆10, 1955). "Mystery Train" b/w "I Forgot to Remember to Forget" (Sun 223; c☆1, 1955). "Heartbreak Hotel" b/w "I Was the One" (RCA Victor 47-6420; c☆1, r☆5, ☆1, 1956). "Blue Suede Shoes" (RCA Victor EPA 747; ☆24, 1956). "I Want You, I Need You, I Love You" b/w "My Baby Left Me" (RCA Victor 47-6540; c☆1, r☆10, ☆3, 1956). "Don't Be Cruel" b/w "Hound Dog" (RCA Victor, 47-6604; c☆1, r☆1, ☆1, 1956). "Love Me Tender" b/w "Anyway You Want Me (That's How I Will Be)" (RCA Victor 47-6643; c☆3, r☆4, ☆1, 1956). "Love Me" b/w "When My Blue Moon Turns to Gold Again" (RCA Victor EPA 992; ☆6, 1956). "Poor Boy" (RCA Victor EPA 4006; ☆35, 1956). "Old Shep" (RCA Victor EPA 993; ☆47, 1956). "Too Much" b/w "Playing for Keeps" (RCA Victor 47-6800; c☆5, r☆7, ☆2, 1957). "All Shook Up" b/w "That's When Your Heartaches Begin" (RCA Victor 47-6870; c☆3, r☆1, ☆1, 1957). "(There'll Be) Peace in the Valley" (RCA Victor EPA 4054; ☆39, 1957). "Let Me Be Your Teddy Bear" b/w "Loving You" (RCA Victor 47-7000; c☆1, r☆1, ☆1, 1957). "Jailhouse Rock" b/w "Treat Me Nice" (RCA Victor 47-7035; c☆1, r☆1, ☆1, 1957). "Don't" b/w "I Beg of You" (RCA Victor 47-7150; c☆2, r☆4, ☆1, 1958). "Wear My Ring around Your Neck" b/w "Doncha' Think It's Time" (RCA Victor 47-7240; c☆3, r☆7, ☆3, 1958). "Hard Headed Woman" b/w "Don't Ask Me Why" (RCA Victor 47-7280; c☆2, r☆2, ☆2, 1958). "One Night" b/w "I Got Stung" (RCA Victor 47-7410; c☆24, r☆10, ☆4, 1958). "(Now and Then There's) A Fool Such as I" b/w "I Need Your Love Tonight" (RCA Victor 47-7506; r☆16, ☆2, 1959). "A Big Hunk o' Love" b/w "My Wish Came True" (RCA Victor 47-7600; r☆10, ☆1, 1959). "Stuck on You" b/w "Fame and Fortune" (RCA Victor 47-7740; c☆27, r☆6, ☆1, 1960). "It's Now or Never" b/w "A Mess of Blues" (RCA Victor 47-7777; r☆7, ☆1, 1960). "Are You Lonesome Tonight?" b/w "I Gotta Know" (RCA Victor 47-7810; c☆22, r☆3, ☆1, 1960). "Surrender" b/w "Lonely Man" (RCA Victor 47-7850; ☆1, 1961). "Flaming Star" (RCA Victor LPC-128; ☆14, 1961). "I Feel So Bad" b/w "Wild in the Country" (RCA Victor 47-7880; c☆5, r☆15, ☆5, 1961). "(Marie's the Name) His Latest Flame" b/w "Little Sister" (RCA Victor 47-7908; ☆4, 1961). "Can't Help Falling in Love" b/w "Rock-a-Hula Baby" (RCA Victor 47-7968; ☆2, 1961). "Good Luck Charm" b/w "Anything That's Part of You" (RCA Victor 47-7992; ☆1, 1962). "Follow That Dream" (RCA Victor EPA 4368; ☆15, 1962). "She's Not You" (RCA Victor 47-8041; r☆13, ☆5, 1962). "King of the Whole Wide World" (RCA Victor EPA 4371; ☆30, 1962). "Return to Sender" (RCA Victor 47-8100; r☆5, ☆2, 1962). "One Broken Heart for Sale" (RCA Victor 47-8134; r☆21, ☆11, 1963). "(You're the) Devil in Disguise" (RCA Victor 47-8188; r☆9, ☆3, 1963). "Bossa Nova Baby" b/w "Witchcraft" (RCA Victor 47-8243; r☆20, ☆8, 1963). "Kissin' Cousins" b/w "It Hurts Me" (RCA Victor 47-8307; ☆12, 1964). "Kiss Me Quick" (RCA Victor 447-0639; ☆34, 1964). "What'd I Say" b/w "Viva Las Vegas" (RCA Victor 47-8360; ☆21, 1964). "Such a Night" (RCA Victor 47-8400; ☆16, 1964). "Ask Me" b/w "Ain't That Loving You Baby" (RCA Victor 47-8440; ☆12, 1964). "Do the Clam" (RCA Victor 47-8500; ☆21, 1965). "Crying in the Chapel" (RCA Victor 447-0643; ☆3, 1965). "(Such an) Easy Question" (RCA Victor 47-8585; ☆11, 1965). "I'm Yours" (RCA Victor 47-8657; ☆11, 1965). "Puppet on a String" (RCA Victor 447-0650; ☆14, 1965). "Tell Me Why" (RCA Victor 47-8740; ☆33, 1966). "Frankie and Johnny" b/w "Please Don't Stop Loving Me" (RCA Victor 47-8780; ☆25, 1966). "Love Letters" (RCA Victor 47-8870; ☆19, 1966). "Spinout" b/w "All That I Am" (RCA Victor 47-8941; ☆40, 1966). "Indescribably Blue" (RCA Victor 47-9056; ☆33, 1967). "Big Boss Man" b/w "You Don't Know Me" (RCA Victor 47-9341; ☆38, 1967). "Guitar Man" (RCA Victor 47-9425; ☆43, 1968). "U.S. Male" (RCA Victor 47-9465; ☆28, 1968). "If I Can Dream" (RCA 47-9670; ☆12, 1968). "Memories" (RCA 47-9731; ☆35, 1969). "In the Ghetto" (RCA 47-9741; ☆3, 1969). "Clean Up Your Own Back Yard" (RCA 47-9747; ☆35, 1969). "Suspicious Minds" (RCA 47-9764; ☆1, 1969). "Don't Cry Daddy" (RCA 47-9768; c☆13, ☆6, 1969). "Kentucky Rain" (RCA 47-9791; ☆16, 1970). "The Wonder of You" (RCA 47-9835; ☆9, 1970). "I've Lost You" (RCA 47-9873; ☆32, 1970). "You Don't Have to Say You Love Me" (RCA 47-9916; ☆11, 1970). "I Really Don't Want to Know" (RCA 47-9960; c☆9, ☆21, 1970). "Where Did They Go, Lord" (RCA 47-9980; ☆33, 1971). "I'm Leavin' " (RCA 47-9998; ☆36, 1971). "Until It's Time for You to Go" (RCA 74-0619; ☆40, 1972). "Burning Love" (RCA 74-0769; ☆2, 1972). "Separate Ways" (RCA 74-0815; ☆20, 1972). "Steamroller Blues" b/w "Fool" (RCA 74-1910; c☆31, ☆17, 1973). "Raised on Rock" b/w "For Ol' Times Sake" (RCA 0088; c☆42, ☆41, 1973). "I've Got a Thing about You Baby" b/w "Take Good Care of Her" (RCA 0196; c☆4, ☆39, 1974). "If You Talk in Your Sleep" b/w "Help Me" (RCA 0280; c☆6, ☆17, 1974). "Promised Land" b/w "It's Midnight" (RCA 10074; c☆9, ☆14, 1974). "My Boy" (RCA 10191; c☆14, ☆20, 1975). "T-R-O-U-B-L-E" (RCA 10278; c☆11, ☆35, 1975). "Pieces of My Life" (RCA 10401; c☆33, 1975).

(Chart positions compiled from Joel Whitburn's *Record Research,* based on *Billboard* Pop chart, unless otherwise indicated; r☆ = position on *Billboard* Rhythm and Blues chart; c☆ = position on *Billboard* Country and Western chart.)

The Sound of New Orleans
by Langdon Winner

Tales from American folklore attach a flattering, but totally exaggerated, importance to New Orleans as the wellspring of the nation's musical traditions. Schoolchildren are asked to believe that the lovely city on the Gulf of Mexico was the "home of jazz," "gave birth to the blues," and spread the rudiments of black music in great shovelfuls pitched from steamboats chugging up and down the Mississippi. Hollywood filmmakers of the Fifties liked to portray Louis Armstrong and his Dixieland band parading through nightclubs, as if in the middle of some never-ending odyssey, playing "When the Saints Go Marching In"; regardless of plot or context, the action would stop long enough for the actors to pay homage to old Satchmo and the place where it all supposedly began—New Orleans.

In point of fact, there was no one geographical center that served as the origin for the many strands of music which have sprung from this continent during the past century. The wonder of it is that jazz, blues, and rock and roll have flourished in many different forms and localities across the land. Nevertheless, though the myth of New Orleans is a distortion, there is no denying the magnificence of the city's actual contributions. Among other things, the place has given us the oldest, richest, and most influential continuing tradition of rock and roll playing the music has ever had. A joyous, rambling, uncomplicated feeling for rhythm, melody and lyric ties together the likes of Fats Domino, Huey "Piano" Smith, Little Richard, Lloyd Price, Shirley and Lee, Professor Longhair, Clarence "Frogman" Henry, Ernie K-Doe, Chris Kenner, Lee Dorsey, Dr. John, Allen Toussaint and others as master craftsmen of a special "sound." Within this extraordinary genealogy other notable families—Motown, Stax/Volt, British rock, and reggae—find their ancestry.

New Orleans's vitality as a musical capital reflects the rich diversity of ethnic groups and cultural elements forming its local culture. Founded in 1718 as a French colony, the city was later transferred to Spain, then back to France before it finally became an official part of the United States in the Louisiana Purchase of 1803. Pre-Civil War trade in slaves and cotton brought fabulous wealth to the coffers of this convenient seaport. In its ability to mix elegant high fashion with delights from the haunts of sin and shame, New Orleans soon became notorious as a place where the good life was easily available. Over the years the city became a home for people of remarkably diverse origins—French, African, English, Spanish, Western Indian, Cajun and Creole. From their harmony and conflict arose a distinctive culture, a characteristic food, dress, architecture, language, entertainment and public ritual, which gave New Orleans an exotic atmosphere totally exceptional for an American city.

Rock and roll performers nurtured in this fertile environment had a wealth of musical sources upon which to draw. The fabulous ensemble playing of the black funeral bands, the syn-copated "second line" rhythms of Mardi Gras parades, the rugged country blues from the surrounding Mississippi delta, the raucous chords of barrelhouse piano players, the elegant styles of jazz improvisation—all became underlying elements of New Orleans rock. The first major hit in this genre, Fats Domino's "The Fat Man," is a poorly disguised version of the old barrelhouse standard, "Junker's Blues." Just triple the blues tempo, change the words "Some people call me a junker, because I am loaded all the time," to "They call, they call me the fat man, because I weigh two hundred pounds," and you've got it. In mid-career, Shirley and Lee produced a small hit, "Feel So Good," which they proudly took credit for having written. Actually, of course, the tune is a version of an old standard, "It Feels So Good," which the parade bands had been playing for decades. Again and again, in this tradition a well-established set of riffs, rhythms, tunes and lyrics is cleverly reworked to provide the basis for new songs and new careers.

Typical of the influence this heady mixture has had on rock and roll is the work of a seminal postwar rhythm and blues player, the legendary Professor Longhair. Born Henry Roeland Byrd in Bogalusa in 1918, Longhair transformed the age-old tradition of barrelhouse playing into the foundations for a bass-centered rhythm and blues. Here it happened that an accident of low-life economics became crucial to musical history. Since whorehouses did not bother to keep their pianos well repaired and well tuned, the great barrelhouse pianists—Drive 'Em Down, Sullivan Rock, Kid Stormy Weather, and the latter-day exponent, Champion Jack Dupree—learned how to cover the keyboard with fists and fingers to extort the sound they wanted. Professor Longhair refined this rugged mode of attack, added some Latin rhythms, and sang blues lyrics with a raw, gentle voice. In the late Forties he began performing in New Orleans clubs and had an immediate impact on local audiences and musicians; over the next several years he recorded for Star Talent, Mercury, Atlantic and other labels and in 1950 had a minor R&B hit with "Bald Head." But his lasting influence extends far beyond his limited personal fame.

Already evident in Longhair's work is the essential substratum of all New Orleans rock and roll—a rugged rolling bass riff in which piano, string bass, guitar and saxophone chug along together, powerful but completely carefree. If Sun Records created rock's excited treble, New Orleans provided its solid bass foundations. Weaned on blues and boogie, Crescent City musicians have never been afraid to load up the lower end of the scale with more instrumentation than seems reasonable. On top of that foggy rumble it becomes possible to contrast the higher range of a fine tenor sax or the voice of a good R&B shouter and generate a marvelous tension in the music.

Two of the people most responsible for codifying this approach remain to this day relatively unknown and unheralded:

Lloyd Price and father, cresting; they don't make jackets like Lloyd's anymore, and you can't buy 'em either. (Michael Ochs Archives)

42

Dave Bartholomew and Cosimo Matassa. Bartholomew, trumpet player and bandleader of the best New Orleans R&B group of the late Forties and Fifties, wrote, arranged, and played for Fats Domino and other stars of the period. Son of Louis Bartholomew, a well-known Dixieland tuba player, Dave grew up learning how the sounds of a proper New Orleans group were crafted. In the two decades after World War II he kept a stable of first-class musicians together blowing in clubs like the Dew Drop Inn and Club Tijuana as well as in countless recording sessions. Earl Palmer, master of bass-drum syncopation and possibly the most inventive drummer rock and roll has ever had, was a mainstay in Bartholomew's organization. Tenor saxophonist Lee Allen, the Lester Young of rock, a superior improviser with a remarkable flair for constructing one-chorus solos precisely appropriate for a given tune, was another continuing presence in the group. Other capable musicians—Alvin "Red" Tyler, tenor; Frank Fields, string bass; Ernest McLean, guitar; Herb Hardesty, tenor; Wendell Duconge, alto; Clarence Ford, baritone and tenor; and Justin Adams, guitar—gave Bartholomew a sound which was extremely tight in the best musical sense yet totally relaxed in the accustomed Crescent City fashion. While Bartholomew's name never became widely known outside New Orleans, the truth is that he was one of the most successful tunesmiths of all time (eclipsed in the rock 'n' roll era of the Fifties only by Jerry Leiber and Mike Stoller). The reason was, of course, that teamed with Domino, he had composed dozens of best-selling tunes.

Another unheralded but nonetheless crucial figure was Cosimo Matassa, owner and chief engineer of J&M studio, where all of the New Orleans groups recorded. Cosimo devised a simple formula for rock recording similar to that used by George Goldner and other early producers: set the dials at some sensible level, turn on the tape machine and let the performers wail. Either one caught the sound live or one did the song over again until it was right. No overdubbing, no electronic manipulation (other than an occasional echo or sound effect) was ever utilized. In the Fifties, performers like Little Richard and Ray Charles flocked to Cosimo's studio in search of that marvelous sound which came from the New Orleans sessionmen, the acoustics of the room and the simplicity of Cosimo's control board. Attempts in the Seventies by Dr. John and others to employ much more sophisticated techniques to achieve the same effects proved utterly fruitless: the fullness of electronic embellishment sounds completely hollow when compared to the amazing density of the J&M takes.

First signs of national recognition of the New Orleans style came in 1948 with the success of Roy Brown's "Good Rockin' Tonight" on Deluxe. Although Wynonie Harris's cover version of the song sold more copies, Brown's lugubrious blues vocals and big-band arrangements soon became trend setters in

rhythm and blues. Brown went on to record a series of first-rate minor hits in the early 1950s, and after exerting a profound influence on the vocal styles of B.B. King, Bobby Bland and Jackie Wilson, faded into virtual obscurity.

With the exception of Fats Domino's steadily growing popularity, the early Fifties were fairly modest years for New Orleans performers. Pianists like Paul Gayten and Archibald recorded very good material which failed to catch on with the rhythm and blues audience. Gravelly-voiced Smiley Lewis, heavily influenced by Fats Domino's singing, made a string of records which in retrospect stand out as small gems. But except for "The Bells Are Ringing," briefly a hit in 1952, and the reflected glory of Gale Storm's smash cover of his "I Hear You Knocking" in 1955, Smiley was never able to find listeners for his buzzy, hard-edge singing.

A more successful Domino imitator, Lloyd Price, claimed a hit with "Lawdy Miss Clawdy" on Specialty in 1952. Price made a series of fine records on Specialty in subsequent years, but none with the popular appeal of his first success. Although a capable blues balladeer, Price was at his best in peppy, up-tempo numbers which matched his husky, handsome voice with a hard-charging brass and reed section. Several years later, in 1957–1959, he refined this style in a sequence of national hits on ABC: "Stagger Lee," "Personality," "I'm Gonna Get Married" and others were among the most successful commercial adaptations of the New Orleans métier.

Another extraordinary Specialty artist of the early Fifties was Guitar Slim, whose slow blues, "The Things That I Used to Do," topped the R&B charts in early 1954. Born Eddie Jones in Greenwood, Mississippi, in 1926, Slim was able to synthesize the essence of country blues singing and guitar with a rhythm and blues band backup. Most importantly, he managed to expand the limits of electric blues guitar playing. Comparing Slim's work to that of Jimi Hendrix, New Orleans songwriter Al Reed told blues historian John Broven: "He had an electric sound like you never heard and they would open the club doors wide so that the sound could just go in and out of the club and he would draw people off the street. Big passing automobiles would stop and just listen to this guy play and watch him walk." As the decade went on, Guitar Slim's star fell into eclipse. Moving to Atco Records in 1957, he was unable to match the sound and success of his early work. Slim died a young man of 32 in 1959, the victim of ill health, drink, and undeserved neglect.

The great breakthrough year for New Orleans finally came in 1955, the point at which R&B finished its metamorphosis into rock and roll and began to win a huge national audience. It was then that Fats Domino's gentle Creole voice began to be heard by Northern teenagers increasingly able to distinguish the genuine music in songs like "Ain't It a Shame" from Pat Boone's pale, cleaned-up imitations. It was then also that the wonderful, wild Little Richard, backed by a great Crescent City

Huey "Piano" Smith, Boss of the 88s in the New Orleans of the Fifties, turned to better things in the Seventies. Or so it would seem. (Greg Shaw/'Who Put the Bomp')

studio band, unleashed "Tutti-Frutti" on an American public that had never heard anything like it. Over the next five years the first generation of New Orleans rock performers had dozens of national hits which, along with innovations out of New York, Philadelphia, Chicago, Memphis and Texas, totally transformed the popular music penetrating the everyday lives of Americans.

Most popular of the New Orleans-based performers were, of course, Fats Domino, Little Richard and Lloyd Price, each with his string of best sellers. But other artists of lesser standing had their moments in the spotlight as well. Characteristic of the second-level New Orleans artists of this period was a tendency to sing novelty songs and to employ musical gimmicks to catch the listener's ear. The jokes and goofing on the records are sometimes fun, sometimes totally annoying. New Orleans rock is so fundamentally solid that the layers of nonsense often get in the way of what the listener wants to hear.

One master of this musical mummery, Clarence "Frogman" Henry, made a tiny dent in the hit parade in 1956 with a catchy tune, "Ain't Got No Home," cut with Paul Gayten's band. In the song, Clarence bemoans the modern condition of rootlessness and anomie, using falsettos to mimic a woman's voice and a frog's. Tibetan monks traditionally sang by inhaling rather than exhaling, a technique enabling a single voice to produce as many as three notes at once. As he inhaled to croak the part of the frog, Clarence Henry rediscovered this fruitful but seldom used musical approach. In the early Sixties the Frogman (minus the frog voice) returned to national promi-

nence with the ballads "I Don't Know Why, but I Do" and "You Always Hurt the One You Love." Clarence Henry still performs in New Orleans clubs, one of the most accessible of the performers of the old school.

Another act in which the tension between pure talent and obvious contrivance played a central role was the male/female duo Shirley and Lee. Plucked off the streets of the Latin Quarter by Eddie Mesner of Aladdin Records in the early Fifties, young teenagers Shirley Goodman and Leonard Lee were billed as the "Sweethearts of the Blues." After their original success in 1952 with a doo-wop song, "I'm Gone," they made a continuing series of records which described the ecstasy and turmoil of a young couple in the throes of first romance—"Shirley Come Back to Me," "Shirley's Back," "Lee Goofed," and others with the same theme. Even more important to their success than the convenient boy/girl device, however, was the bizarre, alluring quality of Shirley Goodman's voice. When Shirley sings, her natural voice goes simultaneously sharp and flat. Each note is an average of tones, a half-step up and a half-step down. There is no strain or contortion of her vocal cords to achieve this effect. It's simply what comes out. "My voice is a gimmick rather than a singing voice," Shirley commented recently. "I've tried to change it many times; I used to go out and scream and scream trying to force it to go down. But that only made it stranger than before."

Shirley and Lee soared to national fame in 1956 with "Let the Good Times Roll." A clever merry-go-round riff played by a hot J&M studio band sets the tune in motion. Lee's pleasant, orthodox blues vocal carries the first two choruses solo. Then on the third time around Shirley steps forward. "Come on, baby, let the good times roll/Come on, baby, let me thrill your soul." The listener isn't sure whether to take the record back as defective, have the phonograph repaired, or just pay closer attention. Although it reached no higher than Number 27 on the *Billboard* lists, "Let the Good Times Roll" stayed a hit long enough to sell a million copies and has been remade in countless versions during the two decades since. Unfortunately, Shirley and Lee never were able to find a suitable followup. "I Feel Good," "That's What I Wanna Do," and "Rock All Nite" were interesting, well-produced songs with a fine groove, but none of them enjoyed the sales of their one smash hit. Perhaps their sound was just a little too "black," a little too roughhewn to win the permanent favors of the white record-buying public.

Shirley and Lee eventually fell back to the rhythm and blues circuit and continued to perform as a team until 1963. Leonard Lee has now given up music altogether and works for a U.S. government poverty agency. Shirley's still-incredible voice surfaced again as the lead in the colossal disco hit of 1975, "Shame, Shame, Shame." Few if any of the fans who enjoyed this ebullient dance number realized that the Shirley of Shirley and Company was the same woman whose voice had scandalized popular music two decades earlier.

The ultimate extension of New Orleans music's playful dynamism during this period was achieved by the most wonderful of second-level groups, Huey "Piano" Smith and the Clowns. Since the late Forties, Smith had been a journeyman keyboard wizard in the bands of Guitar Slim and Earl King and had played on dozens of recording sessions with Smiley Lewis, Shirley and Lee and others. With the founding of Johnny Vincent's Ace Records in Jackson, Mississippi, Huey was given a chance to show his stuff. A lazy, loping ditty called "Rockin' Pneumonia and the Boogie Woogie Flu," reached the middle of the Top 100 in August 1957. Several months later the Clowns' fabulous two-sided hit, "Don't You Just Know It" b/w "High Blood Pressure," captured Number Nine on the charts.

All of Smith's singles on Ace carry the same basic format. A heavily accented left-hand piano is set against a low, growling saxophone section. Above that, human voices of varying degrees of freakiness wail away as best they can with lyrics containing as little intelligible verbal content as possible. The poignant hook line in "Don't You Just Know It"—"gooba, gooba, gooba, gooba"—is about as profound as the message ever gets. Sounds, not words, were Huey's forte. His organization featured some of the finest instrumentalists in rock, including Lee Allen, Red Tyler and drummer Charles "Hungry" Williams, and a collection of the wildest singers going. Matched with the gruff talking bass of Billy Roosevelt and shrill squeals of Gerri Hall was the elegant master of nasalized lead vocals, Bobby Marchan (whom many fans mistakenly believed to be Huey Smith). The Clowns' ability to mix comic voices, piano and saxophone produced what may have been the most exciting rock 'n' roll band of its time.

Although Smith and his group soon ran short of good material and began to slip from national popularity, they did appear on a record which stands today as the finest example of pure romping, stomping New Orleans rock ever made—Frankie Ford's "Sea Cruise." In this hit of early 1959, all of the elements of a sound which had been evolving for a decade are carried to their logical extremes. The New Orleans horns finally cook like their lives depend on it. The piano prances along, reaching the very essence of boogie-woogie. The lead vocal finally achieves the perfect mix of pure joke and pure hysteria: "Old man rhythm gets in my shoes/It's no use sitting and singing the blues." White pretty boy Frankie Ford—Ace's first attempt to find a teen idol—sings the tune in a style heavily indebted to Bobby Marchan. In the background, overdubbed foghorns add a deranged emphasis. *Bwammmp! Bwammmmmmmp! Bwammmmmmmmmmmmmp!* Completely out of control, threatening to take over the whole damned song, the foghorns are definitely necessary; another version of the song which Huey Smith did without them missed the boat completely. What we have in the foghorns is the perfect embodiment of the sound

New Orleans hornmen had been after for years. The Queen Mary as the ultimate baritone sax!

As the 1950s drew to a close, it was becoming clear that the music of the first generation of New Orleans performers was wearing dangerously thin. Ace Records' Jimmy Clanton wooed white audiences with sweet pap like "Just a Dream," "Go, Jimmy, Go," and "Venus in Blue Jeans" and became a crashing bore. A host of once-successful artists floundered and were no longer able to discover formulas which could sell records. A sign of the vitality of New Orleans as a rock tradition was its ability at this point to transform its foundations, retain its integrity, and advance to a whole new stage. The person most crucial to this remarkable renewal was a young, quiet, almost compulsively shy pianist, writer and producer, Allen Toussaint.

As a teenager, Toussaint hung around studios and clubs copying musicians' licks and learning the trade. He idolized Professor Longhair and succeeded in mastering all of the tricks of classic New Orleans piano. After a time he was asked to play in sessions for Fats Domino and other senior performers. Young Toussaint, the word got out, was a "natural," a man who played rhythm and blues as easily as breathing.

In 1960, while still in his early 20s, Toussaint became the producer, arranger and bandleader for newly formed Minit Records. By the summer of that year he had already scored his first hit, "Ooh Poo Pah Doo" by Jessie Hill. The song features Hill's crazed shouting on simple, yes, even idiotic lyrics. In the background the band moves along through an ambling, cleverly syncopated pattern, a deliberate contrast to the unrestrained madness of the vocal. Toussaint's trademark, then as now, is a lively but light-handed background riff. The horns enter and leave to punctuate the lyric rather than keep up a sustained, rocking flow. Often the drummer applies the brushes rather than attack with Earl Palmer-style crackling sticks. The hard-edge thrusting of earlier New Orleans bands is completely gone. With a group of fine studio musicians—Roy Montrell, guitar; Chuck Badie, bass; Nat Perrilliat, tenor; Clarence Ford, baritone; James Black, drums—Toussaint chose a much more mellow approach.

Another characteristic of Toussaint's production is the use of ingenious hook lines, often delivered at a pause in the music at the end of a chorus. Two superior examples of this device became hits in spring 1961: Ernie K-Doe's "Mother-In-Law" and Chris Kenner's "I Like It like That." Ernest Kador (K-Doe) has a sharp, sparkling voice, not unlike a latter-day Bobby Marchan. In his only big hit, one of the few New Orleans songs to reach Number One, he complains of the tribulations of domestic life: "If she'd leave us alone/ We could have a happy home/ Sent from down below . . ." The music stops and foggy-voiced Benny Spellman chimes in, "Mutha-in-law."

"I Like It like That" finds a male chorus trading lines with reedy-voiced Chris Kenner, who moans whimsically, "Come on, come on, let me show you where it's at." Kenner: "The name of the place is . . . " Chorus: "I like it like that." A little jewel in the Crescent City genre, the tune begins with a brief piano signature, a nod of acknowledgment to Huey Smith.

In the salad days of 1961–1963 Toussaint produced dozens of wonderful songs on the Minit, Instant, A.F.O. and Fury labels. "Ya Ya," Number Seven in September 1961, featured the creamy soft tones of Lee Dorsey singing the extraordinarily dumb lines, "Sittin' in la la/Waitin' for my ya ya." Barbara George scored with "I Know" later the same year. Chris Kenner had a second hit with "Land of 1000 Dances" in 1963. With varying degrees of commercial success, Toussaint also worked with Aaron Neville, Irma Thomas, Benny Spellman, Eskew Reeder, Diamond Joe and Allen Orange. Traces of his influence are also evident on the marvelous anthem to rock 'n' roll, "It Will Stand," a small hit by the Showmen in late 1961.

With Toussaint's departure into the army in 1963, New Orleans fell into a musical doldrums. In the following year the best it could muster was the dazzlingly insipid "Chapel of Love" by the Dixie Cups, which climbed, Lord knows how, to Number One in the country. Not until 1965, when Toussaint left uniform and teamed up again with Lee Dorsey, was the music put back on its feet. With more mature, more complex arrangements than they had employed earlier, Dorsey and Toussaint released a series of hits: "Ride Your Pony" (1965); "Get Out of My Life Woman," "Working in the Coal Mine," and "Holy Cow" (1966); and "Everything I Do Gonna Be Funky" (1969). These and other less well known songs amount to the New Orleans version of mid-Sixties soul music.

As New Orleans rock approaches its fourth decade, it is difficult to tell whether the music is at last completely exhausted or merely waiting for another burst of enthusiasm. The warhorses of the Forties and Fifties have retired or been enshrined as officially designated "oldies." Allen Toussaint still commands great respect as a producer on the national scene and continues to record interesting, New Orleans-style albums with Lee Dorsey, the Meters and under his own name. A Los Angelesized revival of everything weird in the Latin Quarter arrived in the late Sixties in the form of Dr. John the Night Tripper. Under his real name, Mac Rebennack, the doctor was present as a peripheral figure in some of the less important moments in Fifties recordings. His *Gumbo* album on Atlantic and occasional flashes in other performances recapture some of the tunes and feelings of the old masters. But neither Dr. John's decadence nor Allen Toussaint's enduring brilliance give much hope that the sound will be capable of yet another transfiguration.

New Orleans's great contribution to rock and roll represents the vitality of a local environment in which things could grow and blossom at their own speed. Against the forces of an ex-panding, homogenizing national culture, the music was able to maintain its integrity and breathe freely. Its performers were not so much stars as they were master craftsmen of a special indigenous art. Educated in ways of playing passed on from generation to generation, they enjoyed the special nourishment which only a strong tradition can bring.

Discography

1950–1965

Paul Gayten and Annie Laurie, "I'll Never Be Free" (Regal 3258; r☆8, 1950). **Archibald,** "Stack-a'-Lee" (Imperial 5068; r☆10, 1950). **Roy Brown,** "Hard Luck Blues" (Deluxe 3304; r☆1, 1950). **Larry Darnell,** "I Love My Baby" (Regal 3274; r☆4, 1950). **Roy Byrd (Professor Longhair),** "Bald Head" (Mercury 8175; r☆5, 1950). **Roy Brown,** "Love Don't Love Nobody" (Deluxe 3306; r☆2, 1950). "Cadillac Baby" b/w "Long about Sundown" ((Deluxe 3308; r☆6, 1950). **Larry Darnell,** "Oh Babe" (Regal 3298; r☆5, 1950). **Roy Brown,** "Big Town" (Deluxe 3318; r☆8, 1951). **Lloyd Price,** "Lawdy Miss Clawdy" (Specialty 428; r☆1, 1952). **Smiley Lewis,** "The Bells Are Ringing" (Imperial 5194; r☆10, 1952). **Lloyd Price,** "Oooh-Oooh-Oooh" b/w "Restless Heart" (Specialty 440; r☆5, 1952). **Shirley and Lee,** "I'm Gone" (Aladdin 3153; r☆2, 1953). **Lloyd Price,** "Ain't It a Shame" (Specialty 452; r☆7, 1953). **Guitar Slim,** "The Things I Used to Do" (Specialty 482; r☆1, 1954). **Spiders,** "I Didn't Want to Do It" b/w "You're the One" (Imperial 5265; r☆3, 1954). **Earl King,** "Don't Take It So Hard" (King 4780; r☆13, 1955). **Shirley and Lee,** "Feel So Good" (Aladdin 3289; r☆5, 1955). **Smiley Lewis,** "I Hear You Knocking" (Imperial 5356; r☆2, 1955). **Spiders,** "Witchcraft" (Imperial 5366; r☆7, 1955). **Shirley and Lee,** "Let the Good Times Roll" (Aladdin 3325; ☆27, r☆2, 1956). "I Feel Good" (Aladdin 3338; ☆38, r☆5, 1956). **Clarence "Frog Man" Henry,** "Ain't Got No Home" (Argo 5259; ☆30, r☆3, 1956). **Lloyd Price,** "Just Because," (ABC-Paramount 9792; ☆29, r☆4, 1957). **Annie Laurie,** "It Hurts to Be in Love" (Deluxe 6107; ☆61, r☆3, 1957). **Huey "Piano" Smith and the Clowns,** "Rocking Pneumonia and the Boogie Woogie Flu" (Ace 530; ☆52, r☆9, 1957). **Lee Allen and his Band,** "Walkin' with Mr. Lee" (Ember 1027; ☆54, 1958). **Huey "Piano" Smith and the Clowns,** "Don't You Just Know It" (Ace 545; ☆9, r☆4, 1958). **Jimmy Clanton,** "Just a Dream" (Ace 546; ☆4, r☆1, 1958). **Huey "Piano" Smith and the Clowns,** "Don't You Know Yockomo" (Ace 553; ☆56, 1958). **Lloyd Price,** "Stagger Lee" (ABC-Paramount 9972; ☆1, r☆1, 1958). **Frankie Ford,** "Sea Cruise" (Ace 554; ☆14, r☆11, 1959). **Lloyd Price,** "Where Were You (on Our Wedding Day)" (ABC-Paramount 9997; ☆23, r☆4, 1959). "Personality" (ABC-Paramount 10018; ☆2, r☆1, 1959). "I'm Gonna Get Married" (ABC-Paramount 10032; ☆3, r☆1, 1959). **Jivin' Gene,** "Breaking Up Is Hard to Do" (Mercury 71485; ☆69, 1959). **Paul Gayten,** "The Hunch" (Anna 1106; ☆68, 1959). **Frankie Ford,** "Come into My Heart" b/w "Wont'cha Come Home" (ABC-Paramount 10062; ☆20, r☆2, 1959). **Frankie Ford,** "Time after Time" (Ace 580; ☆75, 1960). **Elton Anderson,** "Secret of Love" (Mercury 71542; ☆88, r☆22, 1960). **Lloyd Price,** "Lady Luck" b/w "Never Let Me Go" (ABC-Paramount 10075; ☆14, r☆3, 1960). **Jessie Hill,** "Ooh Poo Pah Doo—Part II" (Minit 607; ☆28, r☆3, 1960). **Lloyd Price,** "No Ifs—No Ands" (ABC-Paramount 10102; ☆40, r☆16, 1960). **Bobby Marchan,** "There's Something on Your Mind" (Fire 1022; ☆31, r☆1, 1960). **Lloyd Price,** "Question" (ABC-Paramount 10123; ☆19, r☆5, 1960). **Shirley and Lee,** "Let the Good Times Roll" (Warwick 581; ☆48, 1960). **Joe Jones,** "You Talk Too Much" (Ric 972; ☆3, r☆9, 1960). **Aaron Neville,** "Over You" (Minit 612; r☆21, 1960). **James Booker,** "Gonzo" (Peacock 1697; ☆43, r☆3, 1960). **Clarence "Frog Man" Henry,** "I Don't Know Why (but I Do)" (Argo 5378; ☆4, r☆9, 1961). **Joe Jones,** "California Sun" (Roulette 4344; ☆89, 1961). **Joe Barry,** "I'm a Fool to Care" (Smash 1702; ☆24, r☆15, 1961). **Ernie K-Doe,** "Mother-In-Law" (Minit 623; ☆1, r☆1, 1961). **Clarence "Frog Man" Henry,** "You Always Hurt the One You Love" (Argo 5388; ☆12, r☆11, 1961). **Chris Kenner,** "I Like It like That" (Instant 3229; ☆2, r☆2, 1961). **Ernie K-Doe,** "Te-Ta-Te-Ta-Ta" (Minit 627; ☆53, r☆21, 1961). **Clarence "Frog Man" Henry,** "Lonely Street" (Argo 5395; ☆57, r☆19, 1961). **Lee Dorsey,** "Ya Ya" (Fury 1053; ☆7, r☆1, 1961). **Barbara George,** "I Know" (AFO 302; ☆3, r☆1, 1961). **Showmen,** "It Will Stand" (Minit 632; r☆61, 1961). **Lee Dorsey,** "Do-Re-Mi" (Fury 1056; ☆27, r☆22, 1962). **Huey "Piano" Smith and the Clowns,** "Pop-Eye" (Ace 649; ☆51, 1962). **Barbara George,** "You Talk about Love" (AFO 304; ☆46, 1962). **Earl King,** "Always a First Time" (Imperial 5811; r☆17, 1962). **Benny Spellman,** "Lipstick Traces" (Minit 644; ☆80, r☆28, 1962). **Barbara Lynn,** "You'll Lose a Good Thing" (Jamie 1220; ☆8, r☆1, 1962). "You're Gonna Need Me" (Jamie 1240; ☆65, r☆13, 1962). **Chris Kenner,** "Land of 1000 Dances" (Instant 3252; ☆77, 1963). **Betty Harris,** "Cry to Me" (Jubilee 5456; ☆23, r☆10, 1963). **Lloyd Price,** "Misty" (Double-L 722; ☆21, r☆11, 1963). **Dixie Cups,** "Chapel of Love" (Red Bird 10-001; ☆1, 1964). **Alvin Robinson,** "Something You Got" (Tiger 104; ☆52, 1964). **Barbara Lynn,** "Oh! Baby" (Jamie 1277; ☆69, 1964). **Dixie Cups,** "People Say" (Red Bird 10-006; ☆12, 1964). "You Should Have Seen the Way He Looked at Me" (Red Bird 10-012; ☆39, 1964). "Iko Iko" (Red Bird 10-024; ☆20, r☆20, 1965). **Lee Dorsey,** "Ride Your Pony" (Amy 927; ☆28, r☆7, 1965).

(Omitting hits by Fats Domino and Little Richard. Compiled from Joel Whitburn's *Record Research,* based on *Billboard* Pop and Rhythm and Blues charts.)

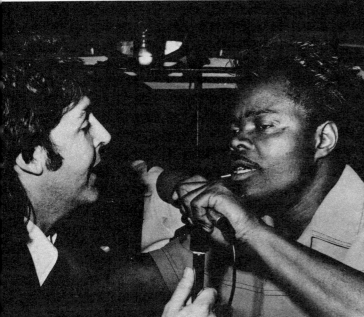

The WILD Sound of New Orleans by TOUSAN

RCA VICTOR
LPM-1767

Fats Domino
by Peter Guralnick

hristened Antoine Domino upon his birth on February 26th, 1928, in the Crescent City of New Orleans, "Fats" Domino was the most comfortable of the rock 'n' roll founders. He came unequipped with the usual iconography; he was never a sex symbol. He did not threaten the established order. He was neither a herald of the new age, like Elvis Presley, nor a scuffed-up leftover of the old, like Big Joe Turner. He was simply the most consistent, predictable hitmaker of them all over a period of nearly 20 years, selling more than 65 million records, earning—depending on whose claim you believe—more gold records (15, 18, 22) than anyone except Elvis and the Beatles. He was a performer of great charm but little charisma, the interpreter, if not the creator, of a music that is instantly recognizable, dominated by a warm vocal style and a thick, chunky, boogie-woogie-based New Orleans-flavored piano. He was a reassuring artist, all of whose records were put across in the same lazily inimitable fashion—a fashion that was undoubtedly informed with stylishness and wit, but that possessed none of the flash, none of the passion and outrageousness of Chuck Berry or Little Richard, Elvis or Jerry Lee Lewis.

It missed this passion, this sense of desperate release, primarily because Fats Domino was not breaking away from a tradition (hillbilly in the case of the white performers, jump blues in the case of the black): he was sustaining it. The New Orleans tradition goes back, of course, to the evolution of jazz in the Vieux Carré at the turn of the century, and carries through the great jazz names as well as celebrated whorehouse pianists like Kid Stormy Weather, Sullivan Rock, Drive 'Em Down. It is a tradition in which distinctions of musical genre are not easily made and one in which the boogie-woogie piano styles of non-New Orleans residents like Pine Top Smith, Jimmy Yancey, and Albert Ammons mix with the light, almost whimsical second-line, or syncopated, beat which permeates all of New Orleans music, from funeral marches to traditional jazz to the rhythm and blues with which Fats Domino began his career.

Fats Domino was born into a musical family. His father was a well-known violinist, and his brother-in-law, Harrison Verrett, some 20 years older than Fats, was a familiar figure in the city and mainstay for years in Fats's band on guitar. It was Verrett who taught Fats how to play piano by marking the keys for his nine-year-old brother-in-law and showing him the progressions. Once he learned how to play, music seems to have become the consuming interest in Domino's life, for he quit school at 14, went to work in a factory, and began playing the clubs at night. It was in one of those clubs, the Hideaway, that Dave Bartholomew, a trumpet player, bandleader, and fledgling entrepreneur, first heard the 21-year-old Fats Domino. He was local A&R man for the West Coast-based Imperial Records, and he soon arranged a session, backing Fats with his own band. The result was "The Fat Man," Fats's first hit and eventually (four years after it was released, in 1953) one of his first million-sellers.

There is nothing so very revolutionary, or even startling, about "The Fat Man." Like its flip side, "Detroit City Blues," it is a conventional enough blues, in this case eight-bar, based on Champion Jack Dupree's 1940 recording of "Junker Blues," which in turn was based on the traditional New Orleans treatment of the "Stag-o-Lee" melodic family (Lloyd Price's landmark 1952 crossover, "Lawdy Miss Clawdy," on which Fats Domino played piano, is another example, as, of course, is Price's Number One rock 'n' roll hit from 1958, "Stagger Lee"). The instrumentation is typical of the period, with riffing saxes, trumpet, full-bodied guitar, bass, and drums, and the boogie-woogie piano part could well have been played by any one of the legendary New Orleans pianists (Salvador Doucette, Huey "Piano" Smith, Archibald, Clarence "Frogman" Henry, or even Professor Longhair, the inspiration for them all), each more or less contemporaneous with Fats, all of whom could, and often did, imitate each other's styles almost flawlessly. Dave Bartholomew's charts are clear, punchy, and unadventurous. And the vocal, while featuring, it is true, Fats's unique buglelike falsetto waa-waaing, and pitched a little higher than on later Fats Domino recordings, is distinguished most not by any emotional intensity but by a sense of warmth, good humor, and an almost disarming simplicity.

In short, "The Fat Man" was a classic Fats Domino record, bringing together not only all the musical elements (instrumentation, blues form, production) but the very musicians, arranger, studio engineer (Cosimo Matassa), and cowriters (Domino-Bartholomew) who were to figure on nearly every one of Fats's hits for the next 20 years. It displayed as well those same qualities of gentle self-deprecation and reassuring familiarity which were to continue to serve Fats well; the setting, while slightly bluesier and rhythmically less regular than his later hits, reflects most of all the personality of the singer. There is no sign of strain, and you can almost picture the young Fats Domino characteristically cocking his head to one side, grinning in that shy ingratiating way, and leaning into the microphone to declare with no apparent self-consciousness, "They call, they call me the fat man/Because I weigh 200 pounds."

It wasn't until 1955 that Fats Domino officially crossed the color line with "Ain't It a Shame," but his records always sold in numbers (between 500,000 and a million) that belied his appeal to a strictly black audience. Perhaps this was because his blues were not very cutting, or perhaps it was because his lyrics, even when they had a serious intent ("Going home tomorrow/I can't stand your evil ways"), were tossed off with such deferential charm, with none of the implicit threat of raw blues singers like Muddy Waters or Howlin' Wolf. In any case it is obvious that Fats Domino had a wider appeal than any R&B artist of the time. According to Dave Bartholomew, "We

*Fats Domino celebrates 25 years
of performing ('Phonograph Record' magazine)*

Over the years virtually nothing changed. Strings were added, and Fats surmounted them. Standards were introduced, and "Blueberry Hill" became his biggest hit. The piano was confined mostly to right-hand triplets, the beat was accentuated with hand claps and tighter rhythms, and the feel remained the same. Fats left Imperial and signed with ABC in 1963. The hits slowed down, and Fats switched to Mercury in 1965, enjoying little success but cutting a live album which showed that the sound in any case hadn't altered. Even after fashion had passed him by, he came back with a 1968 hit, the Beatles' "Lady Madonna," and a relatively successful *Fats Is Back* LP. Removed from the trumped-up hysteria of the rock 'n' roll revival, his live shows continued to be a series of genial reunions, in which with a twist of his body, a flash of his chubby jeweled pinky, a shy winsome smile, or a discreet upward rolling of the eyes, Fats could evoke the charm of an era, convey his simple pleasure simply to be there and entertain.

Lately you don't hear so much from Fats. Perhaps he is simply played out, with those hundreds of songs, that vast repertoire of absolutely consistent product, forming a weight which makes it impossible to go forward. And, too, they say that the bands he fronts nowadays—after death, retirement, and disastrous road accidents have taken their toll—are pale imitations of the old days. Maybe so. But it's hard to believe that Fats will not come ambling back someday, slipping into the charts with another lazy, childlike, softly phrased, boogie-woogie accented, rock-solid hit. Regardless, Cosimo Matassa, the studio owner and engineer who oversaw the rise and fall of the New Orleans sound from the beginning, has long since provided a perfect epitaph. "Domino, he was creative," said Cosimo. "No matter what he does comes through. He could be singing the national anthem, you'd still know by the time he said two words it was him, obviously, unmistakably, and pleasurably him."

Discography

"The Fat Man" (Imperial 5058; r☆6, 1950). "Every Night About This Time" (Imperial 5099; r☆5, 1950). "Rockin' Chair" (Imperial 5145; r☆9, 1951). "Goin' Home" (Imperial 5180; r☆1, 1952). "How Long" (Imperial 5209; r☆9, 1952). "Goin' to the River" (Imperial 5231; r☆2, 1953). "Please Don't Leave Me" (Imperial 5240; r☆5, 1953). "Rose Mary" (Imperial 5251; r☆10, 1953). "Something's Wrong" (Imperial 5262; r☆6, 1953). "You Done Me Wrong" (Imperial 5272; r☆10, 1954). "Don't You Know" (Imperial 5340; r☆12, 1955). "Ain't It a Shame" (Imperial 5348; r☆1, ☆16, 1955). "All by Myself" (Imperial 5357; r☆3, 1955). "Poor Me" (Imperial 5369; r☆3, 1955). "Bo Weevil" (Imperial 5375; r☆6, ☆35, 1956). "I'm in Love Again" (Imperial 5386; r☆1, ☆5, 1956). "When My Dreamboat Comes Home" (Imperial 5396; r☆6, ☆22, 1956). "Blueberry Hill" (Imperial 5407; r☆1, ☆4, 1956). "Blue Monday" (Imperial 5417; r☆1, ☆9, 1956). "I'm Walkin'" (Imperial 5428; r☆1, ☆5, 1957). "Valley of Tears" (Imperial 5442; r☆4, ☆13, 1957). "Wait and See" (Imperial 5467; r☆14, ☆27, 1957). "Sick and Tired" (Imperial 5515; r☆15, ☆30, 1958). "Little Mary" (Imperial 5526; r☆15, ☆49, 1958). "Whole Lotta Loving" (Imperial 5553; r☆2, ☆6, 1958). "Telling Lies" (Imperial 5569; r☆13, ☆50, 1959). "I'm Ready" (Imperial 5585; r☆7, ☆16, 1959). "I Want to Walk You Home" (Imperial 5606; r☆1, ☆8, 1959). "Be My Guest" (Imperial 5629; r☆2, ☆8, 1959). "Walking to New Orleans" (Imperial 5675; r☆2, ☆6, 1960). "Three Nights a Week" (Imperial 5687; r☆8, ☆15, 1960). "My Girl Josephine" (Imperial 5704; r☆7, ☆14, 1960). "What a Price" (Imperial 5723; r☆7, ☆22, 1961). "It Keeps Rainin'" (Imperial 5753; r☆18, ☆23, 1961). "Let the Four Winds Blow" (Imperial 5764; r☆2, ☆15, 1961). "What a Party" (Imperial 5779; ☆22, 1961). "You Win Again" (Imperial 5816; ☆22, 1962).

(Chart positions taken from Joel Whitburn's *Record Research*, compiled from *Billboard* Pop chart, unless otherwise indicated; r☆ = position on *Billboard* Rhythm and Blues chart.)

all thought of him as a country and western singer. Not real downhearted, but he always had that flavor, not the gutbucket sound." It is little wonder, then, that Fats should have crossed over so easily when the new rock and roll market was solidified.

"Ain't It a Shame," "I'm in Love Again," "Blueberry Hill," "Blue Monday," "I'm Walkin'," "Whole Lotta Loving," "I'm Gonna Be a Wheel Some Day," "Be My Guest," "Walking to New Orleans," "My Girl Josephine," "Let the Four Winds Blow": it is a familiar litany—and not due to Fats's efforts alone, either. The songs, with their clean arrangements, simple melodies, casual feel, and catchy lyrics, were an invitation to white covers, and performers like Ricky Nelson, Pat Boone, even Elvis Presley tried their hand often and successfully at a style that was ready-made for co-optation.

Through the years the Domino-Bartholomew partnership continued, both in the studio and on the authorship of songs.

Little Richard

by Langdon Winner

As the needle touches the vinyl, there is a brief moment of silence. Then: "A WOP BOP ALU BOP A WOP BAM BOOM!" Has any record ever brought a more outrageous surprise?

A scant few voices made the difference in determining how rock 'n' roll sounds, and why it is so powerfully different from other kinds of music. On an autumn day in New Orleans in 1955, an unknown, struggling young blues singer named Richard Penniman suddenly found a voice which set America on its ear. In an unprecedented burst of sighs, moans, screams, whoos, and breathless panting, Little Richard opened whole continents of energy and expression for others to explore. Along with Elvis, Fats Domino, Chuck Berry and Buddy Holly, Richard's work defined what rock 'n' roll was all about. That he himself was able to lay claim to only a small corner of the territory he helped pioneer makes small difference now. Those who came after—the Beatles, the Rolling Stones, Creedence Clearwater, and countless others—carry his legacy in every song. Any list of rock immortals which does not include Little Richard near the top has gotten too sophisticated.

Richard Penniman was born December 5th, 1935, in Macon, Georgia, one of 12 children in his family. According to the story he now tells, his grandfather and two uncles were preachers, his father a seller of bootleg whiskey. As a boy, Richard sang gospel music and learned to play piano in a neighborhood church. But his growing hunger for music was thwarted by his parents. "I came from a family where my people didn't like rhythm and blues. Bing Crosby, 'Pennies from Heaven,' Ella Fitzgerald, was all I heard. And I knew there was something that could be louder than that, but I didn't know where to find it. And I found it was me."

Evidently, he made this discovery at a very young age. On one occasion Richard ran away from home to join one of the traveling medicine circuses working the South during that period. By the time Richard was 13, his father had become so disgusted with the boy's noise, strange clothing and wild antics that he threw him out of the house. Black music often bestows the name "Little" upon performers who show their style and talent early on. Some who earned this title—Little Esther Phillips and Little Stevie Wonder, for example—later dropped it as they sought a more mature public image. It is significant that Penniman never abandoned his "Little" and that the outrageous figure we saw at the birth of rock and roll and now see at the onset of middle age was already showing his "thing" in the streets, churches and clubs of Macon in the late Forties.

After Richard had been booted from his home, he went to live with a white couple, Ann and Johnny Johnson, who ran a Macon night spot, the Tick Tock Club. The Johnsons took care of him, put him back in school and let him perform in their club. To this day, Little Richard gives them credit for being second parents and for giving him his chance. The song "Miss Ann" is, according to Penniman, for and about Ann Johnson.

In 1951, at age 16, Richard performed at an audition organized by Daddy Zenas Sears of WGST in Atlanta and won a recording contract with RCA Victor. During the next two years, Richard cut eight sides for RCA. The songs from this period—"Every Hour," "Get Rich Quick," "Ain't Nothin' Happening," and others—are skillfully done small-band jump blues numbers in the style of Roy Brown. Richard's voice and habit of wavering around a note before hitting it are clearly developed even though there is little particularly original or exciting about the tunes.

Richard's next recordings were made in Houston around 1954, on Don Robey's Peacock label, with the Tempo Toppers and the Dueces of Rhythm, two backup groups handling vocals and instrumentals. Tunes from this period show Little Richard approaching his later rock 'n' roll breakthrough from the direction of orthodox rhythm and blues. In an easygoing doo-wop swing he croons, "Ain't that good news; I'm wild about the blues." There is a great deal of fun in songs like "Rice, Red Beans and Turnip Greens" and "Fool at the Wheel," but none of the raw power that marks his later work. In early 1955, Penniman went on to record four sides with the Johnny Otis Orchestra, also on the Peacock label. None of these early efforts on RCA and Peacock sold well.

Down on his luck, Penniman made a demo tape of rhythm and blues songs and mailed it to Art Rupe of Specialty Records in Los Angeles. According to one story, he then went back to Macon, washed dishes in a Greyhound bus depot and waited seven months before hearing from Specialty. Rupe found considerable promise in the tapes. He had been scouting the musical scene in New Orleans and thought it would be a fine idea to have a voice as sharp as Penniman's backed by a solid Crescent City rhythm section. He hired Bumps Blackwell as producer and booked Cosimo Matassa's J&M Studios for a session. On September 14th, 1955, the musicians gathered for what was destined to be a crucial turning point in American music.

Along with Elvis Presley's early sides for Sun Records, Little Richard's first day with Specialty gives us the chance to say, "Rock 'n' roll begins right here." Ironically, all the tunes from that first session, with the exception of one, are painfully dull: Richard is still trying to wring mileage out of an uninspiring rhythm and blues idiom. Then, almost as an afterthought, the players turn to a song based on an obscene ditty Richard liked to wail during the breaks. Revised for lyrical purity by New Orleans songwriter Dorothy La Bostrie, "Tutti-Frutti" leaps out as something audacious and new. Suddenly, all of the restraints and vanities of imitation are gone from Richard's singing. What we hear is a kind of comic madness which requires a gleeful, bombastic voice, chaotic piano playing and hard charging drums, guitars and saxophones. "I've got a gal/

Six inches of hair in July 1965, and that's not all
... the Handsomest Man in Rock 'n' Roll. ('Sepia' magazine)

52

Named Daisy/ She almost drives me crazy/ Whoooooo . . . " At long last Little Richard found (or, perhaps more accurately, stumbled into) his groove.

"Tutti-Frutti" was exciting enough to get played on white pop music stations, innocuous enough to prevent it from getting banned. For youngsters who had never heard black performers sing at full throttle, the effect was hypnotizing. Even though the words had been cleaned up, the pure sexual excitement of the song came through as plain as day—everyone knew that behind all that foolishness lurked a turn-on somewhere. Parents who might well tolerate Elvis Presley balked at the prospect of having Little Richard howl on the family phonograph. Yet the record soon sold 500,000 copies and had an impact far beyond its sales. Other black performers of the era, like Screamin' Jay Hawkins, may have been wilder and more exotic; but Richard succeeded in building strong ties to an audience that included hordes of white as well as black kids.

During his amazing rise to stardom, Little Richard cut about three dozen sides for Specialty, many of which became rock 'n' roll classics. "Long Tall Sally," "Slippin' and Slidin'," "Rip It Up," "Ready Teddy," "The Girl Can't Help It," "Send Me Some Lovin'," "Jenny, Jenny," "Miss Ann," "Keep A Knockin'," "Good Golly, Miss Molly," "Ooh! My Soul" and "True, Fine Mama" were all successful on the pop charts and established Little Richard as one of the leading forces in the revolution which had overtaken American pop music. Some of his songs employed a great New Orleans band—Earl Palmer (drums), Lee Allen (tenor sax), Alvin "Red" Tyler (baritone sax), Frank Fields (bass), and guitarists Edgar Blanchard, Justin Adams or Ernest McLean; other cuts used Los Angeles studio musicians capable of putting down equally hard-rocking sax and guitar riffs. (Whether or not Richard himself played piano on all of his hits is still a subject of controversy; according to his producer, Bumps Blackwell, there were four different piano players— Huey "Piano" Smith, James Booker, Edward Frank and Warren Myles, a suggestion Penniman himself vehemently denies.)

Complementing Richard's recordings from this period is his work in three motion pictures, each of which betrays a different side of the star's ebullient personality. All of them feature Little Richard standing at the piano in front of his band singing (actually lip-syncing) his hits. The first, *Don't Knock the Rock*, shows Richard as the Great God Pan, a combination of imp and clown. When he sings "He duck back in the alley," Richard spins away from the piano and dives back as if to hit the note right on time. With the saxophonist blowing a chorus while kneeling on the grand piano, Richard puts his foot up on the lid and begins exaggerated hip and body undulations— acceptable in public only under the guise of rock 'n' roll dance.

The Girl Can't Help It, released in December 1956, shows a totally different Richard—a serious, somber, vaguely threat-ening figure standing at the piano staring out into space. He looms as a great black force seeking his essential contact with the world, the rock 'n' roll equivalent of a blues singer haunted by dark obsessions.

Richard's last film, *Mister Rock and Roll*, adds yet another dimension to our understanding of what the man is about. Here we find him reeling about the stage rolling his eyes in a coy, beguiling pose which later fashion would term "gay." He wears a sweet but totally maniacal smile. There's more than a faint hint of something demented in his manner. Then the camera zooms in for a close-up. Can it be? Little Richard is wearing mascara! Those who think that Penniman's camp antics were born of a later period should take a closer look at this intriguing segment.

In 1957, at the very peak of his fame and less than a year and a half after his meteoric rise had begun, Little Richard suddenly quit rock 'n' roll and disappeared from the scene. Specialty Records did its best to conceal the fact, and continued to release records from his earlier sessions, including "Keep A Knockin'," which recording engineers pieced together from a short take Richard and his road band had blasted out at a Washington D.C., radio station in 1957. But essentially, Richard's career as a rock 'n' roller of the first rank was over. He withdrew into a world of religious study, evangelism and gospel singing, only to reemerge seven years later.

As is true of almost all aspects of Little Richard's career, the story of his decision to retire is shrouded in myth. The most popular account of the circumstances, one which Richard himself tells in widely differing versions, places the turning point at a powerful conversion experience which seized him on tour in Australia. A horrifying dream showed him the Apocalypse and the ugly stain of his own damnation. On an airplane flight soon after (which may or may not have been threatened by a fire on board), Richard prayed to God to hold that plane in the air. Evidently, the Lord in His infinite wisdom obliged. When Richard reached safety, he threw his jewelry into the harbor at Sydney, Australia, and vowed to cease his evil ways. He quit rock recording and touring and enrolled in Oakwood College, a bible school in Huntsville, Alabama, where he studied prophecy, revelation and God's message for our troubled times. From there he began a career which he hoped would make him a major force on the American evangelical circuit. A song he recorded somewhat later tells the story:

I'm quittin' show business; I want to go straight.
I'm going to serve my Lord, before it's too late.
If I die, while I'm in my sin,
I know that Jesus won't let me in.
I'm quittin' show business, I want to go straight.

Whether or not one believes this story, the fact is that Richard went the better part of a decade without offering a rock 'n' roll song under his own name. In the late Fifties, he appeared

anonymously on some lackluster remakes of Fats Domino hits done by his former road band, the Upsetters, on Little Star. But otherwise all of his records and public performances were pure gospel. Moving from one label to another—Coral, End, Crown, Mercury—Richard cut dozens of sides which comprise a rarely heard second Penniman opus. The earliest of these recordings show Richard trying to conceal his rock 'n' roll identity altogether. His voice presents itself in a mood of subdued reverence or in the unrestrained hysteria of a Sunday meeting. While most of the material from his religious period is undistinguished at best, there are a few great songs. One of them on Mercury, "He Got What He Wanted (but He Lost What He Had)," contains a doubly ironic commentary on Richard's own conversion experience. As a brassy big band blares in the background, he recites the sins of Judas, Adam and Eve and other Biblical figures and preaches that what is offered in temptation leads us to sacrifice the blessings we had all along. At some level the man obviously believed it.

Lamentably, Little Richard was never able to join Billy Graham and Oral Roberts in the world of evangelical chart-busters. And in 1964, stimulated by the success of the Beatles and more than a little jealous of their liberal use of his licks, Penniman finally returned to the world of pop music. Taking up exactly where he left off, he cut a tune on Specialty Records, "Bama Lama Bama Loo," which has much the same kinetic drive and childlike foolishness of his mid-Fifties work. The song attracted enough attention to put it in the 80s on the *Billboard* Hot 100. But tastes had changed; any continuation of this anachronistic approach seemed ridiculous.

From this point, Little Richard's career became a series of frustrated comeback attempts. Shifting from Vee-Jay to Modern, Okeh and Brunswick, he issued a stream of dreadful remakes of his own and other people's oldies. Occasionally, there were flashes of brilliance. In 1965, he worked up a powerful new single for Vee-Jay, "I Don't Know What You've Got but It's Got Me," a Don Covay song expressing the desperation of a man whose woman is cheating on him. A slow blues spiced with gospel-style preaching, the song suggests that the Lord's message is ultimately one of betrayal, abandonment and utter loss. Richard's beautifully agonized singing, comparable to the approach which made Otis Redding famous a short while later, suggests the beginning of an interesting new phase. The record, however, fell stillborn from the plastic presses.

It is not as if Richard was never given an adequate second chance. A major recording contract with Reprise in the early Seventies enabled him to release three albums of new material—*The Rill Thing, King of Rock and Roll* and *Second Coming*. Indeed, each of these records had its moments; Richard's extraordinary voice can still belt out a song as well as ever. But the albums ooze a kind of "getting with the kids and their groovy out-of-sight soul beat" overproduction which makes them barely listenable. The solid center of gravity that once

held it all together had vanished. Richard's wildness just seemed flaky.

At the same time that the "Georgia Peach" was making his bid on Reprise, he also regained a certain notoriety by appearing on late-night television talk shows. "They won't forget me," he would tell friends before he went on. He was right about that. Sporting mirror-cloth costumes with long capes, dangling frills and hideous pancake makeup, Penniman made himself a spectacle by whooping it up, talking out of turn and running through the audience screaming, "I am the most beautiful thing in show business!" The crowning moment came when he actually displaced Johnny Carson from behind Carson's sacred little desk. As his former fans watched in dismay, many wondered whether it might not have been better for the man to have stayed in the church, in the closet, or both.

Little Richard still performs in occasional oldies revivals around the U.S. and Europe in which he makes a virtue of *not* having his act together. Babbling on at length between songs (perhaps to catch his breath at the onset of middle age), bawling out his bands for no apparent reason, Penniman appears to enjoy putting his audiences on edge with schizy pranks. There is no denying either his greatness as a musical spirit or his total desperation at being unable to achieve popularity again. It is ironic that the very qualities which once made him a lovable prime mover in the music—his wild, unrestrained, unformed, joyful passion—now block his access to the title that he has always believed rightfully his—the King of Rock 'n' Roll.

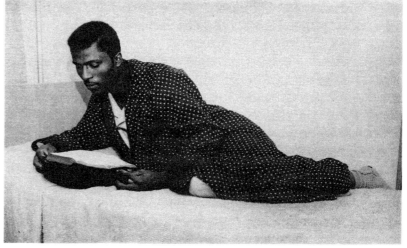

Discography

"Tutti-Frutti" (Specialty 561; ☆21, r☆2, 1955). "Long Tall Sally" b/w "Slippin' and Slidin' " (Specialty 572; ☆13, r☆1, 1956). "Rip It Up" b/w "Reddy Teddy" (Specialty 579; ☆27, r☆1, 1956). "She's Got It" (Specialty 584; r☆15, 1956). "The Girl Can't Help It" (Specialty 591; ☆49, r☆11, 1957). "Lucille" b/w "Send Me Some Lovin' " (Specialty 598; ☆27, r☆2, 1957). "Jenny, Jenny" b/w "Miss Ann" (Specialty 606; ☆14, r☆2, 1957). "Keep A Knockin' " (Specialty 611; ☆8, r☆5, 1957). "Good Golly, Miss Molly" (Specialty 624; ☆10, r☆6, 1958). "Ooh! My Soul" b/w "True, Fine Mama" (Specialty 633; ☆35, r☆15, 1958). "Baby Face" (Specialty 645; ☆41, r☆12, 1958). "I Don't Know What You've Got but It's Got Me" (Vee-Jay 698; ☆92, r☆12, 1965). "Freedom Blues" (Reprise 0907; ☆47, r☆28, 1970).

(Chart positions compiled from Joel Whitburn's *Record Research*, based on *Billboard* Pop charts, unless otherwise indicated; r☆ = position on *Billboard* Rhythm and Blues charts.)

Chuck Berry

by Robert Christgau

Chuck Berry is the greatest of the rock and rollers. Elvis competes with Frank Sinatra, Little Richard camps his way to self-negation, Fats Domino looks old, and Jerry Lee Lewis looks down his noble honker at all those who refuse to understand that Jerry Lee has chosen to become a great country singer. But for a fee—which went up markedly after the freak success of "My Ding-a-Ling," his first certified million-seller, in 1972, and has now diminished again—Chuck Berry will hop on a plane with his guitar and go play some rock and roll. He is the symbol of the music—the first man elected to a Rock Music Hall of Fame that exists thus far only in the projections of television profiteers; the man invited to come steal the show at the 1975 Grammys, although he has never been nominated for one himself, not even in the rock and roll or rhythm and blues categories. More important, he is also the music's substance—he taught George Harrison and Keith Richard to play guitar long before he met either, and his songs are still claimed as encores by everyone from folkies to heavy-metal kids. But Chuck Berry isn't merely the greatest of the rock and rollers, or rather, there's nothing mere about it. Say rather that unless we can somehow recycle the concept of the great artist so that it supports Chuck Berry as well as it does Marcel Proust, we might as well trash it altogether.

As with Charlie Chaplin or Walt Kelly or the Beatles, Chuck Berry's greatness doesn't depend entirely on the greatness or originality of his oeuvre. The body of his top-quality work isn't exactly vast, comprising three or perhaps four dozen songs that synthesize two related traditions: blues, and country and western. Although in some respects Berry's rock and roll is simpler and more vulgar than either of its musical sources, its simplicity and vulgarity are defensible in the snootiest high-art terms—how about "instinctive minimalism" or "demotic voice"? But his case doesn't rest on such defenses. It would be perverse to argue that his songs are in themselves as rich as, say, *Remembrance of Things Past*. Their richness is rather a function of their active relationship with an audience—a complex relationship that shifts every time a song enters a new context, club or album or radio or mass singalong. Where Proust wrote about a dying subculture from a cork-lined room, Berry helped give life to a subculture, and both he and it change every time they confront each other. Even "My Ding-a-Ling," a fourth-grade wee-wee joke that used to mortify true believers at college concerts, permitted a lot of 12-year-olds new insight into the moribund concept of "dirty" when it hit the airwaves; the song changed again when an oldies crowd became as children to shout along with Uncle Chuck the night he received his gold record at Madison Square Garden. And what happened to "Brown Eyed Handsome Man," never a hit among whites, when Berry sang it at interracial rock and roll concerts in Northern cities in the Fifties? How many black kids took "eyed" as code for "skinned"? How many whites? How did

that make them feel about each other, and about the song? And did any of that change the song itself?

Berry's own intentions, of course, remain a mystery. Typically, this public artist is an obsessively private person who has been known to drive reporters from his own amusement park, and the sketches of his life overlap and contradict each other. The way I tell it, Berry was born into a lower middle-class colored family in St. Louis in 1926. He was so quick and ambitious that he both served time in reform school on a robbery conviction and acquired a degree in hairdressing and cosmetology before taking a job on an auto assembly line to support a wife and kids. Yet his speed and ambition persisted. By 1953 he was working as a beautician and leading a three-piece blues group on a regular weekend gig. His gimmick was to cut the blues with country-influenced humorous narrative songs. These were rare in the black music of the time, although they had been common enough before phonograph records crystallized the blues form, and although Louis Jordan, a hero of Berry's, had been doing something vaguely similar in front of white audiences for years.

In 1955, Berry recorded two of his songs on a borrowed machine—"Wee Wee Hours," a blues that he and his pianist, Johnnie Johnson, hoped to sell, and an adapted country tune called "Ida Red." He traveled to Chicago and met Muddy Waters, the uncle of the blues, who sent him on to Leonard Chess of Chess Records. Chess liked "Wee Wee Hours" but flipped for "Ida Red," which was renamed "Maybellene," a hairdresser's dream, and forwarded to Alan Freed. Having mysteriously acquired one-third of the writer's credit with another DJ, Freed played "Maybellene" quite a lot, and it became one of the first nationwide rock 'n' roll hits.

At that time, any fair-minded person would have judged this process exploitative and pecuniary. A blues musician comes to a blues label to promote a blues song—"It was 'Wee Wee Hours' we was proud of, that was *our* music," says Johnnie Johnson—but the owner of the label decides he wants to push a novelty: "The big beat, cars, and young love. It was a trend and we jumped on it," Chess has said. The owner then trades away a third of the blues singer's creative sweat to the symbol of payola, who hypes the novelty song into commercial success and leaves the artist in a quandary. Does he stick with his art, thus forgoing the first real recognition he's ever had, or does he pander to popular taste?

The question is loaded, of course. "Ida Red" was Chuck Berry's music as much as "Wee Wee Hours," which in retrospect seems rather uninspired. In fact, maybe the integrity problem went the other way. Maybe Johnson was afraid that the innovations of "Ida Red"—country guitar lines adapted to blues-style picking, with the ceaseless legato of his own piano adding rhythmic excitement to the steady backbeat—were too far out to sell. What happened instead was that Berry's limited but brilliant vocabulary of guitar riffs quickly came to epito-

mize rock 'n' roll. Ultimately, every great white guitar group of the early Sixties imitated Berry's style, and Johnson's piano technique was almost as influential. In other words, it turned out that Berry and Johnson weren't basically bluesmen at all. Through some magic combination of inspiration and cultural destiny, they had hit upon something more contemporary than blues, and a young audience, for whom the Depression was one more thing that bugged their parents, understood this better than the musicians themselves. Leonard Chess simply functioned as a music businessman should, though only rarely does one combine the courage and insight (and opportunity) to pull it off, even once. Chess became a surrogate audience, picking up on new music and making sure that it received enough exposure for everyone else to pick up on it, too.

Obviously, Chuck Berry wasn't racked with doubt about artistic compromise. A good blues single usually sold around 10,000 copies and a big rhythm and blues hit might go into the hundreds of thousands, but "Maybellene" probably moved a million, even if Chess never sponsored the audit to prove it. Berry had achieved a grip on the white audience and the solid future it could promise, and, remarkably, he had in no way diluted his genius to do it. On the contrary, that was his genius. He would never have fulfilled himself if he hadn't explored his relationship to the white world—a relationship which was much different for him, an urban black man who was used to machines and had never known brutal poverty, than it was for, say, Muddy Waters.

Berry was the first blues-based performer to successfully reclaim guitar tricks that country and western innovators had appropriated from black people and adapted to their own uses 25 or 50 years before. By adding blues tone to some fast country runs, and yoking them to a rhythm and blues beat and some unembarrassed electrification, he created an instrumental style with biracial appeal. Alternating guitar chords augmented the beat while Berry sang in an insouciant tenor that, while recognizably Afro-American in accent, stayed clear of the melisma and blurred overtones of blues singing, both of which enter only at carefully premeditated moments. His few detractors still complain about the repetitiveness of this style, but they miss the point. Repetition without tedium is the backbone of rock and roll, and the components of Berry's music proved so durable that they still provoke instant excitement at concerts two decades later. And in any case, the instrumental repetition was counterbalanced by unprecedented and virtually unduplicated verbal variety.

Chuck Berry is the greatest rock lyricist this side of Bob Dylan, and sometimes I prefer him to Dylan. Both communicate an abundance of the childlike delight in linguistic discovery that page poets are supposed to convey and too often don't, but Berry's most ambitious lyrics, unlike Dylan's, never seem pretentious or forced. True, his language is ersatz and barbaric, full of mispronounced foreignisms and advertising coinages, but then, so was Whitman's. Like Whitman, Berry is excessive because he is totally immersed in America—the America of Melville and the Edsel, burlesque and installment-plan funerals, pemmican and pomade. Unlike Whitman, though, he doesn't quite permit you to take him seriously—he can't really think it's pronounced "a la carty," can he? He is a little surreal. How else can a black man as sensitive as Chuck Berry respond to the affluence of white America—an affluence suddenly his for the taking.

Chuck Berry is not only a little surreal but also a little schizy; even after he committed himself to rock 'n' roll story songs, relegating the bluesman in him to B sides and album fillers, he found his persona split in two. In three of the four singles that followed "Maybellene," he amplified the black half of his artistic personality, the brown-eyed handsome man who always came up short in his quest for the small-time hedonism America promises everyone. By implication, Brown Eyes' sharp sense of life's nettlesome and even oppressive details provided a kind of salvation by humor, especially in "Too Much Monkey Business," a catalog of hassles that included work, school and the army. But the white teenagers who were the only audience with the cultural experience to respond to Berry's art weren't buying this kind of salvation, not en masse. They wanted something more optimistic and more specific to themselves; of the four singles that followed "Maybellene," only "Roll Over Beethoven," which introduced Berry's other half, the rock 'n' roller, achieved any real success. Chuck got the message. His next release, "School Day," was another complaint song, but this time the complaints were explicitly adolescent and were relieved by the direct action of the rock 'n' roller. In fact, the song has been construed as a prophecy of the Free Speech Movement: "Close your books, get out of your seat/Down the halls and into the street."

It has become a cliché to attribute the rise of rock and roll to a new parallelism between white teenagers and black Americans; a common "alienation" and even "suffering" are often cited. As with most clichés, this one has its basis in fact—teenagers in the Fifties certainly showed an unprecedented consciousness of themselves as a circumscribed group, though how much that had to do with marketing refinements and how much with the Bomb remains unresolved. In any case, Chuck Berry's history points up the limits of this notion. For Berry was closer to white teenagers both economically (that reform school stint suggests a JD exploit, albeit combined with a racist judicial system) and in spirit (he shares his penchant for youthfulness with Satchel Paige but not Henry Aaron, with Leslie Fiedler but not Norman Podhoretz) than the average black man. And even at that, he had to make a conscious (not to

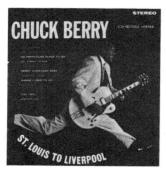    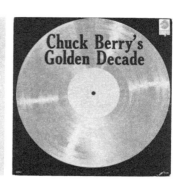

say calculated) leap of the imagination to reach them, and sometimes fell short.

Although he scored lots of minor hits, Chuck Berry made only three additional *Billboard* Top Ten singles in the Fifties—"Rock and Roll Music," "Sweet Little Sixteen," and "Johnny B. Goode"—and every one of them ignored Brown Eyes for the assertive, optimistic, and somewhat simpleminded rock 'n' roller. In a pattern common among popular artists, his truest and most personal work didn't flop, but it wasn't overwhelmingly popular either. For such artists, the audience can be like a drug. A little of it is so good for them that they assume a lot of it would be even better, but instead the big dose saps their autonomy, often so subtly that they don't notice it. For Chuck Berry, the craving for overwhelming popularity proved slightly dangerous. At the same time that he was enlivening his best songs with faintly Latin rhythms, which he was convinced were the coming thing, he was also writing silly exercises with titles like "Hey Pedro." Nevertheless, his pursuit of the market also worked a communion with his audience, with whom he continued to have an instinctive rapport remarkable in a 30-year-old black man. For there is also a sense in which the popular artist is a drug for the audience, and a doctor, too—he has to know how much of his vital essence he can administer at one time, and in what compound.

The reason Berry's rock 'n' roller was capable of such insightful excursions into the teen psyche—"Sweet Little Sixteen," a celebration of everything lovely about fanhood; or "Almost Grown," a basically unalienated first-person expression of teen rebellion that Sixties youth-cult pundits should have taken seriously—was that he shared a crucial American value with the humorous Brown Eyes. That value was fun. Even among rock critics, who ought to know better, fun doesn't have much of a rep, so that they commiserate with someone like LaVern Baker, a second-rate blues and gospel singer who felt she was selling her soul every time she launched into a first-rate whoop of nonsense like "Jim Dandy" or "Bumble Bee." But fun was what adolescent revolt had to be about—inebriated affluence versus the hangover of the work ethic. It was the only practicable value in the Peter Pan utopia of the American dream. Because black music had always thrived on exuberance—not just the otherworldly transport of gospel, but the candidly physical good times of great pop blues singers like Washboard Sam, who is most often dismissed as a lightweight by the heavy blues critics—it turned into the perfect vehicle for generational convulsion. Black musicians, however, had rarely achieved an optimism that was cultural as well as personal—those few who did, like Louis Armstrong, left themselves open to charges of Tomming. Chuck Berry never Tommed. The trouble he'd seen just made his sly, bad-boy voice and the splits and waddles of his stage show that much more credible.

Then, late in 1959, fun turned into trouble. Berry had imported a Spanish-speaking Apache prostitute he'd picked up in El Paso to check hats in his St. Louis nightclub, and then fired her. She went to the police, and Berry was indicted under the Mann Act. After two trials, the first so blatantly racist that it was disallowed, he went to prison for two years. When he got out, in 1964, he and his wife had separated, apparently a major tragedy for him. The Beatles and the Rolling Stones had paid him such explicit and appropriate tribute that his career was probably in better shape after his jail term than before, but he couldn't capitalize. He had a few hits—"Nadine" and "No Particular Place to Go" (John Lennon is one of many who believe they were written before he went in)—but the well was dry. Between 1965 and 1970 he didn't release one even passable new song, and he died as a recording artist.

In late 1966, Berry left Chess for a big advance from Mercury Records. The legends of his money woes at Chess are numerous, but apparently the Chess brothers knew how to record him—the stuff he produced himself for Mercury was terrible. Working alone with pickup bands, he still performed a great deal, mostly to make money for Berry Park, a recreation haven 30 miles from St. Louis. And as he toured, he found that something had happened to his old audience—it was getting older, with troubles of its own, and it dug blues. At auditoriums like the Fillmore, where he did a disappointing live LP with the Steve Miller Blues Band, Chuck was more than willing to stretch out on a blues. One of his favorites was from Elmore James: "When things go wrong, wrong with you, it hurts me too."

By 1970, he was back home at Chess, and suddenly his new audience called forth a miracle. Berry was a natural head—no drugs, no alcohol—and most of his attempts to cash in on hippie talk had been embarrassments. But "Tulane," one of his great-

Below: (1) Chuck Berry onstage in the early Seventies. Opposite: (2) Berry, right, with groupies and Bo Diddley in 1972. (1, Janus Records; 2, Annie Leibovitz)

est story songs, was the perfect fantasy. It was about two dope dealers: "Tulane and Johnny opened a novelty shop/Back under the counter was the cream of the crop." Johnny is nabbed by narcs, but Tulane, his girlfriend, escapes, and Johnny confidently predicts that she will buy off the judge. Apparently she does, for there is a sequel, a blues. In "Have Mercy Judge," Johnny has been caught again, and this time he expects to be sent to "some stony mansion." Berry devotes the last stanza to Tulane, who is "too alive to live alone." The last line makes me wonder just how he felt about his own wife when he went to prison: "Just tell her to live, and I'll forgive her, and even love her more when I come back home."

Taken together, the two songs are Berry's peak, although Leonard Chess would no doubt have vetoed the vocal double-track on "Tulane" that blurs its impact a bit. Remarkably, "Have Mercy Judge" is the first important blues Berry ever wrote, and like all his best work it isn't quite traditional, utilizing an *abc* line structure instead of the usual *aab*. Where did it come from? Is it unreasonable to suspect that part of Berry really was a bluesman all along, and that this time, instead of him going to his audience, his audience came to him and provided the juice for one last masterpiece?

Berry's career would appear closed. He is a rock and roll monument at 50, a pleasing performer whose days of inspiration are over. Sometime in the next 30 years he will probably die, and while his songs have already stuck in the public memory a lot longer than Washboard Sam's, it's likely that most of them will fade away too. So is he, was he, will he be a great artist? It won't be we judging, but perhaps we can think of it this way. Maybe the true measure of his greatness was not whether his songs "lasted"—a term which as of now means persisted through centuries instead of decades—but that he was one of the ones to make us understand that the greatest thing about art is the way it happens between people. I am grateful for aesthetic artifacts, and I suspect that a few of Berry's songs, a few of his recordings, will live on in that way. I only hope that they prove too alive to live alone. If they do, and if by some mishap Berry's name itself is forgotten, that will nevertheless be an entirely apposite kind of triumph for him.

Discography

"Maybellene" (Chess 1604; ☆ 5, r☆ 1, 1955). "Thirty Days" (Chess 1610; r☆ 8, 1955). "No Money Down" (Chess 1615; r☆ 11, 1956). "Roll Over Beethoven" (Chess 1626; r☆ 7, ☆ 29, 1956). "Too Much Monkey Business" b/w "Brown Eyed Handsome Man" (Chess 1635; r☆ 7, 1956). "School Day" (Chess 1653; r☆ 1, ☆ 5, 1957). "Oh Baby Doll" (Chess 1664; ☆ 57, 1957). "Rock and Roll Music" (Chess 1671; ☆ 8, r☆ 6, 1957). "Sweet Little Sixteen" (Chess 1683; r☆ 1, ☆ 2, 1958). "Johnny B. Goode" (Chess 1691; r☆ 5, ☆ 8, 1958). "Carol" (Chess 1700; r☆ 12, ☆ 18, 1958). "Sweet Little Rock and Roll" (Chess 1709; r☆ 13, ☆ 47, 1958). "Anthony Boy" (Chess 1716; ☆ 60, 1959). "Almost Grown" (Chess 1722; r☆ 3, ☆ 32, 1959). "Back in the U.S.A." (Chess 1729; r☆ 16, ☆ 37, 1959). "Too Pooped to Pop" (Chess 1747; r☆ 18, ☆ 42, 1960). "Nadine" (Chess 1883; ☆ 23, 1964). "No Particular Place to Go" (Chess 1898; ☆ 10, 1964). "You Never Can Tell" (Chess 1906; ☆ 14, 1964). "Little Marie" (Chess 1912; ☆ 54, 1964). "Promised Land" (Chess 1916; ☆ 41, 1964). "My Ding-a-Ling" (Chess 2131; ☆ 1, 1972). "Reelin' and Rockin'" (Chess 2136; ☆ 27, 1972).

(Chart positions compiled from Joel Whitburn's *Record Research*, based on *Billboard* Pop chart, unless otherwise indicated; r☆ = position on *Billboard* Rhythm and Blues chart.)

Rockabilly
by Peter Guralnick

Rockabilly is the purest of all rock 'n' roll genres. That is because it never went anywhere. It is preserved in perfect isolation within an indistinct time period, bounded on the one hand by the July 1954 release of Elvis's first record on the yellow Sun label and on the other by the decline and fall of Elvis (his 1958 induction into the Army), Jerry Lee Lewis (his marriage to his 14-year-old cousin, Myra, at about the same time), Carl Perkins (his 1956 car crash and long period of convalescence just subsequent to the sales takeoff of "Blue Suede Shoes," the rockabilly's anthem), and Gene Vincent (the 1960 London taxi accident which killed Eddie Cochran and accentuated a virtually crippling leg injury he had suffered earlier). It was a very brief flourishing, more of feeling than of talent, during which country music almost died, aging hillbilly stars rushed to record in the new style, the major record companies scrambled to learn how to formulize and market an unknown product, and every up-and-coming young singer in the South beat a path to the Memphis door of Sam Phillips's tiny Sun label, where it all began.

The tale of Sun Records is so familiar it hardly needs retelling. How Sam Phillips started out recording the great black blues singers and leasing the results to independents like Chess in Chicago and RPM on the Coast. How Elvis Presley wandered in and paid $3.98, presumably to cut a record for his mother on Phillips's custom recording service. How with the release of "That's All Right," Presley's first record and Sun No. 209, Phillips never looked back, scarcely recorded another black artist, and put together a roster which at one time or another included Presley, Carl Perkins, Jerry Lee Lewis, Johnny Cash, Charlie Rich, Roy Orbison, and such lesser lights, and rockabilly luminaries, as Sonny Burgess, Warren Smith, Onie Wheeler and Malcolm Yelvington.

It was a music of almost classical purity and definition. Perhaps that is why, except for the work of its major practitioners, it holds up so poorly today. It was, to begin with, Southern music. Ricky Nelson could emulate it in California, but the only way he could begin to approach the rockabilly sound was through the hot guitar runs of James Burton, his Louisiana-born lead guitarist. It was not just Southern music either, it was white Southern music and, with the almost sole exception of Wanda Jackson, white Southern *male* music. It was blues-inspired and bluegrass-based, in Carl Perkins's definition, "blues with a country beat." It was "cat music," a secret language for the young seeking to break away from the adult music of their forebears, which—judging by the hillbilly boogie of Hank Williams and Lefty Frizzell—was not always very staid nor even very adult. It was called rockabilly, because it was not the clankety rock of Bill Haley and his Comets nor the hillbilly sound of Roy Acuff and Ernest Tubb but a fusion of the two.

Every genre has its unique requirements. Rockabilly's, however, were more stringent than most. Its rhythm was nervously uptempo, accented on the offbeat, and propelled by a distinctively slapping bass. Instrumentation took its cue from the original trio of Elvis, Scotty and Bill (rhythm guitar, lead guitar and string bass) with drums added later and the honky-tonk piano of Jerry Lee Lewis establishing a whole new strain but one of equal vigor. The sound was always clean, never cluttered, with a kind of thinness and manic energy that was filled by the solid lead of Scotty Moore's guitar or Jerry Lee's piano. The sound was further bolstered by generous use of echo, a homemade technique refined independently by Sam Phillips and Leonard Chess in Chicago with sewer pipes and bathroom acoustics. Critics charged that echo was employed to cover up a multitude of vocal sins—and it did in fact sometimes render lyrics indecipherable—but this was of little moment since the essence of rockabilly lyrics was inspired nonsense and rhythmic patter. Children's games, clothing trends, nursery rhymes, outer-space odysseys—all were legitimate subjects for the spontaneous bop prosody of artists from Carl Perkins ("Put Your Cat Clothes On") to Gene Vincent ("Be-Bop-a-LuLa") to Roy Orbison ("Ooby Dooby") to Charlie Feathers ("Tongue Tied Jill") to Billy Lee Riley and the Little Green Men ("Flyin' Saucers Rock 'n' Roll"). Even vocal technique was something of a constant, with a generation of hiccupers, stutterers, and vibrato-laden warblers, from Elvis's "Baby Let's Play House," through Buddy Holly, up to Freddy Fender and Narvel Felts. It was indeed a music of high spirits, wild rebellion, and almost rigorous classicism.

Its final quality is one which is not so easily appreciated, however, except by the true devotee of the form. That quality is imitation, most kindly seen as *hommage*, but imitation when you come down to it, mimicry of the most slavish and blatant sort.

For rockabilly started and in a sense ended with Elvis Presley. He was the colossus that bestrode its narrow world. Not that he was its most devoted practitioner by any means, nor even necessarily its most inspired. He was, however, undeniably the first, and the influence he exerted over every one of the singers who followed, either directly or by example, is incalculable.

Carl Perkins was a country boy working low-paying gigs and doing a live radio show in Jackson, Tennessee, playing music much the same as that which Elvis was evolving at the time. When Perkins heard Elvis's first record he headed for Memphis and Sam Phillips's studio, where a little over a year later—after Elvis's contract was sold to RCA—he would record "Blue Suede Shoes." Jerry Lee Lewis sold all the eggs from his father's farm and camped out on the Sun doorstep until given an audition. Roy Orbison's first recordings in Clovis, New Mexico, later duplicated on Sun, were fashioned with Elvis very much in mind. Buddy Holly first saw Elvis perform in Lubbock, Texas, and it changed his life and singing style forever. The basis for

Gene Vincent and the Blue Caps circa 1956 (Michael Ochs collection)

Gene Vincent's whole success—deserved though it may have been—was his uncanny resemblance both vocally and visually to a younger, greasier Elvis Presley. Even Ricky Nelson, the only suburban rockabilly (unless you want to count Midwestern-born Californian Eddie Cochran), took his sneer, his stance, and a large part of his repertoire from Elvis Presley. And I'm only speaking of the better known, and more stylistically formed, of the rockabilly artists.

Ray "Caterpillar" Campi, Jackie Lee Waukeen Cochran, Mac Curtis, Peanuts Wilson, the Burnette Brothers, Mack and Ronnie Self, Groovey Joe Poovey, Alvis Wayne, Teddy Reidel, Sleepy La Beef, Sanford Clark—these are truly names from obscurity, and ones for which I have great personal affection. They cultivated the look, the stance, the sound, the part of their more celebrated colleagues. All they lacked was the talent. Rockabilly fanatics will tell you that if you could only hear Johnny Carroll's "Wild Wild Women," if you would just take a listen to the Commodores' or Roy Hall's original versions of "Whole Lot of Shakin' Going On," then the doors of perception would open wide for you and you would recognize the true source behind the legend. It's a nice mythology, and one that has its analogue in every field, but in the case of rockabilly anyway most of the cream rose to the top. Carl Perkins's instrumental brilliance, Jerry Lee's vocal and pianistic acrobatics, Elvis's raw energy, and Gene Vincent's brash tastelessness ("I'm lookin' for a woman with a one-track mind," he sang in a 1956 echo chamber which wreaked havoc with articulation, "a-fuggin' and a-kissin' and a-smoochin' all the time")—these, together with the Sun sound of Sam Phillips's makeshift studio, are the elements for which rockabilly will be remembered.

Today most of the ex-rockabillies have returned to the establishment fold. Some are pumping gas; some, like Sonny Burgess, are traveling salesmen; some are stars; some, like Billy Lee Riley and Warren Smith, are still trying to make it in the music business. Almost all have gone back to the church and to country music. The echoes of their achievement still linger on the radio in nods from Creedence Clearwater, the various ex-Beatles, Elton John, and the renewed success of Narvel Felts, Gary Stewart, and Freddy Fender. And I wonder if rockabilly itself has actually died or if, like the blues, it has just gone underground.

Recently I went to see Charlie Feathers at a little club on Lamar Avenue in Memphis, just up the road from the Eagle's Nest where Elvis started out some 20 years ago. Charlie Feathers's hair is silver now, and his band consists of his daughter, son, son-in-law, and a friend of his son-in-law on drums. The music that he is playing, though, is no different than what he has always played—powerful, vigorous, *crazy* music that animates the beaten-down audience of old men in overalls and bright-eyed factory girls desperately seeking re-

lease from their workaday lives. It's the audience that originally responded to the music, and it doesn't even seem incongruous when a weathered-looking 50-year-old man in a loose-fitting brown suit gets up from his table to do a tuneless but spirited version of Elvis's "Mystery Train." The remembered gestures are letter-perfect, the mood is good-natured and self-deprecating, as he tosses the microphone from hand to hand and flings himself about with wild, hip-swiveling abandon. He gives up the mike self-consciously to a mixture of amusement and acclaim. "I don't care what you say," says the piano player, who does Ernest Tubb imitations, "you get the best music in the world in these little jook joints and holes in the wall. I'm telling the truth, you better believe it, buddy, this is where they always sing from the heart." •

Discography

Johnny Cash, "Cry, Cry, Cry" (Sun 221; ☆14, 1955). **Johnny Cash,** "Folsom Prison Blues" (Sun 232; c☆5, 1956). **Carl Perkins,** "Blue Suede Shoes" (Sun 234; c☆2, r☆2, ☆4, 1956). **Gene Vincent,** "Be-Bop-a-Lula" (Capitol 3450; c☆5, ☆9, 1956). **Roy Orbison,** "Ooby Dooby" (Sun 242; ☆59, 1956). **Carl Perkins,** "Boppin' the Blues" (Sun 243; c☆9, ☆70, 1956). **Johnny Cash,** "I Walk the Line" (Sun 241; c☆2, ☆19, 1956). **Carl Perkins,** "Dixie Fried" b/w "I'm Sorry, I'm Not Sorry" (Sun 249; c☆10, 1956). **Gene Vincent,** "Race with the Devil" (Capitol 3530; ☆96, 1956). **Carl Perkins,** "Your True Love" (Sun 261; c☆13, 1957). **Dale Hawkins,** "Susie-Q" (Checker 863; ☆29, 1957). **Gene Vincent,** "Lotta Lovin' " (Capitol 3763; r☆7, ☆14, 1957). **Johnny Cash,** "Home of the Blues" (Sun 279; c☆5, ☆88, 1957). **Gene Vincent,** "Dance to the Bop" (Capitol 3839; ☆43, 1957). **Johnny Cash,** "Ballad of a Teenage Queen" (Sun 283; c☆1, ☆16, 1958). **Carl Perkins,** "Pink Pedal Pushers" (Columbia 41131; c☆17, ☆91, 1958). **Johnny Cash,** "Guess Things Happen That Way" b/w "Come in Stranger" (Sun 295; c☆1, ☆11, 1958). **Dale Hawkins,** "La-Do-Dada" (Checker 900; ☆32, 1958). **Johnny Cash,** "The Ways of a Woman in Love" (Sun 302; c☆2, ☆24, 1958). **Dale Hawkins,** "A House, a Car and a Wedding Ring" (Checker 906; ☆88, 1958). **Dale Hawkins,** "Class Cutter (Yeah Yeah)" (Checker 916; ☆52, 1959). **Ronnie Hawkins,** "Forty Days" (Roulette 4154; ☆45, 1959). **Ronnie Hawkins,** "Mary Lou" (Roulette 4177; r☆7, ☆26, 1959).
(Omitting hits by Elvis Presley, Jerry Lee Lewis and Buddy Holly. Chart positions taken from Joel Whitburn's *Record Research,* compiled from *Billboard* Pop chart, unless otherwise indicated; c☆ = position on *Billboard* Country and Western chart; r☆ = position on *Billboard* Rhythm and Blues chart.)

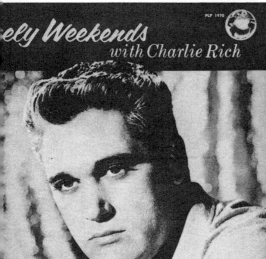

ely Weekends
with Charlie Rich

PLP 1970

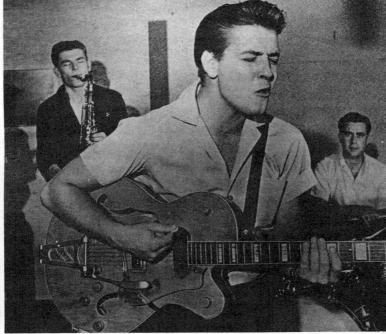

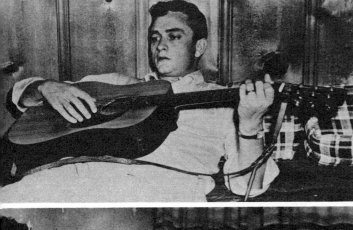

Jerry Lee Lewis
by Jim Miller

Jerry Lee Lewis looks surly. It's 9:30 at the county fair in Cedar Rapids, Iowa, and Lewis, the featured attraction at the fair's auditorium is onstage a half-hour late. He surveys the sparse crowd, his lips snarled like his curly blond hair. He is angry at the disappointing turnout.

It is 1963, and Jerry Lee Lewis is up shit creek. For almost six years, he's been on the road nonstop, mostly in the South, playing one-nighters, trying to recoup some momentum in a career that skidded to a dead stop in 1958, after it became known he married his 14-year-old cousin. Incest, they said; and Jerry Lee has been fighting a losing battle against high-placed hypocrites ever since.

The crowd is restless. To the majority, Jerry Lee Lewis is at best a memory, at worst a washed up has-been. Boredom, not interest, has driven them to gawk at this once-upon-a-time rock 'n' roll star.

Lewis prowls over to his piano from stage right, where he has been silently counting empty seats. He pulls out a gigantic comb from his hip pocket, and, in a trademark gesture, runs the comb through his hair. He swivels a curious half-wiggle of vanity wounded.

The crowd boos. "Music!" yells one. "Queer!" yells another.

Jerry Lee spins around and glares. "*Shaaaaaad*dup ya muuthers," he bellows. Silence.

"This is the *killer,* baby, and *noo*body cuts the Killer. *Nobody.*"

He pauses, and turns back to the piano. And then Jerry Lee Lewis lights into one of the nastiest versions of "Great Balls of Fire" to taunt human ears. "You shake my nerves and you rattle my brain/Too much love drives a man insane . . ."

For the past 20 years, Jerry Lee Lewis has been performing his own brand of rock, country and pop anyplace, anytime and anywhere he gets the money and the opportunity. Although he scored only three Top Ten pop hits, all during the Fifties, his personal style helped define the rock tradition. Out of a genre populated by dime-a-dozen Presley imitators, Lewis emerged a giant, an entertainer gifted with intuitive flair, musical brashness and a genius for self-promotion. Despite daunting obstacles, his ego has let him persevere—and he's not about to let anyone forget it.

The externals of Lewis's career are the stuff of folk legend. Born in Ferriday, Louisiana, near Natchez, Mississippi, in 1935, Lewis performed music professionally from the age of 15. He played what he heard, and what he heard was country swing, rural blues, piano boogies and jump band R&B. When he decided in 1956 to strike out on his own and seek a recording contract, Lewis headed for Memphis to audition for Sam Phillips at Sun Records.

Upon arriving, he found Phillips unavailable, so he cornered Sam's assistant Jack Clement instead. According to Clement, Jerry Lee boasted that "he could play piano like Chet Atkins"—a claim that intrigued Clement (not least, presumably, because Atkins played guitar, not piano). Clement recalled cutting four country tunes that day, although Lewis himself remembers a marathon audition covering "everything from Muddy Waters to 'Silent Night.' "

Whatever the tapes contained, Sam Phillips was duly impressed. Clement had already dispatched Lewis with the standard instructions of the Presley era—"Go learn some rock 'n' roll"—and three weeks later, Jerry Lee was back, for a session that yielded a striding treatment of Ray Price's recent country smash, "Crazy Arms." The song sold well regionally, but didn't dent the national charts.

Lewis's next visit to the studio changed all that. At the tail end of the session during which Lewis had cut "It'll Be Me" as a sequel to "Crazy Arms," Clement told Jerry to play anything he wanted. With the tapes rolling, Jerry Lee and his combo blithely lit into a little ditty called "Whole Lot of Shakin' "—and on one take, Lewis and Clement had their followup. "Whole Lot of Shakin' Going On" went on to sell a million copies; Lewis, catapulted into prominence by television and radio, became an international celebrity.

"Whole Lot of Shakin' " is pure Jerry Lee Lewis from its first pounding chords. The song is delivered over an incessant piano backbeat; Jerry Lee, his voice the very incarnation of nonchalant lust, exploits the hints of lewdness in the lyrics ("Shake it baby, shake") to the hilt.

The public loved it. Suddenly Jerry Lee Lewis, the country kid from Ferriday, Louisiana, was crisscrossing the U.S. on package tours and appearing on Dick Clark's *American Bandstand*, becoming, some said, the successor to Elvis himself. "Whole Lot of Shakin' " went to Number One on both the country-western and rhythm and blues charts, and lingered for 29 weeks on the pop charts, cresting in June of 1957. Subsequent hits, such as "Great Balls of Fire," "Breathless" and "High School Confidential," followed effortlessly.

But in mid-1958, Jerry Lee decided to marry Myra Brown, a sweet young girl who also happened to be his third cousin (it was his third marriage). Industry elders were aghast; no amount of payola, it seemed, could right a taboo once wronged. Overnight, Jerry Lee Lewis's career dried up. Without access to the big tours, the TV shows, the major radio stations, Jerry Lee Lewis became just another entertainer condemned to one-nighters in undreamt-of locales.

There may seem little reason to distinguish Jerry Lee Lewis from a thousand other two-shot hitmakers. But Lewis was different. A natural in an industry filled with calculating mimics, his creativity and consequent impact spilled far beyond the few hits that reached the general public.

Onstage he was a picture of piety dissolved, pounding the piano, scrambling over the instrument's lid—there, like King

A very friendly Jerry Lee, from the jacket of one of his early albums for Sun Records

68

Kong with curly locks, assaulting culture by commanding the summit of his very own white piano, shaking his all-too-long blond hair, as if to mock the well-coiffed mane of a Southern aristocrat.

Hauteur incarnate, Jerry Lee was a talented punk who knew he was talented, and his flamboyant antics conveyed a class resentment that any self-avowed outsider could grasp immediately. It was all a show, of course. Carl Perkins has claimed that Jerry Lee, on his first tour with Perkins and Johnny Cash after "Crazy Arms" had been released, had trouble with shyness. "John and I told him," recalls Perkins, " 'Turn around so they can see you; make a fuss.' So the next night he carried on, stood up, kicked the stool back, and a new Jerry Lee was born."

With a vengeance, Jerry Lee leered his way into the annals of American popular culture. As Waylon Jennings once remarked, "He'll burn a goddamn piano if he has to."

(And, as legend has it, he did once, too. During his heyday in the late Fifties, Lewis used to demand that he close any package tour he appeared on. As writer John Grissim tells the story, "One exception came during a concert tour with Chuck Berry, emceed by Alan Freed. Both Berry and Lewis had million-seller hits on the charts at the time and one night Freed flat-out insisted that Jerry Lee perform first. After a furious argument, Lewis obeyed. The story has it that he blew nonstop rock for a brutal 30 minutes and, during the final "Whole Lot of Shakin'," poured lighter fluid over the piano and threw a match to it. As he stomped off the stage he hollered to the stage crew: 'I'd like to see *any* son of a bitch follow that!' ")

Lewis often seemed on the verge of exploding. His swagger and phrasing exuded an aura of profound lust, the kind of lust that secretly chastises itself as un-Christian and sinful. Therein lay its power: a magic potion of the repressed, right there before millions of American eyes and ears. Lewis's music represented the ungodly miscegenation Presley and Little Richard had only hinted at. A white man with a black soul? Onstage Lewis, unlike Presley, didn't mess much with ballads and hymns. As he admitted in an argument with Sam Phillips early in his career, Lewis saw himself as playing the devil's music—and a true Christian doesn't mix God's music with the devil's.

Presley's early performances had in any case been fastidiously rehearsed, each inflection properly placed. Jerry Lee by contrast always sang with an unquenchable spontaneity, as though he were tapping some primordial wellspring of energy: there are clearly perceptible differences of nuance and phrasing even between two takes of "Great Balls of Fire" cut the same day. His persona, simply, is irrepressible. It emerges on the most benign material, and even in interpretations of songs strongly associated with other performers.

Take "Little Queenie." Originally a sluggish sock hop send-up by Chuck Berry ("There she is again, standin' over by the record machine/Lookin' like the model on the cover of a magazine"), the song was later revived in a grinding version by the Rolling Stones (on *"Get Yer Ya-Ya's Out!"*). In the Stones' recording, Mick Jagger minces his words carefully during the song's spoken interlude: "Now if she'll dance, we can make it—come on, Queenie: let's shake it." But a lumbering tempo and the all-too-familiar guile in his voice give the game away.

Jerry Lee doesn't think twice. With utter self-abandon, he sails through the choruses in a charging uptempo, and then matter-of-factly executes the spoken bit, which any fool, Jerry Lee seems to imply, can see is a come-on, pure and simple.

In themselves, "off-color" sentiments do not a great rock 'n' roll record make, of course. What makes Jerry Lee Lewis great is rather the tension in his persona between worldly sin and salvation, a battle in which sin seems destined inevitably to win. But that is not all: there is also in Lewis's work a parity of means and ends, and a natural economy of musical expression.

The backbone of Lewis's sound is his piano playing, invariably some elementary boogie figure. His solos have always been sheer flash, punctuated by pointless but exhilarating glissando runs. Avoiding the evenly turned figures of a Fats Domino, or the baroque intricacies of a boogie master like Pete Johnson (the great Kansas City jazz pianist), Lewis is content to play crudely with a jerky bravado that matches his vocal unpredictability. He constructs breaks out of the most outrageous elements, hammering triplet chords against prominent, forceful bass lines with the left hand (on some of his early recordings, Lewis performed without an accompanying bass). His piano playing is undisciplined, intuitive and potentially uncontrollable—just like his singing.

Yet as a singer as well as a pianist, Lewis represents something more than licentious maniac. His voice is tempered, polished, with a rounded fullness that hovers, surrounding notes with a barely frenetic halo before engulfing them. His carefully controlled vibrato conveys tension as well as release: his intonation suggests labor, as if he were holding back a scream. But paradoxically the final impression is one of easy mastery. Through his singing, Lewis effortlessly commands a range of moods that other performers (like Jagger) strain for.

His Sun-period band, featuring Roland James on guitar, reinforces the impression of natural mastery. In their own way, Lewis's early Sun recordings even swing, not in the mellow way that Fats Domino swings, but rather in the clipped, urgent, way that Lewis's own piano swings.

The Sun production enhances this overall texture, with a prominent echo smoothing over any rough edges. Although the early records rarely add saxes or an organ and never use strings or a chorus, Sam Phillips's engineering coaxes a fullness out of Lewis's small band; each of the instruments—usually electric guitar, bass and drums accompanying Jerry Lee's piano and

70

Opposite, clockwise from top left:
(1) The teenage rocker supreme; (2) The rocker
grown older; (3) But the arrogance remains; (4 & 5) As does the
dignity; (6) And the show-biz savvy ("Think about it!"); (7) Jerry
Lee with teen-cousin bride, Myra, just married in 1958; (8) As
Iago in 'Catch My Soul,' a Sixties musical version of 'Othello'; (9 & 10)
Jerry Lee over the years; center: (11) Jerry Lee with Myra: "What's
it to ya, punk?" Above: (12) The high-note sweep. (1, Donald
Petri collection; 2, Baron Wolman; 6, John Grissim; 7 & 11, UPI)

singing—assumes a mysterious resonance of its own. Just as with Leonard Chess's production of Little Walter, the judicious use of echo adds depth and a sheen without sacrificing spontaneity or feeling.

Unlike some of his fellow rockers, Lewis did not burn out young; his pride, talent and impenetrable vanity saved him that humiliation. Although he vanished from public view for almost ten years, Jerry Lee continued to present, as one album billed it, "the greatest live show on earth." Finally, when all hope of a successful recording career seemed gone, he made a last bid for renewed popularity.

It worked—but at a price. In 1967, Lewis and Jerry Kennedy, his producer at Mercury (where Jerry Lee has recorded since 1964), surveyed his spectacularly unsuccessful three-year track record. The de facto blacklist that followed his marriage was still in effect, and Lewis's efforts rarely penetrated even the bottom of the trade charts. Only country DJs showed any enthusiasm at all.

So Jerry Lee struck a bargain. "I decided to cut a country record, and then I talked to a lot of jocks," Lewis has explained to John Grissim. "This time I said, 'Look, man, let's get together and draw a line on this stuff—a peace treaty, you know. I'm gonna do "Great Balls of Fire" and "Whole Lot of Shakin'" and "Breathless" and "High School Confidential" and whatever else I wanna do, and I'm also gonna do country stuff onstage. But my records will all be country, not rock. So what do you say we get together and get off this kick.' And they did."

Lewis enjoyed a new career in his reincarnation as a country crooner. Between 1968 and 1973, he scored 12 Top Ten country hits on Mercury/Smash, and when Sun reissued some early Lewis country singles, he added three more Top Ten singles on that label. His country material at Mercury has been strong, and Lewis's performance, on tunes like "What's Made Milwaukee Famous," have been undiluted. But then Jerry Lee Lewis probably couldn't sing even the Lord's Prayer straight: his style is too voracious.

Jerry Lee still sings rock, too. In 1973, he even got another taste of pop chart success, with a remake of "Drinkin' Wine Spo-Dee O'Dee," a 1949 R&B novelty number Lewis first cut at Sun. But his creative days appear numbered. Lewis's limber voice has finally begun to fray around the edges; and his piano playing, once unerring in its flamboyance, has become equally shaky. While he still puts on a terrific (and unpredictable) show, he now seems content to coast on his well-stocked fund of mannerisms.

Rock has never been a profession kind to its old men—and Jerry Lee Lewis, like Elvis, is over 40—but as he mulls over his past, Jerry Lee will find some solace in the knowledge that, after all, he was right all along. In the world of rock 'n' roll, nobody cuts the Killer.

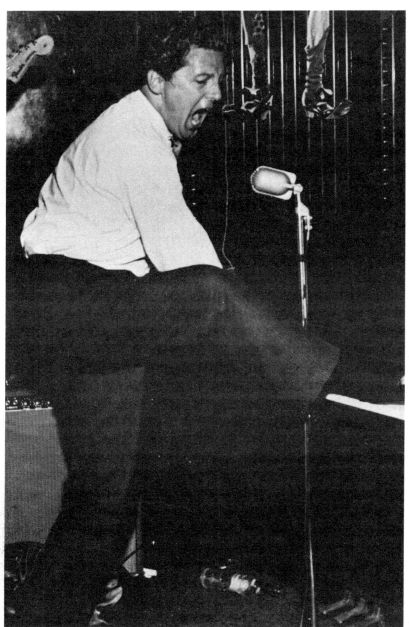

Discography

1957-1975

"Whole Lot of Shakin' Going On" (Sun 267; r☆1, c☆1, ☆3, 1957). "Great Balls of Fire" (Sun 281; r☆3, c☆1, ☆2, 1957). "Breathless" (Sun 288; r☆6, c☆4, ☆7, 1958). "High School Confidential" (Sun 296; r☆16, c☆9, ☆21, 1958). "Break-Up" b/w "I'll Make It All Up to You" (Sun 303; c☆19, ☆52, 1958). "I'll Sail My Ship Alone" (Sun 312; ☆93, 1959). "What'd I Say" (Sun 356; r☆26, c☆27, ☆30, 1961). "Cold Cold Heart" (Sun 364; c☆22, 1961). "Pen and Paper" (Smash 1857; c☆36, 1964). "Another Place, Another Time" (Smash 2146; c☆4, 1968). "What's Made Milwaukee Famous (Has Made a Loser out of Me)" (Smash 2164; c☆2, 1968). "She Still Comes Around" (Smash 2186; c☆2, 1968). "To Make Love Sweeter for You" (Smash 2202; c☆1, 1968). "One Has My Name" (Smash 2224; c☆3, 1969). "Invitation to Your Party" (Sun 1101; c☆6, 1969). "She Even Woke Me Up to Say Goodbye" (Smash 2244; c☆2, 1969). "One Minute Past Eternity" (Sun 1107; c☆2, 1969). "Once More with Feeling" (Smash 2257; c☆2, 1970). "I Can't Seem to Say Goodbye" (Sun 1115; c☆7, 1970). "There Must Be More to Love than This" (Mercury 73099; c☆1, 1970). "Waiting for a Train" (Sun 1119; c☆11, 1970). "Touching Home" (Mercury 73192; c☆3, 1971). "When He Walks on You (like You Walked on Me)" (Mercury 73227; c☆11, 1971). "Would You Take Another Chance on Me" (Mercury 73248; c☆1, 1971). "Drinking Wine Spo-Dee O'Dee" (Mercury 73374; c☆20, ☆41, 1973). "I Can Still Hear the Music in the Restroom" (Mercury 73661; c☆13, 1975). "Boogie Woogie Country Man" (Mercury 76385; c☆24, 1975). "A Damn Good Country Song" (Mercury 73729; c☆68, 1975).
(Chart positions compiled from Joel Whitburn's *Record Research,* based on *Billboard* Pop chart, unless otherwise indicated; r☆ = position on *Billboard* Rhythm and Blues chart; c☆ = position on *Billboard* Country and Western chart.)

The Everly Brothers

by Kit Rachlis

The Everly Brothers were true innocents. From their first hit, "Bye Bye Love" in 1957, to their last, "That's Old Fashioned" five years later, the Everly Brothers sang about love, always love, and always with ingenuous passion and conviction. They never hungered after sex and never sought revenge. Instead they were dreamers, seeking not the ideal woman, but the ideal—or perhaps more accurately, the idealized—relationship. And it was in their wonderful harmonies, which glistened with such delicacy and moved with such buoyancy, that they found the perfect metaphor for that relationship.

The Everly Brothers introduced white country harmony to rock and roll: high tenors with about a third of a note's difference between their voices, they sang in the country duo tradition of the Delmore Brothers and the Louvin Brothers. As the children of Ike and Margaret Everly, a highly respected country and western team, Phil and Don, born in 1939 and 1937, respectively, had been weaned on country music, touring with their parents and appearing on their radio show from the time they were nine and seven years old. In fact, it was their potential as a country act which originally brought them to the attention of Cadence Records in 1957.

Archie Bleyer, president of Cadence, had come to Nashville to work with Wesley Rose in establishing a country and western division to bolster Cadence's flagging sales at a time when the small independent label featured pop singer Andy Williams as its only big name. Rose, with country star Roy Acuff, owned and ran the most prestigious publishing house/management company in the industry. Among the many songwriters Rose had under contract were the Everly Brothers. With the exception of "Thou Shalt Not Steal," a song written by Don and transformed into a hit by vocalist Kitty Wells, the Everly Brothers had little to show for their two years in Nashville. Their one experience in a studio had produced a single for Columbia Records, "The Sun Keeps Shining," which hadn't even reached the lower depths of the C&W charts. Despite their meager record, Bleyer, at Rose's urging, signed the Everly Brothers to a recording contract.

Rose, in turn, introduced Bleyer and the Everly Brothers to Boudleaux Bryant, a highly successful C&W songwriter in the Acuff-Rose stable. One of the tunes Bryant showed them was "Bye Bye Love," a song already rejected by 30 acts. The Everly Brothers, however, liked it and persuaded Bleyer, who (according to Bryant) had expressed some reservations, that they should record the song at their first session. Ten days after its release, "Bye Bye Love" exploded onto the charts, eventually reaching the Number Two spot on the pop listings and Number One on the country charts.

"Bye Bye Love" established the model which the Everly Brothers would follow for the rest of their stay on Cadence. With a pair of acoustic guitars leading the way, the rhythm section of bass, drums, and piano firmly yet unaggressively propelled the song along. The harmonies floated above it all, lightly charting the melody line. It was an almost seamless gown of sound. The Everly Brothers didn't shout or scream. The echo was almost nonexistent. A lone electric guitar provided the ornamental cross-stitching with brief single-note runs. Simultaneously precise, cohesive and effervescent, "Bye Bye Love" had fused country music's obsession for order with the boundless energy of rock and roll.

It's difficult to ascertain who was responsible for the Everly Brothers' sound because their recording sessions were remarkably collective efforts, with the Everlys, Bryant, Rose, Bleyer and the sessionmen all contributing suggestions. What is known, though, is that the sessions were methodically and meticulously run. The Everly Brothers, practicing with a tape machine, would rehearse their vocals two or three days in advance. All arrangements were carefully worked out before entering the studio. The sessionmen, usually including Chet Atkins on guitar and Floyd Cramer on piano, were among Nashville's finest—consummate professionals able to adapt to any performer without sacrificing their individuality.

For as long as they remained on Cadence, the Everly Brothers adhered to that sound with relatively few modifications. As they became more comfortable as rock and rollers, they placed greater emphasis on the drums and electric guitar. Both Chet Atkins and Don Everly, who usually played rhythm guitar, admired Bo Diddley, and increasingly they attempted to incorporate his choppy guitar style into their playing. They experimented by adding strings to "Let It Be Me" and the sound of a screwdriver tapped against a Coke bottle to "Take a Message to Mary." Although they made few radical departures, for all its restrictions the Everly Brothers' formula was remarkably flexible. They rushed headlong into Little Richard's "Rip It Up" with the same ease as they crooned the mawkish sentiments of "Love of My Life." Crucial to their success was an abundance of good songs with strong hooks and catchy melodies—always Bleyer's first priorities. And in Boudleaux Bryant, who wrote many of the Everly Brothers' early hits, Bleyer had a songwriter perfectly suited to the Everlys' skills.

Following the success of "Bye Bye Love," Bryant began tailoring songs specifically to the Everly Brothers' range, harmonies and audience—and what that audience wanted, Bryant presumed, were songs about love. He then proceeded to write some of the most elegantly concise encomiums to romance that rock has ever produced: tender and sensitive, yet rarely yielding to either self-pity or sentimentality. Taken as a whole the songs created an almost hermetically sealed world where only love mattered and only parents ("Wake Up Little Susie" and "Poor Jenny") and school ("Problems") interfered. Unquestionably a simplistic and adolescent world, it assumed that love cured all ills and exorcised all devils. But what saved the Everly Brothers from becoming mere purveyors of Tin Pan Alley pab-

Don and Phil, in the Fifties (courtesy Acuff-Rose)

lum was not the dream itself, but their irrepressible faith in its possibility. Even on songs ostensibly about despair—"Bye Bye Love" and "When Will I Be Loved"—they expressed their eternal resilience and optimism by singing with unabashed exuberance.

For three years on Cadence, the Everly Brothers averaged a Top Ten hit every four months. During the same period (with many of the same songs) they amassed four Number One singles on the country charts. As they progressed, the brothers began to achieve Top Ten success with songs of their own (Don's "['Til] I Kissed You" in 1959 and Phil's "When Will I Be Loved" in 1960). Like their parents, they were troupers and they crisscrossed the country in a continual series of one-night stands. But in 1960 the team that had constructed the Everly Brothers' sound began to fall apart. A bitter fight broke out between the Everly Brothers and Bleyer during negotiations over a new contract—the Everlys were unhappy with their low royalty rate. As a result they left Cadence for Warner Bros. Records. A year later they fired Wesley Rose—who had been acting as both their manager and producer—in a dispute over the arrangement of "Temptation," a single they released in 1961.

The commercial effects of the switch were, if anything, positive. "Cathy's Clown," the pair's first single for Warners, sold over 2 million copies and stands as their all-time best seller. Musically, however, the change in labels and the breakup of their production team marked their decline. Under the stewardship of various producers, their sound became increasingly grandiose, as if to mask their growing lack of assurance. The muted mix and insouciant precision of the Cadence production had always contained the Everly Brothers' maudlin impulses. The hard-edge clarity of their new approach—with horns, piano and backup vocals all competing for attention—magnified their sentimentality, distorted their romanticism. For the first time, their voices began to whine and strain. Without access to Bryant's material (he still worked for Wesley Rose), they resorted to tearjerkers like "Ebony Eyes."

Despite such material, the Everly Brothers continued to produce hits—until the release, in April 1962, of "That's Old Fashioned," which signaled the end. Its very title implied that the Everly Brothers had become an anachronism. Whereas their earlier songs simply assumed their romanticism, "That's Old Fashioned" justified it as if under attack. Supported by a glossy horn arrangement full of uptempo flourishes, they sing with a stridency that exposes their defensiveness: "It's a modern changing world/Everything is moving fast/But when it comes to love/I like what they did in the past."

They never reached the Top Ten again.

The Sixties were not kind to Fifties rock stars, and the Everly Brothers were no exceptions. Don, thanks to "vitamin" treatments from a New York doctor, became hooked on speed, and for the next few years was in and out of sanitariums; before he finally cured himself in 1966, he had attempted suicide. Phil also received the treatments but the effects weren't as serious. During this period, both Don and Phil were divorced from their wives.

They continued, however, to churn out record after record: a C&W album (*The Everly Brothers Sing Great Country Hits*); a couple of R&B albums (*Rock 'n Soul* and *Beat 'n Soul*); an English album (*Two Yanks in England*). Each one was meant to regain the audience they had lost. Each one failed. They had become prisoners of their past, outstripped by the Beach Boys, the Beatles and the Byrds, all of whom had acknowledged their debt to the Everly Brothers. For reasons that remain unclear, the Everlys never actively pursued a country and western career. Instead they played in Las Vegas and became encrusted youthful oldies, biding their time for a possible revival. As their careers floundered, the relationship between the two became increasingly tense.

But the Everly Brothers were not through. In 1968 they released an album called *Roots*, their last magnificent hurrah. Reminiscent of *Songs Our Daddy Taught Us*, an album of traditional songs they had recorded while with Cadence, *Roots* was a self-conscious attempt to retrieve their past. Interjected between the traditional tunes ("Shady Grove," "T for Texas") were snippets of recordings they had made as children on their parents' radio show. Though the album is framed as a documentary, it also revives their Cadence sound and recasts in contemporary rock and roll terms. One can hear simultaneously how the Everly Brothers influenced such groups as the Byrds, and how, in turn, the Byrds were now affecting the Everly Brothers.

The album's centerpiece is their reworking of "I Wonder if I Care as Much," the second song they recorded on Cadence. The original version is too jaunty. Their harmonies gloss over the lyrics, which seem beyond their capabilities. On *Roots* their voices display a new maturity, an added edge and weight. They slow the song down—changing the tempo several times—and break it down into pieces, as if they were rolling it around in their hands and carefully examining it. The song questions their whole career.

> Tears that I have to shed by day
> Give relief and wash away
> The memory of the night before.
> I wonder if I'll suffer more.
> I wonder if I care as much as I did before.

It is perhaps the Everly Brothers' greatest moment—but *Roots* was no more successful in rekindling their career than any of its immediate predecessors. Not long afterward the Everly Brothers left Warners to record for RCA, where they fared no better. Tired, their relationship becoming more acrimonious, they gave their last concert together in July 1973, at the John Wayne Theater in Buena Park, California. Before the concert was over, Phil smashed his guitar on the floor and

Clockwise from right: (1) The cast of the Everly family radio show from the late Forties—from left, Don, Ike, Phil; seated, Margaret; (2) Onstage; (3) Less than clean-cut; (4) A late Sixties incarnation; (5) With Johnny Otis; (6) Two true rockers, late Fifties or early Sixties. (1 & 4, courtesy the Everly Brothers; 2 & 6, courtesy Acuff-Rose; 3, 'Phonograph Record' magazine; 5, Michael Ochs Archives)

walked off the stage. Don finished the last two shows by himself. "The Everly Brothers," he said, "died ten years ago."

The ending, of course, was inevitable—few groups survive intact forever. But it is not without irony that violent divorce was the final image left by the two men who, perhaps more than anybody else, had so well defined what love and affection meant in rock and roll.

Discography

1957–1967

"Bye Bye Love" (Cadence 1315; ☆2, c☆1, r☆5, 1957). "Wake Up Little Susie" (Cadence 1337; ☆1, c☆1, r☆2, 1957). "This Little Girl of Mine" (Cadence 1342; ☆28, c☆4, 1958). "All I Have to Do Is Dream" b/w "Claudette" (Cadence 1348; ☆1, c☆1, r☆1, 1958). "Bird Dog" b/w "Devoted to You" (Cadence 1350; ☆2, c☆1, r☆3, 1958). "Problems" (Cadence 1355; ☆2, c☆17, 1958). "Take a Message to Mary" b/w "Poor Jenny" (Cadence 1364; ☆16, 1959). "('Til) I Kissed You" (Cadence 1369; ☆4, c☆8, r☆22, 1959). "Let It Be Me" (Cadence 1376; ☆7, 1960). "Cathy's Clown" (Warner Bros. 5151; ☆1, r☆1, 1960). "When Will I Be Loved" (Cadence 1380; ☆8, 1960). "So Sad" b/w "Lucille" (Warner Bros. 5163; ☆7, r☆16, 1960). "Walk Right Back" b/w "Ebony Eyes" (Warner Bros. 5199; ☆7, c☆25, r☆25, 1961). "Temptation" (Warner Bros. 5220; ☆27, 1961). "Don't Blame Me" (Warner Bros. 5501; ☆20, 1961). "Crying in the Rain" (Warner Bros. 5250; ☆6, 1962). "That's Old Fashioned" (Warner Bros. 5273; ☆9, 1962). "Don't Ask Me to Be Friends" (Warner Bros. 5297; ☆48, 1962). "Gone, Gone, Gone" (Warner Bros. 5478; ☆31, 1964). "Bowling Green" (Warner Bros. 7020; ☆40, 1967).

(Chart position compiled from Joel Whitburn's *Record Research,* based on *Billboard* Pop chart; r☆ = position on *Billboard* Rhythm and Blues chart; c☆ = position on *Billboard* Country and Western chart.)

Buddy Holly

by Jonathan Cott

According to American mythology, psychopaths and rock 'n' roll stars have almost invisible origins, springing parthenogenetically out of the headlines or onto the record charts as if they had no past. "I taught him once," one of Buddy Holly's high school teachers recalls, "but to be honest, it was only after the news was in the paper about his death that I remembered that he had been in my class. He was a quiet kid—wasn't any great student, but didn't cause any trouble either, you understand. So I really don't remember anything about him."

Killed at the age of 22 on February 3rd, 1959 ("The day the music died"), in the still-memorialized plane crash that also took the lives of the Big Bopper and Ritchie Valens, Buddy Holly was born in Lubbock, Texas, on September 7th, 1936. He made his first appearance onstage when he was five years old, at a local talent show, singing "Down the River of Memories"—a song his mother had taught him—and winning a five-dollar prize for the performance. After forming the Western and Bop band with his high school friends Bob Montgomery and Larry Welborn, he signed with Decca, cut several uncommercial discs, and then, under the supervision of producer Norman Petty in Clovis, New Mexico, made his famous series of recordings, both with his group the Crickets, and as a soloist; between 1957 and 1958, he enjoyed seven Top 40 hits in the United States, and scored several more in England. Late in 1958, he broke with Petty and the Crickets, moved to a Greenwich Village apartment, and married Maria Elena Santiago, a New Yorker whom he proposed to at P.J. Clarke's on their first date.

Buddy Holly was one of the few Fifties rock 'n' roll stars never to have been filmed. So we remember his photographs—all variations of the archetypal high school graduation yearbook picture showing the "shy Texan" in his horn-rimmed glasses. And like one of the figures in a Picasso painting, this conventional image became blurred, transformed through his music into forms and colors. And unique and radiant they were and are. For unlike Bo Diddley (who defined and embodied himself in terms of rhythm), Elvis Presley (who adopted and transmogrified the experiences and values of black sexuality and alienation), or Chuck Berry (who took on and extended Walt Whitman's visionary embrace of American geography), Buddy Holly perfectly, almost obsessively, communicated in song after song his joyful acceptance of "true love ways," his indivertible expectation ("crying, waiting, hoping") of someday finding a love "so rare and true."

Onstage, he came across like a frenetic raver, yet his songs and vocal presentation often belied and went against the grain of this stylized pose. As writer Dave Laing has observed about Holly's rendition of "Rock Around with Ollie Vee": "There is a notable vocal touch on the line 'I'm gonna shake it just a bit *in the middle of the night*,' where the voice suddenly drops an octave for the italicized words. But while Presley manages to get a menacing sexual growl by a similar effect, Buddy Holly comes across here as playful rather than sensual; it is a wink, not a snarl." And it is this playfully ironic, childlike quality that defines and gives the key to Buddy Holly's style.

When adults communicate with infants, they use the language of *baby talk*, exaggerating changes in pitch, speaking almost in singsong, uttering their words more slowly, reduplicating syllables and rhymes, and employing simple sentence structures. It is clear that Buddy Holly absorbed, transformed and revitalized this mode of expression in his use of titles and phrases like "Maybe Baby," "Oh Boy," "oops a daisy," "riddle dee pat," and "hey a hey hey"; in his embellished, rollicking six-syllable delivery of the word "well" at the beginning of "Rave On"; in lines like "Pretty, pretty, pretty, pretty Peggy Sue" (reminding you of a child talking to a little animal in order to tame it) or "You know my love not fade away" (telegraphing its message like a Chinese ideogram); and, most obviously, in his famous "hiccup" signature or in the sudden glides from deep bass to falsetto (and back again), revealing the child inside the man, the man inside the child.

It is Buddy Holly's childlike vocal timbre and phrasing, suggesting the insouciance of a choirboy who doesn't realize his voice is changing, which serves to express his almost prayerful expectancy of a love that will surely come his way . . . because it already exists in his heart. "Take your time," he sings in one of his loveliest songs, "And take mine, too/I have time to spend/Take your time/Go with me through/Times till all times end." The mood of the song makes it seem as if the young singer has all the time in the world, but he is at the same time actually urging his girl to take (seize) the ripened moment of love ("Take your time/I can wait/For all of the love/I know will be mine/If you take your time").

And in "I'm Gonna Love You Too," Buddy Holly—like a little boy confusing the present and the hoped-for future, reality and anticipation—sings: "You're gonna say you've missed me/You're gonna say you'll kiss me/Yes, you're gonna say you'll love me/'Cause I'm gonna love you too." The irrepressible optimism of this song, like the adolescent confidence of "That'll Be the Day" and "Think It Over" or the incantatory trance of "Listen to Me" and "Words of Love," conveys Holly's magical notion that the insistent repetition of one's wishes ("The dreams and wishes you wish/In the night when lights are low"—"Well All Right") is in fact the fulfillment of the wish itself; and, as in ritual, the rapture of song becomes the proof of this magic and, in the end, the magic itself.

In an essay entitled "Pop as Ritual in Modern Culture," the English critic Wilfrid Mellers writes about the Australian aborigines who "make a music consisting of isolated words and phrases—invocations of sun, moon, cloud, and other natural phenomena—yelled against the everlasting drone of the dijiridu and accompanied by the rhythmic beating of sticks. In the

Buddy Holly (Michael Ochs collection)

Left: (1) Holly enjoying happy days with the Crickets; (2) Buddy onstage; (3) The body of Ritchie Valens lies face down in the snow near the wreckage of the plane that also carried Buddy Holly to his death in Clear Lake, Iowa. (1, Ralph J. Gleason collection; 2, John Goddard; 3, UPI)

silent emptiness the aborigine dramatizes the basic fact of his life: the beating of the pulse, the thudding of the heart." And in today's era of sophisticated production techniques, it is important to remember that Holly's most moving songs—whether accompanied by the Crickets, background vocalists or strings—attest to the fact that he was one of the first white rock 'n' roll musicians to keep alive and draw inspiration from the simplest ritual gestures, phrases and forms of musical expression. (Black musicians such as Washboard Sam, Tampa Red, Lonnie Johnson, and Arthur Crudup had earlier created rock and roll out of the barest and most humble instrumental resources. It is also not surprising that the most revelatory "cover" version of Holly's songs are not by bubblegum Holly imitators or English rock artists [the Beatles' "Words of Love" and Blind Faith's "Well All Right" are the exceptions] but by folk and country singers such as Carolyn Hester ["Lonesome Tears"], Tom Paxton ["Love's Made a Fool of You"], and Skeeter Davis ["True Love Ways"].)

Several of Holly's friends recall that some of his most memorable playing occurred in 1956–'57 when he and fellow Cricket Jerry Allison performed regularly at the Lubbock youth center—Holly's vocals and guitar supported only by Allison's drumming. And even later, Holly's rhythm section often consisted of just a tom-tom or jelly. From the slapping-hands-on-knees accompaniment on "Everyday" to the modal plainness and almost shamanistic cymbal drumming on "Well All Right," from the light incantations of "Crying, Waiting, Hoping" to Waylon Jennings's and Slim Corbin's hand-clapping on the original version of "You're the One," Holly's deepest, wisest, and seemingly least complicated songs express the unadorned confrontation of beauty and love with time. Any theory of aesthetics that considers the songs of Don McLean or Harry Chapin to be more subtle or poetically "richer" than the person-to-person utterance of "You're the One" is mawkish at best and dishonest at worst, for the unmediated statement of fact is as complex and significant as reality itself:

You're the one that's a-causing my blues,
You're the one I don't wanna lose,
You're the one that I'd always choose,
You're the one that's a-meant for me.

The women of Fifties rock 'n' roll—about whom songs were written and to whom they were addressed—almost always fell into two categories: the fast and earthy (Lucille, Fannie Mae, Hank Ballard's Annie) and the slow and dreamy (Donna, Denise, and Sheila). In most cases, they were like the emblematic and conventional ladies of the courtly and Petrarchan schools—as interchangeable as hurricanes or spring showers, Party Doll ornaments of the song.

With Peggy Sue, however, Buddy Holly created the first rock and roll folk heroine (Chuck Berry's Johnny B. Goode is her male counterpart). And yet it is difficult to say how Holly did it. Unlike the Sad-Eyed Lady of the Lowlands—whom Bob Dylan fills in as he invents and discovers her—Peggy Sue is hardly there at all. Most Fifties singers let it be known that they liked the way their women walked and talked; sometimes they even let on as to the color of their sweethearts' eyes and hair. But Buddy Holly didn't even give you this much information. Instead, he colluded with his listeners, suggesting that they imagine and create Peggy Sue *for* him: "If you knew Peggy Sue/Then you'd know why I feel blue/About Peggy/My Peggy Sue."

Singing in his characteristically shy, coy, ingenuous tone of voice, Holly seems to let us in on a secret—just as later, in "Peggy Sue Got Married," he continues his complicit arrangement with his listeners, half-pleading with them, and with himself, not to reveal something which he himself must hesitatingly disclose:

Please don't tell—no, no, no—
Don't say that I told you so,
I just heard a rumor from a friend.
I don't say that it's true,
I'll just leave that up to you,
If you don't believe, I'll understand.

You recall a girl that's been
In nearly every song,
This is what I've heard—of course,
The story could be wrong . . .

She's the one, I've been told,
Now she's wearing a band of gold,
Peggy Sue got married not long ago.

In this brilliantly constructed equivocation, Holly asks us to suspend belief (just as, contrarily, Wendy in *Peter Pan* beseeches the children in the audience to give credence to fairies in order to keep them alive) until that inexorable last stanza when we realize that no longer can Holly sing: "You're the one," but only "She's the one, I've been told." He has become one of his own listeners as Peggy Sue vanishes, like Humbert Humbert's Lolita, into the mythology of American Romance.

In his invaluable biography of Buddy Holly, John Goldrosen informs us that Holly originally composed a song called "Cindy Lou," and that Jerry Allison suggested he change the title to the name of Allison's girlfriend (whom Allison married and later divorced). But the Peggy Sue of our hearts continued to live on, making an appearance not only at the living room party in "Splish Splash" but also in Bobby Darin's "Queen of the Hop" and Richie Valens's "Ooh My Head"—finally to be scorned and discarded for a younger rival in the insolent "Barbara Ann": "Played our favorite tune/Danced with Betty Lou/Tried Peggy Sue but I knew she wouldn't do—/Barbara Ann." (Barbara Ann, indeed!)

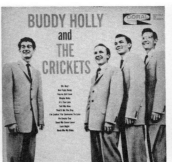

"Love is not love/Which alters when it alteration finds/Or bends with the remover to remove," wrote William Shakespeare. And some of us would like to think that Peggy Sue is still with us, as we keep alive the vibration of her life—and that of her creator—rediscovering her presence in the coded Personal Column message from the English rock group Buddy Holly influenced so strongly:

P.S. I LOVE YOU

"**Y**ou recall a girl that's been in nearly every song," Buddy Holly sang. And it's tempting to imagine that the *idea* of Peggy Sue permeated all of Holly's compositions. Similarly, it is tempting to view all of Holly's recordings as a synchronic rather than a diachronic structure . . . to see them, in other words, as one long song—all the more tempting in that the early Western and Bop demo tapes made by Holly and Bob Montgomery in 1953-'54, as well as the scores of radio and garage tapes which were rediscovered and issued after Holly's death (some untouched, most with overdubbed backings), are among his greatest performances.

His first recordings for Decca—including songs like "Modern Don Juan," "Midnight Shift," "Girl on My Mind," and the first version of "That'll Be the Day"—were either commercial failures or unreleased, and have long been criticized for their poor instrumental balance and overemphasized echo effects. Today, they strike oversatiated ears as some of Holly's freshest and most unpretentious work. Likewise, the often-criticized overdubbed recordings of the slow version of "Slippin' and Slidin'" (backed by the Fireballs), the string-drenched "Love Is Strange," and the version of "Peggy Sue Got Married" overdubbed with New York City studio musicians (in contrast to the forced-ebullient Clovis studio arrangement) are sublime masterpieces, achieving a seemingly effortless clarity. The early Holly/Montgomery recordings of songs like "I Wanna Play House with You" and "Down the Line," as well as this duo's later consummate songwriting collaborations ("Wishing" and "Love's Made a Fool of You"—both recordings featuring the extraordinary lead guitar work of Tommy Allsup), are still too little known. And no one should overlook "Because I Love You," one of Holly's most haunted and haunting ballads—a song which, along with "Love's Made a Fool of You" represents the darker side of Buddy Holly's emotional world.

All of Holly's compositions and performances reflect his amazing capacity to synthesize musical influences as diverse as Hank Williams, Hank Snow, the Louvin Brothers, western swing bands, Elvis Presley, Bo Diddley, Carl Perkins, Tony Williams, Ray Charles, black gospel, and Baptist church tunes. And through Holly, all these musical strands were later taken up and developed in the Sixties.

During the Crickets' first cross-country package tour in 1957, Buddy Holly and Chuck Berry used to spend their time traveling together at the back of the bus, kneeling on the floor and shooting crap with their night's earnings. And on hindsight, it is clear today that it was Holly and Berry who were the major influences on the rock music of the Sixties. But Holly's specific contribution is too often underestimated. He was certainly the main inspiration for the Beatles (think of songs like "I'll Follow the Sun," "Every Little Thing," "I'll Cry Instead," "Here Comes the Sun," and "One after 909"—the last of which is almost an exact imitation of the early Holly/Montgomery recordings), as well as for the entire English Mersey school, the Kinks (think of "I'll Remember" or "Starstruck"), the Hollies (he gave them their name), and Eric Clapton. In the States, of course, he directly influenced singers and groups like Bobby Vee, Tommy Roe, the Bobby Fuller Four, the Everly Brothers, Skeeter Davis, Creedence Clearwater, Tom Paxton and Bob Dylan.

In the words of Malcolm Jones, in an English rock magazine—Holly "scored with a dazzling series of firsts in an era when everyone followed the flock. He was one of the first white rock stars to rely almost exclusively on his own material. The Crickets were probably the first white group to feature the lead/rhythm/bass/drums lineup. He was the first rock singer to double-track his voice and guitar. He was the first to use strings on a rock and roll record. In addition, he popularized the Fender Stratocaster and was probably the only rock star to wear glasses onstage!"

These were no mean accomplishments for a 22-year-old who, as an "unmemorable" high school student six years before his death, had written in an autobiography for his sophomore English course: "My life has been what you might call an uneventful one, and it seems there is not much of interest to tell. . . . I have many hobbies. Some of these are hunting, fishing, leatherwork, reading, painting, and playing western music. I have thought about making a career out of western music if I am good enough but I will just have to wait to see how that turns out. . . . Well, that's my life to the present date, and even though it may seem awful and full of calamities, I'd sure be in a bad shape without it."

As Bob Dylan once confessed: "I just carry that other time around with me. . . . The music of the late Fifties and early Sixties when music was at that root level—that for me is meaningful music. The singers and musicians I grew up with transcend nostalgia—Buddy Holly and Johnny Ace are just as valid to me today as then."

Discography

Crickets, "That'll Be the Day" (Brunswick 55009; r☆2, ☆3, 1957). **Buddy Holly,** "Peggy Sue" (Coral 61885; r☆2, ☆3, 1957). **Crickets,** "Oh, Boy!" (Brunswick 55035; r☆15, ☆10, 1957). **Crickets,** "Maybe Baby" (Brunswick 55053; r☆8, ☆18, 1958). **Buddy Holly,** "Rave On" (Coral 61985; ☆37, 1958). **Crickets,** "Think It Over" (Brunswick 55072; ☆27, 1958). **Buddy Holly,** "Early in the Morning" (Coral 62006; ☆32, 1958). **Buddy Holly,** "Heartbeat" (Coral 62051; ☆82, 1959). **Buddy Holly,** "It Doesn't Matter Anymore" (Coral 62074; ☆13, 1959). (Chart positions taken from Joel Whitburn's *Record Research,* compiled from *Billboard* Pop chart, unless otherwise indicated; r☆ = position on *Billboard* Rhythm and Blues chart.)

Doo-Wop
by Barry Hansen

Of all the musical instruments used on this planet, the all-time favorite is the only one the human race didn't invent—the larynx. No other instrument, be it mbira or Moog, has come close to matching the variety, versatility and impact of the human voice.

The larynx, however, has one terribly frustrating liability: it can only sing one note at a time. This became especially aggravating after moving bass lines and chord changes—what we call harmony—were added to the European musical vocabulary during the early Renaissance.

The rest of the world's musicians and singers managed to get along without harmony until very recently, however Europeans and their American descendants—including the New World blacks whose appropriation of Old World traditions has provided the lion's share of America's musical energy—have always found harmony indispensable.

Rock 'n' roll—despite what its detractors might say—is no exception. Harmonized group vocals have been part of every stage of rock's development. They were especially prominent in the Fifties, when a couple of dozen major vocal groups and more than a thousand obscure ones, comprised chiefly of black singers, created the music that rock 'n' roll connoisseurs still regard as the cream of the cream—at least if one measures the music's worth by the value of the records as collector's items.

No particular name was given to this form of R&B music by the people who made and enjoyed it in the Fifties. Today, we call it "doo-wop," after two of the many characteristic nonsense syllables invented early in the game by the fellows who didn't get to sing lead and got tired of singing nothing but "aaaaah." I'd just as soon call it "sh-boom" or "ookey ook" or "oodly-pop-a-cow pop-a-cow pop-a-cow cow" ("I Promise to Remember," Frankie Lymon and the Teenagers, 1956), but "doo-wop" will do.

Black vocal harmony is as old as America. Some astonishing examples were recorded in the Twenties by the Norfolk Jazz Quartet, a gospel group doing a little backsliding during the jazz age. Everybody's heard the Mills Brothers. For rock 'n' roll purposes, a more important antecedent would be the equally famous Ink Spots, whose ballads, such as "If I Didn't Care" and "My Prayer," featuring lead singer Bill Kenny and talking bassman "Hoppy" Jones, were among the nation's best-selling records in the late Thirties and early Forties.

The Spots gradually faded after Jones died in 1944, but their incredible success gave rise to innumerable imitations. By 1949, two groups had gained national stardom, at least among black listeners: the Ravens, whose bass singer Jimmy Ricks virtually created the role of Mr. Bassman, and the Orioles, whose Sonny Til carried on in the tradition of Bill Kenny. The Orioles' ballad recordings such as "Tell Me So" (1949) added something significant to the Ink Spots' pattern: a wordless falsetto doing a kind of obbligato to the lead vocal. This device,

plus a slightly rougher vocal tone and freer, more prominent background parts, makes "Tell Me So" sound like primeval rock 'n' roll, while the Ink Spots reside securely in rock's *pre*history.

All three pioneer groups, the Ink Spots, Ravens and Orioles, recorded many fast numbers as well, jive tunes done with a restrained, delicate touch that sounds enchanting a quarter century later. By the early Fifties, however, they sounded like pussyfeet. The emerging boppers may have been as sentimental as their older sisters and brothers when it came to the slow stuff at evening's end, but when they wanted to get it on, the Ravens' "Ol' Man River" didn't quite fill the bill anymore. They were replaced by such groups as the Dominoes, the Clovers and the Drifters, who combined liberated gospel-style lead singing with a beat far heftier than any previously heard behind a black vocal group.

The next major figure in our story is Alan Freed, who couldn't sing a note. Freed featured black vocal groups on his radio shows. As sales of group records skyrocketed, every R&B label (plus some that had never before given the music a second thought) was hungry for groups. The bird groups multiplied like rabbits, soon to be joined by insects, flowers and automobiles of every description.

Few of these new groups could do a ballad as sweetly or as smoothly as the Orioles. Few could sell a sexy song with the verve of the Drifters' lead singer Clyde McPhatter. But there was far more demand in the mid-Fifties than those masters could possibly supply, and the cities were packed with aspiring vocal groups. One writer estimates 15,000 groups eventually cut a record apiece. (I'd be tempted to remove at least one zero from that figure, but for legend's sake I'll let it pass.)

The great majority of these records were flops, meaning that relatively few copies of each disc were sold. Back about 1960, when people first began to realize that old rock 'n' roll records were (1) nice and (2) becoming hard to find, certain people (particularly in New York) became devoted enough to the Fifties black vocal group idiom to want to own every record of this type, regardless of musical quality. The scarcest ones—that is, the ones nobody wanted to buy when they first came out—quickly escalated in price, leading rapidly to a subculture that considered old records in terms of price first and music second.

Don't get me wrong—I know many collectors who love this music, even though none of them ever seem to want to play their records all the way through. There's even a certain exhilaration in holding a $500 record, or even a counterfeit replica of one, though that doesn't help the group that put the thing out in 1955 and got dumped on the street when it sold only 83 copies.

Myself, I prefer the hits: by and large, they're better records.

Typically, the popular groups of the Fifties struck a compromise between the Ink Spots/Orioles ballad style and the

The Robins—later the Coasters—circa 1953 (Ralph J. Gleason collection)

The Robins

Exclusive RCA Victor Recording Artists
Hollywood, California.

fervor of the rhythm and gospelers, coming as close to one or both models as their talents allowed. More often than not, their records had one fast side and one slow side.

The Orioles' "Crying in the Chapel" (1953) is often cited as the first R&B record to win a big white audience. Since it was a cover of a country song, I tend to consider it a fluke, lovely fluke though it is. Far more seminal was the Crows' early 1954 coupling of "Gee" and "I Love You So."

This record provided ample confirmation for the many musicians, writers and comedians (such as Stan Freberg) who considered rock 'n' roll artists hopelessly deficient in the basic techniques of musicmaking. On the uptempo "Gee," the lead singer attempts a Clyde McPhatter gospel shout but can produce little more than a croak (or caw, if you please). The equally well beloved B-side, "I love you so," is a woefully discordant ballad, opening with "I love you so/I want you to know/I'm telling you darling/I'll never let you go"—and becoming less articulate as the song proceeds.

So much for the Crows, one might say. But a whole generation, including myself, loved that record. Much has been written and said about rock 'n' roll being sung on street corners by neighborhood kids in the Fifties, and there's no denying that "Gee" and "I Love You So" have a delicious amateurishness to them. The complexity of recording and performing in the Seventies has almost driven that spirit from rock, and it's no small loss.

With Alan Freed as the pusher, "Gee" and contemporaneous songs got thousands of teenage Americans hooked on rock 'n' roll, *nee* rhythm and blues. It wasn't yet a majority taste in 1954, but it was getting there very fast. Group records started coming out at the rate of a couple dozen a week. They ranged from splendidly recorded, aggressively promoted products of major independents like Atlantic and King to things thrown together on home tape recorders, promoted from a phone booth and sold from a car trunk.

The saga of "Earth Angel," the R&B sensation of late 1954, is typical. Often hailed as *the* all-time favorite R&B oldie, "Earth Angel" by the Penguins was originally released early in '54, by Dootone Records of Los Angeles.

Dootone was owned by a south L.A. producer named Dootsie Williams (who later became prosperous via a long series of raunchy comedy LPs by Redd Foxx). Before the Penguins came along, Dootsie had graduated from the car-trunk and phone-booth league, thanks to "party" records by Billy Mitchell and Hattie Noel; but Dootone in 1954 was by no means a major independent, even by R&B standards.

The Penguins, named after the Kool cigarette trademark, were students at Fremont High School in L.A. when Dootsie heard them. Even though he thought they needed more practice, he went ahead and cut two demos and six masters. "Earth

Angel," though listed as one of the latter, could easily pass for the former; its sound is murky, distorted and badly balanced. Dootsie put it out, though, on the B-side of the group's second Dootone release, coupled with "Hey Senorita."

"Senorita" sank without a trace, but "Angel," garage sound and all, lit up the phones wherever it was played. Listeners quickly fell in love with the opening piano lines, melody, lyrics and Cleve Duncan's singing, all of which conveyed true love undiluted by any artistic pretense whatever. It was real people's music—you or your lover could have made it—yet it's sublimely beautiful. For the next ten years, group after group sought to emulate this distillation of pure rock 'n' roll romanticism, free from all artistic trappings such as complex harmonies and clever lyrics.

And what of the Penguins themselves? Lead singer Cleve Duncan told their story in a 1972 issue of *Record Exchanger*, the biggest and most permanent of a host of fanzines dealing with rock 'n' roll and R&B oldies. The Penguins' story could be that of any of a hundred doo-wop groups.

"Earth Angel" hit Number One on the R&B charts, and Number Eight on the pop charts, tying for the latter position with a stiff pop "cover" by the Crew-Cuts. The Penguins played Harlem's Apollo Theatre, the Brooklyn Paramount (with Alan Freed), the Regal in Chicago and most of the other major R&B venues of the time.

They quickly got into a dispute with Dootone, however, over advances on record royalties. In frustration they turned to Buck Ram, who managed their friends the Platters. Ram was able to get the Penguins released from Dootone, and signed with the Mercury label as part of a package deal with the Platters. For the Penguins, the price was high: in a court case, Dootsie Williams wound up with all rights to "Earth Angel."

On Mercury, the Penguins cut some fine sides but failed to produce another big hit. Mercury's enthusiasm waned, and after the first year the company didn't get around to recording the eight sides a year the group's contract called for. The Penguins moved on to Atlantic, but after one unsuccessful Atlantic release they found themselves back in L.A., older, wiser, deep in debt and recording once again for Dootsie Williams.

They remained with Dootsie, hitless, for two years; after one final effort on Sun State Records, the original Penguins disbanded. Since then Cleve has recruited new Penguins on several occasions, one of them a 1963 recording of a song called "Memories of El Monte" written by a young Frank Zappa and Ray Collins. More recently the new Penguins have been heard at rock 'n' roll revival shows, sharing the stage with dozens of other groups, each one with its own bittersweet story to tell about the rush of success and the frustrations of not being able to sustain it.

Of all the doo-wop groups mentioned in the discography for this chapter, only two became long-running pop successes: the Platters and the Coasters. Give an honorable mention to Frankie

THE TEENAGERS

Lymon and the Teenagers. A few others that got into the game early were able to hold loyal R&B audiences for several years without the benefit of a big pop hit: the Spaniels, Moonglows, Five Keys, Charms, Flamingos. For most of the doo-wop groups, it was one or two hits, boom and bust. No other form of commercial entertainment can rival doo-wop music for its dazzling panoply of one-shot acts. Success came much more quickly to a group in the Fifties than it does today, but failure followed even more quickly.

But what glorious one-shots! Here are a few favorites:

"Story Untold" by the Nutmegs. This ballad is totally definitive of doo-wop in mid-1955. Unlike "Earth Angel," it is competently recorded, accompanied by a professional sounding combo. Like "Angel," though, its aim is the expression of romantic sentiments in slow dance tempo uncluttered by any pretense to art. While the background voices perform all the standard functions of their craft, the late Leroy Griffin sings a lead part that manages to be expressive while staying very neutral stylistically, attempting neither the power surges of gospel nor the gloss of a Bill Kenny. The Nutmegs were named after their native Connecticut, the Nutmeg State.

"Speedoo" by the Cadillacs. Despite the great popularity of slow dancing in the Fifties, about half the doo-wop songs that went pop were uptempo. Here, after a bass dominated intro, Earl Carroll (that's Mr. Earl, of course; he later joined the Coasters) takes over this macho manifesto, written by Esther Navarro. The lyrics sound like they were made up on the spot, but the character is well drawn. Did you ever notice that the sax solo is faster than the rest of the record?

"Why Do Fools Fall in Love" by the Teenagers featuring Frankie Lymon. The ill-starred Frankie, who died tragically in 1968, was the premier boy soprano of our time, his rich, round tone dwarfing the bleats of later preteen idols. This song, which Frankie coauthored, is everything you'd expect of the third-prize entry in a junior high poetry contest, but Frankie's pipes and the lively music make it a paean of ecstasy. Bassist Sherman Garnes opens the side with a resonant "eh toom-ah-ta-toom-ah-ta-toom-ah-toh-doh"—spell it any way you like. (Garnes was also the creator of "oodly pop-a-cow cow.") Before Frankie's voice changed, the Teenagers enjoyed an atypically long string of hits, incuding "I Want You to Be My Girl" and "The ABCs of Love." Their "I'm Not a Juvenile Delinquent" was as close as the music ever got to social consciousness.

"In the Still of the Nite" by the Five Satins. A year later than "Story Untold," this makes further progress toward freeing the music from artistic trappings. Most of the vocal counterpoint is abandoned in favor of a simple "shoo-doo-shoo-be-doo" repeated so constantly it becomes a hypnotic hook, while Fred Parris sings the romantic lead in a style even more neutral than Leroy Griffin's. Though this was a relatively modest hit in 1956, it closely rivals "Earth Angel" as the all-time fave oldie today.

"Come Go with Me" by the Dell-Vikings. The first of a long line of racially integrated vocal groups, the Dell-Vikings were with the U.S. Air Force when they recorded "Come Go with Me" in the basement of a Pittsburgh disc jockey's house. After local success on the Fee Bee label the song went national on Dot, the first of several label switches the Dell-Vikings made in what was to be a very confused career. There's nary an original line in the lyrics, as shopworn a satchel of clichés as you could ask for—but the best parts of the record are the parts where the fellows sing only syllables, "dum dum dum dum dum-be-oo-bee." A terrific dance disc.

"Silhouettes" by the Rays. Here by contrast is a highly professional affair, the work of a journeyman group coached by songwriter/producers Frank Slay and Bob Crewe. The lyrics to this ballad of mistaken identity are downright fancy by comparison with those we've just encountered, but the music is as simple and artless as any doo-wopper could wish.

"Get a Job" by the Silhouettes. This song is actually about a guy whose woman is nagging him to get a job, an unusually adult subject for doo-wop. I doubt that very many people noticed, for the "background" singers are the whole show, from the first "byip byip byip byip" to the oft-disputed "sha-na-na" or "sha-da-da," whichever you prefer. An awful lot of socks were worn out to "Get a Job" in 1958.

"Book of Love" by the Monotones. Another supreme one-shot—like the Silhouettes, this group never again had a Top 100 record, though connoisseurs of the bizarre might do well to look up the Monotones' followup attempts, "Legend of Sleepy Hollow" and "Zombi." This record has the simplest and catchiest "hook" of the decade—in a single bass drum beat happening all by itself right in the middle of the chorus.

"Book of Love" was close to the end of the line for classic doo-wop. By 1958, R&B groups were fighting a losing battle for the young record-buyer's 98¢ (up from 89¢ that year) against the young, mostly white artists who were getting saturation exposure on *American Bandstand.*

Two totally dissimilar groups, the Platters and the Coasters, kept the doo-wop tradition going, with modifications. To introduce the first, we go back to 1955, the year "Rock around the Clock" changed the rock audience from a minority to the majority. Easily the second biggest rock event of that year was the emergence of a doo-wop group called the Platters. The Platters debuted on the charts in 1955, after being brought to Mercury, a major national label, by their manager Buck Ram. The Platters were a highly professional group which had been recording for some time on one of the bigger independent labels, Federal. Ram, who had once written songs for the original Ink Spots, had coached the Platters into a modernized reincarnation of the Spots, featuring Tony Williams in the Bill Kenny role. Ram relied on a sturdy rhythm section, with lots of triplets, to bring the music up-to-date.

The Platters' last Federal release had been a Ram-composed ballad called "Only You." The group quickly remade it for Mercury, in the highest of fi. It was an across-the-board smash. "The Great Pretender" was even bigger, becoming the first doo-wop record to hit Number One on the pop charts. After another Ram-composed hit, "You've Got the Magic Touch," the Platters paid true tribute to their roots with "My Prayer," an almost literal reproduction of the Ink Spots' 1939 hit. The Platters went on to become the most successful vocal group of the Fifties.

Closest contenders to the Platters for consistent commercial supremacy was a group that started on the West Coast (whence their name). The Coasters began as the Robins, part of the troupe of veteran bandleader and showman Johnny Otis. The year 1955 found the Robins recording the spectacular "Riot in Cell Block No. 9" and "Smokey Joe's Cafe" for Spark Records, an L.A. label owned by Jerry Leiber and Mike Stoller, who also had written the songs. These enjoyed enough regional success to interest Atlantic Records, which offered Leiber and Stoller a contract to produce similar records for their Atco subsidiary.

This deal was a major milestone for the rock 'n' roll record industry in that it marked the start of independent production, now the *modus operandi* for most rock recording. It also marked the genesis of the Coasters. It seems the Robins had a disagreement; one faction went with Leiber and Stoller while the other retained the Robins name and flew to obscurity on a label called Whippet Records.

The first Coaster record, "Down in Mexico," did well on the R&B market in the spring of '56. The group's real rock 'n' roll fame, however, began with the coupling of "Searchin' " and "Young Blood" which hit the streets in April 1957. Every Top 40 station in America glowed with the sweet funk of these sides. "Young Blood" became the model for a whole series of sly "playlets" (the word is Mike Stoller's) on teenage life and love, all written and produced by Leiber and Stoller.

"Charlie Brown," "Yakety Yak," "Along Came Jones" and "Idol with the Golden Head" are as entertaining today as ever. Though the Coasters' style has no real precedent in the doo-wop mainstream aside from the Robins, the Coasters' records were so often imitated (notably by the Olympics) that they became very much a part of doo-wop's legacy to the 1960s.

The Coasters and the Platters, having in their highly divergent ways established themselves as the fittest, survived into the Sixties. In the meantime, though, classic doo-wop was fading from the airwaves: 1957 was the last vintage year. Ironically, just as classic doo-wop disappeared, we began hearing from the second generation of rock groupdom—white, black and integrated groups who took their inspiration not from the old masters like Bill Kenny or the great showmen like Clyde McPhatter but from the naive, street-corner sound of records like "Earth Angel" and "I Love You So."

Neo-doo-wop, as I like to call this development, produced some of the most awful records of all time. Nostalgia, however, has given some of them a luster no producer could have imagined: "Oh Julie" by the Crescendos, "You" by the Aquatones, "Sorry (I Ran All the Way Home)" by the Impalas, and "You Cheated" in rival versions by the original Slades and the covering Shields. Most successful of all were the Fleetwoods, two girls and a guy who carried on rock 'n' roll's Cadillac tradition by crooning "Come Softly to Me" and "Mr. Blue" in voices as gentle as the drizzles of their native Olympia, Washington.

In 1959, a record from Pittsburgh pointed the way to the future. "Since I Don't Have You" by the Skyliners was one of the first hits that managed to capture the street-corner aura while expanding the horizons of the music with relatively sophisticated harmony, and an elaborately orchestrated production which for a change supported the singers rather than fighting them. Phil Spector, then just getting his producing feet wet with the Teddy Bears, has cited "Since I Don't Have You" as a major inspiration.

The Flamingos, also-rans on the doo-wop scene since the early Fifties, finally soared in 1959 with a similarly adventurous production of the 1934 standard "I Only Have Eyes for You" (doo-vop-she-bop). Meanwhile another bird group, the Falcons, debuted with the much funkier "You're So Fine." Together with other 1959–'60 black groups like the Impressions and the Miracles, and such soloists as Sam Cooke, the Falcons marked a beginning of what we now know as soul music—an idiom that owes a lot to the rhythm and gospel style of Clyde McPhatter but differs from basic doo-wop in owing absolutely nothing to the Ink Spots.

After a fallow year in 1960 (a year in which most of the best-selling singles had only the most tenuous connection with rock of any kind) neo-doo-wop produced a bumper crop in 1961. That year saw not only a huge boom in sales of reissued oldies from the Fifties, but a whole new crop of one-shot groups firmly entrenched in neo-doo-wop style, such as the Capris ("There's a Moon Out Tonight," said to have actually been cut in 1958), the Edsels ("Rama Lama Ding Dong"), the Regents ("Barbara-Ann"), the Marcels, who hit Number One on the pop charts with "Blue Moon," and above all Shep and the Limelites, who after making Number 53 on the charts in 1956 with "A Thousand Miles Away," under the name of the Heartbeats, came back with a Number Two hit in 1961 with the sequel, "Daddy's Home."

In New York City, the neo-doo-wop phenomenon achieved nirvana with the acapella craze. Groups of young blacks, whites and Latins from all over Gotham vied with each other to produce the purest imaginable doo-wop ballads, letting it all hang out with no instrumental accompaniment of any kind. The New York acapella sound (not to be confused with the later unaccompanied soul stylings of the Persuasions) was rarely heard outside Fun City, but immortalized itself with hundreds of 45s, some now nearly as pricey as the original discs from the Fifties.

Despite such fanaticism, neo-doo-wop did not survive the British invasion of 1964 (unless we count the Four Seasons, who owe at least a little to the style). Once again, the sweet sounds faded from the airwaves, to live on in the minds of collectors, the bank accounts of rare record dealers, and the hearts of just about everyone who had the fortune (good or bad) to be young in those times.

Discography

Clovers, "Crawlin'" (Atlantic 989; r☆3, 1953). Du Droppers, "I Wanna Know" (RCA Victor 5229; r☆3, 1953). Vocaleers, "Is It a Dream?" (Red Robin 114; r☆8, 1953). Clovers, "Good Lovin'" (Atlantic 1000; r☆2, 1953). Orioles, "Crying in the Chapel" (Jubilee 5122; r☆1, ☆11, 1953). Spaniels, "Baby It's You" (Chance 141; r☆10, 1953). Spiders, "I Didn't Want to Do It" (Imperial 5256; r☆3, 1954). Clovers, "Lovey Dovey" b/w "Little Mama" (Atlantic 1022; r☆2, 1954). Crows, "Gee" (Rama 5; r☆6, ☆17, 1954). Spaniels, "Goodnite Sweetheart, Goodnite" (Vee-Jay 107; r☆5, 1954). Chords, "Sh-Boom" (Cat 104; r☆3, ☆9, 1954). Clovers, "I've Got My Eyes on You" b/w "Your Cash Ain't Nothin' but Trash" (Atlantic 1035; r☆7, 1954). Charms, "Hearts of Stone" (DeLuxe 6062; r☆1, ☆15, 1954). Moonglows, "Sincerely" (Chess 1581; r☆2, 1954). Penguins, "Earth Angel" (Dootone 348, r☆1, ☆8, 1954). Five Keys, "Ling, Ting, Tong" (Capitol 2945; r☆5, ☆28, 1954). Charms, "Two Hearts" (DeLuxe 6065; r☆9, 1955). Charms, "Ling, Ting, Tong" (DeLuxe 6076; r☆6, ☆26, 1955). Five Keys, "Close Your Eyes" (Capitol 3032; r☆6, 1955). Hearts, "Lonely Nights" (Baton 208; r☆8, 1955). Moonglows, "Most of All" (Chess 1589; r☆11, 1955). Cardinals, "The Door Is Still Open" (Atlantic 1054; r☆10, 1955). Nutmegs, "Story Untold" (Herald 452; r☆2, 1955). Platters, "Only You" (Mercury 70633; r☆1, ☆5, 1955). Jacks, "Why Don't You Write Me?" (RPM 428; r☆4, 1955). El Dorados, "At My Front Door" (Vee-Jay 147; r☆2, ☆21, 1955). Drifters, "Adorable" (Atlantic 1078; r☆5, 1955). Turbans, "When You Dance" (Herald 458; r☆12, ☆33, 1955). Platters, "The Great Pretender" (Mercury 70753; r☆1, ☆1, 1955). Cadillacs, "Speedoo" (Josie 785; r☆3, ☆30, 1955). Clovers, "Devil or Angel" (Atlantic 1083; r☆4, 1956). Frankie Lymon and the Teenagers, "Why Do Fools Fall in Love" (Gee 1002; r☆1, ☆7, 1956). Teen Queens, "Eddie My Love" (RPM 453; r☆3, ☆22, 1956). Flamingos, "I'll Be Home" (Checker 830; r☆10, 1956). Platters, "(You've Got) The Magic Touch" (Mercury 70819; r☆4, ☆4, 1956). Otis Williams and his Charms, "Ivory Tower" (DeLuxe 6093; r☆9, ☆12, 1956). Willows, "Church Bells May Ring" (Melba 102; r☆11, 1956). Frankie Lymon and the Teenagers, "I Want You to Be My Girl" (Gee 1012; r☆3, ☆17, 1956). Cleftones, "Little Girl of Mine" (Gee 1011, r☆8, 1956). Drifters, "Ruby Baby" (Atlantic 1089; r☆13, 1956). Six Teens, "A Casual Look" (Flip 315; r☆7, ☆48, 1956). Clovers, "Love, Love, Love" (Atlantic 1094; r☆10, ☆30, 1956). Platters, "My Prayer" (Mercury 70893; r☆2, ☆1, 1956). Cadets, "Stranded in the Jungle" (Modern 994; r☆4, ☆18, 1956). Five Satins, "In the Still of the Nite" (Ember 1005; r☆4, ☆29, 1956). Frankie Lymon and the Teenagers, "I Promise to Remember" (Gee 1018, ☆10, 1956). Moonglows, "See Saw" (Chess 1629; r☆11, ☆28, 1956). Five Keys, "Out of Sight, out of Mind" (Capitol 3502; ☆27, 1956). Dells, "Oh What a Nite" (Vee-Jay 204; r☆4, 1956), Frankie Lymon and the Teenagers, "The ABCs of Love" (Gee 1022; r☆14, 1956). Heartbeats, "A Thousand Miles Away" (Rama 216; r☆5, 1956). Dell-Vikings, "Come Go with Me" (Dot 15538; r☆3, ☆5, 1957). Diamonds, "Little Darlin'" (Mercury 71060; r☆3, ☆2, 1957). Gladiolas, "Little Darlin'" (Excello 2101; r☆11, ☆41, 1957). Coasters, "Searchin'" b/w "Young Blood" (Atco 6087; r☆1, ☆5, 1957). Johnnie and Joe, "Over the Mountain; across the Sea" (Chess 1654; r☆3, ☆8, 1957). Otis Williams and his Charms, "United" (DeLuxe 6138; r☆5, 1957). Billy Ward and his Dominoes, "Star Dust" (Liberty 55071; r☆5, ☆13, 1957). Frankie Lymon and the Teenagers, "Goody Goody" (Gee 1039; ☆22, 1957). Five Satins, "To the Aisle" (Ember 1019; r☆5, ☆25, 1957). Dell-Vikings, "Whispering Bells" (Dot 15592; r☆5, ☆9, 1957). Bobbettes, "Mr. Lee" (Atlantic 1144; r☆2, ☆6, 1957). Lee Andrews and the Hearts, "Long Lonely Nights" (Chess 1665; r☆45, 1957). Joe Bennett and the Sparkletones, "Black Slacks" (ABC-Paramount 9837; ☆17, 1957). Tune Weavers, "Happy, Happy Birthday Baby" (Checker 872; r☆4, ☆5, 1957). Little Joe and the Thrillers, "Peanuts" (Okeh 7088; r☆23, 1957). Rays, "Silhouettes" (Cameo 117; r☆3, ☆3, 1957). Dubs, "Could This Be Magic" (Gone 5011; ☆24, 1957). Lee Andrews and the Hearts, "Tear Drops" (Chess 1675; r☆13, ☆20, 1957). Danny and the Juniors, "At the Hop" (ABC-Paramount 9871; r☆1, ☆1, 1957). Hollywood Flames, "Buzz-Buzz-Buzz" (Ebb 119; r☆11, ☆11, 1957). Playmates, "Jo-Ann" (Roulette 4037; ☆20, 1958). Silhouettes, "Get a Job" (Ember 1029; r☆1, ☆1, 1958). Diamonds, "The Stroll" (Mercury 71242; r☆7, ☆5, 1958). Crescendos, "Oh Julie" (Nasco 6005; r☆4, ☆5, 1958). Chantels, "Maybe" (End 1005; r☆5, ☆15,.1958). Robert and Johnny, "We Belong Together" (Old Town 1047; r☆18, ☆33, 1958). Pastels, "Been So Long" (Argo 5287; r☆15, ☆24, 1958). Danny and the Juniors, "Rock and Roll Is Here to Stay" (ABC-Paramount 9888; r☆16, ☆19, 1958). Impalas, "Sorry (I Ran All the Way Home)" (Cub 9022; r☆14, ☆2, 1959). Monotones, "Book of Love" (Argo 5290; r☆4, ☆5, 1958). Platters, "Twilight Time" (Mercury 71289; r☆1, ☆1, 1958). Dion and the Belmonts, "I Wonder Why" (Laurie 3013; ☆22, 1958). Lee Andrews and the Hearts, "Try the Impossible" (United Artists 123; ☆33, 1958). Coasters, "Yakety Yak" (Atco 6116; r☆1, ☆1, 1958). Jerry Butler and the Impressions, "For Your Precious Love" (Abner 1013; r☆10, ☆11, 1958). Danleers, "One Summer Night" (Mercury 71322; r☆11, ☆16,

1958). Elegants, "Little Star" (Apt 25005; r☆1, ☆1, 1958). Olympics, "Western Movies" (Demon 1508; r☆7, ☆8, 1958). Jamies, "Summertime, Summertime" (Epic 9281; ☆26, 1958). Little Anthony and the Imperials, "Tears on My Pillow" (End 1027; r☆2, ☆4, 1958). Quin-Tones, "Down the Aisle of Love" (Hunt 321; r☆6, ☆20, 1958). Shields, "You Cheated" (Tender 513; r☆11, ☆15, 1958). Harvey and the Moonglows, "Ten Commandments of Love" (Chess 1705; r☆9, ☆22, 1958). Playmates, "Beep Beep" (Roulette 4115; ☆4, 1958). Cadillacs, "Peek-a-Boo" (Josie 846; r☆20, ☆28, 1958). Platters, "Smoke Gets in Your Eyes" (Mercury 71383; r☆3, ☆1, 1958). Crests, "16 Candles" (Coed 506; r☆4, ☆2, 1959). Coasters, "Charlie Brown" (Atco 6132; r☆2, ☆2, 1959). Flamingos, "Lovers Never Say Goodbye" (End 1035; r☆25, 1959). Skyliners, "Since I Don't Have You" (Calico 103; r☆3, ☆12, 1959). Coasters, "Along Came Jones" (Atco 6141; r☆14, ☆9, 1959). Mystics, "Hushabye" (Laurie 3028; ☆20, 1959). Drifters, "There Goes My Baby" (Atlantic 2025; r☆1, ☆2, 1959). Flamingos, "I Only Have Eyes for You" (End 1046; r☆3, ☆11, 1959). Tempos, "See You in September" (Climax 102; ☆23, 1959). Coasters, "Poison Ivy" (Atco 6146; r☆1, ☆7, 1959). Fireflies, "You Were Mine" (Ribbon 6901; ☆21, 1959). Clovers, "Love Potion No. 9" (United Artists 180; r☆23, ☆23, 1959). Fleetwoods, "Mr. Blue" (Dolton 5; r☆3, ☆1, 1959). Drifters, "Dance with Me" (Atlantic 2040; r☆2, ☆15, 1959). Little Anthony and the Imperials, "Shimmy, Shimmy, Ko-Ko-Bop" (End 1060; r☆14, ☆24, 1959). Platters, "Harbor Lights" (Mercury 71563; r☆15, ☆8, 1960). Drifters, "This Magic Moment" (Atlantic 2050; r☆4, ☆16, 1960). Safaris, "Image of a Girl" (Eldo 101; ☆6, 1960). Olympics, "Big Boy Pete" (Arvee 595; r☆10, ☆50, 1960). Paradons, "Diamonds and Pearls" (Milestone 2003; r☆27, ☆18, 1960). Maurice Williams and the Zodiacs, "Stay" (Herald 552; r☆3, ☆1, 1960). Drifters, "Save the Last Dance for Me" (Atlantic 2071; r☆1, ☆1, 1960). Chimes, "Once in Awhile" (Tag 444; ☆11, 1960). Shells, "Baby Oh Baby" (Johnson 104; ☆21, 1960). Innocents, "Gee Whiz" (Indigo 111, r☆15, ☆28, 1960). Capris, "There's a Moon Out Tonight" (Old Town 1094; r☆11, ☆3, 1961). Tokens, "Tonight I Fell in Love" (Warwick 615; ☆15, 1961). Marcels, "Blue Moon" (Colpix 186; r☆1, ☆1, 1961). Shep and the Limelites, "Daddy's Home" (Hull 740; r☆4, ☆2, 1961). Edsels, "Rama Lama Ding Dong" (Twin 700; ☆21, 1961). Belmonts, "Tell Me Why" (Sabrina 500; ☆18, 1961). Regents, "Barbara-Ann" (Gee 1065; r☆7, ☆13, 1961). Cleftones, "Heart and Soul" (Gee 1064; r☆10, ☆18, 1961). Velvets, "Tonight (Could Be the Night)" (Monument 441; ☆26, 1961). Chanters, "No, No, No" (DeLuxe 6191; r☆9, ☆41, 1961). Spinners, "That's What Girls Are Made For" (Tri-Phi 1001; r☆5, ☆27, 1961). Jive Five, "My True Story" (Beltone 1006; r☆1, ☆3, 1961). Regents, "Runaround" (Gee 1071; r☆30, ☆28, 1961). Little Caesar and the Romans, "Those Oldies but Goodies (Remind Me of You)" (Del Fi 4158; r☆28, ☆9, 1961). Dreamlovers, "When We Get Married" (Heritage 102; ☆10, 1961). Blue Jays, "Lover's Island" (Milestone 2008; ☆31, 1961). Jarmels, "A Little Bit of Soap" (Laurie 3098; r☆7, ☆12, 1961). Dovells, "Bristol Stomp" (Parkway 827; r☆7, ☆2, 1961). Flares, "Foot Stomping—Part I" (Felsted 8624; r☆20, ☆25, 1961). Stereos, "I Really Love You" (Cub 9095; r☆15, ☆29, 1961). Marcels, "Heartaches" (Colpix 612; r☆19, ☆7, 1961). Tokens, "The Lion Sleeps Tonight" (RCA Victor 7954; r☆7, ☆1, 1962). Corsairs, "Smoky Places" (Tuff 1808; r☆10, ☆12, 1962). Sensations, "Let Me In" (Argo 5405; r☆2, ☆4, 1962). Don and Juan, "What's Your Name" (Big Top 3079; ☆7, 1962). Shep and the Limelites, "Our Anniversary" (Hull 748; r☆7, 1962). Jay and the Americans, "She Cried" (United Artists 415; ☆5, 1962). Falcons, "I Found a Love" (Lupine 1003; r☆6, 1962). Volumes, "I Love You" (Chex 1002; ☆22, 1962). Orlons, "The Wah Watusi" (Cameo 218; r☆5, ☆2, 1962). Valentinos, "Lookin' for a Love" (Sar 132; r☆8, 1962). Duprees, "You Belong to Me" (Coed 569; r☆7, 1962). Majors, "A Wonderful Dream" (Imperial 5855; r☆23, ☆22, 1962). Orlons, "Don't Hang Up" (Cameo 231; r☆3, ☆4, 1962). Drifters, "Up on the Roof" (Atlantic 2162; r☆4, ☆5, 1962). Earls, "Remember Then" (Old Town 1130; r☆29, ☆24, 1962). (Chart positions taken from Joel Whitburn's *Record Research*, compiled from *Billboard* Pop chart, unless otherwise indicated; r☆ = position on *Billboard* Rhythm and Blues chart.)

cool, cool **PENGUINS**
DOOTO

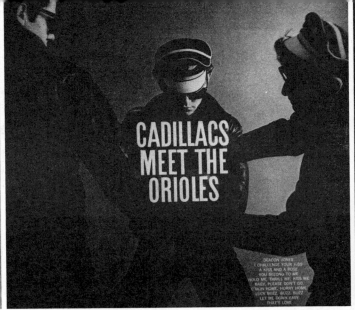

**CADILLACS
MEET THE
ORIOLES**

DEACON JONES
I CHALLENGE YOUR KISS
A KISS AND A ROSE
YOU BELONG TO ME
HOLD ME, THRILL ME, KISS ME
BABY, PLEASE DON'T GO
C'MON HOME, HURRY HOME
LUCKY BUZZ, BUZZ, BUZZ
LET ME DOWN EASY
THAT'S LOVE

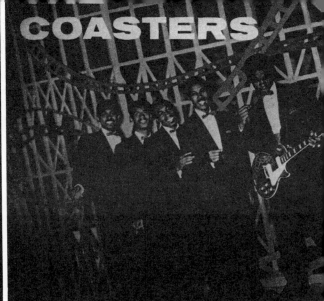

COASTERS

WHIPPET

& featuring
the **robins**

the *Platters*
Federal 651

ONLY YOU
I'LL CRY WHEN YOU'RE GONE
YOU MADE ME CRY
GIVE THANKS
TELL THE WORLD
ROSES OF PICARDY
LOVE ALL NIGHT
MAGGIE DOESN'T WORK HERE ANYMORE
SHAKE IT UP MAMBO
VOO VEE AH BEE
I NEED YOU ALL THE TIME
HEY NOW

TONIGHT-TONIGHT
the **Mellokings**

2Y-8105

THE **5 SATINS SING**

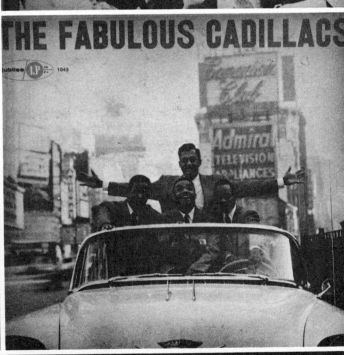

THE FABULOUS CADILLACS
Jubilee LP 1045
Admiral
TELEVISION
APPLIANCES

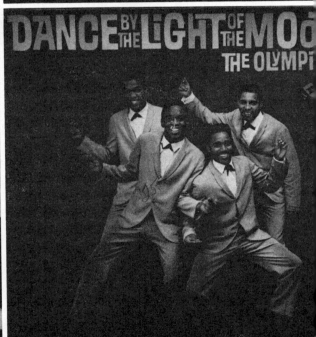

DANCE BY THE **LIGHT** OF THE **MOO**
THE OLYMPI

The Teenagers
GEE
HIGH FIDELITY
GLP 701

featuring

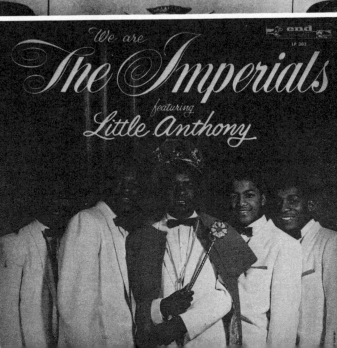

We are
The Imperials
featuring
Little Anthony
end LP 303

**THE CLEFTONES
HEART AND SOUL**

The Rise of Top 40 AM
by John Morthland

It is 1953, and Alan Freed is on the air again for his late night *Moondog Show* on WJW in Cleveland. Over his theme, Todd Rhodes's "Blues for Moon Dog," Freed yips, moans and brays, gearing up for another evening hosting the hottest rhythm and blues show in the land. Slipping on a golf glove, he bangs on a phone book in time to the music—maybe "Money Honey" by the Drifters, or "Shake a Hand" by Faye Adams. Swigging constantly from a trusty bottle of booze, he spins the hits and continues his manic patter throughout the night, spewing forth rhymed jive with the speed and inflections of a Holy Roller at the Pearly Gates.

There had been celebrated disc jockeys before Alan Freed, but never anyone quite so crazed or obsessive. In the early days, the national networks, which dominated radio, programmed live musical broadcasts and adventure and comedy serials; rarely did a mere disc jockey become a star. But in the late Forties, as the networks' attention shifted to television, radio began to open up. While live broadcasts and the serials continued, some listeners interested in drama started watching TV, while the listeners interested in music started flipping the dial to the smaller independent stations—stations too small to afford hiring a live band. The independents had one big advantage over the networks: they usually had a much stronger sense of what music their local audiences liked. As television siphoned off the audience for drama, the independents began to attract audiences for specialized music, from hillbilly to rhythm and blues; whether it was on a record or live didn't much matter.

This was the situation Alan Freed faced when he arrived in Cleveland in 1950. Raised a Methodist in Ohio by a Russian mother and a Welsh Jewish father, he had worked on a number of jobs, although in high school his true goal in life was to front a band of his own (he played trombone). An ear infection contracted during the war years eliminated that possibility. He tried his hand at being a disc jockey, first in Akron where he was a hit with the high school crowd and later on WJW in Cleveland, a "good music" station. At one point he applied for a job at WINS in New York, but was turned down, reportedly because his Midwestern accent was too grating.

That same year Leo Mintz, the biggest local record dealer, hipped Freed to rhythm and blues. Freed was impressed by the number of young people buying these records, so he started programming them. He claims he jumped on rhythm and blues right away; others at his station recall that he approached it cautiously, programming only a little until he was flooded with requests. Freed called the music "rock 'n' roll," eliminating the racial stigma attached to rhythm and blues; though he credited himself with coining the term, it had been common on "race" records for decades—as a metaphor for sexual intercourse. (But Freed *did* apply for a copyright on the term "rock 'n' roll"—and wanted record companies to pay him in order to so describe their product.)

Playing black music by itself did not make Freed such a revolutionary figure; any number of black DJs—"Professor Bop" in Shreveport, "Jocky Jack" Gibson in Atlanta, "Sugar Daddy" in Birmingham—were already doing that. Freed was, however, among the first to program black music for a white audience, and for this he was labeled a "nigger lover" and suffered legal harassment well before his fall in the payola hearings. At the same time, his popularity was skyrocketing.

Other white DJs soon followed Freed's lead: Hunter Hancock in Los Angeles, "Poppa Stoppa" in New Orleans, Gene Nobles in Nashville, Dewey Phillips in Memphis with his *Red Hot and Blues* show. As they attracted more and more white listeners, the bigger stations were forced either to start bopping themselves or go out of business.

In March 1952, Freed sponsored a Moondog Ball in Cleveland featuring top black acts: it drew 25,000 cats and kitties to a hall that held 10,000. The show had to be canceled, but it wasn't the sheer numbers that most upset adults; it was the fact that the crowd was made up equally of whites and blacks, and Cleveland was still a largely segregated city.

In 1954, Freed made a triumphant return to New York, for the princely sum of $75,000 a year; within a few months, he raised WINS to the top of the AM heap. He continued staging shows, now at the Brooklyn Paramount. Opening them himself, he would gyrate onstage in a plaid sports coat, shouting, "Go man go!" to the house band, blowing kisses to the audience. Freed had an emphatic retort for those who scorned his style: "Anyone who says rock 'n' roll is a passing fad or a flash-in-the-pan trend along the music road has *rocks in the head*, dad!"

Freed kept the faith until the bitter end. As rock 'n' roll by whites broke, he programmed the best of it alongside discs by his favorite black artists. And as the record industry began to seize control of the savage new music and tame it down with white "cover" versions of the biggest songs, Freed continued to play only the originals. In this endeavor, he was joined by a few others (some of them black) such as Danny "Cat Man" Stiles in Newark, George "Hound Dog" Lorenz in Buffalo, "Symphony Sid" Torin in Boston, Tommy "Dr. Jive" Smalls in New York, "John R." in Nashville, Al Benson in Chicago, and Peter Potter on the West Coast—to say nothing of Bob "Wolfman Jack" Smith south of the border.

Because he worked for a "pirate" station just across the Mexican border from Del Rio, Texas, the Wolfman didn't have to concern himself with such petty details as wattage limits or sign-off times. On a good night, you could hear him all the way north to Canada, and all the way west to California, so powerful were the station's transmitters. The Wolfman played only the finest blues, occasionally a little hillbilly music, and spent the

In the center, Alan Freed, in 1956, years before the fall. Rock and roll was in its infancy, and with Freed, from left: LaVern Baker, Norman Orleck of 'Cashbox' magazine, Ruth Brown, and Clyde McPhatter (Popsie/N.Y. from the Gleason collection)

Below: Murray the K, the "fifth Beatle," still alive in '68. (Popsie/N.Y.) Opposite, clockwise from top: (1) Symphony Sid Torin leads a gospel sing; (2) Daddy Gene Nobles of WLAC, Nashville, pushing hometown product from Dot Records; (3) Press agent Major Robinson and DJ Tommy Small at a New York rock show, 1955; (4) R&B bandleader Johnny Otis with DJ Hunter Hancock, 1956; (5) The fountain of eternal youth, Dick Clark, directing 'American Bandstand' in the Fifties, but little has changed since; (6) Elvis Presley with the Memphis 'Red, Hot and Blues' show's Dewey Phillips, the first man on Earth to play "That's All Right" and may his name live forever. Center: (7) Wolfman Jack. (1, Gleason collection; 2, Gene Nobles; 3, Popsie/N.Y.; 4, Johnny Otis; 5, Dick Clark; 6, Slate the Bartender; 7, ROLLING STONE)

night howling at the moon between (and during) records, advising listeners to "get yo'self nekkid" and dig the music, all while peddling various snake oils, plastic replicas of Jesus, coffins and inspirational literature. He was assumed to be black, but wasn't; he kept his secret by refusing interviews or public appearances.

The increasing number of white "cover" versions and the popularity of the white teen idols indicated new trends in rock and roll; equally fateful was the upswing in chain ownership of AM stations. Independent stations were on the way out, even as they were providing the most exciting radio on the dial; ironically, the very same wild men who would soon become ensnared in format radio provided the chains with a paradigm of the pop DJ.

The chain owners made no bones about it: radio was a business proposition, plain and simple, and the best way to take the guesswork out of profit making was to refine a basic music-and-news format. KOWH in Omaha (a Storz station) began working within that format in 1949, and by the mid-Fifties the approach had caught on. In order to attract and stabilize both a maximum audience and maximum ad revenue, Storz cultivated a distinctive "sound" by using identification jingles at regular intervals, saturation programming for a few hit records, fast-talking DJs for personality, and a go-go frenzy punctuated only by the hourly news break.

The concept worked, and by the mid-Fifties other Storz stations in New Orleans, Kansas City, and Minneapolis fell into line. Gordon McClendon's stations in Dallas, San Antonio, and Houston followed suit. They were joined by stations in the Gerald Bartell chain, and those licensed to the Plough pharmaceutical firm. At first, Top 40 referred to mainstream pop music, but as rock 'n' roll came to dominate the market, the music was fit, successfully, into the same format.

Of course this meant that disc jockeys were no longer playing their favorite records, but instead were following a programming schedule (based on heavily researched "popularity charts") involving just 40 songs or less, with the Top Ten of those being played even more frequently. They had to read prepared commercials at a certain time—18 minutes of the hour was deemed optimum—and they had to read news off the wire services. While they were often still local stars in their own right, they had to fit themselves into the station's image.

Still, rock 'n' roll radio remained the most vital sound on the airwaves. The DJs shouted with the same intensity as the music they played—they just had to compress their shouts into a shorter time span—and the news itself came off like amphetamine-induced ravings. Perhaps the sense of exhilaration was artificial, but it remained, well . . . exhilarating.

Stations battled each other for ratings, and teenagers had their favorite DJs. Promotion stunts to attract new listeners became valuable tools to the chains. DJs were buried alive; they held contests to see who could stay awake the longest or talk

nonstop the longest; they raced down rivers in bathtubs; they sponsored treasure hunts; they threw money off buildings; they hiked barefoot across deserts; they sat on flagpoles.

Many pioneering DJs kept at it even in the chain format, because there were really no alternatives. Despite their lesser roles, jocks like Jerry Blavatt ("The Geator with the Heator") became stars long after the heyday of the true fire-breathing DJ. Murray the K rode the coattails of the Beatles to stardom, and Wolfman Jack (who never showed his face in public until the Seventies) preserved his outlandish style and his mystique throughout the Sixties, despite a transfer to a southern California pirate.

And while AM Top 40 became ever more conservative, producing such rigid institutions as the Drake chains, the AM dial and Top 40 stations to this day remain a place where sometimes, just sometimes, men can be boys and make a living at it to boot.

The Teen Idols

by Greg Shaw

There are few dates that can be clearly pinpointed as turning points in rock and roll. One would be February 3rd, 1959, when Buddy Holly died, and with him, at least symbolically, rock and roll's first rush of breathless innocence.

By a curious coincidence, Holly's death came at a time when several others of equal prominence in the first generation of rebellious rockers were also exiting the scene. Within a few years Elvis was in the army, Chuck Berry was in jail, Jerry Lee Lewis had been banned from the airwaves, Eddie Cochran was dead, and Gene Vincent had left the country, his popularity on the wane.

This mass exodus left a void that was instantly filled. From the death of Holly to the arrival of the Beatles, pop music fell into the hands of those same old men of the music industry—promoters, radio programmers, A&R men, record executives—who had long sought a means to remove the unpredictability originally inherent in rock, and to bring the phenomenon (or fad, as they considered it) more into line with their own standards and marketing expertise. From the start, industry elders had been intent on "improving" rock and roll. Young rockabilly singers like Carl Dobkins, Terry Noland, and, for that matter, Holly and Presley, were given ballad material; their sound was "cleaned up" with orchestras and choirs. Many disc jockeys, promoters and TV hosts gave preference to clean-cut singers such as Pat Boone. Thus, while audience demand and the efforts of a few crusading DJs were responsible for occasional hard rock or raunchy R&B hits, the years 1959-'63 were, to an overwhelming extent, the era of the Teen Idol: the music left the streets and moved to the studios.

The results of this shift were not, as has often been claimed, altogether dire. In the hands of such inspired craftsmen as Phil Spector, Bert Berns, Neil Sedaka and Carole King, studio pop rose to truly creative heights. The best records of the era were a product of New York's Brill Building. The worst came out of Philadelphia.

As the home of Dick Clark's *American Bandstand*—at this time the national showcase for rock talent—Philadelphia became the hub of the record business. The city had already spawned its share of doo-wop groups and labels, but it was Clark's move to Philadelphia, and the emergence of record companies geared to grooming teen idols from among the local Italian populace for exposure on his show, that put Philadelphia on the musical map.

"Philadelphia," Phil Spector has recalled, "was just the most insane, most dynamite, the most beautiful city in the history of rock and roll and the world." Its energies "were just phenomenal. Everyone you met was raging and racing, 24 hours a day, seven days a week, and existed for nothing but hype. They existed to pull strokes, conjure deals out of nowhere, juggle hits off nothing. Money was a lot of it, of course, but there was something else as well, a real glee involved; a purist's love of hustle for its own sake."

Money was, indeed, a lot of it. The machinery was so well constructed that a good-looking teenager could be spotted on the street (as was Fabian, according to legend), cut a record, and, aided by a few bribed DJs, within a few weeks have a hit on the national charts—no uncertainties, no risks. It was such a blatant racket that in 1960 it came crashing down under government pressure. But while it flourished, the influence of Philadelphia on the musical tastes of young America was staggering, particularly when compared with the actual musical value of the records being promoted.

The Philadelphia sound was the product chiefly of three companies, Cameo-Parkway, Chancellor, and Swan. Each had its house band and arranger, yet the records were virtually interchangeable. Played by bored, middle-aged studio musicians, the music, despite an occasionally tasty saxophone break, at best had an ersatz vivacity. More often, it flaunted the cloying, string-laden blandness that the first rockers had revolted against.

The songs were aimed primarily at teenage girls, the ones in the suburbs who wanted big fluffy candy-colored images of male niceness on which to focus their pubescent dreams. Charming, wholesome dreamboats, the singers were safe and well-mannered, perhaps with a teasing tendency toward wildness. The most convincing and successful of the lot were Bobby Rydell, Fabian and Frankie Avalon.

Rydell was a young man with a boyish smile who loved his mother, liked girls a whole lot, and wanted someday to be a nightclub entertainer. He was a fairly good singer with a friendly sort of adolescent baritone, and in later years he remained popular with the supper club crowd, although his last Top 40 hit was in 1963. But in five years he had more than 20 chart singles, almost all of them Top 40. The earliest, such as "Kissin' Time" and "We Got Love," were the best, depicting a self-contained world of ponytails and transistor radios, centered around high school, where life's greatest concerns were on the order of who would be going with whom to the dance.

The same set of adolescent themes reappeared on many unbelievably trite hits, but none articulated the high school ethos better than Bobby Rydell in "Swingin' School":

Yay yay yay, I go a swingin' school
Where the chicks are hip and the cats are cool.
Well, we dance the greatest and we dress the latest,
Whoa whoa whoa, I go a swingin' school.

Rydell was the mainstay of Cameo Records, a company also renowned for popularizing the Twist, through Chubby Checker, and introducing (by rough count) some 30 new dances during the dance craze of 1960–'64. The label's biggest rival in Philly was Chancellor, built around the prolific output of Fabian and Frankie Avalon.

Paul Anka introduces the new 1960 model
AMI jukebox (Popsie/N.Y.)

Avalon was downright smarmy; Fabian was somewhat better. Well built, slightly oafish, he was discovered by a talent scout who figured looks were the key to rock and roll riches. Fabian was the first to admit he couldn't sing, although he did have a certain native ability. Promoted as the "Tiger Man," Fabian cultivated an image as a rough but safe second Elvis. His hits, like "Tiger," were gruff, but moved along well; one, "Turn Me Loose," by Pomus and Shuman, was actually a fine bluesy number.

While Philadelphia was the center of the Teen Idol business, it by no means held a monopoly. In New York, ABC-Paramount offered stiff competition with Paul Anka, a 16-year-old nasal-voiced composer of teen schmaltz who became an overnight sensation with "Diana" in 1957. Unlike most teen idols he was a genuine prodigy who had been writing and performing at an early age, who traveled to Hollywood from his home in Canada at the age of 14 to record with rhythm and blues musicians, and who continued pushing himself until, by his persistence and precociousness, he became a star. He wrote most of his hits, acted in and composed music for a number of serious films including *The Longest Day,* and possessed a genuine, inborn flair for show business. All the same, his songs were unbelievably mechanical, and lyrically they were pure doggerel. Next to the elegant compositions of his Brill Building contemporaries, what can you say about Anka's couplets?

I'm so young and you're so old
This my darling I've been told
You and I will be as free
As the birds up in the tree
Oh please, stay by me, Diana.

Surprisingly, New York never developed into the kind of teen meat market that Philadelphia had become. Besides Anka, ABC-Paramount (New York's closest equivalent to Cameo-Parkway) had only Teddy Randazzo and Danny and the Juniors. Randazzo never caught on as a teen idol, and the latter were really more typical of the interests of the New York music scene, where street-corner vocal harmony groups, whether black or Italian, ruled the city.

But in Hollywood, it was a different story. Not surprisingly, this city, built on publicity, glamour, fluff and fantasy, became the second home of the teen idol industry. Hollywood talent scouts didn't have to comb the streets looking for pretty faces; this was one commodity the city possessed in surplus. Instead, they looked to the silver screen for young actors and actresses whose already established popularity with millions of viewers would make stupendous record sales a cinch. What chance did a Jodie Sands or a Claudine Clark stand against Annette, the winsome Mouseketeer whose developing bustline had been measured daily by every young male eye in the country?

She couldn't miss, and she didn't. In 1959 and 1960, Annette had eight sizable hit records on Walt Disney's Vista label. Soon every young actor and actress in Hollywood was embarked on a recording career, nearly all of them with some measure of success. Several other Mouseketeers, including Darlene Gillespie, joined Annette; Warner Brothers started a label and began recording such stars as Ed "Kookie" Byrnes, Connie Stevens and Roger Smith (from *Hawaiian Eye* and *77 Sunset Strip*); *The Donna Reed Show* gave us Shelley Fabares and Paul Petersen; and there was Vincent Edwards *(Ben Casey)*, Johnny Crawford *(The Rifleman)*, James Darren (the *Gidget* movies), and numerous others.

Colpix, the record arm of Columbia Pictures, specialized in Teen/Screen idols, and through a fortuitous tie-in with Don Kirshner's Aldon Music in New York, they were able to obtain material written by Carole King and Gerry Goffin, and Barry Mann and Cynthia Weil. While they didn't exactly receive the best work of these writers, Colpix at least had professionally crafted commercial songs to cover up the various vocal inadequacies of their stars. (Kirshner was so impressed with Colpix's ability to combine records with TV that he later went to work for them, creating the Monkees and the Archies.)

Of all the Hollywood teen idols, only one can be said to have any claim to lasting importance—Ricky Nelson. At first glance, he seems like all the rest: a cute face, seen on TV every week, making records and trying to pretend he's Elvis. But Nelson was different; in addition to his moody sex appeal and television sinecure, he also happened to have real talent. He was a fine singer whose personal taste ran to raw rockabilly and blues, and whose band, featuring the brilliant guitarist James Burton, was one of the best in all rock and roll. His records were exceptionally tough and exciting, largely free of intrusive orchestration and studio gimmickry, and his material, whether covers of obscure rockers like "Shirley Lee" or originals written for him by the likes of ex-rockabilly Johnny Burnette or R&B veteran Baker Knight, was on the whole superb.

In truth, Nelson can more closely be compared with an urban rockabilly like Eddie Cochran than with the run-of-the-mill teen idols of his day. Johnny Burnette, best remembered for his teen ballads "Dreamin'" and "You're Sixteen," was another singer whose real roots were in the rockabilly scene of Memphis, where he and his brother Dorsey had started out with a wild trio before moving to Hollywood. Burnette wrote some of Nelson's best songs, and is worshiped today in Europe as one of rock's founding figures.

Apart from Nelson, the most successful west coast teen idol was Bobby Vee, who, like Burnette, began his career in the heart of the country. He grew up in North Dakota, and throughout high school fronted a hard-rocking band called the Shadows. Vee's career really began the night after Buddy Holly's plane crash, when he took his place at the concert Holly had been scheduled to headline in Fargo, North Dakota. Sym-

bolically as well as literally, Bobby Vee personified the new era that had arrived. Though bearing an uncanny vocal resemblance to Holly, Vee was content to crank out the smooth, studio-crafted teen fodder handed him by his producers, chiefly Snuff Garrett. In his high school sweater, there was nothing menacing or primitive about him, no hint of anything black, or Southern, or even from the wrong side of town. He was the boy next door, just like all the other boys and girls next door who peopled the era of the teen idol.

A disproportionate number of the successful teen idols were boys, who supposedly would appeal to adolescent girls, the primary market for this music; indeed, most of the female teen idols also based their appeal on identification with the same audience. Apparently it was felt, rightly or wrongly, that the male audience was more interested in rock's dark and violent side. On the other hand, each of the three most successful female teen idols possessed some special quality that set them apart from their rivals. Annette must surely have sold more records to boys than the average girl singer. The two biggest female stars, however, were Brenda Lee and Connie Francis, both of whom relied on purely musical attributes for their appeal.

Connie Francis, with her mature contralto, never seemed really teenage to me, even when singing about lipstick on collars and guys named Frankie. In fact, she merely used the teen fad to launch a career as a mainstream pop singer, quickly becoming entrenched in Spain and Italy, where she recorded extensively in the native languages. Her early records were perky rockers like "Stupid Cupid," or lush romantic ballads like "Who's Sorry Now," and as pop records they were undeniably good. Connie Francis is said to have had more hit records than any female singer in history, but it wasn't only teenagers who bought them.

Brenda Lee, on the other hand, was essentially a country stylist who was thrust into the role of rock singer, drawing on her roots to come up with a unique sort of female rockabilly style. She started with rock young (her early records list her as "Little Brenda Lee—9 Years Old"), and stayed with it throughout the Sixties (even recording in England with Jimmy Page in 1964).

Today, there are tried and proven formulas for achieving results in most areas of rock, but in those days nobody could say for sure which were the essential ingredients for success in this new, mysterious, and incredibly lucrative field of teenage music. The teen idol era was a product of the assumption that kids were endlessly gullible, utterly tasteless, and dependably aroused by a comely face or a gratuitous mention of "high school" or "bobby sox." This assumption ultimately proved disastrously self-limiting, but not before dozens of teen idols had crooned, croaked and smiled their ways into the Top Ten.

Of the hundreds of would-be teen idols, though, only a handful really had a lasting impact. In addition to those already discussed, there was of course Pat Boone, who began as a safe alternative to Elvis, and is still a safe alternative to just about everything. Others who prospered during this era but really belong more to the mainstream pop tradition include Neil Sedaka, Gene Pitney, Bobby Darin, Tommy Sands, Tony Orlando, and Bobby Vinton.

Some of the runners-up, who enjoyed a hit or two but never quite broke out, included Rod Lauren, Johnny Restivo, Tab Hunter, Jerry Wallace, Adam Wade, Gary Stites, Mark Valentino, Kenny Dino, Mark Dinning, Johnny Tillotson, Ray Peterson, Jimmy Clanton, Bob Crewe and Nick Venet (both of whom gave up promising careers as teen idols to become leading record producers), Mike Clifford, Brian Hyland, Ral Donner, Teddy Randazzo, Curtis Lee, Frankie Sardo, Len Barry, Paul Evans, Larry Finnegan, Jerry Fuller, Clint Miller, Robin Luke, Larry Hall, Bobby Curtola, Deane Hawley and Troy Shondell.

Discography

TEEN IDOLS IN THE TOP TEN, 1955-1963

Pat Boone, "At My Front Door (Crazy Little Mama)" (Dot 15422; ☆7, 1955). "I'll Be Home" (Dot 15443; ☆5, 1956). "I Almost Lost My Mind" (Dot 15472; ☆1, 1956). "Friendly Persuasion" (Dot 15490; ☆8, 1956). "Don't Forbid Me" (Dot 15521; ☆1, 1956). "Why Baby Why" (Dot 15545; ☆6, 1957). "Love Letters in the Sand" (Dot 15570; ☆1, 1957). "April Love" (Dot 15660; ☆1, 1957). "A Wonderful Time Up There" (Dot 15690; ☆10, 1958). "Moody River" (Dot 16209; ☆1, 1961). "Speedy Gonzales" (Dot 16368; ☆6, 1962). **Ricky Nelson,** "A Teenager's Romance" (Verve 10047; ☆8, 1957). "Be-Bop Baby" (Imperial 5463; ☆5, 1957). "Stood Up" (Imperial 5483; ☆5, 1957). "Believe What You Say" (Imperial 5503; ☆8, 1958). "Poor Little Fool" (Imperial 5528; ☆1, 1958). "Lonesome Town" b/w "I Got a Feeling" (Imperial 5545; ☆7, 1958). "Never Be Anyone Else but You" b/w "It's Late" (Imperial 5565; ☆6, 1959). "Sweeter than You" b/w "Just a Little Too Much" (Imperial 5595; ☆9, 1959). "Travelin' Man" b/w "Hello Mary Lou" (Imperial 5741; ☆1, 1961). "Young World" (Imperial 5805; ☆5, 1962). "Teen Age Idol" (Imperial 5864; ☆5, 1962). "It's Up to You" (Imperial 5901; ☆6, 1962). **Paul Anka,** "Diana" (ABC-Paramount 9831; ☆2, 1957). "You Are My Destiny" (ABC-Paramount 9880; ☆7, 1958). "Lonely Boy" (ABC-Paramount 10022; ☆1, 1959). "Put Your Head on My Shoulder" (ABC-Paramount 10040; ☆2, 1959). "It's Time to Cry" (ABC-Paramount 10064; ☆4, 1959). "Puppy Love" (ABC-Paramount 10082; ☆2, 1960). "My Home Town" (ABC-Paramount 10106; ☆8, 1960). "Dance On Little Girl" (ABC-Paramount 10220; ☆10, 1961). **Frankie Avalon,** "Dede Dinah" (Chancellor 1011; ☆7, 1958). "Ginger Bread" (Chancellor 1021; ☆9, 1958). "Venus" (Chancellor 1031; ☆1, 1959). "Bobby Sox to Stockings" b/w "A Boy without a Girl" (Chancellor 1036; ☆8, 1959). "Just Ask Your Heart" (Chancellor 1040; ☆7, 1959). "Why" (Chancellor 1045; ☆1, 1959). **Connie Francis** "Who's Sorry Now" (MGM 12588; ☆4, 1958). "My Happiness" (MGM 12738; ☆2, 1958). "Lipstick on Your Collar" b/w "Frankie" (MGM 12793; ☆5, 1959). "Among My Souvenirs" (MGM 12841; ☆7, 1959). "Mama" (MGM 12878; ☆8, 1960). "Everybody's Somebody's Fool" (MGM 12899; ☆1, 1960). "My Heart Has a Mind of Its Own" (MGM 12923; ☆1, 1960). "Many Tears Ago" (MGM 12964; ☆7, 1960). "Where the Boys Are" (MGM 12971; ☆4, 1961). "Breakin' in a Brand New Broken Heart" (MGM 12995; ☆7, 1961). "Together" (MGM 13019; ☆6, 1961). "When the Boy in Your Arms" (MGM 13051; ☆10, 1961). "Don't Break the Heart That Loves You" (MGM 13059; ☆1, 1962). "Second Hand Love" (MGM 13074; ☆7, 1962). "Vacation" (MGM 13087; ☆9, 1962). **Annette,** "Tall Paul" (Disneyland 118; ☆7, 1959). "O Dio Mio" (Vista 354; ☆10, 1960). **Fabian,** "Turn Me Loose" (Chancellor 1033; ☆9, 1959). "Tiger" (Chancellor 1037; ☆3, 1959). "Hound Dog Man" (Chancellor 1044; ☆9, 1959). **Bobby Rydell,** "We Got Love" (Cameo 169; ☆6, 1959). "Wild One" (Cameo 171; ☆2, 1960). "Swingin' School" (Cameo 175; ☆5, 1960). "Volare" (Cameo 179; ☆4, 1960). "The Cha-Cha-Cha" (Cameo 228; ☆10, 1962). "Forget Him" (Cameo 280; ☆4, 1963). **Brenda Lee,** "Sweet Nothin's" (Decca 30967; ☆4, 1959). "I'm Sorry" b/w "That's All You Gotta Do" (Decca 31093; ☆1, 1960). "I Want to Be Wanted" (Decca 31149; ☆1, 1960). "Emotions" (Decca 31195; ☆7, 1961). "You Can Depend on Me" (Decca 31231; ☆6, 1961). "Dum Dum" (Decca 31272; ☆4, 1961). "Fool #1" (Decca 31309; ☆3, 1961). "Break It to Me Gently" (Decca 31348; ☆4, 1962). "Everybody Loves Me but You" (Decca 31379; ☆6, 1962). "All Alone Am I" (Decca 31424; ☆3, 1962). "Losing You" (Decca 31478; ☆6, 1963). **Bobby Vee,** "Devil or Angel" (Liberty 55270; ☆6, 1960). "Rubber Ball" (Liberty 55287; ☆6, 1960). "Take Good Care of My Baby" (Liberty 55354; ☆1, 1961). "Run To Him" (Liberty 55388; ☆2, 1961). "The Night Has a Thousand Eyes" (Liberty 55521; ☆3, 1962).

(Chart positions compiled from Joel Whitburn's *Record Research*, based on *Billboard* Pop chart.)

HOLD THAT TIGER!

J. FRANK WILSON and the Cavaliers

TELL LAURA I LOVE HER
ONLY THE LONELY
THAT'LL BE THE DAY
YOUNG LOVE
SCHOOL DAYS
OVER THE MOUNTAIN
SEA OF LOVE
KISS AND RUN
SPEAK TO ME

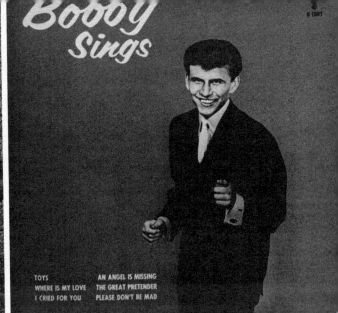

Bobby Sings

TOYS   AN ANGEL IS MISSING
WHERE IS MY LOVE   THE GREAT PRETENDER
I CRIED FOR YOU   PLEASE DON'T BE MAD

Connie Francis sings

Second Hand Love
Don't Break The Heart That Loves You
Breakin' In A Brand New Broken Heart
When The Boy In Your Arms
(Is The Boy In Your Heart)
Together
Baby's First Christmas
Someone Else's Boy
Pretty Little Baby
Dreamboat

Emotions

DECCA

BRENDA LEE

WHEN I FALL IN LOVE   GEORGIA ON MY MIND

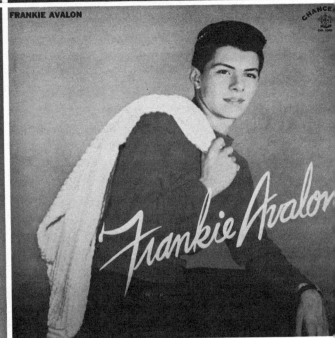

FRANKIE AVALON

Frankie Avalon

Annette

MUSCLE BEACH PARTY

SONGS FROM THE AMERICAN INTERNATIONAL FILM

PLUS
MERLIN JONES
THE SCRAMBLED EGGHEAD

MONAURAL   BV-3314

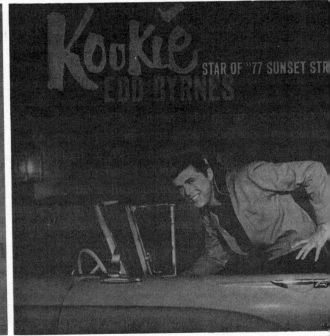

Kookie
EDD BYRNES
STAR OF "77 SUNSET STRIP"

shelley

Shelley Fabares of The Donna Reed Show
Distributed by Screen Gems, Inc.

...includes her great hit "JOHNNY ANGEL"

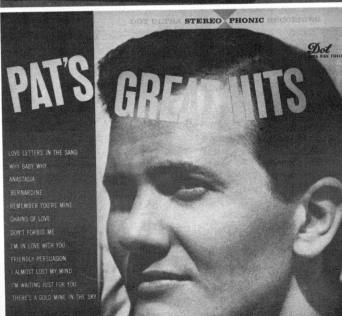

DOT ULTRA **STEREO** PHONIC RECORDING
Dot

PAT'S GREATEST HITS

LOVE LETTERS IN THE SAND
WHY BABY WHY
ANASTASIA
BERNARDINE
REMEMBER YOU'RE MINE
CHAINS OF LOVE
DON'T FORBID ME
I'M IN LOVE WITH YOU
FRIENDLY PERSUASION
I ALMOST LOST MY MIND
I'M WAITING JUST FOR YOU
THERE'S A GOLD MINE IN THE SKY

Annette sings **Anka**

The Payola Scandal
by John Morthland

ayola—the narrow definition: pay (cash or gifts) for radio airplay—has been a factor in radio since the medium's inception. In the Fifties, the practice flourished among rock 'n' roll disc jockeys. Payola padded their frequently paltry salaries, and it helped the new music reach its intended audience, no matter how small the label on which it appeared. By the late Fifties, in fact, a swarm of independent labels recording rock had broken the stranglehold of the majors—in particular Columbia, RCA and Decca—on the sales and airplay of popular records.

These developments displeased not only the older labels, but also the American Society of Composers, Authors and Publishers (ASCAP). In the Thirties and Forties, ASCAP had thrived on the sales of sheet music, piano rolls and recordings of Tin Pan Alley songs; but the advent, in the early Forties, of radio formats geared to recorded music created new conditions in the industry. After a battle between radio stations and ASCAP over royalty payments, the stations decided to boycott recordings registered with ASCAP, and in 1940 began operating their own publishing corporation, Broadcast Music Incorporated (BMI). Since ASCAP tended to ignore music composed by blacks and hillbillies, BMI ended up with a virtual monopoly on songs in those fields—a monopoly strengthened by the fact that many record playing stations catered to regional tastes ignored by the major networks. When rock 'n' roll—at first the music of blacks and hillbillies—broke, BMI was there first, too.

So it was hardly surprising when ASCAP, in 1959, urged a House Legislative Oversight subcommittee chaired by Representative Oren Harris to broaden its investigation of corrupt broadcasting practices—then centered on rigged TV quiz shows—to include the practice of payola in radio. When Representative Harris announced that his subcommittee would probe payola, *Variety* reported that ASCAP songsmiths took credit for switching the spotlight from TV quiz rigging to disc jockey payola. The assumption was that songs copyrighted with BMI would be revealed as having become hits fraudulently, thanks to payola.

Twisted as this logic appears, it was very much in the mainstream of American thinking at the time. From the beginning, rock 'n' roll had been the object of virulent attacks: many insisted that it was a source of a breakdown of morals among youth, that it encouraged miscegenation, that it was a subversive tool of Godless Communism. It was commonly believed the music was so terrible that teenagers listened to it only because they had been tricked into doing so by greedy DJs who pocketed payola and then played a record so often it was imprinted on listeners' impressionable young minds. Many considered rock 'n' roll a passing fad that would soon die out; the payola hearings were in part an attempt to insure this, and thus it was perfectly appropriate to hold those hearings in the election year 1960.

Industry response was swift. In Philadelphia, ABC-TV told *American Bandstand* host Dick Clark either to give up the program or to sell his shares in music-related firms, from record labels to publishing houses. Clark chose the latter course, and signed an affidavit denying any involvement in payola. When Alan Freed, on WABC radio, refused "on principle" to sign a similar affidavit, the station fired him. Other disc jockeys around the country were also dismissed.

Prior to House hearings, the Federal Trade Commission (FTC) filed payola complaints against a number of record manufacturers and distributors, claiming that the practice represented "unfair competition"; the companies had 30 days to file a consent order, or face an FTC examiner. Since a consent order did not constitute an admission of guilt, most labels agreed to eliminate payola. As a result, the independents found themselves back in withering competition with the majors and their superior publicity and distribution networks. In the following years, many of the small companies recording rock folded.

Meanwhile, in New York, District Attorney Frank Hogan announced that his assistant, Joseph Stone, would convene grand jury hearings, and seek misdemeanor commercial bribery charges against culpable DJs.

The House hearings began on February 8th, 1960, and focused on disc jockeys from Cleveland and Boston. The witnesses in the first week were typical of those to follow. David Maynard (WBZ-Boston) admitted taking $6000 in cash and gifts for promoting records—but only at "record hops." Joseph Smith (WILD-Boston) admitted he got royalties on the sales in his area of two recent hit records; between these royalties and other gifts and cash, he had made $8995 in a three-year period, beyond his $117 weekly salary.

Since a major payola issue had been vacations for DJs funded by record companies, another scandal erupted on March 4th, when it was revealed that John C. Doerfer, chairman of the Federal Communications Commission, had himself just enjoyed a six-day junket in Florida, courtesy of the Storer Broadcasting Company. President Eisenhower asked for his resignation, and had it within the week. On the same day, subcommittee member John B. Bennett stated that they should give up on "small-fry DJs" and look into Dick Clark, whom Bennett asserted was "obviously seriously involved in payola."

Clark appeared before the Harris subcommittee at the end of April. To aid in his defense, he hired a statistician, Bernard Goldstein; while admitting that Clark had a personal interest in records representing 27% of the "spins" on *American Bandstand* over a 28-month period, Goldstein argued that these records had in any case what he called a "popularity score" of 23.9, which "proved" that Clark was playing records because listeners wanted to hear them, not because Clark stood to gain financially. Observers were bewildered by Goldstein's computations and correlations, but any doubts about conflict of interest were laid to rest by Clark himself when he testified.

Below, left: (1) Dick Clark shows the kids how it's done. He came out of the payola scandal clean; Right (2) Alan Freed, pictured with Little Richard, center, and Bill Haley, right, took the fall. (1, ABC Television; 2, Michael Ochs Archives)

Speaking in a soft tone, Clark explained how he had given up whole or part interest in 33 businesses since the payola issue had surfaced; he'd become involved in that many businesses, he later said, to take advantage of tax laws. True, he'd profited from his investments. For example, Clark had originally invested $125 in Jamie Records, a Philadelphia label that included Duane Eddy among its acts; he eventually sold his stock for a profit of $11,900. True, he owned rights to 160 songs, 143 of which he claimed had been given to him; but Clark denied ever plugging any of them "consciously." True, Jamie Records had doled out $15,000 worth of payola; but Clark testified that he had never accepted any payola himself.

The subcommittee was charmed although it didn't completely swallow Clark's explanations. At the end of the hearing, Representative Harris called Clark a "fine young man." Their payola probe finished, the subcommittee recommended anti-payola amendments to the Federal Communications Act. The amendments, which became law on September 13th, 1960, prohibited the payment of cash or gifts in exchange for airplay, and held radio stations responsible for any employees who accepted cash or gifts.

Meanwhile, on May 19th, 1960, Joseph Stone's grand jury in New York had handed down commercial bribery informations—the misdemeanor equivalent of an indictment—charging eight men with receiving a total of $116,580 in illegal gratuities. The big name was Alan Freed; he had been the only DJ subpoenaed, and had refused to testify despite an offer of immunity. He was served two informations charging 26 counts.

Freed, the disc jockey most vociferous in his support of rock 'n' roll, took the fall for the scandal. He didn't stand trial until December 1962, when he finally pleaded guilty to two counts of commercial bribery. He was fined $300 and given a six-month suspended sentence. That should have been the end of his troubles, but on March 16th, 1964, he was indicted by another grand jury, this time for income tax evasion. The Internal Revenue Service claimed that he owed $37,920 on unreported income of $56,652 during 1957–1959. Freed was living in Palm Springs at the time; he was a poor man, unemployed and unemployable. At the end of the year, before he was able to answer the new charges, Freed entered a hospital, suffering from uremia. Three weeks later, on January 20th, 1965, he died. He was 43.

Instrumental Groups
by Greg Shaw

No year goes by without a couple of instrumental rock hits, each usually built on a simple riff, a catchy melody or some piece of electronic gimmickry. They're novelty records and their role in rock has been minimal, with the important exception of a brief period in the early Sixties when instrumentals were one of the most vital trends in the music.

Originally, rock instrumentals were provided by the rhythm and blues dance combos that flourished in the early Fifties. These bands usually featured organists or honky-tonk pianists like Cecil Gant and Bill Doggett (who had once served as the boogie specialist in Lionel Hampton's big band), or gutsy sax players such as Joe Houston, Jimmy Beasley, King Curtis, Jimmy Forrest, Lee Allen, Gene Barge, Plas Johnson and Clifford Scott (who played on Doggett's 1956 "Honky Tonk," the first big rock instrumental hit). Bands like Doggett's combo, featuring the influential Billy Butler on guitar, rocked nightly at roadhouses throughout the land, bringing to rock an improvisational approach derived from jazz via boogie-woogie.

Such bands remained popular at dances, but by 1957 black music had become almost purely vocal as far as recording was concerned. White rock, meanwhile, could be divided into two categories: the studio-manufactured teen idols, and the powerful but unpolished rockabilly singers. If rhythm and blues was the genuine teenage music of the big cities, rockabilly represented the grass-roots music of the South. But undiluted rockabilly had little commercial appeal; by the late Fifties, white rock had come to be almost completely monopolized by teen idols and the centralized media machinery that packaged and promoted them.

As if in response to this amputation of rock and roll from its roots, white instrumental bands began appearing in the late Fifties throughout the country, helping to keep the music alive at a local level, directly influencing the English bands which would bring rock out of its doldrums later on in the Sixties.

Instrumental groups were almost without exception a regional phenomenon, a product of the local music scenes that have been the source of virtually every significant innovation in rock and roll. As a general rule, professional musicians in the music capitals—New York, Los Angeles and London—had become insulated from influences outside the music industry, while local bands, playing every night in front of audiences with whom they had a direct rapport, initiated new styles, dances and music developments. The immediacy of this interaction between fans and musicians has been crucial to rock's evolutionary process.

But why instrumental bands, anyway? In the early days of rock, bands had existed to back a singer, usually a Presley imitator (it was easy enough to twitch about and mumble something like "gonna bop-a-bop-a muh a buh-a-buh-a-baby tuh-nite"). A lot of early instrumental groups, such as the Rock-a-Teens, continued to feature vocalists on some numbers, but the rockabilly style of singing was becoming dated, while the new teen ballad style depended on songs and productions crafted in the big studios of New York and Philadelphia. In any case, these bands just wanted to rock, and they played for audiences that just wanted to drink and dance. So why not dispense with the singer altogether?

The earliest instrumental rock hits had featured saxophones, piano or drums—for example, Bill Doggett's "Honky Tonk," Bill Justis's "Raunchy," and Cozy Cole's "Topsy." Toward the end of 1958, guitars, the predominant instruments in rockabilly, gradually took over instrumental rock. The tunes the groups recorded were usually simple, relying on some gimmick to catch the listener's attention (like the bug being swatted in "The Green Mosquito" by the Tune Rockers). Other instrumentals, however, succeeded in creating an intense mood, whether slow and menacing (Link Wray's "Rumble") or wild and frantic (Johnny and the Hurricanes' "Crossfire").

Link Wray was the most volatile and sophisticated guitarist to emerge from this period. He was a powerful, inventive player, doing things with dynamics and rhythm that would later inspire Pete Townshend and Eric Clapton.

The most successful instrumental rocker of the period, however, was Duane Eddy, a young man from Phoenix who developed (with his producer, Lee Hazlewood) a style known as "twangy" guitar: his hits featured a relaxed, bluesy guitar figure played on the bass strings, a raunchy but restrained sax break, and occasional whoops from the band, all set to an easy, loping beat. This formula carried Eddy through nearly 20 top hits, and made him one of America's biggest international stars, especially in England, where instrumentals (popularized by the Shadows, Tornadoes and dozens of other groups) virtually dominated the rock scene. (Holland, Sweden and Japan also elevated instrumentals to a level of importance never matched in the U.S.)

The year 1959 yielded a bumper crop of instrumental hits. By now every American city claimed an instrumental band as hometown favorites. The difficulty of bridging the gap between the simple shuffles a dancing audience liked and the kind of catchy statement required for a Top 40 hit prevented most of them from making the charts more than once—although in those days of free programming, a record could easily be a large hit locally or regionally without denting the national Hot 100. The twist arrived in 1960, and subsequent dance crazes through 1962 provided plenty of work for thousands of these bands, although twist records in general lacked the impact of the best instrumental hits.

By far the most important instrumental band of the era was the Ventures. The pride of Seattle, they were the kingpins of

Top: Johnny and the Hurricanes, 1960. (Popsie/N.Y.) Bottom: Johnny and the Hurricanes, mid-Sixties. Take your pick. (Richard Nader)

Opposite: Duane Eddy, King of Twang, 1958 (Popsie/N.Y.)

the Northwest rock scene that also produced the Wailers, the Frantics, the Viceroys, the Bluenotes, the Sonics, the Dynamics and the Kingsmen. Their music wasn't raunchy like that of the other Northwest groups, however; it was smooth, polished, and technically precise. Their important hits were "Walk—Don't Run" and "Perfidia," both in 1960, but they survived into the Seventies, recording over 50 albums and inspiring legions of guitarists the world over.

If I had to name the most representative group of the period, though, it would have to be Johnny and the Hurricanes. Their story is typical.

The group was started by sax player Johnny Paris while he was still in high school just outside Toledo, Ohio. After a couple years playing dances and nightclubs, a local vocal group asked them to provide backing for an audition in Detroit. The singers flunked the audition, but the Hurricanes so impressed the talent scouts that they signed the group to a contract in 1959.

This management firm, run by Irving Micahnik and Harry Balk (two cigar-chewing record execs), had enormous influence over Detroit's white music scene through various arrangements with local radio stations, clubs and record companies. As with Del Shannon and the other artists they managed, Micahnik and Balk took 20% off the top of the group's earnings, and signed them to their own record label, Twirl, at a one-and-a-half-percent royalty (out of which the band had to pay all recording costs). Twirl then leased the records to Warwick, Big Top and other New York companies at a royalty rate of eight percent, giving the managers a tidy profit. In addition, Balk and Micahnik took credit as composers for most of the group's songs, thereby collecting publishing royalties as well.

This sort of arrangement was common in its day, since teenage musicians knew little about the music business and were easily exploited. It was unfair, of course, but it worked both ways. The artist could at least count on having hit records, which meant they could make money on live appearances.

For the next few years, that's how it worked for Johnny and the Hurricanes. They hit in early 1959 with "Crossfire," a pounding, highly charged rocker that made Number 23 on the *Billboard* charts. Three more hits followed in rapid succession, all hard-rocking takeoffs on well-known melodies: "Red River Rock" was a revamped "Red River Valley," "Reveille Rock" was the military tune, and "Beatnik Fly" was a thinly disguised "Bluetail Fly."

All three would seem to be unlikely candidates for rock and roll hits, but the novelty of such unusual material being done in this style proved a strong commercial asset. Mainly, though, it was the band itself that impressed listeners with its solid, inventive, rousing sound. Paris blew a raspy, wailing tenor sax, and lead solos were also taken by guitarist Dave Yorko and organist Paul Tesluk. With two or three hot solo breaks in each record, and a rock-hard driving beat that never failed, Johnny and the Hurricanes were like some missing link between the

great jazz combos of the Thirties and the Rolling Stones.

Their records continued to make the charts through 1961, though in progressively lower positions. A couple of members left the group, were replaced, and Paris received an offer to come to Germany and headline at the Star Club, Hamburg. So he and the group set sail, remaining in Hamburg for a couple of weeks. There, they were treated as stars and admired by the Beatles, who frequently opened the show for them at the Star Club.

In 1965, after a couple of hitless years, Paris raised enough money to start his own label, Atila, on which the Hurricanes released an album, *Live at the Star Club.* In the early Sixties, the group had sported the cleanest of crew cuts and ducktails, but the new album cover showed them with long Beatles hair and black leather; they were also attempting vocals, and trying, via such wretchedly bad material as "Saga of the Beatles," to capitalize on their association with the Liverpudlians.

The new records stiffed, Paris's label folded, and by 1967, after five albums, more than 20 singles and several million records sold, Paris was left with nothing but a name that would at least guarantee him work locally. Richard Nader's oldies but goodies revue ignored Paris's phone calls for work; he has been forgotten everywhere except in Europe (where albums of Johnny and the Hurricanes hits are compiled regularly), but Paris and his group are still together, playing high schools, bars, nightclubs and whatever other venues Toledo has to offer. He also occasionally works for his uncle's vending machine business. Still waiting for a recording contract to come along, he told an interviewer in 1974:

"I'm closer to my goal now than I was four years ago. It might take a long time; B.B. King did it at 45 or 50, so maybe I got 20 years left. You've got to be after it a long, long time. Then when it comes you've got to know how to handle it. I believe it's going to happen to me someday."

Johnny Paris got more mileage than most out of a career built on a trend that lasted only two years. At the same time he and others of his era proved the continuing viability of elemental rock and roll at the local level.

A few other instrumentalists, including Duane Eddy, the Ventures, Bill Black, the Champs, and Sandy Nelson, continued having hits up through the mid-Sixties. But by 1962, soul records, "girl group" records, and dance novelty vocals were competing for airplay, and instrumentals were once again relegated to the repertoire of amateur dance bands. Their heyday was not quite over yet, however.

Out of the hundreds of leftover instrumental bands still looking for a marketing hook emerged the brief surf music fad of 1963. Dick Dale opened the door with "Let's Go Trippin," a big L.A. hit, while the Beach Boys and Jan and Dean established surfing as the biggest overnight sensation since the twist. During 1961 and 1962, California had developed a large contingent of local instrumental bands playing Dick Dale-style music for

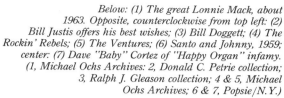

Below: (1) The great Lonnie Mack, about 1963. Opposite, counterclockwise from top left: (2) Bill Justis offers his best wishes; (3) Bill Doggett; (4) The Rockin' Rebels; (5) The Ventures; (6) Santo and Johnny, 1959; center: (7) Dave "Baby" Cortez of "Happy Organ" infamy. (1, Michael Ochs Archives: 2, Donald C. Petrie collection; 3, Ralph J. Gleason collection; 4 & 5, Michael Ochs Archives; 6 & 7, Popsie/N.Y.)

the surfers. By 1963, several of these groups broke nationally with records like "Pipeline" by the Chantays, "Penetration" by the Pyramids and "Wipe Out" by the Surfaris. Across the country, instrumental groups switched over to surf music, from the Astronauts in Denver, to the Wailers in Seattle, to the Trashmen in Minneapolis. The Ventures even returned to the Top Ten with a surf remake of "Walk—Don't Run." But surf music was the last hurrah for instrumental rock as a popular genre; after the British Invasion of 1964, vocals again assumed primacy in white rock.

The instrumental hits had filled a void in the early Sixties. While the primal excesses of rock and roll had been pushed aside by the big labels and the teen idols, the kids couldn't be stopped from rocking; as long as there were local musicians to provide what they couldn't get on the radio, rock and roll in its simplest and most effective form continued to prosper.

Instrumental rock emerged as a distinct idiom with the ability to excite the listener's imagination without the use of words. Admittedly, it's a more limited genre than most; but because the rules are stricter, the results are often more refined, more special, and more memorable than the simple formulas might imply. And though the survival of the local music scenes on which rock depends has appeared doubtful in recent years, I suspect that instrumental rock will make yet another resurgence before the history of rock and roll is completed.

Discography

1956–1965
INSTRUMENTAL ROCK HITS,
(From "Honky Tonk" to "Shotgun")

Bill Doggett, "Honky Tonk" (King 4950; ☆2, 1956). **Bill Doggett,** "Slow Walk" (King 5000; ☆26, 1956). **Bill Justis,** "Raunchy" (Phillips 3519; ☆3, 1957). **Ernie Freeman,** "Raunchy" (Imperial 5474; ☆12, 1957). **Lee Allen and His Band,** "Walkin' with Mr. Lee" (Ember 1027; ☆54, 1958). **Champs,** "Tequila" (Challenge 1016; ☆1, 1958). **Duane Eddy and the Rebels,** "Movin'n'Groovin' " (Jamie 1101; ☆72, 1958). **Link Wray and His Ray Men,** "Rumble" (Cadence 1347; ☆16, 1958). **Champs,** "El Rancho Rock" (Challenge 59007; ☆30, 1958). **Duane Eddy and the Rebels,** "Rebel-'Rouser" (Jamie 1104; ☆6, 1958). **Tune Rockers,** "The Green Mosquito" (United Artists 139; ☆44, 1958). **Duane Eddy and the Rebels,** "Ramrod" (Jamie 1109; ☆28, 1958). **Cozy Cole,** "Topsy II" b/w "Topsy I" (Love 5004; ☆3, 1958). **Duane Eddy and the Rebels,** "Cannonball" (Jamie 1111; ☆15, 1958). **Duane Eddy and the Rebels,** "The Lonely One" (Jamie 1117; ☆23, 1959). **Link Wray and His Ray Men,** "Raw-Hide" (Epic 9300; ☆23, 1959). **Virtues,** "Guitar Boogie Shuffle" (Hunt 324; ☆5, 1959). **Dave 'Baby' Cortez,** "The Happy Organ" (Clock 1009; ☆1, 1959). **Duane Eddy and the Rebels,** "Yep!" (Jamie 1122; ☆30, 1959). **Johnny and the Hurricanes,** "Crossfire" (Warwick 502; ☆23, 1959). **Preston Epps,** "Bongo Rock" (Original Sound 4; ☆14, 1959). **Wailers,** "Tall Cool One" (Golden Crest 518; ☆36, 1959). **Duane Eddy and the Rebels,** "Forty Miles of Bad Road" (Jamie 1126; ☆9, 1959). **Santo and Johnny,** "Sleep Walk" (Canadian American 103; ☆1, 1959). **Johnny and the Hurricanes,** "Red River Rock" (Warwick 509; ☆5, 1959). **Sandy Nelson,** "Teen Beat" (Original Sound 5; ☆4, 1959). **Ernie Fields,** "In the Mood" (Rendezvous 110; ☆4, 1959). **Fireballs,** "Torquay" (Top Rank 2008; ☆39, 1959). **Rock-a-Teens,** "Woo-Hoo" (Roulette 4192; ☆16, 1959). **Duane Eddy and the Rebels,** "Some Kind-a Earthquake" (Jamie 1130; ☆37, 1959). **Johnny and the Hurricanes,** "Reveille Rock" (Warwick 513; ☆25, 1959). **Bill Black's Combo,** "Smokie—Part 2" (Hi 2018; ☆17, 1959). **Santo and Johnny,** "Tear Drop" (Canadian American 107; ☆23, 1959). **Duane Eddy and the Rebels,** "Bonnie Came Back" (Jamie 1144; ☆26, 1960). **Viscounts,** "Harlem Nocturne" (Madison 123; ☆52, 1960). **Fireballs,** "Bulldog" (Top Rank 2026; ☆24, 1960). **Champs,** "Too Much Tequila" (Challenge 59063; ☆30, 1960). **Johnny and the Hurricanes,** "Beatnik Fly" (Warwick 520; ☆15, 1960). **Bill Black's Combo,** "White Silver Sands" (Hi 2021; ☆9, 1960). **Duane Eddy and the Rebels,** "Because They're Young" (Jamie 1156; ☆4, 1960). **Ventures,** "Walk—Don't Run" (Dolton 25; ☆2, 1960). **Bill Black's Combo,** "Don't Be Cruel" (Hi 2026; ☆11, 1960). **Floyd Cramer,** "Last Date" (RCA Victor 7775; ☆2, 1960). **Ventures,** "Perfidia" (Dolton 28; ☆15, 1960). **String-a-Longs,** "Wheels" (Warwick 603; ☆3, 1961). **Ramrods,** "(Ghost) Riders in the Sky" (Amy 813; ☆30, 1961). **Jorgen Ingmann,** "Apache" (Atco 6184; ☆2, 1961). **Ventures,** "Ram-Bunk-Shush" (Dolton 32; ☆29, 1961). **Kokomo,** "Asia Minor" (Felsted 8612; ☆8, 1961). **Floyd Cramer,** "On the Rebound" (RCA Victor 7840; ☆4, 1961). **Ray Charles,** "One Mint Julep" (Impulse 200; ☆8, 1961). **Freddie King,** "Hide Away" (Federal 12401; ☆29, 1961). **B. Bumble and the Stingers,** "Bumble Boogie" (Rendezvous 140; ☆21, 1961). **Frogmen,** "Underwater" (Candix 314; ☆44, 1961). **Philip Upchurch Combo,** "You Can't Sit Down—Part 2" (Boyd 3398; ☆29, 1961). **Fireballs,** "Quite a Party" (Warwick 644; ☆27, 1961). **Mar-Keys,** "Last Night" (Satellite 107; ☆3, 1961). **Duals,** "Stick Shift" (Sue 745; ☆25, 1961). **Sandy Nelson,** "Let There Be Drums" (Imperial 5775; ☆7, 1961). **Dick Dale and the Del-Tones,** "Let's Go Trippin' " (Deltone 5017; ☆60, 1961). **Ace Cannon,** "Tuff" (Hi 2040; ☆17, 1961). **Billy Joe and the Checkmates,** "Percolator (Twist)" (Dore 620; ☆10, 1962). **Marketts,** "Surfer's Stomp" (Liberty 55401; ☆31, 1962). **King Curtis,** "Soul Twist" (Enjoy 1000; ☆17, 1962). **Sandy Nelson,** "Drums Are My Beat" (Imperial 5809; ☆29, 1962). **B. Bumble and the Stingers,** "Nut Rocker" (Rendezvous 166; ☆23, 1962). **Dave 'Baby' Cortez,** "Rinky Dink" (Chess 1829; ☆10, 1962). **Booker T. and the MGs,** "Green Onions" (Stax 127; ☆3, 1962). **Duane Eddy and the Rebelettes,** "(Dance with the) Guitar Man" (RCA Victor 8087; ☆12, 1962). **Jimmy McGriff,** "I've Got a Woman" (Sue 770; ☆20, 1962). **Les Cooper,** "Wiggle Wobble" (Everlast 5019; ☆22, 1962). **Routers,** "Let's Go" (Warner Bros. 5283; ☆19, 1962). **Rebels,** "Wild Weekend" (Swan 4125; ☆8, 1962). **Duane Eddy and the Rebelettes,** "Boss Guitar" (RCA Victor 8131; ☆28, 1963). **Boots Randolph,** "Yakety Sax" (Monument 804; ☆35, 1963). **Chantays,** "Pipeline" (Dot 16440; ☆4, 1963). **Dartells,** "Hot Pastrami" (Dot 16453; ☆11, 1963). **Lonnie Mack,** "Memphis" (Fraternity 906; ☆5, 1963). **Surfaris,** "Wipe Out" (Dot 16479; ☆2, 1963). **Al Casey,** "Surfin' Hootenanny" (Stacy 962; ☆48, 1963). **Jack Nitzsche,** "The Lonely Surfer" (Reprise 20202; ☆39, 1963). **Lonnie Mack,** "Wham!" (Fraternity 912; ☆24, 1963). **Busters,** "Bust Out" (Arlen 735; ☆25, 1963). **Marketts,** "Out of Limits" (Warner Bros. 5391; ☆3, 1963). **Pyramids,** "Penetration" (Best 13002; ☆18, 1964). **King Curtis,** "Soul Serenade" (Capitol 5109; ☆51, 1964). **Ventures,** "Walk-Don't Run '64" (Dolton 96; ☆8, 1964). **Willie Mitchell,** "20-75" (Hi 2075; ☆31, 1964). **Travis Wammack,** "Scratchy" (Ara 204; ☆80, 1964). **Alvin Cash and the Crawlers,** "Twine Time" (Mar-V-Lus 6002; ☆14, 1965). **Davie Allan and the Arrows,** "Apache '65" (Tower 116; ☆64, 1965). **Jr. Walker and the All Stars,** "Shotgun" (Soul 35008; ☆4, 1965).

(Chart positions compiled from Joel Whitburn's *Record Research*, based on *Billboard* Pop chart.)

the webbs

Ray Charles
by Peter Guralnick

Ray Charles: the Genius, the High Priest of Soul. Black, blind, an addict for over 20 years; singer, pianist, composer. For black America he brought the feeling of the church into secular music and crystallized an era. For white America he suggested whole new arenas of experience and served as a symbolic encapsulation of that experience: spontaneous, "natural," and irremediably flawed. To Frank Sinatra he was "the only genius in the business." To Ray Charles: "Art Tatum—he was a genius. And Einstein. Not me."

Ray Charles was born Ray Charles Robinson on September 23rd, 1930, in Albany, Georgia. His family moved to Greenville, Florida, when he was small, and he has vivid memories of his father, his mother, his younger brother, and a neighbor, Wylie Pittman, who started him off on the piano at around the age of five. He can picture all these people, because it was not until he was six, after traumatically witnessing his brother's death by drowning in the tub his mother used for take-in washing, that he began to lose his sight from glaucoma. At seven, his parents enrolled him in the St. Augustine School for the Deaf and the Blind, where he learned to read and write music in braille, score for big bands, and play piano, alto, organ, clarinet and trumpet. His earliest musical influences were Chopin, Sibelius, Artie Shaw and Art Tatum.

He left school at 15, when his mother died (several years after his father's death), and drifted around Florida, making money off his music for the next couple of years. In 1947, he took his savings of $600 and moved as far away as he could get—to Seattle, Washington.

In Seattle he quickly resumed the life he had led in Florida, gigging at places like the Elks Club, the Rocking Chair, the Black and Tan. The music he played was very much in the vein of black popular music of the day—sophisticated cocktail swing, modeled on the King Cole Trio and Johnny Moore's Three Blazers featuring Charles Brown, with an occasional Louis Jordan jump blues thrown in. Piano generally took a decorously bluesy lead, guitar held back and chorded, providing tasteful fills, and bass took the rhythm, while Ray Charles (he didn't want to be Ray Robinson because of Sugar Ray, the great middleweight boxer) sang in a crooning, soothing, conventional nightclub style, as smooth and polished as his mentor, Nat "King" Cole.

Around 1949, Jack Lauderdale of Swing Time Records offered him a chance to record, and he cut his first sides in Los Angeles, debuting with a typical number called "Confession Blues." It didn't do much, and he appeared on a number of West Coast labels until he hit with "Baby, Let Me Hold Your Hand," a Top Ten R&B number in 1951. On the strength of that record he went on the road with blues singer Lowell Fulson who was riding high with his own hit on Swing Time, "Every Day I Have the Blues" (a song B.B. King would later adapt for his theme). Ray Charles played piano for Fulson in the band, which included Stanley Turrentine on tenor and Earl Brown on alto.

When Atlantic took over his Swing Time contract in 1952, the music Charles played was not much different from what he had been playing at the start of his career—a little bluesier perhaps, under Fulson's influence, but still smooth, sophisticated, well-mannered and well-bred. It's hard to say what Ahmet Ertegun, Herb Abramson, and the Atlantic staff saw in Ray Charles at this point. He had made some good derivative records; he was obviously a very capable journeyman musician; but he had showed no hint of originality.

In 1952 and 1953 he did a couple of New York sessions, which yielded a boogie-woogie classic ("Mess Around"), a novelty number ("It Should've Been Me"), and some fine blues ("Losing Hand," "Funny," Lowell Fulson's "Sinner's Prayer"); they demonstrated a harder edge of emotionalism than anything he had previously recorded. In this period he put together a band for Ruth Brown, then at the height of her popularity (and also on Atlantic), and played briefly with Moms Mabley. But it was not until he went to New Orleans in 1953 that he established a musical identity of his own.

There he hooked up with Guitar Slim (real name, Eddie Jones), a bluesman who was extremely popular on the club circuit. According to Jerry Wexler, Charles worked closely with Slim for some time. Then on September 26th Slim had a session for Specialty Records. He cut six or seven titles. One of them was "The Things That I Used to Do," a blues that sold a million copies, going on to become a blues standard. The pianist and arranger on this session was Ray Charles.

Guitar Slim was in many ways the antithesis of all that Ray Charles had sought to become in his musical career to date: crude; untutored; musically unsophisticated; possessed of a primitive, perfervid style that most resembled the gospel shouting of the Baptist Church. Even the melodies and titles of his songs ("Trouble Don't Last," "Reap What You Sow") seemed lifted from the church tradition. To Ray Charles it must have been like a revelation of something he had known all along. The arrangement and mode of Guitar Slim's hit—with gospel changes, horns riffing like a soulful choir, and above all the impassioned, emotionally charged tone of Eddie Jones's voice—were to set the pattern for much of Ray Charles's subsequent success.

In December of 1953 Jerry Wexler and Ahmet Ertegun were in New Orleans to cut Big Joe Turner. "We ran into Ray at Cosimo's famous small studio, and Ray asked us please (!) to do a session with him. . . . This was the landmark session because it had: Ray Charles originals, Ray Charles arrangements, a Ray Charles band." The session produced a fine single, "Don't You Know." The second New Orleans session brought about a moving version of Guitar Slim's "Feelin' Sad," but it was the next session, cut in an Atlanta radio station, which ultimately consolidated the style.

Ray Charles onstage in the early Sixties (Don Paulsen)

Below: Ray Charles, circa 1959 (Atlantic Records)
Opposite: The Raelettes (Ralph J. Gleason collection)

"I've Got a Woman," cut in Atlanta, was the consummate marriage of all the elements which up till then had simply failed to coalesce in Ray Charles's musical makeup. It featured, of course, his strong gospel-based piano, a seven-piece group (sans guitar) that cooked, and a vocal which, in the studio version of the song, only begins to suggest the change that had taken place in Ray Charles; with a full-throated rasp, sudden swoops, falsetto shrieks, and a sense of wild abandon, Charles totally removed himself from the polite music he had made in the past. There was an unrestrained exuberance to the new Ray Charles, a fierce earthiness which, while it would not have been unfamiliar to any follower of gospel music, was almost revolutionary in the world of pop. Big Bill Broonzy was outraged: "He's crying, sanctified. He's mixing the blues with the spirituals. He should be singing in a church." Only Roy Brown, in the Forties, had even suggested this mix of styles, though Little Richard was soon to follow and raise a hopped up version of the same hybrid to undreamt of heights. No one who had listened to the Soul Stirrers or the Five Blind Boys or Professor Alex Bradford could miss the connection, however.

The gospel genesis of "I've Got a Woman" and its enormous popularity set the tone for Ray Charles's subsequent success. The Pilgrim Travelers' "I've Got a New Home" became "Lonely Avenue"; "This Little Girl of Mine" took something from Clara Ward's "This Little Light of Mine" and the Caravans' "What Kind of Man Is This"; "Nobody but You, Lord" was shortened to "Nobody but You." The Raelettes were added as a gospel choir. The sound became increasingly churchy, a deliberate evocation of holiness feeling.

Over the next six years Ray Charles enjoyed a period of extraordinary creativity in which all the various strands of his musical heritage were brought together; and he was given the opportunity to show his true genius which, if it lay more in the realm of assimilation than originality, as can now be seen, was inspired assimilation nonetheless. He did blues and funk; jazz at Newport; revivals of old standards with and without strings; even, in "I'm Movin' On," a good rocking stab at country and western. More than anything else, though, there was the translation of gospel standards into secular success and the creation, in the process, of a whole new phase of black music, one in which artists such as James Brown, Sam Cooke, Solomon Burke, and Otis Redding could take Ray Charles for a model and call upon their own church backgrounds to create what became known as soul music. For Charles himself, the pinnacle of this movement came in 1959 with the enormous success of "What'd I Say," a conventional enough blues riff with Latin rhythm and a gospel feel and six and a half minutes of the most joyous celebration of an utterly profane love. A kind of secular evocation of an actual church service, complete with moans,

groans, and a congregation talking in tongues, the record was banned on many radio stations and was Ray Charles's first million-seller.

In November 1959, on the strength of this success, he signed with ABC Records for a sizable advance and the promise of an economic independence to match the creative freedom he had always enjoyed. In 1962 he cut his landmark country and western album which included two big hits, the biggest of which ("I Can't Stop Loving You") sold over 3 million records. When reporters asked Ray Charles how he had come to invent this new trend, he credited the *Grand Ole Opry,* which he had listened to since he was a child.

For the rest of the Sixties, and up to the present day, he has contented himself with what have come to be virtually MOR albums, broad-based, inoffensive, a sterile mix of heavenly choirs, Beatles hits and nostalgic show tunes, bland arrangements and syrupy strings. Only once in a while, cutting through all the slush, as on "I Don't Need No Doctor" (1966), do you hear that aching, almost painfully raw voice which inspired Joe Cocker, Eric Burdon, Stevie Winwood and a generation of white rockers. In recent years he has seemingly returned to the cocktail music of his youth, the music of Charles Brown and Nat "King" Cole.

I remember seeing Ray Charles several times in the early Sixties. It was always the same. The big band opened with blasting evocations of the swing era—Ray Charles's vocal appearance, in the time-honored fashion of the R&B revue, came only after an intermission. The show ended with an orgiastic performance of "What'd I Say," with Ray Charles writhing puppet-like in a spastic trance and some couple inevitably moved to get up out of their seats and dance. It was at this point, at all the performances I saw, that the cops moved in, the band wound down, and someone led Ray Charles away from his suddenly silent piano to safety backstage. It was great theater, re-creating the revivalistic fervor of his early performances and simultaneously retaining a faint edge of cool, a kind of reserve, which seemed suspicious, brittle, and perhaps even contemptuous.

There is no question that for white audiences Ray Charles was a romantic figure whose first well-publicized heroin bust in 1965 (which led to his commitment to a California sanatorium, a period of cleaning out, and a year-long retirement from performing) did little but extend the image of Billie Holiday, Charlie Parker and Bud Powell, twisted black geniuses whose mythic role it was to die for white people's sins. Ray Charles, however, has always gone his own way. He survived, and he still resists personal, as well as musical, categorization. "I started using stuff when I was 16 and first started in show business," he has said in reference to his habit. "Every experience I've had—good and bad—has taught me something. I was born a poor boy in the South, I'm black, I'm blind, I once fooled around with drugs, but all of it was like going to school—and I've tried to be a good student. I don't regret a damn thing."

Discography

"Baby Let Me Hold Your Hand" (Swing Time 250; r☆7, 1951). "Kiss Me Baby" (Swing Time 274; r☆10, 1952). "It Should've Been Me" (Atlantic 1021; r☆7, 1954). "Don't You Know" (Atlantic 1037; r☆10, 1954). "I've Got a Woman" (Atlantic 1050; r☆2, 1955). "A Fool for You" b/w "This Little Girl of Mine" (Atlantic 1063; r☆2, 1955). "Blackjack" (Atlantic 1076; r☆8, 1955). "Drown in My Own Tears" (Atlantic 1085; r☆2, 1956). "Hallelujah I Love Her So" (Atlantic 1096; r☆5, 1956). "Lonely Avenue" (Atlantic 1108; r☆8, 1956). "Ain't That Love" (Atlantic 1124; r☆11, 1957). "Swanee River Rock" (Atlantic 1154; r☆14, ☆42, 1957). "Rockhouse—Part 2" (Atlantic 2006; r☆14, 1958). "The Right Time" (Atlantic 2010; r☆5, 1959). "That's Enough" (Atlantic 2022; r☆19, 1959). "What'd I Say" (Atlantic 2031; r☆1, ☆6, 1959). "I'm Movin' On" (Atlantic 2043; r☆11, ☆40, 1959). "Don't Let the Sun Catch You Cryin' " (Atlantic 2047; r☆17, 1960). "Just for a Thrill" (Atlantic 2055; r☆16, 1960). "Sticks and Stones" (ABC-Paramount 10118; r☆2, ☆40, 1960). "Tell the Truth" (Atlantic 2068; r☆13, 1960). "Georgia on My Mind" (ABC-Paramount 10135; r☆3, ☆1, 1960). "Ruby" (ABC-Paramount 10164; r☆10, ☆28, 1960). "Them That Got" (ABC-Paramount 10141; r☆10, 1961). "One Mint Julep" (Impulse 200; r☆1, ☆8, 1961). "I've Got News for You" (Impulse 202; r☆8, 1961). "Hit the Road Jack" (ABC-Paramount 10244; r☆1, ☆1, 1961). "Unchain My Heart" (ABC-Paramount 10266; r☆1, ☆9, 1961). "Hide 'Nor Hair" b/w "At the Club" (ABC-Paramount 10314; r☆7, ☆20, 1962). "I Can't Stop Loving You" b/w "Born to Lose" (ABC-Paramount 10330; r☆1, ☆1, 1962). "You Don't Know Me" (ABC-Paramount 10345; r☆5, ☆2, 1962). "You Are My Sunshine" b/w "Your Cheating Heart" (ABC-Paramount 10375; r☆1, ☆7, 1962). "Don't Set Me Free" (ABC-Paramount 10405; r☆9, ☆20, 1963). "Take These Chains from My Heart" (ABC-Paramount 10435; r☆7, ☆8, 1963). "No One" b/w "Without Love (There Is Nothing)" (ABC-Paramount 10453; r☆9, ☆21, 1963). "Busted" b/w "That Lucky Old Sun" (ABC-Paramount 10481; r☆3, ☆4, 1963). "My Heart Cries for You" b/w "Baby, Don't You Cry" (ABC-Paramount 10530; ☆38, 1964). "A Tear Fell" (ABC-Paramount 10571; ☆50, 1964). "Makin' Whoopee" (ABC-Paramount 10609; r☆14, ☆46, 1965). "Crying Time" (ABC-Paramount 10739; r☆5, ☆6, 1966). "Together Again" (ABC-Paramount 10785; r☆10, ☆19, 1966). "Let's Go Get Stoned" (ABC 10808; r☆1, ☆31, 1966). "I Chose to Sing the Blues" (ABC 10840; r☆22, ☆32, 1966). "Here We Go Again" (ABC 10938; r☆5, ☆15, 1967). "In the Heat of the Night" (ABC 10970; r☆21, ☆33, 1967). "Yesterday" (ABC 11009; r☆9, ☆25, 1967). "That's a Lie" (ABC 11045; r☆11, 1968). "Eleanor Rigby" b/w "Understanding" (ABC 11090; r☆13, ☆35, 1968). "Laughin' and Clownin' " (ABC 11259; r☆18, 1970). "If You Were Mine" (ABC 11271; r☆19, ☆41, 1970). "Don't Change on Me" (ABC 11291; r☆13, ☆36, 1971). "Feel So Bad" (ABC 11308; r☆16, 1971).

(Chart positions taken from Joel Whitburn's *Record Research,* compiled from *Billboard* Pop chart, unless otherwise indicated; r☆ = position on *Billboard* Rhythm and Blues chart.)

Sam Cooke

by Joe McEwen

Thousands of screaming, crying, pushing people thronged the area surrounding A.R. Leak's Funeral Home at 7838 So. Cottage Grove in a frantic attempt to view the body of singer Sam Cooke....

"Both chapels, each holding about 300 people, were filled shortly after the doors opened, and the urgency of many to 'get a last look at Sam' resulted in near chaos, with young and old being crushed in the process....

"When the plate glass in a front door of Leak's chapel gave way under the pressure of the crowd, Spencer Leak, a son of A.R. Leak Sr., shouted, "There are just too many of them."

One emotional woman when crushed while attempting to step over the threshold screamed, "Please let me in. I've never seen anything like this in my life."

Cooke's coffin was covered with glass, to the disappointment of many. A blind woman, who came to pay her respects and perhaps "touch" her singing idol, was rammed against a door frame and had to be pulled over the entrance by funeral parlor employees.

—The Chicago Defender,
December 19th, 1964

Sam Cooke died on December 11th, 1964. Gunned down in a Los Angeles motel room under mysterious and unsavory circumstances, he nonetheless died a martyr's death. To black America, he was a hero.

Yet Cooke, a true pioneer of black music, has rarely received the recognition accorded Ray Charles, or such early rock stars as Little Richard and Chuck Berry. The neglect is misleading; Sam Cooke, as much as any R&B artist of the Fifties, paved the way for the soul explosion of the Sixties, influencing performers from Otis Redding to Al Green.

In the beginning, he was black America's favorite gospel singer. Sam Cooke was 20 years old when he replaced R.H. Harris as the lead singer for the Soul Stirrers in 1951. The Soul Stirrers had been one of the most popular gospel groups, thanks largely to Harris, whose quivering tenor was the forerunner of the modern soul falsetto.

It's not hard to imagine the intense pressure Sam must have felt on his first Sunday afternoon with the sextet, as the crowd murmured its displeasure at the Soul Stirrers beginning their program without Harris. From the sanctuary of the group, Sam stepped forward for his first solo, perhaps Professor Alex Bradford's "Jesus Is a Friend until the End." Eyes closed and arms outstretched, Cooke sang without the rasping delivery or broken vowels of older stylists, avoiding the tentative offering of Harris's Roman tenor. Yet his voice, burrowing and soaring through plaintive dirges, exuding a gentle world-weariness, moved the congregation to a standing ovation.

During Cooke's tenure with the group, the Soul Stirrers recorded for Art Rupe's Specialty label. Although Sam's voice always retained the purity of the early days, his gospel records

on Specialty capture his finest vocal moments: he never sang songs that were more erotic or buoyant than the love songs he sang about his Lord. While other gospel singers often let themselves get carried away in the emotion of the moment, Cooke's phrasing was always articulate, never out of control, every word enunciated clearly, even as he growled and clapped (with only a guitar echoing his harsh call), "Were you there/When they crucified my Lord?"

For almost six years, Sam and the Soul Stirrers crisscrossed the country. For the folks flocking to the big halls and storefronts, Cooke's pure, sanctified singing, smooth features and lithe body offered the same combination of religious charisma and sweaty sexuality that Marjoe and the like exploited in the white Bible Belt.

J.W. Alexander, Sam's close friend, manager and business associate, was shrewd enough to realize that if Cooke was having this kind of an effect on the sequestered gospel audience, then there was a whole world out there, more openly sexual and sinful, that had to be ripe for Sam's physical and vocal appeal.

One can guess that Cooke himself was more than eager for the transition. The years on the gospel trail had given Sam the perspective and maturity he needed to tackle pop, and it seemed that he already had the right idea in 1956, when he sat down with his guitar and recorded his first pop song, "Lovable." The record, released under the name of Dale Cooke so as not to offend Sam's gospel following, set the pattern for the pop records that followed. Singing noticeably higher and lighter, Cooke imbued the song with a purity familiar from his church music. Cooke's almost wispy delivery is balanced by a huge, doowah choral backup, and their meeting place is the elusive middle ground Sam staked out most of his career, the place where the soul and feeling of gospel meets the finger-snapping, ascot-wearing ambience of supper club pop.

Specialty's white owner Art Rupe was not happy with Cooke's pop ambitions. When Rupe walked into the studio one night and saw the white choral group Sam and producer Bumps Blackwell were using in their "bleached" approach, he sold Blackwell the right to take Cooke's pop output elsewhere.

Rupe missed a gold mine. The song that came out of that session was "You Send Me." Released as Cooke's next single, it sold 1.7 million copies in 1957 on the tiny Keen label. It was also the catalyst for Cooke's meteoric rise as a pop singer.

J.W. Alexander has claimed he intended from the outset that Sam Cooke would eventually become the kind of idol to black teenage girls that white girls had been used to having for years.

Cooke had been with Keen almost two years when the first and most ambitious of their schemes was realized: Sam signed with RCA, spurning offers from numerous independents and becoming RCA's first major black pop singer, apart from calypso specialist Harry Belafonte.

The move could have been disastrous. Sam still depended on

Sam Cooke circa 1964 (Michael Ochs collection)

114

the R&B market as his base, and RCA was virtually without contacts there. But Cooke and Alexander were counting on the strength of Sam's name to generate black airplay, while the RCA label provided Sam with a seal of legitimacy for the wider white audience.

The first RCA release, a saccharine ditty titled "Teenage Sonata," did reasonably well, but its followup was the venerable "Chain Gang," released in August 1960. From that point on, Cooke was rarely without a Top 40 hit.

"Chain Gang" was a catchy record that never quite rang true, with its male chorus oohing and aahing over clinking steel spike hammers, but "Sad Mood," released in December 1960, was a complete reversal of form, depending more on blues idioms and phrasing. Unlike earlier 45s ("Wonderful World," "Everybody Likes to Cha Cha Cha" and "Only Sixteen"), "Sad Mood" didn't seem to hold obvious appeal to a teen or even pop audience; the surprising commercial success of the record must have indicated to Cooke and his arranger Rene Hall that the market for "soulful" music was wider than they had anticipated.

While his output on Keen centered on light ballads and novelty items, at RCA Cooke began to draw more on blues and gospel arrangements, coupled with popular black slang expressions. The most successful record along these lines was "Bring It On Home to Me," a timeless song built on a simple, laconic piano figure and Sam's weary vocal, echoed in true call-and-response fashion by Lou Rawls. Upon release in the summer of 1962, the song was an instant hit. Perhaps the first record to define the soul experience, it would be one of the most influential songs Cooke ever cut, matched in impact only by the sensual "That's Where It's At."

Unlike his peers—and only Jackie Wilson and Little Willie John came close to rivaling Cooke's vocal virtuosity—Sam's destiny was always firmly within his control, artistically and otherwise. He was one of the first popular black vocalists in 40 years of recording who ran his own publishing company (Kags Music) and his own management firm; he also owned his own record company, Sar/Derby Records, which established itself as a successful independent almost immediately after its first soul release.

Sar, incorporated in 1960 and discontinued shortly after Cooke's death, was at first conceived as a gospel label for the Soul Stirrers, whose popularity had declined after Cooke's departure (Johnnie Taylor was the lead singer for the group at the time). But the sanctity of the label didn't last for long. Within a year, Cooke and Alexander had "turned out" a number of their gospel protégés by having them record the type of blues and soul that Sam seemed most comfortable with as a songwriter and producer. Among Cooke's discoveries were the Womack Brothers, including Bobby Womack, from Cleveland, who be-

came the Valentinos; Billy Preston; Johnnie Taylor; the Sims Twins; Mel Carter (who re-created Sam's early innocence with a song Sam wrote, "When a Boy Falls in Love"); and finally Lou Rawls, whom Cooke and Alexander signed to Herb Alpert and Lou Adler's Shardee label, where it was hoped he would duplicate Sam's pop success.

During his lifetime, Cooke established a public personality of grace and poise, yet the court record of the events surrounding his death is brutal in presentation, and in sharp contrast to the genial public image he presented.

According to the testimony, Cooke, at the time married to his high-school sweetheart Barbara Campbell, had picked up a 22-year-old woman named Elisa Boyer at a party on the night of December 10th. Although he had promised her a ride home, he instead drove her to a motel on South Figueroa in Los Angeles, where he registered the two of them as "Mr. and Mrs. Cooke." Miss Boyer testified that she walked up to the registration desk and asked to be taken home. But Cooke managed to force her into a motel room; there, she claimed, Cooke "began to rip my clothes off." She escaped when Cooke went into the bathroom and fled with Cooke's clothing. According to her testimony, he pursued her, dressed only in a sports coat and shoes. While Elisa Boyer phoned police from a nearby booth, Cooke pounded on the door of the motel's manager, 55-year-old Bertha Franklin; demanding to know Miss Boyer's whereabouts, Cooke allegedly broke the door open and assaulted Mrs. Franklin. During the scuffle, Mrs. Franklin pulled out a .22 caliber pistol and shot Cooke three times. When the wounded singer charged Franklin, the motel manager picked up a stick and clubbed him. By the time police arrived, Sam Cooke was dead.

To most of his white audience, Sam Cooke remained little more than a handsome, well-groomed black man, the quaint bearer of the cha-cha and twist. Across the tracks, on the other hand, his stature was almost comparable with that of Malcolm X and Martin Luther King. His death, like theirs, only enhanced his standing.

He was a black music capitalist at a time when Berry Gordy, later to found Motown, was still writing songs for Jackie Wilson. Yet as Cooke developed, his own music became increasingly blacker, returning to its gospel roots. When Bertha Franklin shot Sam Cooke in that Los Angeles motel, he died his own man, unbought and unbleached.

A few weeks after his death, RCA released "A Change Is Gonna Come." Curtained with shimmering strings and anchored by a dirgelike drumbeat, "Change," like Martin Luther King's final speech, in which he told his followers that he had been to the mountaintop, was appropriately ominous, as if to anticipate the turbulent years facing black America. Dignified and transcendent, it made a fitting final statement from a fallen hero.

Discography

"You Send Me" (Keen 34013; r☆1, ☆1, 1957). "I'll Come Running Back to You" (Specialty 619; r☆7, ☆22, 1957). "(I Love You) for Sentimental Reasons" b/w "Desire Me" (Keen 34002, r☆17, ☆43, 1958). "Lonely Island (Keen 4009; r☆15, ☆39, 1958). "Win Your Love for Me" (Keen 2006; r☆4, ☆33, 1958). "Love You Most of All" (Keen 2008; r☆12, ☆26, 1958). "Everybody Likes to Cha Cha Cha" (Keen 2018; r☆2, ☆31, 1959). "Only Sixteen" (Keen 2022; r☆13, ☆28, 1959). "There, I've Said It Again" (Keen 2105; r☆25, 1959). "Teenage Sonata" (RCA Victor 47–7701; r☆33, ☆50, 1960). "Wonderful World" (Keen 2112; r☆2, ☆12, 1960). "Chain Gang" (RCA Victor 47–7783; r☆2, ☆2, 1960). "Sad Mood" (RCA Victor 47–7816; r☆23, ☆29, 1960). "That's It—I Quit—I'm Movin' On" (RCA Victor 47–7853; r☆25, ☆31, 1961). "Cupid" (RCA Victor 47–7883; r☆20, ☆17, 1961). "Twistin' the Night Away" (RCA Victor 47–7983; r☆1, ☆9, 1962). "Bring It On Home to Me" b/w "Having a Party" (RCA Victor 47–8036; r☆2, ☆13, 1962). "Nothing Can Change This Love" b/w "Somebody Have Mercy" (RCA Victor 47–8088; r☆2, ☆12, 1962). "Send Me Some Lovin'" (RCA Victor 47–8129; r☆2, ☆13, 1963). "Another Saturday Night" (RCA Victor 47–8164; r☆1, ☆10, 1963). "Frankie and Johnny" (RCA Victor 47–8215; r☆4, ☆14, 1963). "Little Red Rooster" (RCA Victor 47–8247; r☆7, ☆11, 1963). "Good News" (RCA Victor 47–8299; ☆11, 1964). "Good Times" b/w "Tennessee Waltz" (RCA Victor 47–8368; ☆11, 1964). "Cousin of Mine" b/w "That's Where It's At" (RCA Victor 47–8426; ☆31, 1964). "Shake" b/w "A Change Is Gonna Come" (RCA Victor 47–8486; r☆2, ☆7, 1965). "It's Got the Whole World Shakin'" (RCA Victor 47–8539; r☆15, ☆41, 1965). "Sugar Dumpling" (RCA Victor 47–8631; r☆18, ☆32, 1965).

(Chart positions taken from Joel Whitburn's *Record Research,* compiled from *Billboard* Pop chart, unless otherwise indicated; r☆ = position on *Billboard* Rhythm and Blues chart.)

Jackie Wilson

by Joe McEwen

oston's Back Bay Theater was jammed to capacity, filled with a noisy, enthusiastic
throng, out to see the latest of the traveling
soul revues. This show promised to be some-
thing special, with a rare visit from Roy Hamilton, the urbane
crooner of "Ebb Tide," and an appearance by Jackie Wilson,
the man responsible for "Lonely Teardrops" and "That's
Why." But as the warmup acts went through their paces, all
was not well backstage; the show's promoter was on the phone
jabbering frantically to Roy Hamilton's agent, who had no idea
where his singer was. It soon became clear that Hamilton
wouldn't show.

Fearful of the wrath of the fevered crowd if one of the headliners failed to appear, the promoter urgently whispered in
Jackie Wilson's ear as he prepared to go on; Wilson, after a
moment's pause, agreed. Bounding onstage, he grabbed the
mike, spun around and raced into a blistering version of
"That's Why." For over an hour, Jackie Wilson played to the
screaming audience, teasing the women clustered in front of
the stage. Suddenly, in the middle of "Shake! Shake! Shake!,"
he jumped into a sea of outstretched arms. With mike in hand,
he attempted to sing, but women, clawing ravenously, shred-
ded his shirt. Finally, Wilson's body disappeared. The theater
was in turmoil; the audience pressed forward, hoping to catch a
glimpse of what was going on. After minutes of pushing and
shoving, the police escorted Wilson to safety. The lights were
turned on and everybody ordered out. No one missed Roy
Hamilton.

In his prime, Jackie Wilson was that kind of performer: he
could stop a show at the drop of a hat—sometimes, without even
trying. A contemporary of James Brown and Sam Cooke, he
made his debut as a solo performer in 1957. The comparison
with two of black music's most influential figures is not unflat-
tering: as a showman, Wilson was the equal of Brown, while as
a vocalist, he could match Cooke's range and then some. Yet
while both Brown and Cooke became wealthy men, honored as
pioneers, Jackie Wilson suffered a checkered and enigmatic
career. Despite his popularity in the late Fifties and early Sixties, his recordings rarely reflected his talent.

And his raw talent was enormous. Born in 1934 in Detroit,
growing up under the influence of Forties blues vocalist Roy
Brown, Wilson's first break came in 1953, when he dropped by
the Fox Theater in Detroit during a rehearsal of Billy Ward and
his Dominoes. The group had recently lost its immensely popular lead singer, Clyde McPhatter, and Ward was looking for a
replacement. Wilson, boasting that he was a better singer than
McPhatter, landed an audition with the group; to Ward's as-
tonishment, his claim proved credible. The brash Detroit teenager became the Dominoes' new lead vocalist.

The Dominoes never quite regained their stride with Wilson
at the helm; though they were able to play Las Vegas and the
Copa on the strength of their earlier hits, it wasn't until 1956

that the Dominoes returned to the charts, with Wilson's flamboyant interpretation of the unlikely "St. Therese of the
Roses." The record gave a temporary shot in the arm to the
Dominoes' faltering fortunes; but Jackie Wilson used "St.
Therese" as a stepping-stone to a solo career. Shortly after its
release, he left Ward to sign with Brunswick, an affiliation he
has maintained to this day.

"Reet Petite," Wilson's first solo effort, was released in 1957.
Penned by a struggling Detroit songwriter named Berry Gordy,
"Reet Petite," a blaring uptempo novelty song, featured Wilson
mimicking Elvis Presley's stuttering, breathless vocal delivery.
For Gordy, the record marked his first hit as a writer (he would
later found Motown); for Wilson, on the other hand, "Reet
Petite" inaugurated an oddly aimless solo recording career
that, in the course of 18 years, would meander through countless musical styles, pitting Wilson against slipshod orchestration and material that was often mediocre if not absurd.

Although Dick Jacobs arranged Wilson's first record, "Reet
Petite," it was Milton DeLugg, an accordionist/bandleader,
who arranged "To Be Loved," the successor to Wilson's smash
debut disc, and several of Wilson's early records. Though De-
Lugg's melodramatic scores and heavy-handed choral accompaniments afflicted most of his productions, Wilson somehow
managed to surmount such obstacles through the sheer power
of his amazing vocals and a knack for knowing what to do with
even the worst of songs. Between 1958 and 1963, Jackie Wilson
was one of black America's most popular vocalists, scoring a
long string of pop and soul hits.

In 1960, Wilson released his biggest single, "Night" backed
with "Doggin' Around," a double-sided hit that defines the
paradox of his recording career. "Doggin' Around" was one of
his rare songs to take a direct, bluesy approach. Though
marred by an obtrusive (and defiantly white-sounding) chorus,
the record is one of Wilson's finest moments: urged on by a
polite blues piano, he soars through the song, stretching and
wrenching notes like a true virtuoso. It is one of the few Jackie
Wilson records from the early Sixties that does not sound
hopelessly dated today.

But while Jackie sang the blues on one side, the flip was pure
schmaltz. Flaunting his operatic range, Wilson crooned
"Night" in his best Mario Lanza style, accompanied by scads of
strings. Wilson obviously enjoyed such showstoppers, though;
by choice, he recorded a number of standards throughout his
career, including a truly transcendent "Danny Boy." Here Wilson exhibited the full extent of his abilities, transforming the
hoary ballad into a stunning display of vocal gymnastics.

While Wilson's recorded material often consisted of dreary
supper club fare, his live performances from the period belonged to another world entirely. At 16, he had been a Golden
Gloves champ, and like James Brown, Wilson put his boxing

Jackie Wilson, 1953 (Popsie/N.Y.)

ability to hair-raising use: splits, spins, slides and one-footed dancing were all part of the show. And his dramatic readings of ballads, complete with knee drops and overdrawn gestures, rarely failed to bring his audience to a state of frenzy. The sexual hysteria helped promote an aura of violence around him, and in 1961, he was shot and seriously wounded by a female friend in a New York hotel.

Though Wilson, in an attempt to keep up with new fashions, cut a few ill-conceived gospel-shout singles in the mid-Sixties, it wasn't until 1966 that his sagging career was temporarily revived, by Carl Davis, the Chicago producer. Davis brought Wilson into the soul era with two quick million-sellers, "Whispers" and "(Your Love Keeps Lifting Me) Higher and Higher," easily Wilson's best later efforts. Sadly, the hits didn't last; Davis couldn't seem to find appropriate material. By 1970, Wilson was an aging, second-rate soul star, unsuccessfully aping contemporary trends and finally consigned to the oldies circuit, as a member of Dick Clark's Good Ol' Rock 'n' Roll revue. Jackie's last album, titled *Nowstalgia,* was a company-conceived tribute to one of Wilson's early idols, Al Jolson.

The path of Jackie Wilson's career is puzzling. Though Berry Gordy wrote Jackie's first few hits and was once a close friend, Wilson never benefited from Gordy's success at Motown. Wilson would have been a logical choice to head the Motown roster, but instead he remained at Brunswick, a label with a dubious reputation and few facilities for promoting his career. Wilson himself has been deliberately hazy in interviews about the specifics of his career: one of the great unfulfilled talents of soul music, he is also proof of the music's exploitative potential.

In October 1975, Jackie Wilson suffered a serious heart attack on the stage of the Latin Casino in Cherry Hill, New Jersey, where he was appearing with the Dick Clark revue. The likelihood is strong that his performance of that night will prove to have been his last.

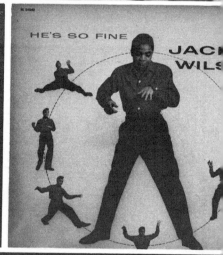

Discography

"Reet Petite" (Brunswick 55024; ☆62, 1957). "To Be Loved" (Brunswick 55052; r☆11, ☆22, 1958). "Lonely Teardrops" (Brunswick 55105; r☆1, ☆7, 1958). "That's Why" (Brunswick 55121; r☆2, ☆13, 1959). "I'll Be Satisfied" (Brunswick 55136; r☆6, ☆20, 1959). "You Better Know It" (Brunswick 55149; r☆1, ☆37, 1959). "Talk That Talk" (Brunswick 55165; r☆3, ☆34, 1959). "Doggin' Around" b/w "Night" (Brunswick 55166; r☆1, ☆4, 1960). "A Woman, a Lover, a Friend" b/w "(You Were Made for) All My Love" (Brunswick 55167; r☆1, ☆12, 1960). "Am I the Man" b/w "Alone at Last" (Brunswick 55170; r☆10, ☆8, 1960). "The Tear of the Year" b/w "My Empty Arms" (Brunswick 55201; r☆10, ☆9, 1961). "Please Tell Me Why" (Brunswick 55208; r☆11, ☆20, 1961). "I'm Comin' On Back to You" (Brunswick 55216; r☆9, ☆19, 1961). "You Don't Know What It Means" b/w "Years from Now" (Brunswick 55219; r☆19, ☆37, 1961). "The Greatest Hurt" (Brunswick 55221; ☆34, 1962). "I Just Can't Help It" (Brunswick 55229; r☆17, 1962). "Baby Workout" (Brunswick 55239; r☆1, ☆5, 1963). "Shake! Shake! Shake!" (Brunswick 55246; r☆21, ☆33, 1963). "Danny Boy" (Brunswick 55277; r☆25, 1965). "No Pity (in the Naked City)" (Brunswick 55280; r☆25, 1965). "Whispers" (Brunswick 55300; r☆5, ☆11, 1966). "I Don't Want to Lose You" (Brunswick 55309; r☆11, 1967). "(Your Love Keeps Lifting Me) Higher and Higher" (Brunswick 55336; r☆1, ☆6, 1967). "Since You Showed Me How to Be Happy" (Brunswick 55354; r☆22, ☆32, 1967). "I Get the Sweetest Feeling" (Brunswick 55381; r☆12, ☆34, 1968). "Helpless" (Brunswick 55418; r☆21, 1969). "This Love Is Real" (Brunswick 55443; r☆9, 1970). "Love Is Funny That Way" (Brunswick 55461; r☆18, 1971).

(Chart positions taken from Joel Whitburn's *Record Research,* compiled from *Billboard* Pop chart, unless otherwise indicated; r☆ = position on *Billboard* Rhythm and Blues chart.)

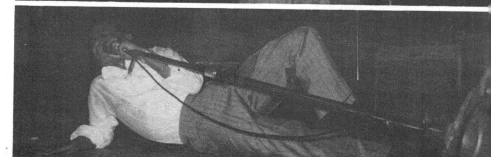

Brill Building Pop
by Greg Shaw

The Brill Building, located at 1619 Broadway in the heart of New York's music district, is in outward appearance indistinguishable from a thousand other old office buildings in midtown Mahattan. Yet since the late Fifties, its name has been synonymous with an approach to rock songwriting that has changed the course of the music.

The fame of the Brill Building is largely due to Aldon Music, a music publishing firm actually located across the street. Formed in 1958 by Al Nevins and Don Kirshner, Aldon mounted a full-scale invasion of the pop charts in the early Sixties. Nevins had previously been a guitar player with the Three Suns, while Kirshner had experience in songwriting, management, publishing and song plugging. They were, in every sense, the right people in the right place at the right time.

Rock and roll had been growing steadily in popularity for several years, and the tastes of its audience were becoming possible to define, if not always to predict; the established music industry, at first baffled by rock and roll, was now searching for means to manipulate it, to make it fit into the old rules they understood. No larger gap could be imagined than that between the sophisticated cocktail music of Tin Pan Alley and the rude street noise of rock and roll, yet it was this very gap that Nevins and Kirshner set out to bridge. Initially, they were merely responding to the overwhelming demand for songs by the thousands of young groups and singers now clogging the studios; most of these performers were recording either old standards or thoroughly inadequate original material—for it was very rare in those days for rock and roll artists to write decent material of their own.

Kirshner's goal was to supply songs for this new market, songs that would meet the highest standards of professionalism while still appealing to a teenage audience. He and Nevins gathered together the best of New York's young writers, some now forgotten (Jack Keller, Gary Sherman, Kenny Karen, Toni Wine, Larry Kolber), others destined for lasting popularity. Among Aldon's first group of then-unknowns were Gerry Goffin, Carole King, Barry Mann, Cynthia Weil, Bobby Darin, Neil Diamond, Howard Greenfield and Neil Sedaka. Aldon's clients were chiefly the large record labels like Columbia, Atlantic, RCA and ABC, which required songs of high quality in great quantity. On the whole, it was Aldon's success in setting a new standard of quality in rock songwriting that insured the firm's preeminence.

Although Aldon employed several songwriting teams, there was a common quality in all their songs that was identifiable as the "Brill Building sound," a term which later came to include other New York writers who aspired to Aldon's standards, such as Jeff Barry and Ellie Greenwich, Doc Pomus and Mort Shuman, and Bert Berns. What all these writers had in common was a genuine empathy with teenagers—their values, interests, emotional needs and slang. What made them different from other rock composers was their professionalism, their respect for the Tin Pan Alley tradition of pop songwriting, established in the Thirties by Cole Porter, George and Ira Gershwin, Rodgers and Hart. There were, of course, more differences than similarities between the Tin Pan Alley tunesmiths and the Brill Building writers. The songs of Cole Porter reflected a brittle, cynical sophistication; those of the Gershwins or Rodgers and Hart often had an abstract quality far removed from the realities of ordinary life. In writing for teenagers in the Fifties, it was necessary that the images be very simple, believable, and immediate, even as the element of fantasy had to be melodramatically overblown.

The music that came out of the Brill Building differed in at least one crucial respect from that being written in Philadelphia. The stock Teen Idol approach was to find singers with faces that could be promoted, then to supply them with whatever songs happened to be around, often written by the leader of the label's studio orchestra. As long as something about high school was mentioned, they figured the kids would buy it. The Brill Building writers took the opposite tack. They tried to understand what the kids wanted and why; knowing that any singer could be promoted on the basis of a strong song, they concentrated on writing songs that would be hits because they were good. Discounting small pockets of creativity in New Orleans and Detroit, the Brill Building accounted for much of the best rock popular between 1959 and 1964.

The majority of Aldon's hit songs were composed by three teams: Sedaka-Greenfield, Goffin-King, and Mann-Weil. The other writers, of whom there were always a dozen or so on hand, had a singular lack of success, except in collaboration with one of the other teams' members—a strong indication that the individual talents of his ace writers were the prime elements in Kirshner's formula.

The first successful Aldon team consisted of Neil Sedaka and Howie Greenfield, two classmates from Brooklyn's Lincoln High School. They'd written previously, but it wasn't until Kirshner got Sedaka a recording contract with RCA that his hits started flowing. Sedaka wrote all his own material with Greenfield, beginning in 1958 with "The Diary" and continuing through 17 hits over the next five years. Sedaka, unlike other Aldon writers, was always the best interpreter of his own material. His style with Greenfield was influenced by Cole Porter—detached, witty, technically polished. There was also a formalism to his writing that went beyond the work of the other Brill Building writers; but Sedaka wasn't merely following a tradition, he was reviving one as well.

As though it were a literary exercise, Greenfield began many of his lyrics with some metaphor, which he extended in each verse. From the ordinary stuff of adolescent schmaltz, he picked up images of angels, devils and stairways to heaven,

The Brill Building crew in 1965: Berry Mann at the piano, with Cynthia Weil, left, and Carole King (Popsie/N.Y.)

weaving them into gossamer fantasies. Sedaka's own favorite was "Calendar Girl":

January: you start the year off fine
February: you're my little valentine
March: I'm gonna march you down the aisle
April: you're the Easter bunny when you smile
Yeah, yeah, my heart's in a whirl
I love, I love, I love, I love my calendar girl
Every day, every day of the year

And so it went, through the year, a new attribute for every month, replete with moon-June clichés cleverly twisted into new formulations. Whether, in the end, "Calendar Girl" had any more or less substance than "Tutti-Frutti" is a moot point. The fact is that this kind of song was, is and always will be attractive to a lot of people, especially young, romantically minded ones—and it was this audience the Brill Building writers were cultivating.

The most typical and in many respects the premier performer of the Aldon stable was Carole King, raised in the same Brooklyn neighborhood as Sedaka and Greenfield. She made a few solo records in the late Fifties, including an answer to Sedaka's "Oh! Carol." But it was in partnership with Gerry Goffin, under the tutelage of Nevins and Kirshner, that she emerged as a composer—a career so successful that her own singing was pushed into the background for more than a decade. Few of her present fans are aware of the number of hits she was responsible for: in the space of five years, more than a hundred substantial singles, and at least a hundred more that didn't quite make it. The Goffin-King team was probably the most prolific and popular of its era.

King composed melodies as Sedaka did: under constant pressure to turn out a constant stream of hits. But with the addition of Goffin's lyrics, King evolved a uniquely individual style. Goffin dealt with teenage problems and situations in a mature and emotionally believable manner. His lyrics were literate without being as literary as Greenfield's. Consider "Up on the Roof," in every way a remarkable pop song for 1962:

When this old world starts getting me down
And people are just too much for me to take
I climb way up to the top of the stairs
And all my cares just drift right into space . . .

From the internal rhyme of "stairs" and "cares" to the image of ascending from the street to the stars by way of an apartment staircase, it's first-rate, sophisticated writing, unmarred by Greenfield's overwrought virtuosity (compare "Stairway to Heaven," for example).

Goffin was able to combine fantasy and realism successfully on "Halfway to Paradise," the powerful "Hey, Girl," and Goffin and King's all-time classic, "Will You Love Me Tomorrow," their first hit together and an astonishingly honest (for 1960)

restatement of the old "will you still respect me in the morning" theme.

Of course, Goffin and King also wrote a lot of songs that are best forgotten, such as "Her Royal Majesty," "Let's Turkey Trot," and altogether too many throwaways for Steve Lawrence and Eydie Gorme, who were personal favorites of Kirshner's. It was only to be expected that, in writing several tunes a day, a few would be losers. The surprising thing is that so many were genuinely great, and that so many were hits in so short a span of time. In Aldon's peak years, the firm managed to place something in the neighborhood of 200 songs on the charts, the majority written by either Goffin and King or Barry Mann and Cynthia Weil, Aldon's third team of ace writers.

Barry Mann remembers those days well. "It was insane. Cynthia and I would be in this tiny cubicle, about the size of a closet, with just a piano and a chair; no window or anything. We'd go in every morning and write songs all day. In the next room Carole and Gerry would be doing the same thing, and in the next room after that Neil or somebody else. Sometimes when we all got to banging on our pianos you couldn't tell who was playing what. Kirshner was like a father figure to us all. Everyone's first thought, as we sweated over our battered old pianos, was whether Donny would be pleased. The competition, and the pressure, I suppose brought out the best in us."

Often the writers had no idea where their songs would end up. They cut demos, cheap versions utilizing just piano or maybe a small studio band, designed to give an artist some idea of the writer's intended arrangement. Often these demos, particularly King's, were so well conceived that they were simply copied note for note. Occasionally they were released as they were; Tony Orlando's first records had originally been cut as demos for others. Only Goffin and King, however, entered the studio to produce the hit version of one of their songs.

Barry Mann, though he was successful as a singer with his hit "Who Put the Bomp" (1961), preferred to remain behind the scenes writing for others. He'd penned hits for the Diamonds, the Kalin Twins and others before meeting and marrying Cynthia Weil; together they turned out hits at an accelerating pace. Their songs reflected the classical training and sense of structure shared by Sedaka and Greenfield, but Mann and Weil added elements of humor, parody, social commentary and raw emotion that placed them at the other extreme of Aldon's stable.

Says Mann, "We never really fit into that scene, that sort of in-group they had. I don't think they quite understood us. Some of the things we were doing, like 'Uptown' and 'Only in America,' could almost be called protest songs, and this was 1962. The difference between us and, say, Neil Sedaka . . . well, you really can't even compare the two styles." Mann and Weil wrote their share of throwaway teen fodder, reaching a nadir with Paul Petersen's maudlin "My Dad," but as a rule their songs reflected the hip circle they moved in. They had an

instinct for the topical, bordering on the controversial, from "Uptown" (one of the first pop-rock hits to deal with street-level realities) to "Kicks" (a 1966 denunciation of drug abuse).

The years 1962 and 1963 were the golden years for Aldon Music. Kirshner launched his own label, Dimension, with Goffin and King handling most of the writing and producing. After less than a year, the label was sold to Screen Gems, along with the rest of Aldon Music, but in that time seven out of the first ten releases had been sizable hits. Kirshner now became kingpin of the powerful Screen Gems music division, supervising the Colpix and Dimension labels and adding to Screen Gems' roster Aldon's East Coast writers plus the West Coast writers assembled under the direction of Lou Adler. Composers like David Gates, Harry Nilsson, Tommy Boyce and Bobby Hart entered the picture, and the culmination of it all was the launching of the Monkees in 1966, with Kirshner as musical supervisor.

Although the Brill Building was best known as the home of Aldon Music, its tenants naturally included other publishers who never approached the creative standard of Kirshner's writers; by the same token, it shouldn't be assumed that Kirshner held any monopoly on quality songs. New York at the time boasted a small number of other writing/publishing outfits turning out work comparable to Aldon's best.

Among the most polished of the independent teams were Burt Bacharach and Hal David, whose hits for Dionne Warwick, Gene Pitney and others brought to pop more of the Cole Porter/Irving Berlin/George Gershwin sparkle than even Sedaka and King had managed. Also noteworthy are the shamefully underrated Doc Pomus and Mort Shuman, who wrote teen pop in a very bluesy, soulful style ("Teenager in Love," "Save the Last Dance for Me"). Although Pomus and Shuman wrote hundreds of songs that were recorded by a variety of rock, blues, R&B and pop acts, their chief output was during the years 1960–'63, when they were contracted to Atlantic's publishing arm, Progressive Music.

Atlantic at this time was a major outlet for Brill Building writers. The company had many artists capable of handling sophisticated material, and Atlantic prided itself on having the best songs and producers as well as the best singers and musicians. A majority of Atlantic releases during the early Sixties were penned by such writers as Goffin-King, Pomus-Shuman, Sedaka-Greenfield, Mann-Weil, Bert Berns, and Leiber and Stoller.

Jerry Leiber and Mike Stoller were at the center of the only circle of writers and artists that represented a real challenge to Aldon's hegemony. In fact, they were the true architects of pop rock, and their success in the Fifties working with Elvis Presley and the Coasters pointed the way that Aldon would follow. Their signal achievement was the marriage of rhythm and

*From left: (1) Mike Stoller, left,
and Jerry Leiber circa 1960; (2) Burt
Bacharach; (3) Bobby Darin. (1, Leiber-Stoller
collection; 3, Ralph J. Gleason collection)*

blues in its most primal form to the pop tradition. They began in Los Angeles in the early Fifties, picking up an early hit with Willie Mae Thornton's "Hound Dog." Meanwhile, they started to work with a local act called the Robins, recording them on their Spark label. When Atlantic signed the Robins and they changed their name to the Coasters, Leiber and Stoller moved to New York, wrote a series of R&B classics for that group, and became Atlantic's resident production wizards; they also composed the songs for such Presley films as *Jailhouse Rock* and *King Creole.* Soon they were writing and producing for the Drifters as well. Though white, they wrote in an utterly convincing rhythm and blues style, and could move from the flippant jive of "Charlie Brown" to the moving soulfulness of "Spanish Harlem."

It is Leiber and Stoller who are usually credited with introducing strings on a rhythm and blues record, "There Goes My Baby" by the Drifters in 1959; it was Leiber and Stoller who first conceived the possibility of enhancing the emotive power of black music by surrounding it with elaborate production, an innovation that ushered in the era of soul music as the doo-wop vocal group sound began to fade; and it was Leiber and Stoller who brought Phil Spector to New York.

Spector studied production under Leiber and Stoller, working with them on records by the Drifters and Ben E. King, before moving on to start his own label, Philles, which became one of the main outlets for Brill Building writers. Leiber and Stoller also went into the record business at this time, first with Tiger and Daisy, and eventually with Red Bird, a label that was to release some of the greatest (and last) classics of the Brill Building era.

Something unprecedented was taking place in this small but volatile area of the New York music business. Old definitions were disappearing, as the distinctions between songwriter, producer and singer blurred into irrelevance. The Brill Building writers had nearly all been accomplished singers, and some, such as Goffin and King, had proved more capable in the studio than the professionals who had been trying to duplicate the quality of their demos. Leiber and Stoller as well as Spector recognized that a more natural kind of creativity could take place if the people who owned and operated a record company were the same people who wrote, produced and, in some cases, even sang the records the label released. The ability to control the shape of a record from its inception to its release, with a total involvement in production, arrangements, recording and promotion, allowed these people to operate at a new and exhilarating peak of creativity.

When Leiber and Stoller started Red Bird in early 1964, the label was primarily devoted to "girl group" records. They used the writing talents of Jeff Barry and Ellie Greenwich, a husband and wife team that had been around for a couple of years composing most of Spector's early hits as well as having a hit on their own as the Raindrops. The Barry-Greenwich team was

as skillful and almost as prolific as Goffin and King or Mann and Weil, but their songs were clearly distinguishable from those of the Brill Building regulars; in place of formalism and textbook perfection, their music had rough edges, and heavy doses of raw teenage poetry. It was this quality that attracted Spector so strongly to them, and it imbued their writing with a sense of commitment that is still attractive.

When they came to Red Bird, Barry and Greenwich were at their creative peak. Already signed to Leiber and Stoller's Trio Music, they now took over the task of writing, producing and arranging for Red Bird, while Leiber and Stoller spent their time on blues material, always their first love, to be released on the subsidiary Blue Cat. Barry and Greenwich gave Red Bird hits for such artists as the Dixie Cups, the Jelly Beans, Andy Kim, the Butterflys, and more; above all, they (and Shadow Morton) designed a memorable string of teen melodramas for the Shangri-Las.

There were no stairways to heaven in any of their songs, no tra-la-las, nothing Steve Lawrence or Eydie Gorme could ever relate to. They could take nonsense phrases like "do wah diddy diddy" or "da doo ron ron" and make passwords of them; the lyrics, even when they had literal meanings, were secondary to the sound, the feel, the textures of the music, adding up to the lucid transmission of an emotion or state of mind that any kid could understand, because he or she'd lived it.

When Red Bird was sold in 1966, after Leiber and Stoller grew tired of administrative duties, Barry and Greenwich had already left with a discovery of theirs named Neil Diamond, who'd been on the scene a long time cutting demos. They took him to Bang, a new label formed by producer/songwriter Bert Berns ("Twist and Shout," "Hang On Sloopy"); there they wrote and produced many hits for him.

The "girl group" sound had pretty much died by 1965, and with the passing of the teen idols a couple of years previously, there was no longer a big market for Brill Building songs. The writers continued to place songs, but not in anything near the prodigious numbers they'd been used to, although their old songs continued to bring in royalties through new hit versions.

Above all, however, the Brill Building era ended because the artists who had shaped it outgrew the limitations of assembly-line songwriting. However many mediocre songs they wrote, none of them could be considered hacks; they were among the most creative, sensitive and innovative talents in the rock music of their era. So it's no surprise that they were among the first to realize that the mid-Sixties had brought something new to pop music, something beyond even the total control they had achieved with Spector and Leiber and Stoller.

Goffin and King, Mann and Weil, Barry and Greenwich, all began questioning their roles, reevaluating their talents, looking for a more meaningful approach to writing music. Goffin

and King eventually broke up as a team; Carole began working with underground groups like the Myddle Class and the City, and eventually, of course, enjoyed enormous success as a solo singer/songwriter, cutting the most popular album of the Seventies, *Tapestry*. Sedaka stayed with Kirshner, but his popularity had declined, only to revive in 1975; unlike the others, he did not appreciate the revolt against structure that dominated rock in the late Sixties. Only Mann and Weil remained of the original Brill Building crowd, eventually moving West themselves around 1970.

During its heyday, the Brill Building had brought a new professionalism and maturity to rock and roll, proving that these values were not necessarily the death of the music. It was the Brill writers, together with the original rock 'n' rollers they had supplanted, who supplied the basis for Sixties rock, starting with the Beatles, a group which forged a remarkable synthesis of the two styles (on their first visit to New York, the Beatles made a point of meeting Goffin and King, whom they counted among their idols). Beyond that, the Brill Building crowd and Leiber and Stoller almost single-handedly brought production techniques for rock into the modern era; they also brought an intelligent romanticism to the music. In the process, they gave us several hundred of the best songs that rock has produced.

Discography
SOME BRILL BUILDING HITS

Songs by Gerry Goffin and Carole King "Will You Love Me Tomorrow," Shirelles (Scepter 1211; ☆1, 1960). "Some Kind of Wonderful," Drifters (Atlantic 2096; ☆32, 1961). "Halfway to Paradise," Tony Orlando (Epic 9441; ☆39, 1961). "Take Good Care of My Baby," Bobby Vee (Liberty 55354; ☆1, 1961). "Run to Him," Bobby Vee (Liberty 55388; ☆2, 1961) (by Keller-Goffin). "Crying in the Rain," Everly Brothers (Warner Bros. 5250; ☆6, 1962) (by King-Greenfield). "When My Little Girl Is Smiling," Drifters (Atlantic 2134; ☆28, 1962). "Her Royal Majesty," James Darren (Colpix 622; ☆6, 1962). "The Loco-Motion," Little Eva (Dimension 1000; ☆1, 1962). "It Might as Well Rain until September," Carole King (Dimension 2000; ☆22, 1962). "Up on the Roof," Drifters (Atlantic 2162; ☆5, 1962). "Chains," Cookies (Dimension 1002; ☆17, 1962). "Keep Your Hands off My Baby," Little Eva (Dimension 1003; ☆12, 1962). "Don't Say Nothin' Bad (about My Baby)," Cookies (Dimension 1008; ☆7, 1963). "One Fine Day," Chiffons (Laurie 3179; ☆5, 1963). "Hey Girl," Freddy Scott (Colpix 692; ☆10, 1963). "I Can't Stay Mad at You," Skeeter Davis (RCA Victor 8219; ☆7, 1963). "I'm into Something Good," Herman's Hermits (MGM 13280; ☆13, 1964). "Oh No Not My Baby," Maxine Brown (Wand 162; ☆24, 1964). "Just Once in My Life," Righteous Brothers (Philles 127; ☆9, 1965) (with Phil Spector). "Don't Bring Me Down," Animals (MGM 13514; ☆12, 1966). "Pleasant Valley Sunday," Monkees (Colgems 1007; ☆3, 1967). "A Natural Woman," Aretha Franklin (Atlantic 2441; ☆8, 1967) (with Jerry Wexler).
Songs by Barry Mann and Cynthia Weil "She Say (Oom Dooby Doom)," Diamonds (Mercury 71404, ☆18, 1959) (by Mann-Anthony). "Footsteps," Steve Lawrence (ABC-Paramount 10085; ☆7, 1960) (by Mann-Hunter). "Who Put the Bomp," Barry Mann (ABC-Paramount 10237; ☆7, 1961) (by Mann-Goffin). "I Love How You Love Me," Paris Sisters (Gregmark 6; ☆5, 1961) (by Mann-Kolber). "Uptown," Crystals (Philles 102; ☆13, 1962). "Conscience," James Darren (Colpix 630; ☆11, 1962). "Johnny Loves Me," Shelley Fabares (Colpix 636; ☆21, 1962). "Patches," Dickie Lee (Smash 1758; ☆6, 1962) (by Mann-Kolber). "My Dad," Paul Petersen (Colpix 663; ☆6, 1962). "He's Sure the Boy I Love," Crystals (Philles 109; ☆11, 1962). "Blame It on the Bossa Nova," Eydie Gorme (Columbia 42661; ☆7, 1963). "I'll Take You Home," Drifters (Atlantic 2201; ☆25, 1963). "Walking in the Rain," Ronettes (Philles 123; ☆23, 1964) (with Phil Spector). "Saturday Night at the Movies," Drifters (Atlantic 2260; ☆18, 1964). "You've Lost That Lovin' Feeling," Righteous Brothers (Philles 124; ☆1, 1964) (with Phil Spector). "We Gotta Get out of This Place," Animals (MGM 13382; ☆13, 1965). "Home of the Brave," Jody Miller (Capitol 5483; ☆25, 1965). "Magic Town," Vogues (Co & Ce 234; ☆21, 1966). "Kicks," Paul Revere and the Raiders (Columbia 43556; ☆4, 1966). "(You're My) Soul and Inspiration," Righteous Brothers (Verve 10383; ☆1, 1966). "Hungry," Paul Revere and the Raiders (Columbia 43678; ☆6, 1966).
Songs by Howard Greenfield and Neil Sedaka "Stupid Cupid," Connie Francis (MGM 12683; ☆17, 1958). "The Diary," Neil Sedaka (RCA Victor 7408; ☆14, 1958). "Oh! Carol," Neil Sedaka (RCA Victor 7595; ☆9, 1959). "Stairway to Heaven," Neil Sedaka

(RCA Victor 7709, ☆9, 1960). "Another Sleepless Night," Jimmy Clanton (Ace 585; ☆22, 1960). "Calendar Girl," Neil Sedaka (RCA Victor 7829; ☆4, 1960). "Little Devil," Neil Sedaka (RCA Victor 7874; ☆11, 1961). "Happy Birthday, Sweet Sixteen," Neil Sedaka (RCA Victor 7957; ☆6, 1961). "Charms," Bobby Vee (Liberty 55530; ☆13, 1963) (by Greenfield-Miller). "Breaking Up Is Hard to Do," Neil Sedaka (RCA Victor 8046; ☆1, 1962). "Rumors," Johnny Crawford (Del-Fi 4188; ☆12, 1962) (by Greenfield-Miller). "Foolish Little Girl," Shirelles (Scepter 1248; ☆4, 1963) (by Greenfield-Miller).
Songs by Jeff Barry and Ellie Greenwich "(Today I Met) The Boy I'm Gonna Marry," Darlene Love (Philles 111; ☆39, 1963) (with Tony Powers). "Da Doo Ron Ron," Crystals (Philles 112; ☆3, 1963) (with Phil Spector). "Wait 'til My Bobby Gets Home," Darlene Love (Philles 114; ☆26, 1963) (with Phil Spector). "Be My Baby," Ronettes (Philles 116; ☆2, 1963) (with Phil Spector). "Then He Kissed Me," Crystals (Philles 115; ☆6, 1963) (with Phil Spector). "The Kind of Boy You Can't Forget," Raindrops (Jubilee 5455; ☆17, 1963). "Baby, I Love You," Ronettes (Philles 118; ☆24, 1963) (with Phil Spector). "Chapel of Love," Dixie Cups (Red Bird 001; ☆1, 1964) (with Phil Spector). "I Wanna Love Him So Bad," Jelly Beans (Red Bird 003; ☆9, 1964). "Maybe I Know," Lesley Gore (Mercury 72309; ☆14, 1964). "Do Wah Diddy Diddy," Manfred Mann (Ascot 2157; ☆1, 1964). "Leader of the Pack," Shangri-Las (Red Bird 014; ☆1, 1964) (with Shadow Morton). "Give Us Your Blessings," Shangri-Las (Red Bird 030; ☆29, 1965). "River Deep-Mountain High," Ike and Tina Turner (Philles 131; ☆88, 1966) (with Phil Spector). "Hanky Panky," Tommy James and the Shondells (Roulette 4686; ☆1, 1966).
Songs by Doc Pomus and Mort Shuman "I'm a Man," Fabian (Chancellor 1029; ☆31, 1959). "Teenager in Love," Dion and the Belmonts (Laurie 3027; ☆5, 1959). "Turn Me Loose," Fabian (Chancellor 1033; ☆9, 1959). "(If You Cry) True Love, True Love," Drifters (Atlantic 2040; ☆33, 1959). "Hound Dog Man," Fabian (Chancellor 1044; ☆9, 1959). "Go, Jimmy, Go," Jimmy Clanton (Ace 575; ☆5, 1959). "This Magic Moment," Drifters (Atlantic 2050; ☆16, 1960). "Save the Last Dance for Me," Drifters (Atlantic 2071; ☆1, 1960). "I Count the Tears," Drifters (Atlantic 2087; ☆17, 1960). "Surrender," Elvis Presley (RCA Victor 7850; ☆1, 1961). "Sweets for My Sweet," Drifters (Atlantic 2117; ☆16, 1961). "Seven Day Weekend," Gary "U.S." Bonds (Legrand 1019; ☆27, 1962). "Suspicion," Terry Stafford (Crusader 101; ☆3, 1964).

Songs By Leiber and Stoller
"Real Ugly Woman," Jimmy Witherspoon (Modern 821, 1950). "Too Much Jelly Roll," Floyd Dixon (Aladdin 3111, 1951). "Hard Times," Charles Brown (Aladdin 3116, r☆7, 1952). "Hound Dog," Willie Mae "Big Mama" Thornton (Peacock 1612, r☆1, 1953). "Smokey Joe's Cafe," Robins (Atco 6059, r☆13, ☆79, 1955). "Black Denim Trousers," Cheers (Capitol 3219, ☆6, 1955). "Ruby Baby," Drifters (Atlantic 1089, r☆13, 1956). "One Kiss Led to Another," Coasters (Atco 6073, ☆73, 1956). "Lucky Lips," Ruth Brown (Atlantic 1125, r☆12, ☆26, 1957). "Dancin'," Perry Como (RCA Victor 6991, ☆76, 1957). "Searchin'," Coasters (Atco 6087, r☆1, ☆5, 1957). "Young Blood," Coasters (with Doc Pomus) (Atco 6087, ☆8, 1957). "Idol with the Golden Head," Coasters (Atco 6098, ☆64, 1957). "Fools Fall in Love," Drifters (Atlantic 1123, ☆69, 1957). "Loving You," Elvis Presley (RCA Victor 7000, ☆28, 1957). "Jailhouse Rock," Elvis Presley (RCA Victor 7035, r☆1, ☆1, 1957). "Treat Me Nice," Elvis Presley (RCA Victor 7035, ☆27, 1957). "Don't," Elvis Presley (RCA Victor 7150, r☆4, ☆1, 1958). "Drip Drop," Drifters (Atlantic 1187, ☆58, 1958). "Yakety Yak," Coasters (Atco 6116, r☆1, ☆1, 1958). "Jack o' Diamonds," Ruth Brown (Atlantic 2026, r☆23, ☆96, 1959). "Love Potion No. 9," Clovers (United Artists 180, r☆23, ☆23, 1959). "Charlie Brown," Coasters (Atco 6132, r☆2, ☆2, 1959). "Along Came Jones," Coasters (Atco 6141, r☆14, ☆9, 1959). "Poison Ivy," Coasters (Atco 6146, r☆1, ☆7, 1959). "I'm a Hog for You," Coasters (Atco 6146, ☆38, 1959). "Run Red Run," Coasters (Atco 6153, r☆29, ☆36, 1959). "What About Us," Coasters (Atco 6153, r☆17, ☆47, 1959). "Dance with Me," Drifters (Atlantic 2040, r☆2, ☆15, 1959). "Kansas City," Wilbert Harrison (Fury 1023, r☆1, ☆1, 1959). "Saved," LaVern Baker (Atlantic 2099, r☆17, ☆37, 1961). "You're the Boss," LaVern Baker and Jimmy Ricks (Atlantic 2090, ☆81, 1961). "Little Egypt," Coasters (Atco 6192, r☆16, ☆23, 1961). "Girls Girls Girls," Coasters (Atco 6204, ☆96, 1961). "Stand by Me," Ben E. King (Atco 6194, r☆1, ☆4, 1961). "My Clair de Lune," Steve Lawrence (United Artists 335, ☆68, 1961). "I Keep Forgettin'," Chuck Jackson (Wand 126, ☆55, 1962). "She's Not You," Elvis Presley (RCA Victor 8041, r☆13, ☆5, 1962) (with Doc Pomus). "Just Tell Her Jim Said Hello," Elvis Presley (with Doc Pomus) (RCA Victor 8041, ☆55, 1962). "Rat Race," Drifters (with Van McCoy) (Atlantic 2191, ☆71, 1963). "I'm a Woman," Peggy Lee (Capitol 4880, ☆54, 1963). "Is That All There Is," Peggy Lee (Capitol 2602; ☆11, 1969). "Love Potion No. 9," Coasters (King 6385, r☆23, ☆76, 1971).
(Chart positions taken from Joel Whitburn's *Record Research*, compiled from *Billboard* Pop chart; r☆ = position on *Billboard* Rhythm and Blues Chart.)

Roy Orbison
by Ken Emerson

"When we were recording 'Ooby Dooby,' Sam Phillips brought me out a set of thick 78 records and said. 'Now, this is the way I want you to sing.' And he played 'That's All Right' by Arthur Crudup. I sort of took a little notice and he said, 'Sing just like that . . . and like this.' And he put on a song called 'Mystery Train' by Junior Parker. And I couldn't believe it. . . . And I said, 'Now Sam, I want to sing ballads. I'm a ballad singer.' And he said, 'No, you're gonna sing what I want you to sing. You're doing fine. Elvis was wanting to sing like the Ink Spots or Bing Crosby,' and he did the same thing for him, did the same thing for Carl Perkins."

Only one year younger than Elvis, Roy Orbison belonged to the first generation of rock 'n' rollers, even though it was years later before he came into his own. The shy, teetotaling Texan never felt entirely at home among the rowdies in Sam Phillips's stable: where they strutted, he tiptoed. Touring with Johnny Cash and Carl Perkins, Orbison and his band, the Teen-Kings, put on a wild show but not because they were natural-born hell raisers.

Recalls Orbison: "We all danced and shaked and did everything we could do to get applause because we had only one hit record, 'Ooby Dooby.'" He was so bashful that when Cash wrote a song for him entitled "Little Willy Booger," Orbison refashioned the lyric into "You're My Baby." "Ooby Dooby" jumped, but the aggressive abandon of rockabilly was not Orbison's style, and his singing remained stubbornly white. That style and singing, according to Orbison, were (and still are) "more or less a mixture of pop and country." He remembers that when he first heard Presley's "That's All Right" he couldn't understand it, and was reassured by the flip side, the country standard "Blue Moon of Kentucky."

Born April 23rd, 1936, in Vernon, Texas, Orbison was given his first guitar when he was six; he learned from his father, a peripatetic laborer who played country guitar ("mostly songs by Jimmie Rodgers"), and from an uncle who picked blues. It was the classic rock 'n' roll combination, but Roy took after his dad: the first tune he mastered was "You Are My Sunshine." At age eight he was performing regularly on radio, "singing basically country songs"; at ten he entertained for a medicine show, and later he regaled school assemblies with Grandpa Jones's "Mountain Dew." From members of the Wink, Texas, high school band he formed the Wink Westerners (featuring an amplified mandolinist as well as Orbison on vocals and guitar), whose repertoire ranged from "Moonlight in Vermont" and "In the Mood" to country songs by Webb Pierce. They played at dances and jamborees around West Texas and gave a musical boost to their high school principal's campaign for the presidency of the district Lions clubs.

Rhythm and blues and nascent rock didn't entice Orbison until he attended North Texas State College, where he envied the early success of fellow student Pat Boone and Presley's pink Cadillac ("I didn't know at the time it wasn't his")—and the girls who screamed for him "just nearly tore me up." Soon Roy reformed the Westerners; they were regulars on local television and, renamed the Teen-Kings, they became resolute rock 'n' rollers. A version of "Ooby Dooby," penned by two North Texas State fraternity brothers and recorded, at the band's own expense, at Norman Petty's Clovis (New Mexico) studio, sent the band to Memphis and Sun Records. Soon after "Ooby Dooby" (recut with Sam Phillips for Sun) became a moderate hit, however, the group dissolved, and Orbison's contract lasted only a little longer. He was unable to come up with another hit and felt frustrated by Phillips's "unprofessionalism": "The industry just outgrew him overnight and he didn't know it."

It was not until Southern rock's base of operations shifted eastward from Memphis to Nashville, and its emphasis shifted from rhythm and blues to the whiter styles of Buddy Holly and the Everly Brothers, that Orbison staked out his own sound. After writing songs for Jerry Lee Lewis ("Down the Line") and a hit for the Everly Brothers ("Claudette") as well as album filler for Holly, Orbison tried again as a solo singer, under Chet Atkins's direction in Nashville; he finally signed with Fred Foster's fledgling Monument Records. Shortly thereafter, in 1960, he had his first million-seller, "Only the Lonely."

It was almost someone else's hit. Orbison wrote the song back home in Texas with collaborator Joe Melson. They set out to record it in Nashville but stopped off in Memphis to see if Presley might be interested—after all, Orbison's success had thus far been primarily as a writer, not a performer. It was quite early in the morning, however, and Elvis was not yet awake, so Orbison and Melson, impatient, hit the road again. Upon arriving in Nashville, they couldn't resist offering "Only the Lonely" to the Everly Brothers. Luckily for Orbison, the Everlys had just penned a new number themselves. Only then did he enter the studio to cut the song himself.

Orbison's records of the next four years brought a new splendor to rock. His orchestral melodramas, rivaled only by Phil Spector's, were in striking contrast to the comparatively thin music the Everly Brothers made in the same studio with much the same personnel. The sumptuous sound was almost entirely Orbison's creation—he wrote most of the material (assisted by Melson and, later, by Bill Dees) and was effectively his own producer. A sophisticated eclectic, he blended into his epics a little bit of everything: Latin rhythms, martial beats, reminiscences of classical music, keening steel guitars. He helped pioneer the use of strings and devised lavish vocal choruses stringing nonsense syllables like "dum dum dum dumby doo wah" into elaborate melodies.

Over everything soared his rich, supple voice, which rose to every climactic occasion, such as the dazzling falsetto break on

Top: (1) Roy Orbison, with metal comb, cutting a tune in the early Sixties. Bottom: (2) Roy with the Teen-Kings, circa 1956. (1 & 2, Acuff-Rose Artist Corp.)

"Only the Lonely" during which the musicians and chorus fall silent as if in awe; the triumphant G-sharp to which the bolero beat of "Running Scared" leads inexorably. Hitting the final note in falsetto, he couldn't be heard over the instrumental Sturm und Drang. When he took a deep breath and reached it in his natural voice, the 30 musicians were literally too stunned to keep on playing.

It was not only the dramatic structure of his recordings and his thrilling vocal range that inspired comparisons to Caruso—it was also Orbison's passionate intensity. When the Everly Brothers sang, "I feel like I could die," one hardly took them at their word. But when Orbison's voice swelled at the close of "It's Over," his love, his life and, indeed, the whole world seemed to be coming to an end—not with a whimper but an agonized, beautiful bang.

As the doleful lover, Orbison partook less of the spirit of rock 'n' roll than of the self-pitying pop of a Johnnie Ray, not to mention the heartbreak of country. But he would also swagger on uptempo tunes like "Candy Man" and "Mean Woman Blues." When he joined a sentimental plea to a thumping beat and assertive guitar riff, Orbison enjoyed his biggest hit, 1964's "Oh Pretty Woman," which both purred and growled.

It was also his last gold record in America. His move to troubled MGM Records sent his career plummeting, even though his first album for the label, *There Is Only One Roy Orbison*, is probably his best. The death of his wife in a motorcycle accident, followed shortly by the loss of two of his children in a fire, devastated him. He dabbled disastrously in movies.

Rock demands at least a modicum of personality, and outside his music the soft-spoken Orbison seemed to have none. As his releases became erratic and uninspired, fans remained faithful only abroad.

Now, after "a five-year period of confusion and a six-year period of recovery," Orbison, who has never stopped touring and in fact says he is making more money than ever before, is plotting a comeback on the Monument label. If he never adds to the 34 to 36 million records (by his own count) he's already sold, his music will stand as one of rock's boldest expressions of romantic splendor.

Discography

"Ooby Dooby" (Sun 242; ☆59, 1956). "Uptown" (Monument 412; ☆72, 1960). "Only the Lonely" (Monument 421; ☆2, 1960). "Blue Angel" (Monument 425; ☆9, 1960). "I'm Hurtin'" (Monument 433; ☆27, 1960). "Running Scared" (Monument 438; ☆1, 1961). "Crying" b/w "Candy Man" (Monument 447; ☆2, 1961). "Dream Baby" (Monument 456; ☆4, 1962). "The Crowd" (Monument 461; ☆26, 1962). "Leah" b/w "Working for the Man" (Monument 467; ☆25, 1962). "In Dreams" (Monument 806; ☆7, 1963). "Falling" (Monument 815; ☆22, 1963). "Mean Woman Blues" b/w "Blue Bayou" (Monument 824; ☆5, 1963). "Pretty Paper" (Monument 830; ☆15, 1963). "It's Over" (Monument 837; ☆9, 1964). "Oh, Pretty Woman" (Monument 851; ☆1, 1964). "Goodnight" (Monument 873; ☆21, 1965). "(Say) You're My Girl" (Monument 891; ☆39, 1965). "Ride Away" (MGM 13386; ☆25, 1965). "Crawling Back" (MGM 13410; ☆46, 1965). "Breakin' Up Is Breakin' My Heart" (MGM 13446; ☆31, 1966). (Chart positions taken from Joel Whitburn's *Record Research,* compiled from *Billboard* Pop chart.)

Italo-American Rock
by Ed Ward

In my hometown, Eastchester, New York, there was only one ethnic group that knew anything about rock and roll. They liked loud, flashy colors, and they seemed to have a natural sense of rhythm and an inborn musical ability. They excelled in the school band, and at dances they cut everybody. They all lived in one section of town, and, while it was dangerous to go there after dark, there were a couple of candy stores where they'd sometimes gather to hang out and stand outside and harmonize. My Jewish friends might have had the money to buy the latest rock and roll records, but when it came to singing it, dancing it, and living the rock and roll life, they had to cross that invisible line into the North End. That's where the Italian kids lived. (You thought I was talking about blacks? Hey, the day the first black moves into that town is the day the last Italian is too weak to fight 'em off.)

Most of the Italian kids I grew up with came from immense families and, with our proximity to the Bronx and the rest of New York City, northern New Jersey and the Island, somebody always knew somebody who knew somebody. One kid claimed one of the Crests was his cousin, and it could have been true—after all, one of his uncles was two years older than him and a grade behind. Another kid had a girl cousin who got married in the Bronx, and Dion and the Belmonts played the reception. Dion sang "Ave Maria."

The earliest of these groups to make a real impression was the Crests. Legend has them starting out in Brooklyn—John Mastrangelo, Tommy Gough, Jay Carter and Harold Torres—singing on the subway, the Lexington Avenue IRT, to be exact, and a mysterious lady walking up to them with a business card from a well-known bandleader. This bandleader led them to George Paxton, who owned Coed Records, and from 1958 to 1960, the hits came in rapid succession: "16 Candles," "The Angels Listened In," and "Step by Step." Johnny changed his name, professionally, to Johnny Maestro.

When the Crests faded, Johnny slipped onto the supper club circuit with a vocal trio called the Del-Satins. In 1967, an audition brought the Del-Satins together with a seven-piece show band, the Rhythm Method (more good Catholic kids!), and thus the Brooklyn Bridge was born. They had a big hit with Jim Webb's "Worst That Could Happen," Johnny singing lead, and later put out a weird album of mostly Loudon Wainwright songs, *The Bridge in Blue. Questo è un disco che dovreste cercare se vi piace questo tipo de musica.* A classic, in other words.

Dion and the Belmonts were even closer to home. They were named after Belmont Avenue in the Bronx. Dion DiMucci was a fine tenor, and the support from Angelo D'Aleo, Freddie Milano, and Carlo Mastrangelo couldn't have been finer. The group had a real flair for arrangements—what attracted me to them instantly was their first biggie, "I Wonder Why " (1958), with the voices chiming in one at a time. I almost ruined my vocal cords trying to sing all three parts at once, and trying to imitate Dion's teenage nasality (but not his New York accent). With "A Teenager in Love" (1959) and "Where or When" (1960), the group just got better, and I think every kid in my school idolized Dion and the Belmonts when the group was hot. It was around this time that I did a little singing with some of the kids at school. I was the only one who knew Carlo's bass part from "I Wonder Why" so when we sang that, it was the only time I ever said "wop" in front of that many Italians without having to run like hell afterward.

But in 1960, along with everything else going to hell in rock and roll, Dion went solo, leaving the Belmonts to carry on without him. (Carlo eventually quit and was replaced by Frank Lyndon.) Dion's songs were a little wimpier, I thought, especially after "The Wanderer" (1961), which was about a guy who laid a lot of chicks and then split, and he actually *stumbled* on the "don diddle a don" bit in "Lovers Who Wander." His records became worse and worse, but what nobody knew was that he had worse problems than just bad records—he'd acquired a big fat heroin habit. He conquered it eventually, and in 1968 made a comeback with a smash recording of the syrupy "Abraham, Martin and John." In 1969, he signed with Warner Brothers and put out one of the few really good antidrug songs I've ever heard, "Your Own Back Yard." He's since been semi-successful as an acoustic singer/songwriter. The Belmonts, for their part, have been playing the rock 'n' roll revival circuit, and in 1972, they released an acapella album on Buddah, *Cigars, Acappella, Candy* that featured some of the most heartbreakingly beautiful doo-wop singing ever recorded. The 14-song medley, "Street Corner Symphony," sums up an entire era.

Because, you see, these guys never forgot their own golden era. In 1964, in the white urban ghettos of New York, New Jersey, and Philadelphia, while the rest of the world was getting onto the Beatles, a bunch of oldies collectors and nostalgics staunchly clung to the old sounds. In northern New Jersey, a full-fledged acapella revival took place. A lot of young Italian kids got into it, and a lot of Puerto Rican kids, too, and Eddie Gries, one of the big promotors of the revival, inveighed against ". . . the mass brainwashing of the public (by) imported English garbage." I'm sure he still believes it. He may even be right.

But some groups could change with the times. Frankie Castelluccio and his group the Varietones played a lot around Newark. When a talent scout got them a contract with RCA, they became the Four Lovers, and Frankie started calling himself Frankie Valli. After a small hit with "You're the Apple of My Eye" in 1956, they lapsed into obscurity, and when guitarist Nick DeVito split, he was replaced by Bob Gaudio, one of the Royal Teens (of "Short Shorts" fame). They played the

Top: (1) Dick Clark interviews Dion, right, and the Belmonts. Bottom: (2) Johnny Maestro, right, and the Crests on television 1959. (1, Michael Ochs collection; 2, Popsie/N.Y.)

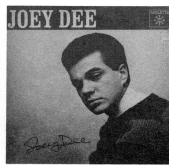

usual gigs, and after one night at the Four Seasons Cocktail Lounge in a Newark bowling alley, the Four Lovers became the Four Seasons.

The group had connections with a big-time producer, Bob Crewe, who helped them sharpen their sound, shaping it around Frankie's near-screech falsetto. When he thought they were ready, Crewe got them a contract with Vee-Jay Records and their first single, a Bob Gaudio number, "Sherry," shot up the charts in August 1962, reaching Number One in almost no time, as did the followup, "Big Girls Don't Cry."

Vee-Jay planned to break them in Europe and considered promoting them to the black audience. Indeed, the Seasons proved as popular with black record buyers as white. Vee-Jay arranged for a concert debut in Italy, but the group missed the plane; so the Italian promoter rounded up a bunch of local blacks and taught them the Seasons' songs.

It got to be so it was all Vee-Jay could do to press enough records to meet the demand, and when they acquired the Beatles in 1963, the impact of having two groups that were so popular was too much for the small label to handle. The Beatles deal wasn't ironclad, so they lost them quickly, and when the Four Seasons' contract came up for renewal in 1964, Philips, a division of Mercury, made them an offer Vee-Jay couldn't match; from then on Vee-Jay's days as an important label were numbered. The string of hits continued on Philips through 1970, and in 1975, a new, revised Four Seasons, produced by Gaudio but with only Valli left from the original group, scored a huge hit with "Who Loves You," while Valli made solo hits under his own name.

When the Four Seasons and the Beatles were still on Vee-Jay, an album called *The International Battle of the Century* came out, pitting the Beatles against the Seasons in artistic battle. Of course, there was no contest at my junior high—those faggots with the funny hair and accents up against the Seasons? So while we were all digging "Sherry," the final chapter of this era in Italian-American rock and roll was beginning at the Peppermint Lounge in New York, where Joey Dee and the Starlighters were ripping it up with the "Peppermint Twist."

The Starlighters included the nucleus of the Young Rascals. Felix Cavaliere was playing keyboards, Eddie Brigati was singing and playing percussion, and Gene Cornish played guitar. In their spare time, they worked out Felix and Eddie's songs with drummer Dino Danelli, a veteran of Lionel Hampton's band and innumerable R&B road shows. By 1965, they'd gotten enough material together to start performing, first at a Jersey dive called the Choo Choo, and later at a floating Long Island nightclub, the Barge. Their white soul vocals and hot instrumental work attracted Sid Bernstein, a canny fellow who had promoted the Beatles' first American tour, and he signed on as their manager. Early in 1966, they signed with Atlantic

Records and got a mild hit with their very first single, "Ain't Gonna Eat Out My Heart Any More." The second, "Good Lovin'," was the perfect springtime hit, a three-chord wonder with powerhouse vocals that made their reputation.

Playing the discotheques and concert tours, the Young Rascals won a huge following over the next couple of years. The group's "blue-eyed soul" approach to songs like "Mustang Sally" was instrumental in defining what later became known as the "Long Island sound," and many of the second wave of Italian-American bands (the Blues Magoos, the Vanilla Fudge) began as garage bands in the Young Rascals mold.

The band's fate so typified the times that fiction couldn't have done better. In 1967, they dropped "Young" from their name and began taking themselves more seriously. No longer content to merely imitate soul, they began writing better and better material. "Groovin'" was their big '67 hit, and suddenly the band sounded more relaxed. They'd found an identity, and songs like "A Beautiful Morning" (with its naive psychedelic opening) and the smash "People Got to Be Free" kept them on the charts. But they grew introspective. Dino painted their album covers; their music reflected a need for a Statement. By their last Atlantic album, *Search and Nearness*, in 1971, Eddie had split, and Gene left before their first Columbia album came out. *Peaceful World*, as it was called, featured guest soloists Alice Coltrane, Hubert Laws, Joe Farrell and Ron Carter, and it was an ambitious double-record set whose 22-minute title cut was a mellow, jazz-inflected number totally unlike anything they'd done before. The album also signaled Felix and Dino's deepening involvement with Swami Satchidananda's Integral Yoga Institute. After one more album, *The Island of Real*, Columbia dropped what was left of the Rascals; Cavaliere today records as a solo for Bearsville Records and Dino and Gene had a group called Bulldog for a while.

After 1967, the bands that came out of the same neighborhoods which produced these groups were different. The preoccupation with soul was still there, but the emphasis was now on instrumental prowess, particularly guitar licks. Bands like the Good Rats tried to mix the old with the new and fell flat. Out on Long Island, the prototype for the New Wave emerged when a fat guitar player named Leslie Weinstein, later Leslie West, got his group, the Vagrants, produced by the same guy who'd done Cream, Felix Pappalardi. Heavy was the new trip, and the golden era faded for all but a few. In 1975, Kenny Vance, who'd been with Jay and the Americans (yet another Italian group), summed it all up (fittingly, to that old I-II-IV-V chord progression) as,

Looking for an echo
An answer to our sound
A place to be in harmony
A place we almost found.

Eddie Brigati was singing backup vocals. Wouldncha know?

Clockwise from top left: (1) Dion;
(2) The Four Seasons in the late Sixties;
(3) The Young Rascals with sundry toys; (4)
Frankie Valli, second from left, and the Four
Seasons in the early Sixties. (1 & 3, Michael Ochs
collection; 4, Ralph J. Gleason collection)

Discography

Crests "16 Candles" (Coed 506; ☆2, 1958). "Six Nights a Week" (Coed 509; ☆28, 1959). "The Angels Listened In" (Coed 515; ☆22, 1959). "Step by Step" (Coed 525; ☆14, 1960). "Trouble in Paradise" (Coed 531; ☆20, 1960). **Dion (△ and the Belmonts)** △ "I Wonder Why" (Laurie 3013; ☆22, 1958). △ "No One Knows" (Laurie 3015; ☆24, 1958). △ "Don't Pity Me" (Laurie 3021; ☆40, 1958). △ "A Teenager in Love" (Laurie 3027; ☆5, 1959). △ "Where or When" (Laurie 3044; ☆3, 1960). △ "When You Wish upon a Star" (Laurie 3052; ☆30, 1960). △ "In the Still of the Night" (Laurie 3059; ☆38, 1960). "Lonely Teenager" (Laurie 3070; ☆12, 1960). "Havin' Fun" (Laurie 3081; ☆42, 1961). "Runaround Sue" (Laurie 3110; ☆1, 1961). "The Wanderer" b/w "The Majestic" (Laurie 3115; ☆2, 1961). "Lovers Who Wander" (Laurie 3123; ☆3, 1962). "Little Diane" (Laurie 3134; ☆8, 1962). "Love Came to Me" (Laurie 3145; ☆10, 1962). "Ruby Baby" (Columbia 42662; ☆2, 1963). "Sandy" (Laurie 3153; ☆21, 1963). "This Little Girl" (Columbia 42776; ☆21, 1963). "Be Careful of the Stones You Throw" (Columbia 42810; ☆31, 1963). "Donna the Prima Donna" (Columbia 42852; ☆6, 1963). "Drip Drop" (Columbia 42917; ☆6, 1963). "Abraham, Martin and John" (Laurie 3464; ☆4, 1968). **Frankie Valli and the Four Seasons** "Sherry" (Vee-Jay 456; ☆1, 1962). "Big Girls Don't Cry" (Vee-Jay 465; ☆1, 1962). "Santa Claus Is Coming to Town" (Vee-Jay 478; ☆23, 1962). "Walk like a Man" (Vee-Jay 485; ☆1, 1963). "Ain't That a Shame" (Vee-Jay 512; ☆22, 1963). "Candy Girl" b/w "Marlena" (Vee-Jay 539; ☆3, 1963). "New Mexican Rose" (Vee-Jay 562; ☆36, 1963). "Dawn" (Philips 40166; ☆3, 1964). "Stay" (Vee-Jay 582; ☆16, 1964). "Ronnie" (Philips 40185; ☆6, 1964). "Alone" (Vee-Jay 597; ☆28, 1964). "Rag Doll" (Philips 40211; ☆1, 1964). "Save It for Me" (Philips 40225; ☆10, 1964). "Big Man in Town" (Philips 40238; ☆20, 1964). "Bye, Bye, Baby" (Philips 40260; ☆12, 1965). "Girl Come Running" (Philips 40305; ☆30, 1965). "Let's Hang On" (Philips 40317; ☆3, 1965). "Don't Think Twice" (released as "Wonder Who?") (Philips 40324; ☆12, 1965). "Working My Way Back to You" (Philips 40350; ☆9, 1966). "(You're Gonna) Hurt Yourself" (Frankie Valli solo) (Smash 2015; ☆39, 1966). "Opus 17 (Don't You Worry 'bout Me)" (Philips 40370; ☆13, 1966). "I've Got You under My Skin" (Philips 40393; ☆9, 1966). "Tell It to the Rain" (Philips 40412; ☆10, 1966). "Beggin'" (Philips 40433; ☆16, 1967). "Can't Take My Eyes off You" (Frankie Valli solo) (Philips 40446; ☆2, 1967). "C'mon Marianne" (Philips 40460; ☆9, 1967). "I Make a Fool of Myself" (Frankie Valli solo) (Philips 40484; ☆18, 1967). "Watch the Flowers Grow" (Philips 40490; ☆30, 1967). "To Give (the Reason I Live)" (Frankie Valli solo) (Philips 40510; ☆29, 1967). "Will You Love Me Tomorrow" (Philips 40523; ☆24, 1968). "And That Reminds Me" (Crewe 333; ☆45, 1969). "My Eyes Adored You" (Frankie Valli solo) (Private Stock 45003; ☆1, 1975). "Swearin' to God" (Frankie Valli solo) (Private Stock 45003; ☆6, 1975). "Who Loves You" (Curb 8122; ☆3, 1975). "Our Day Will Come" (Frankie Valli solo) (Private Stock 45053; ☆11, 1975). **Rascals** "I Ain't Gonna Eat Out My Heart Anymore" (Atlantic 2312; ☆52, 1965). "Good Lovin'" (Atlantic 2321; ☆1, 1966). "You Better Run" (Atlantic 2338; ☆20, 1966). "Come on Up" (Atlantic 2353; ☆43, 1966). "I've Been Lonely Too Long" (Atlantic 2377; ☆16, 1967). "Groovin'" (Atlantic 2401; ☆1, 1967). "A Girl like You" (Atlantic 2424; ☆10, 1967). "How Can I Be Sure" (Atlantic 2438; ☆4, 1967). "It's Wonderful" (Atlantic 2468; ☆20, 1967). "A Beautiful Morning" (Atlantic 2493; ☆3, 1968). "People Got to Be Free" (Atlantic 2493; ☆1, 1968). "A Ray of Hope" (Atlantic 2584; ☆24, 1968). "Heaven" (Atlantic 2599; ☆39, 1969). "See" (Atlantic 2634; ☆27, 1969). "Carry Me Back" (Atlantic 2664; ☆26, 1969).

(Chart positions taken from Joel Whitburn's *Record Research,* compiled from *Billboard* Pop chart.)

THE YOUNG RASCALS

James Brown
by Robert Palmer

Through 1001 nights, 1001 shows, Superbad James Brown keeps on keepin' on. His band locks into a chopping rhythm riff and Brown strides purposefully from the wings, wearing a red jumpsuit with the word SEX stitched across the front. His head jerks to the beat, his hips shimmy, and suddenly he's snaking across the stage on one foot, his other leg windmilling along with his long, limber arms. He does a split, erupts into a pirouette, whirls like a dervish, and ends up at the microphone just in time to shriek "bayba-a-ay" as the band modulates into the introduction to his latest hit. As the Seventies wear on and Brown moves into his mid-40s, the dates become more selective, the act slightly less acrobatic. But the energy, the pandemonium, and the great, rending buzz saw voice remain.

Brown recorded his first single, "Please, Please, Please," in 1956 for the Federal label, a subsidiary of King Records, and during the next few years his grainy gospel voice became a fixture on Southern radio, inexorably affecting the development of rhythm and blues, pulling it away from show business sophistication and back into the orbit of the black churches from which it ultimately derived. The grittiness of Brown's late-Fifties/early-Sixties output—"Think," "Night Train," and "Shout and Shimmy" were a few of the hits—paved the way for the emergence of Otis Redding, Wilson Pickett, and the other soul shouters who followed. For while Ray Charles was already tempering the rawness of his early recordings with uptown sweetening, Brown was injecting some of the hysteria of sanctified church services into each of his releases.

Pervasive as Brown's influence was during the Sixties, he has shaped the music of the Seventies even more profoundly. The chattering choke-rhythm guitars, broken bass patterns, explosive horn bursts, one-chord drones, and evangelical vocal discourses he introduced during the mid-Sixties have become the *lingua franca* of contemporary black pop, the heartbeat of the discotheques, and a primary ingredient in such far-flung musical syntheses as Jamaican reggae and Nigerian Afro-beat. Various producers and arrangers have added lush string arrangements, flugelhorns, bass trombones, and sighing female choruses; Sly Stone, the Isley Brothers, and others have overlaid whining, distorted guitars, wah-wah clarinets, more complex cross-rhythms, or chunkier drumming, according to their tastes. But the basic band tracks—"the wheels of the car," to borrow a metaphor from R&B producer Willie Mitchell—continue to follow Papa James's directions.

Brown knew what and how he wanted to record early on. When Sid Nathan, head of King, refused to let Brown record with his touring band, Brown helped them record for another label as Nat Kendrick and the Swans; the group had a substantial instrumental hit in 1960 with "(Do the) Mashed Potatoes," a dance routine from the Brown stage show. Nathan relented; James Brown records that were both more visceral and commercial followed.

By 1964, the Cincinnati-based King company, which had grown up with band blues, vocal groups, and hillbilly boogie during the late Forties, was functioning more and more like an antique from R&B's golden age, failing to distribute and promote Brown's records on a scale commensurate with his popularity as a live performer. Brown retaliated by forming Fair Deal Productions, and by giving his next set of recordings to Smash, a subsidiary of Mercury. One of the sides included in the package was "Out of Sight," and with Mercury's more thorough and up-to-date distribution network behind it, the record became one of Brown's biggest hits, selling to white listeners as well as to the blacks who had been supporting him for years.

A legal battle with King ensued. Brown held fast, and after a year-long standoff he emerged in complete artistic control of his recording career, and with a deciding voice in the business end of it as well. Almost immediately he released the record that finally made him a superstar and defined the rhythmic direction R&B would take during the next decade, the epochal "Papa's Got a Brand New Bag" (1965). Toward the end of the Sixties, Brown became his own manager, and in 1971 he formed his own record production company, with Polydor as distributor. He had come a long way since the days when Sid Nathan supervised his sessions. Every step had been a battle, but Brown fought hard and, eventually, he won.

What drives a man like Brown, a man who could have retired in 1965 or 1975, but who has kept on trying to outdo himself instead? Perhaps the goal has been forgotten and the struggle itself is the reward. Perhaps it always was. The very beginning was a struggle. Brown was born in 1933 in Georgia; he grew up poorer than poor, picking cotton, shining shoes, dancing for pennies in the streets. Later came reform school, boxing, semiprofessional baseball, and—after a leg injury scotched his ambition to become a big league pitcher—a vocal group, the Famous Flames. The Flames began to attract attention around Macon during the mid-Fifties, signing with King early in 1956 on the strength of "Please, Please, Please." But the first ten singles failed to attract much notice outside Georgia, probably because, as Cliff White writing for *Black Music* has pointed out, they sounded like "a pastiche of the Midnighters, the '5' Royales and Charles Brown with a dash of Little Richard."

In 1958, "Try Me," a laboriously slow, churchy ballad, went to Number 48 in *Billboard*. It wasn't a huge hit, but it enabled Brown and the Flames, the vocal group he now dominated completely, to keep working one-night stands in the South, and to secure the services of a good national booking agent, Ben Bart, Brown's manager-to-be. Soon Brown had a regular road band, an increasingly tight show, and an entire revue, with members of the troupe doubling as opening acts; by 1960, he was attracting a growing audience in the North. In 1963, *The James Brown Show Live at the Apollo* stayed on the *Billboard*

James Brown circa 1956 (Michael Ochs collection)

album charts for 66 weeks, getting as high as Number Two—a virtually unprecedented feat for a hardcore R&B album. Black radio stations played it like a single and, for the first time, anybody anywhere with a few dollars and a phonograph could get a taste of the show that was earning James Brown the nickname "Mr. Dynamite."

It was during this period that Brown earned another reputation, that of the "hardest working man in show business." His rapidly expanding James Brown Revue traveled constantly, crisscrossing the country, playing for all-black audiences which became ever larger and more ecstatic. His band was the toughest, loudest, and most together (as well it should have been, since fluffed notes were reportedly penalized by heavy fines). His clothes were the flashiest, from the shiny suits of the late Fifties to the waist-length jackets with matching vests and supertight pants of the mid-Sixties. His dancing was the wildest, the most spectacularly acrobatic, the most perfectly controlled.

The show itself was programmed down to the last second for maximum impact. During the early Sixties, for example, Brown perfected the finale captured in the 1965 film, *The T.A.M.I. Show*. As he wrenched out the pleading refrain to "Please, Please, Please" he would sink slowly to his knees, writhing to the tune's lugubrious rhythm until finally, still singing, he collapsed in a heap. Famous Flames Bobby Byrd, Bobby Bennett and Lloyd Stallworth would approach him hesitantly. One would produce a purple cape and, reverently draping it over the fallen singer's body, help him to his feet and slowly escort him offstage. Brown, still holding the microphone, would begin to drag his feet, struggle and, after a dramatic pause, shake off the cape and walk deliberately back to stage center. There he would launch into another chorus, only to drop to his knees again, his voice a hoarse sob. The routine was repeated, this time with a gold cape. Once again Brown waited until the last minute, shook off his attendants, returned to the front of the stage, began singing, feigned collapse. Finally, a jet black cape was produced and Brown and the Flames left the stage, while the band played on. The audiences, absolutely spent by Brown's hysterically energetic hour onstage, would shout themselves hoarse for more, wondering all the while how Brown could possibly top what he'd already done. And then Mr. Dynamite would appear, wearing a new suit, a prop suitcase in his hand, propelling himself across the stage on one foot, thumb out as if hitching a ride to the next town.

During this period the most striking thing about Brown's music was his voice, one of the harshest in R&B. His torn and frayed tonal quality wasn't unique; the Sensational Nightingales' Julius Cheeks, who also came from the Southeast, had popularized it some years before. Brown's combination of gospel quartet harmonies with a large, punching horn section and a heavy shuffle beat was more original but, again, hardly unique. But Latin cross-rhythms had crept into some of the records as early as "Good Good Lovin'," and the Brown band's lead guitarist, Jimmy Nolan, had been working on a choked style of rhythm playing which melded beautifully into the band's rhythmic thrust. The bass parts had been growing more and more staccato, in keeping with the increasing percussive orientation of the music, and so had the horn lines. By 1964, these elements had coalesced into a distinctive new sound which caught America off guard.

The change was probably determined, at least in part, by the structure of Brown's new songs. He continued to work in gospel and blues forms, but he also added another kind of composition: Brown would sing a semiimprovised, loosely organized melody that wandered while the band riffed rhythmically on a single chord, the horns tersely punctuating Brown's declamatory phrases. With no chord changes and precious little melodic variety to sustain listener interest, rhythm became everything. Brown and his musicians and arrangers began to treat every instrument and voice in the group as if each were a drum. The horns played single-note bursts that were often sprung against the downbeats. The bass lines were broken up into choppy two- or three-note patterns, a procedure common in Latin music since the Forties but unusual in R&B. Brown's rhythm guitarist choked his guitar strings against the instrument's neck so hard that his playing began to sound like a jagged tin can being scraped with a pocketknife. Only occasionally were the horns, organ or backing vocalists allowed to provide a harmonic continuum by holding a chord.

The chugging push-pull of the Brown band's Brand New Bag was the wave of the future. Its impact was obscured initially by the English invasion, which consisted of white bands covering R&B hits from the previous decade; and by the Memphis sound, which resembled Brown's music in its gospel orientation and harmonic simplicity but had a much more conservative rhythmic bias. By 1968, however, psychedelic rock was replacing the older English R&B styles, and the Memphis sound was becoming diluted. Sly and the Family Stone were purveying a psychedelicized, more rhythmically complex variant of the Brown sound, and Brown himself was at the height of his powers, preaching stream-of-consciousness sermons like "Cold Sweat," "I Can't Stand Myself," and "Say It Loud—I'm Black and I'm Proud," all of them pulsating with polyrhythmic power.

During the late Sixties Brown became a politician of sorts, encouraging black capitalism, hobnobbing with would-be president Hubert Humphrey, touring Africa, entertaining the troops in Vietnam and Korea, urging rioting ghetto youths to cool their passions and build instead of burn. He acquired a large house, a fleet of cars, a jet, several radio stations and other businesses. Militants, suspicious of his vested interest in the system, accused him of Tomming. The ghetto ignored them and bought more and more of his records, even after they had

136

begun to sound alike, as if each were merely another installment in one very long discourse on the state of the nation and the state of mind of its Number One soul brother.

Brown has never been a critics' favorite, principally because of the apparent monotony of so many of his post-1965 recordings. But attacking him for being repetitive is like attacking Africans for being overly fond of drumming. Where the European listener may hear monotonous beating, the African distinguishes subtle polyrhythmic interplay, tonal distinctions among the various drums, the virtuosity of the master drummer, and so on. Similarly, Brown sounds to some European ears like so much harsh shrieking. White Americans have rarely bought his records in large numbers. In fact, he has

never had a Number One pop hit. Only six of his singles have made *Billboard*'s Top Ten, and all of them were released during the years of his most intensive media exposure: 1965–1968. But subsequent Brown singles continued to place high on the R&B charts well into the mid-Seventies.

Characteristically, Brown responded to the rising tide of sweet soul from Philadelphia by sweetening his own recordings with strings, horns and vocal groups. The emergence of the disco fad found him making harder, more aggressive records again, but the public seemed tired of the James Brown formula. For the first time in over ten years, Brown's singles did not get automatic airplay on black radio. But he was still a successful producer of, among other acts, his own backup band, Fred Wesley and the J.B.s, who had several hit singles in a disco dance vein. And he was still a performer capable of communicating sheer frenzy to his followers.

It seems unlikely that anything short of physical collapse will make Brown quit. Apparently he is the same suspicious, hard-pushing, self-absorbed man who built the Famous Flames into a money-making proposition and eventually built an R&B empire for himself. He has loosened up a little. Arrangers Fred Wesley and Dave Mathews now get credit on the back liners of Brown's albums, a gesture of generosity from a man who refused for years to identify any of his arrangers or sidemen to the public. There have been no more of the abusive run-ins with fellow soul singers which made headlines in the black music press.

But the ego games continue. On a recent Brown LP, Hank Ballard, one of his initial inspirations, delivered a demeaning rap exalting Brother James. But criticizing Brown for his ego is like criticizing his music for being repetitive. His fierce determination to get to the top and the hypnotic insistence of his sound made him what he is. What he is, whether you love him or hate him, is Soul Brother Number One.

Discography

"Please, Please, Please" (Federal 12258; r☆6, 1956). "Try Me" (Federal 12337; r☆1, ☆48, 1958). "I Want You So Bad" (Federal 12348; r☆20, 1959). "I'll Go Crazy" (Federal 12369; r☆15, 1960). "Think" b/w "You've Got the Power" (Federal 12370; r☆7, ☆33, 1960). "This Old Heart" (Federal 12378; r☆20, 1960). "Bewildered" (King 5442; r☆8, ☆40, 1961). "I Don't Mind" (King 5466; r☆4, ☆47, 1961). "Baby, You're Right" (King 5524; r☆2, ☆49, 1961). "Just You and Me, Darling" (King 5547; r☆17, 1961). "Lost Someone" (King 5573; r☆2, ☆48, 1961). "Night Train" (King 5614; r☆5, ☆35, 1962). "Shout and Shimmy" (King 5657; r☆16, 1962). "Three Hearts in a Tangle" (King 5701; r☆18, 1962). "Prisoner of Love" (King 5739; r☆6, ☆18, 1963). "Oh Baby, Don't You Weep" (King 5842; ☆23, 1964). "Out of Sight" (Smash 1919; ☆24, 1964). "Papa's Got a Brand New Bag" (King 5999; r☆1, ☆8, 1965). "I Got You (I Feel Good)" (King 6015; r☆1, ☆3, 1965). "Ain't That a Groove" (King 6025; r☆6, ☆42, 1966). "It's a Man's Man's Man's World" (King 6035; r☆1, ☆8, 1966). "Money Won't Change You" (King 6048; r☆11, 1966). "Don't Be a Drop-Out" (King 6056; r☆4, ☆50, 1966). "Bring It Up" (King 6071; r☆7, ☆29, 1967). "Kansas City" (King 6086; r☆21, 1967). "Let Yourself Go" (King 6100; r☆5, ☆46, 1967). "Cold Sweat" (King 6110; r☆1, ☆7, 1967). "Get It Together" (King 6122; r☆11, ☆40, 1967). "There Was a Time" b/w "I Can't Stand Myself" (King 6144; r☆3, ☆28, 1968). "I Got the Feelin' " (King 6155; r☆1, ☆6, 1968). "Licking Stick—Licking Stick" (King 6166; r☆2, ☆14, 1968). "America Is My Home" (King 6112; r☆13, 1968). "I Guess I'll Have to Cry, Cry, Cry" (King 6141; r☆15, 1968). "Say It Loud—I'm Black and I'm Proud" (King 6187; r☆1, ☆10, 1968). "Goodbye My Love" (King 6198; r☆9, ☆31, 1968). "Give It Up or Turnit a Loose" (King 6213; r☆1, ☆15, 1969). "I Don't Want Nobody to Give Me Nothing" (King 6224; r☆3, ☆20, 1969). "The Popcorn" (King 6240; ☆☆11, ☆30, 1969). "Mother Popcorn (Part I)" (King 6245; r☆1, ☆11, 1969). "Lowdown Popcorn" (King 6250; r☆16, ☆41, 1969). "World" (King 6258; r☆8, ☆37, 1969). "Let a Man Come In and Do the Popcorn (Part I)" (King 6255; r☆2, ☆21, 1969). "Ain't It Funky Now" (King 6280; r☆2, ☆24, 1969). "Let a Man Come In and Do the Popcorn (Part II)" (King 6275; r☆6, ☆40, 1969). "It's a New Day" (King 6292; r☆3, ☆32, 1970). "Funky Drummer (Part I)" (King 6290; r☆20, 1970). "Brother Rapp (Part I)" (King 6310; r☆2, ☆32, 1970). "Get Up I Feel like Being a Sex Machine" (King 6318; r☆2, ☆15, 1970). "Super Bad" (King 6329; r☆1, ☆13, 1970). "Get Up, Get into It, Get Involved" (King 6347; r☆4, ☆34, 1971). "Soul Power" (King 6368; r☆3, ☆29, 1971). "I Cried" (King 6363; r☆15, ☆50, 1971). "Escape-ism" (People 2500; r☆6, ☆35, 1971). "Hot Pants (She Got to Use What She Got to Get What She Wants)" (People 2501; r☆1, ☆15, 1971). "Make It Funky" (Polydor 14088; r☆1, ☆22, 1971). "I'm a Greedy Man" (Polydor 14100; r☆7, ☆35, 1971). "Talking Loud and Saying Nothing" (Polydor 14109; r☆1, ☆27, 1972). "King Heroin" (Polydor 14116; r☆6, ☆40, 1972). "There It Is" (Polydor 14125; r☆4, ☆43, 1972). "Honky Tonk" (Polydor 14129; r☆7, ☆44, 1972). "Get on the Good Foot" (Polydor 14139; r☆1, ☆18, 1972). "I Got a Bag of My Own" (Polydor 14153; r☆3, ☆44, 1972). "What My Baby Needs Now Is a Little More Lovin' " (Polydor 14157; r☆17, ☆56, 1972). "I Got Ants in My Pants" (Polydor 14162; r☆4, ☆27, 1973). "Down and Out in N.Y. City" (Polydor 14168; r☆13, ☆50, 1973). "Think" (Polydor 14177; r☆15, ☆77, 1973). "Sexy, Sexy, Sexy" (Polydor 14194; r☆6, ☆50, 1973). "Stoned to the Bone" (Polydor 14210; r☆4, ☆58, 1973). "The Payback—Part I" (Polydor 14223; r☆1, ☆26, 1974). "My Thang" (Polydor 14244; r☆1, ☆29, 1974). "Papa Don't Take No Mess—Part I" (Polydor 14255; r☆1, ☆31, 1974). "Funky President (People It's Bad)/Coldblooded" (Polydor 14258; r☆4, ☆44, 1974). "Reality" (Polydor 14268; r☆19, 1975). "Sex Machine" (Polydor 14270; r☆16, 1975). "Hustle!!! (Dead on It)" (Polydor 14281; r☆11, 1975).

Chart positions taken from Joel Whitburn's *Record Research,* compiled from *Billboard* Pop chart, unless otherwise indicated; r☆ = position on Rhythm and Blues chart.)

The Sound of Chicago
by Joe McEwen

Huddled in a dark corner of the Cabrini Housing Project on Chicago's North Side, five youths struggle to work out the harmonies of a wide-eyed, dreamy love song that three of them have composed. Unlike other numbers in the group's repertoire, this song features no vocal interplay and none of the standard doo-wop harmonies; instead, it is a solo vehicle for a pure and mournful baritone whose deliberate phrasing and dirgelike approach transform the romantic ballad into a somber, religious evocation. The group is the Impressions, the year is 1958, and the song is "For Your Precious Love."

The Impressions formed from the union of two friends, Jerry Butler, 17, and Curtis Mayfield, 15. The two had sung together in church as adolescents, and had traveled with the Northern Jubilee Gospel Singers and the Traveling Souls Spiritualist Church. It was Butler who convinced his friend Mayfield to leave his own struggling group, the Alfatones, and join him, Sam Gooden, and Richard and Arthur Brooks, the remnants of another struggling group, the Roosters.

According to legend, an impressive performance at a swank Chicago fashion show brought the quintet to the attention of Falcon Records, and "For Your Precious Love" was recorded shortly afterward. Butler, setting aside his dreams of becoming a chef or ice sculptor, provided the resonant baritone lead, while Mayfield's fragile tenor wailed innocently in the background.

"For Your Precious Love" was a landmark record. Unlike the harsh South Side blues, which had been transported to Chicago by grown men, "For Your Precious Love" was the music of a new generation that had spent its adolescence in the city, synthesizing music from such diverse sources as the Soul Stirrers, the Ink Spots, the Dells and, of course, the blues. The song can almost be considered the first soul record: in years to come, it provided the inspiration for more fervent performances by Solomon Burke, Jackie Wilson and Tommy Hunt.

"For Your Precious Love," by the Impressions featuring Jerry Butler, was dominated by Butler's virtuoso performance. After two followups failed to catch the public's ear, Butler left the group to attempt a solo career. Without him, the Impressions searched for a comfortable personality, recording several dismal imitations of the Coasters and the Isley Brothers.

While the group floundered, Jerry Butler was having his own problems selling records. In 1960, with the Impressions still struggling, Butler and Mayfield again joined forces to write a song that would not only refurbish Butler's faltering career, but also set the tone for Mayfield's subsequent efforts as a writer and producer. Set to a Brazilianbaion rhythm popularized by the Drifters, "He Will Break Your Heart" featured Mayfield's sparse guitar figures and Butler's dignified vocal pleas, echoed at the refrain by Curtis's wispy tenor. It was the first of several Butler hits fashioned by Mayfield.

The success of these records finally gave Mayfield the impetus to resume his own career with the Impressions. Thanks to his growing reputation as a writer and producer, he landed a contract for the group with ABC-Paramount. The Impressions, now including Sam Gooden's friend Fred Cash as Butler's replacement, were sent to New York under Mayfield's tutelage, and predictably enough it was Mayfield who penned the group's first ABC record. "Gypsy Woman" was a fantasy of longing and desire, with castanets and Mayfield's flamenco strumming setting the mood, while the quintet wove an exotic narrative about "a lovely lady in motion" with eyes "like that of a cat in the dark."

Released late in 1961, "Gypsy Woman" became a national hit. Though Mayfield composed several other songs in a similar vein, including "Minstrel and Queen," an arresting allegory about interracial love, the followups failed to duplicate the success of "Gypsy Woman." Richard and Arthur Brooks opted to stay in New York, but the three remaining Impressions returned to Chicago, hoping for inspiration and still looking for their next hit.

In the meantime, Columbia Records, at the urging of a dapper black A&R man from Chicago named Carl Davis, had reactivated its once mighty "race" label, Okeh. Davis had proven his ability to spot new talent by plucking a group named the Dukays off a Chicago street corner, and fashioning a Number One hit for the lead singer, Eugene Dixon. Dixon was rechristened Gene Chandler (after Davis's favorite actor, Jeff Chandler), and his first record, "Duke of Earl," sold a million copies in a little over a month.

At Okeh, Davis's first major signings were Major Lance and Curtis Mayfield. A scuffling singer and ex-boxer, Lance had come to Davis with Mayfield in hopes of landing a contract. On the strength of a tune called "The Monkey Time" that Curtis had just written, Davis hired Mayfield as Okeh's staff producer, and agreed to let Lance cut the song; he also brought in veteran Johnny Pate to arrange the charts. Davis and Pate discarded Mayfield's strings and beefed up the sound with a stuttering brass section and a percussive bottom. It proved to be the perfect catalyst, giving Mayfield's production an instantly identifiable and catchy stamp.

With Pate's blaring horn intro, Major Lance's reedy vocal and Mayfield's eccentric rhythmic approach, "The Monkey Time" not only became Okeh's first hit in years, but also announced the arrival of a full-fledged Chicago sound.

Pate was immediately called in to help arrange for the Impressions. The first Pate/Impressions single, "Sad, Sad Girl and Boy," was yet another re-creation of the softer Mayfield/Butler sound, but its successor, "It's All Right," released in the fall of 1963, featured a punchier, gospel-styled band track, with boosted bass and a more assertive vocal approach. Unlike the frantic dance songs and intense ballads that had begun to dominate black radio, "It's All Right" combined an understated

Jerry Butler in the early Sixties (Michael Ochs collection)

140

soulfulness with a rhumba beat and updated doo-wop harmonies. The sparse arrangement and elegant sound of the record provided an equally effective counterpoint to the heavily orchestrated Motown singles of the era. Following closely on the heels of "The Monkey Time," "It's All Right" inaugurated a period of Midas-like artistic and commercial success for Curtis Mayfield.

At Okeh, he poured out songs for Billy Butler, Walter Jackson and Major Lance. But it was his collaboration with Gene Chandler (for Constellation) that gave him his most consistent string of hits outside of the Impressions'. While Curtis's Okeh productions were largely cast in the "Monkey Time"/"It's All Right" mold, his work with Chandler took a softer approach.

Chandler was a rather limited vocalist who often sounded like he was singing with a cold. Although his range was narrow, Chandler's style was appealing, distinguished by nasal falsetto swoops that never failed to summon screams from the teenagers at Chicago's Regal Theater. Mayfield composed a series of striking songs for Gene, and it was through Curtis that Chandler became one of black America's favorite balladeers. The high point of their collaboration was "Just Be True," Chandler's biggest hit after "Duke of Earl," which featured aching, deliberate phrasing from the vocalist, an overlay of strings, and Impressions-styled harmony. The effect of the record was galvanic. Chandler's emotional reading perfectly conveyed the vulnerability expressed by the lyric, and the song became a model for his gentle, often wounded persona. Like Major Lance, Chandler enjoyed hit after hit with Mayfield as producer; but when their partnership ended, the hits dried up.

In 1966, Mayfield, hoping to profit more directly from his labors, severed his relationship with Okeh to start his own label, Windy C Records. The company was primarily an outlet for a young teen group, the Five Stairsteps; despite several hits, Mayfield proved less a businessman than a producer, and the venture soon folded. After the collapse of another solo outlet, Mayfield Records, Curtis formed an independent production company, Curtom, with a roster that included the Stairsteps, Major Lance, and eventually the Impressions. Thanks to national distribution from Buddah, the operation survived, though Mayfield never quite matched his earlier work either aesthetically or commercially.

With the Impressions, Mayfield had begun to compose "message" songs. The best, including "People Get Ready" and "We're a Winner," were moving statements, but the worst seemed like clumsy attempts to confront the country's turbulent social developments. When Mayfield left the Impressions in 1970, his best years as a composer were behind him.

Chicago soul nevertheless continued to flourish in other hands. The mid-Sixties Mayfield/Okeh chart eruption had triggered recording activities throughout the city. Chess, which

had been struggling with a roster of dated blues and rock performers, hired writer Billy Davis as arranger and A&R man. Using an orchestrated approach patterned after Motown, Davis had hits with Jackie Ross, Etta James, Fontella Bass, Billy Stewart, Little Milton, and the Radiants. The city's smaller independents, including Twinight, with Syl Johnson, and Onederful! with Otis Clay, tended to feature artists with a bluesier Southern style. While they contributed to the city's reputation as a soul center, for the most part the fortunes of Chicago soul rose and fell with the work of Mayfield and Carl Davis.

Shortly after Mayfield left Okeh, Carl Davis had a feud with the president of Epic/Okeh, Len Levy, over Okeh's musical direction. According to Davis, a spat, stemming from a columnist's reference to him as Okeh's president, brought the conflict to a head, leading to Carl's resignation and the subsequent collapse of Okeh. Davis started his own production company, and after two Jackie Wilson million-sellers, "Whispers" and "(Your Love Keeps Lifting Me) Higher and Higher," he was hired by Brunswick as an executive vice-president.

Working for Brunswick owner Nat Tarnopol, Davis managed to turn up a new batch of Windy City talent. Where Mayfield only fitfully managed to update the uncluttered and honest approach that had been so effective less than a decade earlier, Davis and arrangers Willie Henderson and Sonny Sanders devised a new style directly descended from Mayfield and Pate's original collaborations. Davis had honed his crack Chicago band on records by Mary Wells and Gene Chandler as well as Jackie Wilson, but it wasn't until Tyrone Davis's "Can I Change My Mind" became a national hit in 1968 that the new sound of Chicago emerged.

With brassy flourishes, a relaxed rhythmic lope, and a Davis vocal that owed as much to the big band blues of Bobby Bland as to Jerry Butler, "Can I Change My Mind" sounded almost

anachronistic. Yet the fluid band track and aggressive horns gave the song a freshness lacking in much of the late Sixties soul. Brunswick quickly signed Barbara Acklin, the Young-Holt Trio and the Chi-Lites to benefit from the new Davis/Henderson/Sanders style.

While most of these acts were recorded with a heavy emphasis on Henderson's surging horns, a different tack was taken by the Chi-Lites. Headed by Eugene Record, a former cabdriver turned songwriter, the Chi-Lites sang melancholy ballads as well as protest material modeled after the Temptations. Their strangest hit was "Have You Seen Her," a five-minute song that found lead singer Record painting a picture of a forlorn fellow stumbling through the day pining for his lost love.

Mayfield's decision to leave the Impressions and pursue his own career symbolized the end of an era for Chicago soul. The stately, uplifting harmonies he had developed for the group were replaced in his own music by jagged bass lines, frenetic percussive flourishes, and a more aggressive vocal attack. Though Curtis often sounded strained and brittle as a solo singer, and his own songs were usually didactic rather than poetic, Mayfield's new approach won him a considerable following, culminating in the success of the ambiguous "Superfly" and the more overtly antidrug "Freddie's Dead."

While gospel influences had come to dominate soul by the late Sixties, the restrained, dignified style of Chicago soul stood out; in their heyday, Mayfield and Carl Davis crafted some of the purest and most sanctified pop ever to grace Top 40 radio. By the mid-Seventies, however, only the apparently infinite flow of Tyrone Davis singles bore any real resemblance to this classic "sound of Chicago." But new producers like Leroy Hutson and particularly the Chuck Jackson/Marvin Yancey team, have kept the scene alive. The success in 1975 of Natalie Cole's engaging "This Will Be," produced by Jackson and Yancey, proved that Chicago, while no longer setting distinctive trends, remains a vital center of black music in America.

Discography

△**Jerry Butler,** "Find Another Girl" (Vee-Jay 375; r☆27, ☆10, 1961). **Dee Clark,** "Raindrops" (Vee-Jay 383; r☆3, ☆2, 1961). △**Jerry Butler,** "I'm a Telling You" (Vee-Jay 390; r☆8, ☆25, 1961). △**Impressions,** "Gypsy Woman" (ABC-Paramount 10241; r☆2, ☆20, 1961). **Jerry Butler,** "Moon River" (Vee-Jay 405; r☆14, ☆11, 1961). **Gene Chandler,** "Duke of Earl" (Vee-Jay 416; r☆1, ☆1, 1962). **Jerry Butler,** "Make It Easy on Yourself" (Vee-Jay 451; r☆18, ☆20, 1962). △**Gene Chandler,** "Rainbow" (Vee-Jay 468; r☆11, ☆47, 1963). △**Major Lance,** "The Monkey Time" (Okeh 7175; r☆4, ☆8, 1963). △**Gene Chandler,** "Man's Temptation" (Vee-Jay 536; r☆17, ☆71, 1963). △**Impressions,** "It's All Right" (ABC-Paramount 10487; r☆1, ☆4, 1963). △**Major Lance,** "Hey Little Girl" (Okeh 7181; r☆12, ☆13, 1963). **Betty Everett,** "You're No Good" (Vee-Jay 566; ☆51, 1963). **Jerry Butler,** "Need to Belong" (Vee-Jay 567; ☆31, 1963). △**Impressions,** "Talking about My Baby" (ABC-Paramount 10511; ☆12, 1964). △**Major Lance,** "Um, Um, Um, Um, Um, Um" (Okeh 7187; ☆5, 1964). **Betty Everett,** "The Shoop Shoop Song" (Vee-Jay 585; ☆6, 1964). △**Major Lance,** "The Matador" (Okeh 7191; ☆20, 1964). **Jerry Butler,** "Giving Up on Love" (Vee-Jay 588; ☆56, 1964). △**Impressions,** "I'm So Proud" (ABC-Paramount 10544; ☆14, 1964). △**Impressions,** "Keep on Pushing" (ABC-Paramount 10554; ☆10, 1964). △**Gene Chandler,** "Just Be True" (Constellation 130; ☆19, 1964). **Jerry Butler,** "I Stand Accused" (Vee-Jay 598; ☆61, 1964). **Jackie Ross,** "Selfish One" (Chess 1903; ☆11, 1964). △**Major Lance,** "Rhythm" (Okeh 7203; ☆24, 1964). **Betty Everett and Jerry**

Butler, "Let It Be Me" (Vee-Jay 613; ☆5, 1964). △**Impressions,** "You Must Believe Me" (ABC-Paramount 10581; ☆15, 1964). △**Gene Chandler,** "Bless Our Love" (Constellation 136; ☆39, 1964). △**Walter Jackson,** "It's All Over" (Okeh 7204; ☆67, 1964). △**Gene Chandler,** "What Now" (Constellation 141; r☆18, ☆40, 1965). △**Major Lance,** "Sometimes I Wonder" (Okeh 7209; r☆13, ☆64, 1965). △**Impressions,** "Amen" (ABC-Paramount 10602; r☆17, ☆7, 1965). **Radiants,** "Voice Your Choice" (Chess 1904; r☆16, ☆51, 1965). **Walter Jackson,** "Suddenly I'm All Alone" (Okeh 7215; r☆13, 1965). **Billy Stewart,** "I Do Love You" (Chess 1922; r☆6, ☆26, 1965). **Fontella Bass and Bobby McClure,** "Don't Mess Up a Good Thing" (Checker 1097; r☆5, ☆33, 1965). △**Impressions,** "People Get Ready" (ABC-Paramount 10622; r☆3, ☆14, 1965). △**Gene Chandler,** "Nothing Can Stop Me" (Constellation 149; r☆3, ☆18, 1965). △**Impressions,** "Woman's Got Soul" (ABC-Paramount 10647; r☆9, ☆29, 1965). **Walter Jackson,** "Welcome Home" (Okeh 7219; r☆15, 1965). **Radiants,** "It Ain't No Big Thing" (Chess 1925; r☆14, 1965). △**Billy Butler and the Chanters,** "I Can't Work No Longer" (Okeh 7221; r☆6, ☆60, 1965). **Billy Stewart,** "Sitting in the Park" (Chess 1932; r☆4, ☆24, 1965). **Fontella Bass,** "Rescue Me" (Checker 1120; r☆1, ☆4, 1965). △**Impressions,** "You've Been Cheatin' " (ABC-Paramount 10750; r☆12, ☆33, 1965). **Gene Chandler,** "Rainbow '65" (Constellation 158; r☆2, ☆69, 1965). **Billy Stewart,** "Summertime" (Chess 1966; r☆7, ☆10, 1966). △**Five Stairsteps and Cubie,** "World of Fantasy" (Windy C 602; r☆12, ☆49, 1966). **Jackie Wilson,** "Whispers" (Brunswick 55300; r☆5, ☆11, 1966). **Gene Chandler,** "I Fooled You This Time" (Checker 1155; r☆3, ☆45, 1966). △**Fascinations,** "Girls Are Out to Get You" (Mayfield 7714; r☆13, 1967). **Gene Chandler,** "To Be a Lover" (Checker 1165; r☆9, 1967). **Syl Johnson,** "Come On Sock It to Me" (Twilight 100; r☆12, 1967). **Jackie Wilson,** "(Your Love Keeps Lifting Me) Higher and Higher" (Brunswick 55336; r☆1, ☆6, 1967). △**Impressions,** "We're a Winner" (ABC-Paramount 11022; r☆1, ☆14,

1968). **Dells,** "Stay in My Corner" (Cadet 5612; r☆1, ☆10, 1968). **Barbara Acklin,** "Love Makes a Woman" (Brunswick 55379; r☆3, ☆15, 1968). △**Impressions,** "I Loved and I Lost" (ABC-Paramount 11103; r☆9, ☆61, 1968). △**Impressions,** "Fool for You" (Curtom 1932; r☆3, ☆22, 1968). **Dells,** "Always Together" (Cadet 5621; r☆3, ☆18, 1968). **Young-Holt Unlimited,** "Soulful Strut" (Brunswick 55391; r☆3, ☆3, 1968). **Tyrone Davis,** "Can I Change My Mind" (Dakar 602; r☆1, ☆5, 1968). △**Impressions,** "This Is My Country" (Curtom 1934; r☆8, ☆25, 1968). **Chi-Lites,** "Give It Away" (Brunswick 55398; r☆10, 1969). **Tyrone Davis,** "Is It Something You've Got" (Dakar 605; r☆5, ☆34, 1969). **Dells,** "I Can Sing a Rainbow" (Cadet 5641; r☆5, ☆22, 1969). △**Impressions,** "Choice of Colors" (Curtom 1943; r☆1, ☆21, 1969). **Dells,** "Oh What a Night" (Cadet 5649; r☆1, ☆10, 1969). △**Impressions,** "Say You Love Me" (Curtom 1946; r☆10, ☆58, 1969). **Syl Johnson,** "Is It Because I'm Black" (Twilight 125; r☆11, 1969). **Otis Leavill,** "I Love You" (Dakar 614; r☆10, ☆63, 1969). **Tyrone Davis,** "Turn Back the Hands of Time" (Dakar 616; r☆1, ☆3, 1970). **Dells,** "Open Up My Heart" (Cadet 5667; r☆5, ☆51, 1970). △**Impressions,** "Check Out Your Mind" (Curtom 1951; r☆3, ☆28, 1970). **Gene Chandler,** "Groovy Situation" (Mercury 73083; r☆8, ☆12, 1970). **Tyrone Davis,** "I'll Be Right Here" (Dakar 618; r☆8, 1970). **Garland Green,** "Jealous Kind of Fella" (Uni 55143; r☆5, ☆20, 1970). △**Impressions,** "(Baby) Turn On to Me" (Curtom 1954; r☆6, ☆56, 1970). **Chi-Lites,** "Are You My Woman? (Tell Me So)" (Brunswick 55442; r☆8, 1970). △**Curtis Mayfield,** "(Don't Worry) If There's a Hell Below, We're All Going to Go" (Curtom 1955; r☆3, ☆29, 1970). **Jackie Wilson,** "This Love Is Real" (Brunswick 55443; r☆9, ☆56, 1970). **Tyrone Davis,** "Could I Forget You" (Dakar 623; r☆10, 1971). **Chi-Lites,** "(For God's Sake) Give More Power to the People" (Brunswick 55450; r☆4, ☆26, 1971). **Dells,** "The Love We Had (Stays on My Mind)" (Cadet 5683; r☆8, ☆30, 1971). **Chi-Lites,** "Have You Seen Her" (Brunswick 55462; r☆1, ☆3, 1971).

△ = Record produced by Curtis Mayfield.

(Chart positions taken from Joel Whitburn's *Record Research*, compiled from *Billboard* Pop chart, unless otherwise indicated; r☆ = position on *Billboard* Rhythm and Blues chart [NOTE: *Billboard* did not publish a separate R&B listing during 1964].)

Phil Spector

by Nik Cohn

In Los Angeles I wore a white suit and stayed at the Chateau Marmont, high above Sunset Strip. There was a grand piano and a candelabrum in the lobby and, within an hour of my arrival, persons unknown had sent me a Mexican hooker, name of Angel, who scrubbed my back and cooked me scrambled eggs.

For three days I sat in my room and waited for Phil Spector to contact me. Greta Garbo had once lived in this suite, Myra Breckinridge had looked out through these windows, so I sat and watched the sunsets.

On the third afternoon the phone rang. An unidentified voice asked me if I wished to speak with Mr. Spector. I said that I did. There was a silence. Then the line went dead.

The Chateau was full of corridors and dark corners, Filipino bellhops, aged courtesans. Soon I reached down behind the cooker and came up with a bloodstained silk kimono. I hid it in an air vent and went out to cruise the Strip. When I got back, I looked down from my window, and there was a man with a black moustache, just standing there, motionless.

The phone rang again. This time it was George, Mr. Spector's prime bodyguard. Twenty minutes later he arrived in a black Cadillac, 300 pounds of retired cop, bearded, beringed and heavily holstered, and together we drove off down the Strip, past all the great landmarks, the sacred shrines. Past Dino's and Schwab's and Cyrano's, past the Whiskey. Then past Phil Spector Productions, and on up the hill to El Dorado.

Or, perhaps it wasn't El Dorado, after all. At this distance of time, I can't be sure that it wasn't called Sierra Madre instead, or maybe Besame Mucho or even, who knows, La Paloma. In any case, what matter? It was a mock-Spanish mansion in the classic Hollywood style, all balconies and latticed windows, guard dogs and electronic gates.

As I stepped from the Cadillac, blundering in the dark, I looked up by chance and caught a sudden movement, something shifting behind an upstairs window. A flurry of pink; perhaps a face; nothing more. Wolfhounds snapped and snarled behind a steel-mesh fence. George pushed a sequence of buttons and buzzers, spoke into a mouthpiece, moved us through an electric eye. First one door, then another opened before us. At last we penetrated the mansion.

I was left alone in a very long and high, very cold and empty reception room. Overhead I could hear footsteps moving relentlessly back and forth. Colored lights flashed in the darkness; a door slammed far away.

Everywhere I turned there were pictures of Phil Spector. On coffee tables, around the pool table, stretched across the mantelpiece—Spector with the Teddy Bears, with the Righteous Brothers, with Ike and Tina Turner, with basketball players and karate champions, with Minnesota Fats, with Willie Mosconi, with businessmen, with his mother. In profile, full face, formal or at ease. With companions or, most often, alone.

By the sofa there were three copies of Tom Wolfe's *Kandy-Kolored Tangerine-Flake Streamline Baby,* each with a marker at the chapter on Phil Spector. Underneath there were cuttings from *Time, Life,* ROLLING STONE, each with a marker at the section on Phil Spector. So I sat on the sofa and was idly browsing, when I paused to scratch myself and suddenly there he was, Spector in person, at the far end of the room, on top of a flight of three small stairs, watching me.

At first he did not move. Then I stood up and he came toward me. In close-up, he hardly reached past my shoulder and, even with his gold-rimmed shades, steel-studded wristband and wispy beard, he seemed like a child, maybe ten years old. "Pleased to meet you," he said.

Clearly this wasn't enough. For a very first meeting, something stronger, something altogether more dramatic was called for. So he waited a moment, undecided, and then he gestured round the room, a random sweep that took in the walls, the mansion, the whole of Los Angeles. "Welcome," said Spector, "to Hollywood."

A routine took shape: I sat in my hotel room and every couple of days the phone would ring. Then George picked me up, took me to El Dorado and Spector talked at me. After a few hours, the session ended. Then George drove me back to the Chateau again, and I settled down to wait for the next time.

The idea was that I would eventually write a book. Therefore I crouched over a tape recorder, looking earnest, and Spector kept up a flow of monologue. Footsteps echoed above us, the wolfhounds howled outside the windows and George sat polishing his guns, peaceful in the kitchen. Once I heard a woman singing in another room. Presumably that was Veronica, Ronnie, originally lead singer with the Ronettes, now Spector's second wife. At any rate, she hummed a few bars of "Black Pearl," then cut off dead, halfway through a line, and I never heard her again, nor saw any sign of her existence.

Spector himself, however, was all benevolence. Entombed in his mausoleum, he talked and talked and talked, scarcely pausing for breath. Anecdotes, sermons, remembrances and fantasies poured out of him in a torrent and, in the gaps, he kept me amused with scrapbooks and old snapshots, threw drinks down me until I gagged.

In every detail, he was the perfection of the genial host. One afternoon, like a Jewish mother rampant, he even fixed me a plate of lox and cream cheese on rye, prepared with his own hands, complete with pickles and side salad (Roquefort dressing). Then he sang me old songs, showed me trick shots at pool, almost beat me at pinball. "Fun," he said. And he cackled like a hyena.

Still, I could not relax. Despite all this surface jollity, something in him remained most shadowy, remote beyond reaching. Hunched beside me, with his shades and small child's face, he made me think of a toy—his bones were so birdlike, his voice so shrill. Indeed, he carried such an air of fragility that I was often

Below: Phil Spector, 1969. Bottom:
At a rock and roll conference at Mills College,
Oakland, California, 1969 (Both Baron Wolman)

tempted to lift him up bodily and bounce him on my knee, one hand up his back, like a ventriloquist's dummy.

There was a similar sense of puppeteering when he talked. Time and again, I would catch the whiff of something mechanical, frozen. He would spiel for hours. Jump up and down, wave his arms, flash his hands like torches. Shriek with mock hilarity. Hurl abuse until he was hoarse. But it was all performance, nothing more. Suddenly, without warning, he would grow weary; congeal. Then his limbs would set, as if in rigor mortis, and his eyes snuffed out like candles.

Precisely, the effect was like putting money into a seaside peep show. Pull the lever and he jerked into action, ran through his routines. Let it go again, and he stopped dead.

It was only different when he spoke of his past. Turn him loose in the Fifties, transport him back to Philadelphia or New York, in his golden age, and he flamed. Instantly, he took on true intensity. Outrage and obscenity, crazed invention, labyrinthine sagas tumbled out by the megamot, unstoppable, irresistible, and then there was no doubting him, the full magnificence of his madness. At such moments, one knew precisely how he had happened, how he had become Phil Spector, the all-conquering, in the first place. In memory, he was absolutely heroic. But bring him back to the present, and somehow he expired.

Hard to understand, this collapse. He was still in his late 20s, with money, prestige and great talent, adored and protected at every turn, and he lived exactly as he desired. Yet there was this blankness. It seemed that he had no more great pleasures, no passions, not even all-consuming hatreds. Sometimes he would say he was happy, and he smiled. At other times he shook his head and looked tragic. But mostly he simply sat, and survived, and let time pass.

What was wrong? At 16, at 20, at 24, his drives had been phenomenal. His rage and speed, his sweep of vision, his will—no one in rock had ever moved faster, or been more gifted, or had a more ferocious sense of his own potential. Once he had dared everything; now he seemed to dare nothing. Only the trappings were left—the mansion and the bodyguards, the gold-rimmed shades. Cadillacs and wolfhounds and distant footsteps. The motions of mystique.

So one night, when his soliloquies had run dry and it seemed that there was nothing to be lost, I asked him the truth. Did he feel finished? Was he entirely exhausted? Could anything important lie ahead? Or was his life, in essence, already over?

For a moment he thought about losing his temper. His face scrunched up tight and his mouth opened wide. All his nerve-ends prepared to signal fury. But then he paused, right on the brink, and he drew back. With the first volley of murder already halfway up his gullet, he froze. Let a few seconds pass. Then drew in his head, that skull of an infant gnome, like a hedgehog taking refuge.

"Over," he said, with utmost caution. "How exactly do you mean?"

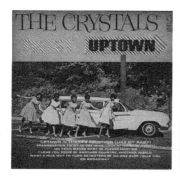 

"Kaput," I replied. "Done with. Complete."

He looked surprised, a mite baffled. Playing for time, he removed his shades and peered past my ear, off into infinity, to signal profound thought. He pondered, reconsidered, delayed. In the end, however, the question must have defeated him, outstripped his range, for he only shrugged his shoulders, and he put his shades back on. "I guess it is," he said, offhand, and we talked about pool instead.

In the first place, more than anything, Phil Spector was a saga of self-invention: a demonstration, on heroic scale, of the possible. Conceive, as a basis, that every life is shaped by two crucial inventions. The first is imposed from outside, at birth and during early childhood, by God, genes, environment, family, initial experience; the second is projected from within, as the life picks up momentum, by force of will and imagination. So we begin by being invented and we progress, if we can, to inventing ourselves.

The decisive element is nerve—how much, precisely, do we *dare?* If we have been invented originally as plain, dumb, insignificant, a loser, will we dare to reinvent ourselves as glamorous, blessed, heroic? If we are cast to obey, will we dare to command? And if we are doomed in any case, as everyone is doomed, will we at least dare to blow ourselves sky-high, in magnificent technorama wipeout, rather than drain away slowly, craven, on our knees?

Phil Spector dared everything.

In his first incarnation, he could hardly have been less promising. He started out in the Bronx: Jewish, shrimpish, twitchy, panic-stricken. A wimp. A runt. His mother crushed and smothered him, his father died when he was nine. Rootless, he was brought out West, to Los Angeles, and that isolated him more than ever. He was close to no one, belonged nowhere, showed gifts for nothing. By the time he entered his teens, he was entirely withdrawn. His mother consumed him alive, girls terrified him. He dreamed that he was being strangled.

At high school he sat apart, stuck away in corners, and he festered. Once he showed me a snapshot taken in his mid-teens, surrounded by a group of classmates, smiling in sunlight. Half a dozen kids in a loose semicircle, golden-fleshed, archetypal Californians. And they slouch and take their ease, they chew gum, they grin, while Phil peeks out, half-hidden, from behind a silver surfer.

It is an image of absolute security. Everyone here has cars, pretty girlfriends, the simplest and safest of futures. But then you glance at Spector and immediately he belongs to another universe. Bad hair, bad skin, bad posture. Focus on his eyes and all you can see is evasion. White flesh in a world of tan, mess in a world of smooth—everything about him is awkward, alien, discomforting, and all the others are looking elsewhere.

That was the premise he worked from. In his first invention,

here, he was hopeless; in his second, he took revenge. All his pent-up energy and rage, his caged passion broke to the surface. Deliberately, he obliterated his roots, wiped out memory, began again from scratch. It was rather like one of those magic drawing pads, where you can draw and erase and draw again as often as you want. Tabula rasa. At one stroke, Spector rubbed out the accumulated doodlings of 17 years, every pattern that others had scribbled upon him. Then he drew for himself; drew his own new being.

In the late Fifties, rock 'n' roll made an obvious context. New and virgin territory, ripe for raiding. The first wild burst of euphoria had just begun to dampen down, there was a temporary hiatus. The natural force of the early rockers had been harnessed and contained by the music industry; now what was needed was a champion, someone to challenge these massed ranks of baldies and cigar-chewing fatties, slay the dragon, wrest away control. Someone with so much force and hunger that he would re-create the whole context, musical, financial, in which rock functioned. Release a true teen holocaust. And that, more or less, is what Phil Spector achieved.

The saga itself was simple. In the beginning, Spector was merely a fan who had a good ear, could play a little guitar and chanced to live in Hollywood, the perfect rock 'n' roll place, at precisely the right moment. He was surrounded by teenage icons, current and future. Annette Funicello, Cher, the budding Fondas. Jan and Dean. Massed spawn of the Sinatras and Martins, the Mitchums, the Kirk Douglases. The collected droppings of a thousand stars.

Spector was duly inspired; blessed by contagion. So he started writing songs. First he achieved "To Know Him, Is to Love Him," a title inspired by his father's epitaph. He took a boy and girl from high school, called them the Teddy Bears, put them into a studio, sold the product to a back-room Los Angeles label, sat back and waited. Sure enough, as if of its own accord, without hustle or the smallest hype, the record hit.

Beatific, Spector went to Philadelphia, which was still the rock 'n' roll mecca in those times; he appeared on *American Bandstand*, made some deals, lost out. Soon he was destitute, right back where he started. But by now the fever was on him; he had caught fire. Having once tasted glory, he could not desist. After a stint as a court reporter he found himself in New York, in the Brill Building, which was just in the process of becoming the new heart of teen dreams, every office overflowing with pimpled, pubescent songwriters, pouring out their anguish in a flood.

It was now 1960; Spector was 19. For months, he made the coffee, ran errands, slept on the tops of desks. Hammered on every door that might imaginably open, hustling in delirium. Begged, blustered, bagged. And finally Atlantic Records gave in, permitted him to produce some sessions.

Now he moved very fast. He created hits for Ray Peterson and Curtis Lee, and he wrote "Spanish Harlem" for Ben E. King. When the royalties came in, he left Atlantic, found some backers and founded his own label, Philles.

In those days, independent labels were mostly small stuff; pimpmobiles without wheels. But Spector flew to Los Angeles, hidden behind shades and an astrakhan coat, swaggering like a pop D.W. Griffiths. On one Friday, renting Gold Star studios, he cut "He's a Rebel" with the Crystals; the following week, he knocked out "Zip-A-Dee Doo-Dah" with a bunch of sessionmen backing Bob B. Soxx and the Blue Jeans. Both were smashes and Philles was made.

Triumphant, he set up New York offices and surrounded himself with assistants, flunkies, bodyguards. Bought himself a custom-made Rolls complete with smoked-glass windows, intercom, bonded bubblegum. And he cut 20 hits within the next three years, the most marvelous teen dreams ever recorded. "Then He Kissed Me" and "Be My Baby," "(Today I Met) the Boy I'm Gonna Marry," "Walking in the Rain," "You've Lost That Lovin' Feeling," "Uptown," "Baby, I Love You," "Da Doo Ron Ron." Heroic combustions, all of them. Soundtracks for a one-shot, one-man millennium.

The noise he made, the so-called "Spector sound," was an apocalypse. Through multitracking, he made his rhythm sections sound like armies, turned the beat into a murderous massed cannonade. No question; his records were the loudest, fiercest, most magnificent explosions that rock had yet produced, or dreamed of. And Spector stood in the center, swamped by all this mayhem, twiddling the knobs, controlling everything, like an infant in charge of Armageddon.

By the time that he passed 21, he was a dollar millionaire. He got married, divorced and married again. His hair grew past his ears, down his neck, almost to his shoulders, and he wore his shades all the time. He strutted, he orated. If someone annoyed him, he called for his bodyguards and ordered vengeance. When he was troubled, he screamed and everybody stopped, took notice. In his high-heeled boots, he stood 5' 7", and the industry called him a genius.

He seemed impregnable. Everything he touched shipped gold; everyone he passed bowed low. He moved to Hollywood, took an office on the Strip, bought El Dorado and cruised in a fleet of cars, all with smoked-glass windows, impenetrable, so that he could see without being seen, rule without being touched.

It was his moment. Then the moment passed. In 1964, the Beatles appeared and, after that, he was no longer the newest and hottest sensation. He still produced hit records, still got his picture in the trade magazines. But his impetus slackened. The industry was busy with other, fresher games, and Spector drew back into shadow.

In 1966, he made "River Deep—Mountain High" with Ike and Tina Turner and it flopped. His very finest record, and his first important failure. So he announced his retirement.

He was then almost 26. Within five years—as artist, businessman and image, as hustler and myth—he had exhausted the fullest potentials of pop. Truthfully, what more was left? Nothing, except to lock the gates of El Dorado and vanish. His journey was completed. Now all that remained was time to kill.

In overall terms of rock history, there were three levels—industrial, creative, stylistic—on which Spector's effect was quite enormous. As a businessman, first of all, it was he, more than anyone, who was responsible for establishing the concept of independence. Before him, mass-market pop had been controlled by a handful of major companies, corporate giants. Their dominance was total; outsiders had little chance. An individual might start his own label and do well enough locally or within a specific market, like R&B or gospel. But if he wanted to be national, he either had to tag on to one of the majors or spend half a lifetime at war.

Spector ripped through all that; refused to be cowed. Almost from the outset, he controlled every aspect of his own enterprise: production, publicity and distribution, hiring and firing, dealing and scamming, artwork, letterheads, office decor, even the color of the toilet paper. He would not be supervised, monopolized; would make no compromise whatever. Afterward, everything came much easier. Spector having made the first breach, it was possible for others to slip through behind him.

That was finance. At the same time, however, he also marked rock's first flirtation with art. Previously there had been great performers, and also a number of natural creators. But Spector was the first to rationalize, the first to comprehend precisely what he was up to. With him, there was immediately a totally new level of sophistication, complexity, musical range.

That could have been fatal. Like all mass media, rock 'n' roll works best off trivia, ephemera, games, and the moment that anyone begins to take it more solemnly he treads on minefields. As performance, rock has been magnificent. Nothing has been better at catching moments, and nothing has carried more impact, more evocative energy. While it lives off flash and outrage, impulse, excess and sweet teen romance, it's perfect. But dabble in art, and instantly it gets overloaded.

Somehow Spector managed it. On one hand, he created his own imaginative universe, which I take to be the test of any true artist. At root, indeed, he was intensely serious. Yet at the same time he never let go of surface folly, of rock's essential ritziness. Simultaneously, he contrived to be subtle and raucous, experimental and corny, pure and strictly commercial. He stole from every source he could—Wagner, Leonard Bernstein, Broadway shows, a thousand or a million other singles, past and present—and was still completely original. Pretentious and funky, earnest and camp. Very complicated indeed, and most beautifully dumb.

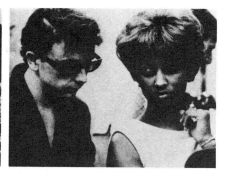

Through this paradox he managed to combine the two great rock 'n' roll romances—rebellion and teen dream—into one. The first meant noise and fury and filth, orgy, musical assassination; the second was sweetest, most perfect innocence. No way for the two to intertwine, or so it seemed. Until Spector jumped up, out of nowhere, and achieved it at one stroke.

In his original songs, by utilizing the massed writers of the Brill Building, he nurtured the purest, the most aching and idyllic of all teen ballads. Into this sound, meanwhile, he poured out his rage and vengeance. Three pianos, half a dozen drummers, rattlers and assorted thumpers, whole battalions of brass and strings, all crashing and smashing away, in deafening, murderous release. So his songs might be pure romance, but his sound was pure slaughter. Together, they meshed as absolute energy.

Money. Music. And then there was Spector as image, where his influence was greatest of all.

Right from the beginning he came on as a guerrilla, dedicated to wholesale riot. When the rest of rock was still stuffed full of crew cuts and natty Italian suits, charm-school smiles, dimples, he was outrageous beyond belief. Grew his hair, draped himself in frills and satins, perched on top of three-inch Cuban heels, sometimes purposely affected a high-pitched lisp. Jangled and shimmered from a dozen bracelets, gold rings, baubles. Leered when he should have beamed, spat when he should have smarmed. Preened and paraded, shameless. The very picture of excess.

Then there were his bodyguards, his limousines, his mansions. His tantrums and his unmitigated gall. For the fact that he had reinvented himself, started again from scratch, did not mean that he wiped out his old neuroses and terrors. It was just that now he turned them to his own use, as engines rather than blockages. At bottom, he was as isolated and estranged, as screwed up as ever. But now he flaunted it, reveled in his own disturbance.

None of his routines was new in itself. Other Americans had grown their hair, been naughty before. Beats had been more extreme, queens more decadent, film directors more ill-tempered, Trotskyites more radical, gangsters more ostentatious and whores more pious. What was special, unparalleled in Spector was simply that he managed to combine so many different forms of provocation and dissent at once, and also that he made them work for him, in mass commercial terms. He was the first of the anarchist/pop millionaires: at last, in him, odium equaled money.

Money, music, image. In each of them, the breakthrough was absolutely basic. Nobody, it's fair to say, ever wrought deeper changes in the way the rock industry looked, felt, behaved. At the time, in the early Sixties, the upheavals seemed cataclysmic; today we take them for granted. Yet, if only one pauses to consider, the achievement becomes more impressive than ever. To come out of a vacuum and force such changes, at such speed, with such totality—even now, it's hard to conceive the force and self-belief it must have taken. Phil Spector, no doubt, was an earthquake.

After "River Deep–Mountain High," when Spector retired in his huff and went up the hill to El Dorado, the idea was not that he would stagnate but that he would now develop in all kinds of new and most scintillating areas. Perhaps he would produce movies, perhaps he'd set up projects with his friend Lenny Bruce, perhaps he would invade Wall Street. He would relax and read and complete his education; travel, and shoot pool, and train the American karate team. Above all, he would go through psychoanalysis, which would release him from his traumas and render him capable of anything, everything. Soon he would be healthier and happier than he had ever been, and he could make a fresh beginning.

It didn't work; it scarcely could. The greatest strength of rock is that it traps the instant. The corollary, almost inevitably, is that it does not last. By its very nature, which is explosion, it is unequipped for abstractions, for profundity or permanence. While he had existed in perpetual motion, Spector had been invincible. The moment he slowed down, he was lost.

Nonetheless, he struggled. He took long and tortuous journeys with himself, his analyst, his mother, his bodyguards, his soul, his past, his possible future. He watched basketball and almost produced *Easy Rider*. He contemplated and rejected a dozen new departures, and he spawned a son. And at the end of all that, after 30 months of solitude, he was bored stiff.

One of the most frightening aspects of boredom is the panic it promotes. People who stay quite calm through riot, tragedy, even death, go berserk in tedium. So Spector, who had thrived under pressure, now could not stand idleness. Quite simply, he made a fatal surrender—he decided to retrace his steps.

He had a favorite dictum, which he told me several times, always in alien contexts, and that was *never repeat*. "You can always come back," he used to say, "But you've got to come back better. If you come back worse, or even the same, you're dead." And promptly he came back worse, or the same.

Instead of returning to Philles, which was his badge of independence, he made a deal with A&M. Perhaps he needed the money, perhaps he was only in need of emotional support. Whichever, it meant that, for the first time since his teens, he became an employee; a hired gun.

Next he signed a group called Checkmates, a supper-soul act from Vegas, and cut a single called "Love Is All I Have to Give." By his own highest standards, it was average, which placed it at least a class above any other record of 1969. The only trouble was, it wasn't new—it was archetypal Phil Spector, technically and musically superlative, but it broke no fresh ground. Accordingly, it didn't hit.

The followup, "Black Pearl," was less exciting but more

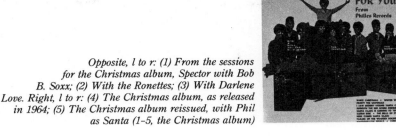

commercial, and it contained one classic teen-dream couplet: "You'll never win a beauty prize, no, they won't pick you/But you're my Miss America, and I love you." As things turned out, it was the last great touch that Spector managed.

"Black Pearl" made the Top 20. So he went back into the studios to cut the obligatory album. Around the same time, I arrived at the Chateau Marmont, and we began to talk.

It was now the summer of 1969, and our conversations lasted several weeks. Between our meetings, meanwhile, Spector went through the motions of hustle. He worked in the studios, set up deals for the future, made large sums of money. However, just like his talk, all this activity seemed somehow spurious, forced. Beneath the hype, I sensed no real hunger. Indeed, the more time I spent around him, the more deeply he seemed paralyzed, and the more I grew convinced that his true moment was gone.

One incident in particular struck me as a perfect symbol.

Down at the Aquarius, at the wrong end of Sunset Boulevard, the producers of *Hair* threw an opening party in the parking lot, late one hot afternoon. All the rich and/or beautiful persons showed up. And so did Spector.

We were still in the Love Age then, and the lot was filled with baubles, bangles, beads. Paraphernalia by numbers—robes and Indian silks, joints in American flag papers, zodiac jackets, patchouli and joss sticks, soul handshakes, handmade Moroccan drums and unwashed feet in sandals. Caftaned musicians from Laurel Canyon tootled away on Arabic flutes and pipes, and long blond girls kept falling over, giggling.

This was the scene Spector stumbled on when he came down from El Dorado, immured behind his smoked windows and his thickest, most impenetrable shades. Cruising by, he told George to drive very slow, rolled his window down six inches and, with utmost caution, he peered out through the slit, took in the tableau.

What he saw was a troupe of girls in semiundress, doing belly dances on a table full of health foods; cross-legged meditators in a circle; the tootlers and thumpers leading an impromptu procession of dancers round the lot, a kind of spaced-out bunny hop; three acid freaks, screaming and laughing uncontrollably, clawing at their eyes, flapping their arms in attempted flight; 200 assorted admen, record executives and publicists, all saying Groovy, Far Out and Too Much; and John Sebastian, standing on one foot like a demented crane, improvising a droned psalm for all humanity.

Spector froze. As though unable to trust his senses, he rolled down his window a few more inches and put his eye still closer to the gap. And that was his undoing, because he was recognized and everyone rushed toward him.

In its own way, this was a major Hollywood event. Since his retirement, Spector had been an almost total recluse. He never appeared in public, cloaked his life in greatest secrecy. So he had acquired near-mythic status as rock's best answer to Howard Hughes, and every move he made, or was rumored to have made, was subject to most furious gossip.

Yet here he was. Live, in person, appearing out of nowhere. The crowd was thrilled, could scarcely believe its luck. Jiggling their beads, jangling their bells in ecstasy, they waved and salaamed, and they brought him their flowers, their joints. Some of them even stripped their clothes off and did a sun dance in celebration. In a sense, after all, Spector was their true founding father. They owed him a great deal: so they rewarded him with adoration.

Spector himself, meanwhile, gazed out at the hordes in a daze, both motionless and expressionless, while they swarmed around his Cadillac and smeared their fingers all over the paintwork. They beamed, he stared. They blew him kisses, and he could not comprehend. Only when a speed freak from the Canyon, naked but for a loincloth, actually put his hand through the lowered window and tried to touch his master's forehead did Phil suddenly come alive and fling himself backward across the seat, shaken by spasms. "George! George!" he squealed, in utter panic. "Get me out of here!"

As the car moved off, he collapsed in a corner, trembling, green faced. Outside a funeral parlor a couple of blocks downtown, he gradually began to recover, subside. In the distance the party continued. The guests capered and flaunted, as though nothing had happened. But Spector did not look back. Eyes half-shut, he seemed drained, entirely spent.

Strange reversal. Very strange indeed. These were his progeny. But now that they confronted him face to face, he could not see the faintest resemblance. "Who were they? I mean, who were those *animals*?" he asked, expecting no answer, and he shook his head slowly, as if in shell shock. Then he wound up his window tight, he headed back for the safety of El Dorado. "My God," he said. "Sweet Lord, what have I done?"

Our book came to nothing. After each meeting, I would take the tapes back to the Chateau and transpose them faithfully, while Angel sucked lollipops. But there was no real point. The contents were always barren.

The time had gone, that was all; I was too late. Already it was impossible to mistake Spector's future, and the vision was soggy, distressing. Having once let go of Philles and allowed himself to be hired, he must automatically lose his uniqueness. Abdicating control, he embarked on yet another invention. And this time, just as in his childhood, his role would be imposed by outsiders, rather than by his own imagination, his inner need.

Naturally, this new self would be colored by his past, his track record. He would never again be seen as runtish or insignificant. On the contrary, he would be a man of substance, revered as a producer, celebrated as a legend. He would be courted and flattered, he would make millions and wield influence, and he would still be a focus for gossip, emulation, envy.

What he wouldn't be, though, was autonomous. He wouldn't transcend all categories, and he would no longer dictate. When he made a record, it would belong less to him than to the performer or the company. It would still be a hit, no doubt. But it would not be Phil Spector.

So it proved. After he had finished with the Checkmates, he moved onward and upward, to the Beatles. He cut "Imagine" with John Lennon and "My Sweet Lord" with George Harrison. In their own context, they were both fine records and, of course, they were monstrous worldwide hits. Superficially, therefore, Spector was right back on top—the number one producer in creation.

The euphoria didn't last. In time, Lennon and Harrison departed, and he could not replace them. When he recorded lesser names, the products failed to sell. In other words, his own presence could no longer guarantee success. Just like any other producer, with the sole exception of his original Philles self, he was dependent on his artists.

That knowledge galled him unbearably. Outraged, despairing, he began to cause scenes, wave his fists at fate. Then he would repent, retreat again into seclusion. But always he was faced by the same eternal problems. What to do next? Where to go?

There were no answers. From time to time, he would go back into the studios, one more time, perhaps with his wife Ronnie, or with Dion. Or he would find some new guru, some miracle healer, to drum up renewed belief in himself. But there was never real fulfillment; not in the end. His myth swamped his present reality, suffocating him.

In spite of that, or because of it, he still stands as the definitive rock 'n' roll saga. No one else had so perfectly caught its potentials, and also its limitations. He'd been everything that pop did best—fast and funny and crazed, full of style and marvelous follies, distinctly heroic; he had also shown just how fast the medium went sour. This was a world made for magnificent flashes, combustions that could never sustain. Get into it two-handed. Stampede right through it and then quit dead, without a backward glance. Don't cruise and don't admire the view. Above all, don't ever stop to think.

On the day I left Los Angeles, I went to say goodbye. In his office, Spector sat surrounded by numberless gold records and told me, for perhaps the third time, how he had chosen the title "To Know Him Is to Love Him." "I took it," he said, "from the words on my grave."

He was standing at the window, looking down at the Strip. For a few seconds he noticed nothing. Just stood there, this tiny, ancient child, with his hair all wisps and his shades refracting silver. Then he heard what he'd said and he turned to face me. He did not look distressed; just puzzled, lost. "Not my grave. I mean my father's," he said. "The words on my father's grave."

Opposite, clockwise from top: (1) Phil Spector with the Checkmates, 1969; (2) The Righteous Brothers; (3) Bob B. Soxx and the Blue Jeans—Darlene Love, center; (4) Phil Spector with the Ronettes and George Harrison. Center: (5) The Ronettes—lead singer and future Spector wife, Ronnie, center. Below: (6) The first teenage millionaire, the early Sixties. (1, A&M Records; 2 & 3, Michael Ochs Archives; 4, Lenny Kaye collection; 5, Original Sound/ collection of Radio KRLA, Los Angeles)

Discography

RECORDS PRODUCED BY PHIL SPECTOR, 1958–1969

Teddy Bears, "To Know Him Is to Love Him" (Dore 503; ☆1, 1958). **Ray Peterson,** "Corinna, Corinna" (Dunes 2002; ☆9, 1960). **Paris Sisters,** "Be My Boy" (Gregmark 2; ☆56, 1961). **Curtis Lee,** "Pretty Little Angel Eyes" (Dunes 2007; ☆7, 1961). **Paris Sisters,** "I Love How You Love Me" (Gregmark 6; ☆5, 1961). **Gene Pitney,** "Every Breath I Take" (Musicor 1011; ☆42, 1961). **Curtis Lee,** "Under the Moon of Love" (Dunes 2008; ☆46, 1961). **Crystals,** "There's No Other (like My Baby)" (Philles 100; ☆20, 1961). **Ray Peterson,** "I Could Have Loved You So Well" (Dunes 2009; ☆57, 1961). **Paris Sisters,** "He Knows I Love Him Too Much" (Gregmark 10; ☆34, 1962). **Crystals,** "Uptown" (Philles 102; ☆13, 1962). **Connie Francis,** "Second Hand Love" (MGM 13074; ☆7, 1962). **Crystals,** "He Hit Me (and It Felt like a Kiss)" (Philles 105). **"He's a Rebel"** (Philles 106; ☆1, 1962). **Bob B. Soxx and the Blue Jeans,** "Zip-a-Dee Doo-Dah" (Philles 107; ☆8, 1962). **Crystals,** "He's Sure the Boy I Love" (Philles 109; ☆11, 1962). **Alley Cats,** "Puddin n' Tain" (Philles 108; ☆43, 1963). **Bob B. Soxx and the Blue Jeans,** "Why Do Lovers Break Each Other's Heart" (Philles 110; ☆38, 1963). **Darlene Love,** "(Today I Met) The Boy I'm Gonna Marry" (Philles 111; ☆39, 1963). **Crystals,** "Da Doo Ron Ron" (Philles 112; ☆3, 1963). **Bob B. Soxx and the Blue Jeans,** "Not Too Young to Get Married" (Philles 113; ☆63, 1963). **Darlene Love,** "Wait 'Til My Bobby Gets Home" (Philles 114; ☆26, 1963). **Crystals,** "Then He Kissed Me" (Philles 115; ☆6, 1963). **Ronettes,** "Be My Baby" (Philles 116; ☆2, 1963). **Darlene Love,** "A Fine Fine Boy" (Philles 117; ☆53, 1963). **Ronettes,** "Baby, I Love You" (Philles 118; ☆24, 1963). **Crystals,** "Little Boy" (Philles 119; ☆92, 1964). **Ronettes,** "(The Best Part of) Breakin' Up" (Philles 120; ☆39, 1964). "Do I Love You" (Philles 121; ☆34, 1964). **Crystals,** "All Grown Up" (Philles 122; ☆98, 1964). **Ronettes,** "Walking in the Rain" (Philles 123; ☆23, 1964). **Righteous Brothers,** "You've Lost That Lovin' Feelin'" (Philles 124; ☆1, 1964). **Ronettes,** "Born to Be Together" (Philles 126; ☆52, 1965). **Righteous Brothers,** "Just Once in My Life" (Philles 127; ☆9, 1965). **Ronettes,** "Is This What I Get for Loving You?" (Philles 128; ☆75, 1965). **Righteous Brothers,** "Unchained Melody" (Philles 129; ☆4, 1965). "Ebb Tide" (Philles 130; ☆5, 1965). **Ike and Tina Turner,** "River Deep—Mountain High" (Philles 131; ☆88, 1966). **Checkmates,** "Love Is All I Have to Give" (A & M 1039; ☆65, 1969). **Sonny Charles and the Checkmates, Ltd.,** "Black Pearl" (A & M 1053; ☆13, 1969). "Proud Mary" (A & M 1127; ☆69, 1969).

Although uncredited, Spector claims to have produced the following records: **Ben E. King,** "Spanish Harlem" (Atco 6185; ☆10, 1961). "Stand by Me" (Atco 6194; ☆4, 1961). "Amor" (Atco 6203; ☆18, 1961). **Nino Tempo and April Stevens,** "Deep Purple" (Atco 6273; ☆1, 1963). "Whispering" (Atco 6281; ☆11, 1963). (Chart positions compiled from Joel Whitburn's *Record Research*, based on *Billboard* Pop chart.)

The Girl Groups
by Greil Marcus

Of all the genres of rock and roll, girl group rock is likely the warmest and the most affecting. The style flourished between 1958 and 1965, fallow years for rock and roll, and it flourished for the same reasons much of the rest of the music of the time grew tame, predictable, and dull.

Girl group rock was producers' music; the songs came out of the Brill Building, written by contract songwriters (Carole King, herself once a member of an early Fifties girl group under her real name, Carol Klein; Gerry Goffin; Ellie Greenwich; Barry Mann; etc.). The "artists" had no "creative freedom." Yet when we look back, we find that the worst of the rock and roll made under such circumstances was made by male singers; the records made by girls are, all in all, glorious. Why? Perhaps it is because the males were singing rock and roll only as a stopover on the road to Vegas, as a trying-out for the security of a nightclub act. The girls, on the other hand, were aimed at teenagers; no thought seems to have been given to smoothing out their music in hopes of attracting "a broader audience." In other words, bets were not hedged. And so, if you were looking for rock and roll between Elvis and the Beatles, girl groups gave you the genuine article.

The form stretches from the classic broken hearts of the Chantels, the first major group, through Rosie and the Originals, the Shirelles, the Marvelettes (the only true "girl" group on Motown), Little Eva, the Chiffons, countless lesser groups like the Angels, the Cookies, the Toys, Claudine Clark (a solo singer, working in the style), the Sensations, the Jaynetts. The form reaches its height with the Spector groups—the Crystals, the Ronettes, and Darlene Love backed by the Crystals—and with the blazing, hokey teen morality plays of the Shangri-Las. Within that listing is emotion of staggering intensity, unforgettable melodies, great humor, a good deal of rage, and a lot more struggle—the struggle, one might think, of the singer—a young girl, black as likely as not—against the domination of her white, male producer. The relationship between singer and producer was dependent; almost none of the great lead singers of girl group rock—Arlene Smith of the Chantels, Shirley Allston of the Shirelles, Darlene Love of the Crystals—achieved even minimal success outside of the direction of the producer originally responsible for her.

Still, it was music of celebration—of simple joy, of innocence, of sex, of life itself, at times—but most often it was a celebration of The Boy. The Boy is the central mythic figure in the lyrics of girl group rock. He is shadowy: the boy who'll love walking in the rain, the fine fine boy, the leader of the pack, the angel baby. He is irresistible—and almost never macho. He is sensitive. He must be pursued. How to reach him? "You can call me up and have a date, any old time," grinned the Marvelettes: "Beechwood 4-5789." "I met him on a Sunday and my heart stood still," sang Darlene Love in the Crystal's magnificent "Da Doo Ron Ron," but really, she only caught a glimpse of him—

"somebody" *else* had to tell her "that his name was Bill." The theme then, is little more than a variation on the Search for Perfect Love and the Attempt to Bring It Home to Meet Mom and Dad (even in the Shangri-La's hits—"Leader of the Pack," "I Can Never Go Home Anymore"—where Mom and Dad won't let it in the house).

The music was perhaps the most carefully, beautifully crafted in all of rock and roll—one reason why none of the 20 or so best records in the genre have dated in the years since they were made. Spector's sound was of course the apotheosis of this approach, of producers' music; but even George Goldner's original productions with the Chantels, which underlie all that followed ("Without George Goldner," said Spector, "there would have been no rock and roll"), are pristine, larger-than-life, taking over a listener and for three minutes driving everything but that sound out of the listener's world. In between Spector and Goldner are some of the more memorable moments in all of rock and roll: the piano on "One Fine Day"; Claudine Clark screaming "I SEE THE PARTY LIGHTS!" with unfathomable passion; the unbelievably sexual syncopation of the Shirelles' "Tonight's the Night"; the pile-driving force of "Da Doo Ron Ron"; the good smile of the Crystal's "He's Sure the Boy I Love," a smile that stretched all across America in 1963, the year that record became a hit.

It was utopian stuff—a utopia of love between a boy and a girl, a utopia of feeling, of sentiment, of desire most of all. That the crassest conditions the recording industry has been able to contrive led to emotionally rich music is a good chapter in someone's thesis on Art and Capitalism, but it happened. That utopian spirit has stayed with those who partook of it—the formal style of girl group rock has passed, but the aesthetic, the spirit of the thing, is there to hear in John Lennon, Bruce Springsteen, Patti Smith, the Three Degrees, Bette Midler. As remnants and impersonators of the old groups make the grimy rounds of the oldies concerts, perhaps they find amusement in the fact that their music, never intended to be more than a round dollar with a hole in it, has lasted.

To sum it up, to sum up the scores of records that were made; the dozens of groups that formed and scattered; the many venal or paternal producers, some like Goldner dead now, some like Spector, still young men with no worlds left to conquer; the songwriters still grinding out the songs or, like Carole King, with the careers of their own—perhaps to sum it all up, one record will do: Phil Spector's "A Fine Fine Boy," a Darlene Love single that barely scraped the charts in 1963. It overwhelms. Its momentum is unbreakable, the backup singing full of delight and wisdom and humor, and the vocal is—well, it is that utopia of feeling. It is Darlene, telling us about her fine fine

The Marvelettes (Ralph J. Gleason collection)

154

boy. She's full of pride; most of girl group rock is music of pain
and longing, of pining away, but there isn't a hint of that here.
Darlene has what she wants and she knows what he's worth—
after about ten seconds, so do you, and you'll never forget it.
Church bells ring (that's not a metaphor; they *do*) and the whole
disc seems to physically jump. It never stops. And the message?
What does girl group rock say? What does it come down to?
What is its mystery of life? "He even takes me places and buys
me things/But love is more important than a diamond ring."

Discography

Chantels, "Maybe" (End 1005; ☆15, 1958). **Chantels,** "Every Night" (End 1015; ☆40, 1958). **Shirelles,** "I Met Him on a Sunday" (Decca 30588; ☆50, 1958). **Chantels,** "I Love You So" (End 1020; ☆42, 1958). **Shirelles,** "Tonight's the Night" (Scepter 1208; ☆39, 1960). **Kathy Young and the Innocents,** "A Thousand Stars" (Indigo 108; ☆3, 1960). **Shirelles,** "Will You Love Me Tomorrow" (Scepter 1211; ☆1, 1960). **Rosie and the Originals,** "Angel Baby" (Highland 1011; ☆5, 1960). **Shirelles,** "Dedicated to the One I Love" (Scepter 1203; ☆3, 1961). **Shirelles,** "Mama Said" (Scepter 1217; ☆4, 1961). **Paris Sisters,** "I Love How You Love Me" (Gregmark 6; ☆5, 1961). **Marvelettes,** "Please Mr. Postman" (Tamla 54046; ☆1, 1961). **Chantels,** "Look in My Eyes" (Carlton 555; ☆14, 1961). **Angels,** "'Till" (Caprice 107; ☆14, 1961). **Crystals,** "There's No Other" (Philles 100; ☆20, 1961). **Shirelles,** "Baby It's You" (Scepter 1227; ☆8, 1961). **Sensations,** "Let Me In" (Argo 5405; ☆4, 1962). **Crystals,** "Uptown" (Philles 102; ☆13, 1962). **Shirelles,** "Soldier Boy" (Scepter 1228; ☆1, 1962). **Marvelettes,** "Playboy" (Tamla 54060; ☆7, 1962). **Claudine Clark,** "Party Lights" (Chancellor 1113; ☆5, 1962). **Marvelettes,** "Beechwood 4-5789" (Tamla 54060; ☆17, 1962). **Crystals,** "He's a Rebel" (Philles 106; ☆1, 1962). **Cookies,** "Chains" (Dimension 1002; ☆17, 1962). **Exciters,** "Tell Him" (United Artists 544; ☆4, 1962). **Crystals,** "He's Sure the Boy I Love" (Philles 109; ☆11, 1962). **Chiffons,** "He's So Fine" (Laurie 3152; ☆1, 1963). **Shirelles,** "Foolish Little Girl" (Scepter 1248; ☆4, 1963). **Cookies,** "Don't Say Nothin' Bad (about My Baby)" (Dimension 1008; ☆7, 1963). **Darlene Love,** "(Today I Met) The Boy I'm Gonna Marry" (Philles 111, ☆39, 1963). **Crystals,** "Da Doo Ron Ron" (Philles 112; ☆3, 1963). **Lesley Gore,** "It's My Party" (Mercury 72119; ☆1, 1963). **Chiffons,** "One Fine Day" (Laurie 3179; ☆5, 1963). **Lesley Gore,** "Judy's Turn to Cry" (Mercury 72143; ☆5, 1963). **Angels,** "My Boyfriend's Back" (Smash 1834; ☆1, 1963). **Crystals,** "Then He Kissed Me" (Philles 115; ☆6, 1963). **Raindrops,** "The Kind of Boy You Can't Forget" (Jubilee 5455; ☆17, 1963). **Ronettes,** "Be My Baby" (Philles 116; ☆2, 1963). **Jaynetts,** "Sally Go 'Round the Roses" (Tuff 369; ☆2, 1963). **Lesley Gore,** "She's a Fool" (Mercury 72180; ☆5, 1963). **Angels,** "I Adore Him" (Smash 1854; ☆25, 1963). **Darlene Love,** "A Fine Fine Boy" (Philles 117; ☆53, 1963). **Ronettes,** "Baby, I Love You" (Philles 118; ☆24, 1963). **Lesley Gore,** "You Don't Own Me" (Mercury 72206; ☆2, 1963). **Dixie Cups,** "Chapel of Love" (Red Bird 10-001; ☆1, 1964). **Jelly Beans,** "I Wanna Love Him So Bad" (Red Bird 10-003; ☆9, 1964). **Patty and the Emblems,** "Mixed-Up Shook-Up Girl" (Herald 590; ☆37, 1964). **Dixie Cups,** "People Say" (Red Bird 10-006; ☆12, 1964). **Shangri-Las,** "Remember (Walkin' in the Sand)" (Red Bird 10-008; ☆5, 1964). **Shangri-Las,** "Leader of the Pack" (Red Bird 10-014; ☆1, 1964). **Ronettes,** "Walking in the Rain" (Philles 123; ☆23, 1964). **Shangri-Las,** "Give Him a Great Big Kiss" (Red Bird 10-018; ☆18, 1964). **Ad Libs,** "The Boy from New York City" (Blue Cat 102; ☆8, 1965). **Dixie Cups,** "Iko Iko" (Red Bird 10-017; ☆20, 1965). **Shangri-Las,** "Give Us Your Blessings" (Red Bird 10-030; ☆29, 1965). **Toys,** "A Lover's Concerto" (Dyno Voice 209; ☆2, 1965). **Shangri-Las,** "I Can Never Go Home Anymore" (Red Bird 10-043; ☆6, 1965).

(Chart positions taken from Joel Whitburn's *Record Research,* compiled from *Billboard* Pop chart.)

The Beach Boys
by Jim Miller

Gone are the white Levis, tennies and striped shirts. Gone too are the odes to affluent hedonism, replaced by a host of ecologic, mystic and poetic preoccupations. Yet despite the beards, beads and plugs for TM, the Beach Boys, after 15 years in the business, remain identifiably the Beach Boys. Alone among white American rock groups, their ingenuity has sustained them over a decade, at times shaping, at times ignoring the whims of passing fancy.

The elements of their style are by now legend: the vocals, densely clustered or moving in counterpoint, simultaneously frail and precise; the compositions, some complex, others elementary, some anthemlike, others confessional, some a catalog of clichés, others a revision of rock orthodoxy.

In the Sixties, when they were at the height of their original popularity, the Beach Boys propagated their own variant on the American dream, painting a dazzling picture of beaches, parties and endless summers, a paradise of escape into private as often as shared pleasures. Yet by the late Sixties, the band was articulating, with less success, a disenchantment with that suburban ethos, and a search for transcendence. It has been a curious trek from hot rods and high times to religion and conservation; yet through it all, the Beach Boys have remained wed to the California that Chuck Berry once called the "promised land"—and their resurgent popularity says as much about the potency of that chimera as it does about the Beach Boys.

They were winners from the start: "Surfin'," their first release on a local L.A. label, made the city's charts in 1961. At a time when rock had become a game for Tin Pan Alley pros, the Beach Boys were very much a family affair: Brian Wilson, 19, his brother Dennis, 17, and Carl, at 15 the youngest Wilson, formed the original group, together with cousin Mike Love and their Hawthorne neighbor, Alan Jardine.

In surfing, the Beach Boys had hit upon a potent image. Leisure, mobility and privacy—it was the suburban myth transported to the Pacific Ocean, but rendered heroic. There had been "surf bands" (such as Dick Dale's) in California before the Beach Boys, but these bands played a homogeneous brand of instrumental rock, crossed with rhythm and blues; the Beach Boys, with their neatly trimmed harmonies, were projecting a world view.

"Surfin' Safari," the group's first national hit on Capitol, launched surf music as a fad; by "Surfin' U.S.A.," the Beach Boys' followup in early 1963, the group had perfected a style. Working off a cop from Chuck Berry's "Sweet Little Sixteen," Brian and Mike contrived a set of lyrics that revealed no small flair for constructing teen utopias ("If everybody had an ocean . . ."); and the music itself was no less striking. While the blanched vocals harked back to the Four Preps, the guitars had the crude drive of a high school band; coming in the midst of teen idols, Brill Building pop and seductive "girl groups," the first Beach Boys hits managed to sound raunchy and vital, yet

clean, somehow safe—for here was a rock and roll band aspiring to the instrumental sleekness of the Ventures, the lyric sophistication of Chuck Berry, and the vocal expertise of some weird cross between the Lettermen and Frankie Lymon and the Teenagers.

Surfin' U.S.A., the group's second album, sold extraordinarily well at a time when singles were still the barometer of pop success. When the Beach Boys returned to the studio, it was under the tutelage of Brian Wilson, who became the band's producer. The Beach Boys thus were one of the first rock groups with studio control; and to a large extent, their history is the story of the records Brian made.

He was not your average rock and roll star. Moody and withdrawn, Brian never quite fit the carefree stereotype the early Beach Boys so carefully cultivated. Onstage, he smiled a lot, but looked awkward; the show focused on the mugging of Mike and Carl, and the athletic sex appeal of Dennis. In the safety of the studio, on the other hand, he was the group's dominant voice, always plotting fresh departures and refining old ideas, rarely content to recycle a tried and true formula. Like his idol Phil Spector, he came to be considered something of an oddball genius.

The first LP he produced for the Beach Boys, *Surfer Girl,* hinted at things to come. For the first time, Brian used his falsetto extensively, sharing lead vocals with Mike Love, whose nasal drone propelled all of the group's early uptempo hits. The group's harmonies veered toward the modern voicings of the Four Freshmen, and the success of "Surfer Girl," a cool ballad, enabled Brian to fill the album with similarly romantic fare, tied to surfing in name only. More importantly, Brian let a little of himself be expressed; on "In My Room," his pure falsetto, soaring over violins (another innovation), carried a message of suburban-bred agoraphobia at variance with (although not unrelated to) the Beach Boys' official posture of nonstop kicks: "There's a world where I can go/And tell my secrets to/In my room. . . . "

Throughout this early period, the Beach Boys refined their sound. On straight rockers, they sang tight harmonies behind Love's lead, with Carl contributing crisp, if rudimentary, guitar lines; on the ballads, Brian played his falsetto off against lush, jazz-tinged voicings, often using (for rock) unorthodox harmonic structures. At the same time, the group's pursuit of Fun, whether on a surfboard or in a car, set them apart and assured them of an audience, no matter how restrictive the specific motifs—although surfing, cars and the California locale all became emblematic, of course.

California—in 1963, it was the one place west of the Mississippi where everyone wanted to be. Rich and fast, cars, women, one suburban plot for everyone: a sea of happy humanity sandwiched between frosty mountains and toasty beaches, all an

The Beach Boys in the mid-Sixties

easy drive down the freeway. But was it that simple and bright? Behind the pursuit of fun, you might hear a hint of tedium, or a realization that each day blemished the pristine Youth this culture coveted. Brian Wilson understood this perfectly, and, characteristically, made it attractive and not a little heroic, as in "I Get Around," in which he expresses sheer frustration: "I'm gettin' bugged drivin' up and down the same old strip. . . . " His business was the revitalization of myths he wished were true and knew were false. The hollowness, properly dressed up as adolescent yearning, could itself be marketed in "teen feel" pop songs.

Brian Wilson in any case was after something more than simple celebrations of suburbia. Throughout 1963, Phil Spector's Crystals and Ronettes recordings poured epic crescendos of sound into three-minute singles. The resonance and self-conscious imagery of Spector's records caught Brian's ear. From 1964 to *Pet Sounds* (May 1966), he dedicated himself to duplicating that oceanic sound. He would wed the Beach Boys' own harmonic expertise to Spector's use of layered percussion and orchestration. But Brian was not after mere imitation; the same impacted density would amplify his own lyrical themes. Suburban values wouldn't be abandoned—they'd be rendered profound, their ambiguities expressed.

"Fun, Fun, Fun" and "Don't Worry Baby" marked the break. "Don't Worry," ostensibly about a drag race, represented an earnest confession of insecurity: "Well, it's been buildin' up inside of me for, oh, I don't know how long/I don't know why, but I keep thinkin' something's bound to go wrong." The vocal arrangement underlined this vulnerability at every turn, casting the lyric's anxiety against a soothing expanse of overdubbed harmony parts. The Beach Boys were beginning to push pop conventions to their limits.

Meanwhile, hit followed hit, each marking some small advance over its predecessor. After "I Get Around," a brilliant teen anthem mounted with unorthodox chord changes, the singles toyed with an ever broader palette of colors. "Dance, Dance, Dance" was the most successful musically, an unabashed rocker driven by Spectoresque percussion (sleigh bells, castanets, tambourine). But "When I Grow Up (to Be a Man)" stands as Brian's most touching work of the period. Its sad queries ("Will I dig the same things that turned me on as a kid?") formed an admission of the ephemerality of youth, the passage of time underlined by the tolling of years on the refrain ("16, 17").

By 1965, "California Girls" and *Summer Days (and Summer Nights)*, Brian's style had fully developed. The group's last unadulterated fling at summer in the suburbs, *Summer Days* included such highlights as "Let Him Run Wild," a cyclical construct that recalled Holland-Dozier-Holland at Motown as much as it evoked Phil Spector. Brian had tamed the studio,

just as the group had mastered his daunting arrangements.

Yet Brian increasingly played the recluse, dropping all concert dates with the band to concentrate on composing and producing. Commercially, the Beach Boys stayed on top, churning out virtually flawless singles, which, after "Surfin' U.S.A.," almost always reached the Top 30 nationally. Brian Wilson, however, wasn't looking back.

Not without regret, the Beach Boys, presumably at Brian's behest, abandoned their search for the perpetual followup. Perhaps, as some have claimed, Brian Wilson was consumed by a desire to better the Beatles; or perhaps, more simply, he was intent on working out the music already in his mind. Whatever the reasons, Wilson now focused all of his energy on creating an album that would fully reflect the Beach Boys' capabilities, by elaborating a new intricacy and a new seriousness of intent.

Their next album, *Pet Sounds,* ushered in a turbulent period for the group. While "Wouldn't It Be Nice," the opening cut, presented Brian's fantasy of marital bliss, the rest of the record vented Wilson's obsession with isolation, cataloging a forlorn quest for security. The whole enterprise, which smacked slightly of song cycle pretensions, was streaked with regret and romantic languor: "I had to prove that I could make it alone now/But that's not me." But it worked; sweetening each cut with everything from chamber strings to a lonesome koto, Wilson distilled a potent brew, both confessional and maudlin, in the melodramatic fashion of Paul Anka. The Beach Boys have never quite recaptured the sustained brilliance of Brian's settings for these songs: and it was his music that carried the lyrics and made them evocative rather than trite.

The record's conclusion was pessimistic, charting the inevitability of change. By closing the cycle on a note of resignation ("Where did your long hair go?/Where is the little girl I used to know?"), "Caroline, No" revealed the emptiness of Brian's daydream on "Wouldn't It Be Nice." Unfortunately, such expressions of adolescent angst were not everybody's cup of tea: compared to previous Beach Boy albums, *Pet Sounds* sold poorly.

As if to prove the Beach Boys could still cut a happy-go-lucky Top 40 single, Brian countered with "Good Vibrations," a foray into full-fledged psychedelia. Through dozens of overdubs and six months of painstaking work, the group created their biggest hit to date.

It was Brian Wilson's finest hour as a producer. Opening over muted bass, organ triplets and a brace of flutes, Carl's lead vocal lent the song a hushed intimacy; and the voicings on the refrain were scored over a rapidly bowed bass and theremin, the song's "psychedelic" ingredient. In midstream, harpsichord, jew's-harp, tambourine, sleigh bells and thickly carpeted vocals swirled into a retard—and suddenly "Good Vibrations" became a meditation for organ, breathy vocals and possibly wind chimes (Brian's penchant for weird per-

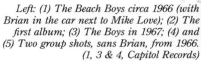

Left: (1) The Beach Boys circa 1966 (with Brian in the car next to Mike Love); (2) The first album; (3) The Boys in 1967; (4) and (5) Two group shots, sans Brian, from 1966. (1, 3 & 4, Capitol Records)

cussion reached new heights here).

Not satisfied with this symphonic million-seller, Wilson pressed on. In 1967 he and lyricist Van Dyke Parks were hard at work on a new, more humorous song cycle. The work was to be called *Smile*, and would include a four-part suite on the elements, as well as "Heroes and Villains," "Vegetables," "Cabinessence" and "Surf's Up." Designed as Brian's crowning achievement, *Smile* would supposedly place the Beach Boys right next to the Beatles in the pantheon of arty rock.

But personality problems had begun to take their toll. As legend has it, Brian, suddenly paranoid, destroyed most of the album's laboriously assembled vocal tracks. The group began objecting to Brian's increasing eccentricity, and Brian himself was reportedly depressed by the appearance of *Sgt. Pepper*. *Smile* finally collapsed under the accumulated pressures.

In its wake, the Beach Boys issued an abridged version of "Heroes and Villians," and *Smiley Smile*, a substitute for *Smile*. Long on parched humor and short on ambitious new music, the album was anticlimactic, to put it mildly. It was also the first album produced by the Beach Boys collectively.

Smiley and its successor, *Wild Honey*, marked a turning point for the Beach Boys. In its heyday, the band had dominated the charts thanks to Brian's skill at cutting hit singles; since the early songs were composed by a performing member of a performing group, they could be successfully re-created onstage. But starting with *Pet Sounds*, the music's complexity virtually precluded live performance; even worse, many of the new lyrics hardly hinted at the sunny fare Beach Boy fans expected. Perhaps sensing defeat in his effort to broaden the group's scope, Brian retreated; after *Wild Honey*, his contributions diminished, often taking the shape of writing three or four tunes for an album.

A few scattered tracks like "Darlin'" and "Do It Again" dented the Top 20 in 1967 and 1968; and in Europe, the Beach Boys' popularity continued unabated. But the days of coasting on the charts were over.

Unhappy with their Capitol contract, the band played out their last two years with the label. On albums like *Friends*, it almost seemed as if they were attempting, defiantly, to be uncommercial. A return to *Smiley's* dryness, minus the weirdness, *Friends* cast the Beach Boys as auteurs: coming from anybody else, the album would have been embarrassing; coming from them, it had the ring of autobiographical truth.

Brian, in the songs he contributed to the venture, returned to the suburban themes that have always preoccupied him; only now, the good life appeared as an exercise in ennui: "I get a lot of thoughts in the mornin'," sang Brian in "Busy Doin' Nothin'," "I write 'em all down/If it wasn't for that, I'd forget 'em in a while." At their best, the Beach Boys have never flinched before their own banality. "Busy Doin' Nothin'," for

example, featured an entire verse devoted to dialing a telephone and not getting an answer. It is one of Brian's most subtle lyrical conquests.

Friends, when set against the success of "Do It Again," a summer-fun rehash, illustrated the band's dilemma. On the one hand, by milking familiar formulas, they could still command an audience; on the other hand, whenever they released a personal statement, or experimental material, the group found themselves performing in a vacuum.

With the expiration of their Capitol contract in 1969, the Beach Boys thus faced several questions. Should they disband in the face of sporadic sales and indifferent response? Should they change their name, a liability in "hip" circles, and aim exclusively at the burgeoning market for "progressive rock"? Or should they continue as before, retain their original name and identity, and record whatever material they felt appropriate?

The answers came in 1970. The Beach Boys signed with Reprise Records, reactivated their own Brother Records logo (which had appeared on *Smiley Smile's* label), played the Big Sur Folk Festival, and issued *Sunflower*, their strongest album since *Pet Sounds*. In name, style and sound, they remained the Beach Boys.

In the five years since, the group has reestablished a loyal following among a new generation, and emerged as one of the biggest live acts in the U.S. In addition, they have continued to record new original material, with fitful public response.

Surf's Up, released in 1971, epitomized the post-*Pet Sounds* Beach Boys. On such tracks as "Long Promised Road," Carl Wilson emerged as Brian's heir apparent, a composer with an intuitive grasp of the Beach Boys' style. But *Surf's Up* also contained large doses of puffery, pretentiousness and ecological nonsense. Truth to tell, the Beach Boys had evolved into an accomplished, idiosyncratic but sometimes sterile ensemble, at least in the studio.

On the road it was a different story. Although the band had been a concert draw in the mid-Sixties, its skid on the charts had brought a virtual halt to touring. The group's pact with Reprise, however, dictated a new strategy: since most of America hadn't heard them since the Sixties, or had never heard them, the Beach Boys decided to return to the road and perfect their live performance. Initially, they labored over contemporary material, finally mastering such difficult songs as "Wouldn't It Be Nice."

But it was the surfing and car songs that brought audiences to their feet. At first the group persisted in largely performing recent material, but as the crowds grew, the pressure to concentrate on the oldies became irresistible. Eventually, in 1974, they found themselves blessed with a million-selling Number One album. They were back on top. There was only one small problem: *Endless Summer*, their first gold record since "Good Vibrations," consisted entirely of tracks cut before 1965.

Opposite: Brian Wilson with wife Marilyn, a singer whom he produced as one-half of the vocal group Spring (Earl Leaf). Below: The Beach Boys in 1971 (clockwise from top left: Brian, Mike Love, Al Jardine, Bruce Johnston, Dennis Wilson, and, in the center, Carl Wilson). (Annie Leibovitz)

To Brian, the problem must have seemed particularly acute. On the one hand, he now composed moody, introspective miniature operas, like " 'Til I Die" on *Surf's Up*—although he was reportedly reluctant to release the song, because it wasn't "fun." On the other hand, he was still capable of writing happy-go-lucky songs like those behind the Beach Boys' initial popularity, as "Marcella" on *Carl and the Passions* showed. Unfortunately, almost all of his writing had become baroque, condensed, difficult to execute forcefully, and, apparently, difficult for an audience to hear. They wanted the cheerful values of the early Sixties reaffirmed, resoundingly, in the compelling and straightforward fashion of the early hits. What Brian for his part wanted was considerably less clear: perhaps just to trundle around the house and run the Radiant Radish, his organic-foods shop in Hollywood.

Buried by a tidal wave of nostalgia, and more or less abandoned by Brian, their greatest creative asset, the Beach Boys had little choice but to embrace their past. Hooking up with Jim Guercio, managing and marketing mastermind for Chicago, they triumphantly toured to sellout crowds. But in the meantime, little new material emerged from the studios.

Ironically, Brian Wilson remains the group's guiding light. It is Brian's old songs that the band plays night after night; and it is Brian's new songs that stand out on the later Beach Boy albums. Indeed, the Beach Boys remain beholden to a style bequeathed them by Brian. From the nasal raunch of "Surfin' Safari" to the convoluted elegance of "Surf's Up," that style has become a nearly autonomous fund of favored themes, production tricks and chord progressions. In tacit acknowledgment of his continued preeminence, even in absentia, 1973's *Holland* opened and closed with a new song by Brian Wilson.

But the future remains uncertain. For one thing, Brian by the end of 1975 had yet to resume an active role within the group despite persistent rumors to the contrary; for another, the group is almost exclusively identified in the public's mind with its hits from the early Sixties. Like Chuck Berry, the Beach Boys lyrically and musically reflect an era; yet like the Beatles, the band has matured and progressed within the confines of a unique style. In many respects, they are the most innovative white rock and roll band the United States has ever seen. But whether they will ever be able to lead their audience beyond the uncomplicated suburban utopia their early hits so brilliantly depicted is another question entirely.

Discography

Singles

"Surfin' " (Candix 331; ☆75, 1962). "Surfin' Safari" (Capitol 4777; ☆14, 1962). "Ten Little Indians" (Capitol 4880; ☆49, 1962). "Surfin' U.S.A." b/w "Shut Down" (Capitol 4932; ☆3, 1963). "Surfer Girl" b/w "Little Deuce Coupe" (Capitol 5009; ☆7, 1963). "Be True to Your School" b/w "In My Room" (Capitol 5069; ☆6, 1963). "Fun, Fun, Fun" (Capitol 5118; ☆5, 1964). "I Get Around" b/w "Don't Worry Baby" (Capitol 5174; ☆1, 1964). "When I Grow Up (to Be a Man)" (Capitol 5245; ☆9, 1964). "Wendy" (Capitol E.P. 5267; ☆44, 1964). "Dance, Dance, Dance" (Capitol 5306; ☆8, 1964). "Do You Wanna Dance?" (Capitol 5372; ☆12, 1965). "Help Me, Rhonda" (Capitol 5395; ☆1, 1965). "California Girls" (Capitol 5464; ☆3, 1965). "The Little Girl I Once Knew" (Capitol 5540; ☆20, 1965). "Barbara Ann" (Capitol 5561; ☆2, 1966). "Sloop John B" (Capitol 5602; ☆3, 1966).

"Wouldn't It Be Nice" b/w "God Only Knows" (Capitol 5706; ☆8, 1966). "Good Vibrations" (Capitol 5676; ☆1, 1966). "Heroes and Villains" (Brother 1001; ☆12, 1967). "Wild Honey" (Capitol 2028; ☆31, 1967). "Darlin' " (Capitol 2068; ☆19, 1967). "Friends" (Capitol 2160; ☆47, 1968). "Do It Again" (Capitol 2239; ☆20, 1968). "I Can Hear Music" (Capitol 2432; ☆24, 1969). "Break Away" (Capitol 2530; ☆63, 1969). "Add Some Music to Your Day" (Reprise 0894; ☆64, 1970). "Long Promised Road" (Brother/Reprise 1047; ☆89, 1971). "Sail On Sailor" (Brother 1138; ☆79, 1973). "Surfin' U.S.A." (Capitol 3924; ☆36, 1974.)

Albums

Surfin' Safari (Capitol 1808; ☆32, 1962). *Surfin' U.S.A.* (Capitol 1890; ☆2, 1963). *Surfer Girl* (Capitol 1981; ☆7, 1963). *Little Deuce Coupe* (Capitol 1998; ☆4, 1963). *Shut Down—Vol. 2* (Capitol 2027; ☆13, 1964). *All Summer Long* (Capitol 2110; ☆4, 1964). *The Beach Boys' Concert* (Capitol 2198; ☆1, 1964). *The Beach Boys Today* (Capitol 2269; ☆4, 1965). *Summer Days (and Summer Nights)* (Capitol 2354; ☆2, 1965). *The Beach Boys' Party* (Capitol 2398; ☆6, 1965). *Pet Sounds* (Capitol 2458; ☆10, 1966). *Best of the Beach Boys—Vol. 1* (Capitol 2545; ☆8, 1966). *Best of the Beach Boys—Vol. 2* (Capitol 2706; ☆50, 1967). *Smiley Smile* (Brother 9001; ☆41, 1967). *Wild Honey* (Capitol 2859; ☆24, 1967). *Friends* (Capitol 2895; ☆126, 1968). *Best of the Beach Boys—Vol. 3* (Capitol 2945; ☆153, 1968). *20/20* (Capitol 133; ☆68, 1969). *Close Up* (Capitol 253; ☆136, 1969). *Sunflower* (Reprise 6382; ☆151, 1970). *Surf's Up* (Reprise 6453; ☆29, 1971). *Pet Sounds/Carl and the Passions "So Tough"* (Reprise 2083; ☆50, 1972). *Holland* (Reprise 2118; ☆36, 1973). *The Beach Boys in Concert* (Reprise 6484; ☆25, 1973). *Endless Summer* (Capitol 11307; ☆1, 1974). *Spirit of America* (Capitol 11384; ☆8, 1975). *Good Vibrations: Best of the Beach Boys* (Reprise 6484/Brother 2223; ☆25, 1975). *20/20 and Wild Honey* (Reprise 2166; ☆50, 1974). *Friends and Smiley Smile* (Reprise 2167; ☆125, 1974).
(Chart positions taken from Joel Whitburn's *Record Research,* compiled from *Billboard* Pop and LPs charts.)

The British Invasion
by Lester Bangs

For an event so crucial in the history of pop music, the "British invasion" produced little of enduring worth. Out of it all, only the music of the Beatles, the Rolling Stones, the Who and the Kinks have lasted; the Searchers, Herman's Hermits, Gerry and the Pacemakers and all the rest today seem quainter than doo-wop—curious relics of a consumers' fever that has long since palled. The reason they seem quaint is that they were, by and large, junk: perfect expressions of the pop aesthetic of a disposable culture. Which is all right. In the fatuity of their enthusiasm lay their very charm.

Consider the time, early 1964. America—perhaps young America in particular—had just lost a president who had seemed a godlike embodiment of national ideals, who had been a youth-cult superstar himself. We were down, we needed a shot of cultural speed, something high, fast, loud and superficial to fill the gap; we needed a fling after the wake. It was no accident that the Beatles had their overwhelmingly successful Ed Sullivan show debut shortly after JFK was shot (the date was February 9th, 1964).

In retrospect, it seems obvious that this elevation of our mood had to come from outside the parameters of America's own musical culture, if only because the folk music which then dominated American pop was so tied to the crushed dreams of the New Frontier. Rock and roll itself was present, but shapeless; we did have Phil Spector, and the Beach Boys and the Four Seasons, but it took the influx of the British Beatles and a thousand trashy imitators to truly bring us together.

The British accomplished this in part by resurrecting music we had ignored, forgotten or discarded, recycling it in a shinier, more feckless and yet more raucous form. The fact that much of this music had originally been written and performed by American blacks made it that much more of a sure thing, but this was not quite a replay of Pat Boone rendering Little Richard palatable to a white audience. In even the limpest, wimpiest Liverpudlian retread of an American R&B oldie, there was at least the promise, the yearning, that both performers and audience might get loose, shake 'em on down, and run wild in the streets, as we of course eventually did.

As for the creators of the music—the "beat" groups and the English audiences that gave them their original support—both were fighting their ways out of their own cultural vacuum. England in the Fifties never really enjoyed a rock and roll juvenile delinquent subculture on the scale of that of America; it was an older society, locked in by class and tradition, and what "rockers" the kids got from their own kind were groomed until pale and proper, calculated not to offend the older listeners of the BBC's *Light Programme*: Cliff Richard, Adam Faith, Tommy Steele. Also big with English pop audiences in the mid and late Fifties were skiffle—a tame brand of pop folk music of which Lonnie Donegan's "Rock Island Line" was the most memorable example—and trad (traditional jazz), a wa-tered down re-creation of New Orleans jazz displayed on such American hits as Mr. Acker Bilk's "Stranger on the Shore."

It was a pallid scene, but there was a youth underground forming in England that anticipated the explosion to come even as it clung to the recent American past. The teddy boys, like their American JD counterparts, greased their hair up and combed it down into a British version of the American "waterfall," which, with a more prurient precision, they called the "elephant's trunk." At first they fed on images of James Dean, Marlon Brando and Elvis, and then, of rock 'n' rollers like Chuck Berry and Little Richard. Later, the teds would mutate into the rockers, a curious early-Sixties tribe of teenage reactionaries who believed that absolutely nothing good had happened musically (or probably in any other sense) since 1959, which by 1964 quite naturally put them in almost constant war with the foppish, pill-popping mods, whose heroes were the Stones, the Who, and the Small Faces.

Teddy boy types swelled many of the groups in Liverpool circa 1959, groups which favored trad, skiffle, or Johnny and the Hurricanes-styled instrumental rock (in emulation of Cliff Richard's backing band, the Shadows, one of the few successful British groups of the time). The influx of the teds brought a shift in musical content: trad and skiffle were dropped (though most local clubs still barred rock). Like the Beatles, a semipro performing unit since the mid-Fifties that had little time for anything but solid rock, the Liverpool bands turned to Elvis, Little Richard, Chuck Berry, Buddy Holly, and American "girl groups" for their material, and suddenly there was a full-blown scene in this brutal, grimy town on the Mersey river. The scene found its nexus in the Cavern, a dive that was almost alone in making the switch from trad to rock, and provided a showcase for the Beatles (who were discovered there by their future manager, Brian Epstein, in November 1961), Rory Storm and the Hurricanes (with their drummer Ringo Starr, who would replace Pete Best in the Beatles in 1962), Gerry and the Pacemakers, and the Swinging Blue Jeans.

There was a boom on, and Liverpool was too small, and its clubs too restrictive, to contain it. Many of the groups, the Beatles included, began to play clubs in Hamburg, Germany, beginning in 1960, and in many ways Hamburg was where the Liverpudlians' sense of themselves as protagonists in an outrageous musical renaissance got off the ground.

Hamburg was a crucible, a proving ground, a place where groups were required to play loud and fast and raw all night, hour after hour, using stimulants to maintain the pace, forcing members of the band who had thought they could not sing to take the mike when the leader's lungs gave out. Things got wild, and the sound took on a mania that became a crucial factor in the coming assault on the United States. It may in fact have been the deciding factor, since by any rational—not to mention purist—standard, most of the beat-group reworkings of

Gerry Marsden of Gerry and the Pacemakers (Gleason collection)

black American R&B and rock and roll were sloppy, mindlessly frenetic, inept in the extreme; a lot of noise with very little behind it except the enthusiasm of the players. And that, I submit, was what was good about it, if any musical yardsticks must be applied: it proved, as mindless Fifties American groups had proved before and punk rockers have proved since, that rock and roll at its core is merely a bunch of raving shit, its utterly hysterical transience and intrinsic worthlessness the not-quite-paradoxical source of its vitality.

Note that no one, absolutely no one, has ever made any grand claims for the British invasion groups such as those advanced for the art rockers of the late Sixties and early Seventies; nobody has argued that "Ferry Cross the Mersey," like, say, *Sgt. Pepper's Lonely Hearts Club Band* or *Electric Ladyland*, is a masterpiece rivaling Beethoven that will survive the ages. Forget it! It was all "yeah, yeah, yeah!" and that was what made the moment precious. Well, no, actually there was a little more involved than "yeah, yeah, yeah!" There were drums that went BOOM BOOM BOOM, and rhythm guitars (which, as in most great rock and roll from the Rolling Stones on down, predominated) that went chunka-chunka chunk.

So the British invasion was more important as an event, as a *mood*, than as music; but the groups that made it in the United States (out of countless numbers that tried and failed) provide the various colors that comprise that mood, and are certainly a part of history even if almost no one listens to their records anymore. And out of that initial Liverpool explosion, these names belong to a yesterday that all rock and roll fans of the time share: the Searchers, Billy J. Kramer and the Dakotas, the Swinging Blue Jeans, and Gerry and the Pacemakers.

The Searchers will live in memory if only for "Needles and Pins," a cover of a Jackie DeShannon song prominent for what must have been the first appearance of the ringing guitar riff which became a stock item in the folk rock of the Byrds, the Leaves, Love, et al. In contrast to many of their contemporaries, the Searchers' image was relatively clean-cut, and so was their music: their close harmonies and glittering guitar lines never got too raw, even on copies of American R&B like "Hully Gully" and "What'd I Say." Although they had emerged from the same Liverpool/Hamburg axis that produced wilder kin, the Searchers held back; and it was precisely the gentleness and general musical tidiness of their best work—"Needles and Pins," "Someday We're Gonna Love Again," "When You Walk in the Room"—that made them both prophets of folk rock and, ultimately, washouts in the age of Beatlemania.

The Merseybeat sound at its wildest and most ephemeral was defined by the Swinging Blue Jeans, whose "Hippy Hippy Shake" was one of the most unforgettable raveups of its time and also the group's only major hit. Most of their repertoire consisted of covers of American oldies, and they slipped into obscurity almost instantly. Still, it remains a curious paradox that of all the groups to come out of the Liverpool/Hamburg scene, these one-hit wonders caught the fever of that scene better than anyone else but the Beatles. It appears, though, that the raving mania of Liverpool was somewhat homogenized for U.S. consumption; the two remaining standout acts from that time and place were Billy J. Kramer and Gerry and the Pacemakers, neither exactly what you would call feverish. Kramer was actually a throwback to the decidedly white ballad crooners of the pre-Beatles era, and in spite of demonstrable talents in that idiom, his short-lived popularity in the days of the craze seems largely attributable to the fact that the Beatles wrote a few songs for him, and also shared Brian Epstein, a brilliant manager and promoter who probably deserves a bigger chunk of this narrative all to himself. In any case, Kramer's two big hits were both smoothies: "Little Children" and "Bad to Me." After about a year he faded from the scene.

Gerry and the Pacemakers, also under the Epstein wing, were a bit hotter, both in terms of hits and Anglomania. They looked just about as twerpy as humanly possible, their hair was very short, and their biggest hits were irresistibly saccharine ballads like "Ferry Cross the Mersey" and "Don't Let the Sun Catch You Crying," which certainly bore no resemblance to the song of the same name recorded by Ray Charles. In some of their other hits like "How Do You Do It" and "I Like It," as well as in the filler on their albums, you hear Mersey-sound garbage at its pinnacle: innocuous but raucous, a cloying clatter that in many ways defined the era. Like many (perhaps most) of the other Liverpool groups, the Pacemakers had no funk, no soul, no danger, and talent that could be measured in dollops, but they were having the time of their lives and it was infectious and that was all that mattered anyway.

Once the Liverpool explosion had established not only the scene in that city but the possibility of a whole rock renaissance emanating from Britain—in 1963 and 1964—record companies began to search in earnest for new talent, scouring the Isles for bands and city scenes. Manchester provided one of the few authentic examples of the latter, producing the Hollies, Wayne Fontana and the Mindbenders, and Freddie and the Dreamers. The Hollies, of course, are still going strong—in fact, there are some who believe they've done their best work in the Seventies. A case could easily be made that they are more consistent now than ever (although when a band changes personnel as often as the Hollies have, it seems as if it hardly matters); from early albums like *Beat Group* through the Creedence Clearwater Revival—influenced "Long Cool Woman in a Black Dress" they remained resolutely trendy and unnervingly erratic. During the British invasion, they were mostly just bad, grinding out sloppy covers of "Stay," "Do You Love Me," "Lucille" and "Memphis" in the most shamelessly churn-'em-up, bash-'em-out Liverpudlian manner. "I'm Alive" remains an obscure

classic from this period, but the Hollies never really found their groove nor dented the U.S. Top Ten until "Bus Stop" in '66.

Wayne Fontana and the Mindbenders may have been a one-shot group, but what a shot. "The Game of Love," with its heavy bass, "Louie Louie" chording, Bo Diddley break and Fontana's rich, wailing vocals, was an instant classic, a perfect example of the rock and roll band of no apparent distinction but with a masterpiece in them anyway. On the flip side of the dialectic you might find a Freddie and the Dreamers, who had no masterpiece but a plentitude of talentless idiocy and enough persistence to get four albums and one film soundtrack (accompanying their now-forgotten version of *A Hard Day's Night*, *Seaside Swingers*) released in the U.S., plus various other LPs for which they may or may not have been given full credit and which they shared with other certifiable nonentity bands which may or may not have been even less talented than they were. What is worth pointing out is that Freddie and the Dreamers were not merely some promoter's concoction, but an actual group who were, after the Beatles broke, the first non-Epstein Merseybeat band to claim a Top Five hit in England. As has been pointed out by other writers, the Dreamers looked as thuggish as Freddie looked dippy, and the band's fame rested primarily on a tie-in with a "dance" called the Freddie (all you had to do was wave both arms and kick both feet out slightly, with a vacant look in your eyes) which in turn tied in with such hits as "I'm Telling You Now" and "Do the Freddie." Like Sam the Sham and the Pharaohs of "Wooly Bully" fame, Freddie and the Dreamers represented a triumph of rock as cretinous swill, and as such should be not only respected, but given their place in history.

Many listeners felt, and no doubt still feel, that the same applies to the Dave Clark Five, but here even I, a connoisseur of garbage, must demur. Of course, their albums were uniformly bad; of course, as *Time* so pithily put it at the time, their singles were primarily distinguished by an "air hammer" beat. But that's just another way of saying BIG beat, and all the Dave Clark Five singles were marked by a loud, thick yet expansive, wall-of-sound production that made them not only distinctive in their day, but ensured that they would sound exciting—more than mere period pieces—to this day. And that's something that can be said of almost none of the hits of their contemporaries. "Glad All Over," "Bits and Pieces," "Can't You See That She's Mine," "Because," "Catch Us if You Can"—if you remember those titles, as you surely do if you listened to the radio or bought records in 1964–'65—if you disparaged or even actively hated the DC5 in their heyday, don't they sound better now, don't they seem vital; don't they seem like pure, mainstream pop-rock? Sure, they were crude and of course they weren't even a bit hip, but in their churning crassness there was a shout of joy and a sense of fun. Clark himself sang, composed, played

drums, produced and even managed the group—which has, over the years, been severely underrated not only as a consistent singles machine, but, as writer Mike Saunders once put it, as "excellent producers of good, healthy, enjoyable schlock."

Speaking of schlock, in a survey such as this there is no getting around Herman's Hermits, who epitomized the Kleenex texture of their age almost as brilliantly as Freddie and the Dreamers. Consider again the evocative power of mere song titles: "Mrs. Brown You've Got a Lovely Daughter," or "I'm Henry VIII, I Am," Herman's hit version of Ray Davies's "Dandy," or "I'm into Something Good"—catchy and downright huggable, thanks, in the last case, to songwriters Carole King and Gerry Goffin. One must realize that the Hermits hit our shores during a time—mid-'64—when the Beatles appeared to be slipping a bit: there were actually some weeks in which the Fab Four failed to appear in the Top Ten, and a few Cassandras were beginning to smirk that the British invasion might be a mere flash in the pan and all those faggy long-haired creeps could go right back where they came from. Meanwhile, the Rolling Stones were coming on from the other corner with their dirty would-you-let-your-daughter image, not to mention *their* smirks and the great high school controversy over whether the lines "Baby better come back, maybe next week/ 'Cause you see I'm on a losin' streak" meant that the girl in "(I Can't Get No) Satisfaction" was menstruating.

Clearly there was a gap here, with imminent threat to the new order implicit from both sides, and into this gap bounced ... who else but cute, cuddly, baby-faced, buck-toothed Peter "Herman" Noone. I can recall a comment by the Hermits' manager to the effect that with the waning of initial Anglomania, it was becoming obvious that there were only three enduring talents in the marketplace: the Beatles, the Stones, and Herman's Hermits. And indeed, the group did last long enough to have a string of hits. In recent years, however, Herman himself has been seen covering David Bowie's "Oh! You Pretty Things," with negligible buyer turnout.

Not all of the invasion bands were as close to candy floss as the Hermits, of course, but many of those more talented had a harder time staying afloat. In the case of the Zombies, this amounted almost to tragedy. Their great hit, "She's Not There," was a gem, with its orgasmic signs and dramatic falsetto vocal rushing forward into a bitter electric piano solo; the followup, "Tell Her No," while more of a standard Beatles cop, was almost as good. But a rush-released U.S. album was followed by a series of fine singles that uniformly bombed—the Zombies were apparently cursed by their own musical adventurousness, and a pop audience that simply was not ready for stuff like "I Want You Back Again," the group's fourth single, a violently (albeit falsetto) sung tale of romantic angst couched in a jazz waltz, with the ghostly "Remember When I Loved Her" on the flip. Failure of this sort of material on both sides of the Atlantic compelled the Zombies to pack it in by 1967, but

before doing so they cut one last album. The result was *Odessey* (sic!) *and Oracle*, a pop masterpiece which produced their Number Three hit, "Time of the Season." It was a classic case of too much too late; the group had disintegrated by the time the single took over the charts. In the end, it sold 2 million copies.

* * *

The blues revivalists, mostly out of London, were also important to the British invasion, though their impact was not felt until after the first assault: the Alexis Korner finishing school, John Mayall's Bluesbreakers, the Stones, and the Yardbirds. But as they were purists, or thought they were, we will leave them to bask in their purity, unsullied by the garbage which has comprised the subject matter of this chapter. Leave them, that is, except for the Animals and Manfred Mann, because like the Stones and unlike most of the other blues revivalists, the Animals and Manfred's men could only have been purists in the privacy of their conceits. For one thing, they both had AM hits in America in 1964, and in those days, purism simply did not survive popularity. Manfred Mann, who came originally from South Africa, may have put stuff like Howlin' Wolf's "Smokestack Lightning" or Muddy Waters's "I'm Your Hoochie Coochie Man" on his first album, and then as now (see his Seventies Earth Band product) he was trying for the great jazz-rock fusion, but for all that Mann's first two U.S. hits, "Do Wah Diddy Diddy" and "Sha La La," were, respectively, a Jeff Barry/Ellie Greenwich tune and a Shirelles cover—in other words, pure only in that they were pure pop. No matter; they clicked, and Manfred was one of the only British rockers with the balls to hit these shores with a beard, which, given his horn-rimmed specs, caused him to look less like a cerebral jazz cat than a befuddled college professor.

Which was someone for whom Eric Burdon could never have been mistaken. With his Newcastle-on-Tyne workingman's scowl, his backup Animals—who could have passed for shop clerks—and his doubtless magnificent collection of American R&B records, Eric Burdon was certifiably only one thing: short. And, like many short people, he looked to scale the heights, to become in the few years allotted to him something he was, at birth, not: a Negro. Whether he ever succeeded is a question best left to medical research; in any case, it is particularly irrelevant since Negroes themselves turned into black people and Eric seems not to have been able to make the transition. What is certain, and germane, is that the Animals made some of the finest British R&B covers of the mid-Sixties, particularly their boiling versions of "House of the Rising Sun" and John Lee Hooker's "Boom Boom." The boil was as much attributable to Alan Price's organ work as to Burdon's voice, and "House" went on to become a new standard rendition of an old standard composition, such a brilliant rearrangement that it was later imitated almost note for note with similar worldwide success by a troupe of Michigan no-talents called Frijid Pink.

The Animals were among the most gifted and beloved of British invasion bands; after the original group split, Alan Price went on to a British hit with a wildly Bached up jazz version of Screamin' Jay Hawkins's "I Put a Spell on You," while Burdon distinguished himself both as the leader of several fine bands (under the all-purpose Animals moniker) and as an ersatz social commentator ("White Houses," "San Franciscan Nights"—which he inexplicably thought were "warm," "Sky Pilot," "Monterey," and finally "Soledad," this last a duet with bluesman Jimmy Witherspoon). Burdon held on until the early Seventies, when he partially realized his lifelong ambition by leading a predominantly black band called War, with whom he scored his last hit, "Spill the Wine." In 1971, War left Eric in the dust and funkified up the charts with such staggering soul mystery as "Slippin' into Darkness." Like Manfred Mann, Eric is still working on a comeback (when last spotted he had reassembled the original Animals), even if his voice isn't the instrument of hog-calling power it once was.

If Eric does make it again, he will be one of the very few people mentioned in this chapter capable, or deserving, of such an achievement. The central irony of this chapter of rock history is that out of so much worthless music was carved nothing less than the first renaissance of rock and roll. It might legitimately be asked whether more than a handful of British invasion bands would have made the States, and rock history, if they hadn't ridden in on the Beatles' coattails, but perhaps it really doesn't matter. For all of its innocence, its excitement and sense of discovery, this seems a far more appropriate question: didn't we all get more kicks than we'd ever dreamed possible? And wasn't it a grand time to be alive?

Discography

1964–1965

Dusty Springfield, "I Only Want to Be with You" (Philips 40162; ☆12, 1964). **Dave Clark Five,** "Glad All Over" (Epic 9656; ☆6, 1964). **Searchers,** "Needles and Pins" (Kapp 577; ☆13, 1964). **Swinging Blue Jeans,** "Hippy Hippy Shake" (Imperial 66021; ☆24, 1964). **Billy J. Kramer,** "Little Children" b/w "Bad to Me" (Imperial 66027; ☆7, 1964). **Dave Clark Five,** "Bits and Pieces" (Epic 9671; ☆4, 1964). **Bachelors,** "Diane" (London 9639; ☆10, 1964). **Peter and Gordon,** "A World without Love" (Capitol 5175; ☆1, 1964). **Searchers,** "Sugar and Spice" (Liberty 55689; ☆44, 1964). **Dave Clark Five,** "Do You Love Me" (Epic 9678; ☆11, 1964). **Searchers,** "Don't Throw Your Love Away" (Kapp 593; ☆16, 1964). **Gerry and the Pacemakers,** "Don't Let the Sun Catch You Crying" (Laurie 3251; ☆4, 1964). **Chad Stuart and Jeremy Clyde,** "Yesterday's Gone" (World Artists 1021; ☆21, 1964). **Dave Clark Five,** "Can't You See That She's Mine" (Epic 9692; ☆4, 1964). **Dusty Springfield,** "Wishin' and Hopin'" (Philips 40207; ☆6, 1964). **Peter and Gordon,** "Nobody I Know" (Capitol 5211; ☆12, 1964). **Cilla Black,** "You're My World" (Capitol 5196; ☆26, 1964). **Gerry and the Pacemakers,** "How Do You Do It" (Laurie 3261; ☆9, 1964). **Animals,** "The House of the Rising Sun" (MGM 13264; ☆1, 1964). **Dave Clark Five,** "Because" (Epic 9704; ☆3, 1964). **Chad Stuart and Jeremy Clyde,** "A Summer Song" (World Artists 1027; ☆7, 1964). **Manfred Mann,** "Do Wah Diddy Diddy" (Ascot 2157; ☆1, 1964). **Nashville Teens,** "Tobacco Road" (London 9689; ☆14, 1964). **Honeycombs,** "Have I the Right" (Interphon 7707; ☆5, 1964). **Gerry and the Pacemakers,** "I Like It" (Laurie 3271; ☆17, 1964). **Animals,** "I'm Crying" (MGM 13274; ☆19, 1964). **Dave Clark Five,** "Everybody Knows" (Epic 9722; ☆15, 1964). **Peter and Gordon,** "I Don't Want to See You Again" (Capitol 5272; ☆16, 1964). **Herman's Hermits,** "I'm into Something Good" (MGM 13280; ☆13, 1964). **Zombies,** "She's Not There" (Parrot 9695; ☆2, 1964). **Manfred Mann,** "Sha La La" (Ascot 2165; ☆12, 1964). **Dave Clark Five,** "Any Way You Want It" (Epic 9739; ☆14, 1964). **Searchers,** "Love Potion Number Nine" (Kapp 27; ☆3, 1964). **Petula Clark,** "Downtown" (Warner Bros. 5494; ☆1, 1964). **Gerry and the Pacemakers,** "I'll Be There" (Laurie 3279; ☆14, 1964). **Peter and Gordon,** "I Go to Pieces" (Capitol 5335; ☆9, 1965).

Zombies, "Tell Her No" (Parrot 9723; ☆6, 1965). **Herman's Hermits,** "Can't You Hear My Heartbeat" (MGM 13310; ☆2, 1965). **Gerry and the Pacemakers,** "Ferry Cross the Mersey" (Laurie 3284; ☆6, 1965). **Animals,** "Don't Let Me Be Misunderstood" (MGM 13311; ☆15, 1965). **George Fame,** "Yeh, Yeh" (Imperial 66086; ☆21, 1965). **Moody Blues,** "Go Now!" (London 9726; ☆10, 1965). **Searchers,** "Bumble Bee" (Kapp 49; ☆21, 1965). **Freddie and the Dreamers,** "I'm Telling You Now" (Tower 125; ☆1, 1965). **Petula Clark,** "I Know a Place" (Warner Bros. 5612; ☆3, 1965). **Wayne Fontana and the Mindbenders,** "Game of Love" (Fontana 1509; ☆1, 1965). **Herman's Hermits,** "Silhouettes" (MGM 13332; ☆5, 1965). **Tom Jones,** "It's Not Unusual" (Parrot 9737; ☆10, 1965). **Peter and Gordon,** "True Love Ways" (Capitol 5406, ☆14, 1965). **Freddie and the Dreamers,** "Do the Freddie" (Mercury 72428; ☆18, 1965). **Herman's Hermits,** "Mrs. Brown You've Got a Lovely Daughter" (MGM 13341; ☆1, 1965). **Yardbirds,** "For Your Love" (Epic 9790; ☆6, 1965). **Ian Whitcomb,** "You Turn Me On" (Tower 134; ☆8, 1965). **Donovan,** "Catch the Wind" (Hickory 1309; ☆23, 1965). **Herman's Hermits,** "Wonderful World" (MGM 13354; ☆4, 1965). **Them,** "Here Comes the Night" (Parrot 9749; ☆24, 1965). **Dave Clark Five,** "I Like It Like That" (Epic 9811; ☆7, 1965). **Herman's Hermits,** "I'm Henry VIII, I Am" (MGM 13367; ☆1, 1965). **Yardbirds,** "Heart Full of Soul" (Epic 9823; ☆9, 1965). **Animals,** "We Gotta Get Out of This Place" (MGM 13382; ☆13, 1965). **Dave Clark Five,** "Catch Us if You Can" (Epic 9833; ☆4, 1965). **Herman's Hermits,** "Just a Little Bit Better" (MGM 13398; ☆7, 1965). **Jonathan King,** "Everyone's Gone to the Moon" (Parrot 9774; ☆17, 1965). **Silkie,** "You've Got to Hide Your Love Away" (Fontana 1525; ☆10, 1965). **Walker Brothers,** "Make It Easy on Yourself" (Smash 2009; ☆16, 1965). **Yardbirds,** "I'm a Man" (Epic 9857; ☆17, 1965). **Them,** "Mystic Eyes" (Parrot 9796; ☆33, 1965). **Dave Clark Five,** "Over and Over" (Epic 9863; ☆1, 1965). **Hollies,** "Look Through Any Window" (Imperial 66134; ☆32, 1965). **Herman's Hermits,** "A Must to Avoid" (MGM 13437; ☆8, 1965). **Petula Clark,** "My Love" (Warner Bros. 5684; ☆1, 1965).

(Omitting hits by the Beatles, Rolling Stones, Kinks, and Who. Compiled from Joel Whitburn's *Record Research*, based on *Billboard* Pop chart.)

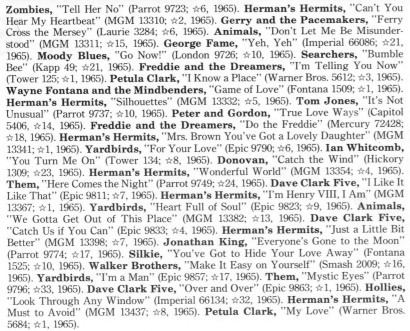

The Beatles
by Greil Marcus

The blues is a chair, not a design for a chair, or a better chair . . . it is the first chair. It is a chair for sitting on, not chairs for looking at or being appreciated. You sit on that music. . . . We didn't sound like anybody else, that's all. I mean we didn't sound like the black musicians because we weren't black. And because we were brought up on a different kind of music and atmosphere, and so 'Please Please Me' and 'From Me to You' and all those were our version of the chair. We were building our own chairs."

—John Lennon, 1970, *Lennon Remembers: The Rolling Stone Interviews*

[ONE VERSION OF THE CHAIR]

1940: John Lennon and Richard Starkey (Ringo Starr) born, to working-class families in Liverpool, England (as are Paul McCartney and George Harrison, in 1942 and 1943, respectively).

1953–'54: Rock and roll, formerly "race" music, begins breakthrough into white America.

1955: January—Bill Haley's "Shake, Rattle and Roll" (a white American cover of a song by black bluesman Joe Turner) makes British charts. June—John, almost 15, playing with his rock/skiffle group, the Quarrymen, meets Paul, almost 13, at Liverpool church social. Their partnership begins. [Some sources date this meeting in 1956.]

1956–'57: First English Elvis release. American rock hits and British rock imitators proliferate in England. John favors Elvis ("Nothing really affected me until . . . "); Paul, Little Richard. They perform with Quarrymen, write songs, appear occasionally as a duo ("The Nurk Twins").

1958: George, a 15-year-old guitarist influenced by Chet Atkins, Buddy Holly, and Scotty Moore, joins Quarrymen; group name changed to Johnny and the Moondogs (later Silver Beatles, after Buddy Holly's Crickets, then to Beatles).

1959: Stu Sutcliffe, Liverpool art student, joins Silver Beatles on bass.

1960: Liverpool "Merseybeat" scene forming on Beatles' model (emphasis on rhythm and big beat). Pete Best, a drummer, is added, as Beatles leave for first of many all-night gigs in Hamburg, Germany.

1961: Beatles commute between Hamburg and Liverpool's Cavern; record "My Bonnie" in Germany. Sutcliffe leaves group to paint. November—Brian Epstein, Liverpool record-store owner, seeks out Beatles at Cavern, his interest cued by request for "My Bonnie." December—Epstein becomes Beatles' manager.

1962: Epstein writes to journalist that his group "would one day be bigger than Elvis," becoming only manager in rock and roll history to use this line and be right. January—Beatles fail audition with Decca, win poll as top group in Liverpool. April—Sutcliffe dies of brain tumor. August—Beatles signed to

EMI, but Capitol refuses American option. In move still shrouded in mystery, John, Paul, George and Epstein replace Best with Ringo Starr, drummer for Liverpool "beat" (after "Merseybeat") group Rory Storm and the Hurricanes (Storm later dies in apparent double suicide with mother). Final Beatles lineup: John, rhythm guitar (harmonica, organ, piano); Paul, bass (piano, organ, guitar); George, lead guitar; Ringo, drums. October—"Love Me Do," written by John and Paul in 1957, released in U.K., peaks at Number 21.

1963: January—"Please Please Me" released, reaches Number One. "Beatlemania" hits Britain. Mass hysteria reigns among youth. February—"Please Please Me" released in U.S. on Vee-Jay label, no chart action. May—*Please Please Me*, Beatles' first album, released in U.K., holds Number One spot for 30 consecutive weeks, replaced by *With the Beatles*, which remains at Number One for an additional 22. "From Me to You" released in U.S., reaches Number 116 in August, drops off chart two weeks later, falling short of Del Shannon's version of same tune, released in June, which peaks at Number 77. July—first Beatles album released in U.S. on Vee-Jay as *Introducing the Beatles*. No chart action.

1964: January—"I Want to Hold Your Hand" released in U.S. on Capitol with $50,000 in publicity from label; reaches Number One February 1st (January 17th in *Cashbox*). February—Beatles appear on Ed Sullivan show. April—Beatles assume first, second, third, fourth and fifth positions on *Billboard* singles charts; *Meet the Beatles*, Capitol's version of *With the Beatles*, becomes best-selling LP in history up to that time. "Beatlemania" hits U.S. Mass hysteria reigns among youth. DJs claim "fifth Beatle" status. British Invasion begins. August—Beatle film, *A Hard Day's Night*, opens to extraordinary critical and popular acclaim; first major American tour begins. December—Ringo tonsillectomy inspires worldwide vigil.

1965: Beatles gain fourth, fifth and sixth Number One LPs, followed by *Rubber Soul*, hailed as artistic breakthrough, in December. American response to British rock renaissance includes Byrds, Lovin' Spoonful, Dylan's move to rock, beginnings of San Francisco sound, and the Monkees. August—second film, *Help!*, released.

1966: Dylan's *Blonde on Blonde*, Rolling Stones' *Aftermath* and Beatles' *Revolver* (hailed as "avant-garde," showing influence of Motown, Mamas and Papas, and Timothy Leary) all released, as Big Three of rock attempt to top each other. August—Beatles make what will be last concert appearance, in San Francisco: return to England to make album to top all toppers. John meets Yoko Ono, avant-garde conceptual artist. Age of media psychedelia—dope, love, peace, Eastern religion—begins.

1967: February—Beatles release "Strawberry Fields Forever," hailed as "psychedelic" because of backward music at

Beatlemania, Liverpool, early Sixties (Photo Trends)

Below: Ringo and Paul with Del Shannon, whose 1963 version of "From Me to You" represented the first entry of a Beatles song onto the American charts. ('Phonograph Record' magazine/Cerf)

fade. June—on eve of San Francisco's projected mass hippie Summer of Love influx, Beatles release *Sgt. Pepper's Lonely Hearts Club Band*, superpsychedelic LP that tops all toppers. Paul announces Beatle LSD use. August—Brian Epstein dies of pill overdose. Beatles, on retreat with Maharishi Mahesh Yogi, Eastern religionist, announce they will manage themselves. Gleam appears in religionist's third eye. December—Beatle TV film, *Magical Mystery Tour*, bombs in Britain; first real Beatle failure.

1968: February—Beatles leave for India to receive instruction from Maharishi. Beatles complain of bad food; Ringo leaves early. May—John and Paul hold press conference in U.S. to sever relationship with Maharishi and launch Apple Corps., Ltd., new company meant to handle Beatles affairs and aid deserving artists. Move subsequently proves disastrous. November—Beatles release *The Beatles* (the "white album") with mostly solo vocals.

1969: John and Yoko marry. Yoko seeks "fifth Beatle" status. Beatles decide to "get back" by recording "roots" album in order to recapture fading sense of combined self; *Abbey Road* appears instead. John forms Plastic Ono Band with Yoko on vocals; releases include "Give Peace a Chance."

1970: Paul releases solo LP, with self as sole if not solo musician; press kit includes self-interview critical of other Beatles. April—Paul announces departure from Beatles. May—Beatles, effectively defunct, release "get back" LP as *Let It Be*, with accompanying *Let It Be* film. December—Paul sues to dissolve Beatles.

1970-1975: Beatles pursue individual careers with good financial but erratic artistic success. Paul forms new band, Wings, with wife Linda Eastman. John and Yoko release albums focusing on primal therapy, politics, self, and old rock and roll. Ringo makes movies and hit singles. George organizes Concert for Bangladesh (1971) and seeks better way.

1976: Wings begin first American tour. EMI rereleases 23 Beatle singles in U.K.; all make charts. Rumors of one-shot Beatle reunion spread, spurred by alleged $30- to $50-million guarantee. Beatles equivocate. Pressure mounts.

[ANOTHER VERSION OF THE CHAIR]

"We were driving through Colorado [and] we had the radio on and eight of the Top Ten songs were Beatles songs. In Colorado! 'I Want to Hold Your Hand,' all those early ones.

"They were doing things nobody was doing. Their chords were outrageous, just outrageous, and their harmonies made it all valid. . . . But I kept it to myself that I really dug them. Everybody else thought they were for the teenyboppers, that they were gonna pass right away. But it was obvious to me that they had staying power. I knew they were pointing the direction where music had to go . . . in my head, the Beatles were *it*. In Colorado, I started thinking but it was so far out I couldn't deal with it—eight in the top ten.

"It seemed to me a definite line was being drawn. This was something that never happened before."

—Bob Dylan, 1971
Anthony Scaduto's *Bob Dylan*

On February 9th, 1964, I was in college in California, a rock and roll fan with creeping amnesia. I remembered Chuck Berry but not the guitar solo in "Johnny B. Goode." The excitement, the sense of being caught up in something much bigger than your own private taste, had disappeared from rock years before. There was still good stuff on the radio—there had been "Heat Wave" by a group called Martha and the Vandellas the summer before, "Be True to Your School" by the Beach Boys a few months after that, and even "On Broadway" by the Drifters—but in 1963 all of it seemed drowned out by Jimmy Gilmer's "Sugar Shack," the Number One song of the year and perhaps the worst excuse for itself rock and roll had yet produced. Rock and roll—the radio—felt dull and stupid, a dead end.

There had been an item in the paper that day about a British rock and roll group which was to appear on *The Ed Sullivan Show* that night: "The Beatles" (a photo too—were those wigs, or what?). I was curious—I didn't know they had rock and roll in England—so I went down to a commons room where there was a TV set, expecting an argument from whoever was there about which channel to watch.

Four hundred people sat transfixed as the Beatles sang "I Want to Hold Your Hand," and when the song was over the crowd exploded. People looked at the faces (and the hair) of John, Paul, George and Ringo and said Yes (and who could have predicted that a few extra inches of hair would suddenly seem so right, so necessary? Brian Epstein?); they heard the

Beatles' sound and said Yes to that too. What was going on? And where had all those people come from?

Back at the radio I caught "I Saw Her Standing There" and was instantly convinced it was the most exciting rock and roll I'd ever heard (with Paul's one/two/three/*fuck!* opening—how in the world did they expect to get away with that?). Someone from down the hall appeared with a copy of the actual record—you could just go out and *buy* this stuff?—and announced with great fake solemnity that it was the first 45 he'd purchased since "All Shook Up." Someone else—who played a 12-string guitar and as far as I knew listened to nothing but Odetta—began to muse that "even as a generation had been brought together by the Five Satins' 'In the Still of the Nite,' it could be that it would be brought together again—by the Beatles." He really talked like that; what was more amazing, he talked like that when a few hours before he had never heard of the Beatles.

The next weeks went by in a blur. People began to grow their hair (one acquaintance argued with great vehemence that it was physically impossible for male hair—at least, *normal* male hair—to grow to Beatle length); some affected British (or, when they could pull it off, Liverpool) accents. A friend got his hands on a British Beatles album unavailable in the U.S. and made a considerable amount of money charging people for the chance to hear John Lennon sing "Money (That's What I Want)"—at two bucks a shot. Excitement wasn't in the air; it was the air.

A few days after that first performance on the Sullivan show I spent the evening with some friends in a cafe in my hometown. It was, or anyway had been, a folk club. This night they played only *Meet the Beatles*. The music, snaking through the dark, suddenly spooky room, was instantly recognizable and like nothing we had ever heard. It was joyous, threatening, absurd, arrogant, determined, innocent and tough, and it drew the line of which Dylan was to speak. "This was something that never happened before."

It was, as Lester Bangs says in his survey of the British Invasion, not simply a matter of music, but of event. Dylan had heard the Beatles in New York before his Colorado revelation; I had first heard them on the radio in early 1963, when "Please Please Me" was released in the U.S., liked the record, disliked the followup, then forgot the group altogether. It was only in the context of the Beatles event that their music was perceived for what it was.

The event was a pop explosion; the second, and thus far the last, that rock and roll has produced.

A pop explosion is an irresistible cultural explosion that cuts across lines of class and race (in terms of sources, if not allegiance), and, most crucially, divides society itself by age. The surface of daily life (walk, talk, dress, symbolism, heroes, family affairs) is affected with such force that deep and substantive changes in the way large numbers of people think and act take place. Pop explosions must link up with, and accelerate, broad shifts in sexual behavior, economic aspirations, and political

beliefs; a pervasive sense of chaos, such as that which hit England in 1963 with the Profumo scandal, and the U.S. in the mid-Sixties with the civil rights movement, the Kennedy assassination, and later the Vietnam war, doesn't hurt.

Now, it has been argued, by British critic George Melly, that a pop explosion merely "turns revolt into a style" (poet Thom Gunn's line on Elvis, originally), but in fact pop explosions can provide the enthusiasm, the optimism, and the group identity that make mass political participation possible; a pop explosion is more than a change in style even if it is far less than a revolution, though it can look like either one—depending on who is looking, and when. (Not that "changing the world" in the political sense of the term is never a "goal" of a pop explosion, if such an event can be said to have a goal beyond good times; still, a pop explosion changes the world by affecting the moment, which means that the world retains the capacity to change back, momentarily.)

Enormous energy—the energy of frustration, desire, repression, adolescence, sex, ambition—finds an object in a pop explosion, and that energy is focused on, organized by, and released by a single, holistic cultural entity. This entity must itself be capable of easy, instantaneous and varied imitation and extension, in a thousand ways at once; it must embody, suggest, affirm and legitimize new possibilities on all fronts even as it outstrips them. This is a fancy way of saying that the capacity for fad must be utterly profound.

And, at its heart, a pop explosion attaches the individual to a group—the fan to an audience, the solitary to a generation—in essence, *forms* a group and creates new loyalties—while at the same time it increases one's ability to respond to a particular pop artifact, or a thousand of them, with an intensity that verges on lunacy. Ringo's shout of "All right, George!" just before the guitar in "Boys" becomes a matter of indefinable and indefensible significance; styles on Carnaby Street outdo the pace of the pop charts and change literally by the hour. Yet within it all is some principle of shape, of continuity, of value.

This principle was the Beatles. As was so often pointed out in the mid-Sixties, the sum of the Beatles was greater than the parts, but the parts were so distinctive and attractive that the group itself could be all things to all people, more or less; you did not have to love them all to love the group, but you could not love one without loving the group, and this was why the Beatles became bigger than Elvis; this was what had never happened before. And so it began. The past was felt to dissolve, the future was conceivable only as an expansion of the present, and the present was defined absolutely by its expansive novelty. Towering above Bob Dylan, the Rolling Stones, a score of British groups, American groups, Mary Quant, the Who, whatever and whoever sprung up day by day, the Beatles seemed not only to symbolize but to contain it all—to make history by anticipating it.

The first pop explosion, beginning in 1955 and 1956, began to yield to normalcy by about 1957. The Beatles event, beyond all expectations save perhaps their own, intensified not only in momentum but in magnetism, reaching more and more people with greater and greater mythic and emotional power, for at least four years. The Beatles affected not only the feel but the quality of life—they deepened it, sharpened it, brightened it, not merely as a factor in the cultural scheme, but as a presence. The Beatles affected not only the quality of life—they affected its worth.

Their event reached its height, and in many ways its effective end, with the release of *Sgt. Pepper* on June 2nd, 1967. For months, rumors had swept the pop world that the Beatles were engaged in an historic project that would sum up, and transcend, all that had been accomplished in the previous four years. In February a single, "Penny Lane"/"Strawberry Fields Forever" was released (if this extraordinary music was merely a taste of what the Beatles were up to, what would the album be like?) and then, in the spring, tapes leaked out. A strange, maddening song called "A Day in the Life Of" was played on the radio and quickly withdrawn. Tension and speculation grew. It was said (correctly) that the new LP had taken 700 hours to record, as opposed to 12 hours for the Beatles' first; that it included astonishingly experimental techniques, huge orchestras, 100-voice choirs. Stories began to appear not only in the pop press but in the daily papers. The record, unheard, was everywhere.

Then the announcement was made. The record would be released for airplay on Sunday midnight, one week before appearing in the stores; any station putting the disc on the air even one minute before the assigned air time would find all forthcoming prerelease airing privileges forever withheld. The fact that many stations habitually went off the air at Sunday midnight in order to service their transmitters, was of no consequence—or perhaps, from the perspective of Brian Epstein and the Beatles, it was a challenge. At any rate, the stations stayed on. They played the record all night and all the next day, vying to see which station could play it the longest, putting in calls to John and Paul in London that never went through, tracking every last second of the endless final chord of "A Day in the Life" (no "Of," as it turned out), generating an unprecedented sense of public euphoria, excitement, satisfaction, and joy.

Almost immediately, *Sgt. Pepper* was certified as proof that the Beatles' music—or at least this album—was Art. But what mattered was the conscious creation of event—the way in which the summing-up-the-spirit-of-the-times style of the music (which for the most part has not survived its time) was perfectly congruent with the organizing-the-spirit-of-the-times manner in which the album was released and received. Which

is to say that *Sgt. Pepper*, as the most brilliantly orchestrated manipulation of a cultural audience in pop history, was nothing less than a small pop explosion in and of itself. The music was not great art; the event, in its intensification of the ability to respond, was.

"The closest Western Civilization has come to unity since the Congress of Vienna in 1815 was the week the *Sgt. Pepper* album was released," Langdon Winner wrote in 1968. "In every city in Europe and America the stereo systems and the radio played, 'What would you think if I sang out of tune . . . Woke up, got out of bed . . . looked much older, and the bag across her shoulder . . . in the sky with diamonds, Lucy in the . . .' and everyone listened. At the time I happened to be driving across country on Interstate 80. In each city where I stopped for gas or food—Laramie, Ogallala, Moline, South Bend—the melodies wafted in from some far-off transistor radio or portable hi-fi. It was the most amazing thing I've ever heard. For a brief while the irreparably fragmented consciousness of the West was unified, at least in the minds of the young."

And so it seemed as if the world really did turn around the Beatles, even if the truth was that this music, as opposed to this event, represented that point at which the Beatles began to be formed more by the times than the other way around. In the next few months Brian Epstein would die, and the Beatles, who had unified the young, would themselves begin to fragment—anticipating, as usual, the fragmentation that in years to come would separate the audience they had created. Still, if *Sgt. Pepper* was an ending, it was an ending that has never been matched. It was perhaps in the nature of the game that it would be all downhill from there.

[A THIRD VERSION OF THE CHAIR]

Or, what about the music. Since the Beatles disbanded a virtual consensus among rock critics has emerged to argue that the music of the Beatles, enjoyable as it may have been, stands now as distinctly inferior to that of the Stones, Dylan, or even the Byrds or the Beach Boys; the Beatles are conventionally portrayed as imitative, lightweights, yea-sayers, softies, ordinary musicians, vaguely unhip, unimaginative lyrically, and, above all, "clever"—that is, merely clever. You know—the Beatles just wanted to hold your hand, while the Stones wanted to pillage your town. Etc.

There is some truth to this argument. While Andrew Loog Oldham, the Stones' manager, urged his boys to flaunt their rebellion, Epstein had the four mop tops clean up their act; he got rid of their grease-and-leather Cavern image and put the Fab Four into matching stage suits. Rebellion was fine as long as tactics were restricted to wit; pissing on a garage (or, as some Stones legends have it, a garage attendant) was definitely out. The Stones wrote from an insistently sexual and aggressive blues tradition; the Beatles worked mostly in the more

polite and circumscribed milieu of pop, as defined not only by rock tunesmiths Carole King and Gerry Goffin but by the earlier professional romanticists of Tin Pan Alley. The Beatles' optimism prevailed even when they tried to sound desperate ("Help!"), which sometimes made them sound sappy; the Stones' sullenness prevailed even when they affected optimism ("We Love You"), which usually made them sound all the more attractive.

Which only proves, I think, that comparisons of the Beatles and the Stones (or Dylan or Elvis or any other true titan of rock) are pointless. I cannot make an argument that the Beatles were better at being the Stones than the Stones were (though I can point out that it was the Beatles who opened up the turf the Stones took as their own—there was no possibility of a Left until the Beatles created the Center). The argument that seems to emerge from a close listening to the Beatles' music, on the other hand, is this one: by 1962 the Beatles' mastery of rock and roll was such that it was inevitable they would change the form simply by addressing themselves to it. Unlike the Stones or Dylan, the Beatles came up *through* rock; as they went on, extending (if not deepening) their mastery, they defined rock, to the degree that it made sense to speak of "Yesterday," a ballad accompanied only by acoustic guitar and strings, as "rock and roll," simply because the disc was credited to the Beatles. And unlike Dylan, and possibly the Stones, at least until 1966, the Beatles had no fall-back position. They were rock and roll or they were nothing. As such, they were, at their best, the best.

Their pop explosion, after all, was not kicked off simply by assassination and PR. You could hear it, and what you heard was a rock and roll group that combined elements of the music that you were used to hearing only in pieces. That is, the form of the Beatles contained the forms of rock and roll itself. The Beatles combined the harmonic range and implicit equality of the Fifties vocal group (the Dell-Vikings, say) with the flash of a rockabilly band (the Crickets or Gene Vincent's Blue Caps) with the aggressive and unique personalities of the classic rock stars (Elvis, Little Richard) with the homey this-could-be-you manner of later rock stars (Everly Brothers, Holly, Eddie Cochran) with the endlessly inventive songwriting touch of the Brill Building, and delivered it all with the grace of the Miracles, the physicality of "Louie Louie," and the absurd enthusiasm of Gary "U.S." Bonds. Three of the Beatles wrote, all sang lead, and they played their own music; in sum, they communicated (and generically insisted upon) absolute involvement (it was only after the Beatles that "rock groups" had to make their own records and write their own songs). Rock, which in the course of the Fifties had changed from a personal inspiration and affirmation to a process that allowed the most marginal of commitments, became, in the shape of the Beatles, a way of life.

Consider the Beatles' history. In 1955, John and Paul were playing something approximating rock and roll before they had ever heard of Elvis Presley (the same probably cannot be said of Buddy Holly); they seem to have written their first hit before they heard "That'll Be the Day" (even if "Love Me Do" would not be released until almost four years after Holly's death). In other words, when the Beatles signed with EMI they were not merely in touch with their roots; in a significant and probably unique sense, they were their roots. They were not only a product of the pre-Beatles era of rock, they were a version of it. Accompanying the shock of novelty so many experienced on first exposure to the Beatles in 1963 or '64 was a shock of recognition, which bespoke the Beatles' connection to the whole history of rock and roll up to that time: the Beatles had absorbed that history because—year by year, playing and listening and writing, in Liverpool and on the bottoms of British tours and in Hamburg—they had, albeit invisibly, made it.

No one else could touch *this* sort of mastery, and the result was that elusive rock treasure, *a new sound*—and a new sound that could not be exhausted in the course of one brief flurry on the charts. That sound was best captured in the Beatles' 1963 recordings of "Please Please Me," "I Saw Her Standing There," their version of the Shirelles' "Boys," the incandescent "There's a Place," "It Won't Be Long," "All I've Got to Do," "She Loves You," "I Want to Hold Your Hand," "All My Loving," George's brooding "Don't Bother Me," "Little Child," and their cover of Barrett Strong's "Money," plus such 1964 cuts as "A Hard Day's Night," "Anytime at All," "I Should Have Known Better," "Things We Said Today," "I'll Be Back," "No Reply," "Eight Days a Week," "Every Little Thing," and "What You're Doing."

The beat, first of all, was not big, it was enormous. The entire performance orchestrated it, was built around it (listen to "There's a Place"). At the same time, there was a lightness to almost every tune, a floating quality, a kind of lyrical attack that shaped but did not lessen the rhythmic power of the numbers. This quality, which can be heard in its most spectacular form in the segues in and out of the middle eight, was perhaps the most important thing John and Paul learned from Goffin-King (and from Ellie Greenwich, Jeff Barry and Phil Spector); it was written right into the compositions, and put across through head arrangements and in the use of rock group dynamics so fluid and intelligent that for years they made nearly everything else on the radio sound faintly stupid (listen to "Every Little Thing," "Anytime at All," "What You're Doing").

Though none of the Beatles made anything of formal instrumental virtuosity—Eric Clapton would bring on *that* era—the playing on the records could take your breath away (Ringo's drumming on "There's a Place," or the piano rumble, supported by bass, drums and rhythm guitar, that cues the vocal on "What You're Doing"). But more than anything else it was the singing that made these records what they were. John and

Paul's vocals—and the four Beatles' unpredictable screams, yeah-yeah-yeahs, and head-to-head oooos—communicated urgency first and foremost. Regardless of lyrics, the singers made demands, reached, got, went after more, blew away all that stood before them. They were exhilarated, exuberant, joyous; but all that joy was rooted in determination, as if those nihilistic nights in Hamburg had not just added an edge to the Beatles' music but had lighted a fire in their hearts. In 1964, the freshness of the Beatles' vocal assault was the sound of pure novelty; today, one hears a lovely, naked emotion in those early vocals, a refusal to kid around, to cut the corners of feeling, and a will to say it all, that was not to be heard in rock and roll from any other white performer until Bob Dylan released "Like a Rolling Stone" in the summer of 1965. This spirit surfaced in more obvious form later—consciously and with great craftsmanship, in "Strawberry Fields Forever," "I Am the Walrus," "Yer Blues" and "I'm So Tired"—but it was there from the beginning. In a sense it was the beginning.

Of these first recordings, it may be that "Money," an unforgiving triumph of the intensity of which rock and roll at its strongest is capable, was the greatest. (All votes for "There's a Place" will be counted, however; in some ways the best of the Beatles throughout their career was either a synthesis or a refinement of these two recordings.) Linked to the rock past, "Money" made Barrett Strong's 1960 original sound quaint; Strong's version of the song (not to mention the Stones') is to the Beatles' as Ricky Nelson's "Stood Up" is to "Hound Dog."

Surging forward after a quick, ominous piano opening, the lead vocal was all John. He sang with a greater fury than possessed him before or since (the wails of *John Lennon/Plastic Ono Band*, the 1970 "primal scream" LP, are contrived by comparison), and with a clarity and insistence he may not have matched until that same post-Beatles album, with the last few lines of "God" perhaps the most sublime singing in all of rock and roll. It was an insistence aimed not inward but at the world itself ("I came out of the fuckin' sticks to take over the world," John was to say later); just as only the deaf, or the dead, could resist the utopianism of Paul's vocal on "All My Loving," only a fool could listen to John sing "The best things in life are free/ But you can keep 'em for the birds and bees," or hear him explode in the final choruses with "Now give me money—a lotta money—*I want to be free!*," and not believe that every word was the truth. Add to this the screams, the blistering double oooos, and the chants of "That's . . . what I want" (the menace of the claim is in the pause), all from Paul and George in a manner of complete dementia; the unbelievable metallic harshness of the band; and a total performance that for all the control inherent in a classically simple rock structure sounds ready to blow up in a listener's face at any moment, and the result is a record that keeps virtually every promise rock and roll ever made (the rest of them were kept by "There's a Place," "Eight Days a Week," and "What You're Doing").

Mixing the lyricism of "There's a Place" and the force of "Money," the Beatles' mastery of rock in their first two years of recording was absolute. Without really testing the limits of the form as they had worked it out in the early Sixties, they continued to prove that mastery through 1965, with "Ticket to Ride," the brilliant "Help!," its little-known flip side, "I'm Down" (an astonishing piece of hard rock with a crazed Little Richard vocal from Paul), and "Day Tripper." Still, given Dylan, the Stones, and the Byrds, there was no question that other rockers were testing the Beatles' limits, even if they were not, and so at the end of 1965 the Beatles turned around and dumped *Rubber Soul* on the market.

Though it can be argued that the Beatles' first four LPs, in their British configurations *(Please Please Me, With the Beatles, A Hard Day's Night* and *Beatles for Sale)* were as good as *Rubber Soul*, it may not be worth the trouble. *Rubber Soul* was an album *made* as an album; with the exception of "Michelle" (which, to be fair, paid the bills for years to come), every cut was an inspiration, something new and remarkable in and of itself.

In terms of lyrics, the Beatles were still writing about love, but this was a new kind of love: contingent, scary, and vital in a way that countenanced ambiguities and doubts earlier songs had skimmed right over. "In My Life" was as moving and precise a song about friendship as rock has produced; "Girl," though deceptively straightforward, was a good deal more sophisticated than Dylan's "Just like a Woman."

If the emotional touch was harder, the musical touch was lighter. This music was seduction, not assault; the force was all beneath the surface, in the dynamics of "I'm Looking through You" (which were so striking that many fans delighted in listening to the stereo version of the tune with the vocal track turned off) and in the other numbers just mentioned. It was the Beatles' most attractive album, perhaps their glossiest, and at the same time their most deeply satisfying. To this listener, it was unquestionably their best.

From this point on the story is not so clear. What was clear, though, what was clear in retrospect even on *Rubber Soul*, was that John and Paul were no longer the songwriting team they had once been. Consistently, John's songs described struggle, while Paul's denied it; Paul wrote and sang the A sides, John the Bs. Mapping out the directions that have governed their careers since the Beatles disbanded, John was already cultivating his rebellion and his anger; Paul was making his Decision for Pop; George was making his Decision for Krishna; and Ringo was having his house painted. All of the Beatles were attaching themselves to the fads and passions of the time, to drugs, transcendence, coats of many colors, the paraphernalia of psychedelia. And as the Beatles became one with the times, merging with them rather than standing above them, they became, musically and in every other way, harder to see truly.

The wholeness of the group, the music, and the very idea of the Beatles began to break up, even as "The Beatles," as cultural icons, media personalities, and phenomena, became more exciting than ever. Thus at the time it was obvious that *Revolver*, released in 1966, was better than *Rubber Soul*, just as it was obvious *Sgt. Pepper* was better than both put together. The times carried the imperative of such a choice—though it was not really a choice at all, but rather a sort of faceless necessity. The only road, after all, was onward.

Such a choice does not seem so obvious now, and of course the necessity has faded. *Revolver* retains the flash its title promised, but little of the soul its predecessor delivered. Compared to either, *Sgt. Pepper* appears playful but contrived, less a summing up of its era than a concession to it.

In the final two and a half years of Beatle groupdom, the four remained charming with "All You Need Is Love"; took a fall with *Magical Mystery Tour*; offered a stunning preview of post-Beatles music with the white album; wrapped up their career with the erratic, overly professional *Abbey Road*; and stumbled off the stage they had raised with a botched release of the antiprofessional *Let It Be*.

Out of that sad ending several recordings stand with the best the Beatles ever made. Save Paul's shimmering "Penny Lane," and his bruising "Helter Skelter," all were John's work, and in truth they may have little of the Beatles—the Beatles as something more than four people who sang and played—in them. Still, to this writer, "Strawberry Fields Forever," "I Am the Walrus," "Yer Blues," "I'm So Tired" and "Don't Let Me Down" are each richer than *Sgt. Pepper*'s best cut, "A Day in the Life"; in every case, John seemed to be getting closer to the essentials of his soul, which might be identified as a refusal to settle for anything short of perfection combined with a clear understanding that perfection does not exist—a dilemma that, given the history of the Beatles era and the years since, is something more than one man's hangup.

[THE CHAIR IN PIECES]

Since 1970, the Beatles have carried on, and it has taken real courage to resist the calls, increasingly intense, to accept a certain defeat and reunite for one last time, or perhaps for longer than that. I think the truth is that the Beatles have accepted that they cannot, in any form, become what they were. John and Paul particularly are engaged in the ultimate pop process of reinventing themselves, and in a manner that defies, or redefines, pop, since pop calls in the moment and their efforts will likely last their whole lives. Today, the Beatles oscillate between genius and self-parody, and only one who does not understand the game that is being played would hope for some final, perfect synthesis. Perhaps what matters is that symbolically or in action, the Beatles, who saved the game close to 15 years ago, have no alternative but to work to keep it going.

[THE CHAIR RECALLED]

"[The blues] is a chair, not a design for a chair, or a better chair . . . it is the first chair. It is a chair for sitting on, not chairs for looking at or being appreciated. You sit on that music. . . . We didn't sound like anybody else, that's all. I mean we didn't sound like the black musicians because we weren't black. And because we were brought up on a different kind of music and atmosphere, and so 'Please Please Me' and 'From Me to You' and all those were our version of the chair. We were building our own chairs." —John Lennon, 1970

Discography

American Singles
"I Want to Hold Your Hand" b/w "I Saw Her Standing There" (Capitol 5112; ☆1, 1964). "She Loves You" (Swan 4152; ☆1, 1964). "Please Please Me" b/w "From Me to You" (Vee-Jay 581; ☆3, 1964). "My Bonnie" (with Tony Sheridan) (MGM 13213; ☆26, 1964). "Twist and Shout" (Tollie 9001; ☆2, 1964). "Can't Buy Me Love" b/w "You Can't Do That" (Capitol 5150; ☆1, 1964). "Do You Want to Know a Secret" b/w "Thank You Girl" (Vee-Jay 587; ☆2, 1964). "Love Me Do" b/w "P.S. I Love You" (Tollie 9008; ☆1, 1964). "A Hard Day's Night" b/w "I Should Have Known Better" (Capitol 5222; ☆1, 1964). "Ain't She Sweet" (Atco 6308; ☆19, 1964). "And I Love Her" b/w "If I Fell" (Capitol 5235; ☆12, 1964). "I'll Cry Instead" (Capitol 5234; ☆25, 1964). "Matchbox" b/w "Slow Down" (Capitol 5255; ☆17, 1964). "I Feel Fine" b/w "She's a Woman" (Capitol 5327; ☆1, 1964). "Eight Days a Week" b/w "I Don't Want to Spoil the Party" (Capitol 5371; ☆1, 1965). "Ticket to Ride" b/w "Yes It Is" (Capitol 5407; ☆1, 1965). "Help!" (Capitol 5476; ☆1, 1965). "Yesterday" b/w "Act Naturally" (Capitol 5498; ☆1, 1965). "We Can Work It Out" b/w "Day Tripper" (Capitol 5555; ☆1, 1965). "Nowhere Man" (Capitol 5587; ☆3, 1966). "Paperback Writer" b/w "Rain" (Capitol 5651; ☆1, 1966). "Yellow Submarine" b/w "Eleanor Rigby" (Capitol 5715; ☆2, 1966). "Penny Lane" b/w "Strawberry Fields Forever" (Capitol 5810; ☆1, 1967). "All You Need Is Love" b/w "Baby You're a Rich Man" (Capitol 5964; ☆1, 1967). "Hello Goodbye" b/w "I Am the Walrus" (Capitol 2056; ☆1, 1967). "Lady Madonna" (Capitol 2138; ☆4, 1968). "Hey Jude" b/w "Revolution" (Apple 2276; ☆1, 1968). "Get Back" b/w "Don't Let Me Down" (with Billy Preston) (Apple 2490; ☆1, 1969). "The Ballad of John and Yoko" (Apple 2531; ☆8, 1969). "Come Together" b/w "Something" (Apple 2654; ☆1, 1969). "Let It Be" (Apple 2764; ☆1, 1970). "The Long and Winding Road" b/w "For You Blue" (Apple 2832; ☆1, 1970).

American Albums
Meet the Beatles! (Capitol 2047; ☆1, 1964). *Introducing . . . the Beatles* (Vee-Jay 1062; ☆2, 1964). *The Beatles* (with Tony Sheridan and their Guests) (MGM 4215; ☆68, 1964). *The Beatles' Second Album* (Capitol 2080; ☆1, 1964). *A Hard Day's Night* (United Artists 3366; ☆1, 1964). *Something New* (Capitol 2108; ☆2, 1964). *The Beatles' Story* (Capitol 2222; ☆7, 1964). *Beatles '65* (Capitol 2228; ☆1, 1965). *The Early Beatles* (Capitol 2309; ☆43, 1965). *Beatles VI* (Capitol 2358; ☆1, 1965). *Help!* (Capitol 2386; ☆1, 1965). *Rubber Soul* (Capitol 2442; ☆1, 1965). *"Yesterday" . . . and Today* (Capitol 2553; ☆1, 1966). *Revolver* (Capitol 2576; ☆1, 1966). *Sgt. Pepper's Lonely Hearts Club Band* (Capitol 2653; ☆1, 1967). *Magical Mystery Tour* (Capitol 2835; ☆1, 1967). *The Beatles* (Apple 101; ☆1, 1968). *Yellow Submarine* (Apple 153; ☆2, 1969). *Abbey Road* (Apple 383; ☆1, 1969). *Hey Jude* (Apple 385; ☆2, 1970). *In the Beginning* (featuring Tony Sheridan) (Polydor 4504; ☆117, 1970). *Let It Be* (Apple 34001; ☆1, 1970.) *The Beatles/1962-1966* (Apple 3403; ☆3, 1973). *The Beatles/1967-1970* (Apple 3404; ☆1, 1973).

SOLO ALBUMS BY EX-BEATLES

Paul McCartney
McCartney (Apple 3363; ☆1, 1970). *Ram* (Apple 3375; ☆2, 1971). *Wild Life* (Apple 3386; ☆10, 1971). *Red Rose Speedway* (Apple 3409; ☆1, 1973). *Band on the Run* (Apple 3415; ☆1, 1973). *Venus and Mars* (Capitol 11419; ☆1, 1975).

John Lennon
Two Virgins (Tetragrammaton 5001; ☆124, 1969). *Unfinished Music No. 2: Music with the Lions* (Zapple 3357; ☆174, 1969). *Wedding Album* (Apple 3361; ☆178, 1969). *Live Peace in Toronto 1969* (Apple 3362; ☆10, 1970). *John Lennon/Plastic Ono Band* (Apple 3372; ☆6, 1970). *Imagine* (Apple 3379; ☆1, 1971). *Some Time in New York City* (Apple 3392; ☆48, 1972). *Mind Games* (Apple 3414; ☆9, 1973). *Walls and Bridges* (Apple 3416; ☆1, 1974). *Rock 'n' Roll* (Apple 3419; ☆6, 1975). *Shaved Fish* (Apple 3421; ☆12, 1975).

George Harrison
Wonderwall Music (Apple 3350; ☆49, 1969). *Electronic Sound* (Zapple 3358; ☆191, 1969). *All Things Must Pass* (Apple 3385; ☆1, 1970). *The Concert for Bangla Desh* (Apple 3385; ☆2, 1972). *Living in the Material World* (Apple 3410; ☆1, 1973). *Dark Horse* (Apple 3418; ☆4, 1974). *Extra Texture (Read All about It)* (Apple 3420; ☆8, 1975).

Ringo Starr
Sentimental Journey (Apple 3365; ☆22, 1970). *Beaucoups of Blues* (Apple 3368; ☆65, 1970). *Ringo* (Apple 3413; ☆2, 1973). *Goodnight Vienna* (Apple 3417; ☆8, 1974). *Blast from Your Past* (Apple 3422; ☆30, 1975).
(Chart positions compiled from Joel Whitburn's *Record Research*, based on *Billboard* Pop and LPs charts.)

The Rolling Stones
by Robert Christgau

Mick Jagger was never a rocker. He wasn't a mod, either. He was a bohemian, an antiutopian version of what Americans called a folkie. That is, he was attracted to music of a certain innocence as only a fairly classy—and sophisticated—person can be. Unlike John Lennon and Paul McCartney (and Bob Dylan), his ambitions weren't kindled by Elvis Presley; his angry, low-rent mien was no more a reflection of his economic fate than his stardom was a means for him to escape it.

Something similar went for all the Rolling Stones. "What can a poor boy do/Except sing for a rock and roll band?" was the way they opted out of the political involvement that most young rebels found unavoidable in the late Sixties. But not only weren't they poor boys when they played that song, they never had been—except voluntarily, which is different. Only two of them—bassist Bill Wyman, the son of a bricklayer, and drummer Charlie Watts, the son of a lorry driver—came from working-class backgrounds, and both were improving their day-job lots dramatically by the time they joined the Stones. The other three, the group's spiritual nucleus through the scuffling days, were in it strictly for the art. Lead guitarist Keith Richard, although he grew up fairly poor, revolted against his parents' genteel middle-class pretensions; rhythm guitarist and all-purpose eclectic Brian Jones came from a musical family headed by an aeronautical engineer and wandered the Continent after leaving a posh school; and Mick himself, the son of a medium-successful educator, did not quit the London School of Economics until after the band became a going proposition in 1963. This is not to say the Stones were rich kids; only Brian qualified as what Americans would call upper middle-class. Nor is it to underestimate the dreariness of the London suburbs or the rigidity of the English class hierarchy. But due partly to their own posturing, the Stones are often perceived as working class, and that is a major distortion.

Working class is more like Elvis and the Beatles, who loved rock and roll at least partly because rock and roll was a way to *make it.* Their propulsive upward mobility thus became inextricably joined with the energy of the music they created; their will to be rich and famous was both heroic and naive, a key ingredient of the projected naturalness that was essential to Elvis, and the projected innocence that was essential to the Beatles. For disapproving elders to dismiss this naturalness/innocence as mere vulgarity—without observing, as Dwight Macdonald did about Elvis, that genuine vulgarity has its advantages in earthiness—represented more than a "generation gap." It was open-and-shut snobbery, motivated like most snobbery by class fear.

With the Stones all of this was more complicated. Their devotion to music itself was purer, but insofar as they wanted to be rich-and-famous—and they did, especially Mick, who had always been into money, and Brian, a notoriety junkie—they were neither heroic nor naive, just ambitious. And insofar as

they wanted to be earthy—which was a conscious ambition too, rather than something they came by naturally or (God knows) innocently—they risked a vulgarity that was mere indeed. Inspired by the coaching of Andrew Loog Oldham, the publicist/manager who undertook the creation of the Stones in their own image starting in the spring of 1963, they *chose* to be vulgar-aggressively, as a stance, to counteract the dreariness and rigidity of their middle-class suburban mess of pottage. Perhaps they aspired to the earthiness of the grandfather who passes wind because he doesn't fancy the bother of holding it in, but in the very aspiration they recalled the grandson who farts for the sheer joyous annoyance value of it—and then calls it youth culture.

It would be quicker, of course, to suggest that they sought only to live up to the earthiness of the rhythm and blues music they lived for. But although there's no doubt that Brian, Mick, and Keith were passionate about hard-to-find black records that were as crude and esoteric by the standards of English pop and beat fans as they were crude and commercial by the standards of old-bohemian English blues and jazz cultists, the Stones have never been very specific about just what that passion meant emotionally. Only their affinities are clear. Elmore James was Brian's man, while Keith loved Chuck Berry, but they by no means defined the group's poles: one of the laborers in the rhythm section, Charlie, had jazzier tastes than Brian, while the other, Bill, was working in a straight rock and roll group when he joined the Stones in late 1962 or early 1963. Mick's preferences, predictably enough, were shiftier; as he once told Jonathan Cott: "We were blues purists who liked ever-so-commercial things but never did them onstage because we were so horrible and so aware of being blues purists, you know what I mean?"

What he means, one surmises, is that the Stones' artiness never deadened their taste for certain commercially fermented blues-based songs—not as long as the songs were pithy and hummable and would induce people to dance when played loudly. But by mocking the blues purist in himself he elides "purism"'s image potential. Symbols of the English "R&B" movement—thought in 1963 to be challenging beat (and hence the Beatles) among British teenagers—the Stones had it both ways. Their first big British hit, that winter, was Lennon and McCartney's "I Wanna Be Your Man." They scoffed virtuously at the notion of "a British-composed R&B number," but wrote their own tunes almost from the start, and ranged as far pop as "Under the Boardwalk" and Buddy Holly in their early recordings.

It is sometimes argued that such modulations of sensibility belie the group's artistic integrity; in fact, however, the Stones' willingness to "exploit" and "compromise" their own bohemian proclivities meant only that they assumed a pop aesthetic.

Mick Jagger, late Sixties (Ethan Russell)

Most artists believe they ought to be rich-and-famous on their own very idiosyncratic terms—the Stones happened to be right. To sing about "half-assed games" on the AM radio (on Bobby Womack's "It's All Over Now") or glower out hirsute and tieless from the Sunday entertainment pages was integrity aplenty in 1964.

Perhaps most important, the Stones obviously cared about the quality of the music they played. If this music recalled any single antecedent it was Chuck Berry, but never with his total commitment to fun. It was fast and metallic, most bluesish in its strict understatement. Clean and sharp—especially in contrast to the gleeful modified chaos of the Beatles—this striking but never overbearing music was an ideal vocal setting, and if it was the guitars and percussion that established the band's presence, it was the vocals, and the vocalist, that defined it. Quite often Jagger chose a light, saucy pop timbre that was also reminiscent of Berry, but something in his voice left a ranker overall impression—something slippery yet unmistakable, as lubricious and as rubbery as his famous lips. (For a simple example, listen to his tone of voice on most of "I'm a King Bee"—and then to his half-playful, half-ominous pronunciation on the word "buzz" in "I can buzz better baby/When your man is gone.") Nor was this just a matter of being sexy. Just as there was a pointed astringency to the band's music, caustic where Chuck Berry was consciously ebullient—listen to the acerbic tinniness of Keith's lead lines, or to Brian's droning rhythm parts, or to the way the added percussion lags behind the beat—so there was a hurtful tinge to Mick's singing, especially on the slow, murky originals ("Tell Me," "Heart of Stone," or "Time Is on My Side," composed by Jerry Ragavoy but defined by the Stones) that served the group's change-of-pace needs the way ballads did the Beatles'.

The Stones' high-decibel, high-speed approach was rock and roll, not rhythm and blues. Nevertheless, they did admittedly appropriate many of the essential trappings of their music—like hooks and solos—from black sources. Jagger, however—despite his rhythmic canniness and cheerful willingness to ape a drawl—was no more a blues stylist *or* a blues thief than Bob Dylan or Paul McCartney. He simply customized certain details of blues phrasing and enunciation into components of a vocal style of protean originality.

Although pinning down the voice of a compulsive ironist like Jagger is impossible by definition, it is perhaps most notable for a youthful petulance that has faded only gradually. His drawl recalls Christopher Robin as often as it does Howlin' Wolf; his mewling nasality might have been copped from a Cockney five-year-old. Jagger's petulance offends some people, who wonder how this whiner—a perpetual adolescent at best—can pretend to mean the adult words he sings. But that ignores the self-confidence that coexists with the petulance—Jagger's very grown-up assurance not that he'll get what he wants, but that he has every reason to ask for it. Even worse, it ignores the fact that Meaning It is definitely not what the Stones are about. Jagger didn't so much sing Muddy Waters's "I Just Want to Make Love to You" as get it over with, and although he did really seem to wish us "Good Times," he made the prospect sound doubtful where Sam Cooke enjoyed the wish itself.

It seems unlikely that at this point any of the Stones were conscious about this. All of them, Jagger included, were attracted to the gruff, eloquent directness of so much black music; relatively speaking, they became natural, expressive, sexy, and so forth by playing it. What set them apart was Jagger's instinctive understanding that this achievement was relative—that there was a Heisenberg paradox built into the way he appreciated the virtues of this music—and his genius at expressing that as well. The aggressiveness and sexuality of the form were his, but the sincerity was beyond him—partly because he was white and English, and especially because he was Mick Jagger. He loved the blues for their sincerity, yet their sincerity was the ultimate object of his pervasive anger. He wanted what he couldn't have and felt detached even from his own desire; he accepted his inability to sing from as deep in his heart as Sam Cooke, he sometimes reveled in it, but he wasn't sure he liked it, not deep in his heart. "An empty heart/ Is like an empty life," he sang in one of his early lyrics, adding nuance to qualification as always, so that even as it adhered to all the lost-love conventions, the song evoked the most basic condition of his existence.

Jagger is obsessed with distance. He forces the Stones' music to gaze across (and down) the generation gap and the money gap and the feeling gap and the meaning gap. But then, powered by the other Stones—all of them, like most of the Stones' fans, somewhat more simple-minded than Jagger—the music leaps, so that as a totality it challenges that frustrating, ubiquitous, perhaps metaphysical margin between reach and grasp that presents itself so sharply to human beings with the leisure to think about it. This dual commitment to irony and ecstasy makes the Stones exemplary modernists. Without a doubt, it has been their readiness to leap that has won the Stones their following—no one has ever rocked on out with more ecstatic energy. But it is their realism, bordering at its most suspect on cynicism, that makes all that energy interesting, and ensures that their following will never be as huge as that of the high-spirited Beatles (or of a technocosmic doom show like Led Zeppelin, either). After all, not everyone wants to be reminded that it is salutary to think and have fun at the same time. But that is what it means to get up and boogie to "Street Fighting Man," or to party to a paean as steeped in irony as "Brown Sugar."

Jagger's distance from the Afro part of his Afro-American musical heritage was especially liberating for white Ameri-

cans. Whereas for Elvis and those natives who followed him the blues bore an inescapable load of racial envy and fear, Mick's involvement was primarily aesthetic. Since as his English blues preceptor, Alexis Korner, once remarked, Jagger's chief worry was whether the music was "performed properly," he betrayed no embarrassment about being white. Not all Englishmen were so uninhibited—an obsessive like Eric Burdon (of the Animals) emulated black Southern intonations sedulously. But Jagger got off on being a white person singing black songs, and he put that across. His mocking, extravagant elocution, as wild as his hair and the way he pranced around the stage, was more than vaguely self-amused, achieving a power that compared to that of its origins because it was true to itself.

For the English audience, however, the Stones' distance from the U.S.A. itself was edifying. Because the English were far enough from American affluence and mass culture to perceive them as sources of vitality rather than of oppression, a natural perspective was commonly built into all Beatle-era rock and roll, but whereas for the Beatles it manifested itself innocently—in fun, silliness, play—the Stones' version was weirder oddball and therefore more sophisticated. They wove a mythology of America around R&B novelties like "Route 66" and "Down Home Girl," and then exaggerated every eccentricity with some vocal moue or instrumental underline. The image of the States that resulted was droll, surreal, maybe a little scary—fascinating, but no hamburger cornucopia.

It was also a cleverly differentiated musical product that rose to number-two status in England upon the release of the first Stones album in mid-1964. In the U.S., however, the Stones were number two only in publicity, with sales well behind the Dave Clark Five and Herman's Hermits and just slightly ahead of arty rivals like the Animals and the Kinks for the first year and a half of British Invasion. Then came their seventh U.S. single, "(I Can't Get No) Satisfaction." It was the perfect Stones paradox—the lyrics denied what the music delivered, with the vocal sitting on the fence—and it dominated the summer of 1965, securing a pop audience half of which was content to shout "I can't get no" while the other half decided that the third verse was about a girl who wouldn't put out during her period.

By then the Stones were Mick and Keith's band, although opening for Alexis Korner at London's Marquee Club in early 1963 they had been "Brian Jones and Mick Jagger and the Rollin' Stones." As vain and exhibitionistic onstage as Jagger, Jones later boasted of having been the group's "undisputed leader," a status he maintained, as Al Aronowitz observed, until it was "worthwhile for someone to dispute." Jones wanted to be a star so much he took it for granted; his relationship to the audience was self-indulgent and self-deceiving. But since outrage was essential to Jagger, Richard and Oldham's prod-

uct—aggro-sex image mongering, lyrics both indecipherable and censorable, and the longest hair known to civilization—and since Brian was the most genuinely outrageous (and crazy) (and generous) (and cruel) of the Stones, he remained essential over and above his musical input. He was the one people remembered after Mick—especially the teenybopper girls who were still the Stones' most visible contingent.

The Stones got the teenyboppers because Oldham was sharp enough to extend Little Richard's First Law of Youth Culture to his scruffy band—he attracted the kids by driving their parents up the wall. But although we can assume Oldham initiated his campaign of world conquest in a spirit of benign, profiteering manipulation, something more was in store. The bohemian-revolutionary vanguard, like the Diggers, who in the mid-Sixties welcomed the Stones to San Francisco as brothers in struggle, were even more symbolic (if less numerous) than that proliferating network of hip collegiate Stones fans heir to a beatnik myth that had passed from media consciousness when San Francisco's bohemian community moved from North Beach to the Haight, none of these fans really knowing how many hundreds of thousands of arty allies they had across the country. Call them predropouts because dropping out then barely knew its name. Soon, in their fashion, they would consider the Diggers and do likewise, just as the Stones' teen hordes would consider *them* and do likewise later on. What it all portended was just what parents had always feared from rock and roll, especially from this ugly group: youth apocalypse.

I remember the first time I ever saw the Stones perform, at the Forum in Montreal in October 1965. I purchased my tickets on the day of the show, and even from deep in the balcony got more from Mick's dancing around the "droogy" stance of the others than I did from the music, which was muffled by the hockey rink P.A. and rendered all but inaudible by the ululations of the teenaged girls around me. It was only afterward, when I happened to walk past the bus terminal, that I glimpsed what had really just happened. There in the station were hundreds of youths, all speaking French, waiting to complete their pilgrimage by plunging back into the cold of northern Quebec. I had never seen so much long hair in one place in my life.

What was about to happen was an unprecedented contradiction in terms, mass bohemianism, and this is where the idea of "pop" became key. Pop is what the mod Oldham shared with the bohemian Stones, and what they in turn shared with the teenyboppers. Applied first to low-priced classical concerts and then to Tin Pan Alley product, the word was beginning to achieve more general cultural currency by the mid-Fifties, when London-based visual artists like Eduardo Paolozzi were proposing that a schlock form (e.g., science fiction pulp) might nurture "a higher order of imagination" than a nominally experimental one (e.g., little magazine). Shocking.

Youths like the Stones—who had never known a nonelectric

culture, and who were no more wary of distribution and exposure in the modern media bath than they were of their own amps—automatically assumed what older avant-gardists formulated with such difficulty. Their pop sensibility led them to a decidedly nonslumming bohemianism—more unpretentious and déclassé than the bohemianism of the Twenties and before. This was the gift of mass culture, compulsory education (especially English art-school routing) and consumer capitalism to five young men who comprise a social sample that would have been most unlikely, statistically, to group around the arts 40 years before. Not that the Stones were untainted by avant-garde snobbishness—in their project of rebellious self-definition, exclusivity was a given. They never figured they'd spearhead a mass movement that went anywhere but record stores. That mass potential, however, was built into their penchant for pop itself.

There were solid economic reasons for the rise of mass bohemianism. Juxtapose a 20-year rise in real income to the contradiction in which the straight-and-narrow worker/producer is required to turn into a hedonistic consumer off-hours, and perhaps countless kids, rather than assuming their production function on schedule, will choose to "fulfill themselves" outside the job market. But, traditionally, bohemian self-fulfillment has been achieved through, or at least in the presence of, art. Only popular culture could have rendered art accessible—in the excitement and inspiration (and self-congratulation) of its perception and the self-realization (or fantasy) of its creation—not just to well-raised well-offs but to the broad range of less statusy war babies who in fact made the hippie movement the relatively cross-class phenomenon it was. And for all these kids, popular culture meant rock and roll, the art form created by and for their hedonistic consumption. In turn, rock and roll meant the Rolling Stones.

Of course, it also meant the Beatles and Bob Dylan and the Who and the Grateful Dead—and Grand Funk Railroad. But the Beatles' appeal was too broad—parents liked them. Dylan's was too narrow—as an American bohemian, he remained suspicious of mass culture, and stayed virtually out of sight from mid-1966 until the hippie thing was done with. The Who and the Dead hit a little too late to qualify as myths; they also proved a little too committed to the mass and the bohemianism, respectively, to challenge the Stones' breadth. And Grand Funk and so many others simply couldn't match the Stones' art.

From "Satisfaction" to the end of the decade, the Stones' aesthetic stature became more heroic. Their R&B phase began with two very good albums that culminated in a classic third, *The Rolling Stones Now!* Then came their long middle period, beginning with two very good transitional LPs—*Out of Our Heads* and *December's Children (and Everybody's),* both of which contained many R&B covers but sold on the strength of their originals—that seemed slightly thin only when compared to those that followed. *Aftermath, Between the Buttons, Beggar's Banquet* and *Let It Bleed* are all among the greatest rock albums, and *Flowers*, although it includes three previously released album cuts, sounds every bit as valid on its own. Furthermore, although the 3-D/psychedelic/year-in-the-making response to *Sgt. Pepper's Lonely Hearts Club Band, Their Satanic Majesties Request,* is remembered as a washout, the tunes prove remarkably solid and the concept legitimate in its tongue-in-cheekness. I would rank it as a first-rate oddity, and note that the title alone was the single greatest image manipulation in the Stones' whole media-happy story.

After "Satisfaction" it was no longer satisfying to accuse the Stones of imitation; after *Aftermath*, their music came almost entirely out of their heads. Blues-based hard rock it remained, with an eventual return to one black classic per album, but its texture was permanently enriched. As Brian daubed on occult instrumental colors (dulcimer, sitar, marimbas and bells, on *Aftermath* alone) and Charlie molded jazz chops to rock forms and Bill's bass gathered wit and Keith rocked roughly on, the group as a whole learned to respect and exploit (never revere) studio nuance. In the fall of 1967, they announced a split from Oldham, whose image-making services had become superfluous and whose record-producing capabilities they have since disparaged. They were making mature, resonant music by then—they could permit their pace changes some lyricism now, there was warmth as well as white heat, and Mick's voice deepened, shedding some of its impertinence.

By proclamation and by vocal method—he slurs as a matter of conviction, articulating only catchphrases—Jagger belittles his own lyrics, an appropriate stance for a literate man who has bet his life on the comparative inexplicitness of music. Nonetheless, Jagger's lyrics were much like the Stones' music, aesthetically: pungent and vernacular ("Who wants yesterday's

papers"); achieving considerable specificity with familiar materials ("You got me running like a cat in a thunderstorm"); and challenging conventional perceptions more by their bite than by any notable eloquence or profundity ("They just get married 'cause there's nothing else to do"). But whereas the Stones' music extended rock and roll usages, Jagger's lyrics often contravened them. He wrote more hate songs than love songs, and related tales of social and political breakdown with untoward glee. The hypocrisy and decay of the upper classes was a fave subject—many songs that seem basically antiwoman (although certainly not all of them) are actually more antirich. He was also capable of genuine gusto about sex (not as often as is thought, but consider the openhearted anticipation of "Goin' Home" or "Let's Spend the Night Together") and wrote the most accurate LSD song ever, "Something Happened to Me Yesterday."

But that was as far as it went. Traditionally, bohemian revolt has been aimed at nothing more fundamental than puritan morality and genteel culture. That's the way it was with the hippies, certainly, and that's the way it was with the Stones. They did show a class animus—even though it wasn't proletariat-versus-bourgeoisie ("Salt of the Earth" evokes that struggle no less sensitively than it evokes Jagger's distance from it), but rather the old enmity between the freemen of democratic England and its peerage—and a penchant for generalized social criticism. They earned their "political" aura. But their most passionate commitments were to sex, dope, and lavish autonomy. Granted, this looked revolutionary enough to get them into plenty of trouble. The dope-bust harassment/persecution of individual Stones did keep the group from touring the States between 1966 and 1969. But their money and power prevailed; in the end, their absence and their apparent martyrdom only augmented their myth and their careers.

Throughout this time, the Stones were heroes of mass bohemianism. They lived the life of art, their art got better all the time, and as it got better, remarkably enough, it reached more people. But although their art survives, its heroic quality does not; the Stones betray all the flaws of the counterculture they half-wittingly and -willingly symbolized. Their sex was too often sexist, their expanded consciousness too often a sordid escape; their rebellion was rooted in impulse to the exclusion of all habits of sacrifice, and their relationship to fame had little to do with the responsibilities of leadership, or of allegiance.

Not that leadership was Mick's—or any ironist's—kind of thing. All he wanted was to have his ego massaged by his public or bathed in luxurious privacy as his own whim dictated. This he got, but it wasn't all roses—it was also dead flowers. Early on, in "Play with Fire" or "Back Street Girl," say, he had attacked decadence with a sneer—it was something that happened to others, especially the idle rich. By "Live with Me," or "Dancing with Mr. D.," the implication was that Mick's life of pop star luxury was turning him into a decadent himself.

But if Mick was a decadent, he was also a professional. His project of radical self-definition flourished where so many others failed. Most bohemians can find ways to waste themselves—it's often fun for a while, and it's certainly easy. But the bohemian art hero has a polar option—he or she can persist and make a career out of it, becoming more exemplary as his or her success becomes more unduplicable. His talent, his resilience, his sure pop instinct, and a boom market in creativity all contributed to Jagger's singular preeminence. Among the many who couldn't match up was Brian Jones. Originally the key to the Stones' rebel-purist image (and reality), he proved to be the group's natural decadent. Despite what those who consider Mick a prick suspect, it is rather unlikely that Brian was forced out of the group because his attraction to the bizarre endangered Mick's self-aggrandizing aesthetic calculations. Quite simply, he seems to have fucked and doped himself past all usefulness. Brian was one of the damned by choice of personality. He drowned in his own swimming pool on July 3rd, 1969.

Two days later the Stones introduced previously hired ex–John Mayall guitarist Mick Taylor at a free concert in Hyde Park that served as Brian's wake, and that November they commenced history's first mythic rock and roll tour. They hadn't swept the U.S.—or anywhere—in three years; the world had changed, or so it seemed; Woodstock hung in the air like a rainbow. It seemed only fitting to climax all that long-haired pomp and circumstance with yet another celebration of communal freeness. The result was Altamont—one murdered; total dead: four; 300,000 bummed out. It seems more a chilling metaphor than a literal disaster in retrospect, as much the Grateful Dead's fault as the Stones'. But the Stones are stuck with it—if it is typical of their genius that their responsibility is difficult to pinpoint, it is typical of their burden that everyone who's into blame blames them anyway.

But in the end that's typical of their genius too, for it means that whatever the specifics—pinpointing *is* always difficult—the Stones acknowledge their complicity in a world in which evil exists. Above all, they are anything but utopians. They never made very convincing hippies because hippie just wasn't their thing. Jagger's taste for ecstatic community was tempered by that awareness of limits that always assured the Stones their formal acuteness. A successful artist may epitomize his or her audience, but that is a process of rarefaction— it doesn't mean conforming to the great mean, even of the time's bohemianism. So while it is true that the Stones' flaws and the counterculture's show a certain congruence, ultimately Mick is congruent to nothing—he always leaves himself an out. He doesn't condone the Midnight Rambler or Mister Jimmy, he just lays them bare. His gift is to make clear that even if the truth doesn't make you free, it needn't sap your will or your energy either. As with most bohemian rebels, his politics are indirect. He provides the information. The audience must then decide what to do with it.

And yet that is perhaps too kind. Somewhere inside, the Stones knew that any undertaking as utopian as Altamont was doomed by definition. If their audience didn't understand it that way, it was because the Stones themselves, in all their multileveled contradiction, were unwilling to come out and tell them. They would suggest it, yes, embody it, but they wouldn't make it plain, because the nature of the Truth is that it isn't plain. If a male fan wants to take Mick's struggle with male persona as an invitation to midnight rambling, well, that's the nature of the game.

After Altamont, the Stones played with a vengeance. *Sticky Fingers*, in April 1971, appeared to trifle with decadence just when some retribution seemed called for, and on its two masterpieces, it definitely did. "Moonlight Mile" re-created all the paradoxical distances inherent in erotic love with a power worthy of Yeats, yet could also be interpreted as a cocaine song; "Brown Sugar," in which (if you listen with care to a rocker so compelling that it discourages exegesis) Jagger links his own music to the slave trade, exploits the racial and sexual contradictions of his stance even as it explores them. *Exile on Main St.*, released in conjunction with the 1972 American tour, was decadent in a more realized way: weary and complicated, barely afloat in its own drudgery, with Mick's voice submerged under layers of studio murk, it piled all the old themes—sex as power, sex as love, sex as pleasure, distance, craziness, release—on top of an obsession with time that was more than appropriate in men pushing 30 who were still committed to what was once considered youth music. It stands as the most consistently dense and various music they've ever made.

Arguably, those two albums are the Stones' summit. It is now as long since Altamont as it was between Altamont and the Stones' recording debut, and the Stones, their halfhearted fantasies of a new cultural order long since forgotten, have found their refuge in professionalism. *Sticky Fingers* and *Exile on Main St.* both featured Mick Taylor, a young veteran of the rock-concert tradition of the boogieing jam, and session hornmen Bobby Keys and Jim Price; in a way they are both (*Exile* especially) triumphs of Taylor/Keys/Price-style musicianly craft over the kind of pop-hero mongering that can produce an Altamont. But if that's so, then *Goat's Head Soup* and *It's Only Rock 'n Roll* are mere product, musicianly craft at its unheroic norm, terrific by the standards of Foghat or the Doobie Brothers but a nadir for the Stones. Even the peaks—"Starfucker" ("Star Star") and "If You Don't Rock Me," respectively—had déjà entendu musical and lyrical themes, and it's hard to imagine the Stones putting their names on tunes as tritely portentous as "Dancing with Mr. D." or "Time Waits for No One" in their prepro days. Only rock and roll indeed.

A similar distinction can be drawn between the 1972 and 1975 tours. In '72 the mood was friendly; "Sympathy for the Devil" was not performed; the gentle Taylor wafted through the proceedings; and Mick undercut his fabled demonism by playing the clown, the village idiot, the marionette. Very professional, yet their most rocking show ever. In 1975, with ex-Face Ron Wood aboard in place of Taylor, they worked even harder, but rather than celebrating professionalism they succumbed to it. Jagger's hyperactive stamina was an athletic marvel, but his moves often looked forced, and although Wood and Richard often combined for a certain bumptious dirtiness, the musical energy seemed forced as well. The 1976 album, *Black and Blue*, put the Stones' recent failures in context, however. It was no masterpiece, but it was rock and roll that didn't deserve an "only," a genuine if derivative departure that showed off artistic professionalism at its best—creative ups and downs that can engross an attentive audience. Not what we want, maybe, but what we can use.

Only rock and roll? The Stones are the proof of the form. When the guitars and the drums and the voice come together in those elementary patters that no one else has ever quite managed to simulate, the most undeniable excitement is a virtually automatic result. To insist that this excitement doesn't reach you is not to articulate an aesthetic judgment but to assert a rather uninteresting crotchet of taste. It is to boast that you don't like rock and roll itself.

Discography
1964–1975

American Singles
"Not Fade Away" (London 9657; ☆48, 1964). "Tell Me (You're Coming Back)" (London 9682; ☆24, 1964). "It's All Over Now" (London 9687; ☆26, 1964). "Time Is on My Side" (London 9708; ☆6, 1964). "Heart of Stone" (London 9725; ☆19, 1965). "The Last Time" (London 9741; ☆9, 1965). "(I Can't Get No) Satisfaction" (London 9766; ☆1, 1965). "Get Off of My Cloud" (London 9792; ☆1, 1965). "As Tears Go By" (London 9808; ☆6, 1965). "19th Nervous Breakdown" (London 9823; ☆2, 1966). "Paint It Black" (London 901; ☆1, 1966). "Mother's Little Helper" b/w "Lady Jane" (London 902; ☆8, 1966). "Have You Seen Your Mother, Baby, Standing in the Shadow" (London 903; ☆9, 1966). "Ruby Tuesday" b/w "Let's Spend the Night Together" (London 904; ☆1, 1967). "Dandelion" b/w "We Love You" (London 905; ☆14, 1967). "She's a Rainbow" (London 906; ☆25, 1967). "Jumpin' Jack Flash" (London 908; ☆3, 1968). "Street Fighting Man" (London 909; ☆48, 1968). "Honky Tonk Women" (London 910; ☆1, 1969). "Brown Sugar" (Rolling Stones 19100; ☆1, 1971). "Wild Horses" (Rolling Stones 19101; ☆28, 1971). "Tumbling Dice" (Rolling Stones 19103; ☆7, 1972). "Happy" (Rolling Stones 19104; ☆22, 1972). "You Can't Always Get What You Want" (London 910; ☆42, 1973). "Angie" (Rolling Stones 19105; ☆1, 1973). "Doo Doo Doo Doo Doo (Heartbreaker)" (Rolling Stones 19109; ☆15, 1974). "It's Only Rock 'n' Roll (but I Like It)" (Rolling Stones 19301; ☆16, 1974). "Ain't Too Proud to Beg" (Rolling Stones 19302; ☆17, 1974). "I Don't Know Why" (Abkco 4701; ☆42, 1975). "Out of Time" (Abkco 4702; ☆81, 1975).
American Albums
The Rolling Stones (London 375; ☆11, 1964). *12 X 5* (London 402, ☆3, 1964). *The Rolling Stones, Now!* (London, 420; ☆5, 1965). *Out of Our Heads* (London 429; ☆1, 1965). *December's Children (and Everybody's)* (London 451; ☆4, 1965. *Big Hits (High Tide and Green Grass)* (London 1; ☆3, 1966). *Aftermath* (London 476; ☆2, 1966). *Got Live if You Want It!* (London 493; ☆6, 1966). *Between the Buttons* (London 499; ☆2, 1967). *Flowers* (London 509; ☆3, 1967). *Their Satanic Majesties Request* (London 2; ☆2, 1967). *Beggar's Banquet* (London 539; ☆5, 1968). *Through the Past Darkly (Big Hits Vol. 2)* (London 3; ☆2, 1969). *Let It Bleed* (London 4; ☆3, 1969). *"Get Yer Ya-Ya's Out!"* (London 5; ☆6, 1970). *Sticky Fingers* (Rolling Stones 59100; ☆1, 1971). *Hot Rocks 1964–1971* (London 606/7; ☆4, 1972). *Exile on Main St.* (Rolling Stones 2900; ☆1, 1972). *More Hot Rocks (Big Hits and Fazed Cookies)* (London 626/7; ☆9, 1972). *Goat's Head Soup* (Rolling Stones 59101; ☆1, 1973). *It's Only Rock 'n' Roll* (Rolling Stones 79101; ☆1, 1974). *Metamorphosis* (Abkco 1; ☆8, 1975). *Made in the Shade* (Rolling Stones 79102; ☆6, 1975). *Black and Blue* (Rolling Stones 79104; ☆1, 1976).
(Chart positions compiled from Joel Whitburn's *Record Research*, based on *Billboard* Pop and LPs charts.)

The Sound of Texas

by Ed Ward

Texas has a little bit of everything, and its music reflects its diversity as well as its size. Spaniards, Germans, Anglos, Czechs, Chicanos, Blacks—each has played a part in shaping the popular music of the Lone Star State.

Western swing, the first distinctively Texan music to gain national popularity (in the late Thirties), was as polyglot as it was unmistakable. A hybrid of big band jazz and Anglo-American reels, it transformed the course of American country music. The idiom's best-known exponent, Bob Wills, introduced drums, electric guitar and a horn section into country and western, and his successors, such as Ernest Tubb, made honky-tonk dance tunes one of the staples of modern Nashville.

Texas musicians also played a major role in setting the course of black music, from the early recordings of "Ragtime Texas" Henry Thomas, with his archaic panpipe-accompanied songs, to the postwar hits of T-Bone Walker with his influential electric guitar stylings. The first stronghold for rhythm and blues in Texas was Houston, the home of Don D. Robey's Duke and Peacock labels. For nearly a quarter of a century, starting in the early Fifties, Robey released black popular music on Duke, and black gospel music on Peacock. Peacock boasted one of the strongest rosters in the field, with gospel stars like the Dixie Hummingbirds and the Mighty Clouds of Joy, while Duke relied largely on the drawing power of its two big names, Bobby "Blue" Bland and Junior Parker.

Throughout the late Fifties and early Sixties, these two urbane stylists, both of them graduates of the Memphis blues scene of the late Forties and early Fifties, almost single-handedly kept the blues alive as a popular form. Bland in particular enjoyed a long string of hits ("Farther Up the Road," "I Pity the Fool," "Turn on Your Lovelight") which showcased his gravelly voice on moody ballads as well as shouting blues (one of Bland's idols was Perry Como). Parker by contrast stuck closer to the style of Chicago blues, although he, too, managed to score hits with brisk, uptempo shuffles like "Next Time You See Me" and soulful ballads like "Driving Wheel." Other Duke-Peacock artists included Willie Mae "Big Mama" Thornton, whose original "Hound Dog" in 1953 inspired you-know-who; Johnny Ace, an immensely popular balladeer until his death (reportedly while playing Russian roulette) on Christmas Eve 1954; and O.V. Wright, an early exponent of soul in the Sixties who later became one of the first singers produced by Willie Mitchell in Memphis.

While rhythm and blues together with country and western flourished in Texas throughout the Fifties, the region's rock scene was thin, if vital. There wasn't much rockabilly around, although Buddy Knox, Jimmy Bowen, and especially Buddy Holly made their marks nationally with an understated "Tex-Mex" blend of country rock. Beaumont's Moon Mullican, "King of the Hillbilly Piano Players" and a key influence on Jerry Lee Lewis, tried his hand at rock in the mid-Fifties, as did

George Jones; neither met with much success outside of the country market. But the first wave of Texas rock only really arrived with Houston producer Huey P. "Crazy Cajun" Meaux, who started producing records in 1959, working out of his barbershop in Winnie. Meaux's first hits were Jivin' Gene's "Breaking Up Is Hard to Do" and Joe Barry's "I'm a Fool to Care," followed by Barbara Lynn's "You'll Lose a Good Thing" and Roy Head's "Treat Her Right" (released on Don Robey's Backbeat label). All were ultimately leased to larger labels, but Meaux's outlook was basically regional—and specifically Cajun—so many of his early efforts, cut in Ville Platte, Louisiana, or at Cosimo Matassa's studio in New Orleans, never got beyond the Texas-Louisiana area.

Still, the combination of Cajun style and Texas talent kept Meaux on the national charts. In 1963, he was riding high: "I had Dale and Grace at Number One," he recalls, "Sunny and the Sunliners' 'Talk to Me,' and eight or nine other records on the different charts in one week, and then the Beatles came along and wiped me off the fuckin' map." Not to be outdone by a bunch of upstart limeys, Meaux headed for San Antonio, his car crammed with Thunderbird wine and every Beatles record he could find; once there, he locked himself in a motel room, vowing not to leave until he had discovered the secret formula. His conclusion: "The beat was *on the beat,* just like a Cajun two-step." His solution: to call up a San Antonio kid named Doug Sahm, who'd been badgering Meaux to record him. "I tole him, git me a tune, grow some fuckin' hair, and let's go cut some of this shit."

Sahm lost no time in assembling a crack band of some of San Antonio's finest musicians, including keyboard player Augie Meyers; billed as "The Sir Douglas Quintet," and promoted by Meaux as a new English group, they had a hit on their first try, "She's About a Mover." The sham was quickly exposed, but not until the band was well established. Unfortunately, a marijuana setup in Corpus Christi abruptly terminated their Texas career. Bedeviled by legal harassments and attracted by the lure of San Francisco, Sahm turned his back on the Longhorn State. Working out of San Francisco, he recorded several delightful albums for Mercury, as well as another hit single, "Mendocino."

Meanwhile, Meaux had set himself up with a new recording studio and a corporation, and had found a new performer, Billy Joe (B.J.) Thomas, a young Houstonian who fronted a show band called the Triumphs. The Triumphs cut an excellent R&B/pop album for Meaux, but Thomas resisted adding a version of Hank Williams's "I'm So Lonesome I Could Cry"—however, he later agreed to placate what he assumed were Meaux's countrified sensibilities. Huey jumped on the track as a single, and when it shot to the top, he had another star on his hands.

Clockwise from left top: (1) Huey Meaux, center, with Sunny Ozuna— of Sunny and the Sunliners—and unidentified companion; (2) Jivin' Gene and the Jokers; (3) Bobby Bland, circa 1960; (4) Sir Douglas Quintet in mod threads, 1965. Center: (5) Junior Parker, early Sixties photo. (4, Ralph J. Gleason collection)

A trip to the 1966 Country Music Disc Jockey's Convention in Nashville proved to be his undoing. Meaux's partner gave a teenage girl a lift to the convention, where she proceeded to set up shop as a prostitute, keeping a diary the whole time. When she returned to Texas, the diary was confiscated by federal officials in connection with another crime she had committed, and Meaux was subsequently indicted, along with his partner, for conspiracy to violate the Mann Act. Meaux did 14 months in prison, an experience that so embittered him that he didn't find his way back to the pop charts for six more years, until, in 1975, "Before the Next Teardrop Falls," a record Meaux cut with Chicano singer Freddy Fender, became a giant country and pop hit.

By the late Sixties, the Texas rock scene Meaux had revitalized was a shambles. Most of the state's native talent had headed for the West Coast, where the drug laws were more liberal and the opportunities to record more abundant. In San Francisco, such Texans as Janis Joplin (from Port Arthur), Doug Sahm, and various members of Mother Earth and the Steve Miller Band held forth; and in Los Angeles, the Bobby Fuller Four had a hit with "I Fought the Law," cut in an updated Tex-Mex vein.

Those who stayed either ended up in trouble or languished in obscurity until being "discovered." In 1966 and 1967, the region briefly sprouted a host of "psychedelic" bands, recorded by International Artists, a Houston-based label. The most prominent among these Lone Star acid rockers was the Austin-based 13th Floor Elevator; but the group, hounded by narcotics agents, never really broke nationally, and their lead singer, Roky Erickson, ended up spending three years at Rusk State Hospital, a mental institution. Other Texas talent fared better. Soon after ROLLING STONE published an article on the Texas rock scene singling out an obscure local guitarist, Johnny Winter, Winter was plucked from the state, handed a fat contract, and sent out on the road to superstardom. It was a route later retraced by such blues-based Texas acts as ZZ Top, one of the most popular boogie bands of the Seventies.

Unfortunately, neither Winter nor ZZ Top evidenced much of the country/blues/Cajun/Tex-Mex crossbreeding that has been the distinctive hallmark of Texas popular music. ZZ Top could have come from anywhere.

But down in Austin, Willie Nelson, a veteran of the Nashville songwriting wars, proved to be the catalyst for a whole new development in Texas music, once again in the area of country music. Nelson had moved back home to Texas after his Nashville house burned down, and he liked it so much that he decided to stay. In Austin, he met Eddie Wilson, a former PR man for the Texas beer industry, who had rented a former National Guard armory and rechristened it "Armadillo World Headquarters." Wilson knew that local longhairs were getting into country music, and that Willie Nelson, a closet liberal, was a hero to almost every political faction in town; he also figured that a Nelson concert would unite these factions, and so in July 1972, he tried out the idea of a country-rock concert, headlined by Nelson, at Armadillo World Headquarters. It was a wild success.

Similar concerts followed, and Nelson himself inaugurated an annual 4th of July festival. These events featured a wide range of Texas talent, running the gamut from the rock of Augie Meyers's Western Head Band to the hard-edge country and western of Waylon Jennings, from the country oriented pop of singer/songwriter Jerry Jeff Walker to the resurrected western swing of Asleep at the Wheel.

The success of this "progressive country" movement can largely be traced to the Texan love of tradition, a love that cuts across the barriers of age and culture. Although little progressive country has been heard outside the state, Texans take pride in the fact that their scene has attracted similarly minded performers from around the country. The country music "outlaws," as some call Nelson and Jennings, are—as Texas popular musicians almost always have done—pumping new blood into an old form.

Discography

Bobby Bland, "Lead Me On" (Duke 318; r☆9, 1960). **Bobby Bland,** "Cry Cry Cry" (Duke 327; r☆9, 1960). **Bobby Bland,** "I Pity the Fool" (Duke 332; r☆1, ☆46, 1961). **Joe Barry,** "I'm a Fool to Care" (Smash 1702; r☆15, ☆24, 1961). **Little Junior Parker,** "Driving Wheel" (Duke 335; r☆5, 1961). **Bobby Bland,** "Don't Cry No More" (Duke 340; r☆2, 1961). **Little Junior Parker,** "In the Dark" (Duke 341; r☆7, 1961). **Bobby Bland,** "Turn On Your Love Light" (Duke 344; r☆2, ☆28, 1961). **Bobby Bland,** "Ain't That Loving You" (Duke 338; r☆9, 1962). **Little Junior Parker,** "Annie Get Your Yo-Yo" (Duke 345; r☆6, 1962). **Barbara Lynn,** "You'll Lose a Good Thing" (Jamie 1220; r☆1, ☆8, 1962). **Bobby Bland,** "Stormy Monday Blues" (Duke 355; r☆5, ☆43, 1962). **Bobby Bland,** "That's the Way Love Is" b/w "Call on Me" (Duke 360; r☆1, ☆22, 1963). **Sunny and the Sunglows,** "Talk to Me" (Tear Drop 3014; r☆12, ☆11, 1963). **Dale and Grace,** "I'm Leaving It Up to You" (Montel 921; r☆6, ☆1, 1963). **Sunny and the Sunliners,** "Rags to Riches" (Tear Drop 3022; ☆45, 1963). **Dale and Grace,** "Stop and Think It Over" (Montel 922; ☆8, 1964). **Bobby Bland,** "Ain't Nothing You Can Do" (Duke 375; ☆20, 1964). **Bobby Bland,** "Share Your Love with Me" (Duke 377; ☆42, 1964). **Bobby Bland,** "Ain't Doing Too Bad" (Duke 383; ☆49, 1964). **Sir Douglas Quintet,** "She's About a Mover" (Tribe 8308; ☆13, 1965). **O.V. Wright,** "You're Gonna Make Me Cry" (Backbeat 548; r☆6, 1965). **Bobby Bland,** "These Hands (Small but Mighty)" (Duke 385; r☆4, 1965). **Roy Head,** "Treat Her Right" (Backbeat 546; r☆2, ☆2, 1965). **Bobby Bland,** "I'm Too Far Gone (to Turn Around)" (Duke 393; r☆8, 1966). **Sir Douglas Quintet,** "The Rains Came" (Tribe 8314; ☆31, 1966). **Bobby Fuller Four,** "I Fought the Law" (Mustang 3014; ☆9, 1966). **B.J. Thomas,** "I'm So Lonesome I Could Cry" (Scepter 12129; ☆8, 1966). **Bobby Fuller Four,** "Love's Made a Fool of You" (Mustang 3016; ☆26, 1966). **B.J. Thomas,** "Mama" (Scepter 12139; ☆22, 1966). **Bobby Bland,** "Good Time Charlie" (Duke 402; r☆6, 1966). **Bobby Bland,** "Poverty" (Duke 407; r☆9, 1966). **O.V. Wright,** "Eight Men, Four Women" (Backbeat 580; r☆4, 1967).

(Chart positions taken from Joel Whitburn's *Record Research,* compiled from *Billboard* Pop chart, unless otherwise indicated; r☆ = position on *Billboard* Rhythm and Blues chart.)

Soul

by Peter Guralnick

The business of soul music was salvation. "There's a song that I sing," preached Solomon Burke in the aptly named "Everybody Needs Somebody to Love," "and I believe if everybody was to sing this song, it would save the whole world." "I'm not singing this song for myself now," James Brown declared in his celebrated live version of "Lost Someone." "I'm singing it for you, too." Both the mood and the message were unashamedly apocalyptic, as the music borrowed not only from the gospel changes which Ray Charles (followed in short order by both Brown and Sam Cooke) had introduced into rhythm and blues but from the iconography of the church as well.

James Brown, tottering offstage, clothed in his royal cloak, staged a drama of personal redemption every night. Wilson Pickett, an ex-Violinaire and an extravagant admirer of the Reverend Julius Cheeks, electrified audiences with his throaty cries, raspy screams, and clumsy holiness dance. Sam Cooke brought the achingly sweet harmonies of the famous Soul Stirrers and the urbane manner of the successful preacher to a lay congregation. Otis Redding maintained that same well-fed dignity with his shiny suits and dramatically halting diction, while Joe Tex, the master rapper, ironically enough ordained as a Muslim minister after his popularity had passed, personified the slick deacon who has been a figure in black mythology since slavery time. And Solomon Burke—King Solomon—a licensed mortician, a minister in his own family's House of God for All People since he was 12, dispensed his secular message like a bishop bestowing blessings on a starved and clamoring multitude. Soul music was indeed a serious business.

It was a peculiarly good-hearted and optimistic sort of music, and it is no accident that its popularity was limited to the early and middle Sixties, a time when awakening black pride went hand in hand with civil rights activism and racial progress seemed more real than illusory. It may have been liberal "good-will" which caused soul to make such a dent in the popular charts (plus the discovery by groups like the Rolling Stones of artists such as Solomon Burke and Otis Redding). The music itself sprang from the deepest wellsprings of the black experience in this country—an experience that revealed a people so resourceful in their adaptation to an alien culture and an alien environment as to create a richly expressive language of their own, from which white society continues to draw today. It was this language that was the basis for soul music, and in this sense soul must be seen as a kind of conscious anachronism, a prideful return to roots which sought in its own way to reverse a century-old impulse toward assimilation into the so-called mainstream of white society.

In this sense it can also be seen why soul music—with its insistence on a unified tradition, stylistic purity and a determinedly down-home approach—was doomed to early extinction. Like the Chicago blues style which developed in the late Forties, and even the white rockabilly sound which came out of

Memphis in the Fifties, it was music of too singular a purpose to adapt to changing trends and styles. In an even closer parallel to blues and rockabilly, nearly all the artists who joined to create this common style came under the aegis of a single record company. With blues it was Chicago's Chess Records; with rockabilly Sam Phillips's tiny Sun label in Memphis. In the case of soul, Atlantic was the label. Atlantic vice-president Jerry Wexler was catalyst, and Solomon Burke, Otis Redding, Wilson Pickett and Joe Tex were the chief protagonists in the evolution of a style. It is an intricate and fascinating story which can only be sketched out in these pages.

Soul started, in a sense, with the 1961 success of Solomon Burke's "Just out of Reach." Ray Charles, of course, had already enjoyed enormous success (also on Atlantic), as had James Brown and Sam Cooke—primarily in a pop vein. Each of these singers, though, could be looked upon as an isolated phenomenon; it was only with the coming together of Burke and Atlantic Records that you could begin to see anything even resembling a movement.

Solomon Burke had recorded for a number of years for Apollo, in both gospel and secular modes, but it wasn't until his second Atlantic release that he was to achieve any degree of success. Oddly enough it was with a country song, though this is not so odd in Jerry Wexler's view. "The changes, the structure, the whole feel are just about identical in gospel and country music." This is a perception Ray Charles would capitalize on just months later for ABC Records, but Solomon Burke—with his smooth, lush voice, his suggestion of a barely suppressed power, and his easy mastery of all the gospel effects from impassioned sermonizing to lullingly melodic interludes to rumbling bass notes—was just as well equipped to prove it. In any case he enjoyed considerable success in 1961 and 1962, but it was with his fifth big hit on Atlantic in 1963 that he consolidated his style.

"One day," says Jerry Wexler, "a tape came in from Detroit with eight songs on it. One of the songs was 'If You Need Me,' which was the only one that impressed me. The singer on the demo was Wilson Pickett."

What happened next is both interesting and historically significant. "If You Need Me" is a classic of the soul genre, with a fervent message, sincere spoken passage, and strict gospel changes. Atlantic bought the publishing rights immediately but somehow neglected to purchase rights to the demo. They recorded Solomon's impassioned interpretation, put it in the can, and then before it was even released discovered that Pickett's original master was being marketed by Lloyd Price and Harold Logan. Jerry Wexler tried frantically to block the release, because "I would say that Pickett's record has the edge

over ours." When he failed, "I went to work on that record. That record put me back into promotion, got me back into the studio, into the excitement of the record business, everything." It also got Solomon Burke a big hit, and it even brought Wilson Pickett to Atlantic eventually. Two years later, "Pickett himself comes into the office with a tape under his arm. I said, 'Man, aren't you sore?' And he said, 'That's in the past.' "

Pickett, the Wicked Pickett, was a much more volatile singer than Solomon Burke, more overtly emotional, perhaps more viscerally exciting, less controlled in his use of vocal and dramatic effects. After a couple of singles which didn't do anything, Wexler took Pickett down to the Memphis studio of Stax Records which in the first six months of 1965 had already recorded "That's How Strong My Love Is," "Mr. Pitiful," "I've Been Loving You Too Long," and "Respect," all by the relatively unknown Macon singer, and one-time Little Richard imitator, Otis Redding. Atlantic had had a distribution deal with Stax since 1960, which meant that Booker T. and the MGs, Rufus and Carla Thomas, William Bell, and later Sam and Dave would all be connected in one way or another with Atlantic Records. As part of that deal, Otis Redding's first album even appeared on the Atlantic subsidiary, Atco, and working arrangements between Atlantic and Stax were very close. To Jerry Wexler's ear, Stax had the hard-edge sound he was looking for in Wilson Pickett. He was evidently right. Pickett and guitarist Steve Cropper sat down to work out a rhythmic idea Pickett had been carrying around in his head for some time. The result was "In the Midnight Hour," one of the biggest soul hits of all time.

Ironically enough, there were only three or four more Atlantic sessions at the Stax studio. Whether due to the success of Pickett's single, or to a more complicated business disagreement, Stax barred Atlantic artists from coming in and cutting records from that point on. The result was that Jerry Wexler cast about for another soulful location and eventually settled on a little studio in Florence, Alabama, properly called Fame Studios, but better known as Muscle Shoals, after a slightly less obscure neighboring town. Fame in the early Sixties had enjoyed considerable success with independent leasing arrangements on Arthur Alexander and Jimmy Hughes (who appeared on their own Fame label). They enjoyed even greater success with Joe Tex, still another gospel-oriented singer with strong Southern roots who came to Atlantic through Buddy Killens's Dial Records, which switched distribution to Atlantic toward the end of 1964.

Joe Tex was a journeyman musician who had been hovering on the edge of the business for ten years when he came to Muscle Shoals. He had recorded in every variety of style, from rock 'n' roll to James Brown's "crying" blues, but it was in Muscle Shoals that he found a groove of his own. Not as sober as Solomon Burke nor as unrestrained as Wilson Pickett, he introduced an element of worldliness in the sly asides and epigrammatic wit which crept into heartfelt preachments like "Hold What You've Got" and "Don't Make Your Children Pay" as well as later comic sermons like "Skinny Legs and All."

His success at Muscle Shoals was only duplicated by Wilson Pickett, who, starting with his January 1966 session, produced "Land of 1000 Dances" and "Mustang Sally," worthy successors to "In the Midnight Hour," and a host of later hits. (Muscle Shoals itself is a whole other story, but it should be noted that Rick Hall's Fame studio, and its equally renowned offshoot Muscle Shoals Sound, set the standard for production in what was left of the soul era and remains to this day a source of some of the finest, and funkiest, music to come out of the South.) It was shortly after Pickett's first session that Fame's studio musicians cut a record behind an unknown local singer named Percy Sledge. That record was "When a Man Loves a Woman," which, with its Bach-like organ, soaring vocal, and frequently imitated church feel might be defined as the quintessential soul sound. Then in February 1967, Jerry Wexler brought down a newly signed artist for her first Atlantic recording session. This was an artist for whom everyone had been predicting stardom ever since she first started recording commercially seven years earlier; although she had been in the business all her life she had never, it was said, lived up to her potential. The artist was Aretha Franklin; the session produced her epochal recordings, "I Never Loved a Man (the Way I Love You)" and "Do Right Woman—Do Right Man."

That in a way was the end of the soul era proper. Not that it vanished in a puff of smoke. Certainly artists like Wilson Pickett, Joe Tex, and even Solomon Burke in his sporadic comebacks continued to enjoy considerable popularity. Nor was Aretha's style any radical departure from the soul sound that had preceded it. Reared in the church, she was as down-home and funky, as plain-spoken and spiritually uplifted as any of the soulmen. No, it wasn't so much that Aretha departed from a style as that by her genius she defined it. Her success, both artistic and commercial, swept everything in its wake, and while there have been scattered echoes of the soul era right up to the present day, the sense of common purpose which had animated the movement for three or four years was gone, the almost uniform level of achievement suddenly shattered by the entrance of someone so uniquely gifted, so transcendent in her art that all others were dwarfed by comparison.

Several other factors entered into it, too, of course. Solomon Burke had departed from Atlantic by 1969, Wilson Pickett and Joe Tex by 1973. Stax ended their distribution arrangement with Atlantic in 1968, shortly after Otis Redding died in a plane crash in December of 1967. More than anything else, though, what seems to me to have brought the era of soul to a grinding, unsettling halt was the death of Martin Luther King in April of 1968, following as it did the 1965 assassination of Malcolm X.

The soul movement was predicated too much upon an assumption of good faith to survive the shock of that awakening, and it was succeeded shortly in logical enough fashion by more militant declarations of identity, starting with Soul Brother Number One James Brown's strident anthem, "Say It Loud— I'm Black and I'm Proud."

While it lasted, though, it was a period of remarkable creativity and solidarity. Soul music at its height, like the anonymous church art of the Middle Ages, came to have a stylistic definition of its own. There were soul classics from such obscure artists as Jesse James, Phil Flowers, Freddy Scott, Laura Lee and Aretha's sister Erma as well as better known ones like James Carr, Clarence Carter, and the man who claims to have started it all, Little Richard. There was a Soul Clan organized by Atlantic artist and prolific songwriter Don Covay, and consisting for one session of Covay, Solomon Burke, Otis Redding protégé Arthur Conley, Joe Tex, and Ben E. King. There was a time when you could listen to the radio and hear song after song in the familiar gospel-oriented vein. It came to matter hardly at all which artist was identified with which song, so strong was the style itself, and even the disc jockeys were inspired to join the soul movement with their exhortations,

interpolations, and vivid displays of verbal invention. It was a whole gaudy panoply in which the singer and his audience were equally caught up, an occasion in live performance for celebration and good feeling. And the atmosphere at those Saturday night meetings was not much different than church on Sunday, with an audience which cut across lines of class and age dressed up in their Sunday best and prepared to *testify*. It was a family audience, well mannered, well behaved, spanning three generations, but expecting to work hard, and their shouts, moans, groans and good-natured cries of approval indicated that they expected the singer to work hard, too. For a white outsider it was like being carried along by an ineluctable tide, and the only response possible was to ride helplessly, unself-consciously, somehow comforted by the overwhelming feeling of community. For me that was soul music almost ten years ago.

Discography

SEVEN SOUTHERN SOUL PERFORMERS, 1961–1969

Solomon Burke, "Just out of Reach" (Atlantic 2114; r☆7, ☆24, 1961). "Cry to Me" (Atlantic 2131; r☆5, ☆44, 1962). "I'm Hanging Up My Heart for You" b/w "Down in the Valley" (Atlantic 2147; r☆15, 1962). "If You Need Me" (Atlantic 2185; r☆2, ☆37, 1963). "You're Good for Me" (Atlantic 2205; r☆8, ☆49, 1963). "He'll Have to Go" (Atlantic 2218; ☆51, 1964). "Goodbye Baby (Baby Goodbye)" (Atlantic 2226; ☆33, 1964). "Everybody Needs Somebody to Love" (Atlantic 2241; ☆58, 1964). "The Price" (Atlantic 2259; ☆57, 1964). "Got to Get You off My Mind" (Atlantic 2276; r☆1, ☆22, 1965). "Tonight's the Night" (Atlantic 2288; r☆2, ☆28, 1965). "Someone Is Watching" (Atlantic 2299; r☆24, 1965). "Keep a Light in the Window till I Come Home" (Atlantic 2378; r☆15, 1967). "Take Me (Just as I Am)" (Atlantic 2416; r☆11, ☆49, 1967). "Proud Mary" (Bell 783; r☆15, ☆45, 1969). **Wilson Pickett,** "If You Need Me" (Double-L 713; r☆30, 1963). "It's Too Late" (Double-L 717; r☆7, ☆49, 1963). "In the Midnight Hour" (Atlantic 2289; r☆1, ☆21, 1965). "Don't Fight It" (Atlantic 2306; r☆4, 1965). "634-5789" (Atlantic 2320; r☆1, ☆13, 1966). "Ninety-Nine and a Half" (Atlantic 2334; r☆13, 1966). "Land of 1000 Dances" (Atlantic 2348; r☆1, ☆6, 1966). "Mustang Sally" (Atlantic 2365; r☆6, ☆23, 1966). "Everybody Needs Somebody to Love" (Atlantic 2381; r☆19, ☆29, 1966). "I Found a Love" (Atlantic 2394; r☆6, ☆32, 1967). "Soul Dance Number Three" (Atlantic 2412; r☆10, 1967). "Funky Broadway" (Atlantic 2430; r☆1, ☆8, 1967). "I'm in Love" b/w "Stag-o-Lee" (Atlantic 2448; r☆4, ☆22, 1967). "Jealous Love" (Atlantic 2484; r☆18, ☆50, 1968). "She's Lookin' Good" (Atlantic 2504; r☆7, ☆15, 1968). "I'm a Midnight Mover" (Atlantic 2528; r☆6, ☆24, 1968). "I Found a True Love" (Atlantic 2558; r☆11, ☆42, 1968). "A Man and a Half" (Atlantic 2575; r☆20, ☆42, 1968). "Hey Jude" (Atlantic 2591; r☆13, ☆23, 1969). "Mini-Skirt Minnie" (Atlantic 2611; r☆19, ☆50, 1969). "You Keep Me Hanging On" (Atlantic 2682; r☆16, 1969). **Don Covay and the Good-timers,** "Mercy, Mercy" (Rosemart 801; ☆35, 1964). "Please Do Something" (Atlantic 2286; r☆21, 1965). "Seesaw" (Atlantic 2301; r☆5, ☆44, 1965). **Joe Tex,** "Hold What You've Got" (Dial 4001; r☆2, ☆5, 1964). "You Got What It Takes" b/w "You Better Get It" (Dial 4003; r☆10, ☆46, 1965). "A Woman Can Change a Man" (Dial 4006; r☆12, 1965). "One Monkey Don't Stop No Show" (Dial 4011; r☆20, 1965). "I Want to (Do Everything for You)" (Dial 4016; r☆1, ☆23, 1965). "A Sweet Woman like You" (Dial 4022; r☆1, ☆29, 1965). "The Love You Save" (Dial 4026; r☆2, 1965). "S.Y.S.L.J.F.M. (The Letter Song)" (Dial 4028; r☆9, ☆39, 1966). "I Believe I'm Gonna Make It" (Dial 4033; r☆8, 1966). "I've Got to Do a Little Bit Better" (Dial 4045; r☆20, 1966). "Papa Was Too" (Dial 4051; r☆15, ☆44, 1966). "Show Me" (Dial 4055; r☆24, ☆35, 1967). "Skinny Legs and All" (Dial 4063; r☆2, ☆10, 1967). "Men Are Gettin' Scarce" (Dial 4069; r☆7, ☆33, 1968). "Keep the One You Got" (Dial 4083; r☆13, 1968). "Buying a Book" (Dial 4090; r☆10, ☆47, 1969). **Joe Simon,** "Let's Do It Over" (Vee-Jay 694; r☆13, 1965). "Teenager's Prayer" (Sound Stage 7 2564; r☆11, 1966). "My Special Prayer" (Sound Stage 7 2577; r☆17, 1967). "Nine Pound Steel" (Sound Stage 7 2589; r☆19, 1967). "(You Keep Me) Hangin' On" (Sound Stage 7 2608; r☆11, ☆25, 1968). "The Chokin' Kind" (Sound Stage 7 2628; r☆1, ☆13, 1969). "Baby, Don't Be Looking in My Mind" (Sound Stage 7 2634; r☆16, 1969). **Percy Sledge,** "When a Man Loves a Woman" (Atlantic 2326; r☆1, ☆1, 1966). "Warm and Tender Love" (Atlantic 2342; r☆5, ☆17, 1966). "It Tears Me Up" (Atlantic 2358; r☆7, ☆20, 1966). "Take Time to Know Her" (Atlantic 2490; r☆6, ☆11, 1968). **Clarence Carter,** "Slip Away" (Atlantic 2508; r☆2, ☆6, 1968). "Too Weak to Fight" (Atlantic 2569; r☆3, ☆13, 1968). "Snatching It Back" (Atlantic 2605; r☆4, ☆31, 1969). "The Feeling Is Right" (Atlantic 2642; r☆9, 1969). "Doin' Our Thing" (Atlantic 2660; r☆9, ☆46, 1969).
(Chart positions compiled from Joel Whitburn's *Record Research,* based on *Billboard* Pop chart, unless otherwise indicated; r☆ = position on *Billboard* Rhythm and Blues chart.)

Otis Redding

by Jon Landau

Musicians see themselves in different ways. Some, the rarest, are artists prepared to make any sacrifice to preserve the integrity of their art. Others are poseurs who adopt the artist's stance without the art, who therefore appeal to the segment of the audience that likes to think of itself as being serious but isn't. And then there are those performers who see themselves as entertainers: they make no pretense of aiming at any particular artistic standard, but are openly and honestly concerned with pleasing crowds and being successful. Such a man was Otis Redding.

Redding wanted to be successful and secure. He saw becoming an entertainer as his way out of a dreary lower-class existence first in Dawson, Georgia, where he was born in 1941, and then in Macon, Georgia.

However, given these motivations, Redding still was able to develop a deeply personal, intimate style that was not nearly as commercial as it might have been, indicating that Redding did not commit himself to doing only that which would make him popular. He couldn't. He didn't have the ability to see which way the wind was blowing, and to head in that direction. His understanding of music was not something he could put on or take off, depending on chart trends. He was truly a "folk" artist; he couldn't escape the musical climate which surrounded him all his life, and out of which he created his own music.

Wanting to make good is characteristic of all soul artists, partly because they tend to have similar backgrounds, James Brown as much as Wilson Pickett as much as Redding himself. All are from rural parts of the South. Their musical influences are limited to folk, country and western, blues, gospel, and some pop. And they have to fasten together their own styles from this limited background—limitations which often preclude the possibility of true flexibility. They have no choice but to put all they know into the one form of music through which they have chosen to express themselves. The lack of intellectuality and detachment inherent in this expression accounts for the resultant intimacy of the music. Soul music approaches folk music in its lack of self-consciousness. And it is art, even though the artist may not seek to do anything beyond entertain.

Otis Redding based a good deal of his style on two important predecessors: Little Richard, one of his boyhood idols, and Sam Cooke. During Redding's childhood years in Georgia, Little Richard was creating his dynamic, shouting kind of R&B and putting it high on the pop charts. Because Richard was also a native of Macon, he made a deep impression on Otis. This influence can be heard most directly on his first album, *Pain in My Heart*, recorded in 1962 and 1963. On it there are several cuts which sound so much like Little Richard it is hard to tell the difference.

It didn't take long for Redding to outgrow his reliance on Little Richard, but he never outgrew his love for Sam Cooke or the influence Cooke's music had on him. Cooke was the top star in his field from 1957, when he had the Number One hit, "You Send Me," until his tragic death in 1964. Redding included Cooke's songs on most of his albums, and one of his most popular numbers in performance was Cooke's "Shake."

Redding's entrance into show business is a straight forward story. He paid his dues early with a group called Johnny Jenkins and the Pinetoppers. In his late teens, he became vocalist of the group and got a lot of experience playing for demanding audiences along the Southern college fraternity circuit. In 1962, Jenkins was to record a number for Atlantic Records without Redding, but he asked Otis to drive him to Memphis where the sessions were scheduled. When Jenkins got through recording, there was still 40 minutes of studio time remaining and Otis got permission to record a tune he had written called "These Arms of Mine." Otis's first release, this record launched him as a solo artist. Memphis became his recording home and he made all his records with the wonderful musicians who played on "These Arms of Mine," namely Booker T. Jones and the MGs, and the horns of the Mar-Keys.

Between 1962 and 1964 Redding recorded a series of soul ballads characterized by unabashedly sentimental lyrics usually begging forgiveness or asking a girlfriend to come home. The titles are revealing: "Pain in My Heart," "Mr. Pitiful" and "That's How Strong My Love Is"—the last, one of Otis's finest recordings. He soon became known as "Mr. Pitiful" and earned a reputation as the leading performer of soul ballads.

Otis's big leap, both as an artist and as a star, came in 1965, a crucial year in pop music marked by the advent of the Rolling Stones. It was also the year modern soul began to take shape. In the summer of '65, Wilson Pickett's "In the Midnight Hour" was climbing the charts (recorded with the same musicians Redding used) and James Brown and the Famous Flames hit with "Papa's Got a Brand New Bag." In addition, the Stones acknowledged the importance of soul music as a basis for the new rock by releasing *Out of Our Heads*, which included their versions of hits by Solomon Burke, Don Covay, Marvin Gaye and Otis. And, finally, the summer of 1965 was when Otis released his own beautiful composition, "Respect."

"Respect" was a smash on the soul charts. Artistically, it was a pounding production which showed off the unrepressed quality of the Memphis sound at its very best. Otis's singing—frantic, powerful and charming—pulled him out of the cul-de-sac of pure soul ballads and, along with his performance on "I've Been Loving You Too Long" (his finest slow song), represented the highest level of artistic development he had attained. "Respect" was the first record which was pure Redding; he was now self-reliant and no longer leaned on anyone else's style.

A publicity shot of Otis Redding from the early Sixties

Although white America waited for Aretha Franklin and 1967 to dig "Respect," the sizable success of Redding's recording in the black market indicated that his greatest hope for making it with pop audiences would be with the faster songs. The slow, eloquent, majestic ballads he sang so well simply required too much patience from a car-radio audience. Otis followed "Respect" with his hyped-up version of "Satisfaction," repaying the Stones the admiration they had shown him. If the white DJs who control suburban radio had given it more airplay, the record could have been a giant hit.

O tis Redding became an extremely popular performer but mainly on the black circuit. He had the ghetto circuit—Harlem and Watts—locked up. He was successful financially and owned a ranch home near Macon. But fame was as important to him as financial reward, as he made clear in his rewrite of the Temptations' "My Girl," where he sings, "I don't need no money, all I need is my fame."

He continued to release soul ballads even though he knew that fast tunes were the key to success in the pop market (as his good friends at Stax, Sam and Dave, proved with their gold record, "Soul Man"). Redding loved his music, and when he talked about it in interviews he was completely articulate. The main feature of modern soul, according to Redding, was the stomp beat. The old-fashioned shuffle was an anachronism; only one of his important records had it—"Shake."

But beyond any musical understanding of the imperatives of his own style, Redding never was confused about his purpose as an entertainer. He believed in communication; every device and technique he created was designed to further his communicative potential. And at the root of Redding's conception of communication was simplicity. Redding's music was always deliberately simple. Direct, unintellectual, honest and concise.

In 1966, Redding's style reached artistic fruition. Late in the year, his album, *The Otis Redding Dictionary of Soul*, was released. The cover was a typically tasteless Stax-Volt rendering, but the record inside was the finest ever to come out of Memphis, truly one of the finest pop records of the decade, and certainly the best example of modern soul ever recorded.

Dictionary of Soul indicated finally that if Otis were to make it outside the regular soul audience, it would have to be because soul music was making it with the pop audience. Redding was not going to change his music. He loved it, had already received recognition for it, and was confident his turn would come. It's doubtful the idea of altering his style to boost record sales ever occurred to him. He had perfected his vocal syntax, his rapport with his sidemen, and his linear, totally committed music. In *Dictionary*, the result of this perfection is evident throughout. Religious in its emotional intensity, it expresses a way of life. Particularly awesome is the consummate skill with which the soul ballads ("You're Still My Baby" and "Try a

Little Tenderness") were performed. He sang the blues like no one else on "Hawg for You," and he breathed new life into the Beatles' "Day Tripper." Here is Redding's blood and guts, and anyone who hears *Dictionary* recognizes its greatness instantly.

While Redding continued to perform almost exclusively for black audiences and to consolidate his status in the soul hierarchy (second only to James Brown in terms of personal popularity), an unusual train of events took place. Soul music, largely through the efforts of Aretha Franklin, began to take over the pop charts. It soon became clear the new wave would be the earthy Memphis soul that Redding had been practicing for the preceding five years. Unfortunately, Otis died in a plane crash December 10th, 1967, before his biggest hit, "(Sittin' on) The Dock of the Bay" was even released.

Redding's friend, guitarist and sometime collaborator, Steve Cropper, best expresses why those who knew Redding felt he was verging on superstardom. In an interview some months before Redding's death, he said: "Otis is the only one I can think of now who does it [sings soul] best. He gets over to the people what he's talking about, and he does it in so few words that if you read them on paper they might not make any sense. But when you hear the way he sings them, you know exactly what he is talking about." Here is the key again: communication. I only saw him perform once, at a revue in Boston. The audience was overwhelmingly black and sat through two and a half hours of mediocre soul music before Redding made his appearance. The crowd was growing restless, having heard too many singers say, "Let me see you clap your hands." Then Redding came on. The first thing he did was say, "Let me see you clap your hands." I immediately forgot the preceding two and half hours and clapped my hands. The audience knew instantly it was in the presence of an absolute master. The band still had not played a single note yet every person in the hall was standing.

Discography

"These Arms of Mine" (Volt 103; r☆20, ☆85, 1963). "That's What My Heart Needs" (Volt 109; r☆27, 1963). "Pain in My Heart" (Volt 112, ☆61, 1963). "Come to Me" (Volt 116; ☆69, 1964). "Security" (Volt 117; ☆97, 1964). "Chained and Bound" (Volt 121; ☆70, 1964). "Mr. Pitiful" b/w "That's How Strong My Love Is" (Volt 124; r☆10, ☆41, 1965). "I've Been Loving You Too Long" (Volt 126; r☆2, ☆21, 1965). "Respect" (Volt 128; r☆4, ☆35, 1965). "I Can't Turn You Loose" b/w "Just One More Day" (Volt 130; r☆11, 1965). "Satisfaction" (Volt 132; r☆4, ☆31, 1966). "My Lover's Prayer" (Volt 136; r☆10, 1966). "Fa-Fa-Fa-Fa-Fa" (Volt 138; r☆12, ☆29, 1966). "Try a Little Tenderness" (Volt 141; r☆4, ☆25, 1966). "I Love You More than Words Can Say" (Volt 146; r☆30, 1967). "Shake" (Volt 149; r☆16, ☆47, 1967). "Glory of Love" (Volt 152; r☆19, 1967). "(Sittin' on) The Dock of the Bay" (Volt 157; r☆1, ☆1, 1968). "The Happy Song (Dum-Dum)" (Volt 163; r☆10, ☆25, 1968). "Amen" (Atco 6592; r☆15, ☆36, 1968). "I've Got Dreams to Remember" (Atco 6612; r☆6, ☆41, 1968). "Papa's Got a Brand New Bag" (Atco 6636; r☆10, ☆21, 1968). "A Lover's Question" (Atco 6654; r☆20, ☆48, 1969). "Love Man" (Atco 6677; r☆17, 1969). "Free Me" (Atco 6700; r☆30, 1969).
Albums
Pain in My Heart (Atco 161; ☆103, 1964). *Soul Ballads* (Volt 411; ☆147, 1965). *Otis Blue* (Volt 412; ☆75, 1965). *The Soul Album* (Volt 413; ☆54, 1966). *The Otis Redding Dictionary of Soul* (Volt 415; ☆73, 1966). *King and Queen* (with Carla Thomas) (Stax 716; ☆36, 1967). *Live in Europe* (Volt 416; ☆32, 1967). *History of Otis Redding* (Volt 418; ☆9, 1967). *The Dock of the Bay* (Volt 419; ☆4, 1968). *The Immortal Otis Redding* (Atco 252; ☆58, 1968). *In Person at the Whiskey A-Go-Go* (Atco 265; ☆82, 1968). *Love Man* (Atco 289; ☆46, 1969). *Tell the Truth* (Atco 333; ☆200, 1970). *Live at Monterey* (with the Jimi Hendrix Experience) (Reprise 2029; ☆16, 1970).
(Chart position taken from Joel Whitburn's *Record Research*, compiled from *Billboard* Pop and LPs charts.)

The Sound of Memphis

by Robert Palmer

A middle-aged ex-minstrel show hoofer named Rufus Thomas was operating eight boilers at a Memphis textile bleaching plant and working afternoons as a disc jockey at black-operated WDIA radio during the summer of 1960. His daughter Carla, an English major at Tennessee A&I in Nashville, was home for vacation, and the two of them decided to make a record for Satellite, a fledgling local label which had released singles by The Vel-tones and Charles Heinz with little success. Carla's experience as a vocalist had been limited to the Teen Tone Singers, a group of students from area high schools, and to occasional solos at P.T.A. meetings. But she had practically grown up in the vaudeville theaters along Beale Street where her father had worked, first as half of the Rufus and Bones minstrel show team, later as a singer, master of ceremonies, and all-around entertainer. Rufus had traveled throughout the South with tent shows and knew what audiences from rural areas liked. He had also made several regionally popular records during the Fifties, most notably "Bear Cat," a Sun single based on Willie Mae Thornton's "Hound Dog."

The Thomases' father-daughter record, "Cause I Love You," did well around Memphis and attracted the attention of Atlantic Records' Jerry Wexler, who arranged to distribute it nationally. Its sales were disappointing, but in September Carla recorded "Gee Whiz (Look at His Eyes)," which shot into the Top Ten when Atlantic released it early in 1961. At this point, Satellite founders Jim Stewart and Estelle Axton changed their company's name to Stax (in order to avoid confusion with a California company named Satellite) and Atlantic took over Stax's distribution and promotion on an exclusive basis. The next few hits were instrumentals by the Mar-Keys, a band that included guitarists Steve Cropper and Charlie Freeman and saxophonist (later producer, singer, and Leon Russell sidekick) Don Nix. Numerous other Memphis musicians were in and out of the Mar-Keys after the group's first hit single, "Last Night," but by 1962 a rhythm section consisting of Cropper, bassist Lewis Steinberg, and drummer Al Jackson Jr. was playing on all of the Mar-Keys' recordings, and on most of Stax's other releases. That summer another vacationing student, Booker T. Jones, joined the three rhythm players as organist and front man after the foursome's "Green Onions" became a national hit for "Booker T. and the MGs."

Soon Rufus Thomas came up with a new hit of his own, "The Dog," and then another, bigger hit, "Walking the Dog." The instrumental backing the Stax musicians provided on these and the company's other early records was simplicity itself. Cropper played choked rhythm guitar and inserted occasional sparse fills. Donald "Duck" Dunn, who had replaced Steinberg, contributed loping, country-flavored bass lines, and Jackson's drumming was a model of restraint and subtle effectiveness. "In some tunes, the straighter you play it the better," Jackson once commented. "You try to stay out of the way because you are selling the tune itself and not the drummer." He might have been speaking for the other three men in the MGs, or for saxophonists Andrew Love and Floyd Newman and trumpeter Wayne Jackson, who took over the Mar-Keys name and eventually incorporated as the Memphis Horns. These three musicians and a few others along the way augmented the MGs on most Stax recordings with spare unison lines, usually created on the spot.

Early in 1965, this writer, an aspiring rock and roll saxophonist fresh from Little Rock, Arkansas, had his first taste of the Memphis studios. It seemed incredible that such an informal and apparently haphazard approach to musicmaking could produce such unified performances, and so many successful records. At Chips Moman's American Recording Studios, where Atlantic sessions for King Curtis and Dusty Springfield would soon be held, the three-track board—actually a standard two-track tape recorder with a second machine ingeniously patched into it—was extremely temperamental. Musicians would show up for scheduled sessions to find Moman, who looked and talked like a country sheriff, and his friend and sessionman, the future soul star Bobby Womack, meticulously reassembling the recording machine, testing connections, and lazily talking shop. "It oughta be ready by the middle of week," Moman would drawl, while Womack grinned in disbelief.

When sessions actually occurred, the American musicians, all of whom looked something like Moman, would drift in singly, dressed like dollar-store branch managers off on a fishing trip. It would take hours to set them up behind baffles in the tiny studio, and to get the microphones properly placed around the drums in the soundproof drum booth, which was virtually a separate room. But once everything was in order, the players would record basic tracks with expeditious precision. Moman sat in the control booth until he was sure he had the sound he wanted, particularly the fat, incredibly "live" drum sound which he pioneered; then he joined the musicians in the studio, contributing letter-perfect rhythm guitar while his bassist, Tommy Cogbill, offhandedly created the lines he would later play to such stunning effect behind Aretha Franklin.

A few days later, the Memphis Horns would arrive at the studio with a bottle of wine. After half the bottle had been consumed over small talk, the musicians would ask to hear the tracks, which might or might not have vocals on them by this time. After a few more drinks, the musicians would siphon into the studio, take out their horns, and quickly tune up. "Okay,"

Clockwise from top: (1) The Mar-Keys, later to separate into the Memphis Horns, and Booker T. and the MGs—standing, Donald "Duck" Dunn, bass; Terry Johnson, drums; Steve Cropper, guitar; Jerry Lee Smith, organ; on floor—Charles Axton, sax; Wayne Jackson, trumpet; Don Nix, sax; (2) Willie Mitchell, Hi Records producer of Al Green, in 1959; (3) Carla Thomas; (4) Don Covay with Jerry Wexler of Atlantic Records; (5) Booker T. and the MGs—"Duck" Dunn, Booker T. Jones, Steve Cropper, Al Jackson. Center: (6) Rufus "Bear Cat" Thomas (1 & 2, Phillip Rauls; 3, Vince Aletti; 4, Fred Lewis; 5, ROLLING STONE; 6, Don Paulsen)

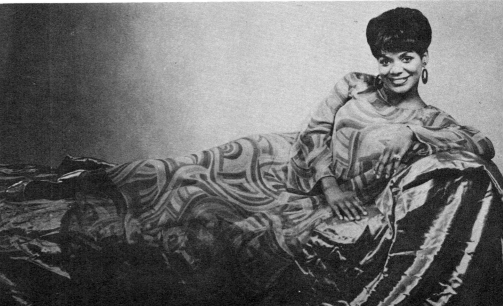

Left, l to r: (1) Carla Thomas; (2) Wilson Pickett; (3) Isaac Hayes. Opposite, l to r: (4) Johnnie Taylor; (5) The Staple Singers; (6) Sam and Dave (1, Michael Ochs Archives; 2, 4, 5, Gleason collection; 3, Enterprise Records; 6, Vince Aletti)

one of them, usually Andrew Love, would say, "DAT dah-dah DAT." The engineer would play back the track and the horns would add a suitably harmonized part which conformed to the syllables Love had suggested. They were so used to playing with each other that they always had acceptable horn lines on tape in two or three takes.

Stax sessions proceeded similarly, though sometimes they were run in a more professional manner. The company's studio musicians were a mixed lot. Around half of them were black, while the others were whites from rural backgrounds. Steve Cropper, for example, had come to Memphis from the Missouri Ozarks. The blend these musicians achieved together could only have happened in Memphis—which had been a Southern melting pot for generations—and perhaps only at a time, the mid-Sixties, when racial integration still seemed to be a believable political goal. But it was facilitated by the similar musical backgrounds of the black and white session players. Many of Stax's black musicians had grown up with country and western music; Isaac Hayes, who arranged and played keyboards when Booker T. Jones was away at school, later remembered that "where I grew up in Tennessee, country music was all you could hear on the radio." The white musicians had lived in close proximity to blacks and had become steeped in blues and R&B, and both whites and blacks had participated in or observed at close hand the same sort of fundamentalist church services which had furnished early training and stylistic models for most of the Stax singers.

William Bell's "You Don't Miss Your Water," one of the company's early Sixties R&B hits, is a perfect illustration of this mix of traditions. The song itself could easily pass for a C&W ballad, but the vocal, piano arpeggios, and organlike chords played by the horns are in a black gospel vein. This combination of white song form, black vocal treatment, simple arrangement, rhythmic restraint, and pure, understated elegance of expression was to characterize most of the classic recordings produced in Memphis during the next few years.

Atlantic Records engineer Tom Dowd traveled to Memphis to participate in an Otis Redding session early in 1965. In July, Jerry Wexler followed him, bringing Atlantic artist Wilson Pickett, a former lead vocalist with the gospel-rooted Falcons from Detroit. Steve Cropper expanded one of Pickett's onstage lines ("wait for the midnight hour, baby") into a sketch for a song, which the singer helped him complete in the studio. "In the Midnight Hour" and the other tunes cut at the session were more than archetypal Memphis R&B: they defined an international soul style. The Beatles and Rolling Stones recorded songs cut in Memphis and emulated Memphis music, and Jamaican, West African, even Ethiopian pop musicians did the same. Around 1967, an English adventurer crossing the Mauritanian desert stumbled into an oasis town which had been visited by few whites and sat down in a cafe just as the local equivalent of a garage band began to play an almost perfect carbon copy of "In the Midnight Hour."

Jerry Wexler took an active role in the "Midnight Hour" sessions. He danced out of the control booth at one point to suggest that Al Jackon shift his drum accents from the weak beats (one and three) to the stronger two and four. Heavily stressed weak beats had been the Stax rhythm section's trademark, so the effect of Wexler's suggestion was not a wholesale accentual shift but an evening-out of rhythmic values which left bassist Duck Dunn free to take a more flowing and melodic role. The musicians liked the innovation and continued to play that way, but their music retained its "lazy," slightly delayed rhythmic quality. "The guys will be playing a tempo and it'll sound like they're going to wind down," Memphis bandleader Willie Mitchell has noted. "And then suddenly they'll kind of sway with it and be right up there on top of the beat. The time isn't like a metronome; it's kind of like shuckin' you, puttin' you on. Even Memphis jazz players play real fast but just a little bit behind the beat, relaxed, lazy-like. It feels good."

"In the Midnight Hour" was released on the Atlantic label, but Stax followed it with hits by Sam and Dave, a Miami-based duo produced by the Isaac Hayes-David Porter team, and with Eddie Floyd's "Knock on Wood" and R&B successes by Carla Thomas, Otis Redding, and Booker T. and the MGs. Redding, the most visceral and distinctive of the Stax vocalists, was beginning to attract a following among white rock critics and fans by 1966, but he had yet to crack the pop Top Ten. It was the Hayes-Porter team that gradually took the commercial lead with their string of Sam and Dave hits, "I Take What I Want," "You Don't Know like I Know," and the epochal "Hold On! I'm a Comin'." Sam Moore and Dave Prater engaged in loose but involving vocal banter and shouted with a churchy intensity that assured their popularity with black audiences. But Hayes and Porter made sure their records would appeal to whites as well as providing catchy melodic hooks, horn lines which were often more memorable than the tunes themselves, and a harder rocking version of the uptempo Memphis dance beat.

In 1967, Sam and Dave's "Soul Man" made it to Number Two on the pop charts, and while other Stax records did not fare as well, the company had enough hits lower down the charts to seem largely responsible for the continuing viability of its parent company, Atlantic. The Stax/Volt Review, with Redding, Carla Thomas, and Booker T. and the MGs, toured Europe to tumultuous acclaim. Redding capped Stax's year of achievement with his triumph at the Monterey Pop Festival. Then, abruptly, he was gone, and his posthumous "(Sittin on) The Dock of the Bay" became the company's first national Number One hit.

In 1968 Stax dissolved its distribution pact with Atlantic. Carla Thomas, Johnnie Taylor, and the newly signed Staple Singers came up with hits, but Sam and Dave ended their partnership. Redding's bright young band, the Bar-Kays, had died with him in the airplane crash, and Stax's new distribution

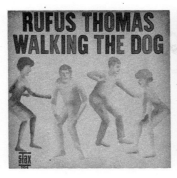

contract with Gulf and Western failed to work out as anticipated. The Stax compound on East McLemore Avenue was still buzzing with activity. Isaac Hayes's *Hot Buttered Soul,* a harbinger of the string-dominated "sweet soul" of the Seventies, was a smash, and on any given day Hayes's Rolls Royce could be seen shining in the company parking lot, which was separated from the rough black neighborhood around it by a barbed wire fence and armed guards.

But Stax had already passed its peak. The members of the original house band had become executives and turned over sessionwork to players who were unable to develop as cohesive a group sound. The younger Stax producers favored orchestral sweetening and more up-to-date band tracks. They diluted the integrity of the original Memphis sound but they were unable to compete effectively with the still more sophisticated R&B recordings being turned out by Motown. The Staple Singers and Isaac Hayes continued to sell records through the early Seventies, but by 1975 both had left, Stax was suing its erstwhile distributor CBS, and the company's board chairman was under indictment for fraud. A few weeks before Christmas 1975, the company's publishing subsidiary, and rights to the biggest hits by Otis Redding and Sam and Dave, were auctioned off to a local bank on the steps of the Shelby County Courthouse.

Stax was not the only local studio to contribute to the Memphis sound during the Sixties. Aretha Franklin's meteoric rise to the top of the pop charts was accomplished with the help of Chips Moman's musicians. At first they recorded with her near Memphis, in Muscle Shoals, Alabama. Later, producer Jerry Wexler began flying them to Miami or New York for sessions.

Hi Records was formed in 1957 and produced successful rockabilly singles by Gene Simmons ("Haunted House"), Murray Kellum ("Long Tall Texan"), and Jerry Jaye ("My Girl Josephine"), as well as a number of "redneck Muzak" hits by ex-Elvis Presley bassist Bill Black and his combo. Willie Mitchell joined the company during the early Sixties and made several instrumental hits of his own. "In 1970," he told this interviewer, "Hi finally gave me the keys to the studio and I started in on the board. For the first time, I could hear what I wanted and get it. The first record I engineered myself was 'Soul Serenade,' the biggest instrumental record I had. Then I started messin' with Ann Peebles, and I found Al Green and Syl Johnson and Otis Clay."

Green was Mitchell's principal success, but he also produced R&B hits with these other singers, including the Ann Peebles classic "I Can't Stand the Rain" (1973). Hi records often sounded uncannily like Stax product of a decade earlier, with their enveloping organ, lean guitar riffs, deliberate drumming (by Al Jackson soundalike Howard Grimes, and sometimes by Jackson himself), and unison horn punctuations (by the Memphis horns). As of 1976, Hi was still carrying on the traditional Memphis sound, but Stax was defunct, Isaac Hayes was involved in films and disco music, Moman and Cogbill had moved to Nashville; only the studios in Muscle Shoals continued to attract outside producers and name talent to the region.

Discography
MEMPHIS SOUL, 1961-1971

Carla Thomas, "Gee Whiz (Look at His Eyes)" (Atlantic 2086; r☆5, ☆10, 1961). **Mar-Keys,** "Last Night" (Satellite 107; r☆2, ☆3, 1961). **Booker T. and the MGs,** "Green Onions" (Stax 127; r☆1, ☆3, 1962). **Carla Thomas,** "I'll Bring It Home to You" (Atlantic 2163; r☆9, ☆41, 1962). **Rufus Thomas,** "The Dog" (Stax 130; r☆22, 1963). **Rufus Thomas,** "Walking the Dog" (Stax 140; r☆5, ☆10, 1963). **Willie Mitchell,** "20-75" (Hi 2075; ☆31, 1964). **James Carr,** "You've Got My Mind Messed Up" (Goldwax 302; r☆7, 1965). **Booker T. and the MGs,** "Boot-Leg" (Stax 169; r☆10, ☆58, 1965). **Wilson Pickett,** "In the Midnight Hour" (Atlantic 2289; r☆1, ☆21, 1965). **Astors,** "Candy" (Stax 170; r☆12, 1965). **Wilson Pickett,** "Don't Fight It" (Atlantic 2306; r☆4, ☆53, 1965). **Sam and Dave,** "You Don't Know like I Know" (Stax 180; r☆7, 1966). **Mad Lads,** "I Want Someone" (Volt 131; r☆10, 1966). **Wilson Pickett,** "634-5789" (Atlantic 2320; r☆1, ☆13, 1966). **Johnnie Taylor,** "I Had a Dream" (Stax 186; r☆19, 1966). **Sam and Dave,** "Hold On! I'm a Comin' " (Stax 189; r☆1, ☆21, 1966). **Carla Thomas,** "Let Me Be Good to You" (Stax 188; r☆11, 1966). **Mable John,** "Your Good Thing (Is About to End)" (Stax 192; r☆6, 1966). **Mad Lads,** "I Want a Girl" (Volt 137; r☆16, 1966). **Johnnie Taylor,** "I Got to Love Somebody's Baby" (Stax 193; r☆15, 1966). **Eddie Floyd,** "Knock on Wood" (Stax 194; r☆1, ☆28, 1966). **Carla Thomas,** "B-A-B-Y" (Stax 195; r☆3, ☆14, 1966). **Booker T. and the MGs,** "My Sweet Potato" (Stax 196; r☆18, 1966). **Sam and Dave,** "Said I Wasn't Gonna Tell Nobody" (Stax 198; r☆8, 1966). **Sam and Dave,** "You Got Me Hummin' " (Stax 204; r☆7, 1966). **James Carr,** "The Dark End of the Street" (Goldwax 317; r☆10, 1967). **Eddie Floyd,** "Raise Your Hand" (Stax 208; r☆16, 1967). **Sam and Dave,** "When Something Is Wrong with My Baby" (Stax 210; r☆2, ☆42, 1967). **Arthur Conley,** "Sweet Soul Music" (Atco 6463; r☆2, ☆2, 1967). **Booker T. and the MGs,** "Hip Hug-Her" (Stax 211; r☆6, ☆37, 1967). **William Bell,** "Everybody Loves a Winner" (Stax 212; r☆18, 1967). **Otis and Carla,** "Tramp" (Stax 216; r☆2, ☆26, 1967). **Bar-Kays,** "Soul Finger" (Volt 148; r☆3, ☆17, 1967). **Arthur Conley,** "Shake, Rattle and Roll" (Atco 6494; r☆20, ☆31, 1967). **Sam and Dave,** "Soothe Me" (Stax 218; r☆16, ☆56, 1967). **Carla Thomas,** "I'll Always Have Faith in You" (Stax 222; r☆11, 1967). **Booker T. and the MGs,** "Groovin' " (Stax 224; r☆10, ☆21, 1967). **Otis and Carla,** "Knock on Wood" (Stax 228; r☆8, ☆30, 1967). **Sam and Dave,** "Soul Man" (Stax 231; r☆1, ☆2, 1967). **King Curtis,** "Memphis Soul Stew" (Atco 6511; r☆6, ☆33, 1967). **James Carr,** "A Man Needs a Woman" (Goldwax 332; r☆16, 1968). **Albert King,** "Cold Feet" (Stax 241; r☆20, 1968). **Sam and Dave,** "I Thank You" (Stax 242; r☆4, ☆9, 1968). **Willie Mitchell,** "Soul Serenade" (Hi 2140; r☆10, ☆23, 1968). **Arthur Conley,** "Funky Street" (Atco 6563; r☆5, ☆14; 1968). **William Bell,** "A Tribute to a King" (Stax 248; r☆16, 1968). **Sam and Dave,** "You Don't Know What You Mean to Me" (Atlantic 2517; r☆20, ☆48, 1968). **Arthur Conley,** "People Sure Act Funny" (Atco 6588; r☆17, ☆58, 1968). **Booker T. and the MGs,** "Soul-Limbo" (Stax 0001; r☆7, ☆17, 1968). **Eddie Floyd,** "I've Never Found a Girl" (Stax 0002; r☆2, ☆40, 1968). **Sam and Dave,** "Can't You Find Another Way" (Atlantic 2540; r☆19, ☆54, 1968). **Judy Clay and William Bell,** "Private Number" (Stax 0005; r☆17, 1968). **Johnnie Taylor,** "Who's Making Love" (Stax 0009; r☆1, ☆5, 1968). **Booker T. and the MGs,** "Hang 'Em High" (Stax 0013; r☆35, ☆9, 1968). **Eddie Floyd,** "Bring It On Home to Me" (Stax 0012; r☆4, ☆17, 1968). **William Bell,** "I Forgot to Be Your Lover" (Stax 0015; r☆10, ☆45, 1968). **Johnnie Taylor,** "Take Care of Your Homework" (Stax 0023; r☆2, ☆20, 1969). **Carla Thomas,** "I Like What You're Doing (to Me)" (Stax 0024; r☆9, ☆49, 1969). **Booker T. and the MGs,** "Time Is Tight" (Stax 0028; r☆7, ☆6, 1969). **Emotions,** "So I Can Love You" (Volt 4010; r☆3, ☆39, 1969). **Johnnie Taylor,** "Testify (I Wonna)" (Stax 0033; r☆4, ☆36, 1969). **Johnnie Taylor,** "I Could Never Be President" (Stax 0046; r☆10, ☆48, 1969). **Isaac Hayes,** "Walk On By" (Enterprise 9003; r☆13, ☆30, 1969). **Soul Children,** "The Sweeter He Is" (Stax 0050; r☆7, ☆52, 1969). **Johnnie Taylor,** "Love Bones" (Stax 0055; r☆4, ☆43, 1969). **Rufus Thomas,** "Do the Funky Chicken" (Stax 0059; r☆5, ☆28, 1970). **Luther Ingram,** "Ain't That Loving You (for More Reasons than One)" (Ko Ko 2105; r☆6, ☆45, 1970). **Johnnie Taylor,** "Steal Away" (Stax 0068; r☆3, ☆37, 1970). **O. V. Wright,** "Ace of Spade" (Back Beat 615; r☆11, ☆54, 1970). **Johnnie Taylor,** "I Am Somebody—Part II" (Stax 0078; r☆4, ☆39, 1970). **Rufus Thomas,** "(Do the) Push and Pull, Part I" (Stax 0079; r☆1, ☆25, 1970). **Staple Singers,** "Heavy Makes You Happy (Sha-Na-Boom Boom)" (Stax 0083; r☆6, ☆27, 1970). **Ann Peebles,** "I Pity the Fool" (Hi 2186; r☆18, ☆45, 1971). **Johnnie Taylor,** "Jody's Got Your Girl and Gone" (Stax 0085; r☆1, ☆28, 1971). **Isaac Hayes,** "Never Can Say Goodbye" (Enterprise 9031; r☆5, ☆22, 1971). **Dramatics,** "Whatcha See Is Whatcha Get" (Volt 4058; r☆3, ☆9, 1971). **Johnnie Taylor,** "Hijackin' Love" (Stax 0096; r☆10, 1971). **Rufus Thomas,** "The Breakdown" (Stax 0098; r☆2, ☆31, 1971). **Staple Singers,** "Respect Yourself" (Stax 0104; r☆2, ☆12, 1971). **Isaac Hayes,** "Theme from 'Shaft' " (Enterprise 9038; r☆2, ☆1, 1971).

(Omitting hits by Otis Redding and Al Green. Chart positions compiled from Joel Whitburn's *Record Research,* based on *Billboard* Pop chart, unless otherwise indicated; r☆ = position on *Billboard* Rhythm and Blues chart.)

Bob Dylan
by Paul Nelson

"Pleasure? I never seek pleasure. There was a time years ago when I sought a lot of pleasure because I'd had a lot of pain. But I found out there was a subtle relationship between pleasure and pain. So now I do what I have to do without looking for pleasure in it."

—Bob Dylan

I knew the feeling.

I had been sitting in the office for days, thinking and rethinking the case, but thoughts about Miranda Abaloni's bright eyes and blue-black hair kept swimming into my mind like the dreams of a kid who's just been told that Christmas is tomorrow, not next week.

Actually it was Cadwallader who had hired me, but I didn't give a damn about him. Somehow the Cadwalladers of this world, though smart enough, all think that life is a debate and if the other guy is human and doesn't talk too well, that kind of makes them his hanging judge.

I kept telling myself the case wasn't a big mistake. It added up all right—hell, it had added up from the very beginning—but I just couldn't figure out why. The more I tried to analyze it, the more it resisted my efforts. I got that nervous feeling on the back of my neck that someone very close was telling me to lay off, that to get too involved with a bogus quest for the white-hot center would be to miss the whole point.

Logic is a funny thing to a private detective. It has nothing to do with facts but rather with intuition—a kind of mathematics without damage. After a few lean years, you learn to trust your hunches and, better yet, to draw occasionally to that inside straight no matter what the book said. Especially if the artist you were investigating—in this case, Bob Dylan—made up new rules each time out in the only worthwhile game in town.

What got to me was that I knew what he was doing but I couldn't explain it, not in words anyway. Arguably I'd had some luck with Dylan before, was not unfamiliar with his circuitous, sporadic manner. He wasn't a classicist and he didn't run with the pack. Instead he played spontaneously, from the heart, stringing together such disparate cards that only the force of his will held his ideas together and kept pretentiousness from breaking down the door. The results he got were amazing, often magical. He'd had some bad years in the late Sixties and early Seventies when he'd tried to run some more or less conventional bluffs, but then who hasn't?

Cadwallader probably.

The office was in the Arbogast Building on Embryo Street off Perelman Square, half a block from the Coma Noodle Corporation, right next to the Ambergris Diner and the Dead Souls Church and Motel.

Miranda Abaloni had first walked into it last Monday afternoon. Since then I hadn't been sleeping too well. She had blue-black hair the color of Sheaffer's Skrip ink, a Mona Lisa mouth as wide as the barrel of a .357 Magnum, and wore dark brown corduroy jeans and khaki Boy Scout shirt which made an instant liar out of its insignia. She looked very healthy.

"Hello," I said.

She asked: "This is the Watchtower Detective Agency, isn't it? You specialize in Bob Dylan?"

I said it was and we did.

When she smiled she was exactly what every adolescent or aging romantic asks for in his letters to Santa. If you wanted to prove there were no God, you would have to find some way to overlook Miranda Abaloni.

Unfortunately there was no way to overlook Gideon Cadwallader, the xanthous young man standing next to her. His stainless-steel eyes vacuumed the room for any trace of class and, finding none, caromed off what I hoped was a savage enough display of my own ocular firepower. The molecules in the office seemed to be bouncing.

"Sit down," I said. "What can I do for you?"

After what passed for the amenities, he told me. Curling back a carnassial upper lip which revealed a grayish-green fang no longer than my little finger, he said: "This young woman whom I am sure you have noticed is Ms. Miranda Abaloni—"

I gave her my best smile.

"My name is Gideon Cadwallader," he said. "I am a member of the Manhattan Institute of Critical Enterprise, the Majorities Enter the War League, the March against Repression, and the Committee to Ruin University Debutantes—for their own good, of course. We—"

It may not be easy to laugh and stare at the same time, but I managed it.

He shot me a look.

"I'm sorry," I said. "I can see you're serious. But my, ah, initial reaction was to laugh."

He appeared slightly mollified. "I don't think it's funny," he said.

"Some people never do," I said. I looked at Ms. Abaloni. "Malcolm Lowry once wrote in a letter: 'Cheerfulness keeps breaking in.' "

"Let us get down to business," said Gideon Cadwallader, and I knew I wasn't going to like what he was about to say. "At the behest of Miranda, that is, Ms. Abaloni, the organizations to which we belong are—I'm not quite sure how to phrase this— 'looking for a hero,' a public figure in which to believe and one who can set the proper sociopolitical standards and yet remain an artist worthy of aesthetic consideration. I am not talking about mere topical songs and their ilk. Ms. Abaloni has suggested, of all people, Bob Dylan, and while I do believe I have driven the wedge of doubt firmly into her underlying perceptions, she insisted we come to you for what she believes may be a valuable report. I concurred. I admire Mr. Dylan—but only to

Bob Dylan at his first Columbia recording session, November 1961 (Michael Ochs Archives)

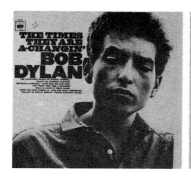   

a point. However, I understand that your devotion is steadfast and that your operatives are experts on the man."

"Yes and no," I said. "The agency's motto isn't 'Mine eyes have seen the glory of the coming of the Lord.' I don't like deification because none of us deserves it. I'd put Dylan, the Rolling Stones, and Jackson Browne at the top because they've changed my life the most. I couldn't live without their music. But it's subjective. And there are others, dozens of others. Why pick out one poor sucker and make an example out of him? Dylan's got his own demons. He probably doesn't give a damn what we think."

Cadwallader looked immensely pleased. He did a little dance with his feet and actually clapped his hands. It sounded like the love song of two dead fish. "Exactly," he said. "Exactly. Worthy as he is, he is not worthy. No one is." His estimation of me had gone up. I liked it better when he hated me.

Miranda Abaloni looked soulfully at the floor.

"On the other hand . . . " I said.

She moved her lovely head.

" . . . if you're determined to proceed with this . . . "

She rolled an elegiac eyeball in my direction. I picked it up and rolled one back.

" . . . there's probably no one better."

She shook her blue-black hair in agreement.

Cadwallader adjusted quickly. Then he looked right at me for a very long time.

I looked at Miranda Abaloni.

I was about to make a fool of myself, and Gideon Cadwallader knew it.

"Bob Dylan. Born Robert Allen Zimmerman on May 24th, 1941, in Duluth, Minnesota. Moved to Hibbing when he was six. Played rock and roll in high school but folk music at the University of Minnesota and in New York City where he also wrote topical songs. Bit of a liar about his background—"

"We know all that," said Cadwallader. "It's dull, except for the part about his being a liar. History should be interpretive."

"When the actor James Byron Dean died at 24 in an automobile crash in 1955, American movies surrendered the mantle of the archetypal sensitive-but-confused teenager to rock and roll. In the early Sixties Dylan claimed the title by emulating Dean and later certified the transferal by naming his firstborn son Jesse Byron Dylan. What Marshall McLuhan would call a hot connection."

"What Gideon Cadwallader would call frivolous pop sociology. Neither James Dean nor Marshall McLuhan is significant here."

I lit a cigarette and tried to think. At least Miranda Abaloni didn't look bored. She didn't look happy but she didn't look bored.

I said: "In the mid-Sixties Dylan's talent evoked such an

intense degree of personal participation from both his admirers and detractors that he could not be permitted so much as a random action. Hungry for a sign, the world used to follow him around, just waiting for him to drop a cigarette butt. When he did they'd sift through the remains, looking for significance. The scary part is they'd find it—and it really would be significant."

"Mystical mumbo jumbo. Undoubtedly the world would be better off were it less enamored of nicotine. Let's have something more specific."

"Cigarette?" I asked.

He just sat there.

"All right," I said. "Interpretive history. Dylan started out as the champ. In the early Sixties, on *Bob Dylan, The Freewheelin' Bob Dylan,* and 1964's *The Times They Are A-Changin'* he knocked out Woody Guthrie, Pete Seeger, the New Lost City Ramblers, Phil Ochs, and quite a few others. Later that year, *Another Side of Bob Dylan* parlayed some highly personal songs into left-right combinations of revolution-evolution that both looked back at folk and protest music and ahead toward rock and roll. He managed at least a draw or a TKO over the Beatles and the Rolling Stones in 1965 with *Bringing It All Back Home, Highway 61 Revisited,* and in 1966 with *Blonde on Blonde—*"

Cadwallader held up his hands in dismay. "I'm sure this is all very interesting," he said. "Do you think we could have it translated from pugilistic to at least pidgin English?"

I handed him a piece of paper with Ellen Willis's writing.

As composer, interpreter, most of all as lyricist, Dylan has made a revolution. He expanded folk idiom into a rich, figurative language, grafted literary and philosophical subtleties onto the protest song, revitalized folk vision by rejecting proletarian and ethnic sentimentality, then all but destroyed pure folk as a contemporary form by merging it with pop. Since then, rock and roll, which was already in the midst of a creative flowering dominated by British rock and Motown, has been transformed.

After he'd read it he handed it to Miranda Abaloni. She read it and handed it to me.

Cadwallader said: "Perhaps we're getting someplace. I could understand that. Does Ms. Willis work with you?"

I shook my head. "I wish she did. The agency usually does its own reports."

"Yes," he said, making it sound like one of the longest words I'd ever heard. Then: "Perhaps we could see one?"

I reached into the files and pulled out some prose about *Highway 61 Revisited, Blonde on Blonde,* and *John Wesley Harding.* I could see the paper had browned to the color of the pages in the Tower edition of *Red Wind.* It looked the same as Miranda Abaloni's Boy Scout shirt. Almost the same.

"Here," I said.

On *Highway 61 Revisited,* Dylan's unyielding and poetic point of view represents a total commitment to the subjective over the objective, the microcosm over the macrocosm, man rather than mankind, problems not Problems. To put it as simply as possible, Dylan's tradition is that of all great artists—he attempts to project, with the highest possible degree of honesty and craftsmanship, a personal vision of the world we live in, knowing full well that unless the personal is achieved, the universal cannot follow.

Not that it's painless. Dylan's concern on *Highway 61 Revisited* is the

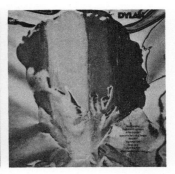

Below, 1966: Al Kooper, Bob Dylan and Sir Douglas, Doug Sahm (Alice Ochs)

classic American Dream—Innocence and Experience—a theme that has haunted American writers from Melville to Mailer. The music of Bob Dylan is the music of illusion and delusion, of men deluded by women, of men and women deluded by surface appearances, a music of the tramp as explorer and the clown as happy victim, where the greatest crimes are lifelessness and the inability to see oneself as a circus performer in the show of life. Thus, in "Ballad of a Thin Man," Dylan will choose the life of emotion rather than the life of reason. And again, in "Tombstone Blues," the outcry against "useless and pointless knowledge."

In "Desolation Row," we find ourselves in a dark, Felliniesque world of clowns and grotesques, but Dylan makes it clear that the tragic man is not the clown per se, but the clown who thinks he is something better. Accept chaos, he says, and advance from there.

"Like a Rolling Stone" is the definitive statement that both personal and artistic fulfillment must come, in the main, by being truly on one's own. Dylan's social adversaries have twisted this to mean something very devious and selfish, but that is not the case at all. Dylan is simply kicking away the props to get to the heart of the matter: self-knowledge. The final chorus . . . is clearly optimistic and triumphant, a soaring of the spirit into a new and more productive present.

Blonde on Blonde—the very title suggests the singularity and duality we expect from Dylan. His music has always carried within it its own unexplained tensions: optimism and pessimism merge amid fragmented reality, yet both terms become finally meaningless because Dylan in the end truly *understands* situations, and once one truly understands anything, there can no longer be mere anger, no longer be moralizing, but only humor and compassion, only pity. And, ultimately, only a kind of shifting contradiction, a duality of emotion, a blonde on blonde, where all relationships can remain one, or become two, or fluctuate from between one and two.

In a Dylan song—"Visions of Johanna" or "Memphis Blues Again," for example—physical objects are no longer merely physical objects but become moral and intellectual properties as well; the whole world is flattened into a plasticity that is cerebral, not physical, and we are free to float with the images in all of their kinetic brilliance.

Released in early 1968, *John Wesley Harding*, the first music Dylan presented to the public after his motorcycle accident in mid-1966, superimposes the literary complexity of both *Highway 61 Revisited* and *Blonde on Blonde* onto the alleged straightforwardness of Dylan's "return to folk music" in a manner rather like certain French directors (Jean-Luc Godard especially) who have taken American genre movies and added layers of 20th-century philosophy to them. It is as if Jean-Paul Sartre were playing the five-string banjo and confining himself to stating all of his theories in words of under four letters. The folk element gains a Kafkaesque chimera and the philosophy a bedrock simplicity which leaves it all but invisible and thus easy to assimilate. While there is no rock and roll here, the warm, inherent mysticism of Southern Mountain music never quite sounded like this before.

Gideon Cadwallader and Miranda Abaloni read for a long time. I just sat and watched them. It was getting dark outside. My teeth were clenched.

Finally Cadwallader said: "Fragmentation without representation may not be tyranny, but neither is it aesthetically or politically sound. Tell me, do men ever delude women? Do you 'accept chaos'?"

I stared at him.

He said: "We don't exactly want the world 'flattened into a cerebral plasticity,' do we? I should think that you, particularly, wouldn't want that. Do you think of yourself as a 'clown'? A 'happy victim'?"

I didn't know what to say.

"Do you think of Ms. Abaloni as a clown? No, certainly not. One should always try to be 'something better,' don't you agree? Perhaps you prefer 'pity.' To be both emotional *and* deluded does not seem wonderful to me. Knowledge is seldom either 'useless' or 'pointless,' and there is a great difference between optimism and pessimism. As a detective you should deal more with facts, less with imagination—they *are*, after all, your business. Is a concern for mankind really that odious? Aren't the sentiments expressed in 'Like a Rolling Stone' a veritable hymn to monomaniacal selfishness? That Dylan can neither maintain nor retain any semblance of a coherent style suggests an identity problem of apocalyptic proportions. The man simply does not know who he is or why he hates both himself and his audience so much. If he does know he is unwilling to tell. I'm afraid I find his fecund fatalism quite appalling. This nonsense about 'duality' sounds like nothing so much as a diagnosis for schizophrenia. Perhaps a chronic inability either to see the world clearly or to come to grips with anything or anyone in it is what Dylan *and* his admirers suffer from."

"That's not what I wrote," I said.

"Isn't it?"

"Those reports are ten years old—"

"—When you loved neither wisely nor too well," Gideon Cadwallader said.

I looked at Miranda Abaloni.

"Don't be too sure," I said.

After they had gone I won't say I wasn't worried. Passion has its potholes, I thought, and I had badly underestimated Cadwallader. No more. Howard Hawks made a movie once called *The Thing.* The Thing was a manlike vegetable from outer space that went around killing people for sustenance. Robert Cornthwaite wanted to keep it alive for science, but Ken Tobey saw that wasn't possible. Both argued so well I never knew who was right. In the end they killed it.

Who was The Thing in this case?

I swung my feet up on the desk, thumbed a match, set fire to a cigarette, stared at the phonograph, and got ready to face the music. I had always prided myself on being a professional, an eye who looked up and straight into all that heaven allowed. In my life there was always a new case, new clients, a few old ones who never left. Thus far I had managed to satisfy most of them—and myself as well—with the proper explanations at the proper time. This go-around I didn't feel half so lucky.

The Basement Tapes was playing. The music, put down in 1967 with the Band, between Dylan's accident and *John Wesley Harding,* was nine years old but it could have been made nine minutes or nine decades ago. It wouldn't have mattered. It had once been illegal, sold under the counter. Hell, even now, on sale free and clear, it wasn't complete—these things never are. It still *sounded* illegal.

"Goin' to Acapulco" came on. The song was about everything it wasn't about as well as what it was about, if you know what I mean. I thought it was probably about Miranda Abaloni. Beauty does that to me sometimes.

What a case, I thought. On the one hand, randiness, roots, memory, archetypal American music and its obsession with mystery and death. On the other, sweet revenge in the form of Gideon Cadwallader wooing the white-hot center with the blowtorch of reason.

I asked myself if I'd ever touched the white-hot center of anything.

He looked particularly smug the next day. Even his sallowness seemed freshly polished, and he beamed like a pale yellow sun coming out of the pollution just to shine on Miranda Abaloni. Who was walking up the hall toward us.

"We'd like to talk about women," he said.

I said: "Here comes one now."

He made a face.

I hit him with a sheaf of reports.

Between 1969 and 1975, Dylan's career slumped badly. After *John Wesley Harding,* he ignored the abyss and tried to convince the world he was just another happily married family man. On *Nashville Skyline* (1969) and *Self-Portrait* (1970), he challenged such country singers as Elvis Presley, Hank Williams, the Everly Brothers, Johnny Cash, Jerry Lee Lewis et al., and, for the first time, got routed. *New Morning* (1970) was a mediocre comeback album, the individuality and ambition apparently gone. It wasn't that he made foolish moves, but no moves at all. *Dylan* (1973) scraped the bottom of the barrel—outtakes released without his consent. Because the expectations for them ran so high, *Planet Waves* and *Before the Flood,* both recorded with the Band in 1974, were the severest disappointments of all. Only 1973's *Pat Garrett and Billy the Kid,* an LP as wrongly underrated as the earlier *Another Side of Bob Dylan,* reinvestigated the old myths, albeit mostly without words. "Knockin' on Heaven's Door" and especially the instrumental, "Final Theme," are well suited for either weddings or funerals.

One of the surprising things about the Dylan/Band *Before the Flood* tour was how impersonal and uninteresting it was, how devoid of urgency and emotional credibility. There are those of us who are possessed and those of us not possessed, and with Dylan possession would seem to be nine-tenths of the law. Dispossessed, he apparently resorted to the delirious pace and pose of a B-movie gangster, sacrificing both stylistic intangibles and the very meaning of the songs for sheer speed in order to create the impression of anger, a handle on which to hang what little real action there was. It sounded fine for a song or two, but the false action soon fostered more effort than effect. Onstage, he seemed absolutely harmless. Did these songs—most of his great ones—no longer mean anything to him or had he simply been away from live performance for too many years? Perhaps he had something else on his mind.

"How easy you make it for me," Cadwallader said. "I need hardly comment on six years of waste. It is odd to equate them with a happy marriage, though. According to you, Dylan would seem better off an aesthetic but antisocial misfit."

"You have a gift for small truths, Cadwallader. But they just won't grow into bigger ones for you because you have no regard for context—and it's that kind of case. Your machine's broken. It's stuck on zero. It subtracts but won't add."

"Tell me, do you think Dylan would consider Ms. Abaloni an 'angel' or a 'bitch'? I believe those are the terms most often used to describe his attitude toward women. Saviors or destroyers—and ne'er the twain shall meet?"

"I think you'd better read the next report," I said.

"Look at her," he said. "Would their union be fire and brimstone, a dark ceremony consummated in some puritanical Midwestern tabernacle, the male cowering in fear and drooling with holiness? Or would he simply send her a postcard from time to time telling her how he wrote 'Sad-Eyed Lady of the Lowlands'?"

"I think their union would probably be lovely," I said.

His marriage rumored troubled, his recent tour and albums treated somewhat indifferently by a less-than-worshipful press, Bob Dylan seems haunted and uncertain again, and that may be very good news. If ironic, such a statement would be both cheap and cruel, but irony has little to do with Dylan's marital situation, however it may turn out, or with the near-total success of 1975's *Blood on the Tracks.* Ambiguousness seems a word more apt for this romantic rethink. When the adventurer Jay Gatsby finally got his Daisy alone, "He knew that when he kissed this girl and forever wed his unutterable visions to her perishable breath, his mind would never romp again like the mind of God." What to do when ambiguity and the realization of the quest prove inseparable? Either crack up or become a sadder, wiser

man. Because he is strong, Bob Dylan has chosen the latter course.

If *Nashville Skyline, New Morning* and *Planet Waves* were essentially about the stable joys of marriage, family, and a happy home in rich bluegrass country, much of *Blood on the Tracks* emanates from a rented room in the dark, bohemian section of town where one can listen to the trains at night. It is to Dylan's great credit that he condemns neither circumstance: like most of us, he dreams of the possibility of a fusion of the two extremes. He began his career as a loner, reveling in the intangibles and uncertainties of his life, but then dropped out of contact and context into the sheltered opulence of rural Woodstock and began sending back platitudes which were as surprising as they were unbelievable. The nadir of this movement was reached with *Planet Waves*, whereon Dylan seemed almost to turn himself inside out in an agonizing and futile effort to convince both us and himself how incredibly content he was. The unintended effect was far from pleasant.

If subterranean tension won out over an overwrought tenderness on *Planet Waves*, the reverse curiously holds true on *Blood on the Tracks*. There is a great deal of personal pain here, and second thoughts abound ("I can change, I swear"), but everything seems deliberately cushioned by myth, distanced by meditative rumination and an artful overview of the lifetimes of ritual staying, leaving, or being told to go which all of us inevitably experience and reexperience. This is the way it is for me now, Dylan appears to be saying, and this is the way it has been and will be again for both of us: something lost, something gained. "Tangled Up in Blue" seems a more than appropriate phrase for this saddest and most beautiful of myths.

Although *Blood on the Tracks* is aptly named, it is hardly the wasteland of pessimism and self-hatred that some critics have claimed. Far from it. The album is vital and alive, its despair tempered throughout with the joy of being a survivor, all senses intact, whose dreams are still made of iron and steel.

"Egotistical, exploitive, and profoundly sexist," said Cadwallader. "Elegant romantic hogwash. We—"

"We?" I looked at Miranda Abaloni and asked: "Have you ever heard 'Ballad in Plain D,' Miss Abaloni? 'To Ramona'? 'Love Minus Zero/No Limit'? 'If You See Her, Say Hello'? 'Sara'?"

She nodded.

"If you were to fall in love with Bob Dylan, Miss Abaloni, and he lucky enough to be in love with you, how much do you think his politics would disturb whatever was good about the relationship?"

Gideon Cadwallader stared.

As she held up her hand, thumb and forefinger extended.

The space between her fingers was barely wide enough to let through any light at all.

I was on my fourth carton of cigarettes. I knew I had to take a shot at it soon, but no man likes to play the fool. There were no truths in this case. I had known that for a long time, that and little else. In death and matters of the heart, we are all of us amateurs, someone once said. Maybe it was me.

Gideon Cadwallader and Miranda Abaloni were reading reports.

Nineteen seventy-five was to be the true beginning of a new era for Bob Dylan, not 1974. All along the watchtower, he had missed it by one. *Blood on the Tracks* and *Desire* (January 1976) were the LPs that convinced us once and for all of his love for his wife Sara; the ubiquitous Rolling Thunder Revue, not the *Before the Flood* tour, made us believe he had not thrown it all away as a live performer. After living for two years in Los Angeles, he returned to the streets of New York City, and as it had 14 years earlier, Manhattan's magic took hold of him. He even looked like the Kid again. In *The Go-Between*, L.P. Hartley wrote: "The past is a foreign country: they do things differently there." Sometimes, but not invariably. For Bob Dylan, the postman always rings twice.

Desire may be a very special album, but it's also Part Two of *Blood on the Tracks*. About that LP Greil Marcus wrote: "At once the tale of an adventurer's war with a woman and with himself, and a shattering attempt to force memory, fantasy, and the terrors of love and death to serve an artist's impulse to redeem disaster by making beauty out of it. . . . [The] songs are as obvious and as unsettling as the weather; no one can fail to understand them, and no one can get to the bottom of them, either. . . . The odyssey of a mythical lover possessed by an affair he can never resolve."

More than any other Dylan album, *Desire* hews to the lifeline, at times seems to be looking right over the edge. Surely one of its themes has to do with the mythopoeic, eternal consequences of a man's actions and/or What Might Have Been. There is real death in these songs, and the acknowledgment of it lurks behind them like some strangely benevolent shadow: "Time is an ocean but it ends at the shore/You may not see me/Tomorrow."

"Sex and death, death and sex," Cadwallader said. "Perhaps we are dealing with the *real* Bob Dylan here. A specious—"

"No," I said slowly, rolling the syllable across my tongue. "No." I bit off the end of the word.

"You don't—"

I said it again. Twice.

Nobody said anything for a while. I let a cigarette burn down between my fingers until it made a small red mark. It had been that kind of caper. The end was very near. I could feel it on the back of my neck. Suddenly I felt very sad.

"He *is* guilty, you know," Cadwallader said. "I think that is significant." Somehow it seemed important to him.

"Fine," I said. "He's guilty. But guilty of what, Cadwallader? Of caring enough to want it all—the myth *and* the reality? You want to destroy one under the guise of protecting the other, and that's such a tiny ambition for a man of your intelligence. Even if you manage it, what have you done? Rid the world of romance? Christ, you can find anyone guilty if that's all you want to do, but someday you'll have to take a stand of your own without checking the book first. Then some bright guy will walk into your office and tell you you're full of it, and then what will you do?"

"You haven't exactly solved the case," he said.

"No," I said thickly. "I haven't solved the case and I don't intend to. No one will ever figure out Dylan the way you want to—somehow it would be indecent. He's tried to hit the longest home runs in the history of rock and roll, and I respect him for that. I don't know what his values are because they keep moving, but I suspect they're at least as good as mine. That's enough for me."

"You're not serious," he said. "You don't expect me to think—"

"I don't care what you think," I said.

I nodded toward the inner office to indicate that I was going in there, and went in there. I picked up a piece of paper about the Rolling Thunder Revue benefit for Rubin Carter, then a prisoner in New Jersey. Dylan had raised a lot of money to free him.

When a man's case is in shambles, he's supposed to do something about it, I kept thinking. It doesn't make any difference what you thought of it. It was your case and you're supposed to do something about it. I gave the report to Cadwallader.

It is 9:57 p.m. Suddenly, Bob Dylan, looking like a cross between a New Mexico gypsy and a glittery New York Doll, is in front of the microphone, lining out "When I Paint My Masterpiece." When Dylan leans triumphantly into a line that isn't even on the recorded version—"It sure has been *one helluva life!*"—I feel a rush of excitement (for him? for me?). On "It Ain't Me Babe," his Chaplinesque harmonica playing drives the crowd into a frenzy. When the harmonica comes out, it's like the real Dylan has arrived.

"The Lonesome Death of Hattie Carroll" is Dylan's best protest song, and he sings it now with a staccato anger and authority so intense and pure that a later rendering of the similar but inferior "Hurricane" is musically, if not politically, anticlimactic. Dylan avoids sentimentality by fusing fire and ice in "Hattie Carroll," and this mixture of rage and severity, when combined with the near-brutal austerity of his singing, somehow suggests a cosmic system of justice so infinite and implacable that the courts and judges of this world seem worth taking seriously only until the purge comes. I can feel it breathing down my neck right now.

I don't know what to say about the trilogy of songs with which Bob Dylan closes the concert. "Sara," "Just like a Woman," and "Knockin' on Heaven's Door," in the context offered here, are so clearly about the Dylans' amorphous marital situation that perhaps the only correct response is to cry—which I almost do, which he almost does. From "Sara, Sara/Don't ever leave me/Don't ever go" to "Yes, I believe it's time for us to quit" to "Mama, take these tears from my eyes," I feel the story of all of our lives—and it's very complicated. Unforgettable would not be too strong a word. It seems significant enough at the time.

I said: "Listen. This isn't a damn bit of good. You'll never understand me, but I'll try once more and then we'll give it up."

He looked worried. His eyes, the color of unset rhinestones, darkened, lightened, got darker again.

"All right," he said.

"Listen. First, when a man has tried to remain whole and tell the truth against all the odds, you get an idea he might be special. It doesn't matter that he makes mistakes, he's still special. Second, it happens we're both in the detective business. Well, when one of your own gets threatened, it's bad business to stand by and let it happen—bad business all around. Third, the songs of Bob Dylan are the hardest, toughest, sweetest, saddest, funniest, wisest songs I know, but I don't always know what they're about. Friendship, sex, death, heroism, learning from others, I guess. History and inevitability are in there too. If there are tests, they've all been passed, and what you're hearing are the results. Serious comedy. Deadpan tragedy. That's—"

He said: "I think—"

"Wait till I'm through and then you can talk. Fourth, I've no reason in God's world to think I can trust you. If I did I'd have to hate all those men and women who aren't afraid to make fools of themselves. Next, I know we need people like you because a world filled with romantics would be a disaster, but a world without them would be worse. That's five of them. The sixth would be that these are inspired times—I respond to myths and so do you. Even you, Cadwallader. You and Miranda Abaloni. But you'll never win her. Even if she wanted you you'd be terrified to fall in love with her because she might not be perfect and one day you might have to do a job on her. Seventh, you can't accept a set of values that takes in loss—and myths need loss. They thrive on it. Allen Ginsberg said of Dylan: 'Who woulda thought he'd say it, so everybody'd finally know him, some soul crying vulnerable caught in a body we all are?

—enough Person revealed to make Whitman's whole nation weep.' And eighth—but that's enough. Maybe some of them are unimportant. I won't argue about that. But look at the number of them. Now on the other side we've got what? All we've got is the fact that you want one hard, clean answer."

"I do," he whispered. "Whether you do or not."

"I don't. I won't play the sap for you. As far as I'm concerned, make him a hero because he's the best failure we've got. I like them like that. You want to solve the case? Get another detective."

"I don't want another detective," said Miranda Abaloni.

I jammed on my hat and we went out into the rain. Together.

Discography

Singles
"Subterranean Homesick Blues" (Columbia 43242; ☆39, 1965). "Like a Rolling Stone" (Columbia 43346; ☆2, 1965). "Positively 4th Street" (Columbia 43389; ☆7, 1965). "Can You Please Crawl Out Your Window" (Columbia 43477; ☆58, 1966). "Rainy Day Women #12 & 35" (Columbia 43592; ☆2, 1966). "I Want You" (Columbia 43683; ☆20, 1966). "Just like a Woman" (Columbia 43792; ☆33, 1966). "Leopard-Skin Pill-Box Hat" (Columbia 44069; ☆81, 1967). "I Threw It All Away" (Columbia 44826; ☆85, 1969). "Lay Lady Lay" (Columbia 44926; ☆7, 1969). "Tonight I'll Be Staying Here with You" (Columbia 45004; ☆50, 1969). "Wigwam" (Columbia 45199; ☆41, 1970). "Watching the River Flow" (Columbia 45409; ☆41, 1971). "George Jackson" (Columbia 45516; ☆33, 1971). "Knockin' on Heaven's Door" (Columbia 45913; ☆12, 1973). "A Fool Such as I" (Columbia 45982; ☆55, 1973). "On a Night like This" (Asylum 11033; ☆44, 1974). "Most Likely You Go Your Way (and I'll Go Mine)" (Asylum 11043; ☆55, 1974). "Tangled Up in Blue" (Columbia 3-10106; ☆31, 1974). "Hurricane (Part I)" (Columbia 3-10245; ☆33, 1975).
Albums
Bob Dylan (Columbia 8579; 1962). *The Freewheelin' Bob Dylan* (Columbia 8786; ☆22, 1963). *The Times They Are A-Changin'* (Columbia 8905; ☆20, 1964). *Another Side of Bob Dylan* (Columbia 8993; ☆43, 1964). *Bringing It All Back Home* (Columbia 9128; ☆6, 1965). *Highway 61 Revisited* (Columbia 9189; ☆3, 1965). *Blonde on Blonde* (Columbia 2-841; ☆9, 1966). *Bob Dylan's Greatest Hits* (Columbia 9463; ☆10, 1967). *John Wesley Harding* (Columbia 9604; ☆2, 1968). *Nashville Skyline* (Columbia 9825; ☆3, 1969). *Self-Portrait* (Columbia 30050; ☆4, 1970). *New Morning* (Columbia 30290; ☆7, 1970). *Bob Dylan's Greatest Hits, Vol. II* (Columbia 31120; ☆14, 1971). *Pat Garrett and Billy the Kid* (Columbia 32460; ☆16, 1973). *Planet Waves* (Asylum 1003; ☆1, 1974). *Dylan* (Columbia 32747; ☆17, 1973). *Before the Flood* (with the Band) (Asylum 201; ☆3, 1974). *Blood on the Tracks* (Columbia 33235; ☆1, 1975). *The Basement Tapes* (with the Band) (Columbia 2-33682; ☆7, 1975). *Desire* (Columbia 33893; ☆1, 1976).
(Chart positions compiled from Joel Whitburn's *Record Research,* based on *Billboard* Pop and LPs charts.)

The Byrds
by Bud Scoppa

The year 1965 was a very good one: the Beatles, the Rolling Stones and Bob Dylan were all at the height of their powers and popularity. It was also the year of the Byrds, L.A.'s answer to London, authors of a new kind of rock—"folk rock," an unlikely blend of Pete Seeger and rock and roll—and L.A. hip, the I-don't-give-a-damn look epitomized by Jim (later Roger) McGuinn's Cheshire smile and sideways nod.

They were an unlikely rock and roll band. McGuinn, a former Chicago folkie, had played guitar for Bobby Darin, Chad Mitchell and Judy Collins before trying to make a living as a solo act, performing Beatles tunes in Greenwich Village cafes; inspired by George Harrison in *A Hard Day's Night*, he decided to master rock on an electric 12-string guitar. David Crosby, a California-bred folk singer who had logged time in coffeehouses himself, joined McGuinn in Los Angeles; so did Chris Hillman, a bluegrass mandolinist who had switched to bass. A singer/songwriter from Missouri named Gene Clark, Dylan fixated but more recently hooked on the Beatles, signed on and was handed a tambourine; Michael Clarke looked the part of a drummer and so was handed a pair of drumsticks. There wasn't a hardcore rocker among them, but they were determined to be a rock and roll band. And so, first as the Beefeaters and then as the Byrds, they became one.

Perhaps it was something intangible in the collective character of the group, or the particular time and place, or something related to their naiveté, but the Byrds pioneered a new approach to rock: it all had to do with the *sound*. Elvis's Sun singles had a sound, as did the Beatles' joyous, head-over-heels hits from 1964 and '65; but in neither the Beatles' nor Elvis's case had the sound been primary, the product of a self-conscious sonic conception. In the liner notes for their first album, McGuinn attempted to explain the Byrds' sound:

"I think the difference is in the mechanical sounds of the time. Like the sound of the airplane in the Forties was a rrrrrrrrooooaaaaaaaahhhhhhhhhh sound and Sinatra and other people sang like that with those sort of overtones. Now we've got the krrrriiiiissssssssshhhhhhhh jet sound, and the kids are singing up in there now. It's the mechanical sounds of the era."

The "mechanical sounds of the era"? The kids are singing "up in there" now? For rock, let alone folk, this was truly bizarre. Admittedly, there's an ironic distance when McGuinn talks about "the kids"; indeed, there's a tongue-in-cheek quality to the entire statement. But irony and facetiousness notwithstanding, McGuinn's statement has the ring of truth, judging from the sound of that first album, *Mr. Tambourine Man*. The blockbuster density of "I'll Feel a Whole Lot Better," with its 12-string symphony and massive chorale was new in rock, as was the strangely pulsating Bo Diddley beat of "Don't Doubt Yourself, Babe." Ballads like "The Bells of Rhymney" and "Chimes of Freedom" were equally majestic, as diamond-sharp cascading guitar notes intertwined with the Byrds' gothic vocal harmonies.

"Mr. Tambourine Man" became a hit in a summer of Top 40 anthems. The Beatles' "Ticket to Ride" and its chimelike guitars set the scene; the venom of the Stones' "(I Can't Get No) Satisfaction" and the snarl of Dylan's "Like a Rolling Stone" followed in an assertively glorious progression. "Mr. Tambourine Man" was the quirkiest: restrained and ambiguous in a way that departed from Dylan's prototype, it was also suggestive and tantalizing, as if those who read between the lines would be let in on a mystic media secret.

The Byrds did it again a few months later, with "Turn! Turn! Turn!," another enigmatic anthem. This one, drawn from a Biblical passage set to music by Pete Seeger, simultaneously urged commitment and acceptance, just as we were learning how to spell "Vietnam." In the meantime, the Byrds had become pied pipers to a generation of L.A. mods who had just discovered drugs, and every few months the band would pack Ciro's or the Trip on Sunset Strip.

After "Turn! Turn! Turn!" the Byrds retreated from national attention, to cut albums aimed at the growing cult for progressive pop and acid rock. *Turn! Turn! Turn!*, their second album, lacked first-rate new material and the fullness and punch of *Tambourine Man*. But the band returned to form for *Fifth Dimension*, released during the summer of 1966. "Eight Miles High," with its ominous bass line, unearthly vocal harmonies, and fiercely electronic 12-string solo inspired by jazzman John Coltrane, was a shattering tour de force. As a single, it had the distinction of being one of the first records widely banned because of its alleged drug references; but hit or not, "Eight Miles High," a hypnotic incantation to "flying," sounded like no rock single before it.

If the Byrds lacked anything, it was sentiment. Their repertoire was short on love songs, and there was a remote quality, a fascination with sheer technique, that suggested the cool precision of hardcore formalists. While there was humanity in this music, it lay by implication in the manipulation of form, in the sound itself. If Dylan *was* the songs he sang, the Byrds were *pilots* of their songs, inscrutable but controlling presences; their ambiguous pose only underlined their preference for detachment over seductiveness.

In this sense, "So You Want to Be a Rock 'n' Roll Star," the opening cut on *Younger than Yesterday*, the Byrds' fourth LP, was delectably ironic. What fleeting stardom the band attained was the result of the sheer power of their early singles. But their identity had become more elusive as their musical conception had become more sophisticated—and to make matters worse, Gene Clark, the band's sole romantic, had left after *Turn! Turn! Turn!* The architect of the group's iconoclasm was McGuinn, a whiz kid who had swapped his slide rule for a 12-string guitar. Compulsively curious, obsessed with electronic gadgetry, McGuinn tinkered with rock and roll as if it were a space-age toy. He also tinkered with the other Byrds, appraising their strengths and weaknesses with disarming

frankness, as if the players were mere cogs in a machine. And yet McGuinn also had the lucidity and assertiveness to tap the special skills of his colleagues: Crosby's knack for harmony singing, Hillman's flair for humming bass lines, Gene Clark's skill as a composer.

Each performer found his skills servicing McGuinn's own ideas; not surprisingly, each in time came to resent McGuinn's control. *Younger than Yesterday* gave the work of both Crosby and Hillman a new prominence, but tensions persisted within the group. By the end of 1967, Crosby was gone.

Undaunted, McGuinn set his stripped down Byrds machine to work on an ambitious new recording project. To construct his magnum opus, he gathered together the most advanced electronic gear of the day, tossed in a string quartet for balance, and hired topflight sessionmen to flesh out the surviving trio of Byrds (McGuinn, Hillman, Michael Clarke).

With the help of producer Gary Usher, he went for absolute tautness in integrating these disparate elements, achieving a sonic totality by cross-fading one track into the next. The resulting album, *The Notorious Byrd Brothers*, sounded airtight; for the first time, McGuinn fully developed the implications of his "krriiiiisssssssshhhhh" concept. While the songs were a mixed lot—topics included speed, childish innocence, the draft, space exploration, and the language of dolphins—the relentless jet-age drone of the album managed to unify the material into a coherent whole.

Although the McGuinn-Hillman Byrds made one more album, the rustic *Sweetheart of the Rodeo* (which helped spark the country-rock revival), that effort was skyjacked from under them by newcomer Gram Parsons. After Michael Clarke faded away and Hillman (according to McGuinn) threw his bass on the floor and walked out for good, the one remaining original

Byrd—McGuinn—hired various musicians to carry on the concept. But except for the late Clarence White, a gifted guitarist, none of them could hit the lofty note McGuinn's conception called for. After several moderately successful tours and a handful of uninspiring albums (excepting one near miss, *Untitled*, which introduced McGuinn's "Chestnut Mare"), McGuinn lost interest and the neo-Byrds crumbled.

For a three-year period, though, from 1965 to 1968, the Byrds were genuine space cowboys, their audacity in the studio second to none, even in that limit-smashing period. McGuinn was one of the great eccentrics of rock and roll, Crosby one of the great loudmouths. And the Byrds transformed the mechanical sounds of an era into a total sonic concept that beguiled the ear, if not the heart.

Discography

Singles

"Mr. Tambourine Man" (Columbia 43271; ☆1, 1965). "All I Really Want to Do" (Columbia 43332; ☆40, 1965). "Turn! Turn! Turn!" (Columbia 43424; ☆1, 1965). "It Won't Be Wrong" b/w "Set You Free This Time" (Columbia 43501; ☆63, 1966). "Eight Miles High" (Columbia 43578; ☆14, 1966). "5D (Fifth Dimension)" (Columbia 43702; ☆44, 1966). "Mr. Spaceman" (Columbia 43766; ☆36, 1966). "So You Want to Be a Rock 'n' Roll Star" (Columbia 43987; ☆29, 1967). "My Back Pages" (Columbia 44054; ☆30, 1967). "Have You Seen Her Face" (Columbia 44157; ☆74, 1967). "Goin' Back" (Columbia 44362; ☆89, 1967). "You Ain't Going Nowhere" (Columbia 44499; ☆74, 1968). "Jesus Is Just Alright" (Columbia 45071; ☆97, 1970).

Albums

Mr. Tambourine Man (Columbia 9172; ☆6, 1965). *Turn! Turn! Turn!* (Columbia 9254; ☆17, 1966). *Fifth Dimension* (Columbia 9349; ☆24, 1966). *Younger than Yesterday* (Columbia 9442; ☆24, 1967). *Greatest Hits* (Columbia 9516; ☆6, 1967). *The Notorious Byrd Brothers* (Columbia 9575; ☆47, 1968). *Sweetheart of the Rodeo* (Columbia 9670; ☆77, 1968). *Dr. Byrds & Mr. Hyde* (Columbia 9755; ☆153, 1969). *Preflyte* (Together 1001; ☆84, 1969). *Ballad of Easy Rider* (Columbia 9942; ☆36, 1969). *(Untitled)* (Columbia 30127; ☆40, 1970). *Byrdmaniax* (Columbia 30640; ☆46, 1971). *Farther Along* (Columbia 31050; ☆152, 1971). *Best of the Byrds—Vol. 2* (Columbia 31795; ☆114, 1972).

Roger McGuinn Solo Albums

Roger McGuinn (Columbia 31946; ☆137, 1973). *Peace on You* (Columbia 32956; ☆92, 1974). *Roger McGuinn and Band* (Columbia 33541; 1975).

(Chart positions compiled from Joel Whitburn's *Record Research*, based on *Billboard* Pop and LPs charts.)

Folk-Rock

by Paul Nelson

During its short-lived heyday in 1965, folk rock was a hastily assembled and transitory frontier junction to and from which several important musical roads were connected. Bordered on one side by the concurrent, multifaceted American folk music and topical song revivals of the late Fifties and early Sixties, and on the other by the onrushing artistic and economic success of New Wave rock and roll, folk rock was the hybrid with which many young urban folk musicians attempted to fuse revered teachings from the past (Woody Guthrie, Leadbelly, the Carter Family, Jimmie Rodgers, Robert Johnson, Hank Williams) with an immediate and more personally relevant knowledge of the present (the Beatles). For at least two or three of folk rock's archetypes—Bob Dylan, the Byrds, the Lovin' Spoonful, the Mamas and the Papas, Donovan, Sonny and Cher—the motto "To thine own self, be true" must have caused considerable schizophrenic reaction at the time, because these artists were rebelling against both the anticommercial snobbery of the folk/topical powers-that-be and, to some degree, their own high estimations of the moral and aesthetic values of traditional music. How to remain true to one's youthful innocence (art without money) while reaching out for viable experience (art with money *and* an audience) was indeed a difficult but thrilling question. In the end more a tenuous artifact than a terminal art form, folk rock boasted a cast of background characters so large and varied that the phrase "et al." must be added to each list of names.

Since the late Fifties, Appalachian musicians such as Roscoe Holcomb, Clarence Ashley, Doc Watson, Bill Monroe, the Stanley Brothers, Frank Proffitt, Dock Boggs, and Horton Barker had often traveled to newfangled schoolhouses for metaphorical and sometimes real square dances, while the blues, rags, and hollers of their black-music counterparts (Sonny Terry and Brownie McGhee, Elizabeth Cotten, Mississippi John Hurt, Muddy Waters, Skip James, Furry Lewis, Fred McDowell, Jesse Fuller, Reverend Gary Davis) were treated with equal respect by a myriad of idealistic white college students and others eager to begin an artistic apprenticeship. Many of the young questers (Ramblin' Jack Elliott, Mike and Peggy Seeger, the New Lost City Ramblers, the Greenbriar Boys, Dave Van Ronk, Dave Ray, John Koerner, Dylan) started by figuratively and often literally worshiping in the churches of their elders, where they learned by practice and imitation the rituals of traditional performing styles. Others—some of whom either couldn't comprehend the complexities of the rural service or rightfully refused to be limited by them—attempted to translate old legends into new myths more accessible to themselves and their citybilly contemporaries: *Bob Dylan*, released in 1962, is the perfect example of a free spirit creatively punching holes in the limits of folk style with one hand while deliriously patching them up again with the other. The Holy Modal Rounders and the Jim Kweskin Jug Band wed urban

absurdity to old-time omniscience in a manner which somehow managed to do justice to both. Judy Collins and Joan Baez took a middle-of-the-road approach by carefully eliminating all meaningful idiosyncrasies from their singing, while such folk groups as the Kingston Trio, the Limeliters, the Chad Mitchell Trio, the Brothers Four, the New Christy Minstrels, and Peter, Paul and Mary simply added a Four Freshmen-cum-Weavers regularity to the Southern Mountain sound, refined the gold from them thar hills, and laughed all the way to the top of the pop charts.

Aesthetic responsibilities and a utopian popularity based upon sociopolitical integrity seemed arduous if not impossible goals for the new breed, many of whom wanted not only to sing songs but to write them, much as the prolific Guthrie had done in the Thirties and Forties. Some found solace in the work of such pioneering Populists as Pete Seeger and the Weavers, artists of optimism who carried at least part of the working-man-as-god thesis into the Sixties. (Indeed, Seeger may have been the original flowerchild.) Their revivalist disciples, the topical songwriters and New Left journalists who published in *Sing Out!* and *Broadside*, extended the radical-liberal tradition of musical politicking while founding a more personal and ultimately more important school—that of the singer/songwriter—which soon preferred its own primal ballads to preachy broadsides. From Phil Ochs, Tom Paxton, Peter La Farge, Eric Andersen, Buffy Sainte-Marie, Len Chandler, and the ubiquitous Dylan came Tim Hardin, Janis Ian, Leonard Cohen, Joni Mitchell, Paul Siebel, Randy Newman, Loudon Wainwright III, Jesse Winchester, and Jackson Browne—and the two lists are all but interchangeable.

If one could characterize many of the most promising artists of the American folk-music and topical-song revivals as politically pugnacious but primarily innocent babes in the woods on their way toward disillusionment and/or maturity in the dark and manly art of rock and roll, then folk rock provided the requisite rite of passage. There, semirecalcitrant teenagers often blissfully bottomed out while recapitulating for a mass market what they felt they had learned about growing up. Like so many double-fold anachronisms, folk rock should have had the strengths of either-or, not the weaknesses of neither-nor; it was almost a virgin but not quite pregnant. Although one can like folk rock, I doubt that one can love it. Too ingratiatingly simpleminded, its easy stance on Uneasy Street now seems neither committed nor individualistic enough to matter much when compared with the monolithic magic of either folk or rock undiluted. While both folk music and rock and roll are too frequently categorized as simple arts, the truth, as Bob Dylan has said, is far from that. His infamous comment about the former—"In that music is the only true, valid death you can feel today off a record player"—also describes the latter. It tells us nothing about folk rock.

Donovan, a flower for your garden (Baron Wolman)

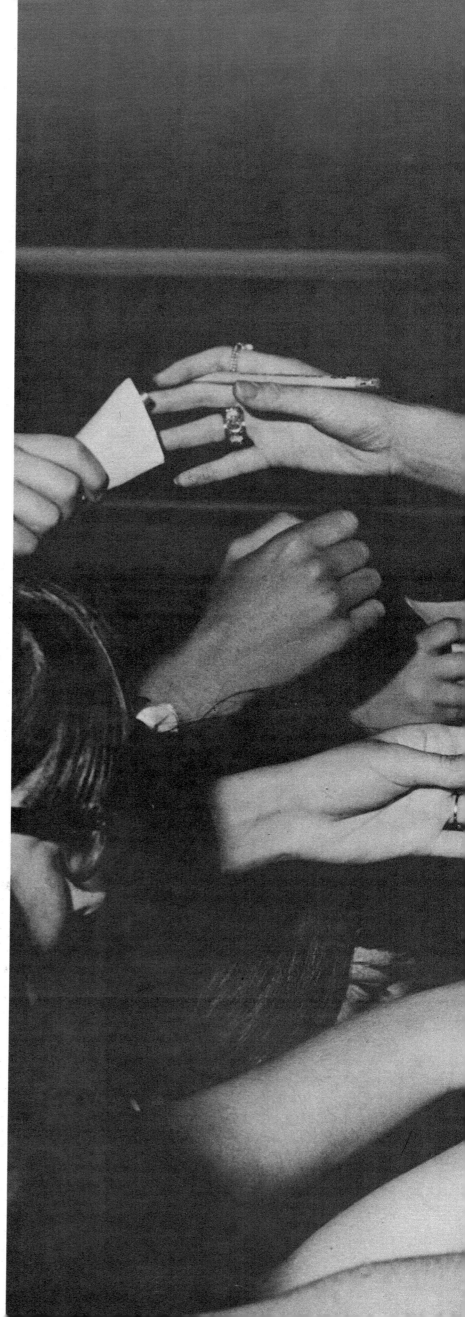

Dylan and the Byrds were the fathers of folk rock, of course,
but the consummation hardly rates more than a footnote in any
legitimate history of rock and roll because neither's career can
be limited to one minor genre, most of whose practitioners
perished after 1966. No matter that some critics have defined
folk rock as a music proliferated by profligate folkies-cum-rock
and rollers who, armed with tambourines and electric 12-
strings, started their transgressive trip by imitating Dylan and
ended it by imitating the Byrds imitating Dylan. Or that many
folk and folk-rock classics were either Dylan songs (Peter, Paul
and Mary's "Blowin' in the Wind," the Byrds' "Mr. Tambourine Man," the Turtles' "It Ain't Me Babe"), reasonable or
unreasonable facsimiles (Simon and Garfunkel's "The Sounds
of Silence," Barry McGuire's "Eve of Destruction"), or likable
but blatant spin-offs (Sonny and Cher's "I Got You Babe").

By the mid-Sixties, Dylan's influence as a
songwriter was so powerful that he almost
single-handedly destroyed both the topical
and folk music revivals when he began to
move from them with 1964's transitional *Another Side of Bob
Dylan* (folk-style music, folk-rock songs), 1965's tentative
Bringing It All Back Home (folk-rock music, rock and roll
songs)—toward "Like a Rolling Stone" and his rock and roll
masterpieces, *Highway 61 Revisited* in 1965 and *Blonde on
Blonde* in 1966. In the summer and fall of 1965, revivalist
purists weaned on the earlier *The Freewheelin' Bob Dylan* and
The Times They Are A-Changin' viciously booed Dylan at the
Newport Folk Festival, in Forest Hills, and in Carnegie Hall for
his homage to the Rolling Stones, but by 1966 the catcalls had
subsided.

Unlike Dylan, the Byrds came at folk rock from both directions (although it must be remembered that Dylan issued a rock
and roll single, "Mixed Up Confusion," in 1962). The band's
"first" album, *Preflyte*, recorded a year before 1965's *Mr. Tambourine Man* but not released until 1969, sounds more like the
Beatles than it does Dylan—Lillian Roxon wasn't far wrong
when she wrote that "*Newsweek* called them Dylanized Beatles
when the whole point was they were Beatlized Dylans." At
their best, the underrated Byrds provided an aural dignity that
is positively Jungian to such mid-Sixties standards as "Mr.
Tambourine Man," "I'll Feel a Whole Lot Better," "The Bells
of Rhymney," "All I Really Want to Do," "Chimes of Freedom," "Turn! Turn! Turn!," "Eight Miles High," "So You
Want to Be a Rock 'n' Roll Star," "My Back Pages," and "Goin'
Back." On "Wasn't Born to Follow," the guitar playing met-
amorphoses perfectly from a Woody Guthrie folk lick into the
spacial electronic phasing that characterized Dylanesque
Roger (nee Jim) McGuinn and the innumerable Byrds and
made them the cowboy-astronaut Carter Family of rock and
roll. The song also supplied folk rock with both a succinct
musical definition and one of its few really magical moments.

Unfortunately, too much of the work of folk rock's major offspring has proven more timely than timeless. The Lovin' Spoonful—a crafty combination of infernal affability, cartoon costumes, rock and roll, and jug-band music—commingled the magic in young girls' hearts with feckless fantasies of escape from the problems of everyday living. John Sebastian's breathy vocals and tie-dye vision were nothing if not pleasant, and his best songs ("Do You Believe in Magic?," "Daydream," "Younger Girl," "Darling Be Home Soon," "Darling Companion," and the surprisingly tough-minded "Summer in the City") can almost make one forget the soft somnolence of most of the band's repertoire. The Mamas and the Papas countered the same difficulties (an elusion of reality, not enough good material) with a similar theme (fleeing to sunny California from cold New York City), but what made the group special was their haunting and sumptuous harmony singing: the message was surely the ultimate vocal massage. "Dedicated to the One I Love," "California Dreamin'," and "Creeque Alley" are fine songs, and "Twelve-Thirty (Young Girls Are Coming to the Canyon)" offers a literal parade of young women—all of whom, one imagines, look exactly like Michelle Phillips—marching from the evil East into luxuriant Los Angeles.

Once considered another Dylan, Scotsman Donovan Leitch failed to parlay an early plethora of exceptional love songs ("Catch the Wind," "Colours," "Josie") into anything more meaningful than his unjustly famous and explicably disastrous psychedelic and flower-power periods. If most of *Mellow Yellow* and *Sunshine Superman* seems merely silly today, the impact of that music on the mid-Sixties was significant. From the vantage point of the present, it is hard not to regard Donovan's career as unnecessarily tragic because, even while he was floating away into the lilac mist, there were traces of a solid and uncommon talent ("Writer in the Sun," "Lalena," "There Is a Mountain," "Atlantis," "Epistle to Derroll"). "I think, therefore I shouldn't think" probably should have been Donovan's motto.

While not really a folk-rock band, the prodigiously talented Buffalo Springfield—Neil Young, Stephen Stills, Richie Furay, Jim Messina, et al.—deserve special mention both for caring enough to preserve the very best qualities of the form and for conscientiously consolidating them into inspired, if idiosyncratic rock and roll. Like the Byrds, the Buffalo could either hang back on a song until all of its somber juices boiled over ("For What It's Worth") or just come right out and say it ("Sit Down, I Think I Love You"). Although the group had a short but troubled career—*Buffalo Springfield* and *Buffalo Springfield Again* (both 1967), *Last Time Around* (1968)—their melodies, not their maladies, linger on in "Mr. Soul," "Bluebird," "Broken Arrow," "I Am a Child" and "Kind Woman."

Although its duration was modestly brief, folk rock furnished an immodest number of previews to coming attractions, some of them important. From the concepts of this cordial genre later emerged the infant and evangelical sound of the Jefferson Airplane and other San Francisco bands, hippies, Scott McKenzie's "San Francisco (Be Sure to Wear Flowers in Your Hair)," flowerchildren, country rock, and the impetus for such diverse groups as the Youngbloods, the not-so-great Crosby, Stills, Nash and Young, the Band, Gram Parsons and the Flying Burrito Brothers, and the Eagles. Not bad for a hybrid.

Discography

Singles
Peter, Paul and Mary, For Lovin' Me" (Warner Bros. 5496; ☆30, 1965). **Bob Dylan,** "Subterranean Homesick Blues" (Columbia 43242; ☆39, 1965). **Donovan,** "Catch the Wind" (Hickory 1309; ☆23, 1965). **Byrds,** "Mr. Tambourine Man" (Columbia 43271; ☆1, 1965). **Cher,** "All I Really Want to Do" (Imperial, 66114; ☆15, 1965). **Byrds,** "All I Really Want to Do" (Columbia 43332; ☆40, 1965). **Sonny and Cher,** "I Got You Babe" (Atco 6359; ☆1, 1965). **Bob Dylan,** "Like a Rolling Stone" (Columbia 43346; ☆2, 1965). **We Five,** "You Were on My Mind" (A&M 770; ☆3, 1965). **Turtles,** "It Ain't Me Babe" (White Whale 222; ☆8, 1965). **Barry McGuire,** "Eve of Destruction" (Dunhill 4009; ☆1, 1965). **Sonny and Cher,** "Baby Don't Go" (Atco 6345; ☆8, 1965). **Lovin' Spoonful,** "Do You Believe in Magic" (Kama Sutra 201; ☆9, 1965). **Sonny,** "Laugh at Me" (Atco 6369; ☆10, 1965). **Sonny and Cher,** "Just You" (Atco 6345; ☆20, 1965). **Joan Baez,** "There But for Fortune" (Vanguard 35031; ☆50, 1965). **Bob Dylan,** "Positively 4th Street" (Columbia 43389; ☆7, 1965). **Sonny and Cher,** "But You're Mine" (Atco 6381; ☆15, 1965). **Byrds,** "Turn! Turn! Turn!" (Columbia 43424; ☆1, 1965). **Turtles,** "Let Me Be" (White Whale 224; ☆29, 1965). **Lovin' Spoonful,** "You Didn't Have to Be So Nice" (Kama Sutra 205; ☆10, 1965). **Bob Dylan,** "Can You Please Crawl Out Your Window" (Columbia 43477; ☆58, 1966). **The Mamas and the Papas,** "California Dreamin' " (Dunhill 4020; ☆4, 1966). **Sonny and Cher,** "What Now My Love" (Atco 6395; ☆14, 1966). **Turtles,** "You Baby" (White Whale 227; ☆20, 1966). **Lovin' Spoonful,** "Daydream" (Kama Sutra 208; ☆2, 1966). **Cher,** "Bang Bang" (Imperial 66160; ☆2, 1966). **The Mamas and the Papas,** "Monday, Monday" (Dunhill 4026; ☆1, 1966). **Byrds,** "Eight Miles High" (Columbia 43578; ☆14, 1966). **Bob Dylan,** "Rainy Day Women # 12 and 35" (Columbia 43592; ☆2, 1966). **Lovin' Spoonful,** "Did You Ever Have to Make Up Your Mind" (Kama Sutra 209; ☆2, 1966). **Leaves,** "Hey Joe" (Mira 222; ☆31, 1966). **Crispian St. Peters,** "The Pied Piper" (Jamie 1320; ☆4, 1966). **Grass Roots,** "Where Were You When I Needed You" (Dunhill 4029; ☆28, 1966). **The Mamas and the Papas,** "I Saw Her Again" (Dunhill 4031; ☆5, 1966). **Bob Dylan,** "I Want You" (Columbia 43683; ☆126, 1966). **Lovin' Spoonful,** "Summer in the City" (Kama Sutra, 211; ☆1, 1966). **Donovan,** "Sunshine Superman" (Epic 10045; ☆1, 1966). **Bob Dylan,** "Just like a Woman" (Columbia 43792; ☆33, 1966). **Bobby Darin,** "If I Were a Carpenter" (Atlantic 2350; ☆8, 1966). **Byrds,** "Mr. Spaceman" (Columbia 43766; ☆36, 1966). **Lovin' Spoonful,** "Rain on the Roof" (Kama Sutra, 216; ☆10, 1966). **The Mamas and the Papas,** "Look through My Window" (Dunhill 4050; ☆24, 1966). **Donovan,** Mellow Yellow" (Epic 10098; ☆2, 1966). **The Mamas and the Papas,** "Words of Love" (Dunhill 4057; ☆5, 1966). **Lovin' Spoonful,** "Nashville Cats" (Kama Sutra 219; ☆8, 1966).
Albums
Donovan
Catch the Wind (Hickory 123; ☆30, 1965). *Fairytales* (Hickory 127; ☆85, 1965). *Sunshine Superman* (Epic 26217; ☆11, 1966). *The Real Donovan* (Hickory 135; ☆96, 1966). *Mellow Yellow* (Epic 26239; ☆14, 1967). *Wear Your Love like Heaven* (Epic 26349; ☆60, 1967). *For Little Ones* (Epic 26350; ☆185, 1968). *A Gift from a Flower to a Garden* (Epic 2-171; ☆19, 1968). *Donovan in Concert* (Epic 26386; ☆18, 1968). *The Hurdy Gurdy Man* (Epic 26420; ☆20, 1968).
Turtles
It Ain't Me Babe (White Whale 7111; ☆98, 1965). *Happy Together* (White Whale 7114; ☆25, 1967). *The Turtles! Golden Hits* (White Whale 7115; ☆7, 1967). *The Turtles Present the Battle of the Bands* (White Whale 7118; ☆128, 1968).
Lovin' Spoonful
Do You Believe in Magic (Kama Sutra 8050; ☆32, 1965). *Daydream* (Kama Sutra 8051; ☆10, 1966). *What's Up, Tiger Lily?* (Kama Sutra 8053; ☆126, 1966). *Hums of the Lovin' Spoonful* (Kama Sutra 8054; ☆14, 1966). *The Best of the Lovin' Spoonful* (Kama Sutra 8056; ☆3, 1967). *You're a Big Boy Now* (Kama Sutra 8058; ☆160, 1967). *Everything Playing* (Kama Sutra 8061; ☆118, 1968). *The Best of the Lovin' Spoonful—Vol. 2* (Kama Sutra 8064; ☆156, 1968).
The Mamas and the Papas
If You Can Believe Your Eyes and Ears (Dunhill 50006; ☆1, 1966). *The Mamas and the Papas* (Dunhill 50010; ☆4, 1966). *The Mamas and the Papas Deliver* (Dunhill 50014; ☆2, 1967). *Farewell to the First Golden Era* (Dunhill 50025; ☆5, 1967). *The Papas and the Mamas* (Dunhill 50031; ☆15, 1968). *The Mamas and the Papas Golden Era—Vol. 2* (Dunhill 50038; ☆53, 1968).
Buffalo Springfield
Buffalo Springfield (Atco 200; ☆80, 1967). *Buffalo Springfield Again* (Atco 226; ☆44, 1967). *Last Time Around* (Atco 256; ☆42, 1968).
(Omitting LPs by Bob Dylan and the Byrds. Chart positions compiled from Joel Whitburn's *Record Research*, based on *Billboard* Pop and LPs charts.)

Motown

by Joe McEwen and Jim Miller

Sandwiched among a row of modest private homes and professional enterprises like Sykes Hernia Control and Your Fair Lady Boutique and Wig Room, the white bungalow at 2648 West Grand Boulevard in Detroit is distinguished only by a large sign proclaiming it HITSVILLE, U.S.A. The two-story frame structure with the angular, jutting picture window, along with a cluster of nearby houses, is the home of Berry Gordy's Motown Records, currently the country's hottest hitmakers.

Shortly after 9 a.m. on a warm morning in June 1965, songwriter/producer Lamont Dozier strolls in, ignoring the company time clock that used to govern his paycheck. Company president Gordy rushes from his office to tell Lamont that Motown needs a quick followup to the Four Tops' "I Can't Help Myself," the label's second Number One pop hit in less than a month (Dozier had helped write and produce the other as well: the Supremes' "Back in My Arms Again"). The Tops had recorded for Columbia before their Motown association, and Gordy explains that the New York label has just released an old record in an attempt to cash in on the group's current success.

Dozier nods and walks down the corridor, past closet-sized offices where groups and producers rehearse material. Lamont's partners, Brian Holland and Eddie Holland, are already in their cubicle, sketching out a preliminary arrangement that bears more than a passing resemblance to the Four Tops' current smash. Lamont Dozier sits down at the piano and smooths out some rough edges in the melody line; all three contribute to the lyric. By noon the song is complete, and the trio take their finished work to the studio, where the Four Tops run down the lyrics while Earl Van Dyke's band negotiates the changes. Later that afternoon, the track will have been recorded and the Tops' voice-over added. Within three days, the record will be on the streets, the pick hit at local soul station WCHB. The Columbia disc is quickly forgotten, and by August "It's the Same Old Song" by the Four Tops hits Number Five on the *Billboard* pop chart.

The success of Motown Records is almost entirely attributable to one man: Berry Gordy. A former boxer and onetime record-store owner, Gordy, through a combination of pugnacious panache, shrewd judgment and good taste, became the mogul of the most profitable black music concern in the world.

It all began in Detroit in the early Fifties. When Gordy's record store specializing in jazz went bankrupt, he decided to redirect his musical moneymaking interests to the burgeoning field of rhythm and blues. While supporting himself with a series of odd jobs, Gordy began writing songs for local R&B acts. At first, his amateur efforts failed miserably; but he soon acquired a local reputation as a songwriter, producer and hustler. In those days, Gordy would write songs for a performer, cut a demo tape, and then take the finished masters to New York, where he would try to peddle his product for a five percent royalty on net sales. Unfortunately, even when somebody purchased his masters, they were never promoted properly; and if they did sell, royalties were rarely accounted for.

It was a tough racket, but Gordy persevered. His first break came in 1957 when Brunswick Records bought a song he had written, called "Reet Petite," for Jackie Wilson. "Reet Petite" was a pop hit, and though his profit only amounted to $1000, several successful followups for Wilson and Brunswick soon established Berry Gordy as Detroit's leading songwriter. But that was not enough: Gordy was determined to produce and market his own music himself.

The Motown mythology has it that Berry Gordy, fresh off an automobile assembly line, borrowed $700 to start his company. In truth, by 1959 Gordy was a prospering songwriter; he first borrowed money, not to start a label, but to go into independent production.

At the time, he had his eye on a local singer named Marv Johnson. Their first joint effort, "Come to Me," was leased to United Artists; although it was only a modest hit (Number 30 on the pop charts), it gave an indication of where Gordy was headed.

The song itself was slight: simple lyrics set to a stock rock chord progression (compare Gordy's smash hit for Wilson, "Lonely Teardrops"). But to accompany Johnson, who followed in the gospel footsteps of Clyde McPhatter and Wilson, Gordy added a churchy female chorus for some call-and-response trades (shades of Ray Charles), and a bubbling male bassman (shades of Clyde McPhatter's "A Lover's Question" on Atlantic). Instrumentally, the record was anchored by a persistent baritone sax and tambourine, with a flute break in the middle (recalling Bobby Day's "Rockin-Robin"). The result was a clean R&B record that sounded as white as it did black.

Gordy perfected this gospel-pop fusion in the months that followed, and by 1960 he'd made two similarly styled Top Ten hits with Johnson, "You Got What It Takes" and "I Love the Way You Love." After leasing yet another hit single, "Money" by Barrett Strong, to Anna, a label owned by his sister, Gordy decided to form his own label: Tammie, soon changed to Tamla Records.

It wasn't surprising that the first Tamla hit of any size belonged to a vocal group called the Miracles. Gordy had discovered the quintet working in Detroit; although initially attracted by the group's only female member, Claudette—the lead singer's girlfriend—Gordy quickly realized the potential of the Miracles' songwriter, Smokey Robinson, who also happened to be the lead singer. He leased a few Miracles sides to Chess Records in 1959, but it was only with "Way Over There" on Tamla in 1960 that the group (and label) began to sell records: 60,000 on that release. In a few months, that would seem like chicken feed.

Smokey Robinson, in action, in 1963: this was soul, this was rock, this was Motown. (Popsie/N.Y.)

*Marvin Gaye, the Prince of Motown: cool,
sexy and built to last (Michael Ochs Archives)*

As a followup to "Way Over There," Robinson came up with a song called "Shop Around." Gordy found the first master too sluggish and called the Miracles back into the studio at three o'clock one morning to cut a new version at a faster tempo. The result was Tamla's first real hit; by January, "Shop Around" had reached Number Two on the pop charts, and Gordy's company was in the black.

The little bungalow on West Grand was teeming with activity as a host of aspiring local singers and songwriters flocked to Gordy's studio. With Robinson and Gordy handling the bulk of composing and producing, Tamla and Gordy's growing family of labels (Motown and Gordy were formed in the next two years, later to be joined by Soul, V.I.P. and Rare Earth) began to log an impressive track record, their hits ranging from Eddie Holland's slick "Jamie" to the Contours' raunchy "Do You Love Me." By the end of 1962, the Gordy roster included Mary Wells, the Marvelettes and Marvin Gaye.

Although several of these acts, particularly Mary Wells and the Marvelettes, made consistent inroads onto the pop charts, Motown's early productions differed markedly in feel and appeal, depending on who was doing the singing. Mary Wells cooed seductive lyrics, the Marvelettes declaimed the "girl group" sound, while Marvin Gaye and the Contours both rasped over rotgut rhythm tracks only one step removed from rural blues and gospel. Motown had hits, all right; but it hadn't quite yet evolved a distinctive sound.

From the beginning, Berry Gordy relied on a handful of dependable writers and producers. In late 1961, he began to expand his staff of writer/producers, and among the new additions was Lamont Dozier, a veteran of the local group scene who toiled in relative anonymity at Motown for a couple of years until he began a creative partnership with Motown cohorts Brian and Eddie Holland. In 1963 the fledgling trio of writers clicked. Working with Martha and the Vandellas, the Holland-Dozier-Holland team set out to refine and systematize the production techniques Gordy had pioneered with Marv Johnson. "Heat Wave," by Martha and the Vandellas inaugurated a three-year stretch that saw H-D-H amass 28 Top 20 pop hits.

As soul producers, they were little short of revolutionary. The trio rarely used standard song forms, opting instead for a simpler, more direct *ababcc* pattern, anchored by an endless refrain of the song's hook line. The effect of this cyclical structure was cumulative, giving records produced by Holland-Dozier-Holland a compulsive momentum; even better, the constant refrains and consistent use of repetition helped make their hits ubiquitous: after you'd heard one, you'd heard them all—and each and every one of them was immediately familiar, subtly distinctive and quite unforgettable.

Lyrically, the H-D-H hits were nothing to write home about. But what mattered was their sense of structure, and the musi-

cal devices the trio used to animate that structure. Following Gordy's lead, they exploited gospelish vocal gestures in a pop context, now defined by their own streamlined approach. If the vocalists provided emotion, the band mounted a nonstop percussive assault highlighted by a "hot" mix, with shrill, hissing cymbals and a booming bass—anything to make a song jump out of a car radio. With tambourines rattling to a blistering 4-4 beat, the H-D-H sound, introduced on "Heat Wave" and perfected on records like the Four Tops' "Reach Out I'll Be There" and the Supremes' "You Can't Hurry Love" (both from 1966), came to epitomize what Motown would call "The Sound of Young America."

"Heat Wave" and the arrival of Holland-Dozier-Holland kicked Motown into high gear. By the late Sixties, Gordy's company had become one of the biggest black-owned corporations in America, as well as one of the most phenomenally successful independent recording ventures in the history of the industry. Motown succeeded beyond anyone's wildest expectations, and did so with black people controlling the company at the technical and business as well as musical and artistic levels.

The reasons behind Motown's popularity are diverse. Overseeing the whole operation was Berry Gordy, who endorsed the old bromide for predictable success: keep it simple. Under his tutelage, Motown's musicians took the concept of formula pop to a new level of sophistication and, thanks to the music's gospel/blues roots, visceral intensity.

The formulas might have quickly become tedious, of course, were it not for the ingenuity of Gordy's stable of producer/songwriters. Smokey Robinson, who handled the Temptations and Mary Wells in addition to the Miracles, was able to transfigure the most banal romantic motifs with clever lyrics and catchy hook lines; Norman Whitfield, who worked extensively with the Temptations as well as Marvin Gaye and Gladys Knight, was able to go beyond R&B clichés with punchy melodies and arrangements; such latecomers as Nickolas Ashford and Valerie Simpson, who produced the Marvin Gaye-Tammi Terrell duets as well as Diana Ross's solo records, were able to amplify secularized gospel lyrics with grandiose orchestra settings; and finally Holland-Dozier-Holland did nothing less than make The Formula a work of art in itself.

And then there was the Motown house band, an unheralded lot of the best R&B musicians in the Sixties. While Booker T. and the MGs helped define the style of Memphis soul, their largely anonymous Motown counterparts were expected to play only what they were told to play. As a result, the Motown rhythm section, which included the late Benny Benjamin on drums, James Jamerson on bass, Joe Messina on guitar, Earl Van Dyke on keyboards, the late James Giddons on percussion and Robert White on guitar, developed a unique dexterity and adaptability; yet a player like Jamerson nonetheless left his own mark on the music (the explosive bass line on Marvin Gaye and Tammi Terrell's "Ain't No Mountain High Enough" could

have come from no one else). Their existence was hardly glamorous, however. Usually paid a flat salary, the Motown musicians toiled in obscurity; where Booker T. and the MGs cut instrumental hits, Earl Van Dyke and the Soul Brothers played small lounges near West Grand for a few dollars, free pizza and the applause of local patrons. In the morning, it was back to the nine-to-five grind.

Indeed, the assembly-line atmosphere had something to do with Motown's success; if nothing else, it enabled Berry Gordy to keep tabs on his empire. He called his direction "quality control"; often, second-string Motown acts would have virtually no public exposure for months at a time while their recordings were polished to Gordy's satisfaction.

Even popular performers found themselves restricted as well as aided by the Motown hit machine. Gordy's innate caution dictated followups that only slightly altered the elements of the previous hit; a formula was mined until it was commercially exhausted. Thus "Heat Wave" reached Number Four on the pop charts; its soundalike successor, "Quicksand," got up to Number Eight—and only after the third go-around, when "Live Wire" stalled at Number 42, did Martha and the Vandellas get the opportunity to try something different.

Gordy's cultivation of Motown's image was equally restrictive. As soon as the company domination of Top 40 pop and soul was clear, Gordy hustled his star acts into "class" venues like the Copa, the Latin Casino, Las Vegas or bust. As if to confer respectability upon his artists, he encouraged albums such as *The Four Tops on Broadway* and *Temptations in a Mellow Mood*. Finally, Gordy devised something called "International Talent Management Incorporated" (I.T.M.I.), a kind of finishing school for Motown stars. I.T.M.I. taught a person how to sit, walk, talk and even how to smoke a cigarette with grace and elegance. Above all, it taught Motown's flock the good manners any adult member of the white middle class would expect to see exhibited at a swank nightclub.

Motown's roots may have been in gospel and blues, but its image was purely one of upward mobility and clean, wholesome fun (Gordy's vision of "Young America"). Motown's stars were groomed to offend no one; the songs they sang were equipped with romantic lyrics that could appeal to practically anyone; and the music itself was rarely demanding, or even aggressive in the tradition of Southern soul. Martha and the Vandellas' "Dancing in the Street" (1964) may have been interpreted by black activist/poet LeRoi Jones as an evocation of revolutionary times, but the closest thing to an overt political statement released by Motown in the mid-Sixties was Stevie Wonder's "Blowin' in the Wind" (1966). (Of course, ever sensitive to changing fashion, Motown eventually hopped on the political—and even psychedelic—bandwagon, with hits like the Temptations' "Psychedelic Shack," 1970, and Edwin Starr's "War," 1970, both Norman Whitfield compositions.)

One statistic gives eloquent testimony to Gordy's success in courting the white market. In 1966, Motown's "hit ratio"—the percentage of records released to make the national charts—was nothing less than 75%. It was an appropriately awesome achievement for a truly astonishing record company.

Although its hits have occasionally been dismissed on grounds of monotony, the truth of the matter is that Motown, even in its assembly-line prime, released a remarkably diverse lot of records, varying in sound, arrangement and feel. While Berry Gordy dictated the overall direction, and the producers and studio musicians stamped the sound, it was the performers themselves who ultimately conveyed the Motown image. Here is a brief guide to the artists who sang the Motown hits (omitting Stevie Wonder, who is discussed elsewhere):

Miracles. Most of Motown's roster consisted of Detroit acts unearthed at local talent shows; here as elsewhere, Smokey Robinson's Miracles set the pattern. When Robinson first approached Gordy late in 1957, most of the group was still in high school; three years later, when "Shop Around" hit, the Miracles' oldest member was barely 21.

During the next ten years, however, the Miracles became a seasoned troupe, while Robinson became one of the most prolific and popular producer/songwriters in the Motown stable. In person, the Miracles' performances were erratic, depending on the state of Smokey's fragile falsetto; by the end of a particularly grueling night, Robinson's voice, always so pure and controlled on record, often sounded frayed. In the studio, on the other hand, Robinson knew few rivals, composing and producing such torchy soul/pop hits as Mary Wells's "My Guy" (1964), the Temptations' "My Girl" (1965), and the Marvelettes' "The Hunter Gets Captured by the Game" (1967).

Smokey was his own best interpreter, and the Miracles remained one of Motown's most consistent groups throughout the Sixties. At the outset, their chief asset was the anguished eroticism conveyed by Robinson's pristine falsetto (listen to "You Can Depend on Me," from 1960). But by the mid-Sixties, Robinson had also blossomed as a composer and lyricist. As writer Charlie Gillett has pointed out, many of his finest lyrics hinged on an apparent contradiction: "I'm a choosy beggar," "I've got sunshine on a cloudy day," "The love I saw in you was just a mirage." Despite a spat of uptempo hits, from "Shop Around" and "Mickey's Monkey" (1963) to "Going to a Go-Go" (1965), the Miracles' forte was ballads. Here Robinson—whether confessing his dependence, as on "You've Really Got a Hold on Me" (1962), or pleading for forgiveness, as on "Ooo Baby Baby" (1965)—could use his voice to transcendent effect. "The Tracks of My Tears" (1965) remains one of the most emotionally demanding Motown singles of the Sixties.

Mary Wells. Just 17 when she auditioned for Berry Gordy in 1960, Mary Wells debuted on Motown with "Bye Bye Baby," a brassy, unrefined shouter. But she didn't really click until early

1962, after she was placed under Smokey Robinson's wing. Their partnership produced four Top Ten pop hits over a two-year span, including "The One Who Really Loves You" and "Two Lovers" (both 1962). A soft, cuddly stylist with just a hint of sassiness, Wells exited Motown shortly after her 21st birthday, lured by a lucrative contract with another label. Although her departure followed her biggest Motown hit ever, "My Guy" (1964), she proved unable to duplicate her success elsewhere.

Marvelettes. Motown's first and only real "girl group" was its most mysterious. Originally a quintet with Gladys Horton as lead, the Marvelettes survived numerous personnel, production and stylistic changes for almost a decade. Although the group was a consistent frontliner only in 1962, when "Please Mr. Postman" and "Playboy" both made the Top Ten, their repertoire of later hits included such gems as Smokey Robinson's suave "Don't Mess with Bill" (1966).

Martha and the Vandellas. Martha Reeves began her career at Motown inauspiciously enough, as a secretary in the A&R department. But Berry Gordy, realizing he had talent sitting right under his nose, sent Martha to work singing with her own group, the Vandellas. They debuted as the backup vocalists for Marvin Gaye on "Stubborn Kind of Fellow," and hit their stride with "Heat Wave" in 1963. Thanks to Reeves's aggressive and flamboyant style, the Vandellas escaped any categorization as an orthodox "girl group"; instead, they recorded some of the toughest mainline rock and roll to come out of Motown.

Reeves's main problem was one of excess, but Holland-Dozier-Holland wrote lyrics that succesfully capitalized on her shrillness: if her love wasn't like a "Live Wire," then she was falling in "Quicksand." Martha spurned, on the other hand, tended to sound forlorn or cross (as on "Love [Makes Me Do Foolish Things]," from 1965). The best Vandellas records were made with H-D-H; but after the atypically infectious "Jimmy Mack" in early 1967, the two teams went their separate ways. The result for Martha and the Vandellas was little short of disastrous. After 1967, the group never made the Top 40 again.

Marvin Gaye. A stage-shy performer who originally fancied himself a jazz singer, Marvin Gaye has been one of Motown's most enigmatic—and consistently popular—acts. First employed by Gordy as a session drummer, he debuted as a vocalist in 1962 with the herky-jerky "Stubborn Kind of Fellow," and proceeded to work with practically every producer in the Motown stable. With Holland-Dozier-Holland, he made "Can I Get a Witness" (1963), a rough-and-tumble gospel/blues track, and "How Sweet It Is (to Be Loved by You)" (1964), a medium-tempo shouter; with Smokey Robinson, he made "I'll Be Doggone" and "Ain't That Peculiar" (both 1965), two of Smokey's most compelling uptempo productions; with Norman Whitfield he made his historic "I Heard It through the Grapevine" (1968), an extraordinarily sophisticated record that nevertheless seemed to go back a good 400 years for the sources of its dark, utterly ominous incantations ("voodoo music," guitarist Mike

Bloomfield once called it). Later, with Ashford and Simpson, Gaye cut a memorable series of duets with the late Tammi Terrell, including "Your Precious Love" (1967) and "You're All I Need to Get By," both majestic, massively orchestrated affirmations of eternal love.

Always one of Motown's most idiosyncratic talents, Gaye entered into a second phase of his career in 1971, with the release of *What's Going On*, a self-composed and -produced song cycle that marked a liberation from Gordy's studio system. (Gaye had previously shown his skill as a songwriter as coauthor of "Dancing in the Streets," and as a writer/producer with the Originals, who cut two gloriously anachronistic hits, "Baby, I'm for Real," 1969, and "The Bells," 1970—both of which betray Gaye's past; he was once a member of the Moonglows, a vintage Fifties vocal group.) Songs like "What's Going On" and "Mercy Mercy Me (the Ecology)" captured a pensive and introspective Gaye, who managed to express the tentative and confused aura of the period; this strain in his work reached its peak with the magnificent "Inner City Blues" (also 1971), which featured a hushed, almost damned sound. Perhaps to cap his career, Gaye followed his more political work with a return, not to "love," but to pure eroticism, with the irresistible "Let's Get It On" (1973), a huge hit with some claim to being the sexiest record Motown ever produced.

Jr. Walker and the All Stars. The sole instrumental star at Motown was Jr. Walker, a veteran of Fifties R&B from Indiana. A gruff but lyrical tenor saxophonist, he specialized in sustained high wails, and his sense of timing was impeccable. Walker's early Motown hits leaned heavily on these instrumental signatures. With a minimum of production, "Shotgun" (1965) established his preeminence as a specialist in hot party discs. Gradually, however, Walker was integrated into the Motown system and encouraged to sing more. An affably raspy vocalist, he performed splendidly on the Holland-Dozier-Holland remake of "How Sweet It Is (to Be Loved by You)" (1966), then cut several string-laden hits, including "What Does It Take (to Win Your Love)" (1969), his last foray into the Top Ten.

Four Tops. Lamont Dozier recalls idolizing the Four Tops in the late Fifties, when the Detroit group was vacillating between R&B and a more sedate Mills Brothers style. He admired the quartet for its professionalism, but above all for its class. Almost five years later the Tops came to Motown. After an early attempt at making the group into bona fide supper-club singers, Holland-Dozier-Holland resurrected the Tops with a sharp midtempo plea called "Baby I Need Your Loving" (1964).

Built around lead singer Levi Stubbs's dramatic, piercing vocal delivery, the Tops/H-D-H hits came nonstop for almost four years. Records like "I Can't Help Myself" (1965) and "Reach Out I'll Be There" (1966) perfectly captured the mid-Sixties Motown sound: tambourines clapped on the off-beat, drummers pounded out indelicate 4-4 rhythms, and imaginative horn and string charts swirled above. Somewhere in the middle was Stubbs, hollering, cajoling and pleading with unflagging intensity. When Holland-Dozier-Holland left Motown, the group fell on hard times. The limitations of Stubbs's voice became increasingly apparent, and, after fitful success, the Tops joined the growing exodus from Motown in the early Seventies.

Temptations. While the Four Tops covered the frenetic side of the Motown sound, and the Miracles monopolized its romantic side, the Temptations quite simply stood as the finest vocal group in Sixties soul: they could outdress, outdance and outsing any competition in sight. It was a quintet distinguished by the breadth and balance of its singing talent, which ran the gamut from David Ruffin's harsh baritone to Eddie Kendricks's wispy falsetto.

The group had been formed in Detroit in the early Sixties, but many members came from the South. Eddie Kendricks had migrated to Detroit from Birmingham, Alabama, in hopes of rebuilding his old group, the Primes, and met Ruffin, a longtime Motor City resident born in Mississippi. The quintet's music reflected its background: of all the Motown acts, the Temptations were the closest to church and gospel roots.

Working primarily with Smokey Robinson and Norman Whitfield, the Temptations enjoyed a number of hits in a variety of styles. At the outset, Kendricks dominated the group, seeing the Tempts through such early R&B hits as "The Way You Do the Things You Do" (Robinson, 1964) and "Girl (Why You Wanna Make Me Blue)" (Whitfield, 1964). After Robinson's "My Girl" (1965), featuring Ruffin, introduced the group to a white audience, Robinson ran through a sequence of ballads pitting Ruffin's raspy voice against violins, a phase climaxing with Smokey's brilliant "Since I Lost My Baby" (1965). But the Temptations only hit their popular peak under Whitfield's tutelage. Unlike Holland-Dozier-Holland, Whitfield had a flair for spacious rhythmic arrangements. He also had the good sense to exploit the Temptations' versatility, moving from the gritty drive of "(I Know) I'm Losing You" (1966) to "You're My Everything" (1967), a melodramatic wall of sound that featured Ruffin and Kendricks swapping leads.

After Ruffin left the group in 1968, Whitfield turned to more declamatory material; influenced by Sly Stone, he brought the Tempts into the psychedelic era ("Cloud Nine," 1968), and began writing didactic social commentary ("Ball of Confusion," from 1970, for example). All these stratagems, however, could scarcely conceal the fact that Ruffin's departure had upset the group's distinctive balance; while the Temptations remained a potent commercial force, they rarely recaptured the glories of their earlier work. Nevertheless, two singles stand out: "I Can't Get Next to You" (1960), a neoclassical throwback to Whitfield's original style, and "Just My Imagination (Running Away with Me)" (1971), a gossamer showcase for Eddie Kendricks, who went solo shortly afterward.

Supremes. Without a doubt, Diana Ross and the Supremes were Berry Gordy's consummate commercial coup. In the span of five years, they amassed 12 Number One pop hits—five in a row after "Where Did Our Love Go" in 1964. A record unrivaled by any other female group in pop, it attests to the skill with which Holland-Dozier-Holland and Gordy packaged the Supremes and their music.

Discovered by Gordy in Detroit, where the trio had grown up together in the Brewster housing project, the Supremes floundered for almost a year until they were hooked up with Holland-Dozier-Holland in 1963. Their first collaboration, "When the Lovelight Starts Shining through His Eyes," a torrid, brassy uptempo track, became a modest pop hit in late 1963.

But H-D-H didn't have quite the right formula for the group down yet. After a followup flopped, they devised a medium-tempo song that accentuated Ross's insouciant delivery; "Where Did Our Love Go," a Number One pop hit in the summer of 1964, set the pattern for the singles that followed. Ross cultivated a nonchalant, almost fey style, while H-D-H turned numerous variations on the theme of lost love. During Holland-Dozier-Holland's tenure with the Supremes, the hits were automatic: between "Where Did Our Love Go" and the end of 1967, the Supremes released 15 singles; with one exception, they all made the Top Ten, and ten of them made Number One.

In a sense, the H-D-H Supremes hits are the purest expression of the Motown sound. The most compliant of Motown's artists, Diana Ross meshed seamlessly with the cyclical structure Holland-Dozier-Holland favored. Her singles resembled one long composition, each new release slightly modifying an element in the overall design, perhaps adding strings or punching the tempo up a notch. By "You Keep Me Hangin' On" (1966), the approach had become so polished that Diana Ross and the Supremes began to sound like an erotic gloss on the assembly-line existence Gordy had adopted in organizing Motown—and in this respect as well, the Supremes were the ultimate embodiment of the Motown ethos.

The key to the Supremes was Ross, who quickly overshadowed her fellow Supremes, visually as well as vocally. Peering with Keane eyes from under a variety of oversized wigs and baroque hairdos, her skinny frame draped in an array of slinky outfits, she was the very picture of the seductive self-pity her lyrics usually articulated ("Nothing but Heartaches"). At the same time, she became a paragon of black respectability; although Gordy found the Supremes "giggly and immature" when he signed them, he soon had reason to be proud of the most illustrious product of his in-house finishing school. By the time Ross left the group in 1969, the Supremes were fixtures on the supper-club circuit. Ross, of course, went on to stardom in the cinema. In 1976, Florence Ballard, one of the other original Supremes, died in Detroit; she had been on and off welfare the last few years.

Gladys Knight and the Pips. Before they came to Motown,

Gladys Knight and the Pips were sporadically popular ballad-eers; after they arrived, Norman Whitfield converted them into consistent hitmakers. On the original "I Heard It through the Grapevine" (1967), Knight was transformed into a fiery hard-edge vocalist, unleashing her scorn with startling fury. But unlike Martha Reeves, Knight was too versatile a singer to be limited to one role; by the early Seventies, the funky persona of Whitfield's productions (such as "The Nitty Gritty," in 1969) had given way to the vulnerable lover of "If I Were Your Woman" (1970). After leaving the label, Knight and the Pips, unlike most Motown alumni, actually consolidated their popularity by reverting to such glossy pop ballads as "Midnight Train to Georgia" (1973).

Jackson 5. "Discovered" by Diana Ross in a Gary, Indiana, club, this quintet of Hoosiers proved to be not only the last great Motown act, but also the last great gasp of Gordy's assembly-line entity. Fronted by the exuberant Michael Jackson, who dipped, spun and moved like a miniature James Brown, the Jackson 5 transcended all barriers of race and age in their appeal; they even hosted a Saturday morning cartoon show for a spell. Unlike many of their prepubescent imitators, however, the J5's talent was strictly for real. As the group matured, so did their music, but though later tracks like "Get It Together" (1973) and "Forever Came Today" (1975) were innovative, tight productions, the best Jackson 5 record remained their first for Motown, "I Want You Back" (1969). Catalyzed by a red-hot performance from ten-year-old Michael, the record explodes off the turntable with an intricate Sly-influenced arrangement featuring some of the toughest bass, drum, piano and guitar playing on any soul record anywhere.

While one facet of the Motown saga is well documented by the consistent popularity of its central acts, a much hazier part of the story has been buried beneath the glitter, purposely obscured to prevent any tarnishing of the corporate image.

To the outside world, Motown seemed like one big happy family. While a number of Motown stars have confirmed the accuracy of this picture in the early Sixties, by the middle of the decade serious problems had begun to appear. The autocratic determination that had carried Gordy's company to the top could not help but foster resentment, especially as Gordy's protégés became used to their status in the limelight.

Yet the company continued to control virtually every relevant detail of a performer's career, dictating the songs to be sung, the producers to be used, the singles to be released, the image to be presented to the public (even Motown's biggest stars remained curiously nondescript; reliable biographical details were few and far between). In financial affairs, Gordy governed his flock with patronizing authority: his younger stars were kept on allowances, ostensibly to help them avoid the pitfalls that had left other nouveau riche R&B stars penniless at 30.

His attitude toward the Supremes was typical. "We had some trouble with them at first," Gordy said in 1966. "You must be very strict with young artists. That instills discipline. But once they get a Number One record, they tend to get more independent. They start spending their money extravagantly.... After a year, they saw their mistakes and came to appreciate our handling of their affairs." Though their yearly income was in the five-figures—record royalties were divided equally—they were on an allowance of $50 a week.

In late 1967, the first major crack appeared in the Motown facade. Holland-Dozier-Holland demanded an accounting of their royalties. Shortly after a suit was initiated, the trio left Motown to form their own label and production firm: a move that neither Motown or H-D-H ever fully recovered from.

But internal dissension was not the only problem plaguing Gordy. By 1968, the industry had begun to catch up with the Motown sound. Without Holland-Dozier-Holland, neither the Supremes nor the Four Tops were able to maintain their popularity. Even worse, the label's new properties were becoming rare; only Gladys Knight and the Jackson 5 were able to match the style and talent of earlier Motown acts. Gordy himself increasingly retreated from company affairs, choosing instead to lavish his attention on Diana Ross, who was being groomed for a career in Hollywood.

In 1971, both Stevie Wonder and Marvin Gaye negotiated contracts giving them artistic control; the same year, the company moved its headquarters from Detroit to Los Angeles. The old studio system was dissolved, and many of the old stars drifted away: by 1975, Martha Reeves, Gladys Knight, the Jackson 5 and the Four Tops had all left. The company's music, with few exceptions, was no longer particularly distinctive; its quality was increasingly erratic. In the unkindest cut of all, Gamble and Huff's Philadelphia combine finally surpassed Motown as the leading purveyors of top-notch assembly-line black pop, using many of the same ingredients that Gordy had parlayed into a corporate empire.

Motown in its heyday, on the other hand, knew no peers. In the end, it was a wholly mechanical style and sound that roared and purred like a well-tuned Porsche. Contrived yet explosive, the very epitome of mass-produced pop yet drenched in the black tradition, the Motown hits of the Sixties revolutionized American popular music. Never again would black performers be confined to the fabled chitlin circuit; never again would black popular music be dismissed as a minority taste. For more than a decade, Berry Gordy and his many talented cohorts managed, with unerring verve and against all the odds, to translate a black idiom into "The Sound of Young America." Aesthetically as well as commercially, Motown's achievement will likely remain unrivaled for years to come.

Motown's Golden Decade

1962-1971

Eddie Holland, "Jamie" (Motown 1021; r☆6, ☆30, January). **Miracles,** "What's So Good about Good-Bye" (Tamla 54053; r☆16, ☆35, January). **Marvelettes,** "Twistin' Postman" (Tamla 54054; r☆13, ☆34, February). †**Mary Wells,** "The One Who Really Loves You" (Motown 1024; r☆2, ☆8, April). **Temptations,** "Dream Come True" (Gordy 7001; r☆22, May). †**Miracles,** "I'll Try Something New" (Tamla 54059; r☆11, ☆39, May). **Marvelettes,** "Playboy" (Tamla 54060; r☆4, ☆7, May). **Marvelettes,** "Beechwood 4-5789" b/w "Someday, Someway" (Tamla 54065; r☆7, ☆17, August). **Contours,** "Do You Love Me" (Gordy 7005; r☆1, ☆3, August). †**Mary Wells,** "You Beat Me to the Punch" (Motown 1032; r☆1, ☆9, September). **Marvin Gaye and the Vandellas,** "Stubborn Kind of Fellow" (Tamla 54068; r☆8, ☆46, October). †**Mary Wells,** "Two Lovers" (Motown 1035; r☆1, ☆7, December). †**Miracles,** "You've Really Got a Hold on Me" (Tamla 54073; r☆1, ☆8, December). **Marvelettes,** "Strange I Know" (Tamla 54072; r☆10, ☆49, December). **Supremes,** "Let Me Go the Right Way" (Motown 1034; r☆26, December).

1963

Contours, "Shake Sherry" (Gordy 7012; r☆21, ☆43, January). **Marvin Gaye,** "Hitch Hike" (Tamla 54075; r☆12, ☆30, February). †**Mary Wells,** "Laughing Boy" (Motown 1039; r☆6, ☆15, March). †**Miracles,** "A Love She Can Count On" (Tamla 54078; r☆21, ☆31, April). ***Martha and the Vandellas,** "Come and Get These Memories" (Gordy 7014; r☆6, ☆29, April). **Marvelettes;** "Locking Up My Heart" b/w "Forever" (Tamla 54077; r☆24, ☆44, May). **Marvin Gaye,** "Pride and Joy" (Tamla 54079; r☆2, ☆10, June). †**Mary Wells,** "Your Old Stand By" (Motown 1042; r☆8, ☆40, June). **Little Stevie Wonder,** "Fingertips–Part 2" (Tamla 54080; r☆1, ☆1, June). **Kim Weston,** "Love Me All the Way" (Tamla 54076; r☆24, July). ***Martha and the Vandellas,** "Heat Wave" (Gordy 7022; r☆1, ☆4, August). ***Miracles,** "Mickey's Monkey" (Tamla 54083; r☆3, ☆8, August). †***Mary Wells,** "What's Easy for Two Is So Hard for One" b/w "You Lost the Sweetest Boy" (Motown 1048; r☆8, ☆22, October). ***Marvin Gaye,** "Can I Get a Witness" (Tamla 54087; r☆15, ☆22, November). †**Marvelettes,** "As Long as I Know He's Mine" (Tamla 54088; ☆47, November). ***Martha and the Vandellas,** "Quicksand" (Gordy 7025; ☆8, November). ***Miracles,** "I Gotta Dance to Keep from Crying" (Tamla 54089; ☆35, November). ***Supremes,** "When the Lovelight Starts Shining through His Eyes" (Motown 1051; ☆23, November).

1964

***Martha and the Vandellas,** "Live Wire" (Gordy 7027; ☆42, February). †**Marvelettes,** "He's a Good Guy" (Tamla 54091; ☆55, February). †**Temptations,** "The Way You Do the Things You Do" (Gordy 7028; ☆11, February). †**Temptations,** "(You Can't Let the Boy Overpower) The Man in You" (Tamla 54092; ☆59, March). ***Marvin Gaye,** "You're a Wonderful One" (Tamla 54093; ☆15, March). †**Mary Wells,** "My Guy" (Motown 1056; ☆1, April). **Contours,** "Can You Do It" (Gordy 7029; ☆41, April). **Martha and the Vandellas,** "In My Lonely Room" (Gordy 7031; ☆44, April). **Brenda Holloway,** "Every Little Bit Hurts" (Tamla 54094; ☆13, May). **Marvin Gaye and Mary Wells,** "What's the Matter with You Baby" b/w "Once upon a Time" (Motown 1057; ☆17, May). **Eddie Holland,** "Just Ain't Enough Love" (Motown 1058; ☆54, May). †**Temptations,** "I'll Be in Trouble" (Gordy 7032; ☆33, May). **Marvin Gaye,** "Try It Baby" (Tamla 54095; ☆15, June). **Stevie Wonder,** "Hey Harmonica Man" (Tamla 54096; ☆29, June). †**Miracles,** "I Like It like That" (Tamla 54098; ☆27, June). †**Marvelettes,** "You're My Remedy" (Tamla 54097; ☆48, July). ***Supremes,** "Where Did Our Love Go" (Motown 1060; ☆1, July). **Brenda Holloway,** "I'll Always Love You" (Tamla 54099; ☆60, August). ***Four Tops,** "Baby I Need Your Loving" (Motown 1062; ☆11, August). **Martha and the Vandellas,** "Dancing in the Street" (Gordy 7033; ☆2, August). **Eddie Holland,** "Candy to Me" (Motown 1063; ☆58, August). ○**Temptations,** "Girl (Why You Wanna Make Me Blue)" (Gordy 7035; ☆26, September). ***Marvin Gaye,** "Baby Don't You Do It" (Tamla 54101; ☆27, September). †**Miracles,** "That's What Love Is Made Of" (Tamla 54102; ☆35, September). ***Supremes,** "Baby Love" (Motown 1066; ☆1, October). **Velvelettes,** "Needle in a Haystack" (V.I.P. 25007; ☆45, October). ○**Marvelettes,** "Too Many Fish in the Sea" (Tamla 54105; r☆15, ☆25, November). ***Four Tops,** "Without the One You Love" (Motown 1069; ☆43, November). ***Supremes,** "Come See about Me" (Motown 1068; r☆3, ☆1, November). **Martha and the Vandellas,** "Wild One" (Gordy 7036; ☆34, December). ***Marvin Gaye,** "How Sweet It Is to Be Loved by You" (Tamla 54107; r☆4, ☆6, December). †**Miracles,** "Come On Do the Jerk" (Tamla 54109; ☆50, December). **Contours,** "Can You Jerk like Me" (Gordy 7037; r☆15, ☆47, December).

1965

†**Temptations,** "My Girl" (Gordy 7038; r☆1, ☆1, January). **Velvelettes,** "He Was Really Sayin' Somethin' " (V.I.P. 25013; r☆21, January). **Four Tops,** "Ask the Lonely" (Motown 1073; r☆9, ☆24, February). **Jr. Walker and the All Stars,** "Shotgun" (Soul 35008; r☆1, ☆4, February). ***Supremes,** "Stop! In the Name of Love" (Motown 1074; r☆2, ☆1, February). ***Martha and the Vandellas,** "Nowhere to Run" (Gordy 7039; r☆5, ☆8, February). †**Brenda Holloway,** "When I'm Gone" (Tamla 54111; r☆12, ☆25, March). **Marvin Gaye,** "I'll Be Doggone" (Tamla 54112; r☆1, ☆8, March). †**Temptations,** "It's Growing" (Gordy 7040; r☆3, ☆18, April). †**Miracles,** "Ooo Baby Baby" (Tamla 54113; r☆4, ☆16, April). ***Supremes,** "Back in My Arms Again" (Motown 1075; r☆1, ☆1, May). ***Four Tops,** "I Can't Help Myself" (Motown 1076; r☆1, ☆1, May). **Jr. Walker and the All Stars,** "Do the Boomerang" (Soul 35012; r☆10, ☆36, June). **Marvelettes,** "I'll Keep Holding On" (Tamla 54116; r☆11, ☆34, June). †**Miracles,** "The Tracks of My Tears" (Tamla 54118; r☆2, ☆16, July). **Spinners,** "I'll Always Love You" (Motown 1078; r☆8, ☆35, July). **Marvin Gaye,** "Pretty Little Baby" (Tamla 54117; r☆16, ☆25, July). †**Temptations,** "Since I Lost My Baby" b/w "You've Got to Earn It" (Gordy 7043; r☆4, ☆17, July). ***Four Tops,** "It's the Same Old Song" (Motown 1081; r☆2, ☆5, August). ***Supremes,** "Nothing but Heartaches" (Motown 1080; r☆6, ☆11, August). **Jr. Walker and the All Stars,** "Shake and Fingerpop" b/w "Cleo's Back" (Soul 35013; r☆7, ☆29, August). †**Contours,** "First I Look at the Purse" (Gordy 7044; r☆12, August). **Marvelettes,** "Danger Heartbreak Dead Ahead" (Tamla 54120; r☆11, September). **Martha and the Vandellas,** "You've Been in Love Too Long" b/w "Love (Makes Me Do Foolish Things)" (Gordy 7045; r☆22, ☆36, September). **Stevie Wonder,** "High Heel Sneakers" (Tamla 54119; r☆30, September). ***Kim Weston,** "Take Me in Your Arms (Rock Me a Little While)" (Gordy 7046; r☆4, ☆50, October). †**Marvin Gaye,** "Ain't That Peculiar" (Tamla 54122; r☆1, ☆8, October). †**Miracles,** "My Girl Has Gone" (Tamla 54123; r☆3, ☆14, October). †**Temptations,** "My Baby" b/w "Don't Look Back" (Gordy 7047; r☆4, ☆13, October). ***Supremes,** "I Hear a Symphony" (Motown 1083; r☆2, ☆1, November). ***Four Tops,** "Something about You" (Motown 1084; r☆9, ☆19, November).

1966

Stevie Wonder, "Uptight (Everything's Alright)" (Tamla 54124; r☆1, ☆3, January). †**Miracles,** "Going to a Go-Go" (Tamla 54127; r☆2, ☆11, January). †**Marvelettes,** "Don't Mess with Bill" (Tamla 54126; r☆3, ☆7, January). ***Supremes,** "My World Is Empty without You" (Motown 1089; r☆10, ☆5, January). **Tammi Terrell,** "I Can't Believe You Love Me" (Motown 1086; r☆27, January). **Jr. Walker and the All Stars,** "Cleo's Mood" (Soul 35017; r☆14, ☆50, January). **Martha and the Vandellas,** "My Baby Loves Me" (Gordy 7048; r☆3, ☆22, February). **Elgins,** "Darling Baby" (V.I.P. 25029; r☆4, February). †**Marvin Gaye,** "One More Heartache" (Tamla 54129; r☆4, ☆29, February). ***Isley Brothers,** "This Old Heart of Mine (Is Weak for You)" (Tamla 54128; r☆6, ☆12, February). ***Four Tops,** "Shake Me, Wake Me (When It's Over)" (Motown 1090; r☆5, ☆18, March). †**Temptations,** "Get Ready" (Gordy 7049; r☆1, ☆29, March). **Kim Weston,** "Helpless" (Gordy 7050; r☆13, March). **Stevie Wonder,** "Nothing's Too Good for My Baby" b/w "With a Child's Heart" (Tamla 54130; r☆4, ☆20, April). **Monitors,** "Greetings (This Is Uncle Sam)" (V.I.P. 25032; r☆21, April). ***Jr. Walker and the All Stars,** "I'm a Road Runner" (Soul 35015; r☆4, ☆20, May). ***Supremes,** "Love Is like an Itching in My Heart" (Motown 1094; r☆7, ☆9, May). †**Marvelettes,** "You're the One" (Tamla 54131; r☆20, ☆48, May). **Spinners,** "Truly Yours," (Motown 1093; r☆16, May). ○**Temptations,** "Ain't Too Proud to Beg" (Gordy 7054; r☆1, ☆13, May). **Tammi Terrell,** "Come On and See Me" (Motown 1095; r☆25, June). †**Marvin Gaye,** "Take This Heart of Mine" (Tamla 54132; r☆16, ☆44, June). **Contours,** "Just a Little Misunderstanding" (Gordy 7052; r☆18, June). **Four Tops,** "Loving You Is Sweeter than Ever" (Motown 1096; r☆12, ☆45, June). **Miracles,** "Whole Lot of Shakin' in My Heart" (Tamla 54134; r☆20, ☆46, June). **Stevie Wonder,** "Blowin' in the Wind" (Tamla 54136; r☆1, ☆9, July). **Jimmy Ruffin,** "What Becomes of the Broken Hearted" (Soul 35022; r☆6, ☆7, August). **Jr. Walker and the All Stars,** "How Sweet It Is (to Be Loved by You)" (Soul 35024; r☆3, ☆18, August). ***Supremes,** "You Can't Hurry Love" (Motown 1097; r☆1, ☆1, August). ○**Temptations,** "Beauty Is Only Skin Deep" (Gordy 7055; r☆1, ☆3, August). ***Marvin Gaye,** "Little Darling, I Need You" (Tamla 54138; r☆10, ☆47, August). ***Four Tops,** "Reach Out I'll Be There" (Motown 1098; r☆1, ☆1, September). ***Elgins,** "Heaven Must Have Sent You" (V.I.P. 25037; r☆9, ☆50, September). ***Supremes,** "You Keep Me Hangin' On" (Motown 1101; r☆1, ☆1, November). ***Martha and the Vandellas,** "I'm Ready for Love" (Gordy 7056; r☆2, ☆9, November). **Stevie Wonder,** "A Place in the Sun" (Tamla 54139; r☆3, ☆9, November). ***Miracles,** "(Come 'Round Here) I'm the One You Need" (Tamla 54140; r☆4, ☆17, November). ○**Temptations,** "(I Know) I'm Losing You" (Gordy 7057; r☆1, ☆8, November). ***Four Tops,** "Standing in the Shadows of Love" (Motown 1102; r☆2, ☆6, December). **Jimmy Ruffin,** "I've Passed This Way Before" (Soul 35027; r☆10, ☆17, December).

1967

Marvin Gaye and Kim Weston, "It Takes Two" (Tamla 54141; r☆4, ☆14, January). †**Marvelettes,** "The Hunter Gets Captured by the Game" (Tamla 54143; r☆2, ☆13, February).* **Supremes,** "Love Is Here and Now You're Gone" (Motown 1103; r☆1, ☆1, February). †**Smokey Robinson and the Miracles,** "The Love I Saw in You Was Just a Mirage" (Tamla 54145; r☆10, ☆20, March). ***Martha and the Vandellas,** "Jimmy Mack" (Gordy 7058; r☆1, ☆10, March). **Jr. Walker and the All Stars,** "Pucker Up Buttercup" (Soul 35030; r☆11, ☆31, March). * **Four Tops,** "Bernadette" (Motown 1104; r☆3, ☆4, March). **Jimmy Ruffin,** "Gonna Give Her All the Love I've Got" (Soul 35032; r☆14, ☆29, April). * **Supremes,** "The Happening" (Motown 1107; r☆12, ☆1, April). **Brenda Holloway,** "Just Look What You've Done" (Tamla 54148; r☆21, April). **Stevie Wonder,** "Hey Love" b/w "Travelin' Man" (Tamla 54147; r☆9, ☆32, May). **Temptations,** "All I Need" (Gordy 7061; r☆2, ☆8, May). **Marvelettes,** "When You're Young and in Love" (Tamla 54150; r☆9, ☆23, May). **Marvin Gaye and Tammi Terrell,** "Ain't No Mountain High Enough" (Tamla 54149; r☆3, ☆19, June). ***Four Tops,** "7 Rooms of Gloom" (Motown 1110; r☆10, ☆14, June). †**Smokey Robinson and the Miracles,** "More Love" (Tamla 54152; r☆5, ☆23, June). **Stevie Wonder,** "I Was Made to Love Her" (Tamla 54151; r☆1, ☆2, June). ***Marvin Gaye,** "Your Unchanging Love" (Tamla 54153; r☆7, ☆33, July). ○**Gladys Knight and the Pips,** "Everybody Needs Love" (Soul 35034; r☆3, ☆39, July). ○**Temptations,** "You're My Everything" (Gordy 7063; r☆3, ☆6, August). ***Diana Ross and the Supremes,** "Reflections" (Motown 1111; r☆4, ☆2, August). **Jimmy Ruffin,** "Don't You Miss Me a Little Bit Baby" (Soul 35035; r☆27, August). **Martha and the Vandellas,** "Love Bug Leave My Heart Alone" (Gordy 7062; r☆14, ☆25, September). ***Four Tops,** "You Keep Running Away" (Motown 1113; r☆7, ☆19, September). ‡**Marvin Gaye and Tammi Terrell,** "Your Precious Love" (Tamla 54156; r☆2, ☆5, September). **Stevie Wonder,**

"I'm Wondering" (Tamla 54157; r☆4, ☆12, October). ○**Temptations,** "(Loneliness Made Me Realize) It's You That I Need" (Gordy 7065; r☆3, ☆14, October). ○**Gladys Knight and the Pips,** "I Heard It through the Grapevine" (Soul 35039; r☆1, ☆2, October). †**Smokey Robinson and the Miracles,** "I Second That Emotion" (Tamla 54159; r☆1, ☆4, November). **Martha Reeves and the Vandellas,** "Honey Chile" (Gordy 7067; r☆5, ☆11, November). *****Diana Ross and the Supremes,** "In and Out of Love" (Motown 1116; r☆16, ☆9, November). *****Jr. Walker and the All Stars,** "Come See about Me" (Soul 35041; r☆8, ☆24, December). ‡**Marvin Gaye and Tammi Terrell,** "If I Could Build My Whole World around You" b/w "If This World Were Mine" (Tamla 54161; r☆2, ☆10, December). †**Marvelettes,** "My Baby Must Be a Magician" (Tamla 54158; r☆8, ☆17, December).

1968

○**Temptations,** "I Wish It Would Rain" (Gordy 7068; r☆1, ☆4, January). **Marvin Gaye,** "You" (Tamla 54160; r☆7, ☆34, February). ○**Gladys Knight and the Pips,** "The End of Our Road" (Soul 35042; r☆5, ☆15, February). *****Four Tops,** "Walk Away Renee" (Motown 1119; r☆15, ☆14, February). †**Smokey Robinson and the Miracles,** "If You Can Want" (Tamla 54162; r☆3, ☆11, March). *****Diana Ross and the Supremes,** "Forever Came Today" (Motown 1122; r☆17, ☆28, March). **Stevie Wonder,** "Shoo-Be-Doo-Be-Doo-Da-Day" (Tamla 54165; r☆1, ☆9, April). **Bobby Taylor and the Vancouvers,** "Does Your Mama Know about Me" (Gordy 7069; r☆5, ☆29, April). **Isley Brothers,** "Take Me in Your Arms (Rock Me a Little While)" (Tamla 54164; r☆22, April). ‡**Marvin Gaye and Tammi Terrell,** "Ain't Nothing like the Real Thing" (Tamla 54163; r☆1, ☆8, April). ○**Temptations,** "I Could Never Love Another (after Loving You)" (Gordy 7072; r☆1, ☆13, May). **Shorty Long,** "Here Comes the Judge" (Soul 35044; r☆4, ☆8, June). †**Smokey Robinson and the Miracles,** "Yester Love" (Tamla 54167; r☆9, ☆31, June). †**Marvelettes,** "Here I Am Baby" (Tamla 54166; r☆14, ☆44, June). ○**Gladys Knight and the Pips,** "It Should Have Been Me" (Soul 35045; r☆9, ☆40, June). **Stevie Wonder,** "You Met Your Match" (Tamla 54168; r☆2, ☆35, August). ‡**Marvin Gaye and Tammi Terrell,** "You're All I Need to Get By" (Tamla 54169; r☆1, ☆7, August). ○**Temptations,** "Please Return Your Love to Me" (Gordy 7074; r☆4, ☆26, August). †**Smokey Robinson and the Miracles,** "Special Occasion" (Tamla 54172; r☆4, ☆26, August). **Jr. Walker and the All Stars,** "Hip City—Part 2" (Soul 35048; r☆7, ☆31, August). ○**Gladys Knight and the Pips,** "I Wish It Would Rain" (Soul 35047; r☆15, ☆41, September). **Marvin Gaye,** "Chained" (Tamla 54170; r☆8, ☆32, September). ‡**Marvelettes,** "Destination: Anywhere" (Tamla 54171; r☆28, October). ‡**Marvin Gaye and Tammi Terrell,** "Keep On Lovin' Me Honey" (Tamla 54173; r☆11, ☆24, October). *****Four Tops,** "I'm in a Different World" (Motown 1132; r☆23, October). **Diana Ross and the Supremes,** "Love Child" (Motown 1135; r☆2, ☆1, October). **Stevie Wonder,** "For Once in My Life" (Tamla 54174; r☆2, ☆2, November). **Bobby Taylor and the Vancouvers,** "Malinda" (Gordy 7079; r☆16, ☆48, November). ○**Temptations,** "Cloud Nine" (Gordy 7081; r☆2, ☆6, November). ○**Marvin Gaye,** "I Heard It through the Grapevine" (Tamla 54176; r☆1, ☆1, November). **Diana Ross and the Supremes and the Temptations,** "I'm Gonna Make You Love Me" (Motown 1137; r☆2, ☆2, December).

1969

†**Smokey Robinson and the Miracles,** "Baby, Baby Don't Cry" (Tamla 54178; r☆3, ☆8, January). **Jr. Walker and the All Stars,** "Home Cookin'" (Soul 35055; r☆19, ☆42, February). **Diana Ross and the Supremes,** "I'm Livin' in Shame" (Motown 1139; r☆8, ☆10, February). ‡**Marvin Gaye and Tammi Terrell,** "Good Lovin' Ain't Easy to Come By" (Tamla 54179; r☆11, ☆30, February). **David Ruffin,** "My Whole World Ended (the Moment You Left Me)" (Motown 1140; r☆2, ☆9, February). **Edwin Starr,** "Twenty-Five Miles" (Gordy 7083; r☆6, ☆6, February). ○**Temptations,** "Run Away Child, Running Wild" (Gordy 7084; r☆1, ☆6, March). ‡**Gladys Knight and the Pips,** "Didn't You Know" (Soul 35057; r☆11, March). **Diana Ross and the Supremes and the Temptations,** "I'll Try Something New" (Motown 1142; r☆8, ☆25, March). **Chuck Jackson,** "(You Can't Let the Boy Overpower) The Man in You" (Motown 1118; r☆27, April). ○**Marvin Gaye,** "Too Busy Thinking about My Baby" (Tamla 54181; r☆1, ☆4, May). ‡**Diana Ross and the Supremes,** "The Composer" (Motown 1146; r☆21, ☆27, May). ○**Temptations,** "Don't Let the Joneses Get You Down" (Gordy 7086; r☆2, ☆20, May). **Jr. Walker and the All Stars,** "What Does It Take (to Win Your Love)" (Soul 35062; r☆1, ☆4, May). **Diana Ross and the Supremes,** "No Matter What Sign You're Are" (Motown 1148; r☆17, ☆31, June). **Stevie Wonder,** "My Cherie Amour" b/w "I Don't Know Why" (Tamla 54180; r☆4, ☆4, June). †**Smokey Robinson and the Miracles,** "Doggone Right" b/w "Here I Go Again" (Tamla 54183; r☆7, ☆32, June). **Edwin Starr,** "I'm Still a Strugglin' Man" (Gordy 7087; r☆27, June). †**Smokey Robinson and the Miracles,** "Abraham, Martin and John" (Tamla 54184; r☆16, ☆33, July). **David Ruffin,** "I've Lost Everything I've Ever Loved" (Motown 1149; r☆11, July). ○**Gladys Knight and the Pips,** "The Nitty Gritty" (Soul 35063; r☆2, ☆19, July). ○**Temptations,** "I Can't Get Next to You" (Gordy 7093; r☆1, ☆1, August). ○**Marvin Gaye,** "That's the Way Love Is" (Tamla 54185; r☆2, ☆7, September). **Originals,** "Baby, I'm for Real" (Soul 35066; r☆1, ☆14, September). ○**Gladys Knight and the Pips,** "Friendship Train" (Soul 35068; r☆2, ☆17, November). **Jr. Walker and the All Stars,** "These Eyes" (Soul 35067; r☆3, ☆16, November). **Stevie Wonder,** "Yester-Me, Yester-You, Yesterday" (Tamla 54188; r☆5, ☆7, November). **Diana Ross and the Supremes,** "Someday We'll Be Together" (Motown 1156; r☆1, ☆1, November). **Jackson 5,** "I Want You Back" (Motown 1157; r☆1, ☆1, November). ‡**Marvin Gaye and Tammi Terrell,** "What You Gave Me"

(Tamla 54187; r☆6, ☆49, December). ○**Four Tops,** "Don't Let Him Take Your Love From Me" (Motown 1159; r☆25, ☆45, December). **David Ruffin,** "I'm So Glad I Fell For You" (Motown 1158; r☆18, December).

1970

○**Marvin Gaye,** "How Can I Forget" (Tamla 54190; r☆18, ☆41, January). ○**Temptations,** "Psychedelic Shack" (Gordy 7096; r☆2, ☆7, January). **Stevie Wonder,** "Never Had a Dream Come True" (Tamla 54191; r☆11, ☆26, February). **Originals,** "The Bells" (Soul 35069; r☆4, ☆12, February). **Jr. Walker and the All Stars,** "Gotta Hold On to This Feeling" (Soul 35070; r☆2, ☆21, February). **Supremes,** "Up the Ladder to the Roof" (Motown 1162; r☆5, ☆10, March). **Jackson 5,** "ABC" (Motown 1163; r☆1, ☆1, March). ○**Gladys Knight and the Pips,** "You Need Love like I Do (Don't You)" (Soul 35071; r☆3, ☆25, April). ‡**Marvin Gaye and Tammi Terrell,** "The Onion Song" (Tamla 54192; r☆18, ☆50, April). ○**Four Tops,** "It's All in the Game" (Motown 1164; r☆6, ☆24, May). **Rare Earth,** "Get Ready" (Rare Earth 5012; r☆20, ☆4, May). ‡**Diana Ross,** "Reach Out and Touch (Somebody's Hand)" (Motown 1165; r☆7, ☆20, May). ○**Temptations,** "Ball of Confusion" (Gordy 7099; r☆2, ☆3, May). ‡**Smokey Robinson and the Miracles,** "Who's Gonna Take the Blame" (Tamla 54194; r☆9, ☆46, June). **Jackson 5,** "The Love You Save" (Motown 1166; r☆1, ☆1, June). ○**Marvin Gaye,** "The End of Our Road" (Tamla 54195; r☆7, ☆40, June). **Stevie Wonder,** "Signed, Sealed, Delivered I'm Yours" (Tamla 54196; r☆1, ☆3, July). ○**Edwin Starr,** "War" (Gordy 7101; r☆3, ☆1, July). **Jr. Walker and the All Stars,** "Do You See My Love (for You Growing)" (Soul 35073; r☆3, ☆32, July). **Spinners,** "It's a Shame" (V.I.P. 25057; r☆4, ☆14, July). ‡**Diana Ross,** "Ain't No Mountain High Enough" (Motown 1169; r☆1, ☆1, August). **Originals,** "We Can Make It Baby" (Soul 35074; r☆20, August). **Rare Earth,** "(I Know) I'm Losing You" (Rare Earth 5017; r☆7, August). **Four Tops,** "Still Water (Love)" (Motown 1170; r☆4, ☆11, September). **Jackson 5,** "I'll Be There" (Motown 1171; r☆1, ☆1, September). ○**Temptations,** "Ungena Za Ulimwengu (Unite the World)" (Gordy 7102; r☆8, ☆33, October). **Stevie Wonder,** "Heaven Help Us All" (Tamla 54200; r☆2, ☆9, October). †**Smokey Robinson and the Miracles,** "The Tears of a Clown" (Tamla 54199; r☆1, ☆1, October). **David and Jimmy Ruffin,** "Stand by Me" (Soul 35076; r☆24, October). **Supremes,** "Stoned Love" (Motown 1172; r☆1, ☆7, November). **Gladys Knight and the Pips,** "If I Were Your Woman" (Soul 35078; r☆1, ☆9, November). ‡**Supremes and Four Tops,** "River Deep—Mountain High" (Motown 1173; r☆7, ☆14, December). ○**Edwin Starr,** "Stop the War Now" (Gordy 7104; r☆5, ☆26, December).

1971

Originals, "God Bless Whoever Sent You" (Soul 35079; r☆14, January). ‡**Diana Ross,** "Remember Me" (Motown 1176; r☆10, ☆16, January). **Four Tops,** "Just Seven Numbers (Can Straighten Out My Life)" (Motown 1175; r☆9, ☆40, January). **Spinners,** "We'll Have It Made" (V.I.P. 25060; r☆20, January). **Jackson 5,** "Mama's Pearl" (Motown 1177; r☆2, ☆2, February). ○**Temptations,** "Just My Imagination (Running Away with Me)" (Gordy 7105; r☆1, ☆1, February). **Marvin Gaye,** "What's Going On" (Tamla 54201; r☆1, ☆2, February). **Stevie Wonder,** "We Can Work It Out" (Tamla 54202; r☆3, ☆13, March). †**Smokey Robinson and the Miracles,** "I Don't Blame You at All" (Tamla 54205; r☆7, ☆18, March). **Jackson 5,** "Never Can Say Goodbye" (Motown 1179; r☆1, ☆2, April). ○**Edwin Starr,** "Funky Music Sho Nuff Turns Me On" (Gordy 7107; r☆6, May). ‡**Diana Ross,** "Reach Out I'll Be There" (Motown 1184; r☆17, ☆29, May). **Supremes,** "Nathan Jones" (Motown 1182; r☆8, ☆16, May). **Gladys Knight and the Pips,** "I Don't Want to Do Wrong" (Soul 35083; r☆2, ☆17, June). ○**Undisputed Truth,** "Smiling Faces Sometimes" (Gordy 7108; r☆2, ☆3, June). **Marvin Gaye,** "Mercy Mercy Me (the Ecology)" (Tamla 54207; r☆1, ☆4, July). **Four Tops,** "In These Changing Times" (Motown 1185; r☆28, July). **Smokey Robinson and the Miracles,** "Crazy about the La La La" (Tamla 54206; r☆20, July). **Jackson 5,** "Maybe Tomorrow" (Motown 1186; r☆3, ☆20, July). **Temptations,** "It's Summer" (Gordy 7109; r☆29, July). **Jr. Walker and the All Stars,** "Take Me Girl, I'm Ready" (Soul 35084; r☆18, ☆50, August). **Stevie Wonder,** "If You Really Love Me" (Tamla 54208; r☆4, ☆8, August). ○**Rare Earth,** "I Just Want to Celebrate" (Rare Earth 5031; r☆30, ☆7, August). ‡**Diana Ross,** "Surrender" (Motown 1188; r☆16, ☆38, September). **Four Tops,** "MacArthur Park (Part II)" (Motown 1189; r☆27, ☆38, September). **Marvin Gaye,** "Inner City Blues (Make Me Wanna Holler)" (Tamla 54209; r☆1, ☆9, October). **Martha Reeves and the Vandellas,** "Bless You" (Gordy 7110; r☆29, October). **Michael Jackson,** "Got to Be There" (Motown 1191; r☆4, ☆4, November). ○**Temptations,** "Superstar (Remember How You Got Where You Are)" (Gordy 7111; r☆8, ☆8, November). †**Smokey Robinson and the Miracles,** "Satisfaction" (Tamla 54211; r☆20, ☆49, November). **Jr. Walker and the All Stars,** "Way Back Home" (Soul 35090; r☆24, December). ○**Undisputed Truth,** "You Make Your Own Heaven and Hell Right Here on Earth" (Gordy 7112; r☆24, December). **Gladys Knight and the Pips,** "Make Me the Woman That You Go Home To" (Soul 35091; r☆3, ☆27, December). **Jackson 5,** "Sugar Daddy" (Motown 1194; r☆3, ☆10, Dec.)

***** = Record produced by Holland-Dozier-Holland
† = Record produced by Smokey Robinson
○ = Record produced by Norman Whitfield
‡ = Record produced by Ashford and Simpson
(Chart positions compiled from Joel Whitburn's *Record Research,* based on *Billboard* Pop and Rhythm and Blues charts. [NOTE: *Billboard* did not publish a separate R&B listing during 1964.])

Aretha Franklin
by Russell Gersten

If, as Robert Christgau once suggested, music is the chief meeting ground between black and white cultures, then Aretha Franklin is a pivotal figure. During her years of preeminence, 1967–'70, she had more going for her than virtually any other black popular musician—phenomenal record sales (nine million-selling singles and three million-selling albums), critical praise verging on hysteria, and massive popular support from both black and white audiences. She played the Apollo and the Fillmore West, appeared with Martin Luther King and won the respect of black poets. She came to symbolize the essence of what used to be called "soul."

Whereas most of her fellow soul singers—James Brown, Joe Tex, the Temptations—were culturally denigrated by some, Aretha was enshrined in an artistic tradition harking back to Bessie Smith and Billie Holiday. Subsequent female singers were compared to her, and her influence extended from Bette Midler to Chaka Khan of Rufus. She got what she asked for in her most popular hit record: respect.

The furor over Aretha has died down during the Seventies. The very excesses that made her so exciting in the Sixties—the melodrama; the running about, screaming and hollering; the gaudiness—began to be treated as embarrassments. People replayed the "Muscle Shoals" classics and thought them overrated. It is sometimes argued that she merely channeled the right energies at the right place and the right time.

But that view is deeply flawed. There is something profound and magical about the woman that references to formal aesthetics do not catch. On "Dr. Feelgood" and "Chain of Fools" she proved she could be a consummate R&B technician when she so desired. Either record could go down in the archives as a perfect example of blues phrasing, vocal control, and refined use of the gospel techniques of note-bending and melisma. But for better or worse, Aretha has always struggled to go beyond the limits of rhythm and blues. At her very first recording session in 1960, her producer, John Hammond, had mapped out four blues and gospel numbers. Aretha demanded that "Over the Rainbow" be included on the session. Seven years later, at her first hardcore soul session, she again fought for the light bossa-nova-based "Don't Let Me Lose This Dream," and gave one of her most memorable performances. Granted, this tendency has led to some of her most embarrassing disasters; it also has led to her greatest achievements—*Young, Gifted and Black*, *I Never Loved a Man the Way I Love You*, and "Day Dreaming."

A deep irony characterizes her career: her great dissatisfaction with what she is, was and will be. This contrasts strongly with the self-assurance and casual machismo of other great soul artists like Otis Redding and Ray Charles. At the peak of her career in 1968, when she had become virtually a legend in her own time, she told a reporter she "was 26," but felt like she "was going on 65."

Her vocal style, with its unexpected two-octave jumps and whoops, evokes a chaotic, unpredictable world, harboring meanings that are never obvious. For example, when blues singer Bobby Bland sang "Share Your Love with Me," he delicately and carefully interpreted the lyrics of the ballad. Aretha's version is disorganized by contrast. She rips the whole thing apart, slurring over key lines and emphasizing the syllables one would least expect. Her attitude is that no mere lyricist is going to tell *her* what the song is about. The moments of ecstasy reached there, and in Sam Cooke's "You Send Me," go well beyond the intentions of the songs' composers. Similarly, the ferocity of "Chain of Fools" is well out of the range of writer Don Covay or producer Jerry Wexler. At her best she shows an understanding of what can happen between two people, displaying a rare delicacy.

* * * *

Her musical career began when, as a young girl, she began singing in her father's church. She could draw on an almost mythical lineage: her father, whom she was always close to, was one of the most popular (and wealthiest) black ministers in the North; her mother was reputedly a great gospel singer; her first musical influences were Clara Ward, James Cleveland and Mahalia Jackson, gospel stars and fellow travelers on the evangelical circuit. After several years on the road with her father, she decided to try the big time of the pop world—New York, and producer John Hammond.

Hammond, the man who had produced and promoted Billie Holiday, Bessie Smith, Charlie Christian, and was soon to do the same for Bob Dylan, was duly impressed by this wild 18-year-old. "An untutored genius," he called her, "the best voice I've heard since Billie Holiday." He promptly signed her up and rushed her into the studio. Yet he was unable to do for her what he had done for the others.

The whys and wherefores are intricate, as is everything connected with her the years she spent at Columbia. The issue is in part sociological; 1960 may not seem like so long ago, but there still was such a thing as "race" music, music made to be distributed almost exclusively in black ghettos. That was the category in which Aretha's first single, "Today I Sing the Blues," was placed. It was a surprising success, considering the limited market. Unfortunately Columbia's A&R head, Mitch Miller (host of the popular "sing-along-with-Mitch" TV show), decided to do her a favor. He was going to make another Nancy Wilson or Nat "King" Cole out of her—a black crooner for the white masses. She got voice lessons, and big-time arrangers (like Bob Mersey, who also worked with Barbra Streisand). He got her big orchestras with violins; she was no longer allowed to accompany herself on piano. She was weaned from her rhythm and blues repertoire and assigned show tunes ("If Ever I Would Leave You"), jazz standards ("God Bless the Child") and Al Jolson tunes ("Rock-A-Bye Your Baby with a Dixie Melody,"

Aretha Franklin ('Sepia' magazine)

African and black nationalist affairs. Thus in 1971 we were confronted with an enigmatic new Aretha Franklin, wearing her natural hair and African clothes, singing tunes like "This Girl's in Love with You" and "Call Me," backed by large violin sections.

In the halcyon days, Franklin's AM hits were generally written by men; her own compositions were relegated to flip sides or album cuts. Now she turned the tables with "Spirit in the Dark" and "Day Dreaming." She flaunted her sensitivity and her aspirations as a poet at her audience, sometimes in an ungainly fashion. When she played the Apollo in 1974, the dancers bowed at her feet before she walked onstage to perform a solo piano medley of her own compositions. On "First Snow in Kokomo," she tackled a subject worthy of Eliot or Yeats—the mysterious processes by which some individuals pull themselves together, while others disintegrate. Her radiant *Young, Gifted and Black* album was a frank exploration of her failed marriage, and fittingly takes its place alongside the disillusioned, confessional work of writers like Doris Lessing or Anaïs Nin.

After *Young, Gifted and Black*, she needed a new direction. She knew she couldn't return to the Lady Soul of the Sixties, and that she had more or less exhausted her autobiographical repertoire. As the Seventies progressed and black music became more producer dominated, she became a culturally displaced figure. Her career deteriorated into a series of comebacks—often glorious ones like "Brand New Me," *Amazing Grace*, and the tour with saxophonist King Curtis (a respected Atlantic veteran who had accompanied Aretha on the label from the outset). Yet each was followed by a corresponding debacle. She developed an obsession with being exactly what she was not: a sophisticate, a great lady, a sexy, slinky Diana Ross type figure. Finally, like a protagonist in an existential novel, she assailed her own body, losing a massive amount of weight, parading onstage in minks and a rhinestone bikini.

Her albums became erratic and a bit bloated; but they almost always contained a couple of brilliant moments—her 1974 resurrection of the old Marvin Gaye-Tammi Terrell "Ain't Nothing like the Real Thing" is a perfect example. Franklin takes upbeat tune at a mournful pace. She sounds distracted and absent-minded during the first half, working at cross-purposes with the lyric. For no apparent reason, she assumes her lover has lost interest in her, and shrieks, "Let's stay together," denoting an unnerving, confusing emotion, given the context of the song. Then swiftly, intuitively, she leaps down an octave and gives a sublime reading of the next line: "I've got some memories to look back on." It's difficult to convey how she gives several meanings simultaneously. First, she indicates that for all of us, no thing, no relationship ever dies, that memory is stronger than reality. On the other hand, she tells us that whatever her current problems, however badly she's messed up now, *she's* got memories to look back on that you can't even

conceive: millions of people screaming at her, reaching out to touch her. And finally it is as if she wishes to confide the simple truth: she was great and unique, she knew it, the world knew it, and nothing can obliterate that truth.

The French filmmaker and critic Jean-Luc Godard put it this way (freely translated): "There are two kinds of artists. Some walk down the streets with their heads up, looking straight ahead. They look and plan and organize, and their work is smart and wise and well developed and sometimes great. This group is always admired.

"Then there's the other type of artist. They walk down the street with their heads down, lost in thought or daydreams. Every so often, they're obliged to lift their heads, always suddenly, embracing their field of vision in a series of rapid, oblique glances. This group *sees*. However confused or eccentric their style, they see with a wonderful clarity."

Aretha fits into the latter category. Long after the mediocre works are forgotten, the beauties of her intuitive, improvisatory work will remain.

Discography

Singles

"Today I Sing the Blues" (Columbia 41793; r☆10, 1960). "Won't Be Long" (Columbia 41923; r☆7, 1961). "Operation Heartbreak" b/w "Rock-a-Bye Your Baby with a Dixie Melody" (Columbia 42157; r☆6, ☆37, 1961). "Runnin' out of Fools" (Columbia 43113; ☆57, 1964). "One Step Ahead" (Columbia 43241; r☆18, 1965). "cry Like a Baby" (Columbia 43827; r☆27, 1966). "I Never Loved a Man (the Way I Love You)" b/w "Do Right Woman—Do Right Man" (Atlantic 2386; r☆1, ☆9, 1967). "Respect" (Atlantic 2403; r☆1, ☆1, 1967). "Lee Cross" (Columbia 44181; r☆31, 1967). "Baby I Love You" (Atlantic 2427; r☆1, ☆4, 1967). "Take a Look" (Columbia 44270; r☆28, 1967). "A Natural Woman" (Atlantic 2441; r☆2, ☆8, 1967). "Chain of Fools" (Atlantic 2464; r☆1, ☆2, 1967). "(Sweet Sweet Baby) Since You've Been Gone" b/w "Ain't No Way" (Atlantic 2486; r☆1, ☆5, 1968). "Think" b/w "You Send Me" (Atlantic 2518; r☆1, ☆7, 1968). "The House That Jack Built" b/w "I Say a Little Prayer" (Atlantic 2546; r☆2, ☆6, 1968). "See Saw" b/w "My Song" (Atlantic 2547; r☆9, ☆14, 1968). "The Weight" b/w "Tracks of My Tears" (Atlantic 2603; r☆3, ☆19, 1969). "I Can't See Myself Leaving You" (Atlantic 2619; r☆3, ☆19, 1969). "Share Your Love with Me" (Atlantic 2650; r☆1, ☆13, 1969). "Eleanor Rigby" (Atlantic 2683; r☆5, ☆17, 1969). "Call Me" (Atlantic 2706; r☆1, ☆13, 1970). "Spirit in the Dark" (Atlantic 2731; r☆3, ☆23, 1970). "Don't Play That Song" (Atlantic 2751; r☆1, ☆11, 1970). "Border Song (Holy Moses)" (Atlantic 2772; r☆5, ☆37, 1970). "You're All I Need to Get By" (Atlantic 2787; r☆3, ☆19, 1971). "Bridge over Troubled Water" b/w "Brand New Me" (Atlantic 2796; r☆1, ☆6, 1971). "Spanish Harlem" (Atlantic 2817; r☆1, ☆2, 1971). "Rock Steady" b/w "Oh Me Oh My" (Atlantic 2838; r☆2, ☆9, 1971). "Day Dreaming" (Atlantic 2866; r☆1, ☆5, 1972). "All the King's Horses" (Atlantic 2883; r☆7, ☆26, 1972). "Master of Eyes" (Atlantic 2941; r☆8, ☆33, 1973). "Angel" (Atlantic 2969; r☆1, ☆20, 1973). "Until You Come Back to Me (That's What I'm Gonna Do)" (Atlantic 2995; r☆1, ☆3, 1973). "I'm in Love" (Atlantic 2999; r☆1, ☆19, 1974). "Ain't Nothing like the Real Thing" (Atlantic 3200; r☆6, ☆47, 1974). "Without Love" (Atlantic 3224; r☆6, ☆45, 1974). "With Everything I Feel in Me" (Atlantic 3249; r☆20, 1975). "Mr. D.J. (5 for the D.J.)" (Atlantic 3289; r☆13, 1975).

Albums

Gospel Soul (Checker 10009). *The Tender, the Moving, the Swinging Aretha Franklin* (Columbia 8676; ☆69, 1962). *Runnin' out of Fools* (Columbia 9081; ☆84, 1964). *Yeah!* (Columbia 9151; ☆101, 1965). *Soul Sister* (Columbia 9321; ☆132, 1966). *I Never Loved a Man the Way I Love You* (Atlantic 8139; ☆2, 1967). *Aretha Franklin's Greatest Hits* (Columbia 9473; ☆94, 1967). *Aretha Arrives* (Atlantic 8150; ☆5, 1967). *Take a Look* (Columbia 9554; ☆173, 1967). *Aretha: Lady Soul* (Atlantic 8176; ☆2, 1968). *Aretha Now* (Atlantic 8186; ☆3, 1968). *Aretha in Paris* (Atlantic 8207; ☆13, 1968). *Aretha Franklin: Soul '69* (Atlantic 8212; ☆15, 1969). *Aretha's Gold* (Atlantic 8227; ☆18, 1969). *This Girl's in Love with You* (Atlantic 8248; ☆17, 1970). *Spirit in the Dark* (Atlantic 8265; ☆25, 1970). *Aretha Live at Fillmore West* (Atlantic 7205; ☆7, 1971). *Aretha's Greatest Hits* (Atlantic 8295; ☆19, 1971). *Young, Gifted and Black* (Atlantic 8213; ☆11, 1972). *Amazing Grace* (with James Cleveland) (Atlantic 2-906; ☆7, 1972). *In the Beginning/The World of Aretha Franklin (1960-1967)* (Columbia 31355; ☆160, 1972). *Hey Now Hey (The Other Side of the Sky)* (Atlantic 7265; ☆30, 1973). *Let Me in Your Life* (Atlantic 7292; ☆14, 1974). *The First 12 Sides* (Columbia 31953; 1973). *With Everything I Feel in Me* (Atlantic 18116; ☆57, 1974). *You* (Atlantic 18151; ☆83, 1975).

(Chart positions taken from Joel Whitburn's *Record Research*, compiled from *Billboard* Pop and LPs charts, except where otherwise indicated; r☆ = position on *Billboard* Rhythm and Blues chart.)

B.B. King
by Peter Guralnick

Almost single-handedly B.B. King introduced the blues to white America. He did so largely through the mid-Sixties British invasion—for while there are many styles of blues guitar (and King is himself heir to a long tradition), it was King's style of rapidly picked single notes, embellishing and extending the vocal but rarely supporting it with full-bodied chords, which prevailed to create a whole blues-tinged vocabulary for modern rock. In the process, King himself even managed to achieve something like widespread popularity with the rock audience.

B.B. King was born Riley B. King on a plantation near Itta Bena, Mississippi, on September 16th, 1925. He got his name, and a good deal of his early fame, from the radio show he did on station WDIA in Memphis from 1948–1952. WDIA, the first major radio outlet in the South to be black operated, if not black owned, was known as the Mother Station of the Negroes; Riley B. King was known as the Beale St. Blues Boy, later shortened to simply B.B.

He came to Memphis from a classic background in the blues. His cousin is Bukka White, the great country bluesman. B.B. sang in gospel quartets as a boy, greatly admired Samuel McCrary and the Fairfield Four, and picked up a little bit of guitar from his aunt's brother-in-law, who was a preacher. It wasn't until he went into the army in 1943 that he started playing blues. When he got out shortly afterward (on a tractor driver's agricultural deferment), he started playing on the streets of nearby Mississippi towns, going just far enough away from home so that his family wouldn't catch him singing the "devil's music." It was Robert Jr. Lockwood, stepson of the legendary Robert Johnson, who helped him refine his T-Bone Walker and Charlie Christian influenced single-string guitar runs. And it was Sonny Boy Williamson, whom Lockwood accompanied in the jook joints and little backcountry plantation halls that made up a bluesman's professional career, who got King started in Memphis. There he met Rufus Thomas, a former vaudevillian and then emcee of the amateur talent contest at the Palace Theater. There, too, he completed his musical education.

B.B. King, more than any of the country bluesmen or even urban singers like Muddy Waters or Howlin' Wolf, is a self-made artist, his style assembled from a variety of sources. These sources include jazz and gospel and country music, and perhaps this eclecticism is the one reason for his unique susceptibility to white adaptation. In any case his music is not, like Muddy's or Wolf's, the product of a local or isolated tradition, the inescapable extension of a long historical line.

Instead, it is comprised of a series of conscious choices. His early music was very much influenced by the wide range of material (everything from R&B to Frank Sinatra, Nat "King" Cole, Vaughn Monroe and Frankie Lane) which he programmed as a disc jockey. To B.B. King, the theme of self-improvement has been a constant one, and he must have seen his radio show not just as a chance to convey his personality in a 15-minute live segment (like Sonny Boy or Wolf, Joe Hill Louis, and numerous other itinerant bluesmen turned disc jockeys), but also as an opportunity to better himself. He got his own two-hour show; he taught himself to speak more "properly"; he widened his frame of musical reference; and he acquired the modest, almost self-deprecating but self-assured manner that serves him to this day.

He started his recording career as a shouter very much in the vein of Roy Brown or Wynonie Harris. He relied heavily on the small-band arrangements (eight- or nine-piece) and riffing horn section of their particular brand of jump blues, over which his voice and guitar would forcefully ripple out—though never simultaneously. His vocals, originally all of the shouter variety, gradually took on more of a gospel hue, as he began to employ the full-throated phlegminess, falsetto effects, and melisma (stretching a single syllable over several notes) of the fervid quartet singer. The kind of material he performed drew heavily from the declamatory style of Louis Jordan. As for his guitar playing—well, in later years he was to point to Django Reinhardt and Charlie Christian as key influences, and it may well have been through Robert Lockwood or on his radio show that he was exposed to a considerable amount of their music—but most of his solos were pure T-Bone Walker and Lonnie Johnson: liquid, mellow, relying almost exclusively on the single string runs which they had popularized in the blues.

His first recordings were made in 1949, but his first big hit came in 1951 with "3 O'Clock Blues." Like nearly all of his later hits, "3 O'Clock" was not original with B.B. King but a very popular song for its composer, Lowell Fulson, some two years earlier. "Every Day I Have the Blues" came from Joe Williams via Fulson and Memphis Slim, "Sweet Sixteen" from Big Joe Turner, even "Sweet Little Angel," the song with which he has been most identified, from Tampa Red via Robert Nighthawk. It's all somewhat academic. Unlike many of his contemporaries, B.B. King had a wide-ranging curiosity and an extensive frame of reference. On each song he put his individual stamp.

Success meant the same thing for B.B. King as it did for any black R&B artist of the time: an endless round of one-nighters in joints not much better than the country shacks in which he had started out, culminating in 342 engagements in 1956 alone. After the Fifties, his popularity waned (he left in his wake a handful of Kings—Albert, Freddie, Earl, Little B.B., B.B. Junior), and in the Sixties, the era of soul, he frequently shared the bill with Bobby "Blue" Bland—a singer who had come up behind him in Memphis, had in fact started out as his driver—in a touring Battle of the Blues. Then around 1966, he was discovered by the white rock audience, thanks to the efforts of such influential guitarists as Mike Bloomfield and Eric Clapton. By

B.B. King in the mid-Fifties (Promotions Consolidated)

238

1969, he was a fixture at rock ballrooms like the Fillmores and was wearing his hair natural. In late 1969, he had his first (and only) Top 20 pop hit with "The Thrill Is Gone."

Today he is something of an institution. He has passed through adulation and emerged on the other side, if not without incident, then without overwhelmingly adverse effects. He has fathered a whole generation of rock guitarists from Bloomfield and Clapton to Jimmy Page, Jimi Hendrix and Alvin Lee. His goal over the years has continued to be self-improvement and a more widespread recognition of the blues. He has studied the Schillinger Method of Musical Composition, gotten his pilot's license, and appeared on network TV shows. Over and over in interviews he has stressed, "If Frank Sinatra can be tops in his field, Nat 'King' Cole in his, Bach and Beethoven in theirs, why can't I be great and known for it in blues? Because I don't know anybody else have kept as constant study, working as I have for 21 years, in blues." Today he plays Las Vegas. He has realized his ambition.

Discography

"3 O'Clock Blues" (RPM 339; r☆1, 1951). "You Know I Love You" (RPM 363; r☆1, 1952). "Story from My Heart and Soul" (RPM 374; r☆9, 1952). "Woke Up This Morning" (RPM 380; r☆5, 1953). "Please Love Me" (RPM 386; r☆2, 1953). "Please Hurry Home" (RPM 391; r☆8, 1953). "You Upset Me Baby" b/w "Whole Lotta Love" (RPM 416; r☆2, 1954). "Every Day I Have the Blues" b/w "Sneakin' Around" (RPM 421; r☆10, 1955). "Ten Long Years" (RPM 437; r☆12, 1955). "Crying Won't Help You" (RPM 451; r☆15, 1956). "Sweet Little Angel" b/w "Bad Luck" (RPM 468; r☆6, 1956). "On My Word of Honor" (RPM 479; r☆11, 1956). "Troubles, Troubles, Troubles" (RPM 492; r☆13, 1957). "You've Been an Angel" b/w "Please Accept My Love" (Kent 315; r☆9, 1958). "Sweet Sixteen" (Kent 330, r☆2, 1960). "Got a Right to Love My Baby" (Kent 333; r☆8, 1960). "Partin' Time" (Kent 346; r☆8, 1960). "Someday" b/w "Peace of Mind" (Kent 360; r☆7, 1961). "Gonna Miss You Around Here" (Kent 372; r☆17, 1962). "Rock Me Baby" (Kent 393; ☆34, 1964). "Don't Answer the Door" (ABC-Paramount 10856; r☆2, 1966). "The Jungle" (Kent 462; r☆17, 1967). "Paying the Cost to the Boss" (BluesWay 61015; r☆10, ☆39, 1968). "Why I Sing the Blues" (BluesWay 61024; r☆13, 1969). "Just a Little Love" (BluesWay 61029; r☆15, 1969). "The Thrill Is Gone" (BluesWay 61032; r☆3, ☆15, 1970). "So Excited" (BluesWay 61035; r☆14, 1970). "Hummingbird" (ABC 11268; r☆25, ☆48, 1970). "Chains and Things" (ABC 11280; r☆6, ☆45, 1970). "Ask Me No Questions" (ABC 11290; r☆18, ☆40, 1971). "Ain't Nobody Home" (ABC 11316; r☆28, ☆46, 1971).

Chart positions taken from Joël Whitburn's *Record Research,* compiled from *Billboard* Pop chart, unless otherwise indicated; r☆ = position on *Billboard* Rhythm and Blues chart.)

The Blues Revival
by Ed Ward

Records by black American bluesmen began to appear in Britain after the end of the second World War; some were British pressings leased by English jazz labels that presumably thought the music was jazz. Other blues discs were left behind by American GIs and sold in secondhand stores; still more came through the mails to kids like Mick Jagger who sent away to Chess Records in Chicago.

The principal "black music" trend in England in the Fifties, however, was "trad" jazz, a pallid but enthusiastic attempt to re-create the Chicago and New Orleans styles of the Twenties. The big name in trad was Chris Barber, who in the mid-Fifties began importing blues singers such as John Lee Hooker and Muddy Waters to play in his live programs. During these years Barber's band also occasionally included Alexis Korner and Cyril Davies, Englishmen who had been playing Sonny Terry-Brownie McGhee style blues together since 1953. Korner and Davies played in an R&B unit within the band, which was enlarged in 1960, when a youth named Brian Jones joined them on slide guitar. In 1962, when the threesome, calling themselves Blues Incorporated, left Barber, they had built up a sizable following.

The blues was catching on. The blues, the *purity* of the blues, the *folk poetry* of the blues—all of it became something like a religion with musicians and fans, partly as a reaction against the insipid British pop music of the time and partly as a reaction against the cultish stuffiness of the trad jazz scene. Blues Incorporated was the transitional band, and it served as an incubator for literally dozens of young musicians who later went on to rock and roll fame. Among them were several of the Rolling Stones.

The Stones were the first broadly popular and musically effective British blues group, a distinction they earned by mixing Slim Harpo and Muddy Waters with uptown R&B and Chuck Berry. Purists themselves in the beginning, the Stones outraged the folk/poetry crowd and were commonly accused of betraying the blues. In fact, they saw themselves as evangelists.

Dozens of blues groups sprung up in the wake of the Stones' early success; the Yardbirds, likely the best, were typical in that they featured blues in live performance and elaborate pop tricks in the studio. Such gimmickry (as on "For Your Love," 1965) led to the departure of their much-idolized lead guitarist, Eric Clapton, another purist. Clapton joined John Mayall's Bluesbreakers, a band that spawned as many future stars as Korner's original outfit. Among Mayall's alumni were Peter Green (later of Fleetwood Mac), Jack Bruce (of Cream), and Mick Taylor (who replaced Brian Jones in the Stones).

Clapton and Bruce soon departed to form Cream with drummer Ginger Baker—the first British blues group to achieve more than local success since the Stones. After Cream, the blues scene lost its shape. There was Fleetwood Mac, which specialized in Elmore James copies and which, after many per-

sonnel changes, has evolved into a very pleasant pop group; there was Ten Years After starring speed guitarist Alvin Lee and specializing in frenzy; Chicken Shack; the Climax Blues Band; and Savoy Brown, which perhaps has had more personnel shifts than any group in rock. Blues bands continue in and around the British Isles; the best of them is led by Irishman Rory Gallagher, a superb flash guitar player.

On the American side of the Atlantic, the folk music crowd was slower to accept the spectacle of a white kid playing something advertised as blues. The folkies worshiped "authenticity," which meant an aged black man playing an acoustic instrument; in the rush to "rediscover" Thirties bluesmen like Skip James and Mississippi John Hurt, living (and working) legends like Howlin' Wolf and Sonny Boy Williamson were passed over, even though their music was "people's music" if anything was. The folkies allowed a few of their own into the pantheon, but only if they restricted themselves to pre-WW II rural forms: Dave Van Ronk, who brilliantly interpreted finger-picking stylings of the Twenties and Thirties, and John Hammond Jr., whose mush-mouthed imitations of Son House convinced at least a few.

Unconcerned with such limitations were a bunch of young white Chicagoans who had discovered a whole world of music in their own backyard. One was Michael Bloomfield, a nice Jewish boy straight out of the very comfortable upper middle-class. At 16, he had a couple of years of rock behind him, but blues guitar was what he wanted to learn; and to this end he was soon backing older bluesmen on guitar and piano. At the same time, unknown to Bloomfield, a lawyer's son named Paul Butterfield was making a name for himself on the South Side as a freak act: see the white kid play blues harmonica. In general, Bloomfield was playing with blacks for folkies; and Butterfield and his friends were playing for all black audiences.

It was inevitable that they would meet, and after joining the first Paul Butterfield Blues Band as a piano player, Bloomfield turned down Bob Dylan's offer to join his group (Bloomfield played guitar on Dylan's 1965 classic *Highway 61 Revisited*) and stuck with Butterfield, reigning as America's most influential guitarist until the arrival of Eric Clapton in 1967.

Members of the Butterfield Band had backed Dylan at the Newport Folk Festival in 1965, and their first album on Elektra (until then, strictly a folk label) converted many. Their second album, *East-West,* established second guitarist Elvin Bishop, and though the band never sounded as good again (Bloomfield left in 1967, to form the Electric Flag), the band's name was made; in pieces, they continue.

As in England, blues groups were everywhere in short order. Most were terrible and died quick and unlamented deaths. The most interesting was a band put together by two blues collec-

Top: (1) Chuck Berry, backed by the Blues Project, mid-Sixties— from left: Steve Katz, Roy Blumenthal, Al Kooper, Danny Kalb. Bottom: (2) In the mid-Sixties, a very young Michael Bloomfield sits at the foot of a master, John Lee Hooker. (1, Don Paulsen; 2, Ray Flerlage)

Clockwise from top left: (1) Canned Heat out of L.A.—fanatical collectors who took a version of early Delta blues into the Top 40; (2) The original Fleetwood Mac, who worshiped at the shrine of Elmore James—from left: John McVie, Danny Kirwan, Mick Fleetwood, Jeremy Spencer, Peter Green. In 1976, only McVie and Fleetwood remain; (3) Charles Musselwhite, Mississippi harp player who learned his trade in Chicago; (4) Paul Butterfield, harpist, founder of the first important integrated blues band of the Sixties; (5) John Mayall's original Bluesbreakers, the first important British blues band—Mayall, left, Eric Clapton, second from left. Center, left: (6) John Hammond Jr., in the mid-Sixties; right: (7) Rory Gallagher, Irish guitarist extraordinare. (1, 2 & 3, ROLLING STONE; 4, Annie Leibovitz; 5, Robert Stigwood; 6, John Edward Memorial Foundation; 7, David Bieber/Bieber Archives)

tors, Bob Hite and Alan Wilson, called "Canned Heat," after an old Tommy Johnson song. Reaching back to the Twenties for their spirit, yet fully electrified and endlessly preaching "Boogie!," they were capable of memorable music. Wilson's high voice, eerie harmonica and fluid rhythm guitar floated above a grunting rhythm section; the combination brought them two Top 20 hits in 1968, "Going up the Country" and "On the Road Again." Wilson, nearly blind and subject to intense depression, died from a drug overdose in 1970; the band survived him in name only.

Other important musicians of the Sixties included Charlie Musselwhite, a white musician from Memphis who played harp Chicago-style; Nick Gravenites (an excellent singer and songwriter from the Bloomfield/Butterfield crowd) and the strange Blues Project, a New York band whose odd urban reworkings of older blues had an intense local following in 1965.

And there were those who followed in the late Sixties and early Seventies, most of whom either abandoned blues for straight rock and roll, or died: Johnny Winter, the albino guitarist from Texas; Duane Allman from Georgia, who made his professional reputation as a studio guitarist backing established R&B performers; the Allman Brothers Band, a racially mixed powerhouse which included Duane and his brother Gregg, and which was dominant on the concert circuit even after Duane's death in a motorcycle accident; and the J. Geils Band out of Boston, which burst into prominence with a searing debut album in 1971 and has been on the decline ever since.

White blues performers have lacked staying power, but the phenomenon of the white blues "revival" is recurrent; it can be expected whenever mainstream pop music finds itself weighed down by gimmicks. Ironically, when blues is brought into the mainstream, it almost never survives the gimmicks its practitioners seem only too ready to employ.

Discography

John Mayall
Bluesbreakers (London 492; 1967; released in Britain 1965). *A Hard Road* (London 502; 1967; released in Britain 1966). *Crusade* (London 529; ☆136, 1968; released in Britain 1967). *The Blues Alone* (London 534; ☆128, 1968). *Bare Wires* (London 537; ☆59, 1968). *Blues from Laurel Canyon* (London 545; ☆68, 1969). *Looking Back* (London 562; ☆79, 1969). *Turning Point* (Polydor 4004; ☆32, 1969).

Fleetwood Mac
Fleetwood Mac (Epic 26402; ☆198, 1968). *English Rose* (Epic 26446; ☆184, 1969). *Then Play On* (Reprise 6368; ☆109, 1969).

Ten Years After
Ten Years After (Deram 18009; 1968; released in Britain 1967). *Undead* (Deram 18016; ☆115, 1968). *Stonedhenge* (Deram 18021; ☆61, 1969). *Ssssh* (Deram 18029; ☆20, 1969).

Paul Butterfield
The Paul Butterfield Blues Band (Elektra 294; ☆123, 1965). *East-West* (Elektra 315; ☆65, 1966). *The Resurrection of Pigboy Crabshaw* (Elektra 74015; ☆52, 1968). *In My Own Dream* (Elektra 74025; ☆79, 1968). *Keep On Moving* (Elektra 74053; ☆102, 1969).

Canned Heat
Canned Heat (Liberty 7526; ☆76, 1967). *Boogie with Canned Heat* (Liberty 7541; ☆16, 1968). *Living the Blues* (Liberty 27200; ☆18, 1968). *Hallelujah* (Liberty 7618; ☆37, 1969).

(Chart positions compiled from Joel Whitburn's *Record Research*, based on Billboard LPs charts.)

The Sound of San Francisco

by Charles Perry

Everybody knew how rock and roll worked in 1965. You played hits. You wore matching uniforms. You got the Top 40 DJ who controlled the local music scene to take you under his wing and book you into the big high school dances at the armories. In San Francisco, that man was "Big Daddy" Tom Donahue, and he even had a little record label of his own you could record on. If you were very good boys, you might play for the topless dancers at the North Beach nightclubs. Maybe you'd get to record a single. An A&R man would pick your material and you'd record it in a couple of hours at the label's own studio.

Everybody knew this, that is, except some crazy *existencialistas* who were living across the Golden Gate Bridge in the bohemian houseboats of Sausalito, or down the peninsula in the crazy-kid purlieus of Stanford University, or in a little-known San Francisco neighborhood called Haight-Ashbury. They didn't know you had to go through Tom Donahue or you were never going to get a crack at the big time; didn't know how you got a record contract; didn't know how many favors somebody had to owe you to put your record on the air—didn't know, and didn't seem to care. Most of them were folk musicians who had never played a sock hop in their lives, but now they were pursuing rock and roll with an unfathomable sense of mission. They were playing dumps no one had ever heard of, with no thought for tomorrow. They hadn't even thought far ahead enough to join the musicians' union. Crazy *existencialistas*.

Among the greatest *existencialistas* of all were the Charlatans. The founder of the group was a draftsman and designer named George Hunter who neither sang nor played an instrument. When the band performed, he just looked busy with a tambourine or an autoharp. In fact, he'd conceived of the Charlatans less as a band than as a visual trip, an artist's conception of America's answer to the Beatles. Even before their first rehearsal, they'd had hundreds of publicity stills taken exploring the mythic possibilities of the Victorian and Old West costume that impoverished young bohemians in the Haight were fishing out of the secondhand stores.

They had scarcely rehearsed when they were actually offered a gig. Mercifully, the gig was out of town, in Virginia City, Nevada, where they had a chance to pull themselves together as a band. When they came back they found a scene had developed for their brand of hip rocking and rolling: a nightclub specialized in it, and a series of giant dance concerts catered to pot-smoking, LSD-eating hippies. How about that! They slipped back into their Haight-Ashbury home as stars.

They remained the ultimate early-Haight band, true to the style of the original core of artists and students and dope dealers. As the scene expanded and changed, they never got into the novelties of heavy rock or flower power. Their repertoire remained essentially folk material—blues, ballads, good-time jug band tunes—plus a few original numbers and the odd Rolling Stones tune. The Charlatans' trademark was a jaunty, ragtimey rhythm that was of a piece with their style.

Other bands were forming in the Haight. One, which took the name Big Brother and the Holding Company, came out of a series of public jam sessions in the basement of a rooming house. Another, started by a sometime Haight resident named Marty Balin, who owned the city's "folk-rock club," the Matrix, made a debut before the Charlatans returned from Nevada (they sported one of those enigmatic names these bands favored: Jefferson Airplane). Soon there were more bands, mostly comprised of San Francisco State College students: the Mystery Trend, the Final Solution, the Great Society and others.

Over in Sausalito a young guitarist named John Cipollina had admitted being a rocker to his beatnik roommates and found it was okay—in fact, they wanted to be rockers too. Cipollina had spent the early Sixties being snubbed in folk music circles for showing up at hootenannies with an electric guitar, that symbol of "commercialism" and "selling out." But the juice had gone out of the folk-purist ethic; soon the little group of musicians heard that Dino Valenti, a folk balladeer they admired, was interested in starting a rock band. Valenti got busted inconveniently and did a year and a half in jail, leaving the band to pull itself together on its own. They called themselves Quicksilver Messenger Service, an astrological reference to their Virgo-heavy personnel.

In the same crazed vein as other early San Francisco bands, they were weirdos who never expected to make it. When they got paid for their first gig, they laughed all the way home. Cipollina had already been through the rock and roll scene years before and considered himself a failure and a dropout. The band included two other teen-rock dropouts, and a bassist named David Freiberg, who, like Cipollina, had been on the folk scene (in fact, he had once roomed with Paul Kantner, later of Jefferson Airplane, and David Crosby, later of the Byrds).

At the outset, Quicksilver's repertoire consisted of Chicago blues, Rolling Stones numbers, occasional folk items, such as their early crowd-pleaser "Pride of Man," and a legacy of Dino Valenti compositions. Their sound reflected an interest in classical music and a clean, organized, perfectionist tendency. Cipollina's voice and guitar, both marked by a quivering, crystalline vibrato, were the most distinctive parts of the band's early sound.

Quicksilver was one of the first bands to move deep into rural Marin County and "mellow out." Their back-to-nature streak was further amplified when Dino Valenti finally rejoined the group. Unfortunately, Valenti also brought his somewhat affected, whining voice and overbearing manner to the group, which he completely dominated after Cipollina left in 1970.

Quicksilver's counterpart to the south was the Grateful Dead. They were folkies (plus one avant-garde electronic music

The Grateful Dead at the source, circa 1966. From left: Jerry Garcia, Pigpen, Phil Lesh, Bob Weir, Bill Kreutzmann. (Herb Greene)

246

dropout): a former bluegrass banjoist, a blues organist and some others who'd gotten caught up in the corny fun of the jug band craze. Shortly after getting into electrified rock, they'd fallen in with the big action of the Stanford psychedelic scene: the Acid Test LSD parties being put on by the novelist Ken Kesey and his Merry Pranksters. With this background and the early patronage of Owsley Stanley, the famous LSD chemist, the Dead became the most notable acid *existencialistas* on the scene, making decisions and managing their affairs as a huge extended family, without regard for status or conventional chains of command. They had a considerable reputation for playing while stoned, and for taking half an hour to tune up and decide on the next song; their endless versions of "In the Midnight Hour," which went on until everybody decided at the same time to end it, were legend.

The Quick and the Dead had a certain yin-yang relationship. Quicksilver was the drugstore cowboy band, and the Dead the psychedelic Indians, prophets of retribalism. There was even a certain parallel in their musical development, when the Dead switched to a softer, more countrified sound in the Seventies. But the Dead's forte remained middle-tempo rockers with a big, fat, solid sound, dominated by Phil Lesh's strong bass line and Jerry Garcia's bluegrassoid guitar runs, which noodled over it all like a sustained, stoned meditation on the mantra "whatever's right." The sound was particularly rich and full because the Dead, under the influence of the technical perfectionist Owsley, quickly discarded the tinny "public address" sound systems rockers had always used; eventually they had 23 tons of sound equipment in use, and a crew of nine just to put it up and take it down.

For all their psychedelic unpredictability, the Dead remained a working group longer than most. It wasn't until fall 1974 that they disbanded for an indefinite period. Their fans, an unusually loyal lot known as Dead Heads, remained utterly confident of a revival.

These were the original crazies, the gamblers for stakes unknowable. They were a doomed-looking bunch when they surfaced (except, perhaps, for the relatively tidy Airplane). The record company talent scouts who dropped by their little nightclubs and ballrooms felt sorry for these babes in the woods. But things had already started to run their way. The record company reps started getting slipped acid-spiked soda pop and seeing the room turn to taffy . . . and noticing that the music had a certain insidious sense for somebody who saw the Buddha in the tip of his shoe.

As a measure of how ripe the scene was, even Big Daddy Tom Donahue was hip to it. He'd taken LSD, quit his job at the Top 40 station and opened a "psychedelic nightclub" where he held court for about six weeks, before retiring to dream up the idea of psychedelic radio: nonplaylisted, non-Top 40 rock and roll, mostly album cuts, on FM. Donahue was Dino Valenti's manager and had gone so far as to sign up the Great Society for his tiny North Beach label.

The intense excitement of the San Francisco rock scene was something new. It wasn't the old rock and roll sexual tension, simmering with potential violence. It was stoned-out, freak-freely dancing, a naively cheerful scene with the conspiratorial excitement of the secret society of acid eaters. The lyrics and the special sound effects re-created aspects of the psychedelic experience—revelatory roaring, chills of ecstasy, hallucinated wandering, mystico-psychotic wonder. And the musicians, for all the informality they had inherited from the consciously antitheatrical folk music tradition, were the ones standing up and speaking about the Great Unspeakable of the stoned experience. For many in the audience they were thereby prophets, gurus, holy men.

That's a market that doesn't show up every quarter of the fiscal year. But the dances were bringing in good money (Bill Graham's Fillmore ballroom had in fact become a kind of youth cult mecca), and the music turned out to be good business on record as well. San Francisco, through the peculiar tolerance and isolation of its culture, had spawned a uniquely open and confident manifestation of the faith in psychedelic drugs, which made it the national capital of psychedelia. Along with Dylan, the Stones and the Beatles, the San Francisco bands were staples of the turntables of acidhead America.

Once the scene started taking off, the original *existencialistas* were joined by others who wanted in. They were psychedelic believers, maybe, but they weren't creating a scene, they were making something out of it.

One of the first was Country Joe and the Fish. Joe McDonald was a folk singer with one foot in the grand old protest song tradition and the other in the good-time jug band scene. Six months after the first hippie dances in San Francisco he was running a rock band which established itself as the Berkeley acid group. They conscientiously explored LSD and strove to unite the hippies and the local radicals. Joe was famous for wearing protest buttons to hippie functions and flowers to the many political benefits he played.

The Fish in their prime were an entertaining band, with more of a stage act than the San Francisco groups. Joe led football-style fuck cheers; the band sang comic commercials for drugs, wore funny costumes and engaged in mild slapstick. Musically they showed folk roots in the jug band style and the down-and-out poetry and pretty melodies of Joe's hero, Woody Guthrie. Particularly in their early days they experimented with the psychedelic effects of the early Jefferson Airplane.

The Fish were even more mercurial than most San Francisco groups, logging five breakups in five years. After the final break Joe worked for a while double-billing with his wife's theatrical troupe, then fronted a largely female band, then sang

as a single again. By 1975, divorced and being sued for alimony by his feminist wife, he had soured on both drugs and radical politics.

One of the biggest San Francisco groups was dreamed up in Los Angeles. Moby Grape, as it was called, comprised three members of a Seattle band called the Frantics, plus an L.A. folkie and Skip Spence, the Airplane's original drummer (on guitar). With two lead guitars, they had a powerful, churning sound. They were quickly signed up for an album and it was released simultaneously with five singles; lofted by a massive promotion, they made an unprecedented splash in 1967. They quickly became one of the most popular bands in San Francisco, which in itself says a great deal about what was happening to the Haight-Ashbury scene. When the Grape first played the Fillmore at the end of November 1966, the faith that psychedelics were going to save the world had already played itself out for some people. But at the same time the faith was bringing people to the Haight in ever greater numbers. It was time for a band like the Grape, combining the tightness and flash of orthodox rock with the new sensibility.

They were a take-charge band that wowed the Fillmore crowds with their powerful sound and slightly stagy hysteria. Many of their songs were carefully composed, and they were also among the first to clean up and commercialize the psychedelic blues. "Changes!" agonized lead guitarist Jerry Miller, sounding a nebulous note of complaint that was to reverberate in Top 40 charts for years to come. The flashy guitar work, likewise, was a departure from the style of the San Francisco bands back in the days when they played for the archetypal happy hippie dancers. But the Fillmore was too crowded with sightseers for much dancing by now.

The scene was bound to become more professional. The money brought competition, and the innovative dance promoter Bill Graham made a great effort to educate the public taste in San Francisco by importing jazz and blues artists. The concertgoers heard what their idols had been listening to, and the local bands were forced to improve their acts to compete with their models, or fall by the wayside. (The Charlatans fell by the wayside for another reason: the growing taste for "heavy" music. Drummer Dan Hicks then perversely started a drummerless nonrock band, the Hot Licks, to back his dry and ironic lyrics in a mixture of pre-Fifties pop styles.)

The biggest import was the band fronted by Texas-bred Steve Miller, a veteran of the rock scene since his early teens in the Fifties who had been holding down Paul Butterfield's white-blues gig in Chicago. He moved into the Haight in November 1966, and started up a band including members of some of his earlier aggregations from Chicago, his college days and even the old days in Texas, notably including the singer and guitarist Boz Scaggs. By January they were headlining the Avalon Ballroom (the Fillmore's only real rival).

They played Chicago blues, emphasizing not its funky, astringent qualities but the big rhythm, the thundering grandeur, the drama. The vocals were often in disciplined three-part falsetto harmony. Miller's own vocal style was fairly black, with a gutsy delivery that suggested the singer's passion and need were making the words positively explode from his throat. Scaggs had a more intimate style, a choked, artless, confessional delivery he later featured in a band of his own that specialized in ballads.

Miller made no secret of what he was in it for: money, fame and pleasure. Acid had somehow left his sense of ambition intact. And his perfectionism. He held out for a record-breaking advance payment from Capitol Records for his first LP, and a royalty payment about three times what anybody else was getting. It permanently changed the economics of rock and roll.

Miller also started giving his record company orders on how he was going to be recorded. He knew exactly what he wanted, and for his first album he flew to England to get it. It was the beginning of the end for the old company studios, staffed with unsympathetic hacks and outfitted with primitive equipment. As Miller had the best singers on the scene, bar Grace Slick and Marty Balin of the Airplane and Janis Joplin of the later Big Brother, together with the Grateful Dead he pioneered the virgin territory of high-fidelity, carefully recorded rock and roll.

It was 1967, the heyday of the Haight-Ashbury. The number of psychedelic bands in the Bay Area was established to be something between 500 and 1500, both local groups and visitors attracted by the mystique of the New Age community and the lure of the numerous paying gigs. Their names came thick and fast. When the Grateful Dead were estranged from their acid-chemist patron, Owsley began backing an extraordinarily loud, simplistic blues band called Blue Cheer; he even named a brand of LSD after them.

The scene finally collapsed, like a nova collapsing into a dwarf star. One of the last gasps was the incredibly successful group Santana, named for the lead guitarist Carlos Santana. The music was still cosmic, psychedelic stuff—but braced with jazz and Latin influences. Santana became more spiritually oriented after he chose the path of guru Sri Chinmoy. There was the standard rock drummer, but there was also a timbales player on percussion. The rhythms were tight, metallic and Latin, the guitar cast in a jazz and Hendrix vein. The lugubrious, been-stoned-too-long lethargy that the old psychedelic bands had fallen into was completely absent; Santana was as tight and sharp as a patent-leather shoe. The band's very existence signaled the spread of psychedelic culture to working-class and minority youth.

One of the commonplace phrases of the day was the "San Francisco sound." An enterprising promoter even copyrighted the phrase. Musically, the meaning is hard to pin down. Most of the early bands played Rolling Stones tunes, for instance, but

Opposite, clockwise from top: (1) Superimpresario Bill Graham; (2) Quicksilver Messenger Service, from left—Gary Duncan, John Cippolina, Greg Elmore, David Freiberg; (3) It's a Beautiful Day; (4) Owsley Stanley under police custody in 1970; (5) The Grateful Dead circa 1967; (6) Dino Valenti; (7) Dan Hicks in Sausalito; (8) Tracy Nelson; (9) Last days of the Filmore West 1971. Center top: (10) Santana; bottom: (11) Moby Grape with friend. Below top: (12) Steve Miller; bottom: (13) Steve Miller Band, from top—Tim Davis, Lonnie Turner, Steve Miller, Jim Peterman, Boz Scaggs. (2, 'Phonograph Record' magazine; 4, The 'Times Picayune,' New Orleans; 5, 6 & 13, Baron Wolman; 7, Tony Lane; 9, Annie Leibovitz; 11, Columbia Records)

they each played them differently. The blues was at the core of most band's repertoires, but most of the well-known songs from this period are not blues. There was the folk music and country-western end of the spectrum, but with that in the equation, the boundaries of the San Francisco sound become impossibly vague. And in the end, there was Santana and its Afro-Cuban heritage.

There were a few elements common to many of the San Francisco bands, however. One was the attempt to incorporate the musical values of Indian ragas into rock: Indian music had the spiritual prestige of the mystic East, of course, and the droning background, sliding notes and absence of chord changes appealed to the acidhead's desire for tranquillity (and sometimes the musician's desire for something he could play when ripped out of his skull). Allied to this fascination with modal forms was the deliberate introduction of feedback. By playing a guitar close enough to the loudspeakers that the sound itself shook the strings, a guitarist could produce a piercing, shrieking sound that musicians had previously struggled to avoid. The psychedelic musician, on the contrary, was fascinated by the searing noise that resulted, and the apparent spontaneity of its production.

If there was anything else distinctive about the San Francisco sound, it was probably the prevalence of long, jam session versions of rock numbers, both in performance and on record. But the "sound" was less a musical phenomenon than a manner, premised on the simple and straightforward assumption that this was trip music, being played by dopers for other dopers. The intense involvement of the audience in the music, and the musicians in certain aspects of their craft, permanently changed the rock scene, adding elements of seriousness, connoisseurship and psychosis. But the real unifying factor is that it was distinctly the music of a community, and at its best it carried the exuberant, wonderstruck spirit of San Francisco's *existencialistas* to the world.

Discography

Jefferson Airplane, *The Jefferson Airplane Takes Off!* (RCA Victor 3584; ☆128, 1966). **Jefferson Airplane,** *Surrealistic Pillow* (RCA Victor 3766; ☆3, 1967). **Grateful Dead,** *Grateful Dead* (Warner Bros. 1689; ☆73, 1967). **Country Joe and the Fish,** *Country Joe and the Fish* (Vanguard 79244; ☆39, 1967). **Moby Grape,** *Moby Grape* (Columbia 9498; ☆24, 1967). **Big Brother and the Holding Company,** *Big Brother and the Holding Company* (Mainstream 56099; ☆60, 1967). **Sopwith Camel,** *The Sopwith Camel* (Kama Sutra 8060; ☆191, 1967). **Jefferson Airplane,** *After Bathing at Baxters* (RCA Victor 1511; ☆17, 1967). **Country Joe and the Fish,** *I-Feel-like-I'm-Fixin'-to-Die* (Vanguard 79266; ☆67, 1967). **Moby Grape,** *Wow* (Columbia 9613; ☆20, 1968). **Steve Miller Band,** *Children of the Future* (Capitol 2920; ☆134, 1968). **Quicksilver Messenger Service,** *Quicksilver Messenger Service* (Capitol 2904; ☆63, 1968). **Country Joe and The Fish,** *Together* (Vanguard 79277; ☆23, 1968). **Big Brother and the Holding Company,** *Cheap Thrills* (Columbia 9700; ☆1, 1968). **Grateful Dead,** *Anthem of the Sun* (Warner Bros. 1749; ☆87, 1968). **Jefferson Airplane,** *Crown of Creation* (RCA Victor 4058; ☆6, 1968). **Steve Miller Band,** *Sailor* (Capitol 2984; ☆24, 1968). **Mother Earth,** *Living with the Animals* (Mercury 61194; ☆144, 1969). **Moby Grape,** *Moby Grape '69* (Columbia 9696; ☆113, 1969). **Quicksilver Messenger Service,** *Happy Trails* (Capitol 120; ☆27, 1969). **Jefferson Airplane,** *Bless Its Pointed Little Head* (RCA Victor 4133; ☆17, 1969). **Sons of Champlin,** *Loosen Up Naturally* (Capitol 200; ☆137, 1969). **It's a Beautiful Day,** *It's a Beautiful Day* (Columbia 9768; ☆47, 1969). **Country Joe and the Fish,** *Here We Are Again* (Vanguard 79299; ☆48, 1969). **Grateful Dead,** *Aoxomoxoa* (Warner Bros. 1790; ☆73, 1969). **Steve Miller Band,** *Brave New World* (Capitol 184; ☆22, 1969). **Mother Earth,** *Make a*

Joyful Noise (Mercury 61226; ☆95, 1969). **Dan Hicks and His Hot Licks,** *Dan Hicks and His Hot Licks* (Epic 26464; 1969). **Santana,** *Santana* (Columbia 9781; ☆4, 1969). **Janis Joplin,** *I Got Dem Ol' Kozmic Blues Again Mama!* (Columbia 9913; ☆5, 1969). **Boz Scaggs,** *Boz Scaggs* (Atlantic 8239; 1969). **Jefferson Airplane,** *Volunteers* (RCA Victor 4238; ☆13, 1969). **Steve Miller Band,** *Your Saving Grace* (Capitol 331; ☆38, 1969). **Grateful Dead,** *Live/Dead* (Warner Bros. 1830; ☆64, 1970). **Grateful Dead,** *Workingman's Dead* (Warner Bros. 1869; ☆27, 1970). **It's a Beautiful Day,** *Marrying Maiden* (Columbia 1058; ☆28, 1970). **Hot Tuna,** *Hot Tuna* (RCA Victor 4353; ☆30, 1970). **Santana,** *Abraxas* (Columbia 30130; ☆1, 1970). **Big Brother and the Holding Company,** *Be a Brother* (Columbia 30222; ☆134, 1970). **Paul Kantner/Jefferson Starship,** *Blows against the Empire* (RCA Victor 4448; ☆20, 1970). **Grateful Dead,** *American Beauty* (Warner Bros. 1893; ☆30, 1970). **Jefferson Airplane,** *The Worst of Jefferson Airplane* (RCA Victor 4459; ☆12, 1970).

(Chart positions taken from Joel Whitburn's *Record Research,* compiled from *Billboard* LPs chart.)

The Jefferson Airplane

by Charles Perry

JEFFERSON AIRPLANE LOVES YOU, read the bumperstickers. It seemed a little odd in early 1966—a rock band confessing love to every stranger who could read the bumpersticker on the car ahead. But the Psychedelic Age was dawning, and such sentiments soon appeared perfectly reasonable. Love, psychedelically understood, was everywhere; blowing in the wind, for instance. Jefferson Airplane was just letting people know they were of, by and for the acid community.

And they were loved in return. By the summer of 1967, they had two Top Ten singles and their second album was right behind the Beatles' *Sgt. Pepper's Lonely Hearts Club Band*. They were the voice of the Love Generation, of San Francisco, of the Haight-Ashbury.

Like most of the early acid bands, they started as folk rockers. Marty Balin, a young actor turned folkie, had taken the same inspiration from *A Hard Day's Night* as the Byrds and Lovin' Spoonful. He took the nucleus of his folk group—guitarist Paul Kantner and vocalist Signe Toly—and added Jorma Kaukonen, a locally celebrated guitar picker, who happened to know a bassist named Jack Casady. Balin picked Skip Spence, actually a guitarist, to play drums, purely because he "looked like a drummer."

In the beginning they were obviously folkies on a Liverpool trip, wearing moddish clothes and playing clean, early-Beatles guitar band arrangements. It was a tentative sound at first. The guitars mostly played chords, on the beat, with a solemn, chiming quality that reflected the folkie's fascination with sonority (not to mention the professional requirements of playing for the blossoming dance scene at the Fillmore and Avalon ballrooms, or the musicians' unfamiliarity with amplified instruments). Their repertoire included rock-arranged staples of the local coffeehouse circuit, folk blues and ballads, as well as several original songs by Balin, Kantner and Spence. They were the right band at the right time: in 1965, they became the first San Francisco group to land a contract with a major label.

Shortly after their first album was released in September 1966, Spencer Dryden replaced Skip Spence; and Signe Toly, now Signe Anderson and too pregnant to perform, was replaced by Grace Slick from a recently disbanded group called the Great Society. Grace was the decisive change. Signe might have had a richer soprano, but Grace had visual style—she'd put her husband through college by fashion modeling—and an Attitude. From the start her voice had an element of icy fury; when she reached for a high note, it was as if she were zeroing in on something in order to throttle it. She wrote songs of a piece with that voice, songs of scathing sarcasm that led one reviewer to observe that she was the only man-hating songwriter who was also a misogynist. Balin wrote his own share of put-down songs too. Jefferson Airplane loved you, but they gave themselves plenty of room for psychic self-defense.

By the time of *Surrealistic Pillow*, the album that brought the Airplane and the "San Francisco sound" to national prominence in 1967, the group was entering its classic phase. Balin's sobbing vibrato played off Slick's needle-sharp soprano, usually singing at the interval of a fifth: a folk harmony style that gives a hollow, austere sound unlike the sweet, "close" harmony of singing in thirds. The rhythms had grown suppler and more powerful, and the guitars were stretching out in a bluesier, jazzier direction.

If they echoed the Beatles in the beginning, in early '67 they leaned to a gentle Lovin' Spoonful-ish style, though the Airplane was harder rocking and solemn, even exalted, where the Spoonful was mellow and cute. Like the Spoonful they were writing freshly and without condescension about young love, especially about the crisis of confessing love. A classic on the *Surrealistic Pillow* album was "Today." A quiet, early-morningish guitar ostinato backed lyrics confessing apocalyptic passion: "I'm so full of love I could burst apart and start to cry." It was the musical equivalent of one of the apprehensive faces on a Fillmore dance poster.

That was one side of the Airplane's love image. Another was the open evocation of the drug experience. "Take me to a circus tent/Where I can easily pay my rent/And all the other freaks will share my cares" was the story of the Haight-Ashbury for a lot of people. So was the group's first hit, "Somebody to Love": "When the truth is found to be lies/And all the joy within you dies/Don't you want somebody to love?" The words resonate of the Kennedy assassination, the Vietnam war, and the tangled passions of youth, acid-magnified. The Airplane Understood.

That phase reached a natural peak during the Summer of Love in 1967. As the first San Francisco band to surface nationally, they were the one band the flood of out-of-towners had to see. And when they performed, at the Fillmore or outdoors, it was more than a show, it was a love feast and religious initiation, with Grace stalking the stage like a howling lioness, and Marty and Grace exhorting everybody to "Let's Get Together," smile on their brothers, try to love one another . . . right now. It seemed about to happen.

But there were some hard knocks in store, for the band as well as their audience. The Summer of Love ended in drug burnouts and a Haight-Ashbury notable for crude commercialism and violent crime. In 1968 the Airplane were part proprietors of a dance hall in competition with the Fillmore and the Avalon; it went broke. A couple more dreams died at the 1968 Democratic convention in Chicago. By 1969, the Airplane had stopped singing about love; the focus shifted more and more to Grace's increasingly strident voice and Paul Kantner's increasingly politicized lyrics.

The Jefferson Airplane in 1966. From left: Marty Balin, Spencer Dryden, Signe Anderson, Paul Kantner, Jorma Kaukonen, Jack Casady. (Herb Greene)

Clockwise from top left: (1) Jefferson Starship, 1974; (2) Grace Slick posing with pasta wheels; (3) and (4) Jefferson Airplane in their natural habitat. (1, Grunt Records; 2, Baron Wolman; 3 & 4, Annie Leibovitz)

The Airplane as such was coming to an end. Casady and Kaukonen started a group of their own in 1970. In '71, Balin left the group he'd founded. Kantner and Slick put out a series of albums with a large roster of San Francisco musicians, showcasing Kantner's science-fiction visions, eventually taking the name Jefferson Starship. (Ironically, when Balin returned to work with Kantner, Slick and the Starship one result was *Red Octopus*, which became the musicians' first Number One album in 1975.)

As the first big San Francisco band, the Airplane had consciously played the role of pioneers. They fought with their label to include the word "shit" in a lyric even though they risked a boycott by some record chains. Grace, in particular, was provocatively direct in interviews. Indeed, it was the Airplane who first brought the San Francisco hip sensibility to national attention. Back home, the Grateful Dead might embody the purest psychedelic vision; Big Brother and the Holding Company might stand for a kind of dropped-out, no-hope glamour; the Charlatans might exemplify the good-timey antique ambience of the early Haight hip scene. But it was the Airplane who consistently exalted the spirit of a new community, from "Let's Get Together" to "Crown of Creation" and "Volunteers." Throughout, the Airplane embodied the messianism of a generation.

Discography

Singles
Jefferson Airplane, "Somebody to Love" (RCA Victor 9140; ☆5, 1967). "White Rabbit" (RCA Victor 9248; ☆8, 1967). "Ballad of You and Me and Pooneil" (RCA Victor 9297; ☆42, 1967). "Watch Her Ride" (RCA Victor 9389; ☆61, 1967). "Greasy Heart" (RCA Victor 9496; ☆98, 1968). "Crown of Creation" (RCA 9644; ☆64, 1968). "Volunteers" (RCA 0245; ☆65, 1969). "Pretty as You Feel" (Grunt 0500; ☆60, 1971). **Jefferson Starship,** "Ride the Tiger" (Grunt 10080; ☆84, 1974). "Miracles" (Grunt 10367; ☆3, 1975). "Play on Love" (Grunt 10456; ☆49, 1975).

Albums
Jefferson Airplane, *Jefferson Airplane Takes Off!* (RCA Victor 3584; ☆128, 1966). *Surrealistic Pillow* (RCA Victor 3766; ☆3, 1967). *After Bathing at Baxters* (RCA Victor 1511; ☆17, 1967). *Crown of Creation* (RCA Victor 4058; ☆6, 1968). *Bless Its Pointed Little Head* (RCA Victor 4133; ☆17, 1969). *Volunteers* (RCA Victor 4238; ☆13, 1969). *The Worst of Jefferson Airplane* (RCA Victor 4459; ☆12, 1970). *Bark* (Grunt 1001; ☆11, 1971). *Long John Silver* (Grunt 1007; ☆20, 1972). *Thirty Seconds over Winterland* (Grunt 0147; ☆52, 1973). *Early Flight* (Grunt 0437; ☆110, 1974). **Paul Kantner and Jefferson Starship,** *Blows against the Empire* (RCA Victor 4448; ☆20, 1970). **Paul Kantner and Grace Slick,** *Sunfighter* (Grunt 1002; ☆89, 1971). **Jefferson Starship,** *Baron von Tollbooth and the Chrome Nun* (Grunt 0148; 1973). *Dragon Fly* (Grunt 0717; ☆11, 1974). *Red Octopus* (Grunt 0999; ☆1, 1975).
(Chart positions taken from Joel Whitburn's *Record Research,* compiled from *Billboard* Pop and LPs charts.)

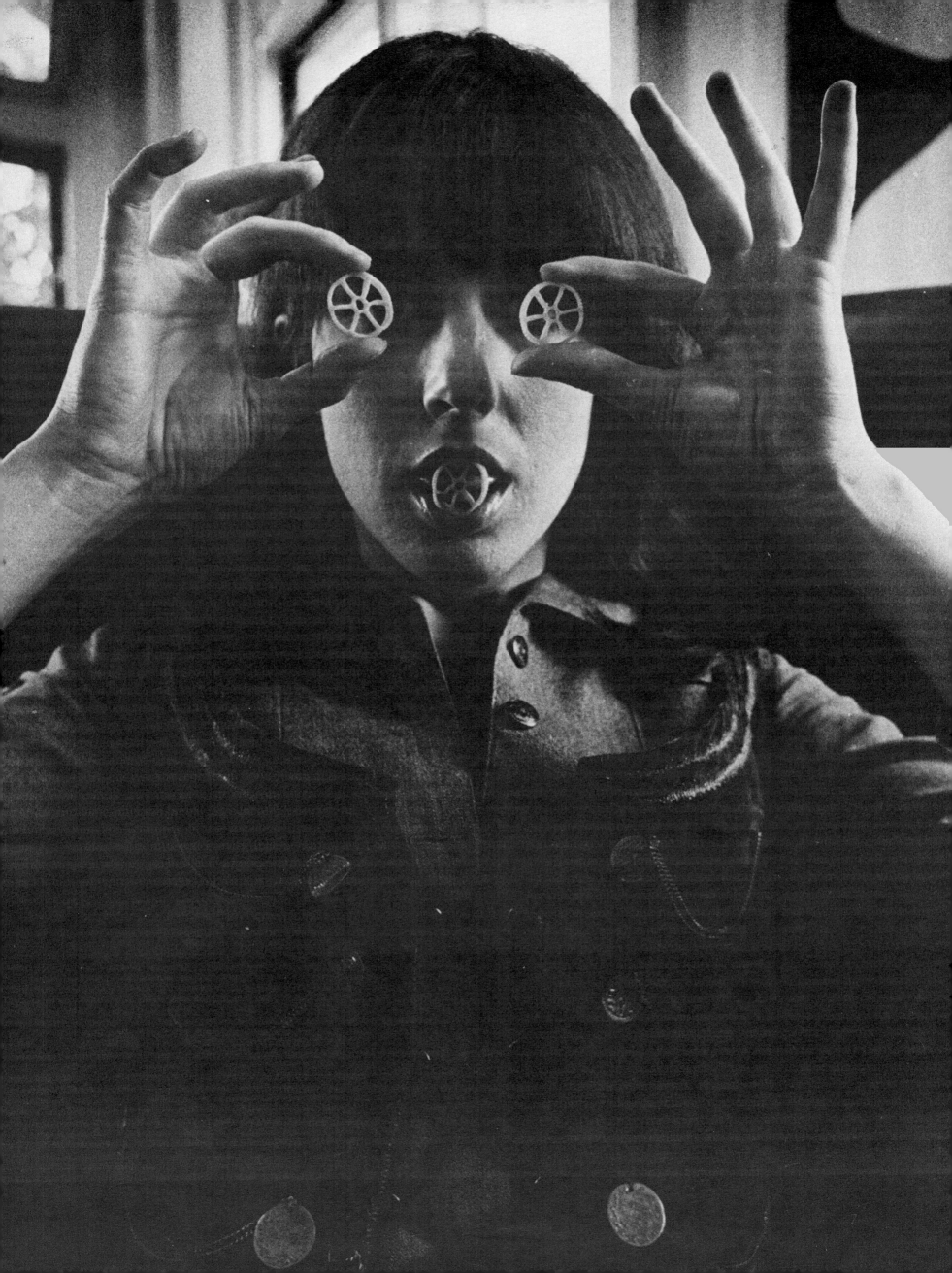

Janis Joplin
by Ellen Willis

anis Joplin was born in 1943 and grew up in Port Arthur, Texas. She began singing in bars and coffeehouses, first locally, then in Austin, where she spent most of a year at the University of Texas. In 1966, she went to San Francisco and got together with a rock band in search of a singer, Big Brother and the Holding Company. The following summer Big Brother performed at the Monterey Pop Festival; Janis got raves from the fans and the critics and from then on she was a star. 'Cheap Thrills', Big Brother's first major album (there had been an early record on a small-time label), came out in July 1968. By then there were tensions between Janis and the group, and she left soon afterward.

With her new backup band she made another album, 'I Got Dem Ol' Kozmic Blues Again Mama!' But the band never quite jelled, and in the spring of 1970, Janis formed another, Full-Tilt Boogie. They spent most of the summer touring, then went to Los Angeles to record an album, 'Pearl'. It was Janis's last. On October 4th, 1970, she died of an overdose of heroin.

* * *

The hippie rock stars of the late Sixties merged two versions of that hardy American myth, the free individual. They were stars, which meant achieving liberation by becoming rich and famous *on their own terms;* and they were, or purported to be, apostles of cultural revolution, a considerably more ambitious and romantic vision of freedom that nevertheless had a similar economic foundation. Young Americans were in a sense the stars of the world, drawing on an overblown prosperity that could afford to indulge all manner of rebellious and experimental behavior. The combination was inherently unstable—Whitman's open road is not, finally, the Hollywood Freeway, and in any case neither stardom nor prosperity could deliver what it seemed to promise. For a fragile historical moment rock transcended those contradictions; in its aftermath our pop heroes found themselves grappling, like the rest of us, with what are probably enduring changes in the white American consciousness—changes that have to do with something very like an awareness of tragedy. It is in this context that Janis Joplin developed as an artist, a celebrity, a rebel, a woman, and it is in this context that she died.

Joplin belonged to that select group of pop figures who mattered as much for themselves as for their music; among American rock performers she was second only to Bob Dylan in importance as a creator/recorder/embodiment of her generation's history and mythology. She was also the only woman to achieve that kind of stature in what was basically a male club, the only Sixties culture hero to make visible and public women's experience of the quest for individual liberation, which was very different from men's. If Janis's favorite metaphors—singing as fucking (a first principle of rock and roll) and fucking as liberation (a first principle of the cultural revolution)—were equally approved by her male peers, the congruence was only on the surface. Underneath—just barely—lurked a feminist (or prefeminist) paradox.

The male-dominated counterculture defined freedom for women almost exclusively in sexual terms. As a result, women endowed the idea of sexual liberation with immense symbolic importance; it became charged with all the secret energy of an as yet suppressed larger rebellion. Yet to express one's rebellion in that limited way was a painfully literal form of submission. Whether or not Janis understood that, her dual persona—lusty hedonist and suffering victim—suggested that she felt it. Dope, another term in her metaphorical equation (getting high as singing as fucking as liberation) was, in its more sinister aspect, a pain-killer and finally a killer. Which is not to say that the good times weren't real, as far as they went. Whatever the limitations of hippie/rock star life, it was better than being a provincial matron—or a lonely weirdo.

For Janis, as for others of us who suffered the worst fate that can befall an adolescent girl in America—*unpopularity*—a crucial aspect of the cultural revolution was its assault on the rigid sexual styles of the Fifties. Joplin's metamorphosis from the ugly duckling of Port Arthur to the peacock of Haight-Ashbury meant, among other things, that a woman who was not conventionally pretty, who had acne and an intermittent weight problem and hair that stuck out, could not only invent her own beauty (just as she invented her wonderful sleazofreak costumes) out of sheer energy, soul, sweetness, arrogance, and a sense of humor, but have that beauty appreciated. Not that Janis merely took advantage of changes in our notions of attractiveness; she herself changed them. It was seeing Janis Joplin that made me resolve, once and for all, not to get my hair straightened. And there was a direct line from that sort of response to those apocryphal burned bras and all that followed.

Direct, but not simple. Janis once crowed, "They're paying me $50,000 a year to be like me." But the truth was that they were paying her to be a personality, and the relation of public personality to private self—something every popular artist has to work out—is especially problematic for a woman. Men are used to playing roles and projecting images in order to compete and succeed. Male celebrities tend to identify with their mask-making, to see it as creative and—more or less—to control it. In contrast, women need images simply to survive. A woman is usually aware, on some level, that men do not allow her to be her "real self," and worse, that the acceptable masks represent men's fantasies, not her own. She can choose the most interesting image available, present it dramatically, individualize it with small elaborations, undercut it with irony. But ultimately she must serve some male fantasy to be loved—and then it will be only the fantasy that is loved anyway. The female celebrity is confronted with this dilemma in its starkest form. Joplin's revolt against conventional femininity was brave and imagina-

Janis Joplin (Herb Greene)

Janis Joplin interviewed at the Landmark Hotel in Hollywood, June 1968 (Lou Mack)

tive, but it also dovetailed with a stereotype—the ballsy, one-of-the-guys chick who is a needy, vulnerable cream puff underneath—cherished by her legions of hip male fans. It may be that she could have pushed beyond it and taken the audience with her; that was one of the possibilities that made her death an artistic as well as human calamity. There is, for instance, the question of her bisexuality. People who knew Janis differ on whether sexual relationships with women were an important part of her life, and I don't know the facts. In any case, a public acknowledgment of bisexual proclivities would not necessarily have contradicted her image; it could easily have been passed off as more pull-out-the-stops hedonism or another manifestation of her all-encompassing need for love. On the other hand, she could have used it to say something new about women and liberation. What makes me wonder is something I always noticed and liked about Janis: unlike most female performers whose act is intensely erotic, she never made me feel as if I were crashing an orgy that consisted of her and the men in the audience. When she got it on at a concert, she got it on with everybody.

Still, the songs she sang assumed heterosexual romance; it was men who made her hurt, who took another little piece of her heart. Watching men groove on Janis, I began to appreciate the resentment many black people feel toward whites who are blues freaks. Janis sang out of her pain as a woman, and men dug it. Yet it was men who caused the pain, and if they stopped causing it they would not have her to dig. In a way, their adulation was the cruelest insult of all. And Janis's response—to sing harder, get higher, be worshiped more—was rebellious, acquiescent, bewildered all at once. When she said, "Onstage I make love to 25,000 people, then I go home alone," she was not merely repeating the cliché of the sad clown or the poor little rich girl. She was noting that the more she gave the less she got, and that honey, it ain't fair.

Like most women singers, Joplin did not write many songs; she mostly interpreted other people's. But she made them her own in a way few singers dare to do. She did not sing them so much as struggle with them, assault them. Some critics complained, not always unfairly, that she strangled them to death, but at her best she whipped them to new life. She had an analogous adversary relationship with the musical form that dominated her imagination—the blues. Blues represented another external structure, one with its own contradictory tradition of sexual affirmation and sexist conservatism. But Janis used blues conventions to reject blues sensibility. To sing the blues is a way of transcending pain by confronting it with dignity, but Janis wanted nothing less than to scream it out of existence. Big Mama Thornton's classic rendition of "Ball and Chain" carefully balances defiance and resignation, toughness

and vulnerability. She almost pities her oppressor: "I know you're gonna miss me, baby . . . You'll find that your whole life will be like mine, all wrapped up in a ball and chain." Her singing conveys, above all, her determination to survive abuse. Janis makes the song into one long frenzied, despairing protest. Why, why, *why,* she asks over and over, like a child unable to comprehend injustice. "It ain't fair . . . this can't be . . . I just wanted to hold you . . . All I ever wanted to do was to love you." The pain is overwhelming her, "draggin' me down . . . maybe, maybe you can help me—c'mon *help me.*" There are similar differences between her recording of "Piece of My Heart" and Erma Franklin's. When Franklin sings it, it is a challenge: no matter what you do to me, I will not let you destroy my ability to be human, to love. Joplin seems rather to be saying, surely if I keep taking this, if I keep setting an example of love and forgiveness, surely he has to understand, change, give me back what I have given.

Her pursuit of pleasure had the same driven quality; what it amounted to was refusal to admit of any limits that would not finally yield to the virtue of persistence—*try just a little bit harder*—and the magic of extremes. This war against limits was largely responsible for the electrifying power of Joplin's early performances; it was what made *Cheap Thrills* a classic, in spite of unevenness and the impossibility of duplicating on a record the excitement of her concerts. After the split with Big Brother, Janis retrenched considerably, perhaps because she simply couldn't maintain that level of intensity, perhaps for other reasons that would have become clear if she had lived. My uncertainty on this point makes me hesitate to be too dogmatic about my conviction that leaving Big Brother was a mistake.

I was a Big Brother fan. I thought they were better musicians than their detractors claimed, but more to the point, technical accomplishment, in itself, was not something I cared about. I thought it was an ominous sign that so many people did care—including Janis. It was, in fact, a sign that the tenuous alliance between mass culture and bohemianism—or, in my original formulation, the fantasy of stardom and the fantasy of cultural revolution—was breaking down. But the breakdown was not as neat as it might appear. For the elitist concept of "good musicianship" was as alien to the holistic, egalitarian spirit of rock and roll as the act of leaving one's group the better to pursue one's individual ambition was alien to the holistic, egalitarian pretensions of the cultural revolutionaries. If Joplin's decision to go it alone was influenced by all the obvious professional/commercial pressures, it also reflected a conflict of values within the counterculture itself—a conflict that foreshadowed its imminent disintegration. And again, Janis's femaleness complicated the issues, raised the stakes. She had less room to maneuver than a man in her position, fewer alternatives to fall back on if she blew it. If she had to choose between fantasies, it made sense for her to go with stardom as far as it would take her.

Discography

Janis Joplin, *I Got Dem Ol' Kozmic Blues Again Mama!*
(Columbia 9913; ☆5, 1969). *Pearl* (Columbia 30322; ☆1, 1971).
Joplin in Concert (Columbia 33160; ☆4, 1972). *Janis Joplin's
Greatest Hits* (Columbia 32168; ☆37, 1973). *Janis* (Soundtrack)
(Columbia 33345; ☆54, 1975).
Big Brother and the Holding Company, *Big Brother and
the Holding Company* (Mainstream 56099; ☆60, 1967). **Big
Brother and the Holding Company,** *Cheap Thrills*
(Columbia 9700; ☆1, 1968).
(Chart positions taken from Joel Whitburn's *Record Research*,
compiled from *Billboard* Pop and LPs charts.)

B ut I wonder if she really had to choose, if her choice was not in some sense a failure of nerve and therefore of greatness. Janis was afraid Big Brother would hold her back, but if she had thought it was important enough, she might have been able to carry them along, make them transcend their limitations. There is more than a semantic difference between a group and a backup band. Janis had to relate to the members of Big Brother as spiritual (not to mention financial) equals even though she had more talent than they, and I can't help suspecting that that was good for her not only emotionally and socially but aesthetically. Committed to the hippie ethic of music-for-the-hell-of-it—if only because there was no possibility of their becoming stars on their own—Big Brother helped Janis sustain the amateur quality that was an integral part of her effect. Their zaniness was a salutary reminder that good times meant silly fun—remember "Caterpillar"?—as well as Dionysiac abandon; it was a relief from Janis's extremism and at the same time a foil for it. At their best moments Big Brother made me think of the Beatles, who weren't (at least in the beginning) such terrific musicians either. Though I'm not quite softheaded enough to imagine that by keeping her group intact Janis Joplin could somehow have prevented or delayed the end of an era, or even saved her own life, it would have been an impressive act of faith. And acts of faith by public figures always have reverberations, one way or another.

Such speculation is of course complicated by the fact that Janis died before she really had a chance to define her post-San Francisco, post-Big Brother self. Her last two albums, like her performances with the ill-fated Kozmic Blues band, had a tentative, transitional feel. She was obviously going through important changes; the best evidence of that was "Me and Bobby McGee," which could be considered her "Dear Landlord." Both formally—as a low-keyed, soft, folkie tune—and substantively—as a lyric that spoke of choices made, regretted and survived, with the distinct implication that compromise could be a positive act—what it expressed would have been heresy to the Janis Joplin of *Cheap Thrills*. "Freedom's just another word for nothing left to lose" is as good an epitaph for the counterculture as any; we'll never know how—or if—Janis meant to go on from there.

Janis Joplin's death, like that of a fighter in the ring, was not exactly an accident. Yet it's too easy to label it either suicide or murder, though it involved elements of both. Call it rather an inherent risk of the game she was playing, a game whose often frivolous rules both hid and revealed a deadly serious struggle. The form that struggle took was incomplete, shortsighted, egotistical, self-destructive. But survivors who give in to the temptation to feel superior to all that are in the end no better than those who romanticize it. Janis was not so much a victim as a casualty. The difference matters.

The Doors

by Lester Bangs

The significance of the Doors should not be underestimated. When you consider the positivist context they discredited through their violence, when you look around at half time in the Seventies and consider the bands and singers that have captured the imagination in the years since—from Alice Cooper to Bryan Ferry—it becomes obvious that Jim Morrison was one of the fathers of contemporary rock. The Stones were dirty but the Doors were *dread*, and the difference is crucial, because dread is the great fact of the Seventies.

Jim Morrison was born on December 8th, 1943, in Melbourne, Florida. He came from a long line of military careerists, and part of his self-hype was that both parents were dead. He studied film at UCLA, hoping to make his own; but soon he drifted out to the Venice beach culture, where transience was a given and acid the drug of preference. A friend later claimed that during this period he ate it constantly, "like candy." Whether that's true or not, it's a fact that one day he ran into keyboard player Ray Manzarek, a passing acquaintance from film school days and a classically trained musician who today looks just like a schoolteacher. But back then, down on the beach, they squatted in the middle of the sand and Morrison recited him "Moonlight Drive."

"When he sang those lines, 'Let's swim to the moon/Let's climb through the tide/Penetrate the evening/That the city sleeps to hide,' " Manzarek has recalled, "I said, that's it. . . . It seemed as though, if we got a group together we could make a million dollars." The Doors as *concept* was created by those two on the beach that day.

The Doors paid what dues mattered in 1966, at crumby clubs on the Strip in L.A. and then at the Whisky A Go Go, where Morrison took off on his poetic/improvisational flights, aloft and hungry until Jac Holzman walked in one night and decided this exhibitionistic debauch was just the act to give Elektra, his slightly fading folkie label, a stake in the electric politics everybody saw building.

Holzman was no fool. *The Doors* (1967) turned out to be one of the best-selling albums of its era, with the hit single "Light My Fire" serving perfectly as the anthem of a generation until "Gimme Shelter" came along to supercede it. But their first real claim to history was probably "The End"; it freaked out producer Paul Rothchild, who waxed metaphysical with Morrison over the Oedipal drama. It had also freaked out the manager of the Whisky, who threw Morrison out of his club. And it was the first major statement of the Doors' perennial themes: dread, violence, guilt without possibility of redemption, the miscarriages of love, and, most of all, death.

Nevertheless, the last time I heard "The End," it sounded funny. Even by *Strange Days*, the second Doors album, it was becoming apparent that the group was limited, and that Morrison's "Lizard King" vision was usually morbid in the most obvious possible way, and thus cheap. The whole nightmare

easily translated into parody—and there was a supremely sad irony here. But when Morrison hit straight and deep—"People are strange when you're a stranger/Faces look ugly when you're alone"—you knew he felt the chill and lived it, and that was perhaps the saddest part. Because in time he became a true clown, picking up the Lizard King cartoon and wearing it like a bib to keep the drunk drool from rolling down to stain his shirt. Meanwhile the audience, oblivious to irony if not entirely to pathos, felt burned as they watched him get drunker and fatter. Pretty soon the word was out all down the line and high school kids were scornful of the Doors; by the time *Waiting For the Sun* was released, the band's stock had dropped to a level just this side of bubblegum, even as Morrison still skirted skid row.

So, with the same desperation that drives millions of far less celebrated alcoholics, Morrison began to flirt with new and more dangerous forms of exhibitionism. Creating havoc on planes, getting arrested in airports. Pushing his way to the stage of the Troubador and raving drunkenly. Onstage at a Doors concert in New Haven, telling the crowd how he and a girl were maced by police in the dressing room; stage suddenly covered with police, the whole thing stupid. But not as stupid as the famous Miami cock-flashing incident. March 1969. A song broken down in the middle, the singer too drunk to even make a pretense of professionalism. Silence as the whole auditorium slips into suspended animation, stop time, maybe a few scattered boos, everybody waiting for the Lizard King to do something crazy. That's what they've come here and paid good money for—a little vicarious insanity, to carry home and nurse, tuck under the pillow you dream on. So Morrison screamed drunkenly, "You wanna see my cock?" and then unzipped, waving his flaccid peter in the air for a couple of still moments . . . well, even if he did stand trial on charges of indecent exposure, public drunkenness, etc., it really wasn't much after all, was it? Christ, I have seen Iggy Stooge vomit or cut himself and bleed on his audiences. Yet this pathetic, petty act was the beginning of the end for Morrison and the Doors.

Meanwhile, the Doors' artistic stock had hit an all-time low with *The Soft Parade,* released in summer 1969, not long after the Miami incident. Relying more and more on brass, strings, and anything else they could bring in, they had not only failed to live up to their original promise—they had (Morrison had) turned what they represented into a joke. *Morrison Hotel,* released in early 1970, redeemed them somewhat, but somehow between Morrison's antics and the whole band's musical slippage the Doors had become a dead issue by the beginning of the Seventies. Morrison was by turns painfully and wryly aware of his own absurdity, and you can hear his humor in the between-song banter and semiimprovised lyrics ("Dead cat in a top hat . . . thinks he's an aristocrat/. . . That's crap") on *Absolutely Live* (1970).

But Jim Morrison had not set out, initially, to be a clown. He had wanted to be a literary figure, even if it was only the Doors'

Top: (1) Jim Morrison. Bottom: (2) The Doors in 1967 enjoying a first taste of success. (1 & 2, Elektra Records)

pop success that allowed publication of his sophomoric jottings in *The Lords and the New Creatures.* In mid-1971, with a bluesy and intermittently successful album called *L.A. Woman* finished, Morrison headed for Paris, home of the French Symbolist poets, birthplace of the Surrealist movement, Céline's misanthropic ellipses, and much else that had undoubtedly inspired him. He probably had some vague idea, like Hemingway and Fitzgerald before him, of finding literary sustenance in that atmosphere, and, like many another frustrated writer before him, he found plenty of booze. He also found death, in a bathtub, of a heart attack, on July 3rd, 1971. He was 27 years old.

Discography

Singles
"Light My Fire" (Elektra 45615; ☆1, 1967). "People Are Strange" (Elektra 45621; ☆12, 1967). "Love Me Two Times" (Elektra 45624; ☆25, 1967). "The Unknown Soldier" (Elektra 45628; ☆39, 1968). "Hello, I Love You" (Elektra 45635; ☆1, 1968). "Touch Me" (Elektra 45646; ☆3, 1968). "Wishful Sinful" (Elektra 45656; ☆44, 1969). "Tell All the People" (Elektra 45663; ☆57, 1969). "Runnin' Blue" (Elektra 45675; ☆64, 1969). "You Make Me Real" (Elektra 45685; ☆50, 1970). "Love Her Madly" (Elektra 45726; ☆11, 1971). "Riders on the Storm" (Elektra 45738; ☆14, 1971).

Albums
The Doors (Elektra 74007; ☆2, 1967). *Strange Days* (Elektra 74014; ☆3, 1967). *Waiting for the Sun* (Elektra 74024; ☆1, 1968). *The Soft Parade* (Elektra 75005; ☆6, 1969). *Morrison Hotel* (Elektra 75007; ☆4, 1970). *Absolutely Live* (Elektra 2-9002; ☆8, 1970). *The Doors-13* (Elektra 74079; ☆25, 1970). *L.A. Woman* (Elektra 75011; ☆9, 1971). *Weird Scenes inside the Gold Mine* (Elektra 2-6001; ☆55, 1972).
(Chart positions taken from Joel Whitburn's *Record Research,* compiled from *Billboard* Pop and LPs charts.)

The Kinks

by Ken Emerson

After a short spell as the Ravens, Ray Davies, kid brother Dave and two friends became the Kinks in 1964, but they might as well have called themselves the Kontradictions. "I Took My Baby Home," the first song they recorded written by Ray, was a bouncy, Beatles-like number which reversed customary sex roles by singing the praises of a female so aggressive that her "hug like a vise" and "high-powered kisses" literally bowled over her cowering lover. Not long thereafter, Ray again assumed a traditionally feminine posture as he beseeched, "Set me free, little girl." Such sexual hide-and-seek culminated much later in the crowning, syntactical ambiguity of "Lola": "But I know what I am and I'm glad I'm a man/And so is Lola." You figure it out.

The Kinks have not contented themselves with the attitudes conventionally espoused by rock and roll, either. Far from urging adolescent rebellion, they have repeatedly sided with parents against the cruelty of their offspring in songs such as "Rosy Won't You Please Come Home" and "Nothing to Say." They have even had the temerity to sing, "God save little shops, china cups and virginity." Even when London was at its most swinging (the Carnaby Street scene was skewered by their "Dedicated Follower of Fashion"), they contrasted two sisters, a harried housewife and her trendy sibling. Rock rarely sympathizes with housewives in curlers, but beleaguered Priscilla, who longs to escape her domestic squalor "just to be free again," yet decides not to, is the heroine here.

Priscilla saw her little children
And then decided she was better off
Than the wayward lass that her sister had been

Still, even as she accepts—and the Kinks condone—her lot, she runs around her home in poignant frustration. Life, as rendered by the Kinks with loving detail unrivaled in pop music, is never simple.

It's never simple because Ray Davies, the Kinks' lead singer, composer and guiding light, seldom is. "No one can penetrate me," he once sang as a half-boast, half-lament, and this would seem to be because he himself can never plumb, or resolve, his ambivalences. On the one hand he's a realist, a pop Balzac with a basically Marxist view of the English society he chronicles; no one else in rock has insisted so on the primacy of class. On the other hand he's a romantic individualist who dreads the gray uniformity a Marxist solution to social problems would impose, so he flees into nostalgia and fantasy. Both satirist and sentimentalist, obsessive poet of food (factuality) and drink (escapism), Ray is divided against himself politically as well as sexually. Seventies albums such as *Preservation Act 2* and *Soap Opera* have been fun-house halls of mirrors in which Ray is refracted as man and woman, capitalist and communist, pop star and normal Norman.

It's less the sophistication of his intellect than the breadth of his compassion that allows Ray to argue both sides of every question, and the outcomes are not answers but suspended judgments. Thus "Autumn Almanac," a British hit single in 1967, both satirizes and celebrates a self-satisfied suburban gardener. On its surface, Davies's "Dandy" (an American hit for Herman's Hermits) admires a free-loving bachelor. But Ray, in his vocal on the Kinks' version (on *Face to Face*), compresses humor, bemused contempt, moral disapprobation and, as he yelps the conclusion, furious envy. Among other things (a psychological study of the singer, for one), "Dandy" is a complex corrective for the banal oversimplifications endemic to rock.

Because, as Ray once sang, "life is so complicated" and offers no solutions capable of satisfying an active mind (or heart), the only options are humor and passive resignation. No one has written so many hymns to laziness as Ray, while the stoicism of "Big Sky" and the sweet acceptance of "Waterloo Sunset" approach philosophical grandeur. The result of such withdrawal, however, is isolation. Ray frequently sings of friends, but they're usually absent, and so are lovers. Loneliness pervades the Kinks' music, lending sad undertones to even their most comic songs.

But there was nothing bittersweet about the pile-driving hits in 1964 and 1965 that first made the Kinks (the Davieses plus Mick Avory on drums and Pete Quaife on bass) famous. "You Really Got Me," "All Day and All of the Night" et al. were amateurishly performed, poorly recorded precursors of heavy metal, but their very nonprofessionalism augmented their raw power. The rudimentary riffs possessed a maddening inevitability and Dave Davies's berserk solos, distorted accelerations of the guitar break on "Louie Louie," were staggering. The Kinks quickly tempered their image with some lovely, wistful ballads ("Tired of Waiting for You," "Set Me Free"), but it was not until late 1965 that Ray Davies's songwriting betrayed a distinct sensibility. "A Well Respected Man" revealed a social satirist whose knack for detail made commentary such as the Beatles' in "Nowhere Man" seem vapid.

On *Face to Face* in 1966, the Kinks came into their own. Ray had decided "to stop writing for other people and start writing for myself," and he emerged as an anecdotist spinning pithy tales of Hawaiian vacations, scrambled party lines, upward (and downward) social mobility, session musicians, housewives and runaways. Because it was essentially homely, Ray's voice sounded extraordinarily human, and his endless sympathy enabled him to become a versatile character actor whose vocals were variously boozy and broad, pinched and dry, tender and poignant. The band stopped bashing but remained just rough enough to communicate an offhand charm. Unfortunately, much of their music from this, their finest period, was overlooked in the U.S.; a dispute with the American musicians' union barred their touring here—but it may very well be that they had turned too idiosyncratically English to interest an audience abroad anyway.

Top: The latter-day Kinks (from left: Ray Davies, Dave Davies, John Gosling, John Dalton, Mick Avory). Bottom: The Kinks circa 1965 (from left: Dave Davies, Pete Quaife, Mick Avory, Ray Davies)

From short satires it was but a small step to a collection unified by a central theme (the pastoral nostalgia of *The Kinks Are the Village Green Preservation Society*) and, from there, the shortest of leaps to an album-long narrative. Written for British television, 1969's *Arthur (or the Decline and Fall of the British Empire)* was neglected in favor of the Who's *Tommy*, but its wit and compassion, both the expanse and specificity of its social panorama, made the Who's vaunted "rock opera" seem, by comparison, a muddled and meager affair. Moreover, with new bassist John Dalton the Kinks had returned to rock.

In 1969, the Kinks also resumed touring the U.S., with little success until the release of "Lola," their last big hit single to date. At first a painfully insecure performer, Ray Davies steadily became more flamboyant onstage, and his thinking grew ever more theatrical. The group added keyboard player John Gosling, and gradually turned into a troupe with a ragtag horn section and a chorus of actor/singers. Albums became soundtracks for elaborate stage shows—plays, really—and sometimes the music suffered. Ray writes few striking tunes these days, presumably because his mind is elsewhere, preoccupied with staging and lyrics. The latter are occasionally belabored, since dramatization, making external and explicit Ray's internal contradictions, requires simplification. Now the ironies lie not so much within individual songs as between them; the sum is more intriguing than its parts. *Preservation Act 2*, the Kinks' best work in this vein, is certainly a glorious whole, and the 1974 tour in which it was showcased afforded the finest *theater* (in the literal sense) rock has yet witnessed.

Throughout their changes, the Kinks have remained extraordinarily consistent. Passing fads have never diverted Ray from mining his seemingly inexhaustible sensibility, which, far more than any musical qualities, is the source of the group's longevity and vitality. Pop music normally thrives on simple statements and sentiments; what distinguishes Ray Davies's group is its human complications—its kinks, if you will.

Discography

American Singles
"You Really Got Me" (Reprise 0306; ☆7, 1964). "All Day and All of the Night" (Reprise 0334; ☆7, 1964). "Tired of Waiting for You" (Reprise 0347; ☆6, 1965). "Set Me Free" (Reprise 0379; ☆23, 1965). "Who'll Be the Next in Line" (Reprise 0366; ☆34, 1965). "A Well Respected Man" (Reprise 0420; ☆13, 1965). "Till the End of the Day" (Reprise 0454; ☆50, 1966). "Dedicated Follower of Fashion" (Reprise 0471; ☆36, 1966). "Sunny Afternoon" (Reprise 0497; ☆14, 1966). "Deadend Street" (Reprise 0540; ☆73, 1967). "Mr. Pleasant" (Reprise 0587; ☆80, 1967). "Victoria" (Reprise 0863; ☆62, 1970). "Lola" (Reprise 0930; ☆9, 1970). "Apeman" (Reprise 0979; ☆45, 1971).

American Albums
You Really Got Me (Reprise 6143; ☆29, 1964). *Kinks-Size* (Reprise 6158; ☆13, 1965). *Kinda Kinks* (Reprise 6173; ☆60, 1965). *Kinks Kinkdom* (Reprise 6184; ☆47, 1965). *The Kink Kontroversy* (Reprise 6197; ☆95, 1966). *The Kinks' Greatest Hits* (Reprise 6217; ☆9, 1966). *Face to Face* (Reprise 6228; ☆135, 1967). *The Live Kinks* (Reprise 6260; ☆162, 1967). *Something Else by the Kinks* (Reprise 6279; ☆153, 1968). *The Kinks Are the Village Green Preservation Society* (Reprise 6327; 1969). *Arthur (or the Decline and Fall of the British Empire)* (Reprise 6366; ☆105, 1969). *Lola vs. Powerman and the Moneygoround* (Reprise 6423; ☆35, 1970). *Muswell Hillbillies* (RCA Victor 4644; ☆100, 1971). *The Kink Kronikles* (Reprise 6454; ☆94, 1972). *Everybody's in Show-Biz* (RCA Victor 6065; ☆70, 1972). *The Great Lost Kinks Album* (Reprise 2127; ☆145, 1973). *Preservation Act 1* (RCA 5002; ☆177, 1973). *Preservation Act 2* (RCA 5040; ☆114, 1974). *Soap Opera* (RCA 5081; ☆51, 1975). *Schoolboys in Disgrace* (RCA 5102; ☆45, 1975).
(Chart positions taken from Joel Whitburn's *Record Research*, compiled from *Billboard* Pop and LPs charts.)

The Who

by Dave Marsh

half-dozen memorable bands emerged from the British Invasion. The Beatles, Rolling Stones, Yardbirds, Kinks, the Animals—each made their contribution to the revivification of rock and roll. But of them all, only the Rolling Stones and the Who have survived to tell the tale with their membership and style relatively intact. And even the Stones have changed from rowdy ravers to sophisticated darlings of the jet set. The Who alone have remained true to the original scruffy rock and roll ideal.

In the mid-Sixties, the Who was the perfect cult group. Known in America only for a few nonhit singles, reputedly involved in such fringe movements as pop art and mod, the bulk of their work was inaccessible. When the group finally arrived for its first American tour in 1967, its audience began to expand, but slowly. It was only with *Tommy* in 1969 that the Who finally gained star status in the U.S.

Ten years ago, it might have seemed impossible that the Who would be counted among the most important rock acts of the era. That they have become such an enormously important phenomenon is due less to any single event than to an accumulation of events, a cumulative style: the smashing of guitars, amps and hotel rooms; leader Pete Townshend's loquaciousness in numerous interviews; his influence as a guitarist on "third generation" and heavy metal bands from Blue Oyster Cult to Aerosmith; singer Roger Daltrey's preeminence as the model of the super sex star; the group's obsession with rock history and rock art; *Tommy*, first as a record, then as a stage show, finally as a film; Woodstock, where Townshend forever sealed the distance between rock stars and political stars by booting Abbie Hoffman off the stage; *Who's Next*, their 1971 masterpiece, where Townshend turned the synthesizer into a great rock rhythm instrument. And most of all, maybe, the tough brag of "My Generation": "Hope I die before I get old." By themselves, these are little more than memorable footnotes. Together, they create Significance. Not necessarily for the right reasons—the truth is more complicated than this—but Significance, nonetheless.

Peter Townshend, Roger Daltrey and John Entwistle all grew up in the same area of London, Shepherd's Bush. (Townshend, in fact, once dated Daltrey's sister.) After grammar school, however, they went their separate ways. Ironically, it was the stolid, retiring bassist Entwistle who gathered them together once more. In 1963, he was playing with a West London group, the Detours, which featured guitarist Roger Daltrey and drummer Doug Sanden. When the band needed a rhythm guitarist, Entwistle thought of Peter Townshend, who had been in his first bands and was then attending art college. Townshend joined; soon after, Daltrey gave up guitar for full-time singing, and the band changed its name to the Who.

It wasn't the group's repertoire that built its reputation. Aside from the formally trained Entwistle, there wasn't a solid musician in the band. But they, and their managers Peter Meaden and Helmut Gordon, were resourceful. The current teenage rage in England was a fashion cult called "mod," and the Who took on this look (which—as working-class kids—they might have done in any case) and projected their philosophy of calculated rebellion, using it to camouflage their fundamental musical limitations.

But Doug Sanden didn't really fit in. He was more than a decade older than the others, and he had the countenance of a convict. Meaden and Gordon made two demands: that the Who sack Sanden and (much less explicably) call themselves the High Numbers. Both stipulations were accepted. As the High Numbers they made one record, "I'm the Face," which didn't go far. The name change didn't last either, but they found the perfect drummer, Keith Moon. He auditioned by destroying a drum kit that had served its previous owner for 20 years without complaint.

Onstage, Daltrey spun his mike like a lariat, stuttered his lyrics in emulation of the amphetamine gobbling mod mob, danced wildly, threw back his head and screamed. Townshend leaped into the air, swung his arm like a windmill, spun his guitar and thrust it before him like a machine gun, building a wailing wall of feedback and distortion. Entwistle stood immobile in a corner away from the cacophony and riot, looking alternately bemused and perplexed.

The final touch to the Who's performance was probably added at the Railway Tavern, a local pub: Townshend stuck his guitar through the low ceiling, breaking the neck. Furious, he smashed it to pieces on the spot, and the band's reputation as rock's autodestruct group was born. Soon the Who's show predictably climaxed in a welter of feedback, with Moon collapsing his drum kit and Townshend pulverizing his guitar, smashing it on the stage and ramming it into his already abused amps. It was expensive, but it helped attract their next managers, Kit Lambert and Chris Stamp, nominally assistant film directors.

Lambert and Stamp arranged a date at the Marquee, the West End's fashionable pop club, and packed it with local mod followers of the band. Their engagement lasted four months. When their first single as the Who came out, a spot on *Ready Steady Go!*, a weekly pop TV show, was offered, and Lambert and Stamp again packed the house with Who buffs.

Lambert and Stamp approached producer Shel Talmy, an American expatriate then having some hits with the Kinks, who agreed to do the Who's first few records. Predictably, the initial pair, "I Can't Explain" and "Anyway Anyhow Anywhere," were essentially higher powered reworkings of the Kinks' basic "Louie Louie" riff, although the latter incorporated feedback. But it was "My Generation," their third single, that would have earned the Who an eternal place in rock history all by itself. The guitar, bass and drums pounded re-

A curious crowd scrutinizes an early free concert by the Who—that's Keith Moon on drums, and a young Peter Townshend on guitar. (Michael Ochs collection)

lentlessly as Daltrey stuttered a Townshend teen-protest lyric which summed up the rock moment:

> *People try to put us d-down*
> *Just because we g-get around*
> *Things they do look awful c-cold*
> *Hope I die before I get old*
> *Talkin' 'bout my generation* ©

The pandemonium continued for three minutes, unrelieved, until it suddenly grew wilder, and the song finished in a burst of feedback, shouts, chants and clanging instruments. No one had ever heard anything like it, and no one ever would again.

"My Generation" was a three-minute revolution. Most of the other British bands were playing extremely derivative music, drawing principally upon American R&B and blues. The Who had their measure of respect for R&B (they included two James Brown tunes on their first album), but their chief influences were the deracinated rock of Eddie Cochran and the Beach Boys; their songs were built from secondary sources, influenced by people who had been influenced by the originators, rather than the originators themselves.

Peter Townshend found a way to expand on both R&B and white rock by playing a wildly propulsive rhythm guitar (influenced heavily by Beach Boy Carl Wilson, Cochran and particularly soul maestro Steve Cropper of Booker T. and the MGs). The style became known as "power chording," because one of its chief characteristics was a full-bodied, heavy, fuzzy tone, often accompanied by feedback or other distortion. Distorted guitar had been used on several 1965 hits—most effectively in the Rolling Stones' "(I Can't Get No) Satisfaction" and the Yardbirds' "I'm a Man"—but always as an effect, not as the focus of the record. On "My Generation," the feedback was the primary technique of a sophisticated, if untutored, arranger.

"My Generation" also made Peter Townshend's skills as a songwriter apparent. The lyric touched everyone who heard it. If the Stones' "Satisfaction" had expressed the individual discontent that was feeding the decade's rock explosion, Townshend's words established just how many people Jagger's dissatisfied "I" spoke for. Taken together, these two songs, the greatest singles of their era, tell us nearly everything we need to know about it.

Four brilliant followups—"A Legal Matter," "Substitute," "The Kids Are Alright," and "I'm a Boy"—established the Who's sound. Townshend generally introduced each number with ringing open chords, exploding the melody line with kinetic riffing: the seeds of the great guitar parts on "I Can See for Miles" and "Pinball Wizard" are already apparent here. But the dominant instrumental motif was crashing drums and the turbulent underpinning of Entwistle's bass. Vocally, Daltrey strutted, shouted and postured, usually to good effect, although there is a significant change on "I'm a Boy," where group harmony is used (apparently as a result of Moon's passion for surf music).

Townshend's lyrics grew more sophisticated. If "My Generation" had essentially been a feat of sloganeering, and "The Kids Are Alright" apparently only a commercially required reprise, the others were inspired. "A Legal Matter" presented a young philanderer squirming out of a marriage. "Substitute," which is a match for any record the group has made, turns the world inside out—Townshend's first great comment on the trap of illusion. Finally, "I'm a Boy" struck a mighty blow against momism with its picture of a young kid forced into premature transvestism.

Musically as well as lyrically, these were singular records. Henceforward, the Who virtually negated their antecedents. If the Beatles' "We Can Work It Out," for instance, could be done as pop rock or (in Stevie Wonder's version) as soul, there was no way to do "Substitute" as anything but hard-driving rock and roll.

Two of these songs were Top 20 hits in Britain, but in America the Who remained virtually unknown. The reason was thought to be the Who's American record label, Decca, which reportedly had almost refused to press "My Generation," mistaking feedback for a defective master. But the real problem was that the group's sound was too hard, and its subject matter too outrageous, for Top 40 radio. And the Who had yet to perform in the States.

When they finally made their U.S. stage debut, it was at Murray the K's Easter 1967 rock pageant at the Brooklyn Paramount. There they eclipsed even Cream, also making their American debut. When "Happy Jack" was released in April, it made Number 24, a welcome circumstance even if it was their worst record to date—more Beach Boys influence.

Happy Jack was also the American title of their second album, which didn't quite work out, principally because of inept songwriting. But the album's final track introduced Townshend's first attempt at extended composition, or, "rock opera." (Townshend says "I'm a Boy" was the first, which is either a joke or a fantasy.) "A Quick One while He's Away" wasn't much—a mélange of music, with atrocious singing and no more story than the three-minute "Legal Matter" or "I'm a Boy"—but it introduced some of the musical themes later used in *Tommy*, particularly the guitar riff and the group singing in the former's final segment.

A tour with Herman's Hermits helped build a following, but the group was badly in debt. Their destructive antics carried over to hotel rooms, and between the booze bills, reparations to America's innkeepers and equipment and costume costs, it was a bad time. Also, the boys weren't getting along: Townshend and Moon came to blows more than once, and the volatility sometimes extended to Roger as well.

Their solution was to keep working. "Pictures of Lily," the followup to "Happy Jack," only made Number 51, principally because its topic was masturbation. In England, Mick Jagger and Keith Richard were sentenced to prison on drug charges, and the next day the Who rush-released a pair of Jagger/Richard songs, "The Last Time"/"Under My Thumb," as a gesture of support, and they promised to do the same thing weekly until the two were released, which they soon were. It is unlikely that the ever-arrogant Jagger and Company would have reciprocated, but the "jail release," as the Who called it, was a token of the emerging solidarity of the rock community.

That community announced itself to the world with the Monterey Pop Festival in June 1967. The Who were one of the big hits of the show, playing at the peak of their form. Only Jimi Hendrix topped them, and he had to burn his guitar to do it.

"I Can See for Miles," the first post-Monterey single, consolidated the year's gains. It put the Beach Boys to rest with a vicious, droning guitar attack coupled with drums that cracked like doom itself. It made Number Nine that fall, the only Top Ten single the Who have ever had.

The album which followed, *The Who Sell Out*, was the most perfect concept album of the concept album era. It places rock in its perfect context—pop radio. The songs are separated by obnoxious commercials, bullying jingles, the whole Top 40 routine. The music is wonderful. Even the hints of orchestration, the occasional brass and ethereal Beach Boys-affected harmony voicings are used to create driving, rock and roll-style effects.

There was also a concept within the concept: a two-part opus, "Rael," which was another step in the formation of rock opera. Its genesis is unclear—apparently, it was intended to be an even longer work—and its story nonexistent, but "Rael" was spectacularly beautiful in a way that "A Quick One" was not.

Most importantly, *The Who Sell Out*, unlike *Sgt. Pepper's Lonely Hearts Club Band*, *Pet Sounds* or *Their Satanic Majesties Request*, was as much rock as it was concept. If there had been any doubt before, it was ended: the Who played only rock and roll, and they played it as well as anyone. All they lacked was mystique, and that wasn't long in coming.

The focus of the group increasingly shifted to Townshend. Although his hawk-nose visage would never replace Daltrey's stud pout as a sex symbol, Townshend was now accepted as a rock spokesman. By far the most articulate of the English rockers, he discussed rock and the scene as a very well informed fan, unabashedly slamming icons he found pompous, hollow or sanctimonious. (He had been doing so all along. "Substitute," for instance, was written as a parody of "19th Nervous Breakdown.")

In keeping with the times, Townshend's thoughts were turning inward. He began to study Meher Baba, the Indian "perfect master" who had lived 44 years without speaking. It was at about the same time, shortly after *Sell Out*, that Townshend conceived his "rock opera," a spiritual allegory tentatively called "Deaf, Dumb and Blind Boy," which spawned *Tommy*.

When the "opera" album was finally released in May 1969, it was seized not only by the rock community but by the straight press as a cultural event. Predictably, however, the coverage of the event missed the substance of the work. Serious music critics were caught up in proving that *Tommy* was not really opera—which was something even a deaf, dumb and blind boy could have perceived. Rock writers were put off by the pretension of the idea, claiming that the Who had lost the spirit of rock.

In fact, *Tommy* recapitulated the Who's most famous musical themes. The two-record length was *Tommy*'s real downfall: the story had no dramatic action, and there simply wasn't enough first-rate music to fill the time. Too much of Townshend's guitar was simply unarranged; a fuller, more orchestral arrangement, like that of "Pinball Wizard," probably would have improved everything. But then the lyrics would have been lost. Rock opera was a real contradiction; and only Peter Townshend's deep commitment to rock could have made *Tommy* as successful as it was. Nonetheless, *Tommy* was an immediate best seller, and remains by far the Who's most commercially successful disc.

Tommy's best moments—"Pinball Wizard," "I'm Free," "Christmas," "Underture," the final "listening to you" bit—came to life onstage. The Who's two-hour presentation of it on their 1969 American tour (and in 1970 at New York's Metropolitan Opera House) found them at their peak. Musically, *Tommy* is the culmination of the era that began with "My Generation," and that's exactly whose story it tells. And that's whose story it was. Townshend's theme was most often seen as guru mongering, but that won't bear analysis; the philosophical question hinges on the disaster of Tommy's leadership. At the end, it is *he* who looks out at the crowd and sings the most beautiful and moving passage of the opera:

> *Listening to you, I get the music*
> *Gazing at you, I get the heat*
> *Following you, I climb the mountain*
> *I get excitement at your feet*

Onstage, particularly since the 1974 tour when the spotlight began to shift from the band to the crowd at this point, there's simply no doubt Tommy has been enlightened by his disciples, as well as vice versa. And that is a nifty, crucial piece of rock criticism. (Ken Russell, of course, opts for the opposite interpretation in his cowardly film.)

As if to bring this home, the Who followed *Tommy* in May 1970, with *Live at Leeds*. Their momentous performance at Woodstock coupled with *Tommy*'s sales in the millions had earned them an audience that, as Townshend put it, "thinks the group's called Tommy and the album is *The Who.*" *Leeds* set things straight. It ranks with the Stones' *"Get Yer Ya-Ya's Out!"* as the greatest live rock music ever put on record.

But *Live at Leeds* was no better than a holding action. Townshend faced a double problem: his "My Generation" epithet ("Hope I die before I get old") had begun to haunt him as he approached 30, and he needed a project that could free the group from the danger of being a one-opera sensation.

Who's Next seemed to solve Townshend's problems. It is the best and most sophisticated version of the Who's music: powerful, clean, driving, fed by marvelous guitar lines and Townshend's synthesizer work (he used the instrument as a singularly effective rock keyboard), and Moon's most controlled drumming. Daltrey handled the finest melodies he had ever been given with a delicacy that belied his vocal limitations.

But *Who's Next* was also a turning point for Townshend as a writer, rock spokesman and thinker. Always obsessed with illusion and role playing—the turn to Baba was a method of dealing with that, just as songs like "Tattoo" and "I'm a Boy" had been—he now became focused on a specific illusory role: the rock star's. Townshend began to use his heroic stature to undercut those who lionized him. In "The Seeker," the first post-*Tommy* single, he had questioned the relevance of counterculture icons like Timothy Leary, Bob Dylan and the Beatles, nearly a year before John Lennon's similar, widely hailed "God." On *Who's Next*, Townshend carried the idea even further, labeling the rock scene "teenage wasteland" in "Baba O'Riley." The album's lovely ballad, "Behind Blue Eyes," foreshadowed doom, and the hit, "Won't Get Fooled Again," held out hope only to the totally smashed.

Although *Who's Next* is a brilliant record, and while the concert tour that coincided with it ranks among the Who's best ever, it was also an omen of new kinds of trouble. Had Townshend been a different kind of artist, he would have jettisoned the rock opera idea altogether. But the Who had been talking for some time of *Lifehouse*, a story about a rock band that finds the lost chord and transforms the universe; although *Lifehouse* was never completed, some of its songs, particularly the theme, "Pure and Easy," were incorporated on *Who's Next*, on *Who Came First*, Townshend's subsequent solo album, and on the 1974 anthology of outtakes, *Odds and Sods*. The project that followed *Who's Next* was another opera, *Quadrophenia*. It is extremely well played, with Townshend's synthesizer leading the way again, and the story held much fascination: a mod tries to recapture the magic of his moment, and ends tragicomically. (The overt concept of double schizophrenia is really secondary.) Jimmy, the mod, had, Townshend said, "made the ultimate mod mistake: bad timing." And, clearly, time itself had become Townshend—and the Who's—central antagonist.

Peter Townshend worshiped mods when he was growing up, because they were freer—morally and intellectually—than he

could ever be. They helped him discover another of his themes: "There's no easy way to be free." *Quadrophenia* is a tribute to them, and also to the Who, mod's quirkiest spinoff. But Townshend's synthesizer parts lacked the impact of those from *Who's Next*, and the material was well out of Daltrey's range. The album is deeply felt, and, in its intensely personal fashion, the perfect proof that Peter Townshend is the greatest auteur of pure rock and roll, but the album, and the concert tour that followed, left many longtime fans wondering if "My Generation" wasn't an artistic prophecy, instead of a boast.

Thus, when *The Who by Numbers* was released in late 1975, it was acclaimed as a return to the basics, "not a concept album." But by now a nonconcept album by the Who was its own concept, and *By Numbers* was infested with an overwhelming concern with aging and with the lack of meaningful success. I could have lived without stardom, Townshend seemed to be saying, but to have gained it and then lost my faith in the *idea* of stardom is too much to bear. This is, I think, the ultimate intellectual rock attitude, and the music, which is the most fundamental since "I Can See for Miles," doesn't take anything away from that. The synthesizer, which since *Who's Next* had become Townshend's trademark instrument, was banished, replaced by Nicky Hopkins's acoustic piano overdubs. The songs were also fundamental; no themes, but plenty of messages. It was, once and for all, a great rock album.

The 1976 concert tour was less successful. In ten years, the Who onstage—where Daltrey is as much in charge as Townshend—have simply not grown, or even changed very much. The guitar smashing is only a memory, the leaps and mike spinning totally pro forma. Daltrey, in what looked like the same fringed outfit he wore at Woodstock, is surly, Townshend more bored than Entwistle, Moon alternately maniacal and ill. The spirit of the music still huddles there somewhere, but it has become lost in the giant hockey arenas the Who resisted playing for so long.

But it ain't over yet. In the Seventies, the Who, like ourselves, stumble on. And if we are all very lucky, we certainly may die before we get old. At least, too old for rock and roll.

Discography

American Singles

"I Can't Explain" (Decca 31725; ☆93, 1965). "My Generation" (Decca 31877; ☆74, 1966). "Happy Jack" (Decca 32114; ☆24, 1967). "Pictures of Lily" (Decca 32156; ☆51, 1967). "I Can See for Miles" (Decca 32206; ☆9, 1967). "Call Me Lightning" (Decca 32288; ☆40, 1968). "Magic Bus" (Decca 32362; ☆25, 1968). "Pinball Wizard" (Decca 32465; ☆19, 1969). "I'm Free" (Decca 32519; ☆37, 1969). "The Seeker" (Decca 32670; ☆44, 1970). "Summertime Blues" (Decca 32708; ☆27, 1970). "See Me, Feel Me" (Decca 32729; ☆12, 1970). "Won't Get Fooled Again" (Decca 32846; ☆15, 1971). "Behind Blue Eyes" (Decca 32888; ☆34, 1971). "Join Together" (Decca 32983; ☆17, 1972). "The Relay" (Track 33041; ☆39, 1972). "Love Reign o'er Me" (MCA 40152; ☆76, 1973). "The Real Me" (MCA 40182; ☆92, 1974). "Squeeze Box" (MCA 40475; ☆17, 1975).

American Albums

The Who Sings My Generation (Decca 74664; 1966). *Happy Jack* (Decca 74892; ☆67, 1967). *The Who Sell Out* (Decca 74950; ☆48, 1968). *Magic Bus—The Who on Tour* (Decca 75064; ☆39, 1968). *Tommy* (Decca 7205; ☆4, 1969). *Live at Leeds* (Decca 79175; ☆4, 1970). *Who's Next* (Decca 79182; ☆4, 1971). *Meaty Beaty Big and Bouncy* (Decca 79184; ☆11, 1971). *Quadrophenia* (MCA 10004; ☆2, 1973). *Odds and Sods* (MCA 2126; ☆15, 1974). *The Who by Numbers* (MCA 2161; ☆8, 1975). (Chart positions compiled from Joel Whitburn's *Record Research,* based on *Billboard* Pop and LPs charts.)

270

Eric Clapton

by Dave Marsh

Eric Clapton was the focal point of the cult that formed around the electric guitar and guitarists during the Sixties; until the advent of Jimi Hendrix, Clapton was the unchallenged master. CLAPTON IS GOD, read the graffiti in London; plenty of aspiring guitarists believed it.

The classic Clapton pose—back to the crowd, head bowed over his instrument, alone with the agony of the blues—suggested a supplicant communing with something inward and elevated. As few white men have, he understood the impulses behind the blues, even if he could not always express them. In a way, his entire career can be seen as a search for a form in which he could express the staple blues emotions—fear, loneliness, anger and humor—in a personally valid way. It was a prototypical Sixties search, and the measure of his accomplishment is that where so many others became sidetracked or fell short, Clapton finally attained his goal.

In retrospect, there is little in his early recordings to substantiate claims of genius—less on the Yardbirds cuts (where he played Chuck Berry riffs with only as much skill as Keith Richard) than on his tracks with John Mayall's Bluesbreakers; there, by playing songs by Chicago and Delta bluesmen like Otis Rush, Robert Johnson and Freddie King, Clapton at least opened up a new world of music to the rock crowd. It was Mayall's evangelizing and Clapton's playing that laid the groundwork for the white blues "revivals" of 1965–'68 in both Britain and America.

Like Mike Bloomfield, who was doing similar work at the same time with Paul Butterfield in America, Clapton did more than merely imitate the Chicago bluesmen. He sped their licks up, indulging in a flashy sort of instrumental showmanship that helped make the blues appealing to rock listeners. Such music, as represented on the first Bluesbreakers LP and on the tracks he cut with Jimmy Page between his stint with Mayall and the formation of Cream, never offered him the opportunity to fully express himself. He was still an English white kid trying to connect with the emotions of older, black Americans.

With Cream, the band he formed in 1966 with bassist Jack Bruce and drummer Ginger Baker, Clapton did find a more personal style, but it wasn't lasting. Cream created the fastest, loudest, most overpowering blues-based rock ever heard, particularly onstage, which is where the group acquired its reputation. But the emphasis was on quantity at the expense of quality. Overlong solos were the order of the day, often to the exclusion of discipline or tastefulness. While the group spawned a seemingly infinite flock of imitators—boogie bands, power trios and heavy metal groups—it is only as an influence that most of Cream's music, so widely hailed at the time, will last. It was a good show, but it wasn't great music.

After Cream broke up in 1968, Clapton and Baker quickly regrouped, joining forces with Steve Winwood of Traffic and Rick Grech of Family to form Blind Faith, the first overt attempt to manufacture a "supergroup"; although the group had been elaborately hyped, its first tour did not sell out, and by late 1969, the band was finished.

But on the Blind Faith tour, Clapton had become involved with the opening act, Delaney and Bonnie and Friends, and when his band folded, he joined them for a tour. Once more a sideman, he was able to relax into their easy mix of country, blues, rock and white gospel. After that, Delaney Bramlett and many of the group's sidemen joined him for his first solo LP, where for the first time he took complete charge of singing and also emerged as a writer. It was a mixed success—only J.J. Cale's "After Midnight" and a pair of collaborations, "Blues Power" (by Clapton with Leon Russell) and "Let It Rain" (with Bonnie Bramlett) really stood out.

Clapton then finally formed his first full-fledged group, Derek and the Dominoes, comprised of several Delaney and Bonnie alumni, and with the band's first album, Clapton finally found his own blues, though it had obviously not been a simple process. For one thing, during the Blind Faith tour, he had been converted to Christianity, an odd choice when most of his musical colleagues were opting for Eastern religions as a means of solace against the terrors and rigors of an intensely public life. But like artists from Tennessee Williams, T.S. Eliot, Little Richard and Jerry Lee Lewis, Clapton found something inspiring in Christianity that simply wasn't available elsewhere. It was undoubtedly a tradition comfortable to Clapton; but he may have also relished the irony of placing God against what had been labeled "devil's music," first in the black community (the blues) and later in the white (rock). Clapton had always had a slightly mystical quality—you can see him nearly as a changeling in the photos on the cover of Atlantic's *History of Eric Clapton*, where he never looks the same way twice.

The association with devil's music must have cut deeper, because Clapton had become thoroughly involved with the legend of Robert Johnson, the greatest of the preelectric bluesmen. Johnson, it was said, had left his Mississippi hometown an incompetent guitarist and singer and returned (from no one knew where) a year later with the enormous talent that distinguished the handful of recordings he made before his death in his mid-20s. Much of Johnson's career parallels Clapton's. Between Mayall and the formation of Cream, Clapton is said to have locked himself in a room for a year, with only his guitar. There he began to develop his own style. It was also well-known that he hardly expected to live until he was 30—in fact, some said he looked forward to dying young. But Clapton lost his faith before Derek and the Dominoes recorded their first and only album, *Layla*. He had become infatuated with Patti Harrison, wife of his good friend George, of the Beatles. When Patti elected to return to her husband, Clapton was crushed—he deserted religion and began shooting heroin.

Eric Clapton in 1974 (David Melhado)

272

Clockwise from top left: (1) Cream circa 1967,
from left—Ginger Baker, Eric Clapton, Jack Bruce;
(2) Eric Clapton on his first American "comeback" tour,
1974; (3) Blind Faith, from left—Steve Winwood, Rich Grech,
Ginger Baker, Clapton; (4) Derek and the Dominos, from
left—Jim Gordon, Carl Radle, Bobby Whitlock, Clapton; (5) Eric
Clapton backstage in 1969; (6) The Yardbirds. (2 & 4,
Atlantic Records; 3, 5 & 6, Robert Stigwood)

The disappointment fueled his next record. The passion is present in standard 12-bar blues like "Have You Ever Loved a Woman," "Nobody Knows You when You're Down and Out," and "Key to the Highway"; in classic rock and roll like Chuck Willis's "It's Too Late"; in originals like "Bell Bottom Blues." It is majestically apparent in a brief, intensely moving version of "Little Wing," Jimi Hendrix's simplest, most poetic song. But it smashes home most forcefully with "Layla," perhaps the most powerful and beautiful song of the Seventies.

There are few moments in the repertoire of recorded rock where a singer or writer has reached so deeply into himself that the effect of hearing them is akin to witnessing a murder, or a suicide: Dylan's "Like a Rolling Stone," the Four Tops' "Reach Out I'll Be There," "Love Child" by the Supremes, "You've Lost That Lovin' Feelin'," Phil Spector's Righteous Brothers hit, Neil Young's *Tonight's the Night*, John Lennon's *Plastic Ono Band*, Roy Orbison's "Running Scared," Bruce Springsteen's "Backstreets"—all are sung and played as though lives depended upon them. To me, "Layla" is the greatest of them all.

It emerges, seven minutes of agony, from an album that is the most assured Clapton has ever made. For three sides the mood has been tranquil. "Little Wing," the breathtaking number that perches at the beginning of that final side, offers a hint of the pain in store, but its effect is soaring, transcendent—we have to imagine the hurt. "Layla," by contrast, opens suddenly, the guitars trumpeting the theme; and then the maelstrom begins. At first, the words seem total gibberish; all that's clear is the awfulness of it all, undiminished on the hundredth hearing:

Let's make the best of the situation
Before I finally go insane
Please don't say we'll never find a way
Or tell me all my love's in vain

There is, I suppose, a certain irony in Clapton's quotation from Robert Johnson ("Love in Vain") in his darkest hour. But it is also fitting in the most direct sense, for with "Layla," Clapton composed his own perfect blues without resorting to the traditional blues form. It's an epiphany few white men have experienced—only Van Morrison's *Astral Weeks* and *Saint Dominic's Preview* seem so rooted in the blues experience while eschewing the 12-bar form. For that reason alone, the song's greatness and its importance to rock history and Clapton's career would be unquestioned. The unguent piano and slide guitar break which follows that final verse only makes what has come before seem all the more intense.

Even such a song could not clear the blood from the floor, but in the first four minutes of "Layla," Eric Clapton nevertheless fulfilled the intention of his first decade of music. He had finally felt the music as deeply as anyone, matched Robert Johnson blow for blow, sorrow for sorrow. Having done so, he dropped from sight for nearly three years.

From the last part of 1971 through 1972, Clapton remained in virtual isolation. In January 1973, Peter Townshend of the Who arranged a London solo concert for him at the Rainbow Theatre. Ostensibly, Clapton was recovering from his addiction but there was also a musical question: where do you go from "Layla"?

Clapton answered the question, or began to, in July 1974, with an album called *461 Ocean Boulevard*, a full-scale tour featuring a band that was as good as it was unheralded, and a ROLLING STONE interview in which he told his story: about drugs, "Layla," the conversion to Christianity, his affair with Patti Harrison (with whom he now lives). But in light of *461*, Clapton's most crucial comment was, "I still pray."

Unlike Peter Townshend or John McLaughlin or George Harrison, Clapton hadn't been thought of as an artist with a specific creed; it was easy to miss the religious implications of his work. But they were there, in the easy feeling of the music, and in the lyrics. The song titles on *461 Ocean Boulevard* told the story: "Please Be with Me," "I Can't Hold Out," "Let It Grow," "Give Me Strength." Clapton was much more supplicant, obviously, than missionary, another thing that differentiated him from the other religiously oriented rock stars. In its way, Christianity influenced *461 Ocean Boulevard* as deeply as Judaism shaped Bob Dylan's *John Wesley Harding*. The tension of the blues was still present, but it was accepted and channeled more calmly. Nor had Clapton succumbed to Christian mores entirely: one of the best numbers on *461* was a reworked version of Johnny Otis's "Willie and the Hand Jive," and he was still capable of reveling in the pure carnality of reggae. The album, in short, wasn't all sweetness and light—even the sexuality had a dark undertone. But then, once possessed by the gloomy spirit of Robert Johnson, it's unlikely that anyone could shake it entirely.

Discography

Sonny Boy Williamson, *Sonny Boy Williamson and the Yardbirds* (Mercury 61071; 1966; released in Britain 1964). **Yardbirds,** *For Your Love* (Epic 26167; ☆96, 1965; Clapton appears on several cuts). *Having a Rave Up with the Yardbirds* (Epic 26177; ☆53, 1965; Clapton appears on side two, recorded live in 1964). *The Yardbirds Featuring Performances by Jeff Beck, Eric Clapton, Jimmy Page* (Epic 30135; ☆155, 1970). **John Mayall,** *Bluesbreakers* (London 492; 1967; released in Britain 1965). **Cream,** *Fresh Cream* (Atco 206; ☆39, 1967; released in Britain 1966). *Disraeli Gears* (Atco 232; ☆4, 1967). *Wheels of Fire* (Atco 700; ☆1, 1968). *Goodbye* (Atco 7001; ☆2, 1969). *Best of Cream* (Atco 291; ☆3, 1969). *Live Cream* (Atco 328; ☆15, 1970). *Live—Vol. 2* (Atco 7005; ☆27, 1972). *Heavy Cream* (Polydor 3502, ☆135, 1972). *Off the Top* (Polydor 5529; 1973). **Delaney and Bonnie and Friends,** *On Tour (with Eric Clapton)* (Atco 326; ☆29, 1970). **Derek and the Dominos,** *Layla* (Atco 704; ☆16, 1970). *In Concert* (RSO 8800; ☆20, 1973).
Eric Clapton, *Eric Clapton* (Atco 329; ☆13, 1970). *History of Eric Clapton* (Atco 803; ☆6, 1972). *Eric Clapton at His Best* (Polydor 3503; ☆87, 1972). *Clapton* (Polydor 5526; ☆67, 1973). *Eric Clapton's Rainbow Concert* (RSO 877; ☆18, 1973). *461 Ocean Boulevard* (RSO 4801; ☆1, 1974). *There's One in Every Crowd* (RSO 4806; ☆21, 1975). *E.C. Was Here* (RSO 4809; ☆20, 1975).
(Chart positions taken from Joel Whitburn's *Record Research,* compiled from *Billboard* LPs chart.)

Jimi Hendrix

by John Morthland

Jimi Hendrix was the flower generation's electric nigger dandy—its king stud and golden calf, its maker of mighty dope music, its most outrageously visible force. That he was also a revolutionary musician—perhaps the only one, in the end, to come out of the whole mid-Sixties psychedelic explosion—was often obscured by that all-consuming image and the most obvious elements of his music, and it led Hendrix to fight many a lonely battle with himself in front of thousands of admirers. Three years and three months after his triumphant performance at the Monterey Pop Festival, he was dead.

As a guitarist, Hendrix quite simply redefined how that instrument could be played, in the same way that Cecil Taylor redefined the piano or John Coltrane the tenor sax. As a songwriter, Hendrix was capable of startling, mystical imagery as well as the down-to-earth sexual allusions of the bluesman. He sang in a wispy voice that at first seemed limited, but proved remarkably effective at conveying nuance and emphasis.

Hendrix came on like gangbusters from the start. He made his American debut at the Monterey Pop Festival in June 1967; appearing on the last of five concerts, he came onstage shortly after the Who had drained the audience with its mod flash and maniacal destructiveness. But Hendrix revved that crowd right back up again. Backed by Englishmen Noel Redding on bass and Mitch Mitchell on drums, he played guitar with his teeth and behind his back. He humped it and caressed it, and finally, to finish off his set, he burned it. He had played exhilarating music throughout, but when it was over everyone buzzed about nothing but that *show;* it was dramatic, it was galvanizing, and though it had alienated a few, the night was obviously Jimi's. Nobody was quite sure where he'd come from, but he had definitely arrived.

Actually, he'd come from Seattle, where he lived an apparently humdrum middle-class black life, listening to Eddie Cochran and blues, learning guitar at 12, playing in local bands for Cokes and burgers, getting in occasional trouble for dating white girls, and ultimately enlisting in the army (in 1959) at 17. By 1963, he was on the chitlin circuit as a backup guitarist, picking up work where he could find it—with Little Richard, the Isley Brothers, Wilson Pickett, Jackie Wilson, King Curtis and others.

Doubtful about his singing voice, he didn't go out on his own until late 1965 or early 1966. He had heard Bob Dylan sing and reasoned that if Dylan could go that far with a lousy voice, so could he. His band was called Jimmy James and the Blue Flames, and they worked the Greenwich Village clubs. Blues bands were increasingly popular in the predominantly white Village club scene, and so Hendrix played mostly blues—a paradoxical situation for a black man trying to break into white music. But he was already beginning to experiment with feedback, fuzz tone, and the like. He soon attracted the attention of John Hammond Jr., who hired Hendrix (still known as Jimmy James) as his guitarist. Other musicians began seeing a lot more of him.

"I was performing with Paul Butterfield, and I was the hotshot guitarist on the block—I thought I was *it,*" Mike Bloomfield told *Guitar Player* magazine. "I went right across the street and saw him. Hendrix knew who I was, and that day, in front of my eyes, he burned me to death. I didn't even get my guitar out. H-bombs were going off, guided missiles were flying—I can't tell you the sounds he was getting out of his instrument. He was getting every sound I was ever to hear him get right there in that room with a Stratocaster, a Twin (amp), a Maestro fuzz tone, and that was all—he was doing it mainly through extreme volume. How he did this, I wish I understood. He just got right up in my face with that axe, and I didn't even want to pick up a guitar for the next year."

Bloomfield wasn't the only listener impressed with Hendrix. After the Animals' former bassist Chas Chandler heard him, he convinced Hendrix to move to England, where Chas promised to make him a star. Hendrix agreed; Chandler and his partner Michael Jeffrey told him to adopt his surname again and fixed him up with Redding and Mitchell, two British journeymen. The three frizzed their hair and dressed in the most outlandish clothes they could find. Working mainly with soul tunes Hendrix must have played a thousand times ("Land of a 1000 Dances," "In the Midnight Hour"), and then with Hendrix originals and a few pop hits of the day ("Hey Joe," "Like a Rolling Stone"), the Jimi Hendrix Experience soon stunned England and then the Continent, setting the stage for their Monterey appearance.

Immediately after that triumph, Hendrix set out to conquer America as the second-billed act to the Monkees, a tour that must have been conceived in a lunatic asylum; the Experience played to deaf teenybop ears for a few dates before Jimi's management bailed him out by announcing (falsely) that he'd been banned by the Daughters of the American Revolution. It hardly mattered, because Hendrix had already accomplished his purpose via the release of the "Purple Haze" single and *Are You Experienced?*, his first album.

The single, with its fuzzed garage band guitar intro, was perfect for that spacey summer of '67: "Scuze me," Jimi demanded, "While I kiss the sky." The album was equally impressive; on it, Hendrix displayed almost the full breadth of his talents. Although his second album (*Axis: Bold as Love*) added a new twist by taking its inspiration from black vocal groups of the Fifties, and the third (*Electric Ladyland*) marked his mastery of the recording-studio-as-additional-instrument, that first album had so much going for it that Hendrix never really surprised anyone with anything he did subsequently.

Are You Experienced? had a multilayered sound, thanks to Mitchell's Elvin Jones-like drumming and Jimi's own arranging

Jimi Hendrix burns his guitar as the Jimi Hendrix Experience makes its American debut at the Monterey Pop Festival, 1967. (Ed Caraeff Photography)

reels. And Beck became one of the first superstars who owed his celebrity to his instrumental prowess.

Leaving the Yardbirds in the hands of latecomer Jimmy Page, who revamped the band before founding Led Zeppelin, Beck in 1967 recruited some estimable talent—Rod Wood, Rod Stewart, Nicky Hopkins—and tried to front a group of his own. But organization was not his forte: he couldn't keep them together nor, since he was interested primarily in improvisatory effects, could he write cogent material. His gifts were too mercurial to be effectively marshaled, and his thunder was soon stolen by the more cohesive Zeppelin, for whom the Jeff Beck Group's blues-based exaggerations served as a blueprint.

While Beck played in the States and became Jeff Who? to his countrymen, other Britishers never left the Isles. As the novelty of English bands wore off and American rock enjoyed a resurgence with Los Angeles folk rock and San Francisco psychedelia, many British groups never made it across the Atlantic, which was America's misfortune as well as theirs. The most notable of the missing-in-action were the Move, whose ponderous rhythms—all rock and no roll—and mordant lyrics made them pop favorites in their homeland. Their songs, beginning with "Night of Fear" in 1967, were oddball: jaunty singalong melodies deliberately encumbered with elephantine bass lines and given a grotesque edge by macabre lyrics about nightmares, brain damage, suicide and the like. Groomed by a sensation-seeking manager much as the Who had been a couple of years before, they dressed as gangsters, smashed televisions onstage and defamed Harold Wilson, who sued for libel and won. As more and more groups cluttered the scene, such outrageousness became necessary to attract attention: Arthur Brown regularly pretended to set fire to his hair; another appeared to plunge needles through his skin. But the Move deserved the hearing they got, for the texture of their music was thick and fascinating, and the madcap irony of Roy Wood, who wrote the songs and sang most of them with a wobbly chirruping smirk, was unique. In the Seventies, Wood became a multiinstrumental archivist, queerly reproducing sounds of the rock 'n' roll past, while two other members of the Move continued with the Electric Light Orchestra, a rock band-cum-string section which has scored several American hits of passing interest.

Only slightly more successful in the U.S. were the Small Faces, whose feverish live performances were especially welcome in England because the Beatles, engrossed in the technology of studio recording, and the Stones, plagued by drug charges and Brian Jones's deterioration, had stopped touring. Steeped in the Stones and the Who (whose mod constituency embraced them), the Faces started out playing inept rhythm and blues. Their first British Top Ten hit, "Sha La La La Lee" (1966), began with Pete Townshend-styled chording, rocked out with a Keith Richard-styled guitar lick, and stole the bass line from Fontella Bass's "Rescue Me." Yet Steve Marriott's freneticism onstage, even if he was merely a pip-squeak poseur, conquered all. By 1967 the Small Faces had mastered not only their instruments but a style of their own, a novel mix of psychedelic whimsy and heavy rock crunch. "Lazy Sunday" (1968), with a comic Cockney vocal, party noises, kazoos (quoting "(I Can't Get No) Satisfaction," no less), whistles, the roar of the ocean and the flushing of a toilet, was typical of the former, while "Tin Soldier" (1967), one of the late Sixties' overlooked great singles, epitomized the latter, with brutal riffs and Marriott's most electrifying shouts. While the Move's humor was queasy, the Small Faces' was high-spirited, and Marriott, originally an actor, became equally adept at lunacy and passion. He left in 1968 to form Humble Pie, with whom he eventually lapsed into the mock soul the Faces had outgrown; the rest of the band carried on with Ron Wood and Rod Stewart, refugees from the Jeff Beck Group who made the Faces, at long last, stars in America.

The Spencer Davis Group began in 1963, much like the Small Faces, but from the start their R&B was tauter, more authentic. The rather pallid Davis was quickly upstaged by teenaged Stevie Winwood, whose imitations of Ray Charles (Marriott's model was Otis Redding) were uncanny. When Winwood switched from guitar to organ, the band captured the American market immediately with "Gimme Some Lovin' " (1966) and one of the most excited and exciting vocals ever recorded by a white man, let alone a white boy (Winwood, who also cowrote the number, was only 17). His yowl seemed to yank him out of his body and the song was wrought up still higher by his wailing organ chords and brother Muff Winwood's hammering bass. Singer, songwriter, guitarist, organist and pianist, Winwood was a one-man show who had no need to share billing with Davis, and soon he holed up with three friends in a Berkshire cottage where, in 1967, Traffic was spawned.

Like Graham Nash, Winwood had become hip—drugs and the ethos they helped usher in had opened his young eyes. Pop professionalism was slick and superficial, so the fact that Chris Wood and Jim Capaldi were mediocre musicians hardly mattered: communal vibes were all-important. Bound together by tenuous feelings rather than by the nuts and bolts of music, Traffic disbanded and reformed countless times. At first Dave Mason, a talented guitarist and songwriter in his own right, helped hold things together with his sense of craft, but after his departure Winwood entered a gradual decline which has yet to be arrested. His best work resulted when he strained against the limits imposed by the pop format or a disciplined collaborator; without such constraints, the tension disappeared and Winwood, his generation's most prodigiously gifted performer, became its most notable burnt-out case, undone by self-indulgence, by a naive faith in amateurism (as if he played so many instruments for fear of becoming too skilled on any one), and by

self-repetition, the fate of those who rely on nebulous emotion rather than concrete musical ideas.

Still, Traffic's first two albums (with Dave Mason) were stunning. The first, *Mr. Fantasy*, was cluttered with psychedelic gimmickry and performed rather raggedly, but its ingenious eclecticism and Winwood's muffled vocals, which seemed to issue from a drugged fog, created a novel, heady ambience. The second, *Traffic*, was one of the decade's masterpieces, not coincidentally because Mason played a major role. Its tone ranged from jovial to desperate but the flawless musicianship never wavered. The band would never do so well again.

Another quick casualty of the drug era was Pink Floyd, whose leader, Syd Barrett, drifted off in a daze after their debut album, released in 1967. The first British group to utilize a light show, the Floyd were psychedelia incarnate, inspired by reports of happenings in San Francisco. They jumbled fairy tales and evocations of outer space, as Richard Wright piled up organ chords from the crypt while Barrett ground out grating guitar lines or reverberated into the ozone amid barrages of boggling special effects. Their music, if it could be called that, was an eldritch assault, but for all their weirdness they didn't entirely neglect singles. No British group, no matter how bizarre, could afford to: albums were too expensive and pocket money too scarce to permit a long-playing market to flourish as it did in America. When Barrett departed, he took his madness and humor with him.

The Nice were psychedelic but with a twist, tossing Bach into the lysergic brew. Bastardizing classical music had been a long-standing pop tradition, but the bravura and impudence of keyboard virtuoso Keith Emerson were unprecedented. As played by Winwood, Brian Auger, Al Kooper, Felix Cavaliere and Matthew Fisher, the organ came into its own as a vehicle for rock in the later Sixties, and Emerson was its Hendrix. The Nice (after guitarist David O'List left) evolved into a power trio along the lines of the Hendrix Experience and Cream. Emerson manhandled his organ, plunged daggers into the keyboard to hold notes while he whipped around to play the piano, and his antics were such that one easily overlooked how adept and imaginative a musician he was. His "Brandenburger," a riot of tubular bells, souped up Bach, orchestral settings and jazzy improvisations, was a dizzying extravaganza, the omnivorous eclecticism of which embodied perfectly the "progressive" rock the Beatles inspired. Emerson's playfulness avoided undue pretension, but not for long: when he moved on to found Emerson, Lake and Palmer, his music turned to pompous bombast.

While the Nice ran amok in the concert hall, Procol Harum haunted the cathedral. They too borrowed from Bach, but from his religious music: "A Whiter Shade of Pale" (1967) set Keith Reid's mumbo-jumbo lyrics (a patchwork of evocative phrases and Dylanish nonsense) to an echo of "Sleepers Awake" and became an international hit that the group, actually formed only after its success, never quite surpassed. The album that

followed, *Procol Harum*, was stately, somber and ominous, the confusion and despair of the words set in ironic contrast to the deliberate architecture of the music and the religiosity of Matthew Fisher's organ and Gary Brooker's gospel-tinged vocals and piano. Reid wrote of questers for revelation—conquistadores and, later, salty dogs—who came home empty-handed if at all, and the band's instrumental majesty made these failures still more pathetic. Very few groups (only the Band, which also exploits the piano/organ combination, comes to mind) have ever produced so fully realized a first album, and Procol Harum—garbled Latin for "far from these things"—has never quite duplicated it. The personnel has changed (guitarist Robin Trower now enjoys a profitable solo career) but Reid and Brooker remain constant, working endless variations on a self-contained sound that is timeless.

At the tail end of the Sixties appeared another, very different British band whose music had much the same stately, architectural feel. But whereas Procol Harum ventured far beyond rock to achieve this, Free was, in some respects, the British Creedence Clearwater Revival, rediscovering something primal in rock that had been forgotten in the rush of Beatles-like resurrections and progressive experimentation. Their moody, moderate tempos and severe simplicity seemed to rebuke the razzledazzle of other bands, and these restraints merely pressurized lead singer Paul Rodgers's passion. Paul Kossoff's guitar sizzled all the more because he kept it under such taut control. The most compelling English vocalist since Stevie Winwood, Rodgers sang with a tense, sexy swagger at first, but as the group, troubled by drugs and illness, disbanded, re-formed, disbanded and reunited again, its music grew even bleaker, culminating in the utter and eloquent despair of 1973's *Heartbreaker*, an album so dire the band had little alternative but to break up for a final time. Rodgers and drummer Simon Kirke are now with Bad Company, one of the most popular British bands of the Seventies.

Discography

Bee Gees, *Bee Gee's 1st* (Atco 223; ☆7, 1967). *Horizontal* (Atco 233; ☆12, 1968). *Idea* (Atco 253; ☆17, 1968). *Rare Precious and Beautiful* (Atco 264; ☆99, 1968). *Odessa* (Atco 702; ☆20, 1969). *Best of Bee Gees* (Atco 292; ☆9, 1969). *Rare Precious and Beautiful—Vol. 2* (Atco 321; ☆100, 1970). *Cucumber Castle* (Atco 327; ☆94, 1970). *2 Years On* (Atco 353; ☆32, 1971). *Trafalgar* (Atco 7003; ☆34, 1971). *To Whom It May Concern* (Atco 7012; ☆35, 1972). *Life in a Tin Can* (RSO 870; ☆69, 1973). *Best of the Bee Gees, Vol. 2* (RSO 875; ☆98, 1973). *Mr. Natural* (RSO 4800; ☆178, 1974). *Main Course* (RSO 4807; ☆14, 1975). **Hollies,** *Hear! Hear!* (Imperial 12299; ☆145, 1966). *Beat Group!* (Imperial 12312; 1966). *Bus Stop* (Imperial 12330; ☆75, 1966). *Stop! Stop! Stop!* (Imperial 12339; ☆91, 1967). *The Hollies' Greatest Hits* (Imperial 12350; ☆11, 1967). *Evolution* (Epic 26315; ☆43, 1967). *Dear Eloise/King Midas in Reverse* (Epic 24344; 1968). *Words and Music by Bob Dylan* (Epic 26447; 1969). *He Ain't Heavy, He's My Brother* (Epic 26538; ☆32, 1970). *Moving Finger* (Epic 30255; ☆183, 1971). *Distant Light* (Epic 30958; ☆21, 1972). *Romany* (Epic 31992; ☆84, 1973). *Hollies* (Epic 32574; ☆28, 1974). *Another Night* (Epic 33387; ☆123, 1975). **Yardbirds,** *For Your Love* (Epic 26167; ☆96, 1965). *Having a Rave Up with the Yardbirds* (Epic 26177; ☆53, 1965). *Over Under Sideways Down* (Epic 26210; ☆52, 1966). *The Yardbirds' Greatest Hits* (Epic 26246; ☆28, 1967). *Little Games* (Epic 26313; ☆80, 1967). *The Yardbirds Featuring Performances by Jeff Beck, Eric Clapton, Jimmy Page* (Epic 30135; ☆155, 1970). **Jeff Beck Group,** *Truth* (Epic 26413; ☆15, 1968). *Beck-Ola* (Epic 26478; ☆15, 1969). *Rough and Ready* (Epic 30973; ☆46, 1971). *Jeff Beck Group* (Epic 31331; ☆19, 1972). **Move,** *Shazam* (A&M 4259; 1970). *Looking On* (Capitol 658; 1971). *Message from the Country* (Capitol 811; 1971). *Split Ends* (United Artists 5666; ☆172, 1973). *The Best of the Move* (A&M 3625; 1973). **Small Faces,** *There Are But Four Small*

Faces (Immediate 52002; ☆178, 1968). *Ogdens' Nut Gone Flake Tobacco* (Immediate 52008; ☆159, 1968). *Early Faces* (Pride 0001; ☆176, 1972). **Spencer Davis Group,** *Gimme Some Lovin'* (United Artists 6578; ☆54, 1967). *I'm a Man* (United Artists 6589; ☆83, 1967). *Greatest Hits* (United Artists 6641; ☆195, 1968). **Traffic,** *Mr. Fantasy* (United Artists 6651; ☆88, 1968). *Traffic* (United Artists 6676; ☆17, 1968). *Last Exit* (United Artists 6702; ☆19, 1969). *Best of Traffic* (United Artists 5500; ☆48, 1970). *John Barleycorn Must Die* (United Artists 5504; ☆5, 1970). *Welcome to the Canteen* (United Artists 5550; ☆26, 1971). *The Low Spark of High Heeled Boys* (Island 9306; ☆7, 1971). *Shoot Out at the Fantasy Factory* (Island 9323; ☆6, 1973). *Traffic—On the Road* (Island 9336; ☆29, 1973). *When the Eagle Flies* (Island 1020; ☆9, 1974). **Pink Floyd,** (With Syd Barrett) *Pink Floyd* (Tower 5093; ☆131, 1967). *Relics* (Harvest 759; ☆152, 1971). **Nice,** *The Thoughts of Emerlist Davjack* (Immediate 52004; 1968). *Ars Longa Vita Brevis* (Immediate 52020; 1969). *Nice* (Immediate 52022; 1969). *Five Bridges Suite* (Mercury 61295; ☆197, 1970). *Elegy* (Mercury 61324; 1971). *Keith Emerson with Nice* (Mercury 6500; ☆152, 1972). **Procol Harum,** *Procol Harum* (Deram 18008; ☆47, 1967). *Shine On Brightly* (A&M 4151; ☆24, 1968). *A Salty Dog* (A&M 4179; ☆32, 1969). *Home* (A&M 4261; ☆34, 1970). *Broken Barricades* (A&M 4294; ☆32, 1971). *Live in Concert with the Edmonton Symphony Orchestra* (A&M 4335; ☆5, 1972). *Grand Hotel* (Chrysalis 1037; ☆21, 1973). *The Best of Procol Harum* (A&M 4401; ☆131, 1973). *Exotic Birds and Fruit* (Chrysalis 1058; ☆86, 1974). *Procol's Ninth* (Chrysalis 1080; ☆52, 1975). **Free,** *Tons of Sobs* (A&M 4198; 1969). *Free* (A&M 4204; 1970). *Fire and Water* (A&M 4268; ☆17, 1970). *Free Highway* (A&M 4287; ☆190, 1971). *Free Live!* (A&M 4306; ☆89, 1971). *Free at Last* (A&M 4349; ☆69, 1972). *Heartbreaker* (Island 9324; ☆47, 1973).
(All albums American. Chart positions compiled from Joel Whitburn's *Record Research,* based on *Billboard* LPs chart.)

285

The Band
by Ed Ward

It might have been a mention in the *Village Voice* that alerted me to the impending release of an album "by Bob Dylan's backup band," but the word had been in the air for some time. The day the odd-looking record, with its weird watercolor cover (painted, as I'd read, by Dylan himself), arrived in the local record store, I picked it up, confident that I had bought something good. If nothing else, it had a couple of new Dylan songs, and in mid-1968, evidence of Dylan's continuing existence was almost an event in itself.

Music from Big Pink sure wasn't a new Dylan album, though. In fact, the Dylan songs weren't even the best things on it: there was a demonic organ workout, "Chest Fever," that far outclassed Procol Harum's experiments; a couple of evocative if opaque songs by pianist Richard Manuel, "In a Station" and "We Can Talk"; and a bouncy number with funny lyrics, called "The Weight" for no good reason at all. The group didn't really call itself anything either, although on the record's spine it said "The Band." *Music from Big Pink* was totally unlike anything my friends and I had ever heard, and everybody wanted to know one thing: who were these guys, anyway?

To some, they were Levon and the Hawks, to others they were the Crackers, and to yet others they were the Canadian Squires. They'd gotten the name the Hawks while touring as Ronnie Hawkins's backup band. Hawkins, an Arkansas rockabilly singer who arrived a little too late (his first records didn't appear until 1959) to latch on to the U.S. rockabilly boom, had lots of spirit but little distinctive talent through which to channel it. Canada, however, was wide-open territory for an energetic rock 'n' roller, and Hawkins moved there with his band of Arkansas boys, including drummer Levon Helm, from Sonny Boy Williamson's hometown of West Helena. The group played the Canadian honky-tonks, coming south now and then, and as the original band members fell prey to homesickness or Hawkins's temper, they were replaced, one by one, with Canadians.

But even Canada catches up with fashion sooner or later, and as the gigs declined for Hawkins, the Hawks decided to strike out on their own. Levon Helm knew he had a good working band around him, so it was with confidence that they spent the next few years touring Canada. Guitarist Jaime Robbie Robertson was developing into one of the dirtiest, most inventive guitarists on either side of the border, while keyboard wizards Richard Manuel and Garth Hudson were extending black gospel music's piano-and-organ texture into something completely unique and Rick Danko played a Motown-inflected bass that was the perfect counterpoint to Helm's loose but snappy drum style. Levon was the best singer, but everybody except Robertson and Hudson took turns on vocals. Perhaps because it had developed in a relative vacuum, their music could scarcely be compared to anybody else's.

After hearing the Hawks in a Toronto bar, John Hammond Jr., the American folk/blues singer, invited them to New York

in 1964 to cut records and work gigs with him. Hammond wasn't the only member of the New York/Greenwich Village folk scene going electric, though, and soon Bob Dylan caught wind of the group. Dylan started jamming with Robbie Robertson and proclaimed him "the only mathematical guitar genius I've ever run into who does not offend my intestinal nervousness with his rear guard sound." Whatever Dylan intended by that, it meant that Robertson and Helm were in Dylan's band (with Harvey Brooks on bass and Al Kooper on organ) when Dylan played his famous Forest Hills gig on August 28th, 1965.

Nobody really seems to know what happened next, but Dylan ended up hiring the Hawks, without Levon. Whether Helm resented Dylan's moving in on his band, or whether he just didn't feel up to it is hard to say, but it was the Hawks minus Helm who toured with Dylan on his 1965–'66 world tour, playing all over Europe, Australia and parts of Asia. The group (with Mickey Jones on drums) was remarkable, as the bootleg recordings of the tour show. People came to see Dylan and went away marveling at his band; by the end of the tour, their place in rock and roll history was secure. They also backed Dylan on a couple of late '65 recording sessions, yielding "Can You Please Crawl Out Your Window," "One of Us Must Know (Sooner or Later)," and a few as yet unreleased tunes, including a magnificent instrumental, "Number One."

Back home in 1966, the Hawks knew the time had come to make a move on their own. They rented a large pink house in West Saugerties, New York, just down the road from Dylan's place near Woodstock. The first thing they did was to get Levon Helm back from Arkansas, where he'd gone while they accompanied Dylan. They wrote some new songs for themselves, and in an improvised recording studio in Big Pink's basement, two distinct sets of tunes began to emerge. On the one hand, there were collaborations with Dylan, the famous "Basement Tapes." Two of the Dylan songs were cowritten with band members: "Tears of Rage" with Richard Manuel, and "Wheel's on Fire" with Rick Danko. The rest, although arranged and accompanied by the band, were pure Dylan.

On the other hand, there were songs earmarked for the band's first album, *Music from Big Pink*, Big Pink being an affectionate name for their house. Capitol Records gave them a contract, neighbor John Simon helped them produce the album, and in the summer of 1968, it was released. It was a revolutionary album in many ways: the emphasis was on ensemble work rather than on the soloing that had previously dominated rock; the melodies, few of them blues based, were delivered by an ensemble that was almost orchestral in scope, yet comprised of only five musicians; the lyrics were elusive, like Dylan's, but with a distinctive and compelling cast: "We can talk about it

Clockwise from top left: (1) Richard Manuel; (2) Rick Danko; (3) The Band as rustic frontiersmen, 1969; (4) Robbie Robertson; (5) Levon Helm, left, with Danko; (6) Danko; (7) Garth Hudson (1, 2, 4, 5, 6 & 7, Baron Wolman; 3, Capitol Records)

now/It's that same old riddle, only start from the middle/I'd fix it but I don't know how/We could try and reason, but you might think it's treason/One voice for all/Echoing around the hall. . ." Enigmatic? You bet—I love this song and I'd *still* like to know what Manuel was writing about.

Big Pink really didn't sell as well as its impact would have you believe, and the Band removed temporarily to Los Angeles to record a second album, simply entitled *The Band.* With its evocative songs of the American frontier and the farming life, *The Band* remains their masterpiece. "Virgil Kane is the name, and I rode on the Danville train," sings Levon in "The Night They Drove Old Dixie Down," and after looking at the cover photos, you'd almost be willing to believe that this song dates from the time in which it is set, the last days of the Civil War.

The Band came out in the fall of 1969, and there was no time more appropriate to the release of such a collection of Americana. The amazing thing about the album was that, without quoting or making direct reference, verbal or musical, to country music, 19th-century parlor and military music, or any of the patriotic poets like Whitman, Sandburg or Lowell, it seemed to evoke all these things and more, entirely on its own terms. I was living in Ohio at the time, in a room with two windows, one overlooking a saloon and the other facing north, where there was nothing but fields and a farmhouse. I could sit for hours, playing *The Band* and looking out one of those two windows. If my experience is anything like typical, I would say that *The Band* helped a lot of people dizzy from the confusion and disorientation of the Sixties feel that the nation was big enough to include them, too.

The Band was the breakthrough. It sold well, enabling the Band to tour for the first time as headliners. Other performers started recording their material (including Joan Baez, who scored a hit off a philistine rewrite of "The Night They Drove Old Dixie Down").

The level of excellence *The Band* set was one the group was unfairly expected to maintain; it is hardly surprising that the next album, *Stage Fright,* was uneven and didn't contain one song with the distinctive stamp of their previous work. It didn't help, either, that the song "Stage Fright" itself was seen by many as a taunt at Dylan who, rumor had it, was considering going on tour again, with the Band backing him, but kept canceling or refusing to finalize his plans. Robbie also turned producer in mid-1970, recording a fine album by singer/songwriter Jessie Winchester.

The Band also cut a tune around this time that could have cracked the Top Ten for them (something they have yet, as of this writing, to do). A version of Marvin Gaye's "Baby Don't You Do It" (composed by Motown's Holland-Dozier-Holland) was recorded to test out the sound at Albert Grossman's brand-new Bearsville recording studio. It sizzles and snaps like the best rock and roll, but it has never been officially released. Too bad.

Their next album, *Cahoots,* was even weaker than *Stage Fright.* The Band was beginning to sound like the many imitators who had sprung up in the wake of its second album, and when the members photographed for *Cahoots'* back cover with their eyes shut, it prompted some to comment that they sounded like they were playing in their sleep. But they closed 1971 by proving, at a New Year's Eve concert at New York's Academy of Music, that they still had life in their collective bones. A recording of the concert, which featured a brass section arranged by Allen Toussaint, was released in 1972 as a double live album, *Rock of Ages,* an excellent set by any standards. Still, *Ages* contained little new material, and the Band's next effort was an oldies album; it seemed as if they were treading water. *Moondog Matinee,* released in 1973, was named for Alan Freed's Cleveland radio show, which, beaming clear channel, could easily have been heard by fledgling Hawks in Toronto. The oldies—Bobby Bland's "Share Your Love with Me," Sam Cooke's "A Change Is Gonna Come" and Junior Parker's "Mystery Train"—were of a higher order than on most such albums, but, good as the album was, I, for one, had almost given up expecting anything new or exciting from the Band again.

Then it was back to the starting line in a big way: an album with Bob Dylan. Not the world's greatest Dylan album or the best backup work the Band ever did, *Planet Waves* betrayed an artist out of touch with his audience. There was only one way out, and late in 1973 Bob Dylan and the Band announced a joint tour. It proved to be the kick in the ass both careers needed. The resulting live album, *Before the Flood,* is such a feast for the ears that it's too rich to get through at one sitting.

Dylan, refreshed, went on to make some excellent records, and even loosened up enough to release *The Basement Tapes* as a double album, including some of the pre-*Big Pink* songs by the Band. The tour also seemed to jar something loose in Robbie Robertson's creative faculties, as evidenced late in 1975 on *Northern Lights—Southern Cross,* the Band's first set of new material since 1971. It was as contemporary as the disco beat of "Forbidden Fruit," as antiquarian as "Acadian Driftwood," a song chronicling the migration of a group of French Canadians. The best Band album since *The Band* itself, it bodes well for the future of the only rock group good enough to be called simply the Band.

Discography

Music from Big Pink (Capitol 2955; ☆30, 1968). *The Band* (Capitol 132; ☆9, 1969). *Stage Fright* (Capitol 425; ☆5, 1970). *Cahoots* (Capitol 651; ☆21, 1971). *Rock of Ages* (Capitol 11045; ☆6, 1972). *Moondog Matinee* (Capitol 11214; ☆28, 1973). *Before the Flood* (with Bob Dylan) (Asylum 201; ☆3, 1974). *The Basement Tapes* (with Bob Dylan) (Columbia 33682; ☆7, 1975). *Northern Lights-Southern Cross* (Capitol 11440; ☆26, 1975). (Chart positions taken from Joel Whitburn's *Record Research,* compiled from *Billboard* LPs chart.)

Sly and the Family Stone

by Dave Marsh

After almost a decade, the image remains static and indelible. Sly and the Family Stone are on-stage, slamming out their music in all their leather, plumed velvet and satin finery. Sly himself is at the piano, fist pounding the air, shouting "I want to take you . . . HIGHER!" and the audience responds with an affirmation of that command. The music explodes; the sweeping rhythms of voice and band pull the energy together in a loose, semimysterious fashion. It's not quite soul, not quite rock and roll, but an epiphanous ritual. Or, depending on where you are sitting, seminal fascism. Nobody's thinking—everyone's grooving. Maybe a remark by Jimi Hendrix describes it best: "Is this love, baby, or is it, uh . . . con-*fu*-sion?"

Sly Stone was, for a while anyway, one of the greatest musical explorers rock has known. Almost single-handedly, he effected a revolution in soul music. With his band, Sly ended the dominion of the sweet basic soul sound practiced by the Stax, Motown and Muscle Shoals rhythm crews; 18 months after his first hit in 1968, "Dance to the Music," everyone was following his lead.

What he'd done was so simple it might have occurred to almost any black kid living in communal late Sixties San Francisco. The antinomian spirit of R&B—recklessness personified—was grafted onto the close-knit, deliberately paced rock band experience; the musical wildness of the rock band then was wedded to the utter discipline of the soul band. The sound was totally integrated, not just musically, but racially and sexually—here was a band in which men and women, black and white, had not one fixed role but many fluid ones. The women played, the men sang; everyone did something unexpected. It might have been only the heap of contradictions it suggests had Sly's talent not been equally unpredictable. As it was, the band lived up to its first proud boast: a Whole New Thing.

Previously, soul records had been conceived as vocal vehicles; even the often brilliant playing of a group like Booker T. and the MGs was merely supportive. Rock bands changed that: in San Francisco music, the vocals were often an afterthought. "Dance to the Music" finally pulverized those polarities by joining them not calmly but brutally—the voice and the music didn't achieve equality; they fought it out for space, right on the disc. The exhortation of the title may have been the whole message to a good deal of those who bought it. But others listened more closely, and what they heard spelled the doom of American R&B's formal stasis.

The impresario of this barely contained cacophony was one Sylvester Stewart, born in Texas, bred a tough street fighter in Vallejo, a factory town on the wrong side of San Francisco Bay. A music theory course in high school inspired him, and he hooked up with local DJ Tom Donahue, then running Autumn Records. There, Sly produced some of the first Bay Area rock and roll records: local, regional and, finally, national hits for bands like the Mojo Men, the Vejtables and the Beau Brum-

mels. When the acid-rock gang itself moved in, Sly moved out—he tried to cut Grace Slick and the Great Society and wound up with one song in 200-odd takes.

He went to work for one of the area's black radio stations. As usual, Sly did things quite differently, interrupting the flow of Stax and Motown singles with Beatles and Dylan tracks, fidgeting with commercials, raising the call-in dedication to a minor art form. In his off-hours, he had a band working in bars—the nucleus of Sly and the Family Stone. It ultimately came to include his brother Freddie, Jerry Martini, Jerry's cousin Gregg Errico, Sly's sister Rose, Cynthia Robinson and Larry Graham.

The pop scene was then at a turning point. Both soul and rock were trapped—the former by its own conventions, the latter by its increasing solemnity as it pursued High Art. Sensing a gap, Sly moved to fill it with his characteristic mixture of calculation, conviction and dumb luck. He made his music with the assurance of a man whose vision requires a new mode. In the songs that followed "Dance to the Music," he toyed with everything from free-form doo-wop—"Hot Fun in the Summertime"—to the basic funk-chant that would be adopted by the next decade's disco groups ("Sing a Simple Song," "Stand!").

He was a philosopher, too, preaching a message of total reconciliation that lived up to the big sound. "Everyday People," "Everybody Is a Star," "Life," "I Want to Take You Higher," and "You Can Make It if You Try"—most of them hits—expressed as well as anything the sentiments of the Haight, and the hopes of the ghetto. For a time, it seemed, Sly's approach could heal all wounds: offer black kids a model for something other than slick, Copacabana-level success; give whites a fairly healthy black star; produce for both a meeting ground where they could work out their mistrust.

In the best songs, Sly promised to work it out for them. "Everyday People" contributed mightily to the hip lexicon—"different strokes for different folks" was Sly's whole ideology—but it was also a taunt and a proclamation. Nobody who heard this record could disbelieve Sly's power; he really might transform rock and roll into some triumph of integration.

But even in a time when a good share of the rock population was flaky enough to believe in chemical salvation, Sly's utopian vision couldn't triumph. The first symptom of trouble was his own increasing eccentricity. Then Sly started to blow gigs—half the thrill of buying a ticket was anticipating whether he would really show. Usually he did, but he missed enough dates—generally without announcement until the seats of an arena were filled—to earn a reputation for irresponsibility.

At Woodstock, only a year and a half from the beginning, the dark underside of his vision began to catch up. "Higher!" became less a slogan of collective triumph than a means for ravishing the crowd. Otis Redding had died a year and a half

Sly Stone, the 'Riotmaster' (Charles Gatewood)

earlier, and the Woodstock generation was looking for a new black hope, someone who could make race a safe issue. With Jimi Hendrix already showing signs of resistance, Sly was the prime candidate.

In January 1970, Sly released the sardonic single, "Thank You Falettinme Be Mice Elf Agan." It was slinky, hip dance music, and no one thought much of it—the weird spelling was to be expected from this maverick. "I Want to Take You Higher," recycled as a single in May, was an afterthought, hardly an event. The gigs continued to be blown, while rumors of drug problems and threats from black political organizations floated around. Sly toured, canceled, recorded, failed to release. Meanwhile, no new music. It looked like the middle stage of a downward spiral: a Whole New Thing had simply petered out.

The spirit of that thing was now dominant, however. Sly's influence had been completely absorbed, and now coursed through the mainstream of soul, affecting rock as well. At Motown, the Jackson 5 and the Temptations carried his banner; in Philadelphia, the Gamble-Huff organization was churning out Sly-derived funk records; in Chicago, Curtis Mayfield, that sweetest of old soul singers, had made his move in the Family Stone's direction. Sly himself may have been in exile from the charts, but in the Hot 100, his music reigned.

In November 1971, he finally released a new album, just in time for Christmas. It was less than a merry affair, however. The title was *There's a Riot Goin' On*, and the title track was precisely timed at no minutes and no seconds. That was the first hint.

The next hint lay in the revulsion felt by many listeners—particularly, it may safely be said, white listeners. Where was the joyous, life-affirming black hero? This music stumbled, faltered, its rhythms hobbled like a heroin roller coaster, its entire tone an affront to the spirit of boogie. Sly had always built his songs from bits and pieces, strange unexpected scraps, parts zipping in—often half-unformed—to *make* a song. But this sounded like the scrap heap, connections unmade.

Then it got scary. "Feel so good/ Feel so good/ Don't wanna move" was what passed for exuberance on this record. It was the aural equivalent of William Burroughs's *Naked Lunch* ("... when everyone sees what is on the end of every fork"). Those who didn't stop listening became fascinated by the resultant chills and despair; even those who didn't want to know couldn't shut them out. *Riot* had not one but three hit singles—"Family Affair," "(You Caught Me) Smilin'" and "Runnin' Away." The idea was beginning to form that maybe *There's a Riot Goin' On* was trying to tell us something.

Well now, as open as it was supposed to be, the white rock crowd had not acquired a reputation for its fondness for a harsh, direct look at the black experience. It was hardly prepared to deal with a black hero who decided to work completely on his own terms; but even if he had to make them up, that's just what Sly was doing. In effect, he took the power of his stardom and shook it in their faces. "Family Affair," the album's biggest hit, was pure bile: "Blood's thicker than the mud." He meant it, too—that three-day mud festival in Woodstock wasn't enough to make him deviate from his true heritage. In the days of Nixon's White House and ODs all around, there wasn't much question where he discovered the blood either. "Muzak with its finger on the trigger," Greil Marcus called *Riot*.

Riot was perfectly timed. Maybe it ignited one of the greatest explosions of pop, or maybe it served simply as a sign. In any event, the airwaves were soon filled with tough black testimony, unbending, seeking its own audience and not caring so very much about the damage done to integrationist sensibilities. The Temptations scored their own experience with "Papa Was a Rollin' Stone" ("and when he died all he left us was alone"). Curtis Mayfield turned in *Super Fly*, a cheap movie soundtrack that came to life on radio as one of the most searing antidrug diatribes ever written. War proclaimed "The World Is a Ghetto," warned against "Slippin' into Darkness." Stevie Wonder excoriated "Superstition." Marvin Gaye simply asked "What's Going On." The O'Jays railed against "Back Stabbers." There was no avoiding this music; it was right there in the Top Ten. You couldn't get in the car and run away from it, because it kept blasting through the static.

These songs had everything to do with America at a time when an election was being stolen. They reflected an almost unspoken acknowledgment of a long list of sins from the murder of Fred Hampton and thousands of Vietnamese to crime in the streets and the everyday robbery at the grocery store, from the loss of simple friendship to the lack of a center in many people's lives. It was the world turned inside out. As if in proof, Sly ended his album with a reprise of "Thank You Falettinme Be Mice Elf Agan." Only this time he called it "Thank You for Talkin' to Me Africa."

The tempo slowed to a heartbeat. Nothing but bass and drums for the first minute, with some occasional jagged interjections from the guitar. Then those awful freeze-frame lyrics:

> *Lookin' at the devil*
> *Grinnin' at his gun*
> *Fingers start shakin'*
> *I begin to run*
> *Bullets start chasin'*
> *I begin to stop*
> *We begin to wrestle*
> *I was on the top*

Here, Sly pulled the trigger. It was torture, but a torture that had been lived out.

Sly was one of the richest black stars. Maybe the richest. His contract with Epic Records provided more than half a million dollars in advances for each album. He lived in plush Holly-

Below, far right: (1) Sly and wheels.
Bottom: (2) Sly and the Family Stone—l to r,
front, Rose Stone, Jerry Martini, Cynthia Robinson;
seated on couch, Freddie Stone, Sly, Gregg Errico,
Larry Graham. (1, Annie Leibovitz; 2, Don Paulsen)

wood comfort—neither drugs, fast cars, women nor fancy clothes were beyond his resources. To blow a gig, he had only to seize a whim. And this is what it came down to: "We begin to wrestle/I was on the top." No one—not even Sly—knew for how long.

Making that music in the studio was one thing. Acting it out onstage was another. In the live show, little of the *Riot* material turned up; maybe it was too difficult to do, but who could believe "Life" or "Higher" after *Riot's* exorcism of jollity? And the scars showed. The idealistic band disintegrated. Members drifted in and out. The music faltered and fell. A year and a half later, with *Fresh*, Sly performed the ultimate copout, epitomized by his final, brilliant, statement: "*Que sera, sera*—whatever will be, will be." The music was still good, in its way, probably better than *Riot*, but it was over. It was a great move, but it was also a marvelously concealed surrender; it took his onstage wedding a year later to sell out Madison Square Garden.

But one still listened with interest to each new record. Still hoped for each new show. No telling when the next *Riot* might begin.

Discography

Singles

"Dance to the Music" (Epic 10256; ☆8, r☆9, 1968). "Life" b/w "M'Lady" (Epic 10353; ☆93; 1968). "Everyday People" b/w "Sing a Simple Song" (Epic 10407; ☆1, r☆1, 1968). "Stand!" b/w "I Want to Take You Higher" (Epic 10450; ☆22, r☆14, 1969). "Hot Fun in the Summertime" (Epic 10497; ☆2, r☆3, 1969). "Thank You Falettinme Be Mice Elf Agin" b/w "Everybody Is a Star" (Epic 10555; ☆1, r☆1, 1970). "Family Affair" (Epic 10805; ☆1, r☆1, 1971). "Runnin' Away" (Epic 10829; r☆15, ☆23, 1972). "Smilin' " (Epic 10850; r☆21, ☆42, 1972). "If You Want Me to Stay" (Epic 11017; r☆3; ☆12, 1973). "Frisky" (Epic 11060; r☆28; ☆79, 1973). "Time for Livin' " (Epic 11140; r☆10, ☆32, 1974). "Loose Booty" (Epic 50033; r☆22, ☆84, 1974). "I Get High on You" (Epic 8-50135; r☆3, ☆52, 1975).

Albums

A Whole New Thing (Epic 30335; 1970). *Dance to the Music* (Epic 26371; ☆142, 1968). *Life* (Epic 26397; ☆195, 1968). *Stand!* (Epic 26456; ☆13, 1969). *Greatest Hits* (Epic 30325; ☆2, 1970). *There's a Riot Goin' On* (Epic 30986; ☆1, 1971). *Fresh* (Epic 32134; ☆7, 1973). *Small Talk* (Epic 32930; ☆15, 1974). *High Energy* (Epic 33462; 1975). *High on You* (Epic 33835; 1975). (Chart positions compiled from Joel Whitburn's *Record Research*, based on *Billboard* Pop and LPs charts, unless otherwise indicated; r☆ = position on *Billboard* Rhythm and Blues charts.)

Van Morrison
by Greil Marcus

In 1961, as a member of a band from Northern Ireland called the Monarchs, Van Morrison toured Germany and sang Ray Charles imitations to homesick American GIs. In 1963 and '64, as the leader of Them, a group working out of Belfast, Morrison began to find his style (a rough mix of American folk blues, R&B, electric rock and roll, Irish poetry declaimed aloud), driving his band through half-hour versions of songs that, cut to two or three minutes, would soon bring him a taste of fame. In 1965, in London, Them scattered, but Morrison recorded under their name with a few remnants of the band and a clutch of British studio musicians, among them guitarist Jimmy Page, later of the Yardbirds and Led Zeppelin. Morrison made two brilliant albums, *Them* (called *The Angry Young Them* in the United Kingdom, it sounded it), and *Them Again.* In 1965 and '66, he scored modest but unforgettable hits on both sides of the Atlantic with four of the most exciting records of the time: "Gloria" (covered by the Chicago punk band the Shadows of Knight, who had the bigger hit in America), "Baby Please Don't Go," "Mystic Eyes" and "Here Comes the Night."

To those who were listening, it was clear that Van Morrison was as intense and imaginative a performer as any to emerge from the first wave of the post-Beatles British Invasion. Yet it was equally clear, to those who saw his early live shows in 1965, that Morrison lacked the flash and the flair for pop stardom possessed by such clearly inferior singers as Keith Relf of the Yardbirds or Eric Burdon of the Animals. Morrison communicated distance, not immediacy; bitterness, not celebration. His music had power, but also subtlety; as a white R&B singer he was a great lyric poet. Without the superb studio band that had played on his records, he seemed unfocused, and his music did not quite come across.

What he lacked in glamour he made up in weirdness. He was small and gloomy, with more black energy than he knew what to do with, the wrong man to meet in a dark alley, or cross on a stage. He did not fit the maracas-shaking mold of the day; instead, in 1965, he recorded a shimmering version of "It's All Over Now, Baby Blue" that in some ways was stronger than Dylan's, and turned the fey Paul Simon composition "Richard Cory" into a bone-chilling horror story. Who was this Irish kid, singing folk songs and R&B with the raw emotion of a country bluesman, but never sounding black?

In 1966 Them broke apart for good, and Morrison took himself to New York under the wing of producer Bert Berns, scoring in 1967 with "Brown Eyed Girl," his first Top Ten single, after which he was promptly forgotten. Brooding and drinking hard, Morrison moved to Boston, where, in an incomprehensible Belfast accent, he pestered late-night DJs for John Lee Hooker sides. Once he was booed off the stage when a group that would later make up part of the J. Geils Band called him out of the audience to front their version of "Gloria." "Don't you know who this is?" Peter Wolf shouted at the hissing crowd. "This man *wrote the song!*"

But they didn't know. In 1967, when you said "Morrison," you meant the Doors, who, one read at the time in *Crawdaddy,* were preparing a treatment of "Gloria" that upon release (it never was released) would surely be greeted by the gathering storm of new rock fans as "a masterpiece."

As if Van Morrison's performance of "Gloria" had ever been anything else.

Bert Berns had tried. He and Morrison had followed "Brown Eyed Girl" with a dark, bluesy album called (with too-late trendy hopes) *Blowin' Your Mind*; the music was well-made (Eric Gale played first-rate guitar), but also morbid. Sales were minimal. The signature track was titled "T.B. Sheets," which was exactly what it was about. Who wanted to listen to an endless song about tuberculosis when the air was filled with the sounds of the Summer of Love?

Morrison returned to Ireland, apparently a burnt-out victim of the pop wars. There he wrote a set of songs about childhood, initiation, sex and death, which finally took form as *Astral Weeks,* a strange, disturbing, exalting album for which there was little precedent in rock and roll history when it was released in November 1968. Tempered by jazz restraint (Connie Kay of the Modern Jazz Quartet played drums, while the great Richard Davis provided the finest bass playing ever to appear on a rock and roll record) and three levels of string arrangements, the disc moved with a rock beat and a rock feel. It was as serious an album as could be imagined, but it soared like an old Drifters 45.

With *Astral Weeks,* Morrison opened the way to a new career, and established himself as a performer who deserved to be ranked with the creators of the very best rock and roll music. He has lived up to that promise.

Astral Weeks did not sell strongly, but it attracted widespread critical attention, and, in some sections of the country (most notably the San Francisco Bay Area), constant airplay on a few of the FM rock stations just then coming to the fore. Both reviews and airplay paid off with subsequent releases, and Morrison achieved a solid if not a mass popularity with *Moondance* (1970) and with singles such as "Domino" (1970) and the wonderful "Wild Night" (1971). He had moved to Woodstock, and he celebrated a pastoral life of domesticity and sexual delight; the hard edge of his early music, and the profound ambiguities of *Astral Weeks,* seemed well behind him. Then he relocated in Marin County, where his wife had grown up and where his popularity was fierce; one more album of good times (his best) followed, *Tupelo Honey* (1971); his domestic paradise fell apart; and his music turned tough once again, with *Saint Dominic's Preview* (1972). Yet Morrison's music has been of a piece.

Van Morrison, performing with Them in the mid-Sixties (Popsie/N.Y.)

294

"When I was very young," the late Ralph J. Gleason wrote in a review of *Moondance*, "I saw a film version of the life of John McCormack, the Irish tenor, playing himself. In it he explained to his accompanist that the element necessary to mark the important voice off from the other good ones was very specific. 'You have to have,' he said, 'the yarrrrragh in your voice.'"

Van Morrison has the yarrrrragh. His career, especially since *Astral Weeks*, can be seen as an attempt to deal with the yarrrrragh: to find music appropriate to it; to bury it; to dig it out; to draw from that sound, that aesthetic (for it is an aesthetic more than it is merely a sound), new tales to tell, or old tales to tell in new ways. The yarrrrragh is Van Morrison's version of Leadbelly, of jazz, of blues, of poetry. It is a mythic incantation, and he will get it, or get close to it, suggest it, with horns (no white man working in popular music can arrange horns with the precision and grace of Van Morrison), strings, in melody, in repetition (railing the same word, or syllable, 10, 20, 30 times until it has taken his song where he wants it to go). To Morrison the yarrrrragh is the gift of the muse and the muse itself. He has even written a song about it: "Listen to the Lion." Across 11 minutes, he sings, chants, moans, cries, pleads, shouts, hollers, whispers, until finally he breaks away from language and speaks in Irish tongues, breaking away from ordinary meaning until he has loosed the lion inside himself. He begins to roar: he has that sound, that yarrrrragh, as he has never had it before. He is not singing it, it is singing him.

That is a mystical description; it is a mystical song. Much of what Morrison has done in the last years has been in this vein (though not obviously; Sri Chinmoy has yet to appear on one of Morrison's LP covers). Certain themes have emerged in Morrison's music, from album to album: an attempt to come to grips with his existence as an Irishman, whose homeland is in flames, who lives safely, if not peacefully, in America; a corresponding will to discover or recapture a mythical homeland, "Caledonia," or Scotland, the place from which his ancestors originally came, ages ago; an attempt to shape and communicate a sense of freedom. All—the resolution of each of these questions—come down to the yarrrrragh, Morrison's sound, which he cannot, it seems, get at will, which is definitely not "a style," which is a gift and a mystery and understood as such. When Morrison touches that sound he is alive as an artist; he is an adventurer in mystic realms, a conqueror, a supplicant, whatever he would be. When he cannot get it—as on *His Band and the Street Choir* or *Tupelo Honey*, when he was likely not looking for it—he is an impeccable, satisfying, altogether masterful musician.

Morrison is heir to a tradition of mysteries, and he knows it. He is a Celt, and at least a spiritual descendant of the Irish prelate St. Brendan, who set out from Ireland 1500 years ago and who, according to legend, reached America itself, and perhaps founded a colony, which disappeared. So there may be a sense in which Morrison can understand that he was always an American (could have been, was meant to be); that his place in America is fated, even if it is unsettled, as he stretches out toward that mythical Caledonia, even believing, sometimes, that in a long and intricate manner, the blues came not from Africa, but from Scotland. That here came from there, that there are no divisions, that all parts of himself are, somehow, linked. Yet this is not a belief, it is a possibility, and the tension remains, driving the urge to wholeness, leading to albums like the incandescent *Veedon Fleece* (1974).

Morrison remains a singer who can be compared to no other performer in the history of rock and roll, a singer who cannot be pinned down, dismissed, nor fitted into anyone's expectations. He is a conundrum: his mysticism, which is, I think, his final strength, is anchored by the day to day reality of the American life he has chosen, which is why his mysticism has nothing in common with the tawdry banalities prevalent in the "spiritual" rock and roll of the Seventies. But of course it is that anchor, that reality, that has brought his mysticism to the surface, that has demanded it. That is, one might think, the way it ought to work. Morrison, it can be seen now, is a man on a quest; it will be a long one, but there are listeners who will be with him for the duration.

Discography

Singles

Them, "Gloria" (Parrot 9727; ☆93, 1965). "Here Comes the Night" (Parrot 9749; ☆24, 1965). "Mystic Eyes" (Parrot 9796 ☆33, 1965).

Van Morrison, "Brown Eyed Girl" (Bang 545; ☆10, 1967). "Domino" (Warner Bros. 7434; ☆9, 1970). "Wild Night" (Warner Bros. 7518; ☆28, 1971). "Tupelo Honey" (Warner Bros. 7543; ☆47, 1972).

Albums

Them, *Them* (Parrot 61005; ☆54, 1965). *Them Again* (Parrot 61008; ☆138, 1966). *Them Featuring Van Morrison* (Parrot 71053; ☆154, 1972). *Backtrackin'* (London 639).

Van Morrison, *Blowin' Your Mind!* (Bang 2189; ☆182, 1967). *The Best of Van Morrison* (Bang 222; 1967). *T.B. Sheets* (Bang 400; ☆181, 1974). *Astral Weeks* (Warner Bros. 1768; 1969). *Moondance* (Warner Bros. 1835; ☆29, 1970). *His Band and the Street Choir* (Warner Bros. 1884; ☆32, 1970). *Tupelo Honey* (Warner Bros. 1950; ☆27, 1971). *Saint Dominic's Preview* (Warner Bros. 2633; ☆15, 1972). *Hard Nose the Highway* (Warner Bros. 2712; ☆27, 1973). *It's Too Late to Stop Now* (Warner Bros. 2760; ☆53, 1974). *Veedon Fleece* (Warner Bros. 2805; ☆53, 1974).

(Chart positions taken from Joel Whitburn's *Record Research*, compiled from *Billboard* Pop and LPs charts.)

Creedence
by Ellen Willis

For two years, 1969 and 1970, Creedence Clearwater Revival—John Fogerty (composer, singer, lead guitarist, arranger, manager, spiritual center); Tom Fogerty (guitarist); Stu Cook (bassist); Doug Clifford (drummer)—was the most popular rock band in America. During those years the group released five of its seven albums and seven (mostly two-sided) hit singles. At a time when the rock audience had already divided into antagonistic subgroups—hardcore rock and roll fans vs hardcore freaks, high school kids vs college students, AM vs FM—Creedence kept us all, dominating Top 40 radio while continuing to be acknowledged as "serious" by the industry/media/fan cabal that arbitrates such matters. Yet for all this ecumenical appeal, Creedence was always somewhat estranged from its generational and musical peers. Its image was of a group stubbornly loyal to unfashionable values. The geographical metaphor will do as well as any: though Creedence shared turf with the acid-rock bands, its roots were not in psychedelic San Francisco or political Berkeley but in El Cerrito, an East Bay suburb with even less cachet, if possible, than Oakland. Its members were not former folkies converted to electric music by Bob Dylan; they had been a rock and roll band ever since high school in El Cerrito, surviving five years of touring as the Blue Velvets, three as the Golliwogs and one more as Creedence before their first gold single, "Proud Mary," put them over the top in January 1969. They were not "underground" or "avant-garde" or into drugs or given to revolutionary rhetoric. They were at home with the short, tight, hit-single aesthetic that most "serious" rock musicians scorned in favor of the feckless, improvisatory aesthetic of the jam.

Despite these divergences, and the reservations about the counterculture that they implied, John Fogerty and his cohorts were very much a part of that culture, iconoclastic freaks but freaks nonetheless. As often as not their songs addressed the issues—political, cultural, musical—that moved the hip community. In response to the spoiled-rich-kid aspect of cultural-revolutionary politics, songs like "Fortunate Son" and "Don't Look Now" insisted on the touchy subject of class—of privilege and the lack of it. "Proud Mary," with the Huck-and-Jim-on-the-Mississippi echoes that lent its lyrics about dropping out a historical dimension, was an implicit critique of the idea that radicals had nothing to learn from American tradition. "Lookin' Out My Back Door" was at once a silly-serious celebration of tripping (with or without chemicals, as you prefer) and a send-up of pretentious visionaries. The band's 11-minute version of "I Heard It through the Grapevine" was a brilliant synthesis of opposing musical ideas; it was effective improvisation and effective rock and roll. The tension between identification and skepticism that informed Creedence's relation to its own subculture had a lot to do with why the group was great—and also with why it eventually fell apart.

Fogerty's dedication to the formula of rock and roll—energy rigidly structured by what were originally commercial constraints—was, in a looser, freer era, as much an aesthetic choice, dictated by temperament, as other musicians' revolt against it. At bottom the choice was a function of Fogerty's populist instincts. Practically it meant that Creedence could reach the mass radio audience. Formally it meant loyalty to rock's plebeian roots, and to its most basic pleasures (Creedence was *the* white American dance band; no one else came close). Fogerty's musical choice had its verbal analogue in his commonsense politics. But here an ambiguity arose. For if Fogerty's sensitivity to the realities of class made him reject the elitist romanticism of Sixties revolutionaries, it often led him into the opposite trap—a fatalism best expressed in his repeated use of rain as a metaphor for social ills. Weather, after all, is something you can't do anything about. Fortunately, Fogerty's lyrics were both compassionate enough and angry enough to take the curse off their pessimism; his persona in songs like "Who'll Stop the Rain" and "Wrote a Song for Everyone" was not the smug liberal secretly happy that he won't have to give up his two cars, but you and me on a bad day. And "Saw the people standing a thousand years in chains/Somebody said it's different now, but look it's just the same" was undeniably truer to most people's reality than "We want the world and we want it NOW!" But it was also undeniably less exciting. If this was not necessarily disastrous in itself, it was nevertheless symptomatic of a serious limitation.

Fogerty's populism and the counterculture's utopianism converged on one important point: being a best-selling rock band was not enough. A serious rock star aspired not only to entertain the public but to alter its consciousness and so in some sense affect history. By the end of the Sixties, the fragmentation of the audience that had coalesced around the Beatles, the Stones and Dylan had made that aspiration increasingly unrealistic. Creedence remained the one band capable of uniting that audience and therefore of penetrating—and transforming—its fantasies. But it didn't happen. Creedence never crossed the line from best-selling rock band to cultural icon. And that failure seemed directly attributable to Fogerty's peculiar virtues.

The great Sixties superstars did not make the pantheon on the strength of their music alone; they, or rather their public images, were also aesthetic objects. Though Fogerty understood this, there was not much he could do about it without being false to himself. He had no affinity for the obvious image-making ploys: flamboyant freakery, messianism, sex, violence. Nor was he a flashy ironist. Instead he projected intelligence, integrity and moderation—not the sort of qualities that inflame either fans or journalists. In certain respects he resembled the solid, sustaining husband who is forever being betrayed for the dashing, undependable lover. It was no accident that my interest in Creedence progressed from warm to obsessive at a time when I was in a state of emotional upheaval

Creedence Clearwater Revival in 1969. From left: Doug Clifford, Stu Cook, John Fogerty, Tom Fogerty (Baron Wolman)

brought on by politics, drugs, writing blocks and problematic personal relationships. It was also a time when I was feeling alienated from my erstwhile favorite rock band, the Rolling Stones, partly because of Altamont, partly because of feminism, but mostly because I was tired of chasing Mick Jagger's mysterious soul through the mazes of fun-house mirrors he had built to protect it. Maybe it was all the politics and all the drugs, but I craved a simpler, more direct, more human connection to rock and roll, and I connected with John Fogerty in a way I never could with Jagger. Yet my realization that Creedence had edged out the Stones on my personal rock chart came long after the fact. The switch happened gradually, easing into my subconscious without the customary *zap*—which says something about the difference between Creedence and the Stones.

I t could be, of course, that none of this really mattered—that the Warholian age of the media artist was irrevocably over, and that Creedence never had a chance. But that was not the way the boys perceived it; they were profoundly demoralized by the celebrity gap. One result was that they became oversensitive to criticism, which consisted mostly of complaints from the diehards of the Bay Area art-rock lobby that Creedence was an uncreative "singles band." They began making defensive comments like "We have something to *say*." Their sixth album, *Pendulum*, released in December 1970, included what Creedence watchers took to be some tentative concessions to Art—stuff like improvised organ music. I liked the album, but it made me uneasy; it seemed to lack Fogerty's usual authority. Later I found out that the rest of the group had been challenging his leadership; they wanted more artistic leeway. In 1971, Tom left the band, and John agreed that Stu and Doug should play an equal part in writing, arranging and performing Creedence's material. Creedence put out only two singles that year. The next album was long in coming, very long by Creedence's previous standards—over a year. When it did come, in the spring of 1972, it was disappointing.

Mardi Gras wasn't bad, just mediocre. Its rock was softened and countrified. More important, Stu Cook and Doug Clifford simply did not write or sing as well as John Fogerty, who contributed only three of the album's songs. Perhaps, given enough time, they would have grown into their new responsibilities. But in October, Creedence Clearwater Revival disbanded. Their situation was hardly unique. It had become a commonplace among political and cultural radicals that leadership was inherently oppressive, and all over the country groups of people who tried to live by an ideology of leaderlessness were disintegrating in bitterness and confusion. In the circumstances of its dissolution, Creedence was, for once, utterly typical of the dissident community to which it so uneasily belonged.

Discography

Singles
"Suzie Q" (Fantasy 616; ☆11, 1968). "I Put a Spell on You" (Fantasy 617; ☆58, 1968). "Proud Mary" b/w "Born on the Bayou" (Fantasy 619; ☆2, 1969). "Bad Moon Rising" b/w "Lodi" (Fantasy 622; ☆2, 1969). "Green River" b/w "Commotion" (Fantasy 625; ☆2, 1969). "Down on the Corner" b/w "Fortunate Son" (Fantasy 634; ☆3, 1969). "Travelin' Band" b/w "Who'll Stop the Rain" (Fantasy 637; ☆2, 1970). "Up Around the Bend" b/w "Run through the Jungle" (Fantasy 641; ☆4, 1970). "Lookin' Out My Back Door" b/w "Long As I Can See the Light" (Fantasy 645; ☆2, 1970). "Have You Ever Seen the Rain" b/w "Hey Tonight" (Fantasy 655; ☆8, 1971). "Sweet Hitch-Hiker" (Fantasy 665; ☆6, 1971). "Someday Never Comes" (Fantasy 676; ☆25, 1972).
Albums
Creedence Clearwater Revival (Fantasy 8382; ☆52, 1968). *Bayou Country* (Fantasy 8387; ☆7, 1969). *Green River* (Fantasy 8393; ☆1, 1969). *Willy and the Poorboys* (Fantasy 8397; ☆3, 1969). *Cosmo's Factory* (Fantasy 8402; ☆1, 1970). *Pendulum* (Fantasy 8410; ☆5, 1970). *Mardi Gras* (Fantasy 9404; ☆12, 1972). *Creedence Gold* (Fantasy 9418; ☆15, 1972). *More Creedence Gold* (Fantasy 9430; ☆61, 1973).
Solo Albums by John Fogerty
Blue Ridge Rangers (Fantasy 9415; 1973). *John Fogerty* (Asylum 1046; ☆78, 1975).
(Chart positions taken from Joel Whitburn's *Record Research,* compiled from *Billboard* Pop and LPs charts.)

The Allman Brothers
by Harper Barnes

The sad thing about the Allman Brothers Band is that, by the time they became really popular, they were no longer very good. The reason, of course, is that on October 29th, 1971, after an album called *The Allman Brothers Band/At the Fillmore East* had just turned gold, Duane Allman was killed in a motorcycle accident near the band's communal home in Macon, Georgia. Musically the band never recovered; commercially of course it not only prospered mightily but spawned a whole school of similar-sounding Southern bands—most prominently Lynyrd Skynyrd—which even now continue to troupe northward like dazed fire ants.

Duane Allman's death did more than deprive the band of one of the great modern rock guitarists—to this writer, the greatest, because he did it all without tricks. Duane's death seemingly also left the group's other "lead" guitarist, Dicky Betts, in an identity crisis: was he a rock singer, a country musician, a jazz guitarist, was he—and this must have been a fearful thought—destined to be nothing more than the man forever possessed by Duane Allman? So far, with the exception of his pleasant "Ramblin Man," Betts has not been much of anything, and that is also sad because there were nights when Duane pushed Betts so high and hard in their jamming duets that one literally could not tell where Betts started and Duane left off.

And sadder still is what Duane's death must have done to his brother, Gregg Allman, rock celebrity, superstar. Because of booze, drugs, loneliness, fear, or whatever, Gregg was left sounding like a ghost. Go back to the first real Allman Brothers record, *The Allman Brothers Band* (released in 1969), and listen to "It's Not My Cross to Bear." Follow Duane's passionate introduction to Gregg's vocal. It is impossible to conceive of the man who sang in that impeccably paced, exquisitely contorted blues voice, a voice that made the record a cult FM hit, as the same wan, apparently burnt-out young man who noodles at keyboards and sings these days as if he were recovering from a combined tonsillectomy and lobotomy.

In their earlier years, the Allman Brothers, with a series of bands under a series of names, played rhythm and blues in that string of honky clubs that stretches like chitlins through the South and Midwest. Their first important success came in 1967 in St. Louis, where they were the Allman Joys, and the biggest thing in town since the days when Ike and Tina Turner played the old Club Riviera.

The Allmans then made it to Los Angeles, under the name of Hourglass, and cut two records for Liberty that even the Allmans did not like. So they went to Muscle Shoals, Alabama, and cut a few tapes on their own.

In the winter of 1968–'69, Rick Hall, who ran Fame Studios near Muscle Shoals, remembered Duane's guitar playing, found him in Florida and called him back to do some session-work with such R&B musicians as Wilson Pickett and King Curtis. Jerry Wexler of Atlantic Records heard Duane's work—with some amazement—and began to use him also.

The best of Duane Allman is contained in his studio work, and a superb sampling of that is available on the first *Duane Allman: An Anthology* album, issued not long after his death.

The anthology includes my favorite 15 seconds in rock music, Duane's lead-in to Aretha Franklin's recording of "The Weight." Duane begins with a masterpiece of misdirection and ends by giving Aretha just what she wanted—a place to take off from. Opening with a drawn-out Delta slide note, lazy, almost forgetful, he brings in a hint of the hard beat to come, leaves a hole of silence for suspense, and plunges ahead with four of the most solid beats any singer could ask for.

There is an amusing, quasi-C&W backing for King Curtis on "Games People Play," Duane's lovely duet with Eric Clapton on "Layla" and many other delights. Most important, perhaps, is Duane's transcendent backing of Boz Scaggs on "Loan Me a Dime," which shows Duane's full range of abilities—from his delicious feel for the almost vocal nature of slow blues obbligatos to his ability to build excitement through a series of rhythmically ascending riffs to his agility at stringing together high-speed runs without approaching cliché.

By the spring of 1969, the Allman Brothers Band had finally formed, apparently on the basis of an extended jam between most of the musicians who were to make it up—Duane, Gregg, Betts, bassist Berry Oakley (who also died in a motorcycle accident eerily similar to Duane's) and the two drummers, Jai Johanny Johanson and Butch Trucks. At its best, the band sounded like a more disciplined version of the Grateful Dead with firmer roots in the Southern blues tradition. It was also unique for having two guitarists as skillful as Betts and Duane Allman, who played counterpoint and intricate ensembles together as well as trading off solos.

As a recording group, the Allmans hit their artistic peak with the live Fillmore East album, taped in March of 1971. It features most of the band's standbys, including a great version of "Statesboro Blues," and must be considered one of the quintessential boogie records. After Duane's death came the big hits: *Eat a Peach*—with some playing by Duane; *Brothers and Sisters*; and even a Top Ten single in 1973, "Ramblin Man." They continue to record sporadically, and remain a popular band, but they have never been able to fill the gap left by Duane's death.

Discography

Allman Brothers Band (Atco 308; ☆188, 1970). *Idlewild South* (Atco 342; ☆38, 1970). *At Fillmore East* (Capricorn 2802; ☆13, 1971). *Eat a Peach* (Capricorn 0102; ☆4, 1972). *Brothers and Sisters* (Capricorn 0111; ☆1, 1973). *Win, Lose or Draw* (Capricorn 0156; ☆5, 1975). *The Road Goes On Forever* (Capricorn 0164; ☆43, 1975).
Solo Albums by Allman Brothers Band Members
Duane Allman, *An Anthology* (Capricorn 0108; ☆28, 1972). *An Anthology, Vol. 2* (Capricorn 0139; ☆49, 1974). **Gregg Allman,** *Laid Back* (Capricorn 0116; ☆13, 1973). *The Gregg Allman Tour* (Capricorn 0141; ☆50, 1974). **Richard Betts,** *Highway Call* (Capricorn 0123; ☆19, 1974).
(Chart positions compiled from Joel Whitburn's *Record Research*, based on *Billboard* LPs charts.)

The Allman Brothers, before the days of doom (Annie Leibovitz)

Heavy Metal
by Lester Bangs

As its detractors have always claimed, heavy-metal rock is nothing more than a bunch of noise; it is not music, it's distortion—and that is precisely why its adherents find it appealing. Of all contemporary rock, it is the genre most closely identified with violence and aggression, rapine and carnage. Heavy metal orchestrates technological nihilism, which may be one reason it seems to be running dry in the mid-Seventies. It's a fast train to nowhere, which may be one reason it seems to feel so good and make so much sense to its fans.

When Eric Burdon sang in "Monterey" of "ten thousand guitars . . . groovin' real loud," he was an unwitting prophet of heavy metal. For its noise is created by electric guitars, filtered through an array of warping devices from fuzztone to wah-wah, cranked several decibels past the pain threshold, loud enough to rebound off the walls of the biggest arenas anywhere. Add the aural image of a battering ram, and you've got a pretty good picture of what heavy metal sounds like.

The forerunners of the heavy-metal style were the British superstar bands of the mid-Sixties. The roots of heavy metal, as a sound and a stance, lie in the Who's "My Generation" and "I Can See for Miles," and in the fuzztone-and-feedback explosions of Eric Clapton, Jeff Beck and Jimmy Page.

Two British superbands—Cream, formed in 1966, and Led Zeppelin, in 1968—drew on the British R&B tradition for their material and on ex-Yardbirds for their personnel. They became two of the most popular rock bands in the world. A whole generation of guitarists was turned around and fired up by Eric Clapton's strenuous (strained, some said) lines with Cream and Jimmy Page's power chording with Zep, not to mention Jimi Hendrix, with his Yardbirds/Who-derived distortions and patently personal banshee wails.

The musical achievements of the countless guitarists who have grown up in the shadow of this triumvirate have ranged from sonic Saint Elmo's fires to electric mud. As with so much rock, however, the distinction between the two often lay somewhere between the ears, brain and nervous system of any given member of the audience: there's a thin line between heavy riffs and lumbering sludge.

Now that we have defined the musical territory in general—brutal guitars, equally thunderous slabs of thick-thudding bass, and the obligatory extended drum solo in concert—we must deal with the oft-raised canard that "all heavy metal groups sound alike."

Wrong. They only sound alike to the untutored ear. True, the dependence upon technology does foster a certain machinelike uniformity (if not precision). True, the vocals of Ozzy Osbourne of Black Sabbath bear more than a passing resemblance to those of Jack Bruce of Cream; those of Deep Purple's Ian Gillan to Led Zeppelin's Robert Plant; and those of Aerosmith's Steven Tyler to, among others, Alice Cooper. True also that the author once stared at a picture of Tyler on an office wall for three

months before he realized it wasn't either Carly Simon or Mick Jagger. But to postulate categorically that all heavy metal bands are the same is utterly ludicrous.

That is why I will now provide a convenient reference guide, for those readers who wish to be able to tell heavy metal bands apart without actually listening to their records.

In the primordial tar pits of 1968, early flurries of metal mutation appeared out of California. Blue Cheer, Iron Butterfly and Black Pearl prophesied worldwide madness to come. The Butterfly were renowned for the 17-minute "In-A-Gadda-Da-Vida," title cut on the best-selling LP in the history of Atlantic Records (at least until Led Zeppelin got off the ground). Blue Cheer were truly ahead of their time; from San Francisco, of all places, this power trio was so loud that a reviewer of one of their early concerts, at a loss for words, called them "Super Druid rock." I once had a friend who owned a record player with a switch that could make his turntable rotate counterclockwise, and thus play his records backward; when we played Blue Cheer's first album, *Vincebus Eruptum*, backward, it sounded exactly the same as usual.

A good deal of this action derived from the remaining smoky wisps of psychedelia and "acid rock"—itself an outgrowth of Yardbirds experimentalism. Over in Britain, the psychedelic imperative sank deep into the fretting fingers of the post-Cream, post-Hendrix bands, resulting not only in the cinematic guitar work and fuzzy lyric imagery which have sustained Led Zeppelin to this day, but in such sub-Zeppelin British kozmik behemoths as Black Sabbath.

Perhaps in reaction, there appeared two other, divergent movements among British metallurgists: some were proles, others noblemen. In the Working Class, we find journeyman bands like Deep Purple, who started out psychedelic (*The Book of Taliesyn* was the title of an early LP) but soon became so meaningless as to defy the easy thematic definition of a Black Sabbath, and changed personnel so many times it didn't matter anyway. The most recent notable addition to the British Working Class is a supergroup by the name of Bad Company, whose stock-in-trade are the most predictable of heavy riffs and rodomontades to the effect that they are "bad men." Ex-Yardbird Jeff Beck also briefly formed a Working Class power trio, with two American ex-members of Vanilla Fudge, called Beck, Bogert and Appice.

With the coming of the Seventies, however, there was a certain feeling that one might as well slouch toward Bethlehem with lace cuffs and powdered nose, so the Aristocratic wing of Anglo-metal was born, its most notable adherents being the aptly named Queen and the crossover act, Sweet, who have also dabbled in bubblegum music with such hits as "Little Willy."

We Americans, of course, have never stood for any of that royalty stuff, and our metal merchants have, for the most part, remained solidly Industrial Working Class even if some of them

Your pal, Alice Cooper (Annie Leibovitz)

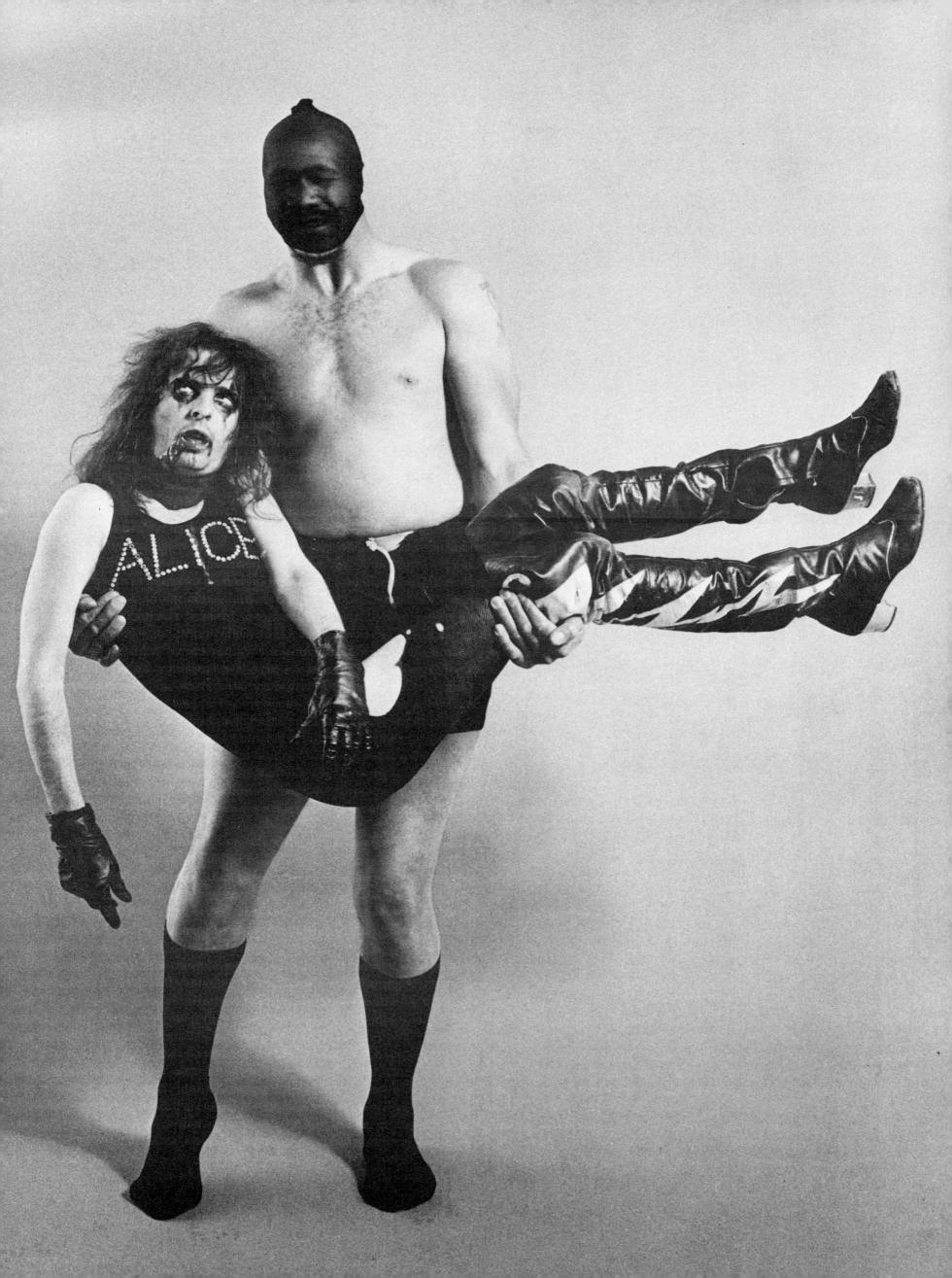

did bathe in mascara. Among the long list of our proletarian partisans are such never-to-be-forgotten bands as Cactus, Mountain (starring Leslie West, who once said in an interview that his life was changed by viewing Eric Clapton in concert with Cream when he—Leslie—was on acid at the Fillmore), the Frost (whose leader Dick Wagner went on to provide anonymous guitar salvage on numerous Alice Cooper albums and tours), Aerosmith, Kiss, Bachman-Turner Overdrive (Canadian division) and the immortal Grand Funk Railroad, who made their debut before 100,000 screaming kids at the Atlanta pop festival in 1969, and went on to become perhaps the first *under*-underground band by being loved all the more fiercely by the teens because they were so roundly hated by all the hip rock critics.

Out of American Working Class metal emerged two subgroups: American Revolutionary and Boogie Bands. The Revolutionary bands believed staunchly in rock and roll as an instrument of social change. The first of them, the MC5, also happened to be one of the best bands this country ever produced, but a series of bad breaks left them stranded in the ozone and Grand Funk—briefly exploiting the same rhetoric, toned down—stepped into their shoes with alacrity. The Boogie Bands by contrast are almost defiantly apolitical (not to mention atonal). Their raison d'être seems to be the eternal reiteration of the simplest riffs, for the sake of "partying." This subgroup includes, among countless others, Black Oak Arkansas (who have also betrayed a pronounced mystical bent), the aforementioned Cactus, and ZZ Top, who wear cowboy hats.

In reaction to all this proletarian/politico/partying, we have had the American Deviates, most of them inspired by that watershed American band of the late Sixties, the Velvet Underground, who thrashed out a whiplash brand of heavy metal in "European Son," "I Heard Her Call My Name" and "Sister Ray." Their most attentive disciples were Detroit's Iggy and the Stooges, who also embodied rock and roll as animal savagery at the most purely atavistic, not to mention nihilistic, level this writer has ever seen. So nihilistic that they just kept on exploding and never achieved the commercial success later engineered in the calculated ploys of Alice Cooper and Kiss, or the less successful Blue Oyster Cult. What all these bands share besides riffs is an interest in rock and roll/heavy metal as transmitter of the sadomasochistic dialectic.

But S&M is only one expression of fixated sexuality. All of rock and roll may be another—the reinforcement and preservation of whatever vestiges of primal infantilism have managed to survive into adolescence, and the glorification of adolescence as the Time of Your Life (yeah, sure). But from Chuck Berry on, rock has provided anthems to teenhood (and teen hoods), has been about teenage frustrations, and there is perhaps no music which more accurately conveys the screaming nerves of pubescent frustration than heavy metal. So we have had the purveyors of what I would call American Teenage Angst Anthems, most notably the Stooges ("I Wanna Be Your Dog"), MC5 ("High School"), Alice Cooper ("I'm Eighteen"), and the Dictators ("Teengenerate"). They are, perhaps, the truest expressions of heavy metal's soul and inspiration.

Then again, it may not make any difference at all in the long run. It is now 1976, and heavy metal seems already to belong to history. Oh, heavy metal records still sell like hot cakes, but somehow Bad Company, Kiss and Aerosmith don't hit the nervous system with quite the same electrode barracuda bite that early Led Zeppelin, MC5 and even Grand Funk had. It is all down to rote now, cyclical permutations of prefab riffs, and another commercial cycle is completed: heavy metal, mutant monster bad boy of Sixties rock, has at last gone middle-of-the-road respectable, terminally predictable, tyrannosaurus tamed into brontosaurus mild-mannered. Which only stands to reason, when one reflects that it was, from inception, a style born from machines and electronic appendages, as much as from human fingers, hearts and minds. Heavy metal has become the foremost victim of a cybernetic revolution spawned by itself—and technology once again closes the gap between frustration and profit.

Discography
1968–1975

Blue Cheer, *Vincebus Eruptum* (Philips 264; ☆11, 1968). **Iron Butterfly,** *Heavy* (Atco 227; ☆78, 1968). **Velvet Underground,** *White Light/White Heat* (Verve 5046; ☆199, 1968). **Iron Butterfly,** *In-a-Gadda-Da-Vida* (Atco 250; ☆4, 1968). **Deep Purple,** *Shades of Deep Purple* (Tetragrammaton 102; ☆24, 1968). **MC5,** *Kick Out the Jams* (Elektra 45648; ☆30, 1969). **Black Pearl,** *Black Pearl* (Atlantic 8220; ☆130, 1969). **Frost,** *Frost Music* (Vanguard 6520; ☆168, 1969). **The Stooges,** *The Stooges* (Elektra 74051; ☆106, 1969). **Mountain,** *Mountain* (Windfall 4500; ☆72, 1969). **Grand Funk Railroad,** *On Time* (Capitol 307; ☆27, 1969). **Grand Funk Railroad,** *Grand Funk* (Capitol 406; ☆11, 1970). **MC5,** *Back in the USA* (Atlantic 8247; ☆137, 1970). **Grand Funk Railroad,** *Closer to Home* (Capitol 471; ☆6, 1970). **Cactus,** *Cactus* (Atco 340; ☆54, 1970). **Black Sabbath,** *Black Sabbath* (Warner Bros. 1871; ☆23, 1970). **Deep Purple,** *Deep Purple in Rock* (Warner Bros. 1877; ☆143, 1970). **Grand Funk Railroad,** *Live Album* (Capitol 633; ☆5, 1970). **Stooges,** *Funhouse* (Elektra 74051; 1970). **Mountain,** *Nantucket Sleighride* (Windfall 5500; ☆16, 1971). **Black Sabbath,** *Paranoid* (Warner Bros. 1887; ☆12, 1971). **Alice Cooper,** *Love It to Death* (Warner Bros. 1883; ☆35, 1971). **Grand Funk Railroad,** *Survival* (Capitol 764; ☆6, 1971). **Black Oak Arkansas,** *Black Oak Arkansas* (Atco 354; ☆127, 1971). **Deep Purple,** *Fireball* (Warner Bros. 2564; ☆32, 1971). **Black Sabbath,** *Master of Reality* (Warner Bros. 2562; ☆8, 1971). **Alice Cooper,** *Killer* (Warner Bros. 2567; ☆21, 1971). **Grand Funk Railroad,** *E Pluribus Funk* (Capitol 853; ☆5, 1971). **Deep Purple,** *Machine Head* (Warner Bros. 2607; ☆7, 1972). **Grand Funk Railroad,** *Mark, Don and Mel 19609-71* (Capitol 11042; ☆17, 1972). **Blue Oyster Cult,** *Blue Oyster Cult* (Columbia 31063; ☆172, 1972). **Uriah Heep,** *Demons and Wizards* (Mercury 630; ☆23, 1972). **Alice Cooper,** *School's Out* (Warner Bros. 2623; ☆2, 1972). **West, Bruce and Laing,** *Why Dontcha* (Columbia 31929; ☆26, 1972). **Uriah Heep,** *The Magician's Birthday* (Mercury 10652; ☆31, 1972). **Deep Purple,** *Who Do We Think We Are!* (Warner Bros. 2678; ☆15, 1973). **Black Oak Arkansas,** *Raunch 'n' Roll/Live* (Atco 7019; ☆90, 1973). **Alice Cooper,** *Billion Dollar Babies* (Warner Bros. 2685; ☆1, 1973). **Deep Purple,** *Made in Japan* (Warner Bros. 2701; ☆6, 1973). **Iggy and the Stooges,** *Raw Power* (Columbia 32111; ☆182, 1973). **Sweet,** *The Sweet* (Bell 1124; ☆191, 1973). **Grand Funk Railroad,** *We're an American Band* (Capitol 11207; ☆2, 1973). **ZZ Top,** *Tres Hombres* (London 631; ☆32, 1973). **Black Oak Arkansas,** *High on the Hog* (Atco 7034; ☆52, 1973). **Queen,** *Queen* (Elektra 75064; ☆83, 1973). **Alice Cooper,** *Muscle of Love* (Warner Bros. 2748; ☆10, 1973). **Deep Purple,** *Burn* (Warner Bros. 2766; ☆9, 1974). **Grand Funk Railroad,** *Shinin' On* (Capitol 11278; ☆5, 1974). **Blue Oyster Cult,** *Secret Treaties* (Columbia 32858; ☆53, 1974). **Queen,** *Queen II* (Elektra 75082; ☆49, 1974). **Alice Cooper,** *Alice Cooper's Greatest Hits* (Warner Bros. 2803; ☆8, 1974). **Queen,** *Sheer Heart Attack* (Elektra 1026; ☆17, 1974). **Blue Oyster Cult,** *On Your Feet or on Your Knees* (Columbia 33371; ☆22, 1975). **Queen,** *Sheer Heart Attack* (Elektra 1026; ☆12, 1975). **Leslie West,** *The Great Fatsby* (RCA 0954; ☆168, 1975). **ZZ Top,** *Fandango* (London 656; ☆10, 1975). **Sweet,** *Desolation Boulevard* (Capitol 11395; ☆25, 1975). **Queen,** *A Night at the Opera* (Elektra 1053; ☆4, 1975).
(Chart positions compiled from Joel Whitburn's *Record Research,* based on *Billboard* LPs charts.)

Led Zeppelin
by Jim Miller

From Hamburg to Hong Kong, Led Zeppelin attracts sellout crowds. Their six albums have all sold more than a million copies each in the United States alone. With total sales topping 12 million, the group ranks with Elton John as one of the most profitable acts of the Seventies. Yet despite their popularity, and the undeniable power of their best music, Led Zeppelin has yet to make much of an impact beyond the relatively narrow confines of the rock culture. Their blunt brand of rock rarely appeals to an older generation that grew up with the Beatles, Stones and Dylan; their media presence has never been unavoidable. Perhaps that's because, on one level, Led Zeppelin represents the final flowering of the Sixties' psychedelic ethic, which casts rock as passive sensory involvement—hardly an aesthetic geared to galvanize the imagination, no matter how broad the music's impact. The band is devoted to no-nonsense musicianship (unlike other acts, they shun most theatrical trappings); they scorn hit singles; they are fond of free-form sonic booms (the break in "Whole Lotta Love") and lovey-dovey rhetoric (lead singer Robert Plant: "Somebody once described me as the original hippie, and that's because of the flowery lyrics, you know, and also because of the buzz we give out"). Led Zeppelin, in short, is an anachronism—and yet it is also the best (and most influential) hard-rock band of the Seventies.

A product of the blues-rock boom in Britain during the late Sixties, Led Zeppelin was founded by guitarist Jimmy Page in 1968, on the model of such bands as Cream, the Jeff Beck group and the Yardbirds, where Page first came to prominence. Page himself was no newcomer. In the mid-Sixties, he had worked sessions with everyone from the Rolling Stones to the Who, reputedly playing on such classics as the Kinks' "You Really Got Me"; he eventually joined the Yardbirds as a bassist, and, later, a second guitarist.

From the outset, Page has been Led Zeppelin's mainspring. Despite vocalist Robert Plant's visibility, it is Page who plots the band's course, not only as lead guitarist, but also as the group's producer. He has been the architect of *the* hard-rock style of the Seventies, perhaps best captured in "Whole Lotta Love" from *Led Zeppelin II.* Page opens with a frenzied fuzz riff, setting a staccato beat; when Plant enters, his voice, contorted and harsh, is framed with reverb, adding yet another element of controlled garble, all of it firmly locked into place by John Bonham's lumbering barrage of drum rolls. The record's excitement comes from the field of tension Page has produced, using more or less simple components; and when the record in midstream collapses into an orgiastic cacophony, it only seems like a logical release. The *sound* of "Whole Lotta Love" says it all: ponderous yet precise, naggingly insistent yet modulated by dynamic contrasts, it gives fresh form to hard rock.

Page's primary concern has always been sound. His playing lacks the lyricism of Eric Clapton's, the funk of Jimi Hendrix's, or the rhythmic flair of Peter Townshend's; but of all the virtuoso guitarists of the Sixties, Page, along with Hendrix, has most expanded the instrument's sonic vocabulary. He exhibits a studio musician's knack for functionalism; unlike many of his peers, he rarely overplays, especially on record. Most of his solos instead evidence the restraint and proportioned style of his avowed influences: the brooding, involuted blues lines of Otis Rush; the finely filigreed acoustic approach of British folk artist Bert Jansch; the echoed, subliminally driving accompaniment of Scotty Moore (behind Elvis) and James Burton (behind Ricky Nelson) on early rockabilly records. But Page's signature remains distortion. Avoiding "clean" timbres, Page often pits muddy overtones against a hugely recorded bottom, weaving his guitar in and out of the mix, sometimes echoing Robert Plant's equally distorted screams, sometimes tunneling behind a dryly thudding drum.

Thanks to Page's production, Led Zeppelin quickly outdistanced its competition. Not only was Plant a stronger singer than the Yardbirds' Keith Relf, but Page, in contrast to Cream's trio of superstars, grasped the importance of crafting a coherent ensemble approach. Taking his cues from old Chess and Sun recordings, he used reverb and echo to mold the band into a unit, always accenting the bottom (bass and drums), always aiming at the biggest possible sound. As a result, the best of Led Zeppelin's records sound powerful where Cream tracks like "White Room" sound pale and disjointed.

By the time of *Zo-So* (often known as *Led Zeppelin IV*), released in 1971, the band had broadened its approach to include acoustic and folk-derived material; in addition, the lyrics increasingly reflected Page's fascination with Celtic myths, adding a mysterioso twist to the band's image. These disparate strands came together on "Stairway to Heaven," Zeppelin's resounding masterpiece, and one of the most popular songs of the decade.

Page here works with two contrasting set of timbres. At the outset, his acoustic guitar and Plant's unusually sweet singing set a delicate mood; but as the track evolves, Page builds intensity, gradually adding instruments, and finally "Stairway" comes to a climax with Plant screeching over a bombastic volley of amplified guitar, distorted and loud. In every respect, "Stairway to Heaven" is a signal achievement; it strikes a perfect balance between an almost childish lyricism and swaggering bluster, and it serves up its mystical message with the kind of visceral impact that few rock bands can rival. Best of all, it is subtle without sacrificing the immediacy and excitement of the most basic rock and roll.

Discography

Led Zeppelin (Atlantic 8216; ☆10, 1969). *Led Zeppelin II* (Atlantic 8236; ☆1, 1969). *Led Zeppelin III* (Atlantic 7201; ☆1, 1970). *Led Zeppelin IV* (Atlantic 7208; ☆2, 1971). *Houses of the Holy* (Atlantic 7255; ☆1, 1973). *Physical Graffiti* (Swan Song 2-200; ☆1, 1975). (Chart positions compiled from Joel Whitburn's *Record Research*, based on *Billboard* LPs charts.)

Jimmy Page, with guitar; background: Robert Plant (Neal Preston)

Singer Songwriters
by Janet Maslin

In 1967, *The Graduate* introduced a leading man, neither conventionally handsome nor redeemingly rugged, who accomplished the impossible: short, flat-voiced Dustin Hoffman actually got the girl. And for him, *The Graduate*'s fringe benefits comprised a lot more than Katharine Ross. Only a few years earlier, Hoffman might have been relegated to the asexual netherworld inhabited by hapless character actors; as it was, he made his debut at a time when Hollywood was ready to revise its notions of glamour. Hoffman may not have been one to stop traffic, but he did project an inviting tangle of contradictions—complexity and innocence, shyness and charm, the promise of intimacy belied by a deep-seated reserve. And if such qualities were appealing on film, they were about to become even more attractive in other realms of show business.

The post-*Graduate* crop of singer/songwriters evolved naturally from a variety of preceding musical forms, but they were also—like the new breed of eccentric-looking, highly individualized movie stars—lucky enough to be in the right place at the right time. San Francisco psychedelia was on the wane, and Woodstock, which ostensibly marked a zenith of generational togetherness, was also the beginning of the end. Even the most euphoric of flowerchildren were beginning both to need and fear their solitude, and to feel the strain of artificially imposed selflessness. The time was ripe for reactionary expressions of frustration, confusion, irony, quiet little confidences, and personal declarations of independence. What was most important to these new artists at the outset, though, was presenting one's musical persona with a persuasive semblance of straightforwardness and simplicity.

The mode of the singer/songwriter (or "chirper-cleffer," as *Variety* described Joni Mitchell on one memorable occasion) was always more of a catchall than a legitimate musical genre, but certain vague criteria did serve to unite performers as diverse as Carole King and Cat Stevens, Randy Newman and James Taylor. All of them derived from either Tin Pan Alley (King, Newman, Laura Nyro) or post-Dylan folk music (Mitchell, Taylor, Jackson Browne, Leonard Cohen, Neil Young); Paul Simon drew upon both. All of them could perform effectively as soloists, using either piano or guitar for accompaniment; the generally spare nature of their early arrangements served both to foster an air of directness and to differentiate them from borderline rock and rollers. And the appeal of each of them, at least initially, had far less to do with either singing or songwriting than with the sheer allure of personality.

Indeed, the form's clearest hallmark became a self-absorption complete enough to counterbalance the preceding era's utopian jive. Bob Dylan had laid most of the groundwork for such solipsism, breaking down the folk convention of keeping one's poetic distance; a few of his contemporaries, once the days of direct Dylan-imitating were over, were able to outgrow sloganizing and become interesting narrative singers or first-person balladeers. But Phil Ochs, Eric Andersen, Tom Paxton, Gordon Lightfoot (and even latecomers like Englishman Ralph McTell and expatriate Jesse Winchester) never progressed fully into the confessional realm—they may not have wanted to. Lightfoot, over the years, shaped a more detailed self-portrait than any of these others, but it reflects a cool masculinity, an adult restraint and self-sufficiency that kept him out of the singer/songwriters' ranks. Lightfoot saw himself too clearly, and could live too calmly with what he saw, to make use of a style that depended so heavily on either bemoaning or elaborately evading one's own internal conflicts.

The singer/songwriters' form matured so slyly that few of their debut albums seemed to be about private struggles at all. And by the time James Taylor began playing delicate acoustic tunes to SRO crowds in basketball arenas (during one tour, huge screens and cameras were set up to magnify his every facial expression), the original conception of the direct, confessional troubadour had clearly undergone some modification. It was to be altered even further once the first exaggerated waves of adulation began to subside. In fact, the essence of the best singer/songwriters' work has been change under pressure, a growth toward self-knowledge. Understanding the singer/songwriter's gift involves tracing a pattern of personal evolution (musical growth was, in all but a few cases, a secondary process) rather than isolating the most impressive material. *Court and Spark* (1974) may be Joni Mitchell's finest album, but the continuum that brought her to that point is more exciting than any single effort.

Hindsight helps, of course: when Mitchell made her 1968 recording debut, it would have been difficult to peg her as anything more promising than an obviously gifted but dour and arty poet, more comfortable behind the scenes (supplying material to Judy Collins, Tom Rush, Ian and Sylvia) than she might ever become in the limelight. (Even then, though, Mitchell's versions of her own songs were better than anyone else's; the singer/songwriter is by definition a personality so compelling that the nuances of his or her own renditions can never be outclassed by interpreters with prettier pipes.) But that first record now seems intriguingly disingenuous. Many of the singer/songwriters' early efforts take on this same uneasy feel in retrospect. Mitchell's opening cut, "I Had a King," is a daintily philosophical account of the breakup of her marriage ("There's no one to blame. . .") that is, upon closer scrutiny, surprisingly snide. (Her husband wore drip-dry shirts, she notes in passing.) Yet for all the air of quiet resignation in the lyrics, Mitchell's vocal is baleful, scathing, charged with an anger she cannot bring herself to express directly. Three albums later, in another song about her former spouse ("The Last Time I Saw Richard"), she's still cruel, condemning the man for his drab new wife and his kitchen appliances. But here the resentment is

Joni Mitchell as queen of Los Angeles (Norman Seeff)

overdrawn, almost caricatured, and tempered by a closing note of loneliness that turns this into a richly dramatic interchange, not a mere sideswipe. Lost in memories of their meeting, she suddenly sinks into depression: "I'm gonna blow this damn candle out/I don't want nobody comin' over to my table/I got nothing to talk to anybody about."

Over the course of her first six albums, Mitchell had more than mere temper to contend with; it took her almost that long to understand and accept her dependency upon men, to see her giddy romanticism for what it was worth (and take it lightly), to acknowledge the scope of her ambition and yet somehow keep it under control. Her vocal style also has kept fascinatingly close pace with her emotional evolution; where the first album had a glum, thin-lipped sound on most cuts ("Night in the City" is a gloriously high-spirited exception), *Court and Spark* is exquisitely snug, passionate and yet perfectly controlled. "Same Situation," her finest song thus far, enhances a concise, agonizingly self-aware lyric with a melody that climbs and plummets as dramatically as do the singer's moods, and with the piercingly lovely vocal a work this incisive surely warrants.

If "Same Situation" is Mitchell's most sterling moment (and "For the Roses," the title song from her preceding 1972 album, a close second), it is also an excruciatingly demanding one. "Living on nerves and feelings" as she describes it, may be too much for anyone to bear indefinitely; certainly that seemed true in Mitchell's case when she abruptly changed course after *Court and Spark*, retreating (with 1975's *The Hissing of Summer Lawns*) into coolly detached condemnation of bourgeois and bohemian foibles. This is in many ways (laborious lyrics, experiments with jazz accompaniment) Mitchell's most painstaking album, but it may also have been her easiest, placed at such a comfortable remove from the struggles of the self.

Mitchell's withdrawal may prove to be only temporary; Laura Nyro's looks more like a full-scale retreat. Nyro was never again able to match the furious brilliance of her 1968 *Eli and the Thirteenth Confession,* though two subsequent efforts (*New York Tendaberry* in 1969, *Christmas and the Beads of Sweat* in 1970) found her still trying. After these, she fell back upon a comfortable collection of oldies with Labelle (*Gonna Take a Miracle,* 1971), retired for several years, and returned in 1976 with a slight, serene effort (*Smile*) that made her shift in priorities clear. The Nyro of *Thirteenth Confession* (and even of the highly commercial album that preceded it, though she disliked the conventional arrangements imposed upon her there) was willing to exchange whatever peace of mind then available for complete, frenetic engagement in her music. Indeed, the immersion was so absolute it often rendered her work incomprehensible. But even at her most erratic and obscure ("Farmer Joe" makes inexplicable rhythm changes half a dozen times, never repeating itself or returning to its original melody), Nyro had a desperate intensity that made her as awesome as she was bewildering. At her best she demanded—and deserved—the lis-

tener's full and unquestioning attention; her hothouse hybrid of soul, jazz and show tunes was wholly without precedent, her finesse on a par with her originality. But the fever pitch at which she performed was ultimately as frightening as it was impressive; Nyro wrote songs about going through numerous forms of hell, and punctuated her vocals with screams of terrifying authenticity. Her agonies were all the more moving for the elusiveness of their source. Nyro had a consummate romanticism to match Mitchell's, but helplessness at the hands of men was only the most readily identifiable of the many demons that plagued her.

Neil Young and Leonard Cohen both struggled with their susceptibility to romantic bondage, but neither needed to fight as frantically as their female counterparts. At the outset of his solo career in 1968, after leaving Buffalo Springfield, Young seemed to revel in his own passivity, to enjoy the complete abdication of personal responsibility; if the lilting melodies and careful rhymes of his early work made him attractive, the emotional stance rendered him even more so. Just as Nyro's following seemed principally composed of women, Young struck a responsive chord in many men; his simultaneous abandonment to love and yearning for revenge against that promiscuous Cowgirl in the Sand held a cryptic promise of release. (Unlike Mitchell, Nyro or Cohen, Young never chose to rage against his own vulnerability, although he did know full well how to complain about it; that naive blamelessness made him inviting, too.) With *After the Gold Rush,* 1970, and *Harvest,* 1972, Young seemed to be attaining some modicum of self-knowledge and self-mockery; "A Man Needs a Maid" was an interesting morass of conflicting impulses. And the musical primitivism into which he had by then settled carried a nicely complimentary irony; as Young's ideas about himself grew more tangled, he fought back by offsetting them with clean, lucid instrumentation. But Young was later to carry his primitivism to shrill and ineffectual extremes, eventually running headlong into the imitative fallacy. With *On the Beach,* 1974, *Tonight's the Night* and *Zuma,* both from 1975, Young's progressively more rudimentary music did little more than reiterate the murkiness of his lyrics. His renunciation of artifice was so absolute it left him no room for either drama or tension.

Leonard Cohen's romantic passivity bears some superficial resemblance to Young's, but Cohen explored and toyed with helplessness more cleverly than any of his singer/songwriter compatriots; his wit and sophisticated insight are unparalleled in the genre. The reason is partly circumstantial: Cohen did much of his growing up in private, recording his first album after he had passed 30 and was already established as both a novelist and a poet. As a result, his recorded work makes up in consistency what it lacks in evolutionary excitement; the bleak eloquence of the 1974 *New Skin for the Old Ceremony* album is

Opposite: (1) Andy Warhol with Jackson Browne.
Below: (2) Randy Newman (1, Popsie/N.Y.; 2, Annie Leibovitz)

very much of a piece with 1968's *Leonard Cohen* and the next year's *Songs from a Room*, his first two. The only major shift was in production style, a move away from elaborate attempts to camouflage his vocal shortcomings in favor of a far more effective spareness.

Cohen's lyrics are less savage than his poetry can be, but like his other writing, they are fueled by the wisdom and bitterness of the prisoner. Accepting love's stranglehold as a given, graced with an almost transcendent indifference to humiliation, Cohen could be as dispassionate about himself as he was mercilessly spiteful toward the male rivals, unconquerable women and fatuous innocents he perceived as enemies. But it is above all the anguished blend of passivity and longing that makes Cohen so compelling (and make him far and away the best performer of his own material; Judy Collins's "Suzanne" may have been sweeter, but Collins had no sense of the way in which Suzanne, who "takes you down to her place by the river," could also be "taking" the singer in a deeper, more insidious way). It's hardly coincidental that Cohen's greatest narrative song, "Famous Blue Raincoat," takes the form of a letter to a rival who is at a safe enough remove for Cohen to avoid engaging him in active combat.

Jackson Browne, who gained a reputation as a writer in the late Sixties and first recorded in 1972, is as precise a lyricist as Cohen, fired by an innocence as indomitable as Cohen's carefully considered resignation. While Browne's thematic concerns and paternal machismo link him with the whole coterie of Hollywood barfly-outlaws, his fine-tuned irony and emotional generosity rescue him from the indolent self-pity that weighs down many of the others. (Warren Zevon, whose "Desperadoes under the Eaves" raises the question of how tough a guy sipping margaritas in an air-conditioned hotel can really be, seems possessed of a similar shrewdness.) Though his seductively fluid arrangements have yet to approach a comparable tautness and complexity, Browne's lyrics alternately depict a childish adult and a very paternal child, vacillating poignantly between the two extremes. The resultant confusion has a wonderfully quotidian authenticity; if Joni Mitchell's special gift is for dramatizing internal conflicts, Browne is just as skillful at articulating a lower-key, sometimes even more debilitating, paralysis. He has an astonishing flair for doing justice to seemingly intractable situations; "My Opening Farewell" and "Late for the Sky" both capture dead endings of relationships with enough compassion to render the moments real, and enough indecisiveness to make the singer feel human. Even when he casts himself in the awkward role of visionary ("For Everyman," "Before the Deluge"), Browne reveals a sweet optimism, a disarming callowness that belies his pretensions to authority. Browne writes best about the things most of his fellows understand least well, and he sings with a warm, untrained nasality perfectly suited to his songs' seemingly untenable mood of casual intensity.

Browne's concerns may be singular, but no one's abstruseness comes close to rivaling that of Randy Newman; if Newman qualifies as a singer/songwriter at all it is only by default, because it would be impossible to label him any more accurately. Unlike all the others, he eschews the confessional mode and rarely even employs the first person; when he does wax sincere ("Marie," "Living without You"), he is somehow least convincing. Newman's inimitably wily persona is far better defined by the absurd presumption of efforts like "Political Science" ("Let's drop the big one and see what happens . . . "),

"Rednecks" (a Southerner's backhanded indictment of Northern racism), "Old Man" (the singer informs a senior citizen, in no uncertain terms, that he is expendable) and "God's Song." In this last number the Lord, as played by Newman, ascribes his soft spot for mankind to the endearing foolishness of anyone who actually believes in Him.

Another thing that sets Newman apart is the influence of show tunes and ornate movie scores (three of his uncles were star composers in this latter field) on his work. *Good Old Boys* (1974), his consummate album, features a full orchestra, elaborate arrangements linking different songs, an the unlikely Newman mumble at its center. It defines a convoluted sensibility that, through sarcasm, sentimentality, unexpected shifts of sympathy and a blithe acceptance of the impossible, very nearly manages to perfect the art of self-obfuscation. And yet Randy Newman is as distinct a figure as any of his more accessible colleagues; what makes him so readily identifiable are, perversely enough, his singular methods of evasion.

Paul Simon and Randy Newman are virtually alone among singer/songwriters in their capacity for accompanying highly polished lyrics with music of comparable sophistication. Simon

316

has arrived at this balance by gradually simplifying his lyrics while turning out more and more complex (though never ostentatiously so) melodies, rhymes and internal contradictions. More so than any of his competitors, Simon has learned to use his music as an ironic commentary on lyrics that are sometimes even more elusive than Newman's.

Simon's artistic evolution has followed a pattern not unlike Joni Mitchell's; he has passed from initial delusions of poetic grandeur, out of the shadow of Bob Dylan, and into a shrewdly self-evaluative stage, finally attaining a placid understanding that less is more. Though it's impossible to cite the exact point at which he began to function as a soloist, "Overs" injected Simon and Garfunkel's 1968 *Bookends* album with an unexpected bitterness, an honesty of the sort that Simon's pretensions had not previously permitted. His innate glibness provided a similar stumbling block, even by the time he had begun to record alone; on *Paul Simon*, his first solo album, the cute, deliberately obscure "Me and Julio Down by the Schoolyard" is no match for "Mother and Child Reunion," an equally vague but more likable song that makes no attempt to play hide-and-seek. Simon's best work—"American Tune," "Something So Right," culminating in 1975's *Still Crazy after All These Years*—is his most likably blunt, even when its subject is his stubborn elusiveness. One extraordinarily deft thing about this last album is its use of delicate accents—a change of tense in "I Do It for Your Love," a martial drum in "50 Ways to Leave Your Lover"—to flesh out ideas Simon's natural reticence prevents him from articulating in their entirety.

Reticence, deep unwillingness to expose himself too fully, and an incorrigible need to undermine moments of apparent sincerity have been even more central to James Taylor's persona than to Paul Simon's; Taylor has never gotten beyond the basic tension between what he feels and what he is able to say. Certainly the flirtation with madness, obsessive weather imagery and pretty face that launched his career in 1969 would not have been sufficient to sustain it without the underlying dishonesty that enlivened even his earliest records. Back then, though the incongruous cheer of Taylor's vocals sometimes seemed deliberate ("Knocking 'round the Zoo"), it could just as often feel dangerously inappropriate, out of control ("Rainy Day Man"). Later on, Taylor's most emphatic declarations of love had an interesting way of sounding as if they'd been wrenched out of him—but even then, the degree to which he understood as much was hard to fathom. But *Gorilla*, the excellent effort in 1975 that picked him up out of a lengthy stay in the doldrums, attacked the issue with a refreshing and promising clarity. "Angry Blues" found Taylor delivering the line "I can't help it if I don't feel so good" like the curve ball it was, phrasing it with an impossibly upbeat lilt.

In the early stages of his career, Taylor introduced Carole King as his warmup act; shortly thereafter, he was a bigger star than ever thanks in large part to his having recorded her "You've Got a Friend." If King's following was less vocal than Taylor's in those days, it was also more ecumenical. Carole King was so readily able to appeal to anyone that her *Tapestry* (1971) sold more than 10 million copies and stayed ensconced on the charts for years. In retrospect, it's easy to understand King's enormous popularity: she combined a Brill Building pop facility with inarguably pleasant sentiments ("Sweet Seasons"), uncomplicated imagery ("A Natural Woman"), and just enough romantic disappointment to keep things lively ("It's Too Late"). But King's ultimate lack of staying power attests to the vital importance of personality within the whole singer/songwriter mode. After years of professional experience, King hardly lost her knack for either composing or arranging catchy melodies; she simply ran out of ideas to go with them. Carole King's only engaging album since *Tapestry* has been the children's record *Really Rosie* (1975), a TV score collaboration with illustrator Maurice Sendak, whose nonsense lyrics showed off King at her most comfortable.

Cat Stevens ran into similar problems shortly after *Teaser and the Firecat*, the 1971 album that finally and unfortunately began to make his musings intelligible. Stevens had previously exhibited a charming fairy-tale whimsy ("I built my house of barley rice/Green pepper walls and water ice . . . ") plus an interesting sense of vocal punctuation that his arrangements served to highlight. Like the Linda Lewis of *Lark* (an album that employed Steven's producer as well as several of his regular musicians), he seemed delightfully childish, joyfully obscure. Perhaps the eccentricity grew out of the period of seclusion and recuperation that intervened between Steven's 1967 teen-prodigy British hit ("Matthew and Son") and his (1971) *Mona Bone Jakon* LP. (And perhaps there was a darker element to his secretiveness: "What's my sex, what's my name/All in all it's all the same," went a line from "Tuesday's Dead.") In any case, "Peace Train" (1971) was the first trouble sign, though a strong arrangement helped bury its problematically lamebrained lyrics. Still, it wasn't long before Stevens was trafficking in weary Donovanisms, never able to regain the air of mystery that had once made hearing him an enjoyable challenge.

The original notion of the singer/songwriter was almost as short-lived as the illusion of Cat Stevens's imaginative scope; the initial preoccupation with forthrightness and simplicity quickly gave way to the cult of the complex, sly and wholly self-absorbed individual. (Bob Dylan's version of "Don't Think Twice, It's All Right" went a long way toward pioneering this strain of self-contradiction and duplicity.) But the initial notion, the form that served so many talented individuals as a springboard is still alive, if not well, in the person of John Denver. As a singer/songwriter in the early sense, Denver is a fine illustration of why modification became a necessity. Confessional, direct, projecting unremitting sincerity, Denver is ultimately more unfathomable than all the others put together. And his is

From left: (1) Cat Stevens; (2) Laura Nyro; (3) James Taylor, not in the flesh. Below: (4) Simon and Garfunkel in their Gertrude Stein/Alice B. Toklas period; (5) Carole King (From left: 1, 3 & 4, ROLLING STONE; 2 & 5, Gleason collection)

such a complete, consistent, impenetrable persona that it discourages any efforts at understanding; he's so earnestly human that he lacks any air of humanity. John Denver, despite his ostensible vulnerability, is a far tougher cookie than any of the singer/songwriters who originally defined the genre; not one of them proved to have the kind of personal staying power that could lead to a double date at Lake Tahoe with Frank Sinatra. Thank goodness for that: their frailties are what have made them so strong.

Discography

Joni Mitchell
Joni Mitchell (Reprise 6293; ☆189, 1968). *Clouds* (Reprise 6341; ☆31, 1969). *Ladies of the Canyon* (Reprise 6376; ☆27, 1970). *Blue* (Reprise 2038; ☆15, 1971). *For the Roses* (Asylum 5057; ☆11, 1972). *Court and Spark* (Asylum 1001, ☆2, 1974). *Miles of Aisles* (Asylum 202; ☆2, 1974). *The Hissing of Summer Lawns* (Joni Mitchell and the L.A. Express) (Asylum 1051; ☆4, 1975).

Neil Young
Neil Young (Reprise 6317; 1969). *Everybody Knows This Is Nowhere* (with Crazy Horse) (Reprise 6349; ☆34, 1969). *After the Gold Rush* (Reprise 6383; ☆8, 1970). *Harvest* (Reprise 2032; ☆1, 1972). *Journey through the Past* (soundtrack) (Warner Bros. 6480; ☆45, 1972). *Time Fades Away* (Reprise 2151; ☆22, 1973). *On the Beach* (Reprise 2180; ☆16, 1974). *Tonight's the Night* (Reprise 2221; ☆25, 1975). *Zuma* (with Crazy Horse) (Reprise 2242; ☆25, 1975).

Laura Nyro
More than a New Discovery (Verve/Folkways 3020; 1967). *Eli and the Thirteenth Confession* (Columbia 9626; ☆181, 1968). *New York Tendaberry* (Columbia 9737; ☆32, 1969). *Christmas and the Beads of Sweat* (Columbia 30259; ☆51, 1970). *Gonna Take a Miracle* (Columbia 30987; ☆46, 1971). *The First Songs* (Columbia 31410; ☆97, 1973), *Smile* (Columbia 33912; ☆60, 1976).

Leonard Cohen
Leonard Cohen (Columbia 2733; ☆83, 1968). *Songs from a Room* (Columbia 9767; ☆63, 1969). *Songs of Love and Hate* (Columbia 30103; ☆145, 1971). *Live Songs* (Columbia 31724; ☆156, 1973). *New Skin for the Old Ceremony* (Columbia 33167; 1974). *The Best of Leonard Cohen* (Columbia 34077; 1976).

Jackson Browne
Jackson Browne (Asylum 5051; ☆53, 1972). *For Everyman* (Asylum 5067; ☆43, 1973). *Late for the Sky* (Asylum 1017; ☆14, 1974).

Randy Newman
Randy Newman (Reprise 6286; 1968). *12 Songs* (Reprise 6373; 1970). *Randy Newman/Live* (Reprise 6459; ☆191, 1971). *Sail Away* (Reprise 2064; ☆163, 1972). *Gold Old Boys* (Reprise 2193; ☆36, 1974).

James Taylor
Sweet Baby James (Warner Bros. 1843; ☆3, 1970). *James Taylor* (Apple 3352; ☆62, 1970). *James Taylor and the Original Flying Machine 1967* (Euphoria 2; ☆74; 1971). *Mud Slide Slim and the Blue Horizon* (Warner Bros. 2561; ☆2, 1971). *One Man Dog* (Warner Bros. 2660; ☆4, 1972). *Walking Man* (Warner Bros. 2794; ☆13, 1974). *Gorilla* (Warner Bros. 2866; ☆6, 1975).

Carole King
Writer (Ode 77006; ☆84, 1971). *Tapestry* (Ode 77009; ☆1, 1971). *Music* (Ode 77013; ☆1, 1971). *Rhymes and Reasons* (Ode 77016; ☆2, 1972). *Fantasy* (Ode 77018; ☆6, 1973). *Wrap Around Joy* (Ode 77024; ☆1, 1974). *Really Rosie* (Ode 77027; ☆20, 1975).

Simon and Garfunkel
Wednesday Morning, 3 A.M. (Columbia 9049; ☆30, 1966). *Sounds of Silence* (Columbia 9269; ☆21, 1966). *Parsley, Sage, Rosemary and Thyme* (Columbia 9363; ☆4, 1966). *Bookends* (Columbia 9529; ☆1, 1968). *Bridge over Troubled Water* (Columbia 9914; ☆1, 1970). *Simon and Garfunkel's Greatest Hits* (Columbia 31350; ☆5, 1972).

Paul Simon
Paul Simon (Columbia 30750; ☆4, 1972). *There Goes Rhymin' Simon* (Columbia 32280; ☆2, 1973). *Live Rhymin'—Paul Simon in Concert* (Columbia 32855; ☆33, 1974). *Still Crazy after All These Years* (Columbia 33540; ☆1, 1975).

Cat Stevens
Matthew and Son/New Masters (Deram 18005; ☆173, 1971). *Very Young and Early Songs* (Deram 18061; ☆94, 1972). *Tea for the Tillerman* (A&M 4280; ☆8, 1971). *Mona Bone Jakon* (A&M 4260; ☆164, 1971). *Teaser and the Firecat* (A&M 4313; ☆3, 1971). *Catch Bull at Four* (A&M 4365; ☆1, 1972). *Foreigner* (A&M 4391; ☆3, 1973). *Buddha and the Chocolate Box* (A&M 3623; ☆2, 1974). *Greatest Hits* (A&M 4555; ☆13, 1975). *Numbers: A Pythagorian Theory Tale* (A&M 4555; ☆13, 1975).

(Chart positions compiled from Joel Whitburn's *Record Research*, based on *Billboard* LPs charts.)

Rod Stewart
by Paul Nelson

Born North London, January 10th, 1945, but proud of Scotch ancestry. Working-class parents. Attended school with Kinks Ray and Dave Davies. Played semipro soccer before busking around Europe as beatnik banjo player. Dug graves. Served early musical apprenticeship with bands which included Long John Baldry and Brian Auger. Known as Rod the Mod. Lead singer for the first Jeff Beck Group, 1967–'69. Since then has maintained separate recording career (six solo LPs) while performing as lead singer for the Faces, ersatz Rolling Stones band whose careless rock and roll sounded best in tattoo parlors near bus stations. Despite obvious star quality, tried hard to remain anonymous within group and seemed to need companionship they provided. Became rich in 1971 with third solo album *Every Picture Tells a Story* (hit single: "Maggie May"), and began to worry about flying in airplanes. After the relative failure of fifth solo LP, *Smiler*, used American musicians for the first time in 1975 on *Atlantic Crossing*. Then left the Faces or group disbanded—hard to say which. Early heroes: Ramblin' Jack Elliott, Sam Cooke. Once told me he wouldn't be nervous about meeting Bob Dylan, but would be awestruck in front of Elliott. Hates to lose and will "accidentally" bump your cue if being beaten in game of pool. . . .

To a lot of people, Rod Stewart onstage in mid-strut—blond hair flying, handy with brandy and partial to the broad smile and easy wink—offers as good a definition of the full flash of rock and roll as we are likely to get. He's a wizard at the spotlight game, his long legs quickly laying claim to the private turf of a public master. Behind him, the Faces, the group that provided B-movie backup throughout most of his concert career, careen like well-oiled parts of a perpetual-motion machine gone somewhat daft of purpose, while their leader lines out antics and anthems, holding everything together with the soft-shoe strength and near-total accessibility of his talent and personality. Mick Jagger, Roger Daltrey and even Elton John—the last a pumped up Dr. T.J. Eckleburg on Sunset Boulevard to Stewart's alley-scuffling, eyeballing Gatsby—may be as exciting, but the Rolling Stones and the Who are formal institutions: visceral, more precise, a little threatening and definitely less friendly. Stewart, even in front of tens of thousands, projects an ex-athlete's warmth, sets up towel-snapping camaraderie among the players, and somehow manages to embody both the extrovert, one-of-the-boys hijinks of the macho carouser and the introvert, aw-she'd-probably-never-notice-me-anyway self-consciousness of the shyest kid on the block. Even as we envy his outgoing, big-winner's style, we revel in the knowledge he provides via self-mockery that he can lose as often and as badly as we do.

This swashbuckling Britisher is a bravado specialist who conversely displays a lucid vulnerability as if it were the sharpest, chip-on-the-shoulder belligerence. Langdon Winner has written of him: "The music of Rod Steward helps us to remem-ber many of the small but extremely important experiences of life which our civilization inclines us to forget. . . . He can recall these fragile moments of insight to our minds without destroying their essence. As I listened to *Gasoline Alley* . . . I found myself saying again and again, 'He *can't* understand *that*.' But he does." A rock and roll private investigator, Stewart could have sprung full-blown from the pages of *Black Mask* as one of those likable, melodramatic professionals who, born on the dark side of the tracks, now traverses the neon streets of fabulous dreamworlds with nothing more (and nothing less) than a head filled with the memories of hard experience and a heart full of innocent mush. Even his present-tense, picaresque adventure stories seldom stray far from the melancholy air of sweet remembrance which permeates virtually all of his fatalistic tales of tender but inevitably lost love. To quote film critic Manny Farber, the best Stewart songs "travel like a shamus who knows his city" well and who respects his own raspy, idiosyncratic ability to locate and itemize small niches within larger ones. Once he has arrived at the heart of the matter, Rod Stewart has an uncanny technical flair for establishing the mood of a song at the outset and sustaining that mood until the last listener is convinced. Some of the primary traits of his complex and contradictory persona are those of the thriller hero and romantic pseudogangster who live life lavishly, sampling the finest wines and loveliest women without ever becoming jaded or having to pick up a heavy physical or psychic tab. Doubtless, Stewart could always use his mellifluous charm and grace to circumvent the sterner issues, but brains rather than brawn seems to prevail. In the end, his ferocious brassiness is generally undone by straightforward, heartfelt common sense. Essentially, his art conforms to the same strict moral and aesthetic guidelines set down by the mythopoeic American pulp genres—Appalachian folk music, skiffle, folk rock, rock and roll, rhythm and blues—from which it grew and to which it constantly refers. Like Philip Marlowe, he is as sentimental as the Beatles—but much tougher. Like Sam Spade, he is fully capable of falling in love, then, because of some higher artistic morality, sending over the loved one in the final reel (e.g., his leaving the Jeff Beck Group after two LPs, the Faces after five). Whatever his reasons, he has preferred to do his solo albums—by far his most important work—with handpicked musicians who (except for long-term friends Ron Wood and Mick Waller) usually were not boys from those lusty, often lusterless bands of which he was once a member.

Throughout his career, Stewart has maintained equal and enviable reputations both as a superb songwriter and as a skillful interpreter of material other than his own. On *The Rod Stewart Album*, the artist undoubtedly functions more impressively in the latter role, but on his best records—*Gasoline Alley*, *Every Picture Tells a Story*, *Never a Dull Moment*, *Atlantic Crossing*—the pendulum swings decisively in the other direction. While Stewart's interpretive powers never diminish, sev-

Rod Stewart and friend (Andy Kent)

eral of his own compositions clearly represent the high points of an entire career. Whether he is reveling in luminous licentiousness to the incendiary beat of knockabout rock and roll ("Every Picture Tells a Story," "Lost Paraguayos," "Sailor," "Three Time Loser," "Stone Cold Sober") or sadly reflecting upon some lost woman to the evocative accompaniment of rustic fiddle or ringing mandolin ("Lady Day," "Jo's Lament," "Maggie May," "Mandolin Wind," "You Wear It Well," "Farewell," "Still Love You"), he is always believable, and his plight often sympathetic. Stewart's musical flexibility within the low-budget voluptuousness of his characteristic, filigreed sound is astonishing yet understandable given his moralistic preoccupation with a past which ties tenderized but old-fashioned guilt to a prodigal son's AC/DC desire to return to his more conservative roots ("Don't you think I better get myself back home?") and to flee at all costs the newfangled commitments of the present and future, ("Tearing down the highway in the pouring rain/Escaping from my wedding day"). In such a philosophical predicament, the singer can lament, "It's been so long since I had a good time," while idly contemplating a dose of "Dixie Toot" hedonism which he knows will not provide any real help. Indeed, Stewart's hell-raising sexist would probably be harder to take if he weren't so honest (" 'Cause I ain't forgetting that you were once mine/That I blew it without even trying"), susceptible ("Now I'm not so young and I'm so afraid/To sleep alone for the rest of my days"), and self-deprecating ("Think of me and try not to laugh"). His compassionate love songs scan like the second thoughts of an unsteady protagonist who "get(s) scared when (he) remember(s) too much" because it is central to his nature to nearly always waver in the face of meaningful choice. "True Blue" starts out as an expression of pure anguish ("Just don't know what to do") but ends with the exhilarating roar of the hero's Lamborghini as he drives blithely away from all of his problems, while "Italian Girls" reverses the process, metamorphosing from happy-go-lucky carnality into a delirious day of reckoning when the stunned Stewart realizes that leaving the woman was exactly what he did not want to do. From start ("Gasoline Alley") to finish ("Down in the alley again" in "Stone Cold Sober"), the artist exhibits great humanity but little permanent change. With his shy-guy verities and slapstick/exuberant male truths intact, he remains the consummate introspective rock and roll romantic. Like all good romantics, he unwittingly destroys everything he touches. Only to feel damned sorry about it later.

The same concerns are only somewhat less apparent when Stewart pursues his more restful role as an interpreter. If he had never written a word of his own, he would still deserve a place in the history of popular music for his almost unerring choice of material, the canniness of his production concepts, and the scope of his emotional range as a singer—arguably the finest in rock and roll. Consider the evidence: "Street Fighting Man," "Man of Constant Sorrow," "Only a Hobo," "(I Know)

I'm Losing You," "Tomorrow Is Such a Long Time," "Reason to Believe," "Mama You've Been on My Mind," "I'd Rather Go Blind," "Jealous Guy," "Sailing" and especially "Handbags and Gladrags," "It's All Over Now," "Country Comforts," "Angel," "Twisting the Night Away," and "Drift Away." On "Drift Away," he darkens the mood to catch perfectly the poignant persona of a young man who feels he may have missed something essential in his daredevil ventures and now needs a place to hide out while he reconsiders and reaccepts his shrinking options. To me, Dobie Gray's hit version of a few years ago sounds routine and unemotional when compared with Stewart's striving desperation. When this North Londoner sings, "Oh, give me the beat, boys, to soothe my soul/I want to get lost in your rock and roll," he seems to mean it. I cannot think of another artist who so fully exemplifies Jean Renoir's iridescent and unforgettable credo: "You see, in this world there is one awful thing, and that is that everyone has his reasons." Rod Stewart understands this and makes us understand it, too. I care about him. In the end, quite a lot.

Discography

Rod Stewart, *The Rod Stewart Album* (Mercury 61237; ☆139, 1969). *Gasoline Alley* (Mercury 61264; ☆27, 1970). *Every Picture Tells a Story* (Mercury 609; ☆1, 1971). *Never a Dull Moment* (Mercury 646; ☆2, 1972). *Sing It Again, Rod* (Mercury 680; ☆31, 1973). *Smiler* (Mercury 1017; ☆13, 1974). *Atlantic Crossing* (Warner Bros. 2875; ☆9, 1975). **Jeff Beck Group,** *Truth* (Epic 26413; ☆15, 1968). *Beck-Ola* (Epic 26478; ☆15, 1969). **Small Faces,** *Small Faces—First Step* (Warner Bros. 1851; ☆119, 1970). **Faces,** *Long Player* (Warner Bros. 1892; ☆29, 1971). *A Nod Is as Good as a Wink to a Blind Horse* (Warner Bros. 2574; ☆6, 1971). *Ooh La La* (Warner Bros. 2665; ☆21, 1973). **Rod Stewart and Faces,** *Coast to Coast, Overture and Beginners* (Mercury 697; ☆63, 1974).
(Chart positions taken from Joel Whitburn's *Record Research*, compiled from *Billboard* Pop and LPs charts.)

Art Rock

by John Rockwell

There is a morphology to artistic movements. They begin with a rude and innocent vigor, pass into a healthy adulthoood and finally decline into an overwrought, feeble old age. Something of this process can be observed in the passage of rock and roll from the three-chord primitivism of the Fifties through the burgeoning vitality and experimentation of the Sixties to the hollow emptiness of much of the so-called progressive or "art" rock of the Seventies.

The whole notion of art rock triggers instinctive hostility from those who define rock in terms of the early-middle stages of its morphology. Rock was born as a street rebellion against pretensions and hypocrisy—of Fifties society, Fifties Tin Pan Alley pop, and high art in general ("Roll Over Beethoven"). Thus the very idea of art rock strikes some as a cancer to be battled without quarter, and the present-day reversion to primitivism is in part a rejection of the fancier forms of progressive rock. The trouble is, once consciousness has intruded itself onto the morphological process, it's impossible to obliterate it (except maybe with drugs, and then only temporarily). And so even primitivism, self-consciously assumed, becomes one of the principal vehicles of art rock.

The Beatles' *Sgt. Pepper's Lonely Hearts Club Band* (1967) is often cited as the progenitor of self-conscious experimentation in rock. It was the album that dramatized rock's claim to artistic seriousness to an adult world that had previously dismissed the whole genre as blathering teen entertainment. The Beatles aspired to something really daring and new—an unabashedly eclectic, musically clever (harmonies, rhythms and, above all, arrangements) mélange that could only have been created in the modern recording studio.

One inevitable implication of the whole notion of art rock, anticipated by *Sgt. Pepper,* is that it parallels, imitates, or is inspired by other forms of "higher," more "serious" music. All young artists, it is said, begin by imitating those they admire, and the good ones eventually break loose on their own. Since mature rock musicians are mostly young and tend to be technically limited, their imitations are often blatant. Sometimes, their very lack of technical facility makes their copies bad ones, and hence leads inadvertently to originality.

On the whole imitative art rock has tended to emulate classical music, primarily the 18th- and 19th-century orchestral sorts. The pioneers in this enterprise were the Moody Blues, whose million-selling 1968 album *Days of Future Passed* paired the group with the London Festival Orchestra. Although Moody Blues devotees seemed to think they were getting something higher toned than mere rock, they were kidding themselves: Moody Blues records are mood music, pure and regrettably not so simple. There's nothing wrong with that, of course, except for the miscategorization into something more profound.

The vast majority of the bands that pillage traditional classical music come from Britain. Why British bands feel compelled to quote the classics, however tongue-in-cheek, leads into the murky waters of class and nation analysis. In comparison with the British, Americans tend to be happy apes. Most American rockers wouldn't know a Beethoven symphony if they were run down by one in the middle of a freeway. One result of such ignorance is that American art (music, painting, poetry, films, etc.) can develop untroubled by lame affectations of a cultured sensibility. In Britain, the lower classes—the source of 99% of all British rockers—enjoy no such isolation. The class divisions and the crushing weight of high culture flourish essentially untrammeled. One result is that in London there is a far closer interchange between establishment contemporary classical composers like David Bedford or even Peter Maxwell Davies and the rock world. It also means that rockers seem far more eager to "dignify" their work, to make it acceptable for upper-class approbation, by freighting it with the trappings of classical music. Or, conversely, they are far more intent upon making classical music accessible to their audiences by bastardizing it in a rock context. Or, maybe, they feel the need to parody it to the point of ludicrousness. In all cases, they relate to it with a persistence and intensity that American groups rarely match.

The principal examples here are acts like the Nice; Emerson, Lake and Palmer; Deep Purple; Procol Harum; Renaissance; Yes; and Rick Wakeman. Much of what these groups do is just souped up, oversynthesized, vaguely "progressive" rock of no particular interest or pretensions. But at one time or another all of them have dealt in some form of classical pastiche. Wakeman, classically trained as a pianist at the Royal Academy, is as good an example as any. After serving time as a session pianist for the likes of David Bowie and Cat Stevens, he joined Yes, helping to lead the group into a convoluted pop mysticism. He eventually left Yes, in 1974, to pursue a solo career devoted to such elaborate, portentously titled orchestral narratives as *Journey to the Centre of the Earth* and *The Myths and Legends of King Arthur and the Knights of the Round Table.* These ice-skating epics have their elements of elephantine humor, I suppose. But his classical excursions are dispatched with such a brutal cynicism as to be genuinely appalling.

Even when such groups aren't busily ripping off Grieg their music is operatically arty in the bad sense, through their ponderous appeal to middle-class sensibility and their lame reliance on electronically updated 19th-century vaudeville stage tricks. Too often these pastiches are further burdened by the seemingly irresistible weakness certain sorts of loud, arty British bands have for science fiction art and "poetry." Yes's album covers make the point as well as anything, but such puerile mythologizing—Tolkien for the teenyboppers—pervades much of British pop poetry, and lapses over with insufferable affectation into much of the British electric folk-rock camp, too; think only of Jethro Tull and Cat Stevens.

Eno, wunderkind of the British pop avant-garde (Neal Preston)

Classical borrowings don't have to be limited simply to quotations, however, nor do they have to be bad by definition. The whole craze for "rock operas" of the Kinks/Who variety has produced some fascinating work. Similarly, some of the fairly straightforward heavy-metal groups have colored their music with the judicious application of nonrock styles, to telling effect (the use of Middle Eastern modes and instrumental accents in Led Zeppelin's "Kashmir," for example).

Such use of classical and other nonrock styles and formal ideas blends imperceptibly into all-purpose stylistic eclecticism—the free and often febrile switching among different styles within the same piece. Eclecticism has been more prominent in London than anywhere else, and, at its best, it stops being lamely imitative and enters the realm of creativity.

Numerous British bands fall into the eclectic art rock camp: Genesis, King Crimson, Electric Light Orchestra, Queen, Supertramp, Sparks, 10cc, Gentle Giant, and Be-Bop Deluxe. There are continental bands like Focus, and even some American groups like Kansas that fit here also. Certainly there are differences between these groups, large differences—and there are many more groups that could be listed. But they all share a commitment to unprepared, abrupt transitions from one mood to another. Sometimes the shifts are between tempos, sometimes between levels of volume, sometimes between whole styles of music. The effect in any case is violent, disruptive and nervously tense, and as such no doubt answers the needs of the age as well as anything. At their best (or at their most commercially successful), these groups never lose sight of older rock basics, as with Queen's best work or with Bill Nelson's extraordinary guitar playing in any style you can think of on Be-Bop Deluxe's albums.

The leader of this particular pack, Roxy Music, is discussed elsewhere. But Brian Eno, one of Roxy's original members, merits special attention here. Aside from the quality of his music, which is considerable, Eno is interesting from two points of view: his command of the synthesizer and his relation to others on the London experimental scene.

The synthesizer is a much-abused, much-misunderstood instrument. When played like a souped up electric organ by people like Keith Emerson, Jon Lord (of Deep Purple) or Rick Wakeman, it can sound simply flashy and cheap. If the obligatory drum solo used to be the bane of any self-respecting rock-concert goer's life, the obligatory synthesizer solo, preferably with smoke bomb and laser obbligato, is the current curse. If synthesizers aren't regarded as newfangled organs, they are taken literally, as something that "synthesizes," and we are subjected to Walter Carlos's and Isao Tomita's synthesized versions of the classics (not rock, or even art rock, technically, but certainly appealing to the same market).

What the synthesizer really is, is an instrument with its own characteristics, and those characteristics are just beginning to be explored by rock musicians. When played with the subtlety and discretion of a Stevie Wonder or a Garth Hudson, it can reinforce conventional textures superbly. And when somebody like Eno or Edgar Froese of Tangerine Dream gets hold of it, the synthesizer can create a whole world of its own. Eno's *Discreet Music* (1975), with its title-track first side full of soothing, hypnotic woodwindish sounds, or *No Pussyfooting* (1975) and *Evening Star* (1976), two collaborations with Robert Fripp, ex-King Crimson guitarist, are masterly examples of genuine rock avant-gardism. Of course, they aren't really "rock" in any but the loosest sense: there is no reference back to a blues base, even in attenuated form. But it is music produced by a rock sensibility aimed at a rock audience.

Eno's position within the London avant-garde, and the nature of that avant-garde, are both of interest, too. London, like New York, has a thriving avant-garde musical community that doesn't place much of a premium on formally acquired technique, thus remaining open to fresh infusions of energy from ostensible "amateurs." In London, the experimentation in rock is fostered by British taxation, which forces most of the successful commercial rockers out of the country, leaving the rest to experiment relatively free from Top 40 pressures. This robs the London scene of some potential big-name experimenters like George Harrison (see *Electronic Sound,* 1969) and John Lennon (whose *Two Virgins* with Yoko Ono was another particularly appealing early art-rock entry in 1969).

Still, what's left in the forefront of experimentation is interesting enough. The mere fact that Eno had to leave Roxy Music (quite apart from the question of clashing egos with lead singer Bryan Ferry) indicates the difficulty of pursuing experimentation and commercial success at the same time. The London avant-garde scene, insofar as any outsider can tell, is marked by a fascinating if rather private and sporadic interchange between the classical and pop worlds. So far, the pop stars (Eno, guitarist Phil Manzanera of Roxy, Fripp) have done rather more interesting work than those who have wandered over from a classical background (David Bedford, Stomu Yamash'ta, the Japanese percussionist-turned-rocker). Michael Oldfield fits here to a certain extent, although his work—particularly after his best-selling *Tubular Bells* (1973), which did admittedly have a bland appeal as a reduction of California composer Terry Riley's ideas—is lame beyond recall.

Much of this work, from Oldfield to Eno and even Riley, is head music, and relates to a rather interesting form of avant-garde trance music, which brings us to the subject of drugs. The avant-gardism in rock of the Sixties and Seventies, for all its ultimate debts to surrealism and other vanguard movements from earlier in the century, owes its primary debts to the proliferation of drugs in the Sixties. It would be misleading to overstress this, but just as false to repress it. Marijuana, LSD and other psychedelics, and methedrine or speed, have all had a

profound effect on how music in general, and art rock in particular, was made and perceived. This is not to say that you have to be stoned to play or enjoy this music. But it does mean that the climate and stylistic preoccupations of many varieties of present-day art are built in part on perceptions analogous to the drug experience. Sometimes it only takes a single trip, as with acid, to give you a whole other fix on the world. Certainly for many people, the state of mind of a marijuana high is something that can be meditatively evoked without an actual joint to inhale.

The kind of quiescent, dappled textural shiftings that mark much of American composer La Monte Young's music (Eno was strongly influenced by Young; and John Cale, formerly of the Velvet Underground, worked closely with him) owe something to grass, at least originally: maybe Young has never smoked in his life, but his art could only have germinated in a subculture primed for it by marijuana. And the same is true for the whole acid rock phenomenon.

The pure acid-rockers of the Sixties—from the Byrds to the Jefferson Airplane—don't really concern us here. But Pink Floyd, originally Britain's premier acid-rockers, do. After cutting a couple of British hit singles in 1967, the group concentrated on extended compositions, often with spacey lyrical motifs. *The Dark Side of the Moon* (1973) became one of the most successful albums of the decade, a best seller in Europe and America as well as England. It seems to me that the Floyd has turned out some of the most consistently interesting "head music" of the late Sixties and Seventies. Much of the group's appeal derives from Rick Wright's imaginative use of keyboards; but the whole group has a sense for line and continuity and ritualistic repetition that is quite special, and to dismiss them simply as technically limited is philistine.

In Los Angeles, the drug scene helped spawn the Mothers of Invention, one of the first rock groups to emphasize mixed-media presentations, dubbed "freak-outs" by leader Frank Zappa. Zappa, himself an avowed teetotaler, was forced after the first few L.A. freak-outs in 1967 to disavow the use of drugs at these affairs—naturally to no avail. The Mothers combined social satire, parody of rock 'n' roll oldies, classical references—Zappa regularly paid homage to Edgard Varèse—and a growing taste for vaguely avant-garde jazz improvisation. It has been an influential collage of styles, affecting the work of such diverse musicians as jazz violinist Jean-Luc Ponty, German jazz rocker Klaus Doldinger of Passport, and Beatle Paul McCartney, who once cited the Mothers' first album, *Freak Out*, as a key inspiration for *Sgt. Pepper*.

The psychedelic enthusiasms of the late Sixties, kindled by (among others) Pink Floyd and the Mothers of Invention and centered in San Francisco and London, have found their most sustained resonance in the Seventies in West Germany. Kraftwerk has had the biggest commercial impact in the United States, thanks to the surprising success in 1975 of *Autobahn*. Rather more interesting is Tangerine Dream and its leader Edgar Froese. The group's records and Froese's solo albums are impressionistic extravaganzas, full of gentle washes of electronic color. There is a parallel to Eno's work here. But Eno is a more diverse artist than Froese, and more overtly rock oriented, and in such purely experimental pieces as *Discreet Music* he shows an indebtedness to the structuralist principles of classical composers like Young, Riley (himself an offshoot of the psychedelic/meditative climate of the Bay Area in the Sixties), Steve Reich and Philip Glass. Froese, on the other hand, owes his classical inspirations to such orchestral colorists as Hungarian composer György Ligeti and the electronic music of Karlheinz Stockhausen and Iannis Xenakis. Froese's work seems less interesting than that of his models, but at least his choice of inspirations betrays a certain sophistication, his own pieces have a demonstrable flair, and his sense of performance has a nice theatricality, to judge from reports (cathedral concerts with former Andy Warhol protégé Nico, herself a crucial precursor of the current cult of rock shamanism).

Psychedelic weirdness never caught on very firmly in speedy, street-oriented New York. But if New Yorkers remained on the cynical sidelines of the Summer of Love Sixties, in the Seventies they came triumphantly into their own. The main antecedent to the present-day art rock scene in New York was the Velvet Underground. The band emerged from lower Manhattan's vanguard arts community—Walter De Maria, the artist, played drums with them informally at the beginning—and was only later taken over by Andy Warhol and his crowd, and plugged into "The Exploding Plastic Inevitable," Warhol's traveling mixed-media circus of 1966–'67. Warhol arguably never really understood their music; what he did understand was their overall sensibility, especially lead singer Lou Reed's, and that really was as symptomatic of the band's appeal and influence as anything else. By the time of its breakup in 1969, and in terms of its subsequent impact, the Underground had coalesced around two figures: Reed and John Cale. Reed had and has ambitions as a poet, and it was his writing that defined the stark, cruelly decadent, despairing tone of the band. Cale was classically trained as a violist in London, and moved in avant-garde musical circles (Xenakis at Tanglewood, Young in New York) before gravitating to the world of pop. As such, he really is a London-originated New York precursor of the classical-pop interchange that is going on in London now. His subsequent solo work at its best—a collaboration with Terry Riley called *Church of Anthrax, Paris 1919*, and above all *The Acad-*

Clockwise from top: (1) Frank Zappa of the Mothers, at ease in his backyard; (2) Patti Smith, New York City poet and queen of rock and roll; (3) Yes, so to speak; (4) The Moody Blues; (5) Tangerine Dream. Center: (6) Kraftwerk—is this the future of rock? What would Elvis say? (1, Baron Wolman; 3, 4 & 5, ROLLING STONE; 2, Michael Zagaris; 6, David Bieber Archives)

emy in Peril—indicates a softer, dreamier, more overtly disoriented, meditative sensibility than Reed's, although in his last few albums, Cale has tried for a rocking commercial appeal.

What appalled people about the Underground then and what appalls them about its offshoots today is the defiant simplicity of the music. The point here is that art rock is hardly to be equated with complexity, no matter what British working-class bands enamored of studio fanciness may think. The New Yorkers owe their principal inspiration to the visual arts of the Sixties, and much of that art was concerned with sparse, delicately or violently contrasted juxtapositions of elements, often in the service of some overt structuralist plan. The influence of meditation, maybe drugs and certainly the Orient is obvious here. The markets for such art and its quality (clearly interrelated, but it would be facile to asume automatically that one decline caused the other) have both fallen off, but much of the artistic energy in Manhattan has been taken up in performance art, and part of that art has manifested itself as rock and roll.

The best-known of the contemporary New York art rockers is Patti Smith. Smith is busily trying to downplay that side of her roots at the moment, stressing her kinship with the "kids" and with crazed, antiintellectual rock. But Patti's always been a role player, and to this taste she's playing her just-folks role a little less successfully than she played her former artist role, her superhip rock hanger-on role, or her poetess-priestess role. In fact, her art, as epitomized on her first LP, *Horses* (1975), is a wonderful blend of ritualistic declamation, surrealist imagery and rock basics. And the basics are basic not just because her band can't play anything else. It's because New York artists have long been fascinated with the minimalist, clean-cut energy of rock at its simplest—a fascination reflected in the work of such other contemporary New York bands as Tom Verlaine's Television and Talking Heads.

I began this disquisition by talking about morphologies and self-consciousness, and in some ways the aesthetic behind the New York art rock scene of the past decade brings us full circle.

Looking at rock from a populist standpoint, one can seriously question both its aspirations to high art and the very hegemony of high art itself. Maybe the self-conscious primitives in New York are right: maybe art rock doesn't have to be clever complexity at all. Maybe real art is that which most clearly and directly answers the needs of its audiences. Which, in turn, means that we can prize pure rock and pure pop, from Chuck Berry on, as "art" in no way inferior to that which may entail a more highly formalized technique for its execution. Rock may be part of a far larger process in which art broadens its gestures to encompass an audience made more numerous by the permeation of social equality down into strata heretofore ignored.

There is another, more philosophical side to it. What Warhol and pop artists are trying to tell us—and what composer John Cage has been telling us all along—is that art isn't necessarily a product crafted painstakingly by some mysterious, removed artist-deity, but is whatever you, the perceiver, choose to perceive artistically. A Brillo box isn't suddenly art because Warhol puts a stacked bunch of them in a museum. But by putting them there he encourages you to make your every trip to the supermarket an artistic adventure, and in so doing he has exalted your life. Everybody's an artist if he wants to be, which is really a more radically populist notion than encouraging scholarly studies of the blues. Roll over Beethoven indeed, and make room for us.

Discography

1966-1975

Frank Zappa and the Mothers of Invention
Freak Out (Verve 5005; ☆130, 1967). *Absolutely Free* (Verve 5013; ☆41, 1967). *We're Only in It for the Money* (Verve 5045; ☆30, 1968). *Lumpy Gravy* (Verve 8741; ☆159, 1968). *Cruising with Ruben and the Jets* (Verve 5055; ☆110, 1968). *Uncle Meat* (Bizarre 2024; ☆43, 1969). *Hot Rats* (Bizarre 6356; ☆173, 1969). *Burnt Weeny Sandwich* (Bizarre 6370; ☆94, 1970). *Weasels Ripped My Flesh* (Bizarre 2028; ☆189, 1970). *Chunga's Revenge* (Bizarre 2030; ☆119, 1970). *Fillmore East—June 1971* (Bizarre 2042; ☆38, 1971). *Frank Zappa's 200 Motels* (United Artists 9956; ☆59, 1971). *Just Another Band from L.A.* (Bizarre 2075; ☆85, 1972). *Grand Wazoo* (Bizarre 2093; 1972). *Waka/Jawaka* (Bizarre 2094; ☆152, 1972). *Over-Nite Sensations* (Discreet 2149; ☆32, 1973). *Apostrophe (')* (Discreet 2175; ☆10, 1974). *Roxy and Elsewhere* (Discreet 2202; ☆27, 1974). *One Size Fits All* (Discreet 2216; ☆26, 1975). *Bongo Fury* (Discreet 2234; ☆66, 1975).
Velvet Underground
The Velvet Underground and Nico (Verve 5008; ☆171, 1967). *White Light/White Heat* (Verve 5046; ☆199, 1968). *The Velvet Underground* (MGM 4617; 1969). *Loaded* (Cotillion 9034; 1970). *Live at Max's Kansas City* (Cotillion 9500; 1972). *1969 Velvet Underground Live with Lou Reed* (Mercury 7504; 1974).
Pink Floyd
Pink Floyd (Tower 5093; ☆131, 1967). *A Saucerful of Secrets* (Tower 5131; 1968). *More* (Tower 5169; 1969). *Ummagumma* (Harvest 388; ☆74, 1970). *Atom Heart Mother* (Harvest 382; ☆55, 1970). *Relics* (Harvest 759; ☆152, 1971). *Meddle* (Harvest 832; ☆70, 1971). *Obscured by Clouds* (Harvest 11078; ☆46, 1972). *The Dark Side of the Moon* (Harvest 11163; ☆1, 1973). *Wish You Were Here* (Columbia 33453; ☆1, 1975).
Albums Featuring Eno
Roxy Music, *Roxy Music* (Reprise 2114; 1972). *For Your Pleasure* (Warner Bros. 2696; ☆193, 1973). Fripp/Eno, *No Pussyfooting* (Antilles 7001; 1973). *Here Come the Warm Jets* (Island 9268; ☆151, 1974). *Taking Tiger Mountain by Strategy* (Island 9309; 1974). *Another Green World* (Island 9351; 1975). *Discreet Music* (Obscure 3; 1975).
Chart-Topping Classical Bombast
Moody Blues, *Days of Future Passed* (Deram 18012; ☆3, 1968). *On the Threshold of a Dream* (Deram 18025; ☆20, 1969). *To Our Children's Children's Children* (Threshold 1; ☆14, 1970). *A Question of Balance* (Threshold 3; ☆3, 1970). *Every Good Boy Deserves Favour* (Threshold 5; ☆2, 1971). *Seventh Sojourn* (Threshold 7; ☆1, 1972). **Emerson, Lake and Palmer,** *Emerson, Lake and Palmer* (Cotillion 9040; ☆18, 1971). *Tarkus* (Cotillion 9900, ☆9, 1971). *Pictures at an Exhibition (Mussorgsky)* (Cotillion 6666; ☆10, 1972). *Trilogy* (Cotillion 9903; ☆5, 1972). *Brain Salad Surgery* (Manticore 66669; ☆11, 1973). *Welcome Back, My Friends, to the Show That Never Ends—Ladies and Gentlemen—Emerson, Lake and Palmer* (Manticore 200; ☆4, 1974). **Yes,** *Fragile* (Atlantic 7211; ☆4, 1972). *Close to the Edge* (Atlantic 7244; ☆3, 1972). *Yessongs* (Atlantic 100; ☆12, 1973). *Tales from Topographic Oceans* (Atlantic 908; ☆6, 1974). *Relayer* (Atlantic 18122; ☆5, 1974). **Rick Wakeman,** *Six Wives of Henry VIII* (A&M 4361; ☆30, 1973). *Journey to the Centre of the Earth* (A&M 3621; ☆3, 1974). *Myths and Legends of King Arthur and the Knights of the Round Table* (A&M 4515; ☆21, 1975).
A Sampler of Eclectic Experimentalism
King Crimson, *In the Court of the Crimson King: An Observation by King Crimson* (Atlantic 8245; ☆28, 1969). *In the Wake of Poseidon* (Atlantic 8266; ☆31, 1970). **Genesis,** *Selling England by the Pound* (Charisma 6060; ☆70, 1973). **Gentle Giant,** *The Power and the Glory* (Capitol 11337; ☆78, 1974). **Electric Light Orchestra,** *On the Third Day* (United Artists 188; ☆52, 1974). **10cc,** *Sheet Music* (Auks 53107; ☆81, 1974). **Sparks,** *Kimono My House* (Island 9272; ☆101, 1974). **Be-Bop Deluxe,** *Futurama* (Harvest 11432; 1975). **Supertramp,** *Crime of the Century* (A&M 3647; ☆38, 1974).
German Art-Rock
Tangerine Dream, *Phaedra* (Virgin 13108; ☆196, 1974). *Rubycon* (Virgin 13116; 1975). **Edgar Froese,** *Aqua* (Virgin 13111; 1974). **Kraftwerk,** *Autobahn* (Vertigo 2003; ☆5, 1975).
Arty Primitivism
John Cale, *Vintage Violence* (Columbia 1037; 1970). **Terry Riley and John Cale,** *Church of Anthrax* (Columbia 30131; 1970). **John Cale,** *The Academy in Peril* (Reprise 2079; 1972). *Paris 1919* (Reprise 2131; 1973). *Fear* (Island 9301; 1974). *Slow Dazzle* (Island 9317; 1975). **Patti Smith,** *Horses* (Arista 4066; ☆47, 1975).
(Chart positions compiled from Joel Whitburn's *Record Research,* based on *Billboard* LPs chart. Discographies for Nice and Procol Harum can be found in the "Britain—The Second Wave" discography.)

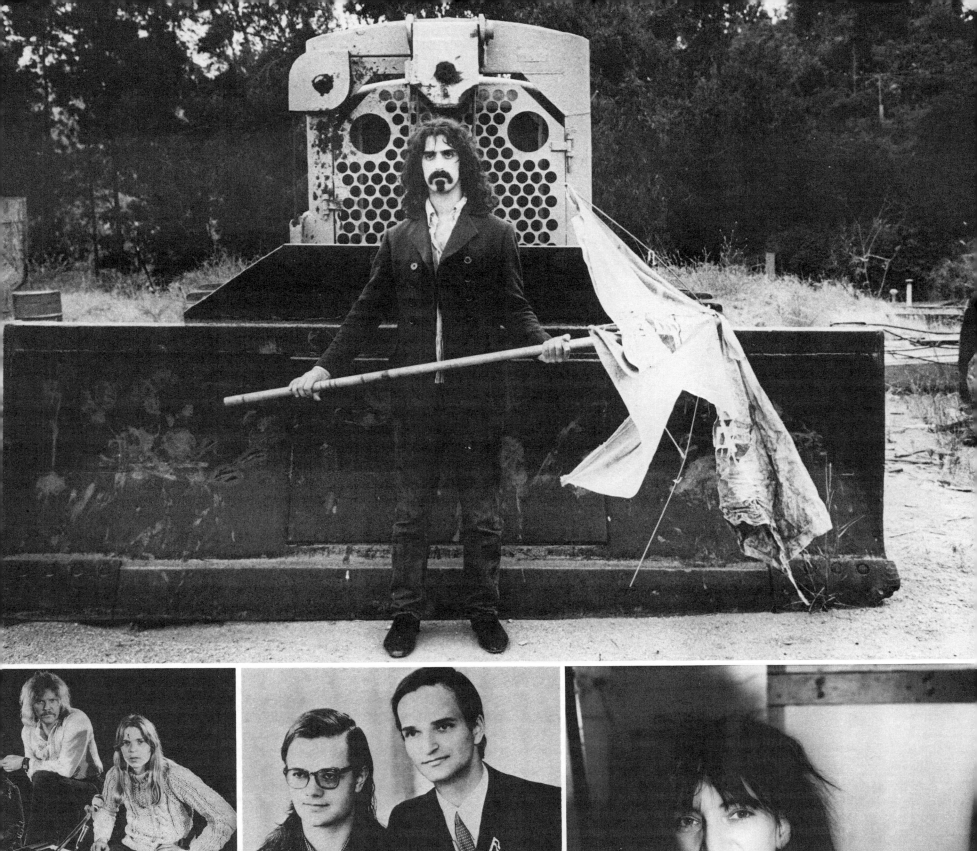

All the Young Dudes
by Paul Nelson

Lou Reed, David Bowie, and Ian Hunter share a similar troubled vision—an outlook of unblinking fatalism that haunts even their legitimate lighter moments. They are all survivors, natural outsiders by unnatural choice or intuitive chance. Like Bob Dylan—a major influence on Reed and Hunter, and the man for whom Bowie wrote a song on *Hunky Dory*—each is a self-conscious mythographer and mythmaker deeply involved in the archetypes of the ultraurban Seventies. The strain of androgyny runs through both Reed and Bowie, although Hunter seems to flirt with it merely momentarily in the title song on Mott the Hoople's *All the Young Dudes* (an album produced by Bowie, who has also produced Reed). Bowie and Hunter perform songs that Reed has written, while Reed and Bowie are the spiritual fathers of such Seventies rock and rollers as Patti Smith, Elliott Murphy, the Modern Lovers, Jonathan Richman, the New York Dolls, Talking Heads, Television, and a veritable host of glitter- and punk-rock bands too numerous to mention.

Lou Reed has been misunderstood too quickly. Perhaps the fact that his curious career continues is more important than what he does with it at any given point, but that career—apparently to the surprise of many—offers far more than death-wish decadence as the basis for cohabitable communication. Lester Bangs has written: "Lou Reed is the guy who gave dignity and poetry and rock and roll to smack, speed, homosexuality, sadomasochism, murder, misogyny, stumblebum passivity, and suicide—and then proceeded to belie all his achievements and return to the mire by turning the whole thing into a monumental bad joke." Yes and no. Had Reed accomplished nothing else, his work with the Velvet Underground in the late Sixties would still have assured him a place in anyone's rock and roll pantheon. "Heroin," "I'm Waiting for the Man," "Venus in Furs," "Some Kinda Love," "White Light/White Heat," and "Sister Ray" still serve as articulate aural nightmares about men and women caught up in the beauty and terror of sexual, street, and drug paranoia, unwilling or unable to move. The message is that city life is rough stuff—it can kill you. Reed, the poet of partial destruction, knows it but never looks away, and somehow finds holiness as well as perversity in both his sinners and his quest.

But those songs, however brilliant, are examples of only the sensational portion of Reed's underground oeuvre (from his erratic later work, one could add "Vicious," parts of *Berlin*, all of the electronic and unlistenable *Metal Machine Music*, and "Kicks")—less than half. More often, the singer's tough-guy stance reflects the dark side of a hard-won sentimentality which rarely goes rotten because it so wants to connect. Most of Reed's tales of Gotham's gay and not-so-gay life ("New Age," "Wild Child," "Walk on the Wild Side," *Coney Island Baby*) are less wasteful than wistful, without a trace of auctorial irony or condescension—Norman Rockwell meets Hieronymus Bosch.

Reed doesn't stop wanting to reshape reality, or at times to celebrate the virtues of love, loyalty, and trust in "I'll Be Your Mirror," "Beginning to See the Light," and "She's My Best Friend." "Rock 'n' Roll," "Sweet Jane," and "We're Gonna Have a Real Good Time Together" tell us that rock and roll saves, and Reed, who is saturated with salvation, proves it with his performances on 1969's *The Velvet Underground*, 1970's *Loaded*, *1969 Velvet Underground Live* released in 1974, and 1976's *Coney Island Baby*, his best albums.

Since leaving the Underground in 1969, Lou Reed's star has shone very brightly commercially (the David Bowie-produced "Walk on the Wild Side" was a big AM hit), less so artistically. For a while, he seemed to lose both his timing and his singing voice—he literally talks his way through the blood-bubbling *Berlin*—and his concerts veered unpredictably from tragic (simulating an injection during "Heroin") to near-terrific (the live *Rock n Roll Animal*). Furthermore, his bizarre behavior and ominous, street-creep image broadened to such comic-strip proportions that people laughed at him, whether he wanted them to or not. Until *Coney Island Baby*, the paucity of much of his newer material was anything but funny.

In his introduction to "I'm Waiting for the Man" on *1969 Velvet Underground Live*, Reed admonishes a Texas audience for allowing the Dallas football team to pile up the score: "We saw your Cowboys today, and they never let Philadelphia even have the ball for a minute. . . . It was ridiculous. I mean, you should give other people just a little chance—in football anyway." If the Velvets—infamous for the violent, hypnotic, dope trance/staccato power of their playing and the seedy, subway vision of Reed's lyrics—can enjoy gridiron drama in the heart of ten-gallon-hat country, surely Lou Reed—once a mixed-up kid from Babylon—can tell everyone who will listen to him in 1976 that "the glory of love might see you through" and that, in high school, he wanted most of all to play football—"for the coach."

There is a more "serious," nonsporting connection between *1969 Velvet Underground Live* and *Coney Island Baby*, however. To capture the correct mood—exactly what is missing from most of his solo LPs—Reed, a master of repetition, has jettisoned most of his sarcastic, Seventies daze to reclaim the intimate style and warmth of some of the songs ("Pale Blue Eyes," "There She Goes Again," "Lisa Says," "Ocean") he loved to sing in the Sixties. *Coney Island Baby* in no way whitewashes the warp and woof of the quintessential monster, but it does restore a much-needed balance and save its creator from further self-parody. The songs—particularly the title cut and "She's My Best Friend"—tackle the themes of friendship, intimidation, and taking stock of one's life and doing something about it. Reed seems more than willing to put his unorthodox lifestyle on the line anytime anyone wants to call him on it, but there is no malice in his challenge and often considerable regret.

Lou Reed, in a mid-Seventies incarnation: yellow hair, black nails (Michael Zagaris)

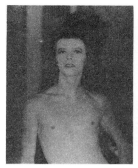

David Bowie, primed for a shipboard romance (Andy Kent)

"Coney Island Baby" is about courage, loss, and the high price an outsider pays for everything. When Lou Reed says, "I'm gonna send this one out for Lou and Rachel/All the kids and P.S. 192/Man, I swear I'd give the whole thing up for you," and talks about "want[ing] to play football for the coach," he isn't just being maudlin. He is expressing the profound dream of the damned—and his loss is given greater intensity because both he and we know that such wishes were impossible from the very beginning. So we reaccept it. And it hurts all over again.

If there is an inherent pretentiousness which Reed usually manages to avoid in the role of romantic outcast, chances are that David Bowie, who first emerged as a star in Britain in 1969, and in the U.S. in 1972, will both seek it out and exploit it. More a masterful manipulator of media than a creditable creative figure, Bowie, whom critic Frank Rose has aptly dubbed "the first space-age bisexual Deco superstar," has fabricated his fame primarily by flitting from one threadbare, mock-serious philosophical stance to another without truly embracing any of them. Sensitive artiste, space baby, glitter queen, neo-Nazi supergod, disco robot, *Cabaret* cadaver—pick any two and then try to figure out whether any real relationship beyond a chic and timely theatricality exists between them. Is there a happy ending? I don't think so.

While a majority of critics would seem to have wagered their superlatives on the Great Pretender's allegedly uncanny intellect, art-rock lyrics, and avant-garde visual flair, this writer has always found that when Bowie is wrestling with what he feels is an obvious major concept, it is time to leave the room. Except for certain songs ("Space Oddity," "The Man Who Sold the World," "Life on Mars?," "Queen Bitch"), one can dismiss almost the whole of *Man of Words, Man of Music* (aka *Space Oddity*), *The Man Who Sold the World*, the overrated *Hunky Dory*, *Pinups*, *David Live*, and *Young Americans*. It's not that Bowie is bad per se—he's not; he's always, ah, interesting—but that too often he is capable merely of the kind of arctic and arid brilliance that characterizes the best—and worst—of Stanley Kubrick. The emotions generally get lost in the icy grandeur, and one remembers only the proper pose, not the precise purpose. As a thinker, Bowie is strictly the Kahlil Gibran of delirious decadence—"fleas the size of rats sucked on rats the size of cats and ten thousand peoploids split into small tribes coveting the highest of the sterile skyscrapers . . . of Love Me Avenue"—with fast-food attitudes and platitudes ("All I have is my love of love—and love is not loving") piled up like so many cybernetic cheeseburgers. In the twilight zone of androgynous sex, he has mastered the art of suggestiveness to such a degree that he serves more as an imaginative harbinger of omnisexual excesses yet to be invented than as a practitioner.

Bowie's first four albums are very derivative of Bob Dylan and the Beatles—"Life on Mars?" sounds exactly like "She's Leaving Home" bred with "A Day in the Life"—and most of his themes are at least symbolically present in the dramatic 1969 British hit "Space Oddity": the astronaut-explorer as an extra-planetary superstar who cannot enjoy his fame because he becomes lost in space and feels "there's nothing I can do." ("Star" and "Fame" are similar but inferior songs.) The underrated *Aladdin Sane* from 1973 is unquestionably Bowie's masterpiece, probably because it is less concerned with cerebral contortions than people, places, and rock and roll music. "Watch That Man" would do the Rolling Stones proud, and "Drive-In Saturday," "Panic in Detroit," "Cracked Actor," and "Time" are both lyrically and musically first-rate. *Station to Station*, parts of *Diamond Dogs*, and even *The Rise and Fall of Ziggy Stardust and the Spiders from Mars* score points with "Word on a Wing," "TVC 15," "Station to Station," "Diamond Dogs," "Rebel Rebel," "Suffragette City," "Rock 'n' Roll Suicide," and especially the personal and passionately sung "Rock 'n' Roll with Me." Like most performers, Bowie is at his best when he cares about something.

At Madison Square Garden on the *Station to Station* tour in 1976, Bowie practiced his art of deliberate illusion and convinced a full house that he really was a natural-born rock and roller like the charismatic Mick Jagger, Rod Stewart, and other athletes of the craft. Backed by a band which played rock and roll and rhythm and blues as if they were a seamless entity invented by the Thin White Duke himself, the artist accomplished his Aryan-as-black-man, whirling-dervish sleight of hand with a will so powerful that no one could resist it. Paradoxically, he was also warmer and more human than I have ever seen him. Of that concert, Robert Christgau has written: "My impression is that . . . this music . . . could define '70s rock the way the Stones defined '60s rock. That may not be an altogether heartwarming hypothesis, for this music runs not only hot but cold. But at least it is not unconducive to life."

Neither are Bette Davis movies, I suppose.

Ian Hunter seems to have reached that point in his life and career where he feels the need to talk to the listener directly about both himself and his politics. He begins his first solo album—1975's *Ian Hunter*—with a spoken "Hallo" and, toward the end, takes over from the music altogether to read what sounds like a late-night page from some haunted diary. On 1976's *All-American Alien Boy*, he is so preoccupied with his recent move from England to America that he abandons many of his usual themes and instead delivers a personal but pedantic state-of-the-union message about both countries, injustice, rock and roll, and his reactions to being an exile on Main Street. "Drunk on wine and wisdom," Hunter, like some contemporary Hamlet-Ulysses, "need[s] someplace to lay [his] weary anger down" because he "feel[s] like [he's] thought a million miles." All of this is not surprising given the artist's 1974 departure from Mott the Hoople (with whom he recorded nine LPs), a

330

concurrent nervous breakdown, and the highly confessional nature of several of his last Mott songs. "Sea Diver," "Hymn for the Dudes," "Ballad of Mott the Hoople," and the extraordinary "I Wish I Was Your Mother" are works so drenched in introspection and relative defeat that it is no wonder he has to talk about it.

From the start with Mott in 1969, Hunter apparently recognized his demons and pursued his recurrent themes of madness, loss of self, redemption, the ultimate cost of sex and rock and roll, and the complex relationship between success and failure. His first song was called "Backsliding Fearlessly"; in "Half Moon Bay," from Mott's first album, the artist realizes that his dreams will never end—but senses "the better half has already played." Both of these early songs are immature and imitative, but the thematic compulsiveness is evident.

On 1972's *Brain Capers*, Hunter weighs in heavily with "Sweet Angeline," the best of his songs about rock and roll women, and "The Journey," a schizophrenic sequel to just about everything that has preceded it. Actually two songs forced into one, "The Journey" artfully combines the singer's concern with madness and loss with the obsession to make someone—in this case, not himself but a woman—believe in herself. Also on the album is the strange, out-of-control "The Moon Upstairs," in which the Hoople berate their audience for being "too fucking slow" and provide a raging, if premature, musical "epitaph."

After such a finale, many wondered what could be left for an obviously talented but troubled band which, up until this point, had not shown the stability to concentrate their strengths into a coherent whole. The answer came with careful reevaluation, a label change, and—most importantly—David Bowie. Bowie immediately channeled Hunter and Mick Ralphs's rock and roll chaos into constructive, comprehensible musical energy, arranged and tightened their songs, had them record Lou Reed's classic "Sweet Jane," and wrote a single for them—"All the Young Dudes," a British hit in 1972. Fame came, but it was apparently a case of too much, too late.

"Sea Diver," Hunter's final song on 1972's *All the Young Dudes* and one of his most telling, could serve as a primer for the anxiety about the meaninglessness of success which comprises much of 1973's *Mott*. The singer's heartbreaking depiction of an almost untenable position ("Ride on, my son . . . ride—until you fail") leads him, in "Ballad of Mott the Hoople," to question the validity of the whole "rock 'n' roll circus." He sees himself "a star . . . on parole" in "All the Way from Memphis," and on *Mott*, seems to feel about rock and roll the way a moth does about a flame: "Rock 'n' roll's a loser's game-it mesmerises and I can't explain." Fully half of Mott's songs reflect a growing dissatisfaction with Hunter's and the group's profession. The LP closes with what is arguably Hunter's finest song, "I Wish I Was Your Mother," in which the singer comes to understand that he cannot prevent his own manic anger and

self-hatred from trying to destroy all of the good qualities he is envious of in the woman he loves.

Ian Hunter lacks the calculated, tragic-triumphant, guitar-textured majesty of both *All the Young Dudes* and *Mott*, but its crafty fusion of ofttimes foreboding, straight-ahead rock and roll ("Once Bitten, Twice Shy," "I Get So Excited") and tense, exhilarating songs of self-redemption carries a considerable, rogue-Lazarus charm of its own. Hunter has always been more concerned with philosophy than sex, with his own perceptions of the world rather than the world itself. In "Boy" and "It Ain't Easy When You Fall," he discards Dionysian revelry for Apollonian self-examination. The singer's predicament worsens ("You're the number one and your hands are shaking"), and Hunter implores, in a case of remarkable self-therapy, "Stand and deliver . . ./Shoot a rocket clean out of your brain," i.e., if one has the courage to take an impossible risk, one may realize one's goals—an altogether different conclusion from that of "Sea Diver," "I Wish I Was Your Mother," and most of the earlier songs.

On *All-American Alien Boy*, Hunter mesmerizes but does not always explain, sometimes preferring to keep a careful aesthetic distance—there is not much rock and roll on the record—between himself and feelings that may run too dangerously deep ("God [Take 1]," "Irene Wilde," "You Nearly Did Me In"). Gone, for the most part, are the angst-filled anthems, and to take their place Hunter has resurrected the stance of John Lennon's *Some Time in New York City*. "Apathy 83" equates Watergate with rock and roll, the Rolling Stones' "Sympathy for the Devil" with apathy, and flatly states: "There ain't no rock 'n' roll no more—just the music of the young/ . . . Just the music of the rich." But just when one thinks that Hunter is floundering, as on the endless list of Indian chiefs from the title song, he shows his self-awareness by saying, "My mouth's exploiting, that's enough of this noise." Depressed or not, Ian Hunter will always be an artist who can take you out with either hand. In the end, those are the only kind who are worth it.

Discography

Lou Reed
Lou Reed (RCA Victor 4701; ☆189, 1972). *Transformer* (RCA Victor 4807; ☆29, 1972). *Berlin* (RCA 0207; ☆98, 1973). *Rock 'n' Roll Animal* (RCA 0472; ☆45, 1974). *Sally Can't Dance* (RCA 0611; ☆10, 1974). *Live* (RCA 0959; ☆62, 1975). *Metal Machine Music* (RCA 1101; 1975).
(For albums with Velvet Underground, see Art Rock discography.)

David Bowie
Hunky Dory (RCA Victor 4623; ☆176, 1972). *The Rise and Fall of Ziggy Stardust and the Spiders from Mars* (RCA Victor 4702; ☆75, 1972). *Space Oddity* (RCA Victor 4813; ☆16, 1972; originally released in Britain 1969). *The Man Who Sold the World* (RCA Victor 4816; ☆105, 1972; originally released in Britain 1970). *Alladin Sane* (RCA Victor 4852; ☆77, 1973). *Images* (London 62819; ☆44, 1973; material originally released in Britain, 1966-67). *Pin Ups* (RCA 0291; ☆23, 1973). *Diamond Dogs* (RCA 0576; ☆5, 1974). *David Live* (RCA 0771; ☆8, 1974). *Young Americans* (RCA 0998; ☆9, 1975).

Mott the Hoople
Mott the Hoople (Atlantic 8258; ☆185, 1970). *Mad Shadows* (Atlantic 8272; 1970). *Wildlife* (Atlantic 8284; 1971). *Brain Capers* (Atlantic 8304; 1972). *All the Young Dudes* (Columbia 31750; ☆89, 1972). *Mott* (Columbia 32425; ☆35, 1973). *The Hoople* (Columbia 32871; ☆28, 1974). *Live* (Columbia 33282; ☆23, 1974). *Drive On* (Columbia 33705; ☆160, 1975). Ian Hunter, *Ian Hunter with Mick Ronson* (Columbia 33480; ☆50, 1975).
(Chart positions compiled from Joel Whitburn's *Record Research*, based on *Billboard* LPs charts.)

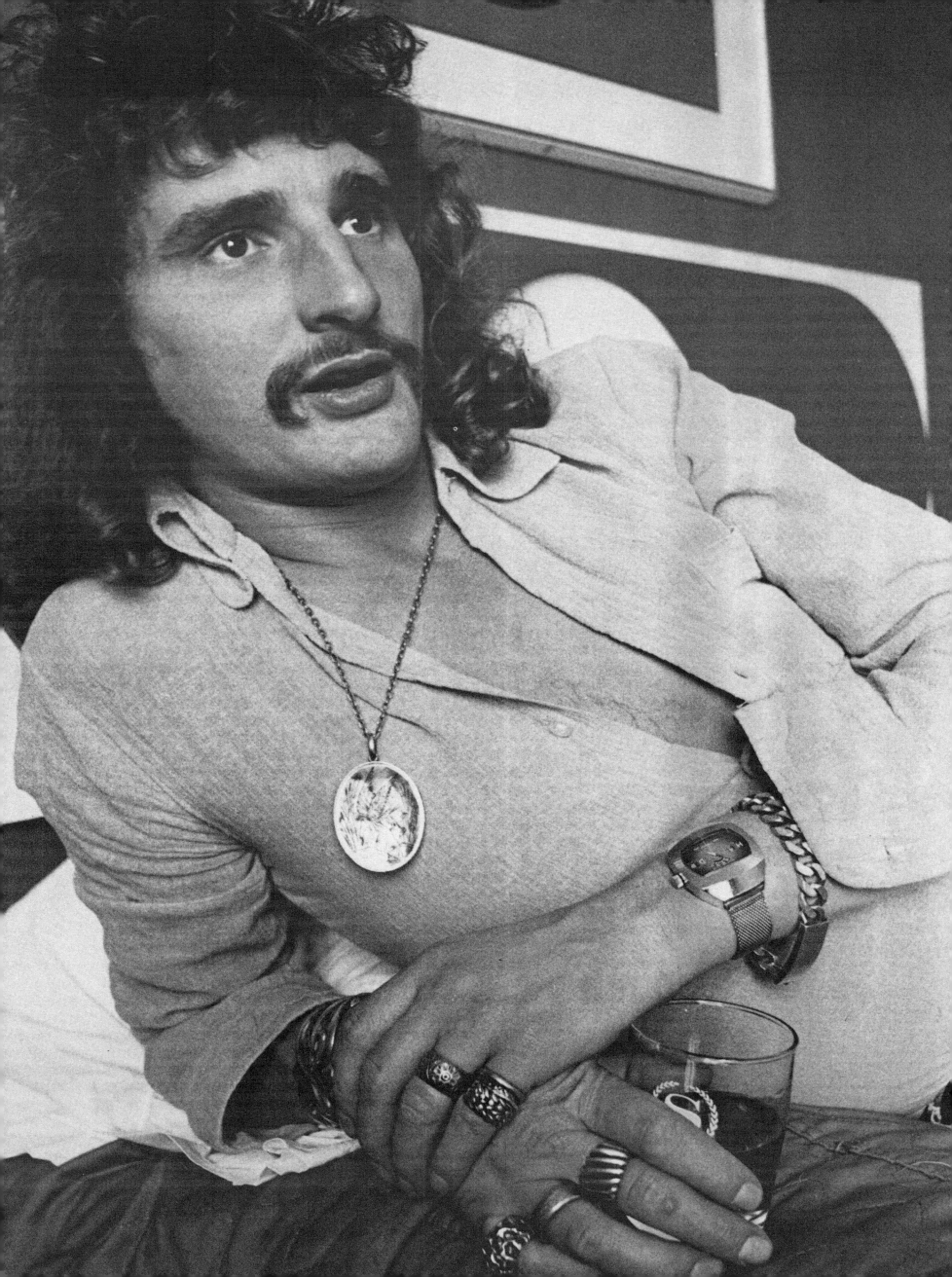

Jazz Rock
by Robert Palmer

Jazz has always been an influence on rock. The bands that toured with Little Richard, Ray Charles, and other black singers during the Fifties invariably included several jazz musicians, and they usually opened shows with bluesy bebop tunes that featured lengthy improvised solos. Such saxophone and organ combos of the Fifties as Bill Doggett's purveyed a related but usually more jazz-based amalgam of improvisation and rhythm and blues. But as a distinct genre of popular music, jazz rock began with the Electric Flag, Blood, Sweat and Tears, and Chicago.

All three bands were distinguished primarily by their use of horns. The Flag, formed in 1967 by white blues musicians Mike Bloomfield, Barry Goldberg and Nick Gravenites, studio bassist Harvey Brooks, and R&B drummer Buddy Miles, billed itself as "An American Music Band"; its stylistic range was broad, but for the most part its horn section played arrangements patterned on those current in the blues and black jazz bands of the Forties and early Fifties. By contrast, the first BS&T album, *Child Is Father to the Man*, featured more ambitious horn arrangements in a Maynard Ferguson/Stan Kenton mold. Chicago made its debut on record in early 1969 (as the Chicago Transit Authority), with horn arrangements closer to MOR pop than to jazz. Despite the horns and jazz trappings, the improvisational content in these groups' recordings was slight (the solos were usually taken by rock guitarists) and improvising, as opposed to embellishing a melody or stringing together stock phrases, is the essence of jazz.

The Flag was the most eclectic and the most visceral of the three bands, but it soon disbanded due to interpersonal problems. BS&T re-formed as a more horn-dominated band after its founder, ex-Blues Project organist and Dylan sideman Al Kooper, went on to other projects. Meanwhile Chicago continued with the same personnel. Both BS&T and Chicago mastered the art of making melodic, relatively low-keyed, marginally rock- and jazz-tinged pop singles, and both turned out gold records. BS&T's string of hits stopped abruptly after *Blood, Sweat and Tears 4* (1971), when a new contingent of horn and rhythm section soloists opted for a more adventurous approach; Chicago, under the firm direction of producer James William Guercio, released eight gold albums in a row.

A number of key jazz musicians were listening to rock during the late Sixties, but not to groups like Chicago and BS&T. Jimi Hendrix and Sly Stone were jazzmen's favorites, the former because of his innovative use of electronics, the latter because of his elaborate rhythmic structures. Soon Miles Davis and some of his sidemen began incorporating rock instrumentation and rhythms into their music, at first cautiously and reflectively, then, beginning with Davis's *Bitches Brew* in 1969, more boldly. *Brew* featured multiple electric keyboards and John McLaughlin's electric guitar in addition to horns, drums and percussion instruments. There was a Sly-like dance beat, but the improvisations were loosely structured around bass lines, scale patterns, or tonal centers. Many fans of Davis's earlier work reacted negatively to the abrupt rhythms, murky textures, and abrasive sonorities of *Bitches Brew,* but after Davis played the Fillmore East and other rock halls, the record became the first jazz-rock crossover, selling well enough to register on the pop charts. Many of the musicians who played on it went on to become important shapers of jazz rock as it developed during the Seventies.

Drummer Tony Williams had left the Davis band several months before *Bitches Brew* was recorded, but he played a crucial role in Davis's developing electric sound by bringing guitarist John McLaughlin to New York from London. McLaughlin joined Tony Williams's group, Lifetime, and played on Davis's *Bitches Brew* and *In a Silent Way*. McLaughlin soon left Lifetime and in 1971, after several moderately successful solo projects, he organized the Mahavishnu Orchestra and recorded *The Inner Mounting Flame*, which turned out to be even more influential than *Bitches Brew*.

Initially, McLaughlin's new sound induced a kind of future shock. There had been plenty of long, loud guitar solos in rock since the emergence of the San Francisco bands, and plenty of electric guitarists in jazz. But McLaughlin was playing long solos with melodic and harmonic substance, not repetitiously juggling blues scales, and he was playing through a bank of amplifiers with his volume controls turned up. Miles Davis had been the first important jazz musician to feature ensemble improvisations on electric instruments, but it was McLaughlin who realized that the new technology demanded the development of new musical forms and new instrumental approaches.

Traditional jazz drumming, for example, was clearly unsuited to the demands of electric music. The timekeeping cymbal, the kit's timbral subtleties, and many other details tended to get lost in the roar. So McLaughlin's drummer, Billy Cobham, reasserted the importance of the snare and bass drum as timekeepers but kept things interesting by adding compound meters derived from Indian music. Traditional jazz ensemble interaction, too, tended to become excessively muddy in an electric context. For all its innovative importance, *Bitches Brew* was often turgid, congested. McLaughlin went back to an earlier jazz device, the idea of soloists trading two- and four-bar statements. And rather than allow for spontaneous interplay, he spiced his compositions with predetermined unison riffs and well-rehearsed counterpoint.

Most of the successful jazz-rock groups that followed the Mahavishnu Orchestra dealt with similar concepts in similar ways. Many of them were spearheaded by former Miles Davis sidemen. Josef Zawinul and Wayne Shorter borrowed more ideas from R&B and encouraged collective improvisation in Weather Report, making it one of the most satisfying of the new bands. Chick Corea's Return to Forever developed a brand

Miles Davis (Baron Wolman)

334

of loud but lyrical music more akin to West Coast rock. Herbie Hancock led a heavily electronic experimental sextet for several years after leaving Davis, but in 1974 he organized a Sly-influenced quintet and recorded *Head Hunters*, which outsold all previous jazz-rock fusion records, placing in the pop Top 20 and spawning a hit single. By the mid-Seventies, these and a few other plugged-in jazzmen dominated the jazz-rock field. The most successful among them were virtual pop stars, able to headline concerts in the halls of their choice almost anywhere in the world, to take as much time as they liked to record, and to appear incestuously on each others' albums despite conflicting contractual obligations. Corea spoke for most of them when he said, "What we're trying to do is to communicate with as many people as possible while retaining our musical integrity."

As electric bands became more and more commercially dominant in the jazz world, however, that integrity was often called into question. "You had jazz bands playing R&B changes and rhythms during the Fifties," a veteran jazzman has observed, "but they didn't make much of a splash. The new groups are doing the same sort of thing with contemporary R&B, but they're copping so much media exposure, people think they're the wave of the future." Well-known jazzmen, feeling pressured by the trend, began making loud, awkward music, without regard for the complexities of handling electronic equipment.

Purists might rage against the mounting tide, but jazz rock by the mid-Seventies was an established idiom. The philosophy of the Columbia Records executives who merchandised it—"Kids who listen to Chicago today will be buying Ornette Coleman records tomorrow"—turned out to be overly simplistic, but jazz in the Seventies *was* more popular than at any time since the Fifties, and not only in its electronic manifestations. Meanwhile, new teenage listeners continued to "discover" the jazz rockers. An 18-year-old at a Corea concert spoke for many of them when he said, "I listen to these guys because, man, they aren't lame like these glitter rock and boogie bands. These guys can really *play*."

Discography

The Electric Flag, *A Long Time Comin'* (Columbia 9597; ☆31, 1968). *The Electric Flag* (Columbia 9714; ☆76, 1969). **Blood, Sweat and Tears,** *Child Is Father to the Man* (Columbia 9619; ☆47, 1968). *Blood, Sweat and Tears* (Columbia 9720; ☆1, 1969). *Blood, Sweat and Tears 3* (Columbia 30090; ☆1, 1970). *B, S and T; 4* (Columbia 30590; ☆10, 1971). *Greatest Hits* (Columbia 31170; ☆19, 1972). *New Blood* (Columbia 31780; ☆32, 1972). **Chicago,** *Chicago Transit Authority* (Columbia 8; ☆17, 1969). *Chicago II* (Columbia 24; ☆4, 1970). *Chicago III* (Columbia 30110; ☆2, 1971). *Chicago at Carnegie Hall* (Columbia 30865; ☆3, 1971). *Chicago V* (Columbia 31102; ☆1, 1972). *Chicago VI* (Columbia 32400; ☆1, 1973). *Chicago VII* (Columbia 32810; ☆1, 1974). *Chicago VIII* (Columbia 33100; ☆1, 1975). *Chicago IX Chicago's Greatest Hits* (Columbia 33900; ☆1, 1975). **Miles Davis,** (Electric) *In a Silent Way* (Columbia 9875; ☆134, 1969). *Bitches Brew* (Columbia 26; ☆35, 1970). *Miles Davis at Fillmore* (Columbia 30038; ☆123, 1970). *Jack Johnson* (Columbia 30455; ☆159, 1971). *Live-Evil* (Columbia 30954; ☆125, 1971). *On the Corner* (Columbia 31906; ☆156, 1972). *In Concert* (Columbia 32092; ☆152, 1973). *Big Fun* (Columbia 32866; ☆179, 1974). *Get Up with It* (Columbia 33236; ☆141, 1975). **John McLaughlin,** (*with The Mahavishnu Orchestra) *Devotion* (Douglas 31568; 1970). **The Inner Mounting Flame* (Columbia 31067; ☆89, 1972). *My Goals Beyond* (Douglas 30766; ☆194, 1972). *Extrapolation* (Polydor 5510; ☆152, 1972). **Birds of Fire* (Columbia 31996; ☆15, 1973). **Between Nothingness and Eternity* (Columbia 32766; ☆41, 1973). **Apocalypse* (Columbia 32957; ☆43, 1974). **Visions of the Emerald Beyond* (Columbia 33411; ☆68, 1975). **Weather Report,** *The Weather Report* (Columbia 30661; ☆191, 1971). *I Sing the Body Electric* (Columbia 31352; ☆147, 1972). *Sweetnighter* (Columbia 32210; ☆85, 1973). *Mysterious Traveller* (Columbia 32494; ☆46, 1974). *Tale Spinnin'* (Columbia 33417; ☆31, 1975). **Chick Corea with Return to Forever,** *Return to Forever* (ECM 1022; 1972). *Light as a Feather* (Polydor 5525; 1973). *Hymn of the Seventh Galaxy* (Polydor 5536; ☆124, 1973). *Where Have I Known You* (Polydor 6509; ☆32, 1974). *No Mystery* (Polydor 6512; ☆39, 1975). **Herbie Hancock,** (Electric). *Mwandishi* (Warner Bros. 1898; 1971). *Crossings* (Warner Bros. 2617; 1972). *Sextant* (Columbia 32212; ☆176, 1973). *Head Hunters* (Columbia 32371; ☆13, 1974). *Thrust* (Columbia 32965; ☆13, 1974). *Man-Child* (Columbia 33812; ☆21, 1975). (Chart positions taken from Joel Whitburn's *Record Research,* compiled from *Billboard* LPs chart.)

Stevie Wonder

by John Rockwell

In rough outline, Stevie Wonder's career goes like this: Born Steveland Judkins (or Morris—his father's name was Judkins, but Wonder says that Morris was on the birth certificate) on May 13th, 1950, in Saginaw, Michigan, he was raised as Steveland Morris in Detroit. At the age of ten, he was introduced by Ronnie White of the Miracles to Berry Gordy's Hitsville, U.S.A. label; his stage name was changed to Little Stevie Wonder at about the same time Hitsville, U.S.A. became Motown. Wonder had his first hit—it went to Number One—in "Fingertips, Pt. 2" in 1963. At that time his audience was consistently integrated: in 1964, the Rolling Stones were his opening act. His adolescence was spent turning out a steady succession of singles and albums, many of which did well on the pop as well as the rhythm and blues charts. But he didn't have another Number One single until "Superstition" in 1972, after the exposure gained from opening for the Stones during their American tour that year. The albums *Music of My Mind*, *Talking Book* (both 1972) and *Innervisions* (1973) were enormous successes both critically and commercially, and sealed Wonder's status as the most influential and acclaimed black musician of the early Seventies. On August 6th, 1973, he was almost killed in an automobile accident on tour in North Carolina. A log from a truck smashed through the front window of the car in which he was a passenger and struck him in the forehead. Already blind from birth, he lost his sense of smell in the accident but apparently emerged otherwise unscathed. In 1974, he won five Grammy awards, then, in 1975, five more, and that August was reported to have signed a seven-year, $13 million contract with Motown, one of the most lucrative in the history of the record business. (It later turned out he didn't actually sign the document until April 1976.) His 1974 album, much of it written before his 1973 accident, was called *Fulfillingness' First Finale*. It would be about two years before the next, long-delayed album appeared, leading to speculation that the "first finale" really was a finale to one stage of Wonder's career.

Even at the peak of his appeal to a general audience, from 1972 to 1974, Wonder occasioned a certain puzzlement. He isn't consistent; he has a distressing predilection for cosmic meanderings and soupy sentimentality. But listening to his albums in sequence is an instructive experience; it indicates that Wonder is perhaps most comfortable as a live performer and that his gifts are more constrained by the confines of the studio than those of some artists, and it suggests that the supposedly sharp break in his career around 1971—when he reached legal maturity and renegotiated his Motown contract to obtain a far-reaching artistic freedom—needs to be partially reevaluated. Certainly the post-1971 Wonder records are more innovative than those that preceded them. But the same polarities in his art can be observed from the beginning.

Wonder's first singles appeared in the fall of 1962, but he didn't make an impact until the summer of 1963, with the "Fingertips" single and the *Little Stevie Wonder, 12 Year Old Genius* album that contained it. Both were distinguished by two things, apart from Wonder's raw talent. First, "Fingertips" and the album were recorded live, which is hardly customary for new artists or hit singles; second, both caught Wonder right at the end of his prepubescence.

The first image of Little Stevie Wonder was of a loose-limbed, tambourine-shaking, harmonica-blowing natural child of music, and it was the image that has defined his large-scale concerts ever since. At Wonder's first major U.S. appearance after his accident, at Madison Square Garden in March 1974, it was the uptempo material that got the biggest cheers and the long, rhapsodic, building, repetitive improvisations that constituted the emotional high points of the night. In particular, his concert version of "Living for the City," with the chorus repeated over and over in terraced levels of intensity, surpassed anything Wonder has ever done on record—and that's not to say he hasn't made wonderful records.

But recording careers are made in the studio, and Wonder's recorded product in his adolescence mostly derived from the Motown hit factory of the Sixties. The fact that his first big hit came when he was 13 meant that Wonder couldn't count on a protracted boy-soprano career like that of Michael Jackson. Almost immediately his voice began to crack, and although his next few albums contain occasional soprano outtakes inserted incongruously into the rest, he was mostly a high baritone/low tenor from then on. His voice now is full of tenor lightness, but he lacks the range to exploit high notes or the desire to cultivate a Smokey Robinson falsetto.

The records of this period are highly variable, ranging from curious emulations of the then popular "surf sound"—he even appeared in two of the surf film epics of that era, *Muscle Beach Party* and *Bikini Beach*—to an inevitable homage to Ray Charles and a Christmas album. The hit singles of his adolescence include punchy R&B—"Uptight (Everything's Alright)," "I Was Made to Love Her"—to brassy pop ("For Once in My Life"), sentimental ballads ("My Cherie Amour"), even a Dylan tune ("Blowin' in the Wind") long before Motown discovered social consciousness.

This is a far more varied output than that of most Motown artists during the Sixties, but Wonder was still deeply enmeshed in the Motown system: the company controlled his publishing, masterminded his arrangements and recording sessions, booked his tours, held his money in trust and doled out an allowance ($2.50 per week when he was 13). Many of the songs Stevie sang were composed by staff writers; those he wrote were generally cocredited to such Motown regulars as Sylvia Moy and Henry Cosby. Just who wrote what in this period remains a mystery. Moy and Cosby, for instance, are credited on "Uptight" along with "S. Judkins," yet Wonder himself once said this was the first song he ever wrote. What is clear is that Motown executives and producers had much to do with how the

338

records actually sounded. "They would have the rhythm worked out," Wonder later recalled, "and I would just come to the sessions and play the piano."

That doesn't mean, however, that some of Wonder's later characteristics weren't already in evidence. There was the childlike ebullience of his fast tunes and the unabashed sentimentality of his slow numbers (no matter that at first he confined himself to the stock banalities of teen-dream love, only later to lap over into universal brotherhood). There was his carnivorous ability to devour diverse influences and put his own stylistic stamp on the results—from the basics of gospel, blues, rhythm and blues and soul to Dylan, the surf sound, jazz, adult white pop, and finally to rock, electronic music and African ethnicity.

Still, by his late teens Wonder had reached a ceiling on what he could accomplish within the traditional Motown strictures. A live album released in early 1970 dramatizes that fact, with its turgid arrangements continually weighing down his inherent gifts. "All I'm trying to do is get myself together," he remarks in the introduction to one song. "All I'm trying to do is do my own thing." *Signed Sealed and Delivered* from later in 1970 was the first album Wonder produced himself, and amounted to a return to his old "Uptight" R&B roots. But the key shift came the next year, when he turned 21 and got control of his $1 million trust fund. His new, laboriously negotiated, 120-page contract was a precedent-shattering event at Motown. The company would continue to distribute his records, but Wonder gained complete artistic freedom, control of his publishing and a far higher royalty rate. *Where I'm Coming From* (1971) only partially fulfilled the promise of this new freedom. But with *Music of My Mind* the next year, Stevie Wonder could be counted as a matured artist.

The maturity expressed itself in several ways. The records weren't "concept albums," but they were conceived as entities, the songs flowing together organically. The lyrics now embraced social, political and mystical concerns, and even his stock love-and-sex themes were deepened to include domesticity and religiousness. Musically, Wonder started to exploit the potential of the modern studio, particularly for overdubbing, with the result that on his recent records he plays most of the instruments, with only occasional guitar solos, horn, string or percussion supplementation and backup singing by others. Most crucially, both the shape and the color of his music had matured. Its shape, no longer bound to the rigid confines of the three-minute hit single, increasingly reflected the expansive spontaneity of his live performances. The music's color was defined above all through Wonder's fascination with Arp and Moog synthesizers, the clavinet and electric pianos and organs. They lent his music, particularly the uptempo material, a twangy insistence that was unmistakably personal without ever lapsing into silly technocratic display.

Although Wonder's big hits remained lively R&B material like "Higher Ground," "Boogie on Reggae Woman," and "You Haven't Done Nothin'," his albums have been largely devoted to balladic ramblings. Some white critics complain about his self-indulgence and bleary universal-love sentimentality. These are unquestionably parts of his nature, but his early records prove they're nothing new.

What is ultimately exciting about Wonder's music—and what makes his potential for growth so much more promising than that of more settled artists—is his unpredictable openness to new sounds and new styles. One imagines that he will keep plugging away, striking the chord of mass popular success every few years and proceeding on his own way in between. Isolated from the "real" world by race and blindness even as he is linked to it by his own extraordinary acuteness, Wonder is probably too original for guaranteed, comfortable mass acceptance. Which, of course, constitutes his ultimate strength.

Discography

Singles
"Never Had a Dream Come True" (Tamla 54191; r☆11, ☆26, 1970). "Signed, Sealed, Delivered I'm Yours" (Tamla 54196; r☆1, ☆3, 1970). "Heaven Help Us All' (Tamla 54200; r☆2, ☆9, 1970). "We Can Work It Out" (Tamla 54202; r☆3, ☆13, 1971). "If You Really Love Me" (Tamla 54208; r☆4, ☆8, 1971). "Superwoman (Where Were You When I Needed You)" (Tamla 54216; r☆13, ☆33, 1972). "Superstition" (Tamla 54226; r☆1, ☆1, 1972). "You Are the Sunshine of My Life" (Tamla 54232; r☆3, ☆1, 1973). "Higher Ground" (Tamla 54235; r☆1, ☆4, 1973). "Living for the City" (Tamla 54242; r☆1, ☆8, 1973). "Don't You Worry 'bout a Thing" (Tamla 54245; r☆2, ☆16, 1974). "You Haven't Done Nothin' " (Tamla 54252; r☆1, ☆1, 1974). "Boogie On Reggae Woman" (Tamla 54254; r☆1, ☆3, 1974).
Albums
Little Stevie Wonder the 12 Year Old Genius (Tamla 240; ☆1, 1963). *Up-Tight* (Tamla 268; ☆33, 1966). *Down to Earth* (Tamla 272; ☆92, 1967). *I Was Made to Love Her* (Tamla 279; ☆45, 1967). *Stevie Wonder's Greatest Hits* (Tamla 282; ☆37, 1968). *For Once in My Life* (Tamla 291; ☆50, 1969). *My Cherie Amour* (Tamla 296; ☆34, 1969). *Stevie Wonder Live* (Tamla 298; ☆81, 1970). *Signed Sealed and Delivered* (Tamla 304; ☆25, 1970). *Where I'm Coming From* (Tamla 308; ☆62, 1971). *Stevie Wonder's Greatest Hits—Vol. 2* (Tamla 313; ☆69, 1971). *Music of My Mind* (Tamla 314; ☆21, 1972). *Talking Book* (Tamla 319; ☆3, 1972). *Innervisions* (Tamla 326; ☆4, 1973). *Fulfillingness' First Finale* (Tamla 332; ☆1, 1974).
(Chart positions compiled from Joel Whitburn's *Record Research*, based on *Billboard* Pop and LPs charts, unless otherwise indicated; r☆ = position on *Billboard* Rhythm and Blues chart.)

The Sound of Philadelphia
by Jim Miller

In 1974, three producers from Philadelphia dominated *Billboard*'s year-end awards. Each year, the magazine ranks records and producers on the basis of sales and airplay, and in 1974, it was Thom Bell, Kenny Gamble and Leon Huff who were the big winners. Bell charted 11 hit singles that year, while Gamble and Huff followed with ten.

All three had recorded their hits in Philadelphia, helping to make it the most influential source of black music in the early Seventies. And at the source stood Gamble and Huff, who, as executives of Philadelphia International, the city's largest label, directed the most lucrative black-owned musical enterprise in the U.S. after Motown.

Philadelphia had not always been a soul center: Kenny Gamble and Leon Huff both cut their teeth on the predominantly white Philly music scene of the early Sixties, a scene revolving around Dick Clark's *American Bandstand.* The Philly-based TV show offered a convenient avenue for plugging current product, and a legion of labels, eager to exploit the *Bandstand* connection, soon popped up. Among them were Chancellor, with Frankie Avalon and Fabian; Swan, with Freddie Cannon and Billie and Lillie; and Cameo-Parkway, with Chubby Checker, the Rays, the Dovells, Bobby Rydell, the Orlons and Dee Dee Sharp (later Mrs. Kenny Gamble).

It was a scene that fostered a flourishing community of musicians who made sessions and swapped ideas, churning out Bobby Rydell tracks by day, jamming at jazz clubs at night. Out of it emerged the key figures in today's Philly scene, including Gamble and Huff, who first made their mark as songwriters, accompanists and performers during this period. Gamble and Thom Bell both worked in a local band called the Romeos, with guitarist Roland Chambers, who eventually became a mainstay of MFSB, the Philadelphia house band. Leon Huff (who was also with the Romeos at one point) was active as a songwriter and producer, participating in Danny and the Juniors' "At the Hop," and Len Barry's "1-2-3" (Barry had been the Dovells' chief vocalist).

By the mid-Sixties, Gamble and Huff had joined forces to produce records. Their first national hit came in 1967, when the Soul Survivors' "Expressway to Your Heart" made the Top Ten. Previously, the duo had scored solid R&B hits with the Intruders, who remain a Gamble and Huff act to this day.

It was with the Intruders that the G&H style first began to jell. Fashioning a series of novelty songs—"Cowboys to Girls," "(Love Is Like a) Baseball Game"—for lead singer "Little Sonny" Brown, who wobbled unpredictably offpitch on each take, the producers focused on homey lyrics ("Love is like a baseball game/Three strikes you're out"), a solid rhythm section, and expert sweetening, usually strings and horns. These records were raunchy, slick and silly simultaneously, mixing spontaneous jive with meticulous production.

But the team first hit their stride in a pathbreaking series of sessions with Jerry Butler, the Chicago soul stylist. Butler, originally lead singer with the Impressions, specialized in mellow ballads, scoring pop hits early in the decade with material by Burt Bacharach ("Make It Easy on Yourself") and Curtis Mayfield ("He Will Break Your Heart"). When he arrived in Philadelphia in 1967 Butler's star was in eclipse, but by fashioning a stunning series of singles over the next two years, Gamble and Huff changed all that. Jerry Butler reemerged as "The Iceman," Mr. Cool set against the driving/shimmering sound of Philadelphia. Instrumentally, that sound, softened for Butler, revolved around a crack rhythm section that included such novel instruments as vibraphone (occasionally used by Motown) and harpsichord, and featuring creamy guitar obligatos, equal parts Wes Montgomery and Curtis Mayfield (a neglected influence in his role as the Impressions' lead guitarist).

The songs, composed by Butler, Gamble and Huff in tandem, struck a vulnerable pose, as Butler sang about loves lost with moving pathos. His silken voice had begun to fray around the edges, but the producers, by forcing Butler to sing in his highest register, exploited his breaking pitch to express the lyrics. Structurally, many of the songs recalled Burt Bacharach's work with Butler and Dionne Warwick. Most cuts phased in the rhythm section gradually, confining the use of full percussion to the choruses. But the complexities of the material did not prevent the studio band (MFSB as we know it today; the same musicians performed on the 1968 chart-topping instrumental "The Horse") from punching out the changes in a fashion owing more to Motown than Bacharach, who had always preferred a polite rhythm section.

But the Butler sessions soon diverged from Motown in rhythmic style and the techniques used to record the section. Instead of the shrill highs and booming bass of the Motown singles, with their hot mix geared to AM airplay, Gamble and Huff strove to clean up the sound, sharply pinpointing each instrument in their increasingly lush arrangements. The guitars, which eschewed the staccato chording characteristic of Motown and James Brown singles, were plugged directly into the studio board, instead of being recorded through amplifiers. Instrumental lines were etched out in the mix, each floating with an almost palpable presence.

By 1969 and "Only the Strong Survive," "Moody Woman," and "What's the Use of Breaking Up," the Gamble-Huff style had been perfected: a classic trio of discs, these singles summarized the duo's achievement as well as pointing toward things to come. Take "Moody Woman." Vibes and marimba, soon joined by an electric guitar sounding like a sitar (a favorite trick, used by Thom Bell as a signature on his Delfonics' hits), bounce off bass drum and hi-hat to open the track, with Butler, backed by female chorus, entering, relaxed, at the middle of his

Kenny Gamble in the early Sixties (CBS Records)

range. On the chorus, on the other hand, Butler strains for the high notes, and drummer Earl Young finally gets to use his full battery of percussion; aided by strings (mixed down, with reverb added), the drummer picks up the track and firmly pushes Butler back into the refrain. Thanks to its structure, the song bristles with channeled energy, building tension in the refrains, releasing it in the choruses.

As the Seventies began, Gamble and Huff were clearly angling for a larger slice of the chart action. In 1968, they had signed an ill-fated deal with the Chess brothers, giving Chess distribution rights for G&H's Neptune label; despite sessions with the O'Jays, yielding such brilliant singles as "One Night Affair" and "Looky Looky (Look at Me Girl)," the label eventually collapsed after Leonard Chess's death. Independent production deals with Spring (Joe Simon's "Drowning in the Sea of Love") and Atlantic (Wilson Pickett's "Don't Let the Green Grass Fool You," Archie Bell's "I Can't Stop Dancing" and Dusty Springfield's "Brand New Me") kept Gamble and Huff in hits, but didn't net them the independent label they were obviously after—a label with reliable distribution and plenty of capital, to finance promotion and experimentation in the studios (all that orchestration wasn't cheap).

Finally, in 1971, Gamble and Huff formed Philadelphia International Records under the auspices of CBS (with Clive Davis at the helm, in one of his shrewdest moves to corner the R&B market). With CBS distributing and promoting to the white market, Philadelphia International working black radio stations and media, and Gamble and Huff themselves recording their most commercial material to date, the label became an instant success. Singles poured out of Philly's Sigma Sound studios, and several promptly crossed over to the pop charts, going on to sell a million copies. Billy Paul crooned about "Mrs. Jones"; the O'Jays indicted the "Back Stabbers"; Harold Melvin and the Blue Notes offered "If You Don't Know Me by Now."

For these records, Gamble and Huff further refined their sound. Earl Young's drums were recorded with an astonishing fullness, the hi-hat swishing, the bass drum thumping, the snare crackling; meanwhile, the rest of the rhythm section—usually Ronnie Baker on bass, Roland Chambers and Norman Harris on guitar, and Vince Montana on vibes—improvised an instrumental track, aiming at a groove with an irresistible undertow. Although sweetening gave the Philly sound a candied veneer, the rhythm track, alive and kicking, belied claims that Gamble and Huff churned out nothing but fluff.

Leon Huff has explained the procedure he and Gamble follow in the studio: "We have about two sessions a week. If we book a day we'll be lucky if we cut three tracks. We put down the rhythm track first. Our sound stems from the feeling of the musicians; you know everybody down there is in a relaxed atmosphere, they're not pressured to play. . . . The warmness shows in the grooves, the mechanical feeling is not there, it's more of a free type of thing. But the professionalism is there. You see, we have been playing together so long, everybody knows what the next guy's doing."

As it emerged in the Seventies, the Philly sound abandoned the blunt 2-4 that had characterized the classic Motown singles (such as "Dancing in the Street"). In its stead arose the streamlined pulse of MFSB, a beat that has helped define the contemporary disco style, through such singles as "Love Train," "I'll Always Love My Mama," "TSOP" and "Bad Luck."

Gamble and Huff's two major groups of the early Seventies, Harold Melvin and the Blue Notes, and the O'Jays, presented divergent images. Theodore Pendergrass, the Blue Notes' former lead singer (he left in 1976), played the suffering soul, losing loves, alienating friends, getting raw deals; he moaned a lot. The O'Jays complained about the world, too, in a series of "protest" lyrics, but they also sang about successful love affairs; less bluesy than Melvin, they came on assertive and brassy. Theodore Pendergrass was an intransigent stylist, unlike the O'Jays' Eddie Levert, but both singers were capable of cutting through thickets of orchestration. If the O'Jays had a fault, it was their versatility; they were too malleable to resist full-blown production assaults. For their part, Gamble and Huff themselves had a tendency to round off the rough edges that Motown, in its heyday, had left intact.

An urbane glossiness is the leading characteristic of the entire Philadelphia school. In their wake, Gamble and Huff have left a flourishing band of slick-minded producers, most of them using Sigma Sound and the same batch of musicians. Session guitarist Norman Harris produces Blue Magic; local impresario Stan Watson has worked with the Delfonics and First Choice; veteran R&B producer Dave Crawford records the gospel group the Mighty Clouds of Joy in Philadelphia; and even David Bowie cut *Young Americans* at Sigma Sound.

While most of Philly's producers hew close to formulas, a few stand out as pioneers (such as Thom Bell) or eccentrics (such as Bunny Sigler). Apart from Gamble and Huff, Bell (who has done numerous arrangements for G&H) is the most noteworthy—and successful—of the lot.

His first hit came in 1968 with the Delfonics' "La-La Means I Love You." A subtle orchestrator and lyric composer, Bell from the outset favored ballads with seamless string arrangements, garnished by woodwinds and French horns. On cuts like "Didn't I (Blow Your Mind This Time)," he created symphonic miniatures within a sweet soul format.

In the Seventies, Bell perfected his approach with the Stylistics, a falsetto-led group cast in the Delfonics mold, and the Spinners, a more orthodox quintet of Motown veterans. Both

groups were often saddled with banal lyrics, but Bell at his best, on singles like the Spinners' "I'll Be Around" and the Stylistics' "Make Up to Break Up," projected a genuine feeling of warmth, conveyed through sophisticated compositions and scores. Bell is a nonpareil producer of pop soul, and the true heir of Burt Bacharach.

Other Philadelphia figures pursued a more idiosyncratic course. Bunny Sigler, for example, indulged onstage in outrageous theatrics, and brought an offbeat imaginativeness to his productions for Philadelphia International. He composed straight ballads for the O'Jays, and recorded several himself ("Regina," "Keep Smilin' "); on the other hand, he worked in a funky streetwise vein, producing Archie Bell and the Drells, and cutting a lovely, slow-drag remake of "Love Train."

TheTrammps, darlings of the discos, followed a similarly idiosyncratic course. Founded by drummer Earl Young as an outlet for his performing ambitions, the group was coproduced by Young and fellow session musicians Ronnie Baker and Norman Harris. A loose and light musical showcase, the band cut Baker originals like "Where Do We Go from Here," as well as updating such oldies as "Zing Went the Strings of My Heart" (modeled after the Coasters' arrangement). Lead singer Jimmy Ellis, a dexterous tenor, played the straight man to Young, a basso profundo, and a ham to boot. The result was some of the most good-natured music to emerge from Philadelphia.

When the disco scene exploded in 1974, most of the Philadelphia producers and groups found themselves in the right place at the right time. Unfortunately, the fad has rendered the Philly formulas about as fresh as the jingles for Wrigley's Doublemint gum. The formulas still sell records, but they rarely create vital recordings; a producer like Bell (who now lives in Seattle, Washington) seems locked into cream-puff soul, and even Gamble and Huff have trouble resisting five-minute tags to songs that ought to clock in at three.

For a spell, the biggest threat to the scene seemed to be legal. When the first indictments in the payola probe of 1975 were announced, prominent among those implicated were Kenny Gamble and Leon Huff. The indictments accused Philadelphia International of peddling influence, favors and money in exchange for air play. Early in 1976, the charges against Huff were dismissed, but Gamble was fined $2500.

Payola or no—and the rules of the game have never been partial to independent labels, especially if they happen to be black owned and operated—Gamble, Huff and Bell, along with their countless progeny, have transfigured the sound of black music in America, a feat accomplished through musical innovation as much as shrewd manipulation. Architects of a new style in dance music, Top 40 hitmakers of a proven caliber, creative artists in a cutthroat field—Gamble and Huff, and Thom Bell, are to the Seventies what Holland-Dozier-Holland and Smokey Robinson were to the Sixties: the preeminent soul producers of the decade.

Discography

△ **Intruders,** "Together" (Gamble 205; r☆9, ☆48, 1967). △ **Soul Survivors,** "Expressway to Your Heart" (Crimson 1010; r☆3, ☆4, 1967). **Barbara Mason,** "Oh, How It Hurts" (Arctic 137, r☆11, 1968). △ **Jerry Butler,** "Lost" (Mercury 72764; r☆15, 1968). ○ **Delfonics,** "La-La Means I Love You" (Philly Groove 150; r☆2, ☆4, 1968). △ **Intruders,** "Cowboys to Girls" (Gamble 214; r☆1, ☆6, 1968). △ **Jerry Butler,** "Never Give You Up" (Mercury 72789; r☆4, ☆20, 1968). ○ **Delfonics,** "I'm Sorry" (Philly Groove 151, r☆15, ☆42, 1968). **Cliff Nobles and Co.,** "The Horse" (Phil L.A. of Soul 313; r☆2, ☆2, 1968). △ **Intruders,** "(Love Is like a) Baseball Game" (Gamble 217; r☆4, ☆26, 1968). △ **Archie Bell and the Drells,** "I Can't Stop Dancing" (Atlantic 2534; r☆5, ☆9, 1968). △ **Jerry Butler,** "Hey, Western Union Man" (Mercury 72850; r☆1, ☆16, 1968). **Archie Bell and the Drells,** "Do the Choo Choo" (Atlantic 2559; r☆5, ☆44, 1968). △ **Intruders,** "Slow Drag" (Gamble 221; r☆12, 1968). △ **Jerry Butler,** "Are You Happy" (Mercury 72876; r☆9, ☆39, 1968). ○ **Delfonics,** "Ready or Not Here I Come" (Philly Groove 154; r☆14, ☆35, 1968). △ **Archie Bell and the Drells,** "There's Gonna Be a Showdown" (Atlantic 2583; r☆6, ☆21, 1969). △ **Jerry Butler,** "Only the Strong Survive" (Mercury 72898; r☆1, ☆4, 1969). △ **Jerry Butler,** "Moody Woman" (Mercury 72929; r☆3, ☆24, 1969). △ **Archie Bell and the Drells,** "Girl You're Too Young" (Atlantic 2644; r☆13, 1969). △ **O'Jays,** "One Night Affair" (Neptune 12, r☆15, 1969). ○ **Delfonics,** "You Got Yours and I'll Get Mine" (Philly Groove 157, r☆6, ☆40, 1969). △ **Intruders,** "Sad Girl" (Gamble 235; r☆14, ☆47, 1969). △ **Jerry Butler,** "What's the Use of Breaking Up" (Mercury 72960; r☆4, ☆20, 1969). △ **Dusty Springfield,** "A Brand New Me" (Atlantic 2685; ☆24, 1969). △ **Jerry Butler,** "Don't Let Love Hang You Up" (Mercury 72991; r☆12, ☆44, 1969). **Eddie Holman,** "Hey There Lonely Girl" (ABC 11240; r☆4, ☆2, 1969). ○ **Delfonics,** "Didn't I (Blow Your Mind This Time)" (Philly Groove 161; r☆3, ☆10, 1970). △ **O'Jays,** "Deeper (in Love with You)" (Neptune 22; r☆21, 1970). △ **Jerry Butler,** "I Could Write a Book" (Mercury 73045; r☆15, ☆46, 1970). △ **Intruders,** "When We Get Married" (Gamble 4004; r☆8, ☆45, 1970). ○ **Delfonics,** "Trying to Make a Fool of Me" (Philly Groove 162; r☆8, ☆40, 1970). △ **O'Jays,** "Looky Looky (Look at Me Girl)" (Neptune 31; r☆17, 1970). ○ **Delfonics,** "When You Get Right Down to It" (Philly Groove 163; r☆12, 1970). △ **Wilson Pickett,** "Engine Number 9" (Atlantic 2765; r☆3, ☆14, 1970). **Stylistics,** "You're a Big Girl Now" (Avco Embassy 4555; r☆7, 1971). △ **Wilson Pickett,** "Don't Let the Green Grass Fool You" (Atlantic 2781; r☆2, ☆17, 1971). △ **Intruders,** "I'm Girl Scouting" (Gamble 4009; r☆16, 1971). **Brenda and the Tabulations,** "Right on the Tip of My Tongue" (Top & Bottom 407; r☆10, ☆23, 1971). △ **Ebonys,** "You're the Reason Why" (Philadelphia International 3503; r☆10, 1971). ○ **Stylistics,** "Stop, Look, Listen (to Your Heart)" (Avco Embassy 4572; r☆6, ☆39, 1971). **Delfonics,** "Hey! Love" (Philly Groove 166; r☆9, 1971). △ **Intruders,** "I Bet He Don't Love You (like I Love You)" (Gamble 4016; r☆20, 1971). **Delfonics,** "Walk Right Up to the Sun" (Philly Groove 169; r☆13, 1971). ○ **Stylistics,** "You Are Everything" (Avco 4581; r☆10, ☆9, 1971). △ **Joe Simon,** "Drowning in the Sea of Love" (Spring 120; r☆3, ☆11, 1971). ○ **Stylistics,** "Betcha By Golly, Wow" (Avco 4591; r☆2, ☆3, 1972). △ **Joe Simon,** "Pool of Bad Luck" (Spring 124; r☆13, ☆42, 1972). **Delfonics,** "Tell Me This Is a Dream" (Philly Groove 172, r☆15, 1972). **Barbara Mason,** "Bed and Board" (Buddah 296; r☆24, 1972). △ **Harold Melvin and the Blue Notes,** "I Miss You" (Philadelphia International 3516; r☆7, ☆58, 1972). ○ **Stylistics,** "People Make the World Go Round" (Avco 4595; r☆6, ☆25, 1972). **Trammps,** "Zing Went the Strings of My Heart" (Buddah 306; r☆17, ☆ 64, 1972). △ **Joe Simon,** "Power of Love" (Spring 128; r☆1, ☆11, 1972). △ **O'Jays,** "Back Stabbers" (Philadelphia International 3517; r☆1, ☆3, 1972). △ **Intruders,** "(Win, Place or Show) She's a Winner" (Gamble 672, r☆12, 1972). ○ **Spinners,** "I'll Be Around" (Atlantic 2904; r☆1, ☆3, 1972). **Eddie Holman,** "My Mind Keeps Telling Me" (GSF 6873; r☆20, 1972). △ **Johnny Williams,** "Slow Motion (Part I)" (Philadelphia International 3518; r☆12, 1972). △ **Harold Melvin and the Blue Notes,** "If You Don't Know Me by Now" (Philadelphia International 3520; r☆1, ☆3, 1972). ○ **Stylistics,** "I'm Stone in Love with You" (Avco 4603; r☆4, ☆10, 1972). △ **Billy Paul,** "Me and Mrs. Jones" (Philadelphia International 3521; r☆1, ☆1, 1972). △ **O'Jays,** "992 Arguments" (Philadelphia International 3522; r☆13, ☆57, 1972). ○ **Spinners,** "Could It Be I'm Falling in Love" (Atlantic 2927; r☆1, ☆4, 1972). △ **O'Jays,** "Love Train" (Philadelphia International 3524; r☆1, ☆1, 1973). ○ **Stylistics,** "Break Up to Make Up" (Avco 4611; r☆5, ☆5, 1973). △**Harold Melvin and the Blue Notes,** "Yesterday I Had the Blues" (Philadelphia International 3525; r☆12, ☆63, 1973). **First Choice,** "Armed and Extremely Dangerous" (Philly Groove 175; r☆11, ☆28, 1973). ○ **Spinners,** "One of a Kind (Love Affair)" (Atlantic 2962; r☆1, ☆11, 1973). **Delfonics,** "I Don't Want to Make You Wait" (Philly Groove; r☆22, 1973). △ **Ebonys,** "It's Forever" (Philadelphia International 3529; r☆14, 1973). △ **Intruders,** "I'll Always Love My Mama" (Gamble 2506; r☆6, ☆36, 1973). ○ **Stylistics,** "You'll Never Get to Heaven if You Break My Heart" (Avco 4618; r☆8, ☆23, 1973). △ **O'Jays,** "Time to Get Down" (Philadelphia International 3531; r☆2, ☆33, 1973). **Jackie Moore,** "Sweet Charlie Babe" (Atlantic 2956; r☆15, ☆42, 1973). ○ **Spinners,** "Ghetto Child" (Atlantic 2973; r☆4, ☆29, 1973). **Eddie Holman,** "My Mind Keeps Telling Me" (GSF 6873; r☆20, 1973). △ **Harold Melvin and the Blue Notes,** "Yesterday I Had the Blues" (Philadelphia International 3533; r☆1, ☆7, 1973). △ **Intruders,** "I Wanna Know Your Name" (Gamble 2508; r☆9, ☆60, 1973). ○ **Stylistics,** "Rockin' Roll Baby" (Avco 4625; r☆3, ☆14, 1973). △ **O'Jays,** "Put Your Hands Together" (Philadelphia International 3535; r☆2, ☆10, 1973). ○ **Spinners,** "Mighty Love—Part I" (Atlantic 3006; r☆1, ☆20, 1974). △ **Billy Paul,** "Thanks for

Saving My Life" (Philadelphia International 3538; r☆9, ☆37, 1974). △ **Harold Melvin and the Blue Notes,** "Satisfaction Guaranteed (or Take Your Love Back)" b/w "I'm Weak for You" (Philadelphia International 3543; r☆6, 1974). △ **MFSB,** "TSOP (the Sound of Philadelphia)" (Philadelphia International 3540; r☆1, ☆1, 1974). ○ **Stylistics,** "You Make Me Feel Brand New" (Avco 4634; r☆5, ☆2, 1974). **Blue Magic,** "Sideshow" (Atco 6961; r☆1, ☆8, 1974). △ **O'Jays,** "For the Love of Money" (Philadelphia International 3544; r☆3, ☆9, 1974). ○ **Spinners,** "I'm Coming Home" (Atlantic 3027; r☆1, ☆18, 1974). ○ **Dionne Warwick and the Spinners,** "Then Came You" (Atlantic 3029; r☆2, ☆1, 1974). **First Choice,** "The Player—Part I" (Philly Groove 200; r☆7, 1974). △ **Three Degrees,** "When Will I See You Again" (Philadelphia International 3550; r☆4, ☆2, 1974). ○ **Spinners,** "Love Don't Love Nobody—Part I" (Atlantic 3026; r☆1, ☆15, 1974). **Blue Magic,** "Three Ring Circus" (Atco 7004; r☆5, ☆36, 1974). △ **Harold Melvin and the Blue Notes,** "Where Are All My Friends" (Philadelphia International 3552; r☆8, 1974). △ **O'Jays,** "Sunshine—Part II" (Philadelphia International 3558; ☆17, ☆48, 1974). **Manhattens,** "Don't Take Your Love from Me" (Columbia 3-10045; r☆7, ☆37, 1975). **First Choice,** "Guilty" (Philly Groove 202; r☆19, 1975). △ **Three Degrees,** "I Didn't Know" (Philadelphia International 3561; ☆18, 1975). ○ **Spinners,** "Love Don't Love Nobody—Part I" (Atlantic 3206; r☆7, ☆37, 1975). △ **Harold Melvin and the Blue Notes,** "Bad Luck (Part I)" (Philadelphia International 8-3562; r☆4, ☆15, 1975). △ **O'Jays,** "Give the People What They Want" (Hi 2282; r☆1, ☆45, 1975). ○ **Spinners,** "Sadie" (Atlantic 3268; r☆7, 1975). **Manhattens,** "Hurt" (Columbia 3-10140; r☆10, 1975). △ **MFSB,** "Sexy" (Philadelphia International 8-3567; r☆2, ☆42, 1975). △ **Harold Melvin and Sharon Paige,** "Hope that We Can Be Together Soon" (Philadelphia International 8-3569, r☆1, ☆42, 1975). △ **O'Jays,** "Let Me Make Love to You" (Philadelphia International 8-3558; r☆10, 1975). **People's Choice,** "Do It Any Way You Wanna" (TSOP 8-4769; r☆1, ☆11, 1975). ○ **Spinners,** "They Just Stop It (Games People Play)" (Atlantic 3284; r☆1, ☆5, 1975). △ **O'Jays,** "I Love Music—Part I" (Philadelphia International 3577; r☆1, ☆5, 1975). ○ **Dionne Warwick,** "Once You Hit the Road" (Warner Bros. 8154; r☆5, 1975).

△ = Record produced by Gamble and Huff
○ = Record produced by Thom Bell

(Chart positions taken from Joel Whitburn's *Record Research,* compiled from *Billboard* Pop chart, unless otherwise indicated; r☆ = position on *Billboard* Rhythm and Blues chart.)

345

Al Green
by Robert Christgau

Especially when Al Green is on—which means anytime this intensely self-alienated man can be observed in what feels to him like a role, in performance or offstage or at business—his speech is even more stylized than his singing. It combines three major elements. The *down-home* is rooted in the migrations of Green's growing up, on an Arkansas dirt farm and in the black downtown of Grand Rapids, Michigan. The *ersatz formal*, common among undereducated successes, usually takes a preacherly tone in its black variant; Green's version is more professorial. The *cute*, however, is entirely his own innovation. The man crinkles up his voice as if he's trying out for *Sesame Street*; he drawls like someone affecting a drawl; he hesitates and giggles and murmurs and swallows his words.

Like most great popular singers, Green transmutes and resynthesizes his speech in his singing style, both melting it down until it begins to flow and shoring it up, rhythmically, against its own nervousness. This style then becomes the vehicle for a persona that is modest, even fragile, yet undeniably compelling, a term which in Green's case can mean only one thing: *sexy*. One wants to go to bed with a person who is down-home, ersatz formal, and cute because these qualities have their conventionally attractive counterparts—earthy, self-possessed, vulnerable—and yet are unique in themselves. Combined with Green's physical charms—a lean body and winsome face, plus a warm vocal timbre—all this makes for a sex fantasy that is both sweet and original. And not just for women. Green's sexiness is so pervasive that no male who responds to his singing can do so without feeling a jolt that transcends identification.

Of course, we turn on not to a real person but to a persona—a fantasy of a real person that compounds several roles. Moreover, the chemistry is not our own. The Green persona is manufactured—in a process as calculated as a Gatorade assembly line and as natural as the production of sugar in photosynthesis—by Al Green himself. It can be disturbing to realize this, but it is rarely decisive. In October 1974, a woman who had gotten close enough to Al Green to learn that he was nowhere near as self-possessed, earthy, or vulnerable as a fan might hope, persisted in her dreams of marriage anyway. Green rejected her. In retaliation, she attempted to disfigure him with a scalding pot of grits—what an image of the soul music business—and then killed herself. I don't know why the woman continued to love Green; maybe she was still ensnared by the fantasy, or maybe there was something in the reality that continued to satisfy her. Maybe both. For those of us who take pleasure in Green's ability to create fantasies of character in the public drama of his life and in performance because of the genuine pleasure we derive from his music, that's just the way it is.

Green has constructed his persona for the same reason all stars do—to synthesize his need for approval with his need for a firm ego-base. But Green is even less trusting than most stars. He got his professional start as a young teenager, singing lead in a family gospel group, a stint that ended when his father threw him out of the group and the house for listening to Jackie Wilson; his father, perceiving all that Baby Workout as devil's music, couldn't understand that his son had a different kind of religion. "Music engulfs one's soul to exert himself beyond imagination," Green has said. "That music just tripped me out." Later, in 1967, when Green was 20, he and a fellow musician from Grand Rapids made a record called "Back Up Train" that eventually hit Number 41 in *Billboard*. He never got a cent for it. Soon he headed south.

In 1969, in Midland, Texas, Green and a trumpet player named Willie Mitchell were ripped off by the same club owner. Their bond thus cemented, Green accompanied his new acquaintance back to Memphis, where Mitchell was staff producer for Hi Records. Over the next two years, Mitchell constructed a new Memphis sound around a percussive studio style in which even strings were counterpointed rhythmically to the thick, third-beat drumming of Howard Grimes and Al Jackson, ex-Booker T. and the MGs and hence one-fourth of Stax-Volt's original Memphis sound. The signature of this sound was Green's soft-edged, almost indolent phrasing, full of audacious slurs, with his startling falsetto adding an intensity that was suffering soul and sweet pop at the same time. The team's first smash was "Tired of Being Alone," in mid-1971; to date, they have produced eight gold singles and six gold albums. The five albums of Green's great period—which probably ended with *Livin' for You* in November 1973—all flow with an intense consistency, thus earning the dubious appellation "artistic unit." That total has been approached by very few white artists of the decade; among black artists, who had no *Sgt. Pepper* tradition to admonish them when their own LP market established itself, only Aretha Franklin is in Green's class; and none of his peers, black or white—except for Elton John—has showed Green's consistency as a singles artist.

Once again excepting Franklin (who in any case was making minor hits six years before she hooked up with Jerry Wexler in 1967), Green is much the last of the purebred house of soul innovators which seemed to have closed with Otis Redding and Sam and Dave in the mid-Sixties. Although his string of smooth-surfaced hits on man/woman themes tempted those consumers who like their aesthetic differentiation in the large economy size to dismiss his music as black bubblegum, in fact it represented a powerful synthesis and a unique style. The synthesis united the two mainstreams of soul, homogenized cool Detroit-Chicago (near where he grew up and began to record) and greasy get-down Memphis (near where he was born and where he now lives and records). Supported by a respectable variety of hooks and riffs, his vocal musicianship—control of timbre and volume, projection, and especially phrasing—showed a sophisticated instinctive musicianship unprecedented within his genre. His persona was equally original, nonmacho

Al Green, 1973 (Charles Gatewood)

but not long-suffering (Smokey Robinson) or vague (Curtis Mayfield) or button-down (Bill Withers) or wimpy (Russell Thompkins of the Stylistics). He wrote or cowrote most of his own songs, and blended an audacious variety of outside tastes—from the Doors to the Bee Gees, from Hank Williams to Kris Kristofferson, from Roosevelt Sykes to the Temptations, from "God Is Standing By" to "Unchained Melody"— into his own cool-and-creamy sound. Although both music and persona were in a conservative black tradition, it is essential to realize that both were romantic enough, at least in theory, to pass as white pop—and that this is what Green intended.

Because Green's hit singles are so pervasive, even those astonished by his television appearances, where his expressive face makes a startling impression, can't imagine him as a live performer. But Green needs a stage. It's the only place where he can overwhelm his own good taste, providing a subtlety and a power not so easily available to the listener over the car radio—until Green has been seen live just once. The male soul star is expected to come onstage, as Green has said, "in some superman machine suit that glitters and lights up," but Green's conservative flash is both sexier and more subversive. Not only are his clothes tailored to show off the lithe eloquence of his body; they also make that body accessible. There was even a time when he would appear carrying a shoulder bag and looking slightly rumpled, as if he'd just gotten off a Greyhound, and he always performs with a layer of fuzz on his face, making it impossible to tell whether he's growing a beard or just neglected to shave.

Green shares almost nothing with old studs like Wilson Pickett's man-and-a-half or new studs like chesty Teddy Pendergrass. Yet unlike black lover boy Barry White, who sells his deep-voiced solidity like so much pomade, Green definitely does exploit his own immense physical attractiveness. He is exciting, not just secure. Every time he draws back from the microphone so that his trademarked high moans can waft unamplified over the arena, he works his savvy, diffident style of sexual confidence on everyone who strains toward the stage to hear. Every time he laughs mischievously at the passion elicited by his boyish come-on, he shares a joke about the pleasures of the tease. His interplay with the band is a model of generous authority; his interplay with the crowd a dream of self-possessed appeal. Only as the climactic riff sets in does he finally begin to stride and belt, and even though he doesn't quite muster the power of a soul man-and-a-half, the audience is more than fulfilled.

Yet this epiphany is a qualified one. For us, its failure is in its aesthetic spirit—especially compared to great predecessors like Sam Cooke and Otis Redding, Green lacks any sense of openness. For Green himself, the failure is commercial, for his control has never achieved the mass interracial success he in-

tended. When it looked as if he might make it, the climactic riff went with a song called "Love and Happiness," a playful euphemism for good sex and all the things that go with it. Now that he is settled back into the role of second-level black hero, with the same reputation for general unreliability that has afflicted so many great soul innovators past their commercial prime, the show topper is "Take Me to the River," which is unclear in a mystical rather than a euphemistic way.

You get the feeling with many soul singers that the spiritual root of their music (call it God) and its emotional referent (by which I mean sex) coexist at the center of their musical conception. Perhaps it is appropriate that Green, as the last of the great soul men, should have apotheosized this confusing synthesis at its most extreme. In a rambling lyric that refers to his musical past (the phrase "sweet 16" is a title from *Livin' for You*) and is tinged with the paranoia that has lately become more explicit in his work, he seems to beg for a sexual deliverance that is identical to a country baptism. He demands to have his feet on the ground and to walk in the water. Perhaps it is the final tragedy of soul music that all its creators have hoped to do just that, and almost none of them have really managed it.

Discography

Singles

"Back Up Train" (Al Green and the Soul Mates) (Hot Line 15,000; r☆5, ☆41, 1967). "You Say It" (Hi 2172; r☆28, 1970). "Right Now, Right Now" (Hi 2177; r☆23, 1970). "I Can't Get Next to You" (Hi 2182; r☆11, ☆60, 1970). "Driving Wheel" (Hi 2188; r☆46, 1971). "Tired of Being Alone" (Hi 2194; r☆7, ☆11, 1971). "Let's Stay Together" (Hi 2202; r☆1, ☆1, 1971). "Look at What You've Done for Me" (Hi 2211; r☆2, ☆4, 1972). "I'm Still in Love with You" (Hi 2216; r☆1, ☆3, 1972). "You Ought to Be with Me" (Hi 2227; r☆1, ☆3, 1972). "Guilty" (Bell 45,258; r☆29, ☆69, 1972). "Hot Wire" (Bell 45,305; ☆71, 1973). "Call Me (Come Back Home)" (Hi 2235; r☆2, ☆10, 1973). "Here I Am (Come and Take Me)" (Hi 2247; r☆2, ☆10, 1973). "Livin' for You" (Hi 2257; r☆1, ☆19, 1973). "Let's Get Married" (Hi 2262; r☆3, ☆32, 1974). "Sha-La-La (Make Me Happy)" (Hi 2274; r☆2, ☆7, 1974). "L-O-V-E (Love)" (Hi 2282; r☆1, ☆13, 1975). "Oh Me, Oh My (Dream in My Arms)" (Hi 2288; r☆7, ☆48, 1975). "Full of Fire" (Hi 2300; r☆2, ☆4, 1975).

Albums

Al Green Gets Next to You (Hi 32062; ☆58, 1971). *Let's Stay Together* (Hi 32070; ☆8, 1972). *I'm Still in Love with You* (Hi 32074; ☆4, 1972). *Al Green* (Bell 6076; ☆162, 1972). *Green Is Blues* (Hi 32055; ☆19, 1973). *Call Me* (Hi 32077; ☆10, 1973). *Livin' for You* (Hi 32082; ☆24, 1973). *Al Green Explores Your Mind* (Hi 32087; ☆15, 1974). *Greatest Hits* (Hi 32089; ☆17, 1975). *Al Green Is Love* (Hi 32092; ☆28, 1975).
(Chart positions taken from Joel Whitburn's *Record Research*, compiled from *Billboard* Pop chart, unless otherwise indicated; r☆ = position on *Billboard* Rhythm and Blues chart.)

Rock Films
by Greil Marcus

The first rock and roll movies had little or nothing to do with rock and roll music, and everything to do with the rock and roll ethos—with defining teenagers as a dissatisfied, self-consciously distinct group within American society as a whole. *The Wild One* (1953, directed by Laslo Benedek) predated the general emergence of rock by about a year, but what mattered was that the movie, like the music that was to follow, affirmed the action taking place on the fringes of American life and culture, while ignoring—or assaulting—the mainstream. The identification teenagers made between Marlon Brando's bitter lone-wolf biker (Girl: "What're you rebelling against?" Brando: "Whatta ya got?") and the Elvis Presley of two years later was not only automatic, it was correct.

Then, in 1955, *Rebel without a Cause* (directed by Nicholas Ray) gave us James Dean, the mixed-up-kid-as-existential-hero (shortly, with his death in a classically "meaningless" auto accident, he would serve as the mixed-up-kid-as-martyr—an icon the mythic force of which has yet to completely burn out). Dean, in *Rebel* (and as the "bad" son in *East of Eden*, released that same year), seems in retrospect to stand for, not the rock and roll star, but the rock and roll listener; if Brando symbolized the visceral power the first rock heroes would have to convey, Dean represented the deep and unfocused needs of the audience rock and roll would reach. Both men, though strictly nonrock figures (Brando first expressed himself on rock and roll when Bob Dylan toured with the Hawks in 1965; Dean liked jazz and played bongos), were crucial to defining what rock meant. As music, rock and roll would have taken shape without them; as culture, it very well may not have.

Also released in 1955 was *The Blackboard Jungle* (directed by Richard Brooks). It had a prerock setting (the high school rumblers were into Perry Como, not Little Richard), a well-honed good-boy-goes-bad-goes-good story line, and, most importantly, it had Bill Haley and His Comets' "Rock around the Clock" on the soundtrack. Suddenly, the festering connections between rock and roll, teenage rebellion, juvenile delinquency, and other assorted horrors were made explicit. From Cleveland to Liverpool, the response was the same: chaos. Kids poured into the theaters, slashed the seats, rocked the balconies, they *liked it.*

Something else was made explicit: rock sold movies. Without missing a beat producers watered down plots and pushed the music forward. A seemingly endless series of quickies hit the cinemas: *Rock around the Clock* (1956), *Don't Knock the Rock* (1957), *Rock, Pretty Baby* (1957), *Rock around the World* (1957), *Let's Rock* (1958), *Hot Rod Gang* (1958), and many more. Commonly featured were Bill Haley, Fats Domino, Alan Freed (notably in *Mister Rock and Roll*), Frankie Lymon *(Rock, Rock, Rock)*, Chuck Berry (*Go, Johnny, Go*—though "Johnny" turned out to be Jimmy Clanton, not Mr. B. Goode), and the Platters—along with dozens of assorted titans, pygmies, has-beens, and never-weres.

Plots were not complex. To quote rock historian Mike Daly: "... The kids are putting on the Seniors' Hop and somehow they get all these great rock 'n' roll stars to appear from out of nowhere and play for them for nothing (oh sure, yeah) but the parents and the school committee won't let them put it on because it's bad or something and somehow the big crisis is resolved and near the end Bill Haley or somebody is playing and the kids are all bopping away and the parents are standing around watching, supervising, and the camera shifts to the parents' feet and their toes are tapping, you know, and they're snapping their fingers and their heads are bobbing back and forth, looking at each other and saying: 'Gee, this music ain't so bad after all, is it? Kinda catchy.' "

Out of this limited milieu came countless memorable musical performances, and two first-rate movies.

The Girl Can't Help It (1956, directed by Frank Tashlin) opened with a towering rendition by Little Richard of the now-classic title song; the story centered, hilariously, on the music business, which was presented as controlled from top to bottom by warring mobsters. It was a freewheeling flick: a major Hollywood bandleader, playing himself and using his own name, was portrayed as being under personal contract to one of the hoods; Tashlin's setup of Jayne Mansfield strolling along a street with two huge milk bottles clutched to her breasts represented a landmark in rock-film tastelessness unsurpassed until Ken Russell drowned Ann-Margret in baked beans in his much-ballyhooed production of Pete Townshend's *Tommy* (1975). With all this and more going on, Tashlin still found time for classic performances by Gene Vincent, Eddie Cochran, the Platters, and two more tunes by Little Richard.

Then there was *Jailhouse Rock* (1957, directed by Richard Thorpe), Elvis's third movie. (*Love Me Tender* and *Loving You* had preceded; the exciting *King Creole* would follow. After that, Elvis's movies, picking up again with *Flaming Star* in 1960, would have only the most marginal relationship to rock and roll; they became *Elvis movies*, a genre unto itself.) *Jailhouse Rock* stands as Elvis's finest film, thanks to his utterly convincing portrayal of the violence-prone young rockabilly singer, Vince Everett, and to Jerry Leiber and Mike Stoller's sizzling set of soundtrack tunes. The flick played off Elvis's humble beginnings, his temper, his vanity, his burning ambition, and his magnificent contempt for the highfalutin. One need only recall the scene of Vince—just out of prison, where he had been sent on a manslaughter rap after killing a man in a barroom fight—at the home of his girl's parents, where they and their high-class friends patronize Vince/Elvis with a discussion of modern jazz. "*You're* a musician, Mr. Everett," says a 40-ish woman with undisguised condescension. "What's your opin-

1955: James Dean defines the image of the American teenager for all time with his performance in Nicholas Ray's 'Rebel without a Cause.' (The Bettman Archive)

ion?" "Lady, I don't know what the hell you're talking about," is the immortal Presley response.

And now we must leave the Fifties (but not without noting Jack Arnold's wonderfully sordid 1958 *High School Confidential*, which starred Russ Tamblyn as a junior narc breaking up a teenage dope ring, and featured a cataclysmic assault on the title tune by Jerry Lee Lewis), and leave as well the early Sixties imitations of the Fifties, such as *Don't Knock the Twist* (an unwatchable horror from 1962, starring, of course, Chubby Checker), the various Frankie Avalon-Annette Funicello beach movies, like *Beach Party* (1963), *Beach Blanket Bingo* (1965), and the nicely titled *How to Stuff a Wild Bikini* (1965—some said Kleenex, others cotton), not to mention various other pallid attempts to exploit the youth of America out of their Levi's, and move on to the Beatles—pausing first in brief homage to Kenneth Anger's *Scorpio Rising* (1964).

An astonishingly lurid, hard-hitting work that explored the images of Brando and Dean as magical, homoerotic incantations, *Scorpio Rising* introduced rock and roll into cinema as pure soundtrack, utilizing records to comment on action in a manner that would not even be successfully imitated until years later, with Martin Scorsese's *Who's That Knocking at My Door?* (1968), Perry Henzell's *The Harder They Come* (see below), Scorsese's *Mean Streets* (1973) and George Lucas's *American Graffiti* (1973). Unlike, say, Dennis Hopper with *Easy Rider* (1969), or Antonioni with his unfortunate *Zabriskie Point* (1970), both of whom used rock records to score their movies, Anger, Scorsese, Henzell and Lucas saw the music not as decoration but as essence. One thinks of *Mean Streets*, with a fight played out to the Marvelettes' "Please Mr. Postman," or the dance in the bar to Johnny Ace's "Pledging My Love," foreshadowing doom; one thinks of the way Lucas faded a constant soundtrack of Fifties rock and roll tunes up and down, as if the music never stopped, which of course, in the teenage world he

was presenting, it never did. But in *Scorpio Rising* Anger caught the spirit of the music with a verve no later director has matched, particularly with a shot of Jesus, riding on an ass (taken from Cecil B. DeMille's 1927 *The King of Kings*) accompanied not by the chants of his disciples, but by the Crystals' "He's a Rebel."

Well, the Beatles. In 1964, the group broke internationally, and like pop figures before them, they signed to make a movie. (Earlier, they had shot one extended concert film for British TV, *Around the Beatles*, plus *What's Happening! The Beatles in the U.S.A.*, a 55-minute documentary by the Maysles Brothers, which never went into general release.) No one expected the Beatles' first major cinematic outing to be anything more than a bouncy vehicle for the promotion of Beatle records, Beatle lunchboxes, and Beatle bubblegum cards, and precisely for that reason, *A Hard Day's Night* (1964, directed by Richard Lester) was a shock. The punning wit of the title bespoke the intelligence of the movie: here were the four mop tops, playing themselves in a standard can-they-make-it-to-the-show-on-time story, and they charmed the world. The film, probably more than their music, took the Beatles across social barriers, won them an audience among the intelligentsia, and broadened their hardcore base from teenage girls to rock and roll fans of every description—if rock and roll was about fun, then this movie was rock and roll.

The Beatles on film were, in a word, irresistible. Lines from the movie (Woman: "Are you a mod or a rocker?" Ringo: "A mocker") were used as catchwords among fans for years; scenes were imprinted on a collective memory. It was not uncommon to find people who had seen the film 50 times—in fact, it was almost impossible to find a person who, having seen the film, had seen it only once.

The movie drew on the jump cutting and breakneck pacing of Jean-Luc Godard's *Breathless*, on the superfast, supershiny techniques of TV commercials, and most vitally, it drew on the personalities of the Beatles themselves. For an hour and a half they were alive, funny, quick, iconoclastic and gorgeous, and the pop world fell back before them and created itself again in their image. It was a movie of, and about, innocence: that of the Beatles and that of the audience. Frame by frame, the film sparkled, glowed. Seeing it today, one can hardly help but cry, realizing how completely the world of this film is gone for good.

As with everything else the Beatles touched in the Sixties, *A Hard Day's Night* resulted in new rules and opened up new possibilities. A few traditional pop films followed, such as *Ferry Cross the Mersey* (1965), which starred those sailors in the Beatles' wake, Gerry and the Pacemakers, Cilla Black, and the now-forgotten Fourmost; there was John Boorman's *Having a Wild Weekend* (1965), which starred the Dave Clark Five, and boasts a solid cult reputation, though few saw it in its day. And there was, in 1966 and 1967, *The Monkees* (created by Don Kirshner), that infamous television imitation of *A Hard Day's*

Night and *Help!* (1965), the Beatles' second movie, which was distinguished from the first by color, a weaker script, and a somewhat forced enthusiasm. (The Monkees themselves, desperate for respectability after finding—briefly—careers as artistic frauds, in 1968 made a failed "trip" movie, *Head*, directed by Bob Rafelson, coauthored by Jack Nicholson, and costarring Annette Funicello and Frank Zappa.) The Rolling Stones, eager as always to outdo the Beatles in sophistication (they would not play themselves, they would *act*), took an option on film rights to Anthony Burgess's *Clockwork Orange*, which they never made; considered filming *The Only Lovers Left Alive*, a saga of teenagers loose in post H-bomb/apocalypse England, which they never made either; and, following their drug busts in 1967, flamboyantly shot a few abortive scenes for a planned film about the trial of Oscar Wilde (with Keith as the Judge, and Mick, naturally, as Wilde). But aside from *Charlie Is My Darling*, a spottily released hour-long tour documentary from 1965, the only major appearance of the Stones on film in the mid-Sixties took place when they closed the monumental *T.A.M.I. Show*. It was, some have argued, enough.

The T.A.M.I. Show (1965, directed by Steve Binder, later responsible for Elvis's superb 1968 comeback TV special) was the first great rock performance film, significant not only for the quality of its music but also because it brought together on one screen virtually every strain of rock with a catholicity of taste demonstrated by no subsequent movie.

One year after the Beatles' releases, and before Bob Dylan and folk rock sprung forth to divide audiences by taste and class, there were no serious cracks in the *concept* of pop music—be it Motown, solo singers, English heavies and lightweights, surf music or garage bands, it was *all rock*. And so, kicking off with Jan and Dean skateboarding across L.A. while singing, "They're coming from all over the world," and then segueing into a shot of Diana Ross applying gloss to lips that filled the entire screen, *The T.A.M.I. Show* offered Billy J. Kramer and the Dakotas, Gerry and the Pacemakers trading riffs with Chuck Berry, Lesley Gore, the Supremes, Marvin Gaye, the Miracles, the Barbarians (a Boston group known for "Are You a Boy or Are You a Girl," and for their drummer, Moulty, who had a hook), James Brown, and the Stones. Brown preceded the Stones, and took ten minutes for a staggering version of his No Man Alive Can Make Me Leave the Stage routine; when he finally did leave, even the white, middle-aged studio band stood and applauded him. Jagger couldn't hope to match Brown's dancing, and he didn't try; he minced, pointed and rocked, leading the Stones through a crushing set that finally exploded with "It's All Over Now." *The T.A.M.I. Show* stands as an expression of the power and pluralism of rock and roll at its best.

The T.A.M.I. Show inaugurated an era of performance mov-

ies. In 1966 Phil Spector produced *The Big T.N.T. Show*, an attempted *T.A.M.I.* followup that never caught fire (featured were the Ronettes, Ike and Tina Turner, Bo Diddley, the Byrds, the Lovin' Spoonful, Ray Charles, Donovan, and Joan Baez, who with Spector backing her on piano contributed a horrendous version of "You've Lost That Lovin' Feelin' "). The year 1968 brought *Monterey Pop* (directed by D.A. Pennebaker), a superb color record of the festival that had taken place the previous year, a film that reached its height when it presented Janis Joplin singing "Ball and Chain" with an intensity and artistry she never achieved on record (also included were Otis Redding, the Mamas and the Papas, the Who, Jimi Hendrix, and many more). In 1970 came *Woodstock* (directed by Michael Wadleigh), three hours of footage from the great 1969 gathering, an attractive vision of benign community that effectively utilized split screens to put across memorable performances by the Who, Jimi Hendrix, Santana, Sly and the Family Stone, Ten Years After, and others.

Following the enormous financial success of *Woodstock* came a deluge of straight performance films, as well as many on-tour "documentaries"—the rock version of the backstage musical. The first and best of these, however, came in 1967, with Bob Dylan's *Don't Look Back* (directed by D.A. Pennebaker). A "cinéma vérité" account of Dylan's 1965 tour of England, *Don't Look Back* was a rough, grainy depiction of Dylan's reach for pop stardom, the first close look at a pop figure at work since the Canadian *Lonely Boy* (1964), the story of Paul Anka. There were many unforgettable segments; Dylan, taunting a *Time* interviewer, or a science student, or a guest at a party; Dylan, softly singing "It's All Over Now, Baby Blue" in a hotel room, while a worshipful Donovan looked on; Dylan's manager, Albert Grossman, talking down a scuzzy British agent. For nerve and movement, no later film of this type was to touch it. (In 1966, Pennebaker again shot Dylan on tour in England, this time with the Hawks. Dylan has never permitted the film that resulted, *You Know Something Is Happening*, to be released, but used much of the footage for his own *Eat the Document*. Pennebaker's movie is simply a masterpiece, with indelible scenes of Dylan quietly working out a song with Johnny Cash, sparring viciously with John Lennon, and singing with a power that is almost not to be believed, cupping his hands around the mike, his hair flying, screaming, "How does it *feel?*")

And so the films came, one after the other, most of them sharing the motives of Fifties exploitation movies while lacking their liberating vulgarity: you put a camera on a star, he sang, maybe he mumbled something backstage, jumped in a limousine, looked wasted, and people paid to see it. There was the Beatles' *Let It Be* (1970), released after Paul announced he was leaving, a sad look at their attempts to record what turned out to be their final album (the Beatles had earlier made a cartoon, *Yellow Submarine*, 1968, which was a delight, and a television film, *Magical Mystery Tour*, 1967, which was supposed to be a

delight, and wasn't). There were the Stones, in *One Plus One* (1969), fascinatingly working out "Sympathy for the Devil," while outside the studio London suffered the inspired pop politics of Jean-Luc Godard. There was *The Concert for Bangladesh* (1972), *Soul to Soul* (1971), *Wattstax* (1973), Joe Cocker's *Mad Dogs and Englishmen* (1971), Elvis's *That's the Way It Is* (1970) and *Elvis on Tour* (1972), the disastrous *Farewell of the Cream* (1969, originally released at live concert prices, but not for long), plus numerous filmed concerts, self-promotions, and self-indulgences by Neil Young, Frank Zappa, the Rolling Stones, oldies hustlers, and others. The deaths of Jimi Hendrix and Janis Joplin inspired compilation documentaries ("What was he/she really like?" asks the invisible interviewer). But of all the post-*Woodstock* nonfiction rock and roll movies, probably only two are of enduring interest. Both involved the Rolling Stones.

The first was *Gimme Shelter* (1970, directed by David and Albert Maysles and Charlotte Zwerin), an account of the Stones' 1969 American tour, which ended in the disaster at Altamont. The film was cut to build to the finale, with shots of the preparations for Altamont interspersed with earlier concerts, backstage scenes, and the like. At Altamont, the cameras caught part of the murder of Meredith Hunter, which took place as the Stones played; their performance in the midst of the carnage perpetrated by the Hell's Angels was the best of any they have ever put on film. An extraordinarily compelling film, *Gimme Shelter* failed mostly in that it refused to confront the questions it raised about youth culture and star cults: the Stones were shown as victims, as if the purpose of the film was not to deal with real events, but to absolve those who paid for the film of any responsibility for those events.

Then, in 1972, again touring the States, the Stones hired Robert Frank to make a second movie. The result, *Cocksucker Blues* (so far unreleased), named after a song Jagger sings as the film opens, is *Don't Look Back*, Stones-style: cold-eyed, mean, and revelatory. Frank shot the tour, not its publicity: groupies fucking in airplanes, smack junkies hanging onto the fringes, the Stones cruising a Southern highway as a prisoner's arm waves hopefully at them through the bars of a country jail. Like Godard's *One Plus One*, and unlike *Gimme Shelter* (not to mention *Ladies and Gentlemen: the Rolling Stones*, a straight performance film the Stones substituted for Frank's effort), this was a filmmaker's, not a rock star's, movie, and the result was an increased sense of the complexity of stardom, not to mention its boredom, its triviality, and its horror.

As the mid-Sixties turned the corner, the fictional rock movie, which in terms of theme had not really progressed beyond the Fifties prom-crisis film, made a comeback, beginning perhaps with Antonioni's *Blow-Up* (1966). Not really a rock and roll movie (though a sizzling live performance by the Yardbirds was caught and smoothly integrated into the plot),

Blow-Up was a sometimes accurate, sometimes hopelessly high-minded exposé of the moral emptiness of pop culture in general and swinging London in particular. The problem was, Antonioni captured the shiny vitality of the London scene all too well; in spite of his moralistic intentions, just about everything he put on the screen looked—well, groovy.

Then, as was proper, vulgarity took over, first with *Privilege* (1967), a muddled, hysterical attempt to explore the fascist potential of the music (i.e., big crowds), and with the classic *Wild in the Streets* (1968, directed by Barry Shear), a convincing, often hilarious attempt to explore the fascist potential of youth culture (the kids, after forcing a reduction in the voting age to 14 and electing Christopher Jones, a James Dean lookalike rock singer, president—on the Republican ticket!—put all people over 30 in concentration camps and feed them LSD). The genre went into basic hibernation again (save for a few wild-youth entries and the spate of ghetto westerns that peaked with 1972's *Super Fly* and Curtis Mayfield's accompanying soundtrack) until the release of Perry Henzell's *The Harder They Come* (1972), a brilliant study of a young Jamaican (reggae singer Jimmy Cliff) who comes to Kingston with hopes of reggae stardom and ends up making both the pop charts and the Most Wanted list at the same time. Henzell used the finest reggae yet recorded to comment on the action—most memorable was the scene of Cliff running for his life through the Trenchtown slums as the Maytals chanted out their ferocious version of "Pressure Drop."

There have been fictional films since: *Stardust* (1975) and *That'll Be the Day* (1974), supposedly tough-minded looks at the world of pop stardom that instead betray their own calculating cynicism; and *Tommy*, an overblown, not-unenjoyable rendering of Pete Townshend's Blind, Deaf and Dumb Boy parable. But of all the films that tried to find a story in the world of rock and roll, one stands out, and that is *Performance*.

Performance (1970, directed by Donald Cammell and Nicolas Roeg) starred Mick Jagger as the aging pop star Turner, living in a decaying mansion with two women, Anita Pallenberg and Michel Breton, and James Fox as a hit man on the run from the London mob. Turner, his glory days behind him, spends his days trying to coax the spirit of a dead Mississippi country bluesman out of his synthesizer; Fox arrives, settles on the mansion as a hideout, and begins to trade in his identity for Turner's, a switch Turner is only too happy to make. The movie slammed home with Jagger's "Memo from Turner," a terrifying song that Jagger, as a gangster, sings to a corpulent collection of mob bigwigs; the themes of murder, suicide, sado-masochistic homosexuality, and insanity that had crawled for years beneath the surface of the pop life suddenly came to the surface. This is how it all will end, the movie seemed to call to rock and roll: say your prayers. It is a vision that rock and roll movies, not to mention rock and roll musicians, the Rolling Stones among them, have been dodging ever since.

Elton John
by Robert Christgau

There is something wondrous about Elton John, and something monstrous. The preeminent popular musician of the Seventies seems out of time, untouched by the decade's confusion. Yet he is ravenously contemporary. Although he partakes of none of the defiant irony and isolation that sustain Dylan and Randy Newman and Joni Mitchell and Neil Young, there is no nostalgia about the man either, no namby-pamby religionism or pastoralism, no nuke-fam posturing to comfort the young marrieds; he is not spacey like David Bowie or stuck in a mold like the Stones and the Who and Led Zep. He is just Elton John, moving with the world as only a cynosure can; the most eloquent thing to be said about him is that he is a Rock Star. He consumes music omnivorously—his tastes suggest fuel rather than food—and pursues fame with such single-minded compulsion that to accuse him of escapism sounds silly, like accusing a runaway freight train of antisocial tendencies.

Always the metaphors that arise are mechanical. As the great inheritor of Philadelphia pop-rock, in which rock and roll ceases to be an uncontrolled natural force and turns into a product understood and exploitable, John makes records that are artifacts rather than expressions of a palpably vital individual. Of course, they share this artifactual quality with some of the best popular music of the middle Seventies—the exquisitely crafted recordings of Randy Newman or Paul Simon or Steely Dan, or of the current kings of Philadelphia soul, Gamble and Huff. But with such artists the metaphors are drawn from nature; what they create is like a rare insect preserved in amber. What Elton John creates is more like a Coca-Cola sign.

The world-scale hegemony of Elton's brand of pop emanates from the United States, and like Coca-Cola, which was originally marketed as an elixir, he has become simultaneously more significant and less self-serious. John's glittery outrageousness and rock and roll overdrive have become so pervasive that we tend to forget the wimpiness of his original aspect. The new hopeful's propensity for jumping up and down in front of his piano was duly noted after his U.S. debut at Los Angeles's Troubador Club in 1970, but what stuck out was his eyeglasses—not the spectacles-of-themselves he favors now, but the owlish tortoiseshells that peer off the cover of his first American LP, *Elton John*.

In that year of Sweet Baby James, it was hard not to assume the worst of what was actually a pretty good record. Paul Buckmaster's pervasive strings, the too often inflated and occasionally meaningless banality of Bernie Taupin's lyrics, and the faked-up sensitivity of a voice that at its worst suggested an adenoid in search of a choirmaster all betokened yet another foolish, folkish singer/songwriter, albeit one with two heads. But in fact those arrangements, more astringent than the usual sweetening in any case, also proved dispensable; Taupin's lyrics maintained the kind of 50-50 ratio that can result in a lot of good songs if the music is strong and plentiful; and Elton

possessed a pop-rock voice in the great tradition of Del Shannon and Bobby Vee, as well as the ambition to apotheosize that voice. In other words, that sensitive little LP contained the makings of a rock and roll assembly line.

However unlikely this might have seemed to American observers at the time, it was implicit in the English career of Reg Dwight, which was Elton's name before he decided to destine himself for bigger things. Born in 1947, Reg was a moderately prodigious child pianist who was introduced to rock and roll by his mother and learned less at the Royal Academy of Music than he did in a group called Bluesology. Beginning as a copy band in the London suburbs in 1964, Bluesology moved on to tour with American rock and rollers like Doris Troy and Billy Stewart and eventually came to back the semilegendary Long John Baldry in 1967. Yet Reg was always in pursuit of the eternal more. He tried to land a singer/songwriter gig, but instead landed a partner, fellow reject Bernie Taupin. The two worked solely by mail at first, finally meeting in the flesh at the studios of Dick James, Lennon-McCartney's original publisher, who eventually gave the singer/songwriter team the ten-pound-a-week contract that enabled Reg to quit Baldry and change his name.

According to official legend, John and Taupin tried to grind out pap pop-rock until urged to follow their own noses by the likes of pop-rock kings Roger Greenaway and Roger Cook. What John and Taupin did with this advice, however, becomes understandable only when notions of a muse are put aside. The millions who take their Elton John records at face value still think of Bernie as a conscious artist, half a songpoet; his more reflective admirers like to point out his apparent preoccupation with American imagery and outsider-versus-society themes. Yet although this analysis is not inaccurate statistically, it's aesthetically irrelevant. Most likely, Bernie's writing does reflect genuine personal interests. But he rarely has anything new to say about these interests—or at least anything precise, anything consistent *or* paradoxical. This is just as well for Elton, who needs the sound of the words, not their sense; sense might stanch their flow. It may even be that Bernie's vagueness functions for him the way the dispassion of craft does for pop pros in the tradition of Greenaway and Cook, who must have realized, back at Dick James Music, that for young men like Elton and Bernie, "poetic" imagery and "meaningful" themes were at least a permissible gimmick, probably a personal asset, and possibly a commercial necessity.

Were they necessary? Impossible to tell, although how could Elton have been the complete rocker in this decade without them? In any case, there is no doubt that they were sufficient and then some. Not counting a soundtrack and a live album and a greatest hits and some uncollected singles and an early British LP released six years after the fact, John came up with nine

Opposite: Elton John; Pages 360-361: Elton outside his tour plane, circa 1972. (Both by Annie Leibovitz)

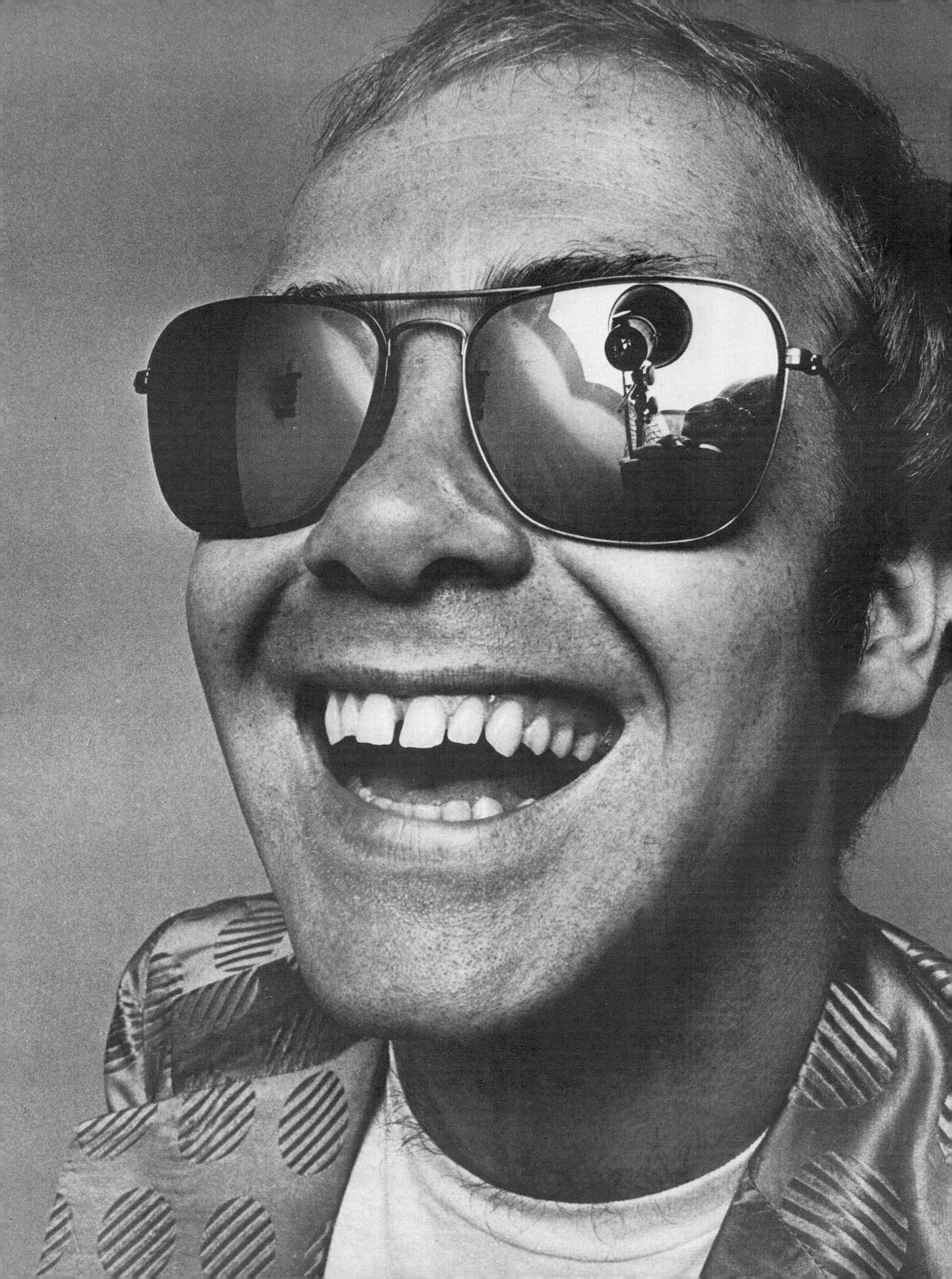

albums (including one double) in the five years following his first visit to America. By the standards established for today's pop, such productivity is gross, proof in itself that Elton must be doing something wrong, and the alacrity with which he works (with a partner whom he rarely sees socially anymore) is equally suspect. The songs begin with Taupin, who will write the lyrics for an album in a two-week flurry, spending perhaps an hour on each one, and forward them to Elton, who works out chords and melody for each lyric unchanged, a process that usually takes less than an hour. Arrangements develop during recording, which takes a few weeks per album at most. John and Taupin both say pop music should be disposable; the way they grind it out, they might pass for a garbage processing plant.

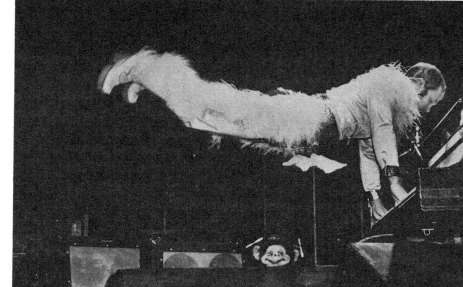

Yet there are few people who like rock and roll, or any pop music, who remain unreached by Elton John. It's not just that he's so pervasive, although that helps; quite simply, the man is a genius. No matter how you deplore his sloppiness, or his one-dimensionality, or his $40,000 worth of rose-colored glasses, you will find yourself humming "Take Me to the Pilot" or "Bennie and the Jets" or "Don't Let the Sun Go Down on Me." Not all of them, perhaps; maybe not any of those three. But the man's gift for the hook—made up whole or assembled from outside sources—is so universal that there is small likelihood one of them hasn't stuck in your pleasure center. Or your craw. Or both.

For a good hook does not guarantee aesthetic merit—it is merely a means to aesthetic merit, and far from foolproof. The chorus of "Take Me to the Pilot" is as compelling a melody as John has ever recorded, but the lyric is gibberish which has drained energy from singers as honest as Ben E. King and Patti LaBelle, and every time the melody leads you to the gibberish there is reason to resent it more. Or again: John's affected pronunciation of the word "discard" ("diszgard") on "Don't Let the Sun" is a kind of hook in itself, and also a turn-off in itself, an aural itch you can't scratch. On the other hand, in "Bennie and the Jets," which is one big hook—as compelling and catchy a performance as John has ever concocted—the way some fairly standard images of pop stardom are given life by the music makes the lyrics completely convincing.

Hooks are integral to hit singles; they are what makes disc jockeys and radio listeners remember a record. The heedless productivity of John's recording habits tends to result in hit singles; one cut or another is bound to be right because the whole process is so hit-or-miss. So when John is praised critically, it is usually as a singles artist. Inevitably, though, some of John's monster singles present him at his most monstrous—not many, granted, but you can't just disregard (or diszgard) those that do. John at his worst is fulsome in both the archaic sense of "copious," "fat," "wanton" and in the modern sense: "offensive

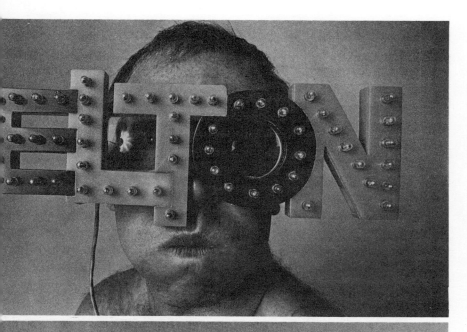

to moral or aesthetic sensibility," "offensive from insincerity or baseness of motive." His rank sentimentality is typified by the semimeaningful "Border Song" or the overripe "Don't Let the Sun"—both included on Elton's otherwise listenable (although stylistically ragged) *Greatest Hits.* But his general slovenliness has its compensations in a kind of postindustrial openness and fecundity, and it is possible to sort out the garbage on that jumble of albums just by analyzing their hook content.

On his two worst albums, *Don't Shoot Me I'm Only the Piano Player* (1973) and (especially) *Madman across the Water* (1971), what few hooks push through are dull or annoying; the same goes for at least half of the double LP, *Goodbye Yellow Brick Road* (1973). The first of the two early LPs is winsome enough, although marred by the aforementioned wimpiness; the other, *Tumbleweed Connection* (1970), continues to sound as flat as it did (to this listener) at the time of its release, although side two saves it from nadirdom. The hooks are much more numerous on *Captain Fantastic and the Brown Dirt Cowboy* (1975), the autobiographical bildungselpee, but the failure of the concept as a whole—Taupin lacks both the honesty and the intellectual discipline to bring it off—diminishes its better parts.

That's six discs gone, some of them pleasantly enough. But what remains is a career's worth of good rock and roll. *Honky Chateau* (1972), album number four, which announced John and Taupin's escape from the excesses of their own romanticism, sounds even crisper today, when we can be sure it wasn't a fluke. Yet although it stands as John's best LP, it remains atypical, the "folk rock" statement that culminates his sensitive phase. The clear break, both aesthetically and professionally, came with the single "Crocodile Rock," included on *Don't Shoot Me,* which unveiled Elton and Bernie's assembly line and put it into overdrive on a road to preeminence which if it wasn't paved with yellow brick was obviously pure gold.

This is why it makes sense to perceive the title track of *Goodbye Yellow Brick Road* as another self-serving enigma even while admitting that the album goes places, including not only "Bennie and the Jets" and John's original Rolling Stones rip-off, the Number One "Saturday Night's Alright for Fighting," but also the unheralded "Your Sister Can't Twist (But She Can Rock 'n' Roll)." This raver is one of John's masterpieces, overlaying surf-sound harmonies and amusement-park organ on an intensified sendup of Danny and the Juniors' "At the Hop," itself the most intense Philadelphia pop-rock record ever made; it proves that rock and roll need not be human to move. The first side of *Caribou* (album seven, 1974) is also mint Elton, leading off with a nastier Rolling Stones rip-off, "The Bitch Is Back," and never letting go. Its moment of transcendence is entitled "Solar Prestige a Gammon": "Solar prestige a gammon/Kool kar kyrie kay salmon/Hair ring molasses abounding/Common lap kitch sardin a poor floundin." And *Rock of the*

Westies (1975) introduces a mostly new Elton John Band that kicks a little more ass than the original. Kenny Passarelli and Roger Pope are tougher and less static than Dee Murray and Nigel Olsson on bass and drums, Caleb Quaye augments Davey Johnstone keenly on guitar, and James Newton Howard adds keyboard touches absent from the boss's rather clunky vocabulary. The result is the best Rolling Stones album since *Exile on Main St.*

It is tempting to conclude that the simplest way to separate good Elton from bad Elton is to assume that good Elton rocks and bad Elton doesn't. But that leaves too many exceptions, not only ballads that work and a lot of in-betweens, but also pointless rockers, a category that includes songs as significant as the rather unfocused, nostalgia-mongering "Crocodile Rock." In fact the truth is that even though Elton seems as indifferent to their quality as Bernie himself does to their specific content, it is only the lyrics which elevate John's music beyond aural diversion. Of course, Elton and Bernie are rarely aware themselves when this happens, favoring ponderous banalities like "Candle in the Wind" ("Hollywood created a superstar/And pain was the price you paid") or "Ticking" ("But blood stained a young hand that never held a gun/And his parents never thought of him as their troubled son") to perfect throwaways like "Your Sister Can't Twist" or "The Bitch Is Back." For the paradox of these new pop pros is that they can create work of genuine aesthetic quality, but this quality is independent of vision and intent; they are such good partners because they share, over and above their commercial energy and a certain expedient sentimentality, a blankness of artistic personality.

Taupin is essential to John because his relative anonymity has saved his superstar mouthpiece from the onanistic know-nothingism of superstar lyrics; he can walk the streets like a real person, so it's no strain for him to write songs that are actually *about* things. Recently the two have even begun to achieve what for them is a certain ironic density. Three songs from *Rock of the Westies* will do as examples: "Grow Some Funk of Your Own," which acknowledges the slumming impulse underlying all south-of-the-border songs in the marimba accent of the band's own funk and the Spanish accent Elton assumes when quoting the avenging boyfriend ("He was so macho," Elton whimpers); "Island Girl," in which the "inappropriate" cheerfulness of the music's ersatz Caribbean inflections, both oral and instrumental, imply a naive racism belied by the impassive but sage cruelty of the lyric's conclusion; and "Street Kids," in which the band's proletarian drive cuts right through Elton's arbitrary ebullience. But it must be reiterated that these effects are probably accidental. For all John and Taupin can be assumed to care, the social issues that arise in their music might as well be moon-June-spoon.

This impartiality carries over into John's singing, which is not interpretive in any ordinary sense of the term. The man has a ballad voice, which is adenoidal and sensitive sounding, and a hard rock voice, which is adenoidal and insensitive sounding, and he can simulate a few surface effects. In its way, his style is quite distinctive—that is, his vocal timbre is unmistakable—but it is indubitably mechanical. Its automatism is acknowledged in that song from *Caribou,* "Solar Prestige a Gammon," which is written entirely in words that only sound like words or can't possibly mean what they seem to mean. Needless to say, John sings it with all his usual cheery conviction, which I assume is his way of telling us something.

If you like, the arrogance of what it tells us is monstrous. That mindless cipher makes untold millions a year; that balding, pudgy robot is an object of pubescent sexual fantasy. But to say that Elton John lacks the lineaments of a conventional artist is not to say he is a cipher; to say that his singing is mechanical is not to declare him a robot. He is a star because people love his music and are immensely attracted to his immense vivacity—both in the media theater of mags and tube and in all the garish fulsomeness of his live shows. He is the true spirit of rock and roll, devoid of all but the most innocent pretensions, as sure a touchstone in this decade as the Beach Boys were in the last. Since his collection of popular records is one of the largest in the world, and he seems to listen to all of them, perhaps it is most apt to steal an image from Greil Marcus and call him Elton John Superfan.

Elton is our tabula rasa—the very sureness of his instinct for sales makes him a kind of one-man zeitgeist. If he can be maudlin or stupid or pleasure-seeking or head-in-the-sand, so can we, and those of us who reject those flaws in ourselves will reject them in him as well. But if he can produce incisive music without even willing it, as seems likely, well, perhaps there is more room for optimism there than there would be in the strivings of a lonely artist. In fact, maybe Elton John isn't out of time at all. Maybe he is one small indication that some things about the times are already all right.

Discography

Singles

"Border Song" (Uni 55246; ☆92, 1970). "Your Song" (Uni 55265; ☆8, 1970). "Friends" (Uni 55277; ☆34, 1971). "Levon" (Uni 55314; ☆24, 1971). "Tiny Dancer" (Uni 55318; ☆41, 1972). "Rocket Man" (Uni 55328; ☆6, 1972). "Honky Cat" (Uni 55343; ☆8, 1972). "Crocodile Rock" (MCA 40000; ☆1, 1972). "Daniel" (MCA 40046; ☆2, 1973). "Saturday Night's Alright for Fighting" (MCA 40105; ☆12, 1973). "Goodbye Yellow Brick Road" (MCA 40148; ☆2, 1973). "Bennie and the Jets" (MCA 40198; r☆15, ☆1, 1974). "Don't Let the Sun Go Down on Me" (MCA 40259; ☆2, 1974). "The Bitch Is Back" (MCA 40297; ☆4, 1974). "Lucy in the Sky with Diamonds" (MCA 40344; ☆1, 1974). "Philadelphia Freedom" (MCA 40364; r☆32, ☆1, 1975). "Someone Saved My Life Tonight" (MCA 40421; ☆4, 1975). "Island Girl" (MCA 40461; ☆1, 1975).

Albums

Elton John (Uni 73090; ☆4, 1970). *Tumbleweed Connection* (Uni 73096; ☆5, 1971). *Friends* (Soundtrack) (Paramount 6004; ☆36, 1971). *11-17-70* (Uni 93105; ☆11, 1971). *Madman across the Water* (Uni 93120; ☆8, 1971). *Honky Chateau* (Uni 93135;' ☆1, 1972). *Don't Shoot Me I'm Only the Piano Player* (MCA 2100; ☆1, 1973). *Goodbye Yellow Brick Road* (MCA 10003; ☆1, 1973). *Caribou* (MCA 2116; ☆1, 1974). *Elton John—Greatest Hits* (MCA 2128; ☆1, 1974). *Empty Sky* (MCA 2130; ☆6, 1975). *Captain Fantastic and the Brown Dirt Cowboy* (MCA 2142; ☆1, 1975). *Rock of the Westies* (MCA 2163; ☆1, 1975). (Chart positions taken from Joel Whitburn's *Record Research*, compiled from *Billboard* Pop and LPs charts.)

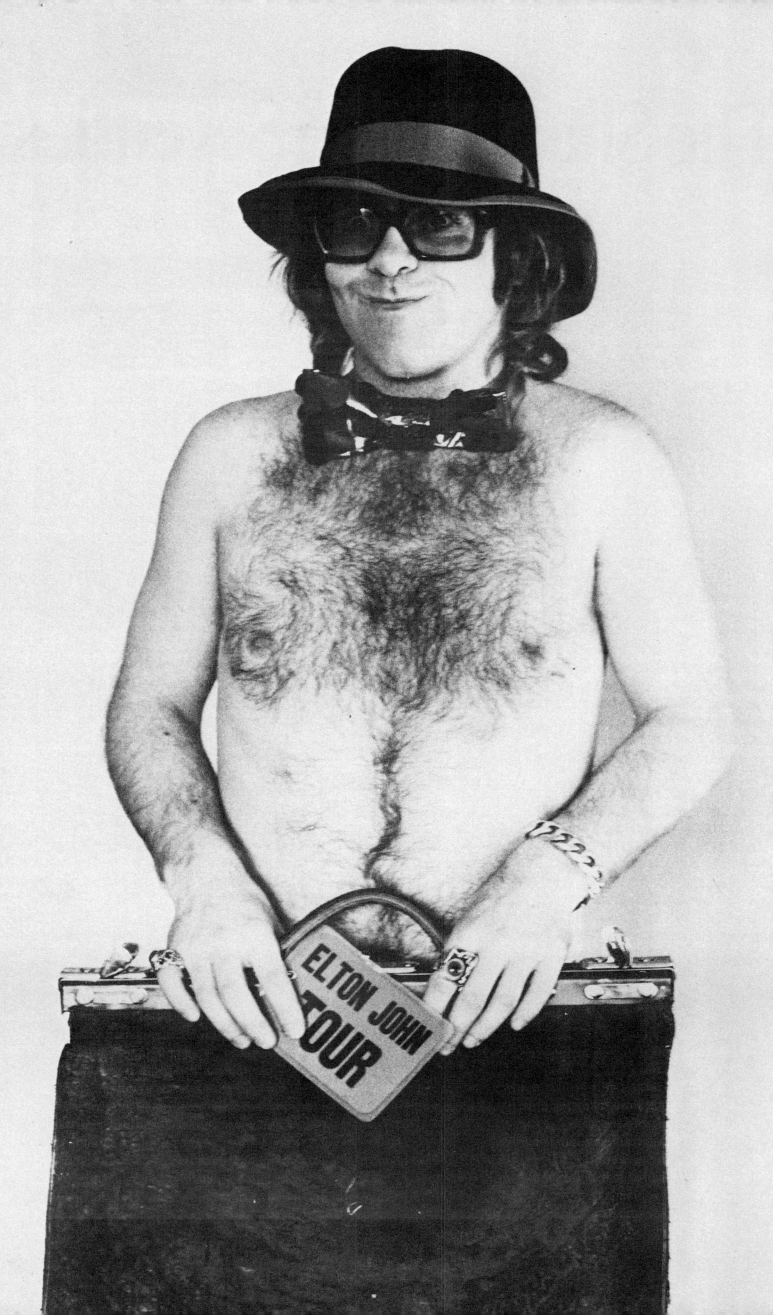

The Shape of the Seventies
by Jim Miller

In the Seventies, disenchantment with rock and roll has become fashionable. The rhetorical question of the previous decade—"Do you believe in magic?"—has met with a resounding response in the negative: as Peter Townshend confessed in the Who's 1975 "Slip Kid," "There's no easy way to be free." Which is true enough. Such demystification, though, has itself proved sterile as often as not; when Neil Young, on Tonight's the Night *(1975), mounted a melodramatic elegy to rock's drug victims, the effect verged unintentionally on parody, as if Young thought the original myths of rock could, inverted, themselves yield an easy truth. That, predictably, has not happened.*

But innocence lost is a saga in itself, and rock in the Seventies has weathered its disillusionment without withering away. As escape and diversion as well as commentary and confrontation, the music has survived, even if it no longer serves as an easy cultural referent. Despite the sense of unfocused drift, rock has continued to span important new genres and bands. Three— Elton John, Al Green, and the sound of Philadelphia—have already been discussed. At least five others deserve close attention: Steely Dan, Roxy Music, disco soul, reggae, and Bruce Springsteen.

Steely Dan

The Thinking Fan's Top 40 band, Steely Dan is the most satisfying new American group of the Seventies. Primarily a studio unit, the Dan was founded in 1972 by Donald Fagen (vocals and keyboards) and Walter Becker (bass), who compose all of the band's material. The two have been associated since the late Sixties; in 1970 and 1971, they worked together backing Jay and the Americans, while attempting to peddle their songs in New York City. When they were signed to ABC records in 1972 by producer Gary Katz, Fagen and Becker assembled the remainder of the group, including Jeff Baxter and Denny Dias, two capable lead guitarists. By the end of 1975, Steely Dan had scored two Top Ten singles, "Do It Again" and "Rikki Don't Lose That Number," and three (out of four) gold albums: *Can't Buy a Thrill*, *Pretzel Logic* and *Katy Lied*.

The band's sound is dominated by Fagen, whose voice, an instrument of narrow range, projects a bruising, nonchalant matter-of-factness, the perfect vessel for sneering put-downs ("Reeling in the Years") or cynical celebrations ("Black Friday"). In the tradition of speaksingers from Dylan to Lou Reed, Fagen has developed a nuanced sense of phrasing that turns technical limitations into an expressive asset.

The lyrics he sings are elusive enough to pass for universal, and evocative enough to identify specific locales and events. Hardly a team of heart-on-the-sleeve confessional writers, they invariably attack their material indirectly, favoring sarcastic portraits and ironic vignettes. The result is oblique, often nasty compositions that are simultaneously intriguing and enigmatic.

The music itself is distinguished by its wit, courting complexity without sacrificing economy. Fagen and Becker rarely let technique dictate their arrangements. Steely Dan's music has a jazz feel: as Walter Becker once put it, "We play rock and roll, but we swing when we play. We want that ongoing flow, that lightness, that forward rush of jazz."

The band's distinctive approach blossomed on *Pretzel Logic* and *Katy Lied*, two of the most brilliant and listenable albums released in the Seventies. With the departure of Baxter for the Doobie Brothers, Steely Dan became almost wholly a creature of Fagen and Becker's imagination. By concentrating on three-minute cuts, they have succeeded in integrating innovative music and cerebral lyrics within a deceptively poppy format— sly subversion for a "million dollar weekend."

Take a song like "Chain Lightning" from *Katy Lied*. A shuffling, shimmering blues line punctuated by a lazy guitar break from Dias, the song seems, in its first verse, to describe a convocation of spiritual cultists: "Don't bother to understand/ Don't question the little man/Be part of the brotherhood/Yes it's chain lightning/It feels so good." The music's arch mellowness belies the lyric; and in the second verse, the gathering has dispersed, and a hip swagger mocks the pieties of roly-poly gurus: "Turn slowly and comb your hair/Don't trouble the midnight air/We're standing just where he stood/It was chain lightning/It feels so . . . good."

Steely Dan is a band very much in control. To this extent, they fall outside the great tradition in rock, for they decline risks and seem to distrust the spontaneity of live performance. They have nevertheless revitalized mainstream rock—and their calculated precision is as symptomatic of the temper of the Seventies as their irony and sarcasm.

Roxy Music

Decadence has been another keynote of rock in the Seventies. Lou Reed has flaunted it, David Bowie has exploited it, the New York Dolls sunk in it. What is different about Roxy Music is the wit with which Bryan Ferry, Roxy's guiding light and lead vocalist, evokes not only decay, but also a last fling in the face of fate.

Ferry approaches decadence, not through tales of self-destruction or redemption, but by depicting romance corrupted. It's easy to moan about heroin, like Lou Reed, or trumpet the coming superman, like Bowie; the prescribed response is either shock, or, if one is inured to such antics, a yawn. But to fashion albums filled with relatively straight love songs that come out sounding like a version of the Decline of the West is no mean feat.

Top: (1) Roxy Music—from left, Andy Mackay, Bryan Ferry, Eddie Jobson, Rick Wills, Phil Manzanera, Paul Thompson. Bottom: (2) Steely Dan—left, Donald Fagen, right, Walter Becker (1, Atlantic Records; 2, ABC Records)

It is as if Ferry ran a cabaret for psychotics, featuring chanteurs in a state of shock. Lyrics, which speak only of *l'amour*, tumble effortlessly, but the novocained lips smack of dementia. Clearly, this is not everybody's cup of tea. Yet Roxy Music has been a hit in Bowiephile Britain ever since their first album was released in 1972.

Initially, the group, formed in 1971 by Ferry, a former art student, featured Brian Eno on synthesizer, as well as Phil Manzanera on guitar and Andy MacKay on sax. Specializing in campy revampings of Fifties styles, garnished by Eno's electronic burps, Roxy found immediate acceptance in England when "Virginia Plain," its first single, became a hit.

After an argument over the band's direction, Eno split in 1973, leaving Ferry to define Roxy's sound; by minimizing the avant-garde veneer, he moved toward a slicker, more basic pop product. On Roxy's last three albums, *Stranded, Country Life* and *Siren,* the group's instrumental attack, spearheaded by MacKay and Manzanera, has been finely honed, without frills.

Torch songs from the crypt—that is the disquieting aspect to Ferry's dandyism: the result is the spectacle of a grown man fluttering in a style not dissimilar to Bobby "Boris" Pickett's on "Monster Mash," cooing about loves lost and "these vintage years." Ferry oscillates unpredictably between camp and deadly seriousness—and when Roxy Music gets serious, they can be scary, even repugnant.

Ferry himself has mastered the role of the sallow blueblood, pitting *l'amour* against *l'ennui.* Yet as he depicts his modern "hero" in a song like "Casanova," the compulsive hedonist is doomed to a life of ephemeral satisfactions. In this context, the most benignly romantic lyrics assume a threatening significance. Eros becomes an uncertain escape, rather than a means of fulfilling desire. In the end, Ferry's *l'amour* is reduced to an idle fantasy; on *Siren,* Ferry explains that he's "just another crazy guy/Playing at love was another high/Just another high." It is precisely this reduction of affection to the level of a narcotic that makes Roxy's music evocative of decadence and which gives the band's persona its cutting edge.

Disco and the Sound of Miami

During the summer of 1973, a crazed instrumental invaded American airwaves; titled "Soul Makossa" by Manu Dibango, an African musician living in Paris, the record, which featured a honking sax skittering across a pounding rhythm section, conjured up some steamy jungle orgy, an impression reinforced by grunts and mumbling. A freak hit, it was a record that would transform the AM singles industry. During the early Seventies, the discotheque scene in New York City, which had flourished during the era of the twist a decade earlier, made a comeback. A new coterie of dancers flocked to lofts and clubs specializing in nonstop recorded music, and a new crew of DJs scouted for records with a big beat, a big sound, or an exotic aura. Although a French import, and the sort of record that is burned in South Carolina, "Soul Makossa" became a favorite with the disco crowd in early 1973; after Atlantic Records picked up American rights, the single became a hit nationwide.

A new route for breaking AM hits was opening up; and a new audience for rhythm and blues dance music was developing. Apart from weird one-shots, the discos drew heavily on soul in the Philadelphia style, as well as singles in a James Brown vein. As the decade progressed, an increasing number of disco-originated hits made the national charts: "Rock the Boat" by the Hues Corporation; "Jungle Boogie" by Kool and the Gang; and "You're the First, the Last, My Everything" by Barry White.

New labels were formed, aimed at the disco market; one-shot hitmakers returned in force, and offbeat records stood an improved chance of making the charts. Best of all, the smaller R&B studios got a new lease on life.

Foremost among these studios is TK, located in Hialeah, Florida. If Philadelphia and New York supplied discos with glossy soul, TK churned out the hardcore funk, becoming the premier Southern soul label of the decade. By the early Seventies, the TK family of labels (Alston, Cat, Glades) had scored a number of regional hits in Florida, and a clutch of pop crossovers: "Clean Up Woman" by Betty Wright, "Funky Nassau" by Beginning of the End, and "Why Can't We Live Together" by Timmy Thomas. Unlike other studios, TK didn't stick to one formula: if TK had a signature, it would be the loping guitars and neo-Caribbean rhythmic feel favored by session guitarist Little Beaver—but "Why Can't We Live Together," for example, featured neither.

The most talented artist in the TK stable is Betty Wright, an original stylist who was only 18 when "Clean Up Woman" was released in 1971. Gifted with a wide range and versatile voice, Wright can shout as well as soothe. She has issued a string of consistent singles during the past few years, ranging from novelty discs modeled after her first hits ("Secretary," "Baby Sitter"), to straightforward soul ("Let Me Be Your Lovemaker," "Shoorah! Shoorah!"). "Where Is the Love," cut in 1974 with KC and the Sunshine Band, threatened to become a disco breakout, but Wright thus far has been frustrated in her attempts to reach a wider audience.

Meanwhile, in 1974 other TK performers began scoring national hits. The most memorable of these, "Rock Your Baby" by George McCrae, was the product of circumstance as much as inspiration. A largely untested songwriting/production team, H.W. Casey and Rick Finch had improvised a sinuous instrumental track, modeled loosely on Bahamian "Junkanoo music." On scouring TK for a suitable vocalist, they discovered McCrae, a lapsed soul performer who was looking after his wife Gwen's career (she would enjoy a Top Ten TK hit in 1975 with "Rockin' Chair"). McCrae, it turned out, had a wavering tenor,

but an earsplitting falsetto. Those vocal ingredients, when added to Casey and Finch's funka nova, catapulted "Rock Your Baby" to the top of the charts in 54 countries, including the United States; it has sold 6.5 million copies worldwide. On the single, McCrae's voice floats in an oceanic echo that seems to engulf his falsetto, while the instrumental track immediately hits a groove that is virtually irresistible.

Other TK acts followed McCrae up the charts. Latimore, an urbane blues stylist given to cocktail keyboard fills, hit with "Let's Straighten It Out"; Little Beaver, a moody vocalist as well as fine guitarist, hit with "Party Down"; and KC and the Sunshine Band, aka H.W. Casey and Rick Finch, hit with "Get Down Tonight," a frantic exercise in redneck soul, launched by an insanely sped-up volley of guitar licks from Finch.

If nothing else, disco has enabled idiosyncratic black music to get national exposure. On the other hand, the ascendance of slick imitation (or real) Philadelphia soul has led to a proliferation of monotonous singles, stuffed with orchestra, echo, and a thump-thump beat; to make matters worse, Gloria Gaynor's success with "Never Can Say Goodbye," originally a hit for the Jackson 5, triggered an avalanche of recycled oldies. The phenomenon that initially challenged the music establishment has become an assembly-line industry in its own right.

Reggae

Throughout the Seventies, the style of Jamaican soul called reggae has intermittently figured on American airwaves, usually in a diluted form: reggae based hits have included Paul Simon's "Mother and Child Reunion," Jimmy Cliff's "Wonderful World, Beautiful People," Johnny Nash's "I Can See Clearly Now" and Eric Clapton's "I Shot the Sheriff." Ironically, the first American reggae hit was one of the most authentic. "Israelites" by Desmond Dekker and the Aces, which made the U.S. Top Ten in early 1969, remains among the most popular reggae discs ever cut, in terms of global sales, and if its pidgin patois and rhythm were a novelty at the time, its lyrics in retrospect seem plain enough: "Get up every morning, slaving for bread, sir/So that every mouth can be fed/Ohh, the Israelites, sir."

Reggae is the most vital adaptation of rhythm and blues since the early days of the Rolling Stones. It began in the early Sixties, when Jamaica's musicians, influenced by New Orleans R&B, evolved their own variant on the Crescent City shuffle, by having the horns riff on the offbeat; the resulting rhythm, which sounded like a Fats Domino record turned inside out, became the trademark of what was called "ska." One ska disc, "My Boy Lollipop" by Millie Small, even became an American hit in 1964.

As ska developed, the prominence of the horns diminished, and the bass and guitar moved into the foreground; the inverted shuffle became syncopated, while the tempo wound

down. "Rock steady" became the local rage in the summer of 1966, when, according to legend, it was too hot to dance fast. Alton Ellis's "Rock Steady," with its sleepy rhythms and cool vocal, set the new trend.

By most accounts, the first record to use the word "reggae" was "Do the Reggay" by the Maytals, released in 1968. With roots in American gospel and soul as well as Jamaican folk music, the Maytals have been transitional figures.

Lyrically, most of the ska and rock steady performers had stuck to stock romantic themes. The Maytals, by contrast, recorded novelty and dance tunes with chanted nonsense verse for lyrics ("Monkey Man"), as well as Christian revivalist anthems ("Loving Spirit," "Revival Reggae"). By updating the mento, Jamaica's indigenous dance form (usually giving two or three lines to a solo singer, alternating with a chanted refrain), the Maytals have been instrumental in resurrecting native musical traditions and imagery. Within the repetitive format of the mento, Toots Hibbert, the Maytals' lead singer, generates an intensity that recalls Otis Redding, Hibbert's American idol.

By the late Sixties, most Jamaican records were being cut with the syncopated lope and prominent bass characteristic of reggae. Yet the music's real distinctiveness came, not from the rhythm, which rock steady had anticipated, but from the performers of the music and the lyrics they sang. In contrast to the revivalist Christianity of the Maytals, most reggae groups espoused Rastafarianism, which in appearance and song conveyed an esoteric cosmology and a fierce pride in being black.

The themes and images of Jamaican music changed. There was "rudie," the hooligan and outsider as hero; and, above all, there was Rasta, the black God (incarnated in the late Emperor Haile Selassie of Ethiopia) who will guide the knowledgeable out of captivity in the white man's Babylon. A new musical world arose, with Rasta at its cosmic source, and Trenchtown, Kingston's ghetto, as its mythic locale.

This world was the subject of Perry Henzell's 1973 film *The Harder They Come*, shot in Jamaica and starring Jimmy Cliff, one of the slicker reggae artists (ironically enough, Cliff is a Black Muslim, not a Rasta). Cliff played an archetypal rudie who made good as a reggae singer, only to be gunned down by white authorities after a desperate odyssey through Trenchtown and the Jamaican countryside.

On record, the same world has been most powerfully evoked by Bob Marley, poet laureate of Rastafarianism and leading light of the Wailers, the most important group reggae has produced. The Wailers were founded around 1964 as a vocal group, featuring Bunny Livingstone and Peter Tosh as well as Marley, the half-caste son of a Jamaican woman and an English captain. The group had a succession of local hits during the Sixties on small labels with names like Coxsone, Wailin' Soul and Tuff Gong; in the late Sixties, Marley met Johnny Nash, and gave him several songs to record, including "Stir It Up," which became a hit for Nash in 1973.

Below: (1) Jimmy Cliff, the Jamaican who starred in 'The Harder They Come' and introduced reggae to the U.S. Though his music has paled in the mid-Seventies, outstripped by that of the Wailers and the Maytals, Cliff's historical importance should not be forgotten. Near left: (2) Bryan Ferry, maestro of Roxy Music. Right, center: (3) Bob Marley of the Wailers (1, Gleason collection; 2, ROLLING STONE; 3, Gleason collection)

Where Toots and the Maytals put on the heat, Marley and the Wailers specialize in the slow burn. Marley, in his brittle vocals, maintains a studied dryness, leaving it to Peter Tosh to add a hint of gruffness (not unlike David Ruffin with the Temptations) while Bunny Livingstone provides falsetto (shades of Curtis Mayfield). Thanks to Lee Perry's echoed production, their hits from the early Seventies on Tuff Gong often sounded like messages from another planet—an effect calculated to underline the otherworldliness of Marley's vision, invoking the one true reality of Rasta.

Most of Marley's compositions hover in a half-haze of mystery, although his metaphors are pungent enough, and the beat compelling enough, to create the impression, even for the attentive outsider, of privileged spiritual access—as if the listener were privy, however indirectly, to a kind of Jamaican gnosticism.

"I Shot the Sheriff" is typical. Introduced by parched rim shots from the drums, the group enters ethereally over muffled guitar and staccato piano: "I shot the sheriff/But I swear it was in self-defense." Marley's taut phrasing accents the song's protest against oppression: "Every day the bucket a go a well/One day the bottom a go drop out."

It is a righteous threat reiterated elsewhere by Marley, although the goal is life, not martyrdom: "Give me the food and let me grow." Typically, the Rasta's pride assaults Mammon's vanity: "If you are a big tree/We are the small ax/Sharpened to cut you down/Ready to cut you down . . ."

In 1973, Marley signed an international contract with Island Records. He has since recorded three fine studio albums, utilizing synthesizer, female choruses and all the paraphernalia of the modern studio; and he has also toured the United States and England. Although the original Wailers disbanded in 1974, Marley continues to produce potent new songs.

In his music and lyrics, Marley lets the mute wisdom within an oppressed people speak, by recollecting the travails of captivity. This message is crucially transmitted by a staccato guitar, a hollow drum, and a bounding bass: for, as Marley put it in "Trenchtown Rock," "One good thing about music/When it hits you feel no pain."

Bruce Springsteen

In 1973, yet another would-be star was introduced to the rock scene. Touted as the latest in a long line of "new" Dylans, Bruce Springsteen, a 23-year-old veteran of the New Jersey bar-band circuit, stirred mild interest among critics and FM listeners, only to retire from the media spotlight, back into the clubs that had been his first home.

It seemed a familiar tale. Throughout the Seventies, new acts arrived on a wave of hype, cut a couple of albums, and then vanished into second-level oblivion. Rarely did the talent merit the hype.

Bruce Springsteen was different. Raised in Asbury Park, a decaying summer resort town on the Jersey coast, he in many respects represented a throwback to the great trashy white R&B bands of the Sixties, such as Mitch Ryder and the Young Rascals. Promoted as a singer/songwriter, he was misunderstood and dismissed. His lyrics often seemed dumb; his first band was saddled with a ham-fisted drummer. He was untidy, effusive, and he looked like a lowlife throwaway.

Throughout 1973 and '74, Springsteen worked the East Coast, whipping his band into shape, gradually attracting fans. Early in 1974, ROLLING STONE writer Jon Landau, curious about Springsteen's cult following in the Boston area, attended a local concert; afterward, in what may be the most quoted quip from a rock critic, he declared in Boston's *Real Paper*, "I saw rock and roll future, and its name is Bruce Springsteen." His records, the word went out, did not accurately reflect his talents: Springsteen had to be seen to be believed.

And indeed those who came to see generally went away converts. Springsteen's label, Columbia, sensed they had a winner, if only Springsteen could cut a strong LP, and tour the nation to support it. With Landau signed on as coproducer, Springsteen entered the studios in April of 1975 to cut his third album (earlier attempts had proven abortive, as Springsteen strained to create a perfect record). That album, *Born to Run*, generated an intensive publicity campaign, and catapulted Springsteen onto the covers of *Time* and *Newsweek*.

If the response to Springsteen says something about the public's (and the media's) hunger for a new rock hero, it also says something about the man's inner drive and talents. Wearing a leather jacket and baggy pants, he fills a stage with unbridled energy, pacing nervously, leading his band through crescendo after crescendo of exhausting climaxes. The sound itself, while raw and purely rock and roll, is also mercilessly tight, and, on a good night, exhilarating: a distillation of every hit from the early Sixties rolled into one cosmic jukebox blaring jangled echoes of Jr. Walker, Phil Spector, Bob Dylan, catalyzed by Springsteen's own guttersnipe vocals, contorted, unafraid to aim for the feeling of the moment.

The sense of déjà vu, which never descends to the level of mere nostalgia, works to Springsteen's benefit: by drawing on the rock and soul tradition, in all its diversity—from rockabilly and surf instrumentals to girl groups and the simplicity of the Stax rhythm section—Springsteen conveys a timeless world of perpetual youth, where all the archetypal characters of the rock 'n' roll world find a home. In the process, he makes that world seem vital again.

His lyrics are central to this conception. He works with a continuing cast that populates the same desolate streets of the "runaway American dream." It is a dream where escape comes hard, in cars and back streets, perhaps in a fleeting snatch of some half-forgotten rock song. There is much to say here, but little to talk about: Springsteen paints vivid characters, but the situations are stock, the action often stale; many songs suggest a soapy retread of *West Side Story*.

In the studio, this obsession takes the shape of piecemeal, track-by-track recording, a painfully slow process that perpetually threatens to shatter the spontaneity of the moment it is intended to trap. What appears onstage as inspired intuition becomes in the studio a meticulous effort at *making* a song; in this sense, Springsteen cuts records like Phil Spector or Brian Wilson, and his obsession becomes one of making the moment an eternity. He may be a primitive, but he sees himself as an artist expressing himself in the only medium he knows.

These are a lot of contradictory impulses for one performer to sustain, and Springsteen does not always succeed; by trying too hard, Springsteen risks pretentiousness and a cold perfectionism. And yet he is too impulsive for that. On *Born to Run*, his vocals project a visceral intensity at odds with the massed sound surrounding them (there are six guitar tracks on "She's the One," for example). "Backstreets," which opens with an eerily echoed passage reminiscent of the Shangri-Las' "Remember (Walkin' in the Sand)," finds Springsteen screaming for his life, as if it might redeem a "love so hard and filled with defeat."

Still, there is something troubling about the trajectory of Springsteen's career. In the search for superstardom, the safest bet is to latch onto something comfortable, familiar—and Springsteen's characters and melodies are nothing if not familiar, despite the original vision behind his renewal of the rock tradition. Such conflicting currents epitomize the ambiguous vitality of rock in the Seventies. In Springsteen's person, we find the contradictory claims of the old and new, and the critic faces the difficult task of discriminating genuine enthusiasm from reflex raves for a talent of recognizable dimensions. Springsteen himself has come to despise the high-pressure publicity surrounding his career; it's impossible to be the "future" of rock and roll, and Springsteen knows it.

That such oracular pronouncements are made, however, and that the desire for a new rock hero can be so effectively exploited, tells us something about the contemporary mechanics of rock, at a time when the music has become self-conscious about its own mythmaking potential.

Springsteen may prove a casualty of an era eager for new illusions, nostalgic for the simpler past rock once reflected, yet wary of false promises and resentful of stampedes to new superstars. The best rock still aspires to tap the temper of its time, to move an audience, and to profit from fulfilling its needs and expectations. Whether it can do so any longer without sacrificing the immediacy of its original impulses is the hard question raised by the orchestrated apotheosis of Bruce Springsteen as a pop hero for the Seventies.

Discography

Steely Dan
Can't Buy a Thrill (ABC 758; ☆17, 1972). *Countdown to Ecstasy* (ABC 779; ☆35, 1973). *Pretzel Logic* (ABC 808, ☆8, 1974). *Katy Lied* (ABC 846; ☆14, 1975).

Roxy Music
Roxy Music (Reprise 2114, 1972). *For Your Pleasure* (Warner Bros. 2696; ☆193, 1973). *Stranded* (Atco 7045; ☆186, 1974). *Country Life* (Atco 106; ☆37, 1975). *Siren* (Atco 127; ☆50, 1975).

The Sound of Miami
Betty Wright "Girls Can't Do What the Guys Do" (Alston 4569; r☆15, ☆33, 1968). "Clean Up Woman" (Alston 4601; r☆2, ☆6, 1971). "Is It You Girl" (Alston 4611; r☆18, 1972). "Baby Sitter" (Alston 4614; r☆6, ☆46, 1972). "It's Hard To Stop (Doing Something When It's Good to You)" (Alston 4617; r☆11, ☆72, 1973). "Let Me Be Your Lovemaker" (Alston 4619; r☆10, ☆55, 1973). "Secretary" (Alston 4622; r☆12, ☆62, 1974). "Shoorah! Shoorah!" (Alston 3711; r☆28, 1974). "Where Is the Love" (Alston 3713; r☆15, 1975). **Timmy Thomas** "Why Can't We Live Together" (Glades 1703; r☆1, ☆3, 1972). "What Can I Tell Her" (Glades 1717; r☆19, 1973). **Beginning of the End** "Funky Nassau—Part I" (Alston 4595; r☆7, ☆15, 1971). **George McCrae** "Rock Your Baby" (TK 1004; r☆1, ☆1, 1974). "I Can't Leave You Alone" (TK 1007; r☆10, ☆50, 1974). "I Get Lifted (TK 1007; r☆8, 1974). **KC and the Sunshine Band** "Blow Your Whistle" (TK 1001; r☆27, 1973). "Sound Your Funky Horn" (TK 1003; r☆21, 1974). "Get Down Tonight" (TK 1009; r☆1, ☆1, 1975). "That's the Way (I Like It)" (TK 1015, r☆1, ☆1, 1975). **Gwen McCrae** "For Your Love" (Cat 1989; r☆17, 1973). "Rockin' Chair" (Cat 1996; r☆1, ☆9, 1975). **Latimore** "Let's Straighten It Out" (Glades 1722; r☆1, ☆31, 1974). **Little Beaver** "Party Down" (Cat 1993; r☆2, 1974). **Clarence Reid** "Nobody but You Babe" (Alston 4574; r☆7, ☆40, 1969). "Funky Party" (Alston 4621; r☆17, 1974).

Reggae
Toots and the Maytals *From the Roots* (Trojan 65 [British import]). *Funky Kingston* (Island 9330; ☆164, 1975). **Bob Marley and the Wailers** *African Herbsman* (Trojan 62 [British import]). *Rasta Revolution* (Trojan 89 [British import]). *Catch a Fire* (Island 9241; ☆171, 1975; originally released 1973). *Burnin'* (Island 9256; ☆151, 1974). *Natty Dread* (Island 9281; ☆92, 1975).

Bruce Springsteen
Greetings from Asbury Park (Columbia 31903; ☆60, 1973). *The Wild, the Innocent and the E Street Shuffle* (Columbia 32432; ☆59, 1973). *Born to Run* (Columbia 33795; ☆3, 1975).
(All chart positions compiled from Joel Whitburn's *Record Research,* based on *Billboard* Pop and LPs charts, unless otherwise indicated; r☆ = position on *Billboard* Rhythm and Blues chart.)

Rock Gallery

Isley Brothers

The Isley Brothers came out of Cincinnati in the mid-Fifties, graduating from gospel to R&B on the Midwestern circuit of black bars and roadhouses. Their first break on the charts came with "Shout" in 1959 on RCA Victor; in the best tradition of frenzied gospel, the million-selling single was a delirious two-sided call-and-response orgy that briefly catapulted the brothers into the national limelight. But it was only in 1962 that the Isleys hit the charts again, this time with "Twist and Shout," the toughest of the twist records (and the source of the Beatles' version). Thus far, the brothers seemed a rotgut R&B band with two great singles to their credit; a stint on Berry Gordy's Tamla label yielded one more hit ("This Old Heart of Mine," #12, 1966), but the Motown machinery couldn't retool for the Isleys, who were carefully following the growing progressive-rock movement. The brothers had moved to Britain, where they experimented with their sound. Their return to the U.S. was triumphant, as "It's Your Thing" got to Number Two in 1969 on the Isley's own label, T-Neck. The group, which always boasted a trio of capable lead singers (Ronald, Kelly and Rudolph Isley) was augmented by younger brother Ernie Isley, a guitarist inspired by Jimi Hendrix. Working in a rockish mode parallel to that of Sly Stone, the Isleys enjoyed consistent success in the Seventies, creating such subtly innovative tracks as "Work to Do" (R&B #11, 1972) and "That Lady" (#6, 1973), a sweetly buzzing cut ignited by Ernie Isley's snaking guitar line.

Jan and Dean

In the academy of surf and music, Jan and Dean played Spike Jones to Brian Wilson's Beethoven. The duo, boyhood chums from L.A., began their career as fans dabbling in rock, scoring their first Top Ten hit in 1958 (with "Jennie Lee," credited to "Jan and Arnie," but sung by Jan, Dean and Arnie Ginsberg—who shortly after left for the navy). For several years, Jan Berry and Dean Torrance led split lives, recording singles like "Baby Talk" (#10, 1959) and "Heart and Soul" (#25, 1961) in a heavily echoed doo-wop style, while pursuing studies in college. In 1963, they met Brian Wilson; his composition, "Surf City," which roared to Number One in 1963, inaugurated a three-year run on the charts for Jan and Dean. On singles like "Dead Man's Curve" (#8, 1964) and "The Little Old Lady (from Pasadena)" (#3, 1964), they essayed their own brand of zany L.A. pop, employing the best studio musicians in town and drawing repeatedly on Brian Wilson, who helped write many of their hits. The duo's career skidded to a halt in April 1966, after Jan Berry was critically injured in an automobile crash. Today Dean Torrance is a graphic designer in Los Angeles, while Jan continues to recover from his accident.

Danny and the Juniors

Danny and the Juniors captured the essence of the *American Bandstand* era. The quartet formed when Danny and friends were high school classmates in Philly; a local entrepreneur caught their act in 1957 and helped the group compose and record a song called "At the Hop" for Singular, a local label. When the disc became a city-wide hit, ABC-Paramount picked up national rights, and watched the record rise to Number One. Unlike many another white Philly act, Danny and the Juniors evinced their own ebullient brand of authenticity; hardly manicured idols, they succeeded solely on the basis of the music they made. And what music: from the opening "bah bah bah bah," each group member chiming in over a charging backbeat piano, to the final resounding "at the hop!," their hit moves relentlessly forward, manically invoking the good times to be had dancing to rock 'n' roll. Like Chuck Berry's finest songs, "At the Hop" encapsulates an entire way of life in a three-minute rush, all the more compelling for the group's breathless enthusiasm. Danny and the Juniors enjoyed some success with their followup, the rather stiff "Rock 'n' Roll Is Here to Stay." But they never again approached their one moment of accidental genius.

Dusty Springfield

Dusty Springfield (real name: Mary O'Brien) first achieved prominence with the Springfields, a trio of British singers prematurely into folk rock (their 1962 version of "Silver Threads and Golden Needles" got to Number 20 in the U.S.). At the end of 1963, the group split up, but Dusty, adapting the trio's moniker, moved on to a solo career at Philips, picking up an early hit with "I Only Want to Be with You" (#12, 1964). Like such peers as Petula Clark and Cilla Black, Dusty was essentially a pop stylist; unlike them, she had a distinctive and totally erotic delivery, built around a wispy voice that moved effortlessly from seductive whispers to passionate shouts (in range, her only peer was Dionne Warwick). Throughout the Sixties, she enjoyed consistent success with singles like "Wishin' and Hopin' " (#6, 1964—originally cut by Warwick), "You

Don't Have to Say You Love Me" (#4, 1966) and "The Look of Love" (#22, 1967). But her consummate achievement was the album *Dusty in Memphis,* produced by Jerry Wexler, et al., featuring Dusty on 11 spectacular songs from the likes of Randy Newman and Goffin-King; the best pop-rock LP of the late Sixties, it contained Dusty's last Top Ten hit in America, "Son-of-a-Preacher Man" (#10, 1968). She has since recorded one fine album with Gamble and Huff in Philadelphia (*A Brand New Me,* 1970) and a number of tracks released on several American and English albums.

Wilbert Harrison

Wilbert Harrison wasn't a one-hit wonder, not quite, even if "Kansas City" may have appeared on more oldies anthologies than any other 45 made in the last 20 years. Born in North Carolina in 1929, Harrison first performed in the early Fifties as a one-man band, and in 1959 cut a new version of Little Willie Littlefield's "K.C. Loving" (written by Jerry Leiber and Mike Stoller), a 1952 R&B hit. As "Kansas City" the disc took off immediately and was instantly covered by other artists, including Little Richard (on whose version the Beatles' later waxing of the tune was based). Wilbert made it to Number One anyway, thanks to a smooth shuffle arrangement and a plaintive man-on-the-street vocal. No sooner here than there, Harrison disappeared from the pop scene to travel a low-rent circuit with the word "HIT!" and a copy of "Kansas City" pasted to the bass drum he carried with him, only to return ten years later with his brilliant "Let's Work Together" (#32, 1969), as infectious and deeply felt a plea for racial understanding as pop music has produced. Harrison followed his second hit with a superb one-man-band album of R&B classics (*Let's Work Together,* Sue Records), a few other LPs that were not superb, and another disappearing act. Still, he may be back.

Del Shannon

Rock and roll has occasionally been praised for its democracy of talent: everybody's a (potential) star, even the kid next door. While this maxim has excused a lot of mediocrity, it also pinpoints the charm of a performer like Del Shannon. Born Charles Westover in Grand Rapids, Michigan, Del was discovered by a local DJ in the early Sixties while performing in the area. In almost any other game, he would have been written off as a modestly talented local boy. But the local rock moguls, ever eager for a quick buck, jumped: on the strength of his roughhewn voice and original composition, Shannon was contracted to Big Top Records, flown to New York and set loose in a studio. Among his first batch of sides was "Runaway," perhaps the most searing teen angst anthem of the early Sixties. The song, taken at a nervous tempo, found Del brooding over a lost love, tensely charting the minor-key chorus in his midrange before exuberantly exploding into a major key release ("I'm a-walking in the rain") and finally unleashing a torrential falsetto on the tag ("I wo-wo-wo-wo-wonder . . . "). Garnished by a berserk organ break at half time, "Runaway" easily cut through the heavily produced Brill Building pop dominating the radio in 1960, going all the way to Number One—an auspicious debut for the kid next door. Over the next three years, Del went on to record several more hits in a similar vein, giving adolescent themes a rare hard edge: his followup, "Hats Off to Larry," got to #5 in '61, to be followed by "Little Town Flirt" (#12, 1962), a remake of Jimmy Jones's "Handy Man" (#22, 1964), and "Keep Searchin' " (#9, 1964). A late Sixties comeback attempt flopped; Shannon remains a star in England.

Chuck Willis

Chuck Willis, who wore a turban and called himself the "King of the Stroll," cut first-rate R&B in the early Fifties on Okeh and made pop hits in the mid-Fifties on Atlantic. Born in Atlanta in 1928, he first gained fame in 1956 with his beautiful "It's Too Late" (covered later by Derek and the Dominos), which he followed in 1957 with "C.C. Rider," an impeccable version of the ancient country blues theme and also Willis's biggest hit. Willis was a tearjerker and a great one; stylistically he owed most to Johnny Ace, the sweet-voiced R&B supplicant who died in 1954. There was little aggression in Willis's music; instead he offered a sort of cosmic world-weariness. So slow, so pretty, so sad, so right. So right, in fact, that when his last hit, the almost unconscionably world-weary "What Am I Living For," entered the charts in 1958, Willis was dead.

Clockwise from top left: (1) Wilbert Harrison,
at the time of "Let's Work Together"; (2) The Isley
Brothers, from the early Sixties; (3) Dusty Springfield; (4) Danny
and the Juniors; (5) Del Shannon; (6) Jan and Dean. Center: (7) Chuck Willis,
"king of the stroll" (1, 3 & 6, ROLLING STONE; 2, Vince Aletti, 4 & 5,
Michael Ochs Archives; 7, collection of Radio KRLA)

Ben E. King and the Drifters

In the summer of 1958, manager George Treadwell was faced with a problem: one of his most popular acts, the Drifters, had just disbanded, after a distinguished five-year career. Loathe to surrender the group name, Treadwell decided to hire a completely new quartet, the Five Crowns of New York, to carry on. Their lead singer was one Benjamin Nelson, who became familiar to rock fans as Ben E. King. With King at the helm, the Drifters enjoyed a major renaissance, thanks in large part to the brilliant production work of Jerry Leiber and Mike Stoller. In 1959, Leiber and Stoller devised a Latin-flavored piece of melodrama called "There Goes My Baby" for the new Drifters' debut on Atlantic. One of the first R&B singles to use strings, the disc eventually sold a million copies, cresting at Number Two. Over the next 18 months, Leiber and Stoller devised a succession of stunning settings for King's suave pleading: "Dance with Me" (#15, 1959), "This Magic Moment" (#16, 1960), "Save the Last Dance for Me" (#1, 1960), culminating in "I Count the Tears" (#17, 1960). All of these records—which sounded like some marvelous marriage of Tchaikovsky, Gershwin and the Penguins—featured swirling orchestral scores and throbbing Latin rhythm sections. The mix was catchy: in effect, the Leiber-Stoller Drifters sessions forged a new orthodoxy in black (and white) popular music. Within a few months, dozens of rock singles were on the radio with strings and a samba sway. At the end of 1960, Ben E. King went on to a successful solo career, cutting such other Leiber-Stoller landmarks as "Spanish Harlem" (coauthored by Phil Spector) and "Stand by Me." The refurbished Drifters, for their part, remained on top with locational hits like "Up on the Roof," "On Broadway" and "Under the Boardwalk," finally scattering into a series of "the *Real* Drifters" revival groups, which haunt the scene to this day.

The Monkees

The consummate artifact of rock consumption was the Monkees, the first major rock band expressly designed, casted, and manufactured for pop stardom. After watching the Beatles tear up America in 1964, Don Kirshner, the mastermind behind the Brill Building pop scene, realized that the Liverpudlians had unleashed a potent—and potentially lucrative—mania that had yet to be fully tapped. In conjunction with Columbia Pictures, he came up with the idea for a TV series modeled after *A Hard Day's Night,* featuring a quartet of mop tops romping about in prime time. Guided by criteria gleaned from pilot scripts and Kirshner's own shrewd sense of the pop marketplace, four Monkees were chosen in auditions. The execs settled on Micky Dolenz and David Jones, two actors who had never played a note, and Peter Tork and Mike Nesmith, two musicians who oozed charm. With discs and material finely crafted by Jeff Barry ("I'm a Believer," #1, 1966) and Tommy Boyce and Bobby Hart ("Last Train to Clarksville," #1, 1966), the quartet sang its way to overnight superstardom, helped mightily along by their TV show, which premiered in September 1966. From there on, it was rough flying through two more years of chart success: in 1967, they came clean in a New York press conference, revealing that none of them played on their records: "We're being passed off as something we aren't." Monkees fans recovered from the shock long enough to buy a few more million albums. Finally in 1968 the group's video series was canceled; their raison d'être removed, the band dissolved, although Nesmith went on to become one of the more eccentric L.A. country rockers.

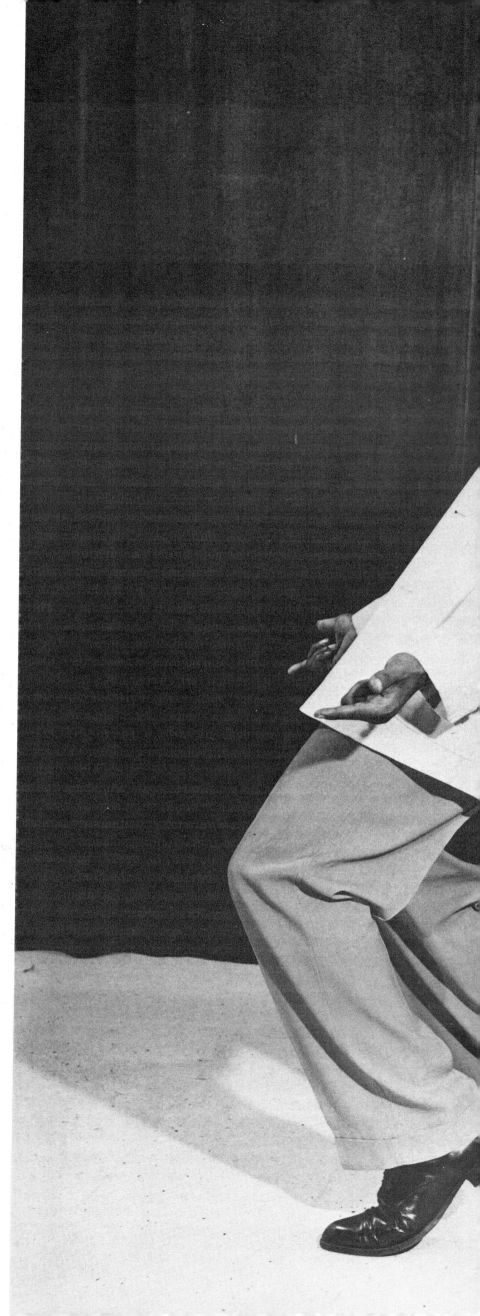

Johnnie and Joe

One-shot hits by obscure performers are the stuff of rock 'n' roll myth, and few performers from the Fifties are more obscure than Johnnie and Joe, who scored one—and only one—hit in 1957 with "Over the Mountain; Across the Sea." Like an unfocused and fading photograph, the record casts a bizarre spell, as the duo wobble their way through a lyric lucid only in its intensity. No other performance from the period is murkier, or more magical, thanks in large part to the disturbing falsetto/moan wavering behind the lead voice, which isn't so rock steady itself. Recently, new light has been cast on the Johnnie and Joe story by writer Norm N. Nite, who tells the following tale: 20-year-old Joe Rivers first heard "Over the Mountain" played by a neighbor in the Bronx who had written it. When Joe decided to record the song, he chose as his partner a friend's daughter, 12-year-old Johnnie Sanders. The home demo they cut was sold to Chess Records, and eventually reached Number Eight. For Johnnie and Joe that was both the beginning and the end.

Bo Diddley

Bo Diddley was the most idiosyncratic of the early rock 'n' rollers. Born in Mississippi (real name: Ellis McDaniel), he was raised on blues in Chicago. Diddley's signature was a snaking rumba rhythm played on his tremoloed electric guitar, accompanied by Jerome Green on maracas. Starting in 1955, Diddley recorded everything from ballads to blues for Chicago's Checker label, but his biggest records were either nonsense songs with his characteristic beat ("Bo Diddley," his first hit in 1955), or novelty discs like "Say Man" (cut in 1958 without Bo's knowledge while he and Jerome were horsing around at a session). Diddley's guitar collection was legendary: every album showed off a different axe (one was carpeted, another square). His stage show was equally renowned. He would pick his guitar with his teeth, play it behind his back, flaunt it as a phallic totem, even set it afire—Jimi Hendrix had nothing on Bo. Although he enjoyed few Top 40 hits, his influence has been pervasive—the Yardbirds covered "I'm a Man," perhaps his best-known blues composition; and the Rolling Stones borrowed the Bo Diddley beat for "Not Fade Away" and "Empty Heart"—and will likely continue to affect the form and the feeling of rock and roll as long as the form and feeling last.

Mitch Ryder and the Detroit Wheels

In late 1965, when inspired rock and roll seemed almost a commonplace on AM radio, Mitch Ryder and the Detroit Wheels weighed in with "Jenny Take a Ride!," a volatile Little Richard retread sent up with electrifying rasps from vocalist Ryder. The band proceeded to release a clutch of singles topped by "Devil with a Blue Dress On" and "Good Golly Miss Molly" (#4, 1966). All featured Ryder's raving R&B vocals (dues paid in full to Wilson Pickett) and, faintly in the background, the Detroit Wheels, one of the hottest white bands of the era. The Wheels were only faintly in the background, as it happens, thanks to producer Bob Crewe, a veteran who had also worked with the Four Seasons; he preferred handclaps to blues licks, and encouraged his boy Mitch to break out as a solo act and sink his teeth into some really meaty material, like "What Now My Love." That was the end. The Detroit Wheels disbanded, while Ryder's career sputtered to a halt. Around 1969, he retreated to Detroit, where he gave rock and roll one last try with the band Detroit: they made one nice album and faded into oblivion. While the echoes of Ryder's music lingered on in the Motor City madness of the MC5 and the guitar sound of Alice Cooper, Mitch now works in a warehouse in Denver.

Captain Beefheart

Of all the freakish acts promoted during the psychedelic euphoria of the late Sixties, only Captain Beefheart stands out as an artist of genius—an appellation most other pretenders stabbed for through a fumbling welter of fuzztone noodling. The Captain—née Don Van Vliet, a native of Glendale, California—enjoyed his first and only local hit in 1966 with a bluesy remake of Bo Diddley's "Diddy Wah Diddy," but his label, A&M, was so nonplussed by the tapes he submitted shortly afterward that they dropped their option on Beefheart. He was the most idiosyncratic of artists in an era that prized idiosyncrasy; yet he was too uncompromising to win the growing audience for personalized rock "art." Beefheart's aesthetic breakthrough came in 1969, after he linked up with high school friend Frank Zappa; Zappa cut Beefheart's *Trout Mask Replica*, capturing Van Vliet's stream-of-consciousness creativity in all its quirky integrity. His sound was all grunts, guitar, lunging rhythms and koan pun lyrics. The glossy psychedelic veneer of his two earlier albums was stripped to showcase Beefheart's unique

ecological vision and his craggy music, equal parts Howlin' Wolf, Albert Ayler and pure Van Vliet. Although the album was an unqualified—and brave—artistic triumph, the Captain's magic was not immediately marketable. Undaunted, Beefheart and his label, Reprise, took his case to the country; for three years, Van Vliet toured regularly with his marvelous Magic Band, playing space blues and earth songs, slowly amassing a hardcore cult following. It was to no avail. Van Vliet kept grasping for more, aiming at the mass audience, subtly diluting his most personal modes of expression. By 1972, Beefheart's momentum had faltered; in 1974, he left Reprise for Mercury, where he released two abysmal stabs at the hit parade. In retrospect, it seems a typical tale of self-destruction, as the innovative energies spontaneously unleashed in a performer in a popular medium become compromised by desire for stardom and a success of orthodox dimensions. But Van Vliet's saga is not quite over; he did a short tour with Frank Zappa and at last report was working on a new solo venture.

Barbara Lewis

Certain pop records are so perfectly turned that it seems only serendipity could explain them. Barbara Lewis's "Hello Stranger" is a prime example. Framed by a soapy organ line, the song is introduced by a male harmony group chanting hypnotically, "Shoo-wop doo-wop, my baby." When Barbara Lewis enters, she purrs in an unforgettable spine-tingling warble, babyish and sexy simultaneously. The track is unencumbered by strings, chorales, or any of the orthodox paraphernalia of a hit single in 1963; yet "Hello Stranger" climbed to Number Three, thanks, perhaps, to the unblemished purity of the interplay between Lewis and the vocal group. While she went on to cut several other memorable hits—"Baby, I'm Yours" (#11, 1965) and "Make Me Your Baby" (#11, 1965)—produced and ornately orchestrated by Bert Berns, her finest hour could not be duplicated or even approached by a full-scale pop onslaught a la Phil Spector. The simplicity behind greatness in rock is sometimes staggering.

Gary "U.S." Bonds

Born Gary Anderson in Jacksonville, Florida, Gary "U.S." Bonds started singing in church as a youngster. In 1960, he met Frank Guida, a producer from Norfolk, Virginia, who had definite ideas of how to cut pop rhythm and blues. Although such dance hits as "New Orleans" (#6, 1960), "Quarter to Three" (#1, 1961), "School Is Out" (#5, 1961) and "Dear Lady Twist" (#9, 1961) always emphasized a bottom-heavy rhythm section and grunting saxophones, Guida's *sound* was his unique ingredient. Rumors had it that Guida recorded Bonds in an open field next to an airport runway while planes took off—and given the blizzard of white noise that accompanied Gary's hits, the story was quite credible. The needle drops down on a perfectly clean pressing only to be overwhelmed by an incredible snap-crackle-and-pop hissing; a lumbering bass drum and echoed handclaps introduce Bonds, who invariably triple-tracked his vocals to a new pitch of garbled frenzy. All of this sonic pandemonium was quite enough to mask the tough R&B basics Bonds and his musicians actually played. Next to Sam Phillips at Sun and Phil Spector at Philles, Guida and Bonds coined the most original sound in rock and roll—something like soulful mud.

Paul Revere and the Raiders

Paul Revere and the Raiders (Paul Revere was the leader's real name) won fame and fortune through a classically circuitous route. Although lead singer Mark Lindsay was a mainstay of the band from the early days, the Raiders originally specialized in such raunchy instrumentals as "Like, Long Hair," a modest hit in 1961. Over the next few years, the band consolidated its following in the Pacific Northwest, finally signing with Columbia in 1963. For starters, the company released the Raiders' "Louie Louie," a remake of the Richard Berry classic, only to see the subsequently released Kingsmen version take chart honors. In '64, the group moved on to San Francisco, where they packed local clubs; from there, it was on to L.A., where they cut two polished classics of punk rock, "Steppin' Out" and "Just like Me" (#11, 1965). The boys with the revolutionary costumes had come to the attention of Dick Clark, then casting a new TV series called *Where the Action Is*, and suddenly the seasoned bar band from Portland, Oregon, was in the thick of the Hollywood production crush. Terry Melcher, a veteran of the first Bryds sessions, began to produce the band, employing L.A.'s blue-chip sessionmen on the instrumental tracks; the best Brill Building tunesmiths were contracted to write for the group. The result was a string of brilliantly contrived hard-rock singles: "Kicks" (#4, 1966), "Hungry" (#6, 1966), "Good Thing" (#4, 1966) and "Him or Me—What's It Gonna Be?" (#5, 1967). Although the Raiders continued to have hits into the Seventies, they only returned to the top with "Indian Reservation," a wretched Number One hit in 1971.

PAUL REVERE +
THE RAIDERS

Index

Contributors

LESTER BANGS was an editor of *Creem* for five years. He has written about rock for ROLLING STONE since 1969, and has also contributed to the *Village Voice*, the *Chicago Tribune*, *Playboy*, *Oui*, *Penthouse*, *Stereo Review*, *Punk* and *Ms.*

HARPER BARNES is a feature writer for the *St. Louis Post-Dispatch*. The editor of the original Boston *Phoenix*, he also has written for the *Atlantic Monthly*, the *Village Voice*, the *Washington Post*, *New Times*, the *Boston Globe* and Boston's *Real Paper*.

ROBERT CHRISTGAU, music editor for the *Village Voice*, is the author of *Any Old Way You Choose It* (Penguin). His articles have appeared in *Esquire*, Long Island's *Newsday*, the *New York Times*, the *Washington Post*, *Creem* and *Cheetah*.

NIK COHN is the author of *Rock from the Beginning* (Stein and Day) and several novels, most recently *King Death* (Harcourt). With the artist Guy Peelaert, he conceived *Rock Dreams* (Popular Library). Currently he is a contributing editor at *New York* magazine.

JONATHAN COTT is the author of *He Dreams What Is Going On in His Head—Ten Years of Writing* (Straight Arrow), a collection of poems, interviews and essays, and *City of 'Earthly Love* (Stonehill), a book of poems. Among his other works are *Stockhausen: Conversations with the Composer* (Simon & Schuster) and an anthology of Victorian children's fantasy stories, *Beyond the Looking Glass* (Stonehill/Bowker). Currently he is an associate editor at ROLLING STONE. He has contributed to the *New York Times*, *American Review*, *Ramparts* and *American Poetry Review*.

KEN EMERSON is an editor of the *Boston Phoenix;* his music reviews have been published in ROLLING STONE, the *Village Voice*, the *New York Times*, the *Boston Globe*, *Creem*, *Fusion* and *Avatar*.

RUSSELL GERSTEN has written about soul for ROLLING STONE, Boston's *Real Paper* and the original Boston *Phoenix*.

PETER GURALNICK is the author of *Feel like Going Home* (Dutton). His articles on blues, country-western and rock and roll have appeared in ROLLING STONE, the *Village Voice*, *Country Music*, *Fusion*, *Creem*, Boston's *Real Paper* and the *Boston Phoenix*.

BARRY HANSEN is familiar to fans of his syndicated radio program of "legendary loony laughin' records" as Dr. Demento. He has written for ROLLING STONE and *Hit Parader*; he compiled the Specialty Records reissue series, and, since 1971, the Warner Brothers "loss leader" double albums. He holds an M.A. in folk music from UCLA, and has taught a course there on the development of rock.

JON LANDAU is the author of *It's Too Late to Stop Now* (Straight Arrow). He has written extensively about rock in the original Boston *Phoenix*, the original *Crawdaddy*, and ROLLING STONE, where he was an associate editor for many years. Currently he is an independent record producer, working with Bruce Springsteen and Jackson Browne, among others.

GREIL MARCUS is the author of *Mystery Train: Images of America in Rock 'n' Roll Music* (Dutton), which was nominated for a National Book Critics' Circle Award in 1975. He has contributed to the *New Yorker*, the *Village Voice*, the *New York Times*, *Creem*, *Take One*, *City* and ROLLING STONE, where he currently writes a column on books.

DAVE MARSH is an associate editor and columnist for ROLLING STONE. Formerly the editor of *Creem*, his work has also appeared in Long Island's *Newsday*, Boston's *Real Paper*, *Penthouse*, *Oui* and *Crawdaddy*. He is the author of Bruce Springsteen's biography, *Born to Run*.

JANET MASLIN is a film and arts critic at *Newsweek*. She has written for the *Boston Phoenix*, *New Times*, the *Village Voice*, ROLLING STONE, *Film Comment* and *Take One*, and she is a member of the National Society of Film Critics.

JOE McEWEN, known to Boston radio listeners as Mr. C, has written about soul for ROLLING STONE, *Phonograph Record* magazine, *Black Music*, the *Boston Phoenix* and Boston's *Real Paper*.

JIM MILLER has contributed to ROLLING STONE, the *Village Voice*, *Creem* and Boston's *Real Paper*, where he was an editor and columnist. He currently teaches political philosophy in the government department at the University of Texas at Austin.

JOHN MORTHLAND has written about music for ROLLING STONE, *Creem*, *Country Music*, Boston's *Real Paper* and Long Island's *Newsday*.

PAUL NELSON has written for ROLLING STONE, the *Village Voice*, *Circus*, the *New York Times*, *Penthouse*, *Creem*, Boston's *Real Paper*, and the *Little Sandy Review*, which he cofounded in 1961. He has also been on the A&R staff of Mercury Records.

ROBERT PALMER is a music critic for the *New York Times*. Formerly a member of Insect Trust, for whom he played saxophone, he has written about jazz and rock for ROLLING STONE, the *Atlantic Monthly*, *Downbeat*, *Ethnomusicology*, *Journal of American Folklore*, the *Black Perspective in Music*, *Black Music*, *Penthouse*, *Oui*, and Boston's *Real Paper*. He has also taught in the music department at Bowdoin College in Maine.

CHARLES PERRY, who has been with the magazine from issue number 11, is an associate editor of ROLLING STONE. He has written for *Playboy*, *Oui*, the San Francisco *Express-Times* and *Rags*.

KIT RACHLIS has written about folk music and rock for ROLLING STONE, the *Village Voice*, Boston's *Real Paper*, the *Boston Phoenix*, *Country Music* and *Creem*.

JOHN ROCKWELL is a music critic for the *New York Times*, and its principle writer on pop. His articles have appeared in ROLLING STONE, the *Oakland Tribune*, the *Los Angeles Times*, *Musical America*, *High Fidelity*, *Opera News*, *Opera Canada*, *Opernwelt*, *Ballet Review*, *Musical Newsletter*, *Music and Musicians* and *Le Monde*. He has a Ph.D. in cultural history from the University of California at Berkeley, where he wrote a dissertation on opera in Berlin in the Twenties.

BUD SCOPPA has contributed to ROLLING STONE, *Phonograph Record* magazine, *Circus*, *Fusion*, and Boston's *Real Paper*. He is the author of *The Byrds* and *The Rock People* (Scholastic). Currently he is a writer in the press department at A&M Records.

GREG SHAW is a senior editor at *Phonograph Record* magazine and the editor/publisher of *Who Put the Bomp*, America's premier rock history magazine (it can be obtained by writing P.O. Box 7112, Burbank, CA, 91510). He has also written for *Mojo Navigator Rock 'n' Roll News*, which he founded in 1966, ROLLING STONE, *Creem*, *Fusion*, *Stereo Review*, *Vibrations*, *Rock*, *Crawdaddy*, *Let It Rock* and *Zig Zag*. He currently helps collate the rock and roll reissues on Sire Records, and is the editor of their rock book series.

ED WARD has written about music for ROLLING STONE, *Creem*, *Phonograph Record* magazine, the *Village Voice*, *Mother Jones*, *Crawdaddy* and Boston's *Real Paper*.

ELLEN WILLIS has been the rock critic for the *New Yorker* since 1968. Her essays on politics, feminism, film and music have appeared in the *New York Review of Books*, ROLLING STONE, *Ramparts*, *New American Review* and *Commentary*. She was a founder of *Redstockings*.

LANGDON WINNER has written about music for ROLLING STONE, *Creem*, and Boston's *Real Paper;* his rock essays have also appeared in the anthology *Rock and Roll Will Stand*. He currently teaches political philosophy in the technology studies program at the Massachusetts Institute of Technology, and is the author of *Autonomous Technology* (MIT).

The discographies supplementing almost every chapter of this book were compiled from Joel Whitburn's *Record Research* books. *Record Research* publishes *Top Pop Records (1940–1955)*, *Top Pop Records (1955–1972)*, *Top LPs (1945–1972)*, *Top Country and Western Records (1949–1971)*, *Top Rhythm and Blues Records (1949–1971)*, *Top Easy Listening Records (1961–1974)* and yearly supplements in each of these categories—based on *Billboard* magazine's weekly charts. The hit records for each artist are listed chronologically along with the date the record entered the chart, the number of weeks it stayed on the chart and the highest position it attained. (These books are available by writing: Record Research, P.O. Box 200, Menomonee Falls, WI 53051.)

PHOTO ACKNOWLEDGMENTS

The editors express their thanks and appreciation for the courtesy and assistance of those who helped provide the photographs, many extremely rare and some never published before, that are included in this book.

Michael Ochs of the Michael Ochs Archives, spent much time guiding us through his collection, and a great many of the album covers shown throughout the book, as well as numerous photos, come from him. Jean Gleason was, as always, gracious and knowledgeable. "Popsie" S. Randolph, now retired in Cave Creek, Arizona, one of the first photographers to cover the music field, has a lifetime of pictures in his files. Collector Fred Lewis, an early DJ on WBCN-FM, and a former manager of the J. Geils Band, is currently a record producer and New England promotion manager for Atlantic Records. John Goddard, collector, photographer and manager of the Village Music Store in Mill Valley, California . . . Alice Ochs, photographer, also from Mill Valley . . . Barbara Carr of Atlantic Records . . . Greg Shaw, editor of *Who Put the Bomp* magazine and an invaluable contributor to this book . . . Vince Aletti, a collector as well as a distinguished critic of black music . . . Martin Cerf of *Phonograph Record* magazine . . . Paul Politi of Art Laboe's Original Sound Records . . . Don Paulsen Photos . . . David Bieber of Bieber Archives in Somerville, Massachusetts . . . *Sepia* magazine . . . *16* magazine . . . *Record Exchanger* magazine . . . *America's Oldies* magazine, Box 2144, Anaheim, California . . . *Record World* magazine . . . Laurie Steinberg of CBS Records . . . Johnny Otis, pioneer of rhythm and blues, author and collector . . . Jess Hansen, coordinator of the Jimi Hendrix Archives, Box 85, Seattle, Washington . . . Don Petri, collector . . . Richard Nader Productions . . . Promotions Consolidated . . . Karen Everly and Acuff-Rose Inc. . . . Evelyn Johnson of Peacock Records . . . Carl Davis of Brunswick Records . . . Billy James of RCA Records . . . Also Janus Records and ABC Records . . . Don Kirshner Enterprises . . . Lance Freed . . . Robert Stigwood Organization . . . Marshall Sehorn . . . James O'Neil of *Living Blues* magazine . . . John Edwards Memorial Foundation . . . Country Music Association.